JAZZ
MILESTONES

BY KEN VAIL

A PICTORIAL CHRONICLE OF
JAZZ 1900-1990

Published by Castle Communications plc,
A29 Barwell Business Park, Leatherhead Road,
Chessington, Surrey KT9 2NY.

Copyright © Ken Vail 1993

ISBN 1 8607405 0 2

Film output by The Copy Centre DAR,
Cambridge, England

Printed and bound in the UK by
Staples Printers Rochester Limited

While the publishers have made every reasonable
effort to trace the copyright owners for any or all of
the photographs in this book, there may be some
omissions of credits for which we apologise.

A foreword by Scott Hamilton

When I was about seven years old, in 1962, a friend of the family gave me a book which was quite unique at the time. It was called *A Pictorial History of Jazz* and was written by Orrin Keepnews and Bill Grauer, who also happened to own Riverside Records.

What made this book so special at the time was that it traced the history of the music with photographs and small captions and very little editorializing. The authors seemed uninterested in giving you their opinions, and seemed to just enjoy showing you the artists themselves in all kinds of situations. I loved this book then, and I still take it out and look at the pictures when I feel nostalgic.

The point of all this is that Ken Vail has come up with a format for a jazz book which is just as revolutionary now as that book was in 1962. Without having to wade through somebody's ideas on who is more important than who, or why, he has given us a chance to see the shape of the music from 1900 to the present, and keep it enjoyable.

I'm sure that I'll enjoy looking through these pages for years to come, and I envy the young person who gets this book as an introduction to jazz.

Photograph: Jay Andersen

3

This book is dedicated to Marian,
whose patience and
encouragement made it possible.

INTRODUCTION

Jazz entered my life in a big way in 1952, when I was thirteen years old. Before that time, through the medium of radio, I had enjoyed recordings by Louis Jordan, Ella Fitzgerald, Louis Armstrong and Fats Waller without realising they were part of the jazz story. By 1952 I was aware of Gerry Mulligan, Charlie Parker and Dizzy Gillespie, but the important names to me were British bandleaders Jack Parnell, Johnny Dankworth, Ronnie Scott and Ted Heath. I had no idea how jazz had evolved and I had nobody to ask as none of my friends were remotely interested. Two books were important in shaping my education.

In 1955, as winner of the school Senior Art Prize, I was allowed a book of my choice. Even today I am amazed that I was smart enough to choose *Hear Me Talkin' To Ya* by Nat Hentoff and Nat Shapiro. The title alone was enough to alarm the headmaster who tried very hard to dissuade me but, thankfully, I was unmoved and spent the next few years devouring this book, reading and re-reading while trying to piece together varying snippets of information and misinformation from other sources. The book told the story of jazz in the words of the musicians who made it, arranged chronologically and without editorial comment. Pictures were added to the words in 1958 when an art school friend gave me a copy of *A Pictorial History of Jazz* by Keepnews and Grauer (yes, the same book that Scott Hamilton found so rewarding).

Together, these two books gave me a basis for an understanding of jazz history as well as a great deal of pleasure, undiminished after 40 years. However, as with most jazz chronologies, they are broken up into styles of convenience with sections encapsulating New Orleans style, swing or bebop etcetera. Unfortunately, real life isn't quite as tidy. The boogie-woogie craze occurred during the swing era of the late Thirties. The birth of bebop and the New Orleans revival happened side-by-side in the Forties. In the Fifties, cool jazz vied with funky hard bop, while today it is possible to hear live jazz in any number of styles.

Jazz Milestones is a chronological look at the history of jazz that attempts to cover the whole spectrum of the music without editorial analysis or comment. Styles, songs, faces and places constantly interact and you are invited to observe the changes in cast and scenery and draw your own conclusions as to who might have been influenced by whom. This book presents the whole mélange and I apologise if space or my personal preference has meant the omission of the reader's favourite recording. All the photographs are, as far as can be ascertained, contemporary with the year in which they are set.

I have many people to thank for their help and encouragement during the making of this book, but especially Hank O'Neal of Chiaroscuro Records who was constantly supportive, and those two wonderful friends of jazz people, Max & Betty Jones, both of whom sadly died before the completion of this book. I am particularly indebted to Charlie Lourie and Michael Cuscuna of Mosaic Editions who supplied photographs by the late Francis Wolff, and also to Rolf Dahlgren, Terry Dash, Brian Foskett, Brian Peerless, David Redfern, Duncan Schiedt and Arthur Zimmerman who opened their photographic collections to me. A special thank you to Karl-Emil Knudsen of Jazz Media ApS, and to Scott Hamilton for his excellent foreword. Thanks also to friends Bob Frost and Grant Elliott for their help, to Anne Beamish and Sally Moon for helping with the print production and to Andy Sharpe and Steve Lay who saved the day when computer crashes threatened both this book and my sanity.

I must not forget the writers and discographers whose work has been both an inspiration and a source of reference. My special thanks to Frank Büchmann-Møller, W. Bruynincx, John Chilton, Frank Driggs, Leonard Feather, Gary Giddins, Ira Gitler, Jorgen Grunnet Jepsen, Gene Lees, Don Marquis, David Meeker, Al Rose, Brian Rust, Phil Schaap, Arnold Shaw, George Simon, Edmond Souchon and, in the words of Max Jones, 'all the labourers in the jazz vineyard'.

Ken Vail, Cambridge, September 1993

1900

Ragtime, the first jazz-related music to achieve popularity, flourishes in America. Scott Joplin (32) has already published *Maple Leaf Rag*, and he moves from Sedalia to St Louis, following his music publisher, John Stark.

In New Orleans, Buddy Bolden (22) is leading his own small band, 'ragging' tunes for dancers in dance halls and amusement parks. King Oliver (15) is playing in a children's brass band and Tony Jackson (24) is the King of Storyville, singing and playing piano in the brothels of the Tenderloin District.

The American recording industry is beginning to take off, following the introduction of the disc gramophone and flat shellac discs in 1897. Ragtime and brass and military bands are popular with the recording companies. Although ragtime is a piano music, the cutting tone of the banjo proves easier to record and banjoists Sylvester 'Vess' Ossman and Fred Van Eps become prolific recording artists.

Eastman Kodak introduce the Brownie Box Camera in this year, making photography affordable to the general public.

BIRTHS
Wilbur De Paris (trombone) 11 January
Harry Roy (clarinet/leader) 12 January
Juan Tizol (trombone) 22 January
Walter Page (bass) 9 February
Wingy Manone (trumpet) 13 February
Jimmy Bertrand (percussion) 24 February
Tiny Parham (piano) 25 February
Joe Robichaux (piano) 8 March
Ernest 'Bass' Hill (bass) 14 March
June Clark (trumpet) 24 March
Ted Heath (trombone/leader) 30 March
Bob Shoffner (trumpet) 4 April
Herb Flemming (trombone) 5 April

Albert Nicholas (clarinet) 27 May
Chester Zardis (bass) 27 May
Tommy Ladnier (trumpet) 28 May
Valaida Snow (trumpet/vocal) 2 June
Paul Mares (trumpet) 15 June
Captain John Handy (alto sax) 24 June
George Lewis (clarinet/leader) 13 July
Don Redman (saxes/composer/arranger) 29 July
Tony Parenti (clarinet) 6 August
Charlie Gaines (trumpet) 8 August
Lucky Millinder (leader) 8 August
Freddie Moore (drums) 20 August
Kid Rena (trumpet) 14 September
Elmer Snowden (banjo) 9 October

Jimmy Harrison (trombone) 17 October
Lawrence Marrero (banjo) 24 October
Joe Watkins (drums) 24 October
Willie Humphrey Jr (clarinet) 29 December
Floyd Casey (drums/washboard)
Al Gandee (trombone)
Charlie 'Big' Green (trombone)
Andrew Hilaire (drums)
Clifford 'Snags' Jones (drums)
Stan King (drums)
Dick Voynow (piano)

COMPOSITIONS
Thomas Broady: *Whistling Rufus*
Abe Holzmann: *Bunch O' Blackberries*
James Weldon Johnson: *In Dahomey*
Scott Joplin: *Swipesey Cake Walk*
J. Bodewalt Lange: *Creole Belles*
Tom Turpin: *A Ragtime Nightmare*

RECORDINGS
Vess Ossman (NYC, 8 January): *Sounds From Africa / Happy-Go-Lucky / An Ethiopian Mardi Gras* (London, 18 May): *Smoky Mokes / A Ragtime Skedaddle / Whistling Rufus* (London, 25 May): *Cotton Blossoms* (NYC, 19 July): *Whistling Rufus / An Ethiopian Mardi Gras / A Bunch Of Rags / A Coon Band Contest*
Sousa's Band (Philadelphia, 9 April): *A Coon Band Contest* (13 April): *Hula Hula Cake Walk / Who Dat Say Chicken In Dis Crowd* (1 October): *At A Georgia Camp Meeting* (2 October): *A Hot Time In The Old Town Tonight* (3 October): *Whistling Rufus*

1901

The Victor Company and Columbia Graphophone Company are founded. Victor issues the first piano rag recording, *Creole Belles*, played by their studio pianist Charles Booth.

10-inch discs are introduced.

Freddie Keppard (12) plays his first job at Spanish Fort, New Orleans, with Johnny Brown's Band.

President McKinley is assassinated (September).

BIRTHS
Claude Jones (trombone) 11 February
Fred Robinson (trombone) 20 February
Sidney Arodin (clarinet) 29 March
Edmond Hall (clarinet) 15 May
Frank Signorelli (piano) 24 May
Frankie Trumbauer (alto sax/C-melody) 30 May
Louis Armstrong (trumpet/leader) 4 August
Phil Napoleon (trumpet) 2 September
Lee Collins (trumpet) 17 October
Danny Polo (saxes) 22 December
Rudy Jackson (clarinet)
Howdy Quicksell (banjo)

COMPOSITIONS
Charles N. Daniels: *Hiawatha*
Abe Holzmann: *Blaze Away / Hunky-Dory*
Scott Joplin: *The Easy Winners / Peacherine Rag / Sunflower Slow Drag*
Walter Wilson & John Queen: *Ain't Dat A Shame*

RECORDINGS
Charles Booth (NYC): *Creole Belles*
Silas Leachman (NYC, 13 May): *I Couldn't Stand To See My Baby Lose* (14 May): *Mr Johnson, Turn Me Loose / Mr Johnson, Don't Get Gay*
Vess Ossman (NYC, 16 May): *Hunky Dory / Rusty Rags*

Right: An aerial view of Storyville, the New Orleans red light district where jazz flourished amid the brothels and saloons.
Inset: The Blue Book was a guide to the establishments and ladies of the District, one of whom is shown wearing the fashionable striped stockings of the period.

1902

Jelly Roll Morton (12) plays in the Tenderloin District in New Orleans. This is the year he claims to have invented jazz.

New Orleans' Lincoln Park opens in July at Carrollton and Forshey Street, and features concerts and dances with the John Robichaux Orchestra, Adam Olivier's Orchestra and the Excelsior Band. Buddy Bolden also plays here, as well as at the adjoining Johnson Park. It is at one of these venues when he points his cornet at the other park and 'calls his children home'.

Emil 'Stalebread' Lacoume is blinded by an eye infection.

BIRTHS
Preston Jackson (trombone) 3 January
Mel Stitzel (piano) 9 January
Putney Dandridge (piano/vocals) 13 January
Benny Waters (saxes) 23 January
Jim Lanigan (bass) 30 January
Lil Hardin (piano) 3 February
Georg Brunis (trombone) 6 February
Joe Tarto (tuba/bass) 22 February
Chauncey Morehouse (drums) 11 March
Leon Roppolo (clarinet) 16 March
Santo Pecora (trombone) 31 March
Monette Moore (vocals) 19 May
Sylvester Ahola (trumpet) 24 May
Jimmie Lunceford (leader) 6 June
Ed Cuffee (trombone) 7 June
Chris Columbus (drums) 17 June
Joe Smith (trumpet) 28 June
Buster Bailey (clarinet) 19 July
Cliff Jackson (piano) 19 July
Omer Simeon (clarinet) 21 July
Luis Russell (piano) 5 August
Lloyd Scott (drums) 22 August
Jerome Don Pasquall (saxes) 20 September
Garvin Bushell (saxes) 25 September
Jimmy Archey (trombone) 12 October
Eddie Lang (guitar) 25 October
Julia Lee (piano, vocals) 31 October
Arthur Schutt (piano) 21 November
Danny Alvin (drums) 29 November
Joe 'Cornbread' Thomas (clarinet) 3 December
Cecil Irwin (saxes) 7 December
Sonny Greer (drums) 13 December
Shirley Clay (trumpet)

COMPOSITIONS
Hughie Cannon: *Bill Bailey, Won't You Please Come Home?*
Tony Jackson: *Naked Dance*
J Rosamond Johnson: *Oh, Didn't He Ramble?*
Scott Joplin: *Elite Syncopations / The Entertainer*
Arthur Pryor: *The Passing Of Ragtime*

RECORDINGS
Vess Ossman (NYC, 27 February): *Creole Belles / A Bunch Of Rags* (NYC, 8 October): *Harmony Moze / Old Plunk's New Coon Medley*
Dan Quinn (NYC, 14 March): *O Didn't He Ramble*
Sousa's Band (Philadelphia, 2 January): *Creole Belles* (Philadelphia, 30 January): *Trombone Sneeze* (Philadelphia, 3 June): *The Passing Of Ragtime* (Philadelphia, 14 August): *At A Georgia Camp Meeting*
The Victor Minstrels (NYC, 13 December): *The Cake-Walk*

1903

12-inch discs are established and, along with 10-inch discs, become the industry standard.

Scott Joplin (35) has his ragtime opera, 'A Guest of Honor' presented in St Louis.

Orville Wright makes the first powered flight at Kitty Hawk, North Carolina in December.

The first Pacific communications cable is opened, and President Roosevelt sends a message around the world.

BIRTHS
Les Hite (alto sax/leader) 13 February
DePriest Wheeler (trombone) 1 March
Bix Beiderbecke (cornet) 10 March
Bubber Miley (trumpet) 3 April
Emmett Hardy (cornet) 12 June
Ben Pollack (drums/leader) 22 June
Charlie Margulis (trumpet) 24 June
Happy Caldwell (tenor sax) 25 July
Hilton Jefferson (alto sax) 30 July
Claude Hopkins (piano) 3 or 24 August
Joe Garland (sanos/arranger) 15 August
Monk Hazel (drums) 15 August
Jimmy Rushing (vocals) 26 August
Joe Venuti (violin) 16 September
Teddy Weatherford (piano) 11 October
Buck Washington (piano/dance) 16 October
Brad Gowans (trombone) 3 December
Matty Malneck (violin) 9 December
Ray Noble (leader/composer/arranger) 17 December
Earl Hines (piano/leader) 28 December

COMPOSITIONS
Scott Joplin: *Weeping Willow / Palm Leaf Rag / A Guest Of Honor*
Eddie Leonard & Eddie Munson: *Ida (Sweet as Apple Cider)*
James Scott: *A Summer Breeze*
Tom Turpin: *St Louis Rag*
Percy Wenrich: *Ashy Africa*

RECORDINGS
Vern Ossman (London, 13 May): *Smoky Mokes / Hiawatha* (London, 16 May): *Harmony Moze* (NYC, 23 October): *Peaceful Henry* (NYC, 5 November): *A Coon Band Contest / An Ethiopian Mardi Gras / Keep Off The Grass*
Charles Prince's Orchestra (NYC, August): *Dixie Girl*
Arthur Pryor's Band (NYC, 24 November): *Mr Black Man* (7 December): *A Coon Band Contest*
Sousa's Band (Philadelphia, 14 August): *Hiawatha* (Philadelphia, 17 August): *A Hot Time In The Old Town Tonight* (Philadelphia, 18 August): *The Passing Of Ragtime*

1904

The St Louis Exposition in St Louis, Missouri, hosts the Olympic Games.

National Ragtime Contest in St Louis.

Bud Scott (guitar) plays with the John Robichaux Band, which also includes Jim Williams (trumpet), Baptiste Delisle (trombone), Dee Dee Chandler (drums) and Henry Kimball (bass).

Tony Jackson (28) joins the Whitman Sisters touring show, returning to New Orleans in the autumn.

The first section of the New York subway system is opened in October. It runs from Brooklyn Bridge to 145th Street & Broadway.

First double-sided records are issued by Odeon.

BIRTHS

Joe 'Tricky Sam' Nanton (trombone) 1 February
Emmanuel Paul (tenor sax) 2 February
Walter Johnson (drums) 18 February
Dede Pierce (trumpet) 18 February
Cié Frazier (drums) 23 February
Jimmy Dorsey (alto sax/leader) 29 February
Glenn Miller (trombone/leader) 1 March
Volly De Faut (clarinet) 14 March
Pete Johnson (piano) 24 March
Sharkey Bonano (trumpet/leader) 9 April
Dave Wilborn (banjo/guitar) 11 April
Russ Morgan (trombone/arranger) 28 April
Bing Crosby (vocals) 2 May
Floyd O'Brien (trombone) 7 May
Fats Waller (piano/vocals) 21 May

Otto 'Toby' Hardwicke (alto sax) 31 May
Leroy Maxey (drums) 6 June
Don Murray (clarinet/saxes) 7 June
Prince Robinson (saxes) 7 June
Bill Rank (trombone) 8 June
Charles Edward Smith (writer) 8 June
Pinetop Smith (piano) 11 June
Adrian Rollini (vibes/bass sax) 28 June
Bill Challis (piano) 8 July
Ikey Robinson (banjo/guitar) 28 July
Bill Coleman (trumpet) 4 August
Jess Stacy (piano) 4 August
Lester Boone (saxes) 12 August
Count Basie (piano/leader) 21 August
Buster Smith (alto sax) 26 August
Floyd Bean (piano) 30 August

Paul Mertz (piano) 1 September
Stump Evans (saxes) 18 October
Louis Bacon (trumpet) 1 November
Art Hodes (piano) 14 November
Coleman Hawkins (tenor sax) 21 November
Horace Henderson (piano) 22 November
Bob McCracken (clarinet) 23 November
Eddie South (violin) 27 November
Jimmy Lytell (clarinet) 1 December
Herman Autrey (trumpet) 4 December
Sinclair Traill (writer/editor) December
Eddie Lang (guitar)
Harlan Leonard (saxes/leader)
Dick McDonough (guitar/banjo)

COMPOSITIONS

Albert Carroll: *Crazy Chord Rag*
George M Cohan: *Give My Regards To Broadway*
Joe Jordan: *Pekin Rag*
Scott Joplin: *The Favorite / The Cascades / The Sycamore / The Chrysanthemum*
Charles Seymour: *Panama Rag*
Barney & Charles Seymour: *St Louis Tickle*
Andrew Sterling: *Meet Me In St Louis, Louis*
Tom Turpin: *The Buffalo Rag*

RECORDINGS

Arthur Pryor's Band (NYC, 23 March): *The St Louis Rag* (21 April): *A Southern Belle*

1905

Buddy Bolden (27) reaches the peak of his popularity. His band includes Willie Cornish (30) on valve trombone, Frank Lewis (35) & Willie Warner (28) on clarinets, Jefferson 'Brock' Mumford (32) on guitar, Jimmy Johnson (21) on bass and Cornelius Tillman (33) on drums.

BIRTHS

Percy Humphrey (trumpet) 13 January
Harold Arlen (composer) 15 February
William Russell (jazz historian) 26 February
Louis Metcalf (trumpet) 28 February
Bertha 'Chippie' Hill (vocals) 15 March
Hal Kemp (alto sax/leader) 27 March
Bernard Addison (guitar) 15 April
Tommy Benford (drums) 19 April
Loring 'Red' Nichols (cornet/leader) 8 May
Dick McPartland (guitar) 18 May
Sidney De Paris (trumpet) 30 May
Adolphus 'Doc' Cheatham (trumpet) 13 June
Don Kirkpatrick (piano/arranger) 17 June
Ray Biondi (guitar) 5 July
Ivie Anderson (vocals) 10 July
Clyde Bernhardt (trombone) 11 July
Nat Towles (bass/leader) 10 August
Jack Teagarden (trombone) 20 August
Alphonso Trent (piano/leader) 24 August
Meade Lux Lewis (piano) 4 September
Tiny Bradshaw (leader) 23 September
Reuben Reeves (trumpet) 25 October
Papa Joe Assunto (trombone) 1 November
Eddie Condon (guitar/leader) 16 November
Tommy Dorsey (trombone/leader) 19 November
Cecil Scott (tenor sax) 22 November
Wayman Carver (saxes) 25 December
Snub Mosley (trombone) 29 December
Arthur Whetsol (trumpet)
Herb Morand (trumpet)
Chelsea Quealey (trumpet)
Dave Nelson (trumpet/piano/leader)

COMPOSITIONS

Warren Edwards: *Peek-A-Boo Rag*
James Reese Europe: *Coon Band Parade*
Scott Joplin: *Bethena*
Joseph Northup: *The Cannonball*
Egbert Van Alstyne / Harry Williams: *In The Shade Of The Old Apple Tree*
Harry Von Tilzer / Andrew B Sterling: *Wait Till The Sun Shines, Nelly*
Percy Wenrich: *Peaches And Cream*
Bert Williams / Alex Rogers: *Nobody*

RECORDINGS

Vess Ossman (NYC, December): *The Buffalo Rag*
Charles Prince's Orchestra (NYC, July): *St Louis Tickle*
Arthur Pryor's Band (NYC, 17 October): *Razzazza Mazzazza*
Sousa's Band (Philadelphia, 25 October): *Silence And Fun – a ragtime oddity*
Victor Dance Band (NYC, 10 April): *The Cakewalk In The Sky*

The Buddy Bolden Band. *Back l to r:* Willie Warner (clarinet), Willie Cornish (valve trombone), Buddy Bolden (cornet), Jimmy Johnson (bass). *Front:* Frank Lewis (clarinet), Brock Mumford (guitar)

Photograph courtesy: *Max Jones*

1906

Buddy Bolden (28) begins having severe headaches (March). He is drinking heavily and is arrested after attacking his mother-in-law. Willie Cornish, Brock Mumford, Jimmy Johnson and Cornelius Tillman all leave the band and are replaced by Frankie Dusen (trombone), Lorenzo Staulz (guitar) and Bob Lyons (bass). Buddy plays his last engagement at a Labor Day parade. His dementia is worsening and he never recovers.

Bunk Johnson (16) plays with the Superior Orchestra which includes

Freddie Keppard (17) and his brother Louis organise the Olympia Orchestra.

14-year-old Clarence Williams moves to New Orleans and earns his living playing piano in restaurants and cabarets.

The San Francisco Earthquake (18 April) is followed by widespread fire.

Race riots in Atlanta, Georgia leave 21 dead. The city is placed under martial law.

COMPOSITIONS
Charles L. Johnson: *Dill Pickles Rag*
Scott Joplin: The Ragtime Dance
Arthur Marshall: *Kinklets*
Jelly Roll Morton: *The King Porter Stomp*
Jean Schwartz: *Chinatown, My Chinatown*
James Scott: *Frog Legs Rag*
Percy Wenrich: *Noodles*

RECORDINGS
Vess Ossman (NYC, 24 January): *Dixie Girl / St Louis Tickle / Koontown Koffee Klatsch* (NYC, 26 January): *The Buffalo Rag / St Louis Tickle / Cannon Ball Rag*

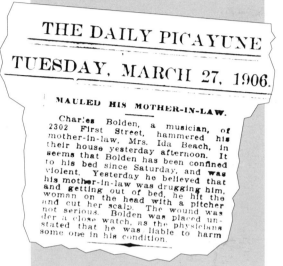

THE DAILY PICAYUNE
TUESDAY, MARCH 27, 1906.

MAULED HIS MOTHER-IN-LAW.

Charles Bolden, a musician, of 2302 First Street, hammered his mother-in-law, Mrs. Ida Beach, in their house yesterday afternoon. It seems that Bolden has been confined to his bed since Saturday, and was violent. Yesterday he believed that his mother-in-law was drugging him, and getting out of bed, he hit the woman on the head with a pitcher and cut her scalp. The wound was not serious. Bolden was placed under a close watch, as the physicians stated that he was liable to harm some one in his condition.

BIRTHS

Frankie Newton (trumpet) 4 January
Wild Bill Davison (cornet) 5 January
Bobby Stark (trumpet) 6 January
Wendell Culley (trumpet) 8 January
Wallace Bishop (drums) 17 February
Sterling Bose (trumpet) 23 February
Barney Bigard (clarinet) 3 March
Frank Teschemacher (saxes) 14 March
Sheldon Hemphill (trumpet) 16 March
George Orendorff (trumpet) 18 March
Pee Wee Russell (clarinet) 27 March
Billy Taylor (bass) 3 April
Fud Livingston (saxes) 10 April
Bud Freeman (tenor sax) 13 April
Little Brother Montgomery (piano/vocals) 18 April
Alex Hill (piano/arranger) 19 April
Ward Pinkett (trumpet) 29 April
Hayes Pillars (tenor sax/leader) 30 April
J.C. Higginbotham (trombone) 11 May
Glen Gray (saxes/leader) 7 June

Edwin Swayze (trumpet) 13 June
Joe Darensbourg (clarinet) 9 July
Vic Dickenson (trombone) 6 August
Eddie Durham (guitar/trombone) 19 August
Manzie Johnson (drums) 19 August
Brick Fleagle (guitar) 22 August
Rod Rodriguez (piano) 10 September
Wilson Myers (bass) 7 October
Freddie Jenkins (trumpet) 10 October
Victoria Spivey (vocals) 15 October
Sandy Williams (trombone) 24 October
Joe Sullivan (piano) 5 November
Pete Brown (alto sax) 9 November
Muggsy Spanier (trumpet) 9 November
Wallace Jones (trumpet) 16 November
Guy Kelly (trumpet) 22 November
George James (tenor sax) 7 December
Gil Rodin (saxes) 9 December
Jack Purvis (trumpet) 11 December
Jesse Crump (piano)
Walter 'Fats' Pichon (piano/vocals/arranger)

1907

Buddy Bolden (29) is arrested (13 March), booked for insanity and sent to the House of Detention. On 5 June he is committed to the Insane Asylum at Jackson, Louisiana where he remains until his death in 1931.

Scott Joplin (39) moves to New York.

Tony Jackson (31) leaves New Orleans for Chicago.

Freddy Keppard (18) organises a band featuring Alphonse Picou (28). He is also working with Frankie Dusen's Eagle Band.

King Oliver (22) playing with the Melrose Brass Band.

Fate Marable (17) begins working on the Mississippi riverboats, sailing out of Little Rock, Arkansas on the steamboat 'J.S.'

The first *Ziegfeld Follies* opens on Broadway.

George Wettling (drums) 28 November
Fred Elizalde (piano) 12 December
Lawrence Lucie (guitar) 18 December
Cab Calloway (vocals/leader) 25 December
Eddie Wilcox (piano) 27 December

COMPOSITIONS
Bernie Adler / Victor H Smalley: *That Lovin' Rag*
C.A.Grimm: *Down South*
Charles L.Johnson: *Fine And Dandy*
Scott Joplin: *Nonpareil / Gladiolus Rag / Rose Leaf Rag / Heliotrope Bouquet*
James Scott: *Kansas City Rag*
Percy Wenrich: *The Smiler / Dixie Darlings*

RECORDINGS
Vess Ossman (NYC, January): *Chicken Chowder* (NYC, 5 February): *Florida Rag* (NYC, March): *Maple Leaf Rag*
Arthur Pryor's Band (NYC, 12 September): *The King of Rags* (19 September): *Darkie's Spring Song*

BIRTHS
Joe Marsala (clarinet) 5 January
Vernon Brown (trombone) 6 January
Benny Morton (trombone) 31 January
Emanuel Sayles (banjo) 31 January
Walter 'Foots' Thomas (tenor sax) 10 February
Harry Dial (drums) 17 February
Charlie Spivak (trumpet) 17 February
Rex Stewart (cornet) 22 February
Harry Gold (saxes) 26 February
Mildred Bailey (vocals) 27 February
Jimmy McPartland (trumpet) 15 March
Herb Hall (clarinet) 28 March
Abe Lincoln (trombone) 29 March
Wilmore 'Slick' Jones (drums) 13 April
Casper Reardon (harp) 15 April
Dave Tough (drums) 26 April
Matty Matlock (clarinet) 27 April
Hayes Alvis (bass) 1 May
Pee Wee Hunt (trombone) 10 May
Rod Cless (clarinet) 20 May
Billie Pierce (vocals/piano) 8 June
Dickie Wells (trombone) 10 June

Nappy Lamare (guitar) 14 June
Sid Phillips (clarinet) 14 June
Gene Sedric (tenor sax) 17 June
Benny Payne (piano/vocals) 18 June
Doc Evans (cornet) 20 June
Lammar Wright Sr (trumpet) 20 June
Jimmy Mundy (tenor sax/arranger) 28 June
Rubberlegs Williams (vocals) 14 July
Johnny Hodges (alto sax) 25 July
Albert Wynn (trombone) 29 July
Lawrence Brown (trombone) 3 August
Benny Carter (alto sax/trumpet/leader) 8 August
Edgar Sampson (saxes/composer/arranger) 31 August
Albert Ammons (piano) 23 September
Edgar Battle (trumpet/arranger) 3 October
Carl Kress (guitar) 20 October
André Ekyan (clarinet) 24 October
Tony Pastor (saxes/leader) 26 October
Rudy Powell (alto sax/clarinet) 28 October
Joe Rushton (clarinet/bass sax) 1 November
Joe Turner (piano) 3 November
Henry 'Hot Lips' Levine (trumpet) 26 November
Frank Melrose (piano/bandleader) 26 November

1908

Nick La Rocca (19) forms his first band in New Orleans with 15-year-old Larry Shields on clarinet.

Freddie Keppard (19) has a band at the Tuxedo Dance Hall.

King Oliver (23) joins the Magnolia Band. Also in the band are Honoré Dutrey (21) on trombone and Pops Foster (16) on bass.

Lulu White builds a saloon on the corner of Basin and Bienville Streets, right next door to her famous Storyville sporting house, Mahogany Hall.

Henry Ford's Model T is introduced on 1st October.

Jack Johnson wins the world heavyweight boxing championship on 26 December, beating Tommy Burns in Sydney, Australia.

BIRTHS
Henry 'Red' Allen (trumpet) 7 January
Teddy McRae (tenor sax/arranger/composer) 22 January
Jerry Blake (saxes) 23 January
Stephane Grappelli (violin) 26 January
Crawford Wethington (saxes) 26 January
Oran 'Hot Lips' Page (trumpet) 27 January
Manny Klein (trumpet) 4 February
Lenny Hayton (piano/arranger) 13 February
Claude Williams (violin) 22 February
Nat Gonella (trumpet) 7 March
Will Hudson (composer/bandleader) 8 March
Johnny Williams (bass) 13 March
Kenneth 'Red' Norvo (vibes) 31 March
Alfred Lion (record producer) 21 April
Avery 'Kid' Howard (trumpet) 22 April
Philippe Brun (trumpet) 29 April
Henderson Chambers (trombone) 1 May
Warren Smith (trombone) 17 May
Gene Gifford (guitar) 31 May
Clarence Hutchenrider (saxes) 13 June
Eli Robinson (trombone) 23 June
Jimmy McLin (guitar) 27 June
Louis Jordan (alto sax/vocals) 8 July
Russell Procope (alto sax) 11 August
Al Morgan (bass) 19 August
Spud Murphy (alto sax/arranger/composer) 19 August
Willie Bryant (vocals/leader) 30 August
Max Kaminsky (trumpet) 7 September
Charlie Beal (piano) 14 September
Kid Sheik Cola (trumpet) 15 September
Alberto Socarras (saxes/flute) 19 September
Sammy Price (piano) 6 October
Alton 'Slim' Moore (trombone) 7 October
Herman Chittison (piano) 15 October
Marshall Stearns (writer) 18 October
Spike Hughes (bass/composer/writer) 19 October
Rollie Culver (drums) 29 October
Bunny Berigan (trumpet) 2 November
Clancy Hayes (banjo) 14 November
Ben Thigpen (drums) 16 November
Keg Johnson (trombone) 19 November
Cladys 'Jabbo' Smith (trumpet) 24 December
Quinn Wilson (bass) 26 December
Jonah Jones (trumpet) 31 December
John Kirby (bass) 31 December
Billy Banks (vocal)
Joe Eldridge (alto sax)
Willie McWashington (drums)

COMPOSITIONS
George Botsford: *Black And White Rag*
Scott Joplin: *Fig Leaf Rag / Sugar Cane / Pineapple Rag*
Charles Lamb: *Sensation Rag*
Theodore F Morse / Edward Madden: *Down In Jungle Town*
Albert Von Tilzer / Jack Norwalk: *Take Me Out To The Ball Game*
Percy Wenrich: *Crab Apples / Memphis Rag*

RECORDINGS
Vess Ossman (NYC, 5 October): *Persian Lamb Rag / A Bunch Of Rags*
Arthur Pryor's Band (NYC, 16 September): *Artful Artie* (NYC, 17 September): *Mr Black Man / That Rag* (NYC, 21 September): *Southern Beauties Rag* (NYC, 22 September): *Georgia Sunset – Cake Walk*

Basin Street, New Orleans. The building on the extreme right is Lulu White's Mahogany Hall. Far left, on the corner of Iberville Street, is Anderson's Saloon. During 1908 railroad passenger sheds were built along Basin Street and these are visible in the photograph on page 12 taken in 1909.

1909

W C Handy (36) composes a campaign song for Edward Crump, the Democrat from Memphis. He calls it *Mr Crump*, but it is retitled and published in 1913 as *Memphis Blues*, probably the first composition to be called a blues.

The National Association for the Advancement of Coloured People (NAACP) is founded by liberal whites to promote the rights of black Americans.

Henry Ford produces 19,000 Model T's, 'in any colour you want as long as it's black'.

BIRTHS
Tab Smith (alto sax) 11 January
Danny Barker (guitar) 13 January
Quentin Jackson (trombone) 13 January
Gene Krupa (drums) 15 January
Ed Lewis (trumpet) 22 January
Irving 'Mouse' Randolph (trumpet) 22 January
Tiny Winters (bass) 24 January
Artie Bernstein (bass) 4 February
Chick Webb (drums) 10 February
Bob Casey (bass) 11 February
Ben Webster (tenor sax) 27 February
Joe Yukl (trombone) 5 March
Herschel Evans (tenor sax) 9 March
Harry Hayes (saxes) 23 March
Marty Marsala (trumpet) 2 April
Hymie Schertzer (alto sax) 2 April
George Dixon (trumpet/saxes) 8 April
Jesse Price (drums) 1 May
T-Bone Walker (guitar/vocals) 22 May
Benny Goodman (clarinet) 30 May
Garland Wilson (piano) 13 June
Ray Bauduc (drums) 18 June
Joe Thomas (tenor sax) 19 June
Arnold Shaw (writer) 28 June
Teddy Buckner (trumpet) 16 July
Cassino Simpson (piano) 23 July
Joe Thomas (trumpet) 24 July
Cedric Wallace (bass) 3 August
Lem Johnson (tenor sax) 6 August
Dan Minor (trombone) 10 August
Claude Thornhill (piano/leader) 10 August
Stuff Smith (violin) 14 August
Paul Webster (trumpet) 24 August
Lester Young (tenor sax) 27 August
Skip Hall (piano) 27 September
Buddy Featherstonhaugh (saxes) 4 October
Art Tatum (piano) 13 October
Herman Chittison (piano) 15 October
Cozy Cole (drums) 17 October
Adelaide Hall (vocals) 20 October
Johnny Mercer (songwriter) 18 November
O'Neil Spencer (drums) 25 November
Kenneth Hollon (tenor sax) 26 November
Teddy Hill (tenor sax/bandleader) 7 December
Cleo Brown (piano/vocals) 8 December
Eddie Barefield (saxes) 12 December
Rudy Williams (saxes)

COMPOSITIONS
Ford Dabney: *Oh! You Devil Rag*
Robert Hoffman: *I'm Alabama Bound*
Scott Joplin: *Wall Street Rag / Country Club / Euphonic Sounds / Paragon Rag / Solace / Pleasant Moments*
Joseph Lamb: *The Excelsior Rag / Ethiopia Rag*
Henry Lodge: *Temptation Rag*
J Russel Robinson: *Sapho Rag*
James Scott: *Great Scott Rag / Sunburst Rag*
Charles Seymour: *Clover Leaf Rag*
Bert Williams / Henry Creamer: *That's-a-Plenty*

RECORDINGS
Vess Ossman (NYC, 2 March): *The Buffalo Rag* (NYC, December): *Moose March*
Charles Prince's Orchestra (NYC, September): *Black and White Rag*
Arthur Pryor's Band (NYC, 8 February): *Dill Pickles Rag* (NYC, 10 February): *Frozen Bill Cake-Walk* (NYC, 30 March): *White Wash Man* (NYC, 31 March): *Pickles and Peppers* (NYC, 7 May): *Sweetmeats – Ragtime March* (NYC, 7 December): *The African 400 (An Educated Rag)* (NYC, 8 December): *Tobasco – A Rag Waltz*
Victor Dance Band (NYC, 15 June): *Black and White Rag*

1910

'Blues' coming into use as a musical term.

James Reese Europe (29) organises the Clef Club in New York.

Oscar Celestin (26) Orchestra begin residency at the newly opened Tuxedo Dance Hall, in Storyville. Across the street, at the 101 Ranch, is 'Big Eye' Louis Nelson (30).

King Oliver (24) begins his professional career as a member of the Eagle Band. He works nights at the 102 Ranch and at the Abadie Cabaret with Richard M Jones.

Halley's Comet passes close to the Earth and is visible across much of the night sky.

Jack Johnson defeats Jim Jeffries in 15 rounds to retain the world heavyweight boxing championship.

BIRTHS

Henry Goodwin (trumpet) 2 January
Jimmy Crawford (drums) 14 January
Sid Catlett (drums) 17 January
Django Reinhardt (guitar) 23 January
Charlie Holmes (alto sax) 27 January
Peanuts Holland (trumpet) 9 February
Paul Bascomb (tenor sax) 12 February
Walter Fuller (trumpet/vocal) 15 February
Al Sears (tenor sax) 22 February
Gene Rodgers (piano) 5 March
Harry Carney (baritone sax) 1 April
Boyce Brown (alto sax) 16 April
Everett Barksdale (guitar) 28 April
Mary Lou Williams (piano) 8 May
Jack Jenney (trombone) 12 May
Artie Shaw (clarinet/leader) 23 May
Pha Terrell (vocals) 25 May
Arthur Trappier (drums) 28 May
Gene Porter (saxes/clarinet) 7 June
Stan Wrightsman (piano) 15 June
Ray McKinley (drums) 18 June
Milt Hinton (bass) 23 June
Shad Collins (trumpet) 27 June
Champion Jack Dupree (piano/vocals) 4 July
Jack Washington (baritone sax) 17 July
Freddie Slack (piano) 7 August
Sammy Weiss (drums) 1 September
Raymond Scott (piano/leader) 10 September
Chu Berry (tenor sax) 13 September
Stanley Dance (writer) 15 September
Billy Exiner (drums) 22 November

Willie Smith (alto sax) 25 November
Armand Hug (piano) 6 December
Budd Johnson (tenor sax) 14 December
John Hammond (record producer/critic) 15 December
Sy Oliver (trumpet) 17 December
Reunald Jones (trumpet) 22 December
Clyde Hart (piano)

COMPOSITIONS

Thornton Allen: *Washington And Lee Swing*
Irving Berlin / Ted Snyder: *Oh, That Beautiful Rag*
Shelton Brooks: *Some of These Days*
Ford Dabney / Cecil Mack: *That Minor Strain*
Scott Joplin: *Stoptime Rag*
Charles Lamb: *Champagne Rag*
J Russel Robinson: *Dynamite Rag*
James Scott: *Grace And Beauty / Hilarity Rag / Ophelia Rag*

RECORDINGS

Vess Ossman (NYC, September): *St Louis Tickle* (NYC, 6 December): *The Smiler Rag*
Charlie Prince's Orchestra (NYC, May): *Temptation Rag / I'm Alabama Bound / Porcupine Rag* (NYC, 27 December): *Tickled to Death*
Arthur Pryor's Band (NYC, 7 June): *Temptation Rag* (NYC, 20 September): *Grizzly Bear Rag*
Fred Van Eps (NYC): *Chatterbox Rag*
Victor Dance Orchestra (NYC, 15 January): *Wild Cherries Rag*

Jack Laine's Reliance Band. L to r: Manuel Mello, Alcide 'Yellow' Nunez, Leonce Mello, Jack Laine, Alfred Laine, Chink Martin, Tim Harris.

Photograph courtesy: *Max Jones*

1911

Bunk Johnson (21) with Frankie Dusen's Eagle Band.

Scott Joplin (43) has his opera 'Treemonisha' presented in New York.

Kid Ory (24) brings his band to New Orleans.

King Oliver (26) replaces Freddie Keppard in the band at Pete Lala's Café. Also in the band are Sidney Bechet (14) and Zue Robertson(20).

Jimmie Noone (16) with Clarence Williams (19) and his Band.

Nick La Rocca (22) and Leon Roppolo, uncle of the NORK clarinettist, in Barocca's Band. Later in the year Nick La Rocca joins the Brunies Brothers Band.

Tony Jackson (35) is back in New Orleans, playing at Frank Early's Café.

Irving Berlin's composition *Alexander's Ragtime Band* is the first song to popularize ragtime outside the Mississippi Delta area.

BIRTHS

Charles Delaunay (writer) 18 January
Michel Warlop (violin) 23 January
Truck Parham (bass) 25 January
Roy Eldridge (trumpet) 30 January
Louis Cottrell Jr (clarinet) 7 March
Heinie Beau (saxes) 8 March
John 'Bugs' Hamilton (trumpet) 8 March
Joe Mooney (accordion) 14 March
Deane Kincaide (arranger/saxes) 18 March
Alton Purnell (piano) 16 April
Johnny Blowers (drums) 21 April
Mario Bauza (trumpet) 28 April
Norma Teagarden (piano) 29 April
Yank Lawson (trumpet) 3 May

Maxine Sullivan (vocals) 13 May
Big Joe Turner (vocals) 18 May
Skeets Herfurt (saxes) 28 May
Dave Matthews (saxes) 6 June
Sanford Gold (piano) 9 June
Babe Russin (tenor sax) 18 June
Eddie Miller (tenor sax) 23 June
Eli Robinson (trombone) 23 June
Cootie Williams (trumpet) 10 July
Bill Dillard (trumpet/vocal) 20 July
Bob Short (tuba) 26 August
Jo Jones (drums) 7 October
Sonny Terry (harmonica) 24 October
Mahalia Jackson (vocals) 26 October
Johnny Richards (composer/arranger) 2 November

Dick Wilson (tenor sax) 11 November
Buck Clayton (trumpet) 12 November
Alvin Burroughs (drums) 21 November
Ernie Caceres (baritone sax) 22 November
Freddie Green (guitar) 31 November
Louis Prima (trumpet/vocals) 7 December
Chuck Gentry (baritone sax) 14 December
Stan Kenton (piano/bandleader) 15 December
Lu Watters (trumpet) 19 December
Cutty Cutshall (trombone) 29 December
Al Cooper (saxes/leader)

COMPOSITIONS

Irving Berlin: *Alexander's Ragtime Band / Everybody's Doing It Now*
Scott Joplin: *Treemonisha (opera) / Felicity Rag*
James Scott: *Quality Rag / The Ragtime Oriole*
Wilbur Sweatman: *Down Home Rag*

RECORDINGS

Charlie Prince's Orchestra (NYC, 6 May): *High Society* (NYC, 7 June): *Red Pepper – A Spicy Rag* (NYC, 4 November): *Ramshackle Rag*
Arthur Pryor's Band (NYC, 5 January): *A Rhinewine Rag* (NYC, 8 May): *Canhanibalmo Rag*
Fred Van Eps (NYC, 31 January): *Rag Pickings / A Ragtime Episode* (NYC, 15 November): *The White Wash Man* (NYC, 19 December): *Red Pepper – A Spicy Rag*
Victor Military Band (NYC, 27 September): *Slippery Place Rag*
Collins & Harlan (NYC, 7 June): *Alexander's Ragtime Band*

STORYVILLE

In 1897, Alderman Sidney Story was instrumental in the ordinance drawn up to confine prostitution in New Orleans to a designated red light area...

'From the South side of Custom Street (Iberville) to the North side of St Louis Street and from the lower or wood side of North Basin Street to the lower or wood side of Robertson Street. And from the upper side of Perdido Street to the lower side of Gravier Street, and from the river side of Franklin Street to the lower, or wood side of Locust Street.'

The area became known as Storyville, although jazzmen generally referred to it as 'The District'. It provided a lot of work for musicians, especially pianists, in the various brothels, clubs, halls and cafés.

The 'Boss' of Storyville was Tom Anderson who ran the Arlington Cafe and Arlington Annex. He published the Blue Book which was a guide to the madams and sporting houses of the district. Among the famous madams were Josie Arlington, Countess Willie Piazza and Lulu White who ran the famous Mahogany Hall at 235 Basin Street.

In October 1917, after America's entry into the First World War, Storyville was closed down at the request of the Navy Department of the Federal Government.

The closure meant a severe loss of work for musicians and many moved on, up the Mississippi, to Chicago.

NEW ORLEANS LANDMARKS

Abadie's
Marais & Bienville Streets (1906–1917)
Tom Anderson's Café
125 North Rampart Street
Anderson's Arlington Annex
Basin & Iberville Streets (1901–1925)
Big 25
Franklin Street near Iberville (1902–50's)
Blum's Café
114 Exchange Alley (1900–1916)
The Budweiser
1017 Iberville Street
also known as the Pup Café, Fern Café and Dance Hall No.2

The Cadillac
342 North Rampart Street (1912–25)
Casino Cabaret
1400 Iberville Street (1907–1913)
Frank Early's Saloon
Franklin & Bienville Streets (1900–1913)
The Entertainers (101 Ranch)
Franklin Street near Iberville (1902–30's)
Butzie Fernandez'
1024 Iberville Street (1905–20's)
Fewclothes Cabaret
Basin Street between Canal & Iberville (1900–1917)
The Frenchman's
Villere & Bienville Streets (1900–1915)
Funky Butt Hall
Perdido Street between Liberty & Franklin (early 1900's)
Pete Lala's
Marais & Iberville Streets (1906–1917)
Lyric Theatre
201 Burgundy Street (–1927)
Mahogany Hall
Basin & Bienville Streets (1903–1949)
Oddfellows Masonic Hall
1116 Perdido Street
Pig Ankle Tonk
Iberville & Franklin Streets (early 1900's)
Poodle Dog Café
Liberty & Bienville Streets (1908–1917)
Red Onion
Julia & South Rampart Streets
Rice's Café
Marais & Iberville Streets (1904–1913)
Spano's
Franklin & Perdido Streets (early 1900's)
Tuxedo Dance Hall
Franklin Street near Bienville (1909–1913)

Below: **The Anderson Annex at the corner of Iberville Street and Basin Street.**

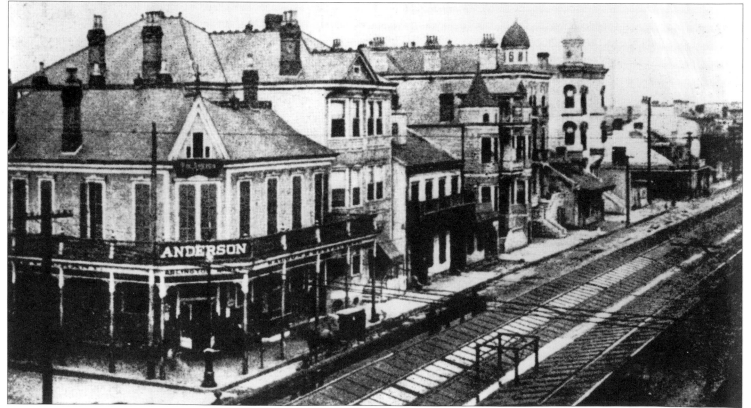

Photograph courtesy: Max Jones

STORYVILLE

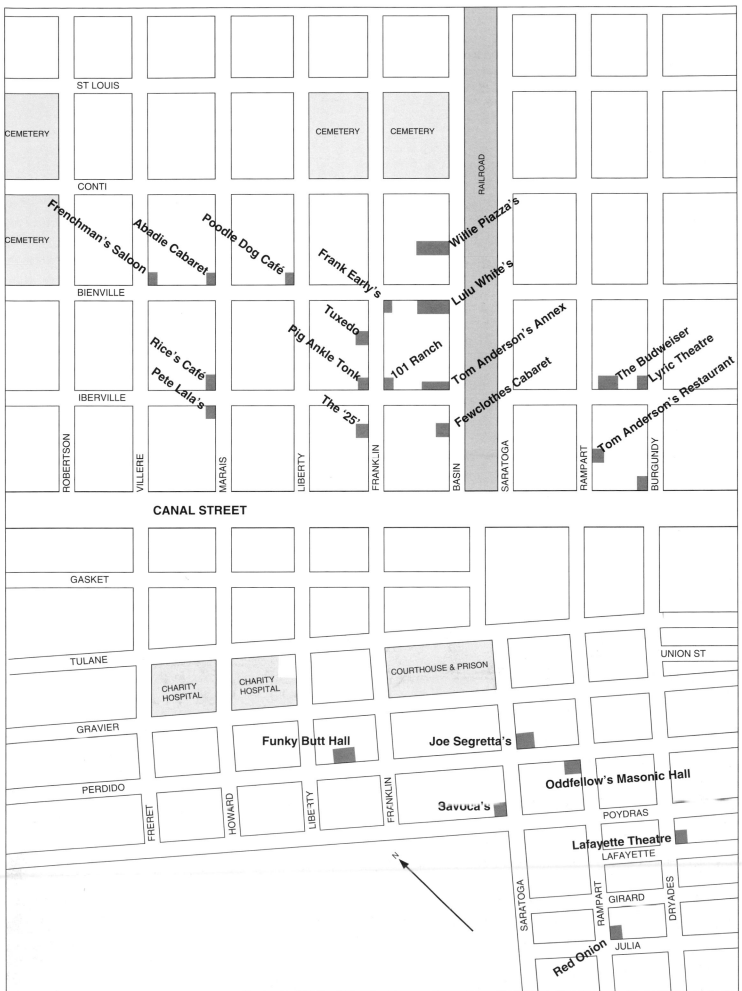

ST LOUIS

CEMETERY

CONTI

CEMETERY

CEMETERY   CEMETERY

CEMETERY

RAILROAD

Frenchman's Saloon

Abadie Cabaret

Poodle Dog Café

Frank Early's

Willie Piazza's

Lulu White's

BIENVILLE

Tuxedo

Pig Ankle Tonk

101 Ranch

Tom Anderson's Annex

Rice's Café

Pete Lala's

Fewclothes Cabaret

The Budweiser

Lyric Theatre

Tom Anderson's Restaurant

IBERVILLE

The '25'

ROBERTSON   VILLERE   MARAIS   LIBERTY   FRANKLIN   BASIN   SARATOGA   RAMPART   BURGUNDY

CANAL STREET

GASKET

TULANE

UNION ST

COURTHOUSE & PRISON

CHARITY
HOSPITAL   CHARITY
HOSPITAL

GRAVIER

Funky Butt Hall   **Joe Segretta's**

Oddfellow's Masonic Hall

PERDIDO

FRERET   HOWARD   LIBERTY   FRANKLIN

3avoca's

POYDRAS

Lafayette Theatre

LAFAYETTE

SARATOGA   RAMPART   GIRARD   DRYADES

N

Red Onion   JULIA

1912

King Oliver (27) joins the Olympia Orchestra under A.J. Piron.

Mutt Carey (21) gets his first job with brother Jack Carey's Crescent Band, which includes Jack Carey (trombone), 15 year old Sidney Bechet (clarinet), Jim Johnson (bass), Charles Moore (guitar) and Ernest Rodgers (drums).

Richard M Jones (20) leads a band at George Fewclothes Cabaret on Basin Street. Also in the band are Freddie Keppard (cornet), Roy Palmer (trombone) and Lawrence Duhé (clarinet).

Louis Armstrong (11) is arrested on New Year's Eve for shooting off a pistol.

The Ragtime fad leads to a series of 'animal' dances including the foxtrot, grizzly bear, turkey trot and the bunny hug.

The Titanic sinks after striking an iceberg off Newfoundland.

BIRTHS

Trummy Young (trombone) 12 January
Bob Zurke (piano) 17 January
Ulysses Livingston (guitar) 29 January
Paul Bascomb (tenor sax) 12 February
Machito (bandleader) 16 February
Hugues Panassié (writer) 27 February
Red Saunders (drums) 2 March
Les Brown (bandleader) 14 March
Lightning Hopkins (guitar/vocals) 15 March
John Levy (bass) 11 April
George Simon (writer/record producer) 9 May
Gil Evans (composer) 13 May
Dave Barbour (guitar) 28 May
Alix Combelle (clarinet/saxes) 15 June
Clarence Profit (piano) 26 June
Johnny Mince (saxes) 8 July
Will Bradley (trombone/leader) 12 July
Nate Kazebier (trumpet) 13 August
Big Chief Russell Moore (trombone) 13 August
Bumps Myers (tenor sax) 22 August
Alvin Alcorn (trumpet) 7 September
Beverly Peer (bass) 7 October
Red Richards (piano) 19 October
Don Byas (tenor sax) 21 October
Franz Jackson (tenor sax) 1 November
Ted Donnelly (trombone) 13 November
Singleton Palmer (bass) 13 November
Tyree Glenn (trombone) 23 November
Teddy Wilson (piano) 24 November
Marshal Royal (alto sax) 5 December
Irving Fazola (clarinet) 10 December
Oscar Moore (guitar) 25 December
Billy Mackel (guitar) 28 December
Toots Mondello (alto sax)
Rudy Rutherford (clarinet)

COMPOSITIONS

Irving Berlin: *When The Midnight Choo-choo Leaves For Alabam*
Ernie Burnett / GeorgeNorton: *My Melancholy Baby*
Ribé Danmark: *The Turkey Trot*
Scott Joplin: *Scott Joplin's New Rag*
Lewis F Muir: *Hitchy-Koo*
J Russel Robinson: *That Eccentric Rag*

RECORDINGS

Charles Prince's Orchestra (NYC, 12 February): *Black Diamond Rag* (30 March): *Cabaret Rag*
Arthur Pryor's Band (NYC, 8 April): *Grizzly Bear Turkey Trot* (NYC, 12 April): *Red Rose Rag*
Fred Van Eps (NYC, 1 May): *Black Diamond Rag* (NYC, 26 July): *Florida Rag*
Victor Dance Orchestra (NYC, 15 February): *The Gaby Glide*
Victor Military Orchestra (NYC, 12 March): *Stomp Dance*

1913

On New Year's Day Louis Armstrong is sent to the Waif's Home.

Tuxedo Dance Hall flourishes in New Orleans Tenderloin District until a gunfight between manager Harry Parker and Billy Phillips of the 101 Ranch. Both men are killed and both establishments are closed down. The police close down five dance halls in all, which has a significant effect on employment for the musicians. The Tuxedo Band reforms as the nucleus of the Original Creole Orchestra, with Freddie Keppard (24), George Bacquet (30), Jimmy Palao (27) and Bill Johnson(39). They leave New Orleans to join an Orpheum Circuit tour that will take them to Chicago and the West Coast.

Clarence Williams (21) becomes manager of a cabaret on Rampart Street.

Sidney Bechet (16) is playing with King Oliver (28).

The Eagle Band includes Bunk Johnson (24), Frankie Dusen and Sidney Bechet.

The word 'jazz' first appears in print in an article by Ernest J Hopkins in the *San Francisco Bulletin*. He defines the word 'jazz' as meaning '*something like life, vigor, energy, effervescence of spirit, joy, pep, magnetism, verve, virility, ebulliency, courage, happiness*'.

Cylinder recordings are discontinued in favour of flat shellac discs.

The Panama Canal is completed in October.

Henry Ford sets up his first automobile assembly line and is soon producing 1000 Model T Fords a day.

Below: **The Onward Brass Band ready to parade. L to r: Manuel Perez, Andrew Kimball, Peter Bocage, Lorenzo Tio Jr, Adolph Alexander, Baby Matthews, Dandy Lewis, Paul Barbarin Sr, Buddy Johnson, Vic Gaspar, Eddie Atkins and Eddie Jackson.**

Photograph Courtesy: *Max Jones*

BIRTHS

Haywood Henry (saxes) 7 or 10 January
Vido Musso (tenor sax) 16 January
Barrett Deems (drums) 1 March
Gene Ramey (bass) 4 April
Lionel Hampton (vibes) 12 April
Earl Bostic (alto sax) 25 April
Karl George (trumpet) 26 April
Squire Gersh (bass) 13 May
Woody Herman (clarinet) 16 May
Pee Wee Erwin (trumpet) 30 May
Jimmy Shirley (guitar) 31 May
Helen Humes (vocals) 23 June
Charlie Teagarden (trumpet) 19 July
George Van Eps (guitar) 7 August
Bob Crosby (bandleader) 23 August
Cliff Leeman (drums) 10 September
Ram Ramirez (piano/composer) 15 September
John Collins (guitar) 20 September
Wally Rose (piano) 2 October
Carmen Mastren (guitar) 6 October
Johnny Best (trumpet) 20 October
Charlie Barnet (saxes) 26 October
Boyd Raeburn (bandleader) 27 October
Andy Gibson (arranger) 6 November
Blue Lu Barker (vocals) 13 November
Gus Johnson (drums) 15 November
Ray Nance (trumpet/violin) 10 December
Don Stovall (alto sax) 12 December

COMPOSITIONS

Bernard Adler: *That Lovin' Rag*
Rev. George Bennard: *The Old Rugged Cross*
Irving Berlin: *That International Rag*
W C Handy / George A Norton: *The Memphis Blues*
Scott Joplin: *Kismet Rag*
Charles Lamb: *American Beauty Rag*
Luckey Roberts: *Junk Man Rag / Pork And Beans*
Chris Smith / Jim Burris: *Ballin' The Jack*
Percy Wenrich: *Ragtime Turkey Trot*

RECORDINGS

Jim Europe's Society Orchestra (NYC, 29 December): *Too Much Mustard / Down Home Rag / Amapa / El Irresistible*
Charles Prince's Orchestra (NYC, 13 January): *Another Rag* (30 July): *Chicago Tickle* (6 October): *The Barbary Rag*
Fred Van Eps (NYC, 6 February): *Whipped Cream* (6 September): *Junk Man Rag*
Victor Military Orchestra (NYC, 6 November): *The Junk Man Rag*

1914

Duke Ellington (15) writes his first composition 'Soda Fountain Rag'.

Louis Armstrong (13) is released from the Waif's Home.

King Oliver (29) and Johnny Dodds (22) are playing in 24 year-old Kid Ory's Band at Pete Lala's. King Oliver is also a member of the Olympia Band.

In Europe, the First World War breaks out in August. The US stays out of the war.

BIRTHS

Kenny Clarke (drums) 9 January
Matt Dennis (songwriter/vocals/piano) 11 February
Teddy Napoleon (piano) 23 January
Tex Beneke (tenor sax) 12 February
Carlo Krahmer (drums) 11 March
Bob Haggart (bass) 13 March
Walt Yoder (bass) 21 April
Sid Weiss (bass) 30 April
Frank Carlson (drums) 5 May
Bobby Plater (alto sax) 13 May
Sun Ra (keyboards) 22 May
Harold 'Shorty' Baker (trumpet) 26 May
Ziggy Elman (trumpet) 26 May
Sing Miller (piano) 17 June
Lem Davis (alto sax) 22 June
Earle Warren (alto sax) 1 July
Billy Eckstine (vocals) 8 July
Billy Kyle (piano) 14 July
Bob Helm (clarinet) 18 July
Erskine Hawkins (trumpet/leader) 26 July
Tommy McQuater (trumpet) 4 September
Dave Bowman (piano) 8 September
Leonard Feather (writer) 13 September
Frank Orchard (trombone) 21 September
Slam Stewart (bass) 21 September
Dave Wilkins (trumpet) 25 September

Marvin Ash (piano) 4 October
Jimmy Powell (alto sax) 24 October
Sabby Lewis (piano/bandleader) 1 November
Jack McVea (tenor sax) 5 November
Sonny Dunham (trumpet) 16 November
Skeeter Best (guitar) 20 November
Coleridge Goode (bass) 29 November
Hal McIntyre (alto sax) 29 November
Eddie Sauter (composer) 2 December
Pat Jenkins (trumpet) 25 December

COMPOSITIONS

Edward B Claypoole: *Ragging The Scale*
W C Handy: *St Louis Blues*
Lew Pollack: *That's-a-Plenty*

RECORDINGS

Jim Europe's Society Orchestra (NYC, 10 February): *You're Here and I'm Here / Castle House Rag / Castle Walk / Congratulations Waltz*
Charles Prince's Orchestra (NYC, 7 July): *That's A Plenty* (24 July): *Memphis Blues*
Fred Van Eps (NYC, 19 March): *Notoriety Rag / Too Much Ginger / The Smiler* (24 July): *Thanks for the Lobster* (4 September): *Old Folks Rag*
Victor Military Band (NYC, 16 February): *Swanee Ripples Rag* (14 April): *Rag-A-Muffin Rag* (15 July): *The Memphis Blues* (25 September): *Ballin' the Jack* (29 November): *Midnight Whirl Rag* (3 December): *Music Box Rag*
Six Brown Brothers (NYC, 20 November): *That Moaning Saxophone Rag*
Felix Arndt (NYC, 20 February): *From Soup to Nuts*

Right: The Original Creole Orchestra, probably the first New Orleans Band to venture north to Chicago. L to r: Eddie Vinson (trombone), Dink Johnson (drums), Freddie Keppard (trumpet), Jimmy Palao (violin), George Bacquet (clarinet), Norwood Williams (guitar) and Bill Johnson (bass).

Photograph Courtesy: *Max Jones*

1915

Jack 'Papa' Laine (42) and his Ragtime Band at Lambs Cafe in Chicago.

King Oliver (30) forms his own band to play at Pete Lala's in New Orleans with Sidney Bechet (18) on clarinet.

Tom Brown (27) and his New Orleans band travel to Chicago to open at Lambs Cafe on 15 May. Presented as Brown's Dixieland Jass Band, the band features Tom Brown (trombone), Raymond Lopez (cornet), Larry Shields (clarinet), Deacon Loyocano (bass) and Billy Lambert (drums).

Jimmie Noone (20) and Buddy Petit (18) lead a band at Frank Early's Café in New Orleans.

The Victor Talking Machine Company launches the Victrola phonograph.

The first transcontinental telephone call is made by Alexander Graham Bell in NYC to Dr Thomas Watson in San Francisco.

The British steamship Lusitania is sunk off Ireland by a German submarine. 114 Americans drown and the indignation contributes to a lobby for US entry into the war.

BIRTHS

Nick Fatool (drums) 2 January
Chano Pozo (conga) 7 January
Keg Purnell (drums) 7 January
Buddy Johnson (piano/leader) 10 January
Frederick Ramsey (writer) 29 January
Bobby Hackett (cornet) 31 January
Gene Schroeder (piano) 5 February
Taft Jordan (trumpet) 15 February
Buddy Tate (tenor sax) 22 February
Scoops Carry (alto sax) 23 February
Ray Perry (violin/alto sax) 25 February
Lee Castle (trumpet) 28 February
Al Hall (bass) 18 March
Sister Rosetta Tharpe (guitar/vocals) 20 March
Hank D'Amico (clarinet) 21 March
Flip Phillips (tenor sax) 26 March
George Chisholm (trombone) 29 March
Muddy Waters (guitar/vocal) 4 April
Billie Holiday (vocal) 7 April
Marlowe Morris (piano/organ) 16 May
Vernon Alley (bass) 26 May
Zeke Zarchy (trumpet) 12 June
Allan Reuss (guitar) 15 June
Milt Buckner (organ) 10 July

Eddie Dougherty (guitar) 17 July
Emmett Berry (trumpet) 23 July
Herbie Haymer (tenor sax) 24 July
George Kelly (tenor sax) 31 July
Harold 'Doc' West (drums) 12 August
Morey Feld (drums) 15 August
Al Hibbler (vocal) 16 August
Murray McEachern (trombone) 16 August
Grachan Moncur (bass) 2 September
Memphis Slim (piano/vocal) 3 September
Al Casey (guitar) 15 September
Lee Wiley (vocal) 9 October
Harry Edison (trumpet) 10 October
Jack Fallon (bass) 13 October
Nellie Lutcher (piano/vocals) 15 October
Chris Griffin (trumpet) 31 October
Billy Bauer (guitar) 14 November
Shorty Sherock (trumpet) 17 November
Gus Bivona (clarinet) 25 November
Dick Vance (trumpet/arranger) 28 November
Billy Strayhorn (piano/composer) 29 November
Brownie McGhee (guitar) 30 November
Eddie Heywood (piano) 4 December
Kansas Fields (drums) 5 December
Frank Sinatra (vocal) 12 December

Photograph Courtesy: *Max Jones*

King Oliver (30) in New Orleans.

Turk Murphy (trombone) 16 December
Cub Teagarden (drums) 16 December
Pete Rugolo (arranger) 25 December
Una Mae Carlisle (piano/vocals) 26 December
Al Klink (tenor sax) 28 December

RECORDINGS

Charles Prince's Orchestra (NYC, 21 October): *The Hesitating Blues* (18 December): *St Louis Blues*
Victor Military Band (NYC, 8 April): *Blame it on the Blues*

1916

Duke Ellington (17) plays his first professional engagement.

Clarence Williams (24) receives a royalty cheque for $1600 from Columbia Records for his song *Brown Skin, Who You For?*

King Oliver (30) and his Band are at the '25' Club in Storyville.

Alcide 'Yellow' Nunez (clarinet), Henry Ragas (piano) and Johnny Stein (drums) are signed up by Chicago promoter Harry James, while playing at the 102 Ranch in Storyville. The band that travels north in March to play at Schiller's Cafe in Chicago as the Dixieland Jass Band, also includes Eddie Edwards (trombone) and Nick La Rocca (cornet) with Tony Sbarbaro (drums) replacing Johnny Stein.

Prohibition spreads, now becoming law in 24 of the United States of America.

BIRTHS

Jay McShann (piano) 12 January
Slim Gaillard (piano/guitar/vocal) 4 January
Milt Raskin (piano) 27 January
Artie Shapiro (bass) 15 January
Jimmy Skidmore (tenor sax) 8 February
Bill Doggett (organ) 16 February
Charlie Fowlkes (baritone sax) 16 February
Svend Asmussen (violin) 28 February
Ina Ray Hutton (bandleader) 13 March
Harry James (trumpet) 15 March
Burt Bales (piano) 20 March
Kenny Kersey (piano) 3 April
Julian Dash (tenor sax) 9 April
Russ Garcia (arranger/trumpet) 12 April
Maurice Purtill (drums) 4 May
Paul Quinichette (tenor sax) 7 May
Moon Mullens (trumpet) 11 May
Skip Martin (saxes) 14 May
Dud Bascomb (trumpet) 16 May
Joe Springer (piano) 22 May
Jerry Gray (composer/arranger) 3 July
Dick Cary (piano/trumpet) 10 July

Sam 'The Man' Taylor (tenor sax) 12 July
Ernie Shepard (bass) 19 July
Paul Moer (piano) 22 July
Charlie Christian (guitar) 29 July
Trigger Alpert (bass) 3 September
Clyde Hurley (bass) 3 September
Cat Anderson (trumpet) 12 September
Helen Ward (vocal) 19 September
Herb Jeffries (vocal) 24 September
Bill Stegmeyer (clarinet) 8 October
Al Killian (trumpet) 15 October
Bill Harris (trombone) 28 October
Ray Conniff (trombone/arranger) 6 November
Joe Bushkin (piano) 7 November
Billy May (trumpet/arranger) 10 November
Don Ewell (piano) 14 November
Al Lucas (bass) 16 November
Norman Keenan (bass) 23 November
Benny Moten (bass) 30 November
Charlie Ventura (saxes) 2 December
Bob Scobey (trumpet) 9 December
Al Drootin (clarinet) 24 December

COMPOSITIONS

J Hubert Blake / Carey Morgan: *Bugle Call Rag*
Raymond Hubbell / John Golden: *Poor Butterfly*
Tony Jackson / Egbert Van Alstyne / Gus Kahn: *Pretty Baby*
Spencer Williams / Roger Graham / Dave Peyton: *I Ain't Got Nobody*

RECORDINGS

Wilbur Sweatman (NYC, December): *My Hawaiian Sunshine / Down Home Rag*
Fred Van Eps (NYC, 25 March): *Hill and Dale* (NYC, 1 June): *Raggin' the Scale* (December): *Pretty Baby / Teasin' the Cat / Down Home Rag*
Victor Military Orchestra (NYC, 2 February): *Bugle Call Rag* (NYC, 15 September): *Hesitation Blues / Kansas City Blues* (NYC, 19 October): *Brown Skin*

Below: Roy Palmer (trombone), the legendary Sugar Johnny (cornet) and Lawrence Duhé (clarinet) on the stage of a South Side theatre in Chicago.

Photograph Courtesy: *Max Jones*

Ragtime vogue wanes and the jazz craze begins.

The United States enter the war in April.

Original Dixieland Jazz Band at Reisenweber's in NYC. In January they make their first recordings

Fate Marable (27) starts his own bands for Mississippi riverboat excursions.

W.C. Handy (44) brings his orchestra to New York.

Wellman Braud (26) moves to Chicago and leads the Original Creole Orchestra at the Pekin Cafe, and later at Dreamland and the De Luxe Cafe. The band includes Lil Hardin (piano), Sugar Johnny (trumpet), Lawrence Duhé (clarinet), Roy Palmer (trombone), Tubby Hall (drums) and Jimmy Palao (violin).

While King Oliver takes a trip to Alabama, Louis Armstrong (16) deputises in the band at Pete Lala's.

Oscar Celestin's Tuxedo Band open at Suburban Gardens in New Orleans.

Armand J Piron Orchestra are appearing at Tranchina's Restaurant, Spanish Fort, New Orleans. The band includes Peter Bocage and John Lindsey.

Storyville is closed down in New Orleans on 12 November.

BIRTHS

Jimmy Maxwell (trumpet) 9 January
Billy Butterfield (trumpet) 14 January
Sandy Block (bass) 16 January
Streamline Ewing (trombone) 19 January
Billy Maxted (piano) 21 January
Pud Brown (saxes) 22 January
Fred Beckett (trombone) 23 January
Avery Parrish (piano) 24 January
Floyd Smith (guitar) 25 January
Junior Raglin (bass) 16 February
Ade Monsbourgh (saxes) 17 February
Tadd Dameron (piano/arranger) 21 February
Max Jones (writer) 28 February
Ralph Gleason (writer) 1 March
Lee Young (drums) 7 March
Nat 'King' Cole (piano/vocal) 17 March
Buster Harding (piano) 19 March
Curly Russell (bass) 19 March
Johnny Guarnieri (piano) 23 March
Bill Finegan (arranger) 3 April
Morty Corb (bass) 10 April
Denzil Best (drums) 27 April
Jimmy Hamilton (clarinet/tenor sax) 25 May

Dave Lambert (vocal) 19 June
Lena Horne (vocal) 30 June
Buddy Rich (drums) 30 June
Tiny Grimes (guitar) 7 July
Lou McGarity (trombone) 22 July
Charlie Shavers (trumpet) 3 August
Velma Middleton (vocal) 1 September
Laurindo Almeida (guitar) 2 September
Johnny Letman (trumpet) 6 September
Jimmy Butts (bass) 24 September
J.C. Heard (drums) 8 October
George Webb (piano) 8 October
Thelonious Monk (piano) 10 October
Dizzy Gillespie (trumpet) 21 October
Carl 'Bama' Warwick (trumpet) 27 October
Howard Rumsey (bass) 7 November
Sonny White (piano) 11 November
Boots Mussulli (saxes) 18 November
Russell Jacquet (trumpet) 4 December
Billy Moore (piano/arranger) 7 December
Eddie 'Cleanhead' Vinson (alto sax/vocal) 18 December
Butch Ballard (drums) 26 December
Freddie Webster (trumpet)

DEATH

Scott Joplin (49) 11 April

FILM

The Good-for-nothing: fictional movie with an appearance by the Original Dixieland Jazz Band.

COMPOSITIONS

Shelton Brooks: *Darktown Strutter's Ball*
W C Handy: *Beale Street Blues*
James F Hanley / Ballard MacDonald: *(Back Home in) Indiana*
Turner Layton / Henry Creamer: *Everybody's Gone Crazy 'Bout The Doggone Blues*
Luckey Roberts: *Rockaway*
Clarence Williams: *You're Some Pretty Doll*

RECORDINGS

Eubie Blake (NYC, August): *Sarah from Sahara / Hungarian Rag / American Jubilee / Jazzin' Around*
W.C. Handy's Orchestra of Memphis (NYC, 21 September): *Fuzzy Wuzzy Rag / Preparedness Blues* (NYC, 22 September): *The Snaky Blues / Ole Miss Rag / That Jazz Dance / The Old Town Pump / Moonlight Blues* (NYC, 24 September): *The Hooking Cow Blues / The Coburn Blues / A Bunch of Blues* (NYC, 25 September): *Those Draftin' Blues / Sweet Child / Livery Stable Blues / The Storybook Ball / Sweet Cookie Mine*
Original Dixieland Jazz Band (NYC, 30 January): *Darktown Strutter's Ball / Indiana* (NYC, 26 February): *Livery Stable Blues / Dixie Jass Band One-Step* (NYC, 17 August): *Barnyard Blues / Ostrich Walk / Tiger Rag* (NYC, 3 September): *At the Jass Band Ball* (NYC, 21 November): *Look at 'em doing it now* (NYC, 24 November): *Oriental Jazz / Reisenweber Rag*
Noble Sissle (NYC, July): *Mammy's Little Choc'late Cullud Chile* (NYC, November): *That's The Kind Of A Baby For Me / He's Always Hanging Around / Mandy Lou*
Wilbur Sweatman & his Jass Band (NYC, March): *Dance and Grow Thin / I Wonder Why / Boogie Rag / Joe Turner Blues / A Bag of Rags / Dancing an American Rag*

Below: **The Original Dixieland Jazz Band in New York. L to r: Tony Sbarbaro, Eddie Edwards, Nick La Rocca, Larry Shields and Henry Ragas.**

Photograph Courtesy: *Duncan P Schiedt Collection*

1918

A devastating influenza epidemic sweeps the United States, reaching its height in October. The epidemic starts in Boston, New York and Philadelphia and spreads to 46 states, causing between 400,000 and 500,000 deaths.

Okeh Records is established.

King Oliver (33) leaves Kid Ory's New Orleans Band and moves to Chicago to join Lawrence Duhe's Band. Louis Armstrong (17) replaces Oliver in Ory's band in the summer, and from November plays evening excursions for Fate Marable on the Streckfus steamers. Louis marries Daisy Parker, a prostitute from Gretna.

The Louisiana Five record in New York for Emerson.

Bunk Johnson (28) plays with P G Lowery's Band.

World War I ends on 11 November.

Below: **21-year-old Sidney Bechet.**

BIRTHS
Harold 'Money' Johnson (trumpet) 23 February
Cliff Smalls (piano) 3 March
Bill Pemberton (bass) 5 March
Red Callender (bass) 6 March
Sam Donahue (tenor sax) 8 March
Howard McGhee (trumpet) 16 March
Sir Charles Thompson (piano) 21 March
Pearl Bailey (vocal) 29 March
Peanuts Hucko (clarinet) 7 April
Johnny Simmen (writer) 7 April
Jimmy Lewis (bass) 11 April
Tony Mottola (guitar) 18 April
Ella Fitzgerald (vocal) 25 April
Carl Pruitt (bass) 3 June
John Simmons (bass) 14 June
Turk Van Lake (guitar) 15 June
Rusty Dedrick (trumpet) 12 July
Hank Jones (piano) 31 July
Eddie Jefferson (vocal) 3 August
Norman Granz (impresario) 6 August
Knocky Parker (piano) 8 August
Arnett Cobb (tenor sax) 10 August
Ike Quebec (tenor sax) 17 August
Eddie Shu (tenor sax) 18 August
Jimmy Rowles (piano) 19 August
Freddie Kohlman (drums) 25 August
Gerald Wilson (trumpet/leader) 4 September
Hubert Rostaing (clarinet/tenor sax) 17 September
Bill Graham (alto sax) 18 September
Tommy Potter (bass) 21 September
Jimmy Blanton (bass) 5 October
Bobby Byrne (trombone) 10 October
Chubby Jackson (bass) 25 October
Wild Bill Davis (organ) 24 November
Joe Williams (vocal) 12 December
John Hardee (tenor sax) 20 December
Panama Francis (drums) 21 December
Eddie Safranski (bass) 25 December
Jimmy Jones (piano) 30 December

COMPOSITIONS
Bob Carleton: *Ja-Da*
Harry Carroll / Joseph McCarthy: *I'm Always Chasing Rainbows*
Eddie Green: *A Good Man Is Hard To Find*
Turner Layton / Henry Creamer: *After You've Gone*
Harold Weeks / Oliver G Wallace: *Hindustan*

RECORDINGS
Louisiana Five (NYC, December): *Heart Sickness Blues / Laughing Blues / A Good Man is Hard to Find*
Original Dixieland Jazz Band (NYC, 18 March): *At the Jazz Band Ball / Ostrich Walk* (NYC, 25 March): *Skeleton Jangle / Tiger Rag* (NYC, 25 June): *Bluin' the Blues / Fidgety Feet / Sensation Rag* (NYC, 17 July): *Mournin' Blues / Clarinet Marmalade Blues / Lazy Daddy*
Wilbur Sweatman's Original Jazz Band (NYC, 29 March): *Regretful Blues / Everybody's Crazy 'Bout the Doggone Blues, But I'm Happy* (NYC, 31 May): *The Darktown Strutter's Ball / Goodbye Alexander* (NYC, 15 June): *Indianola / Oh! You La! La!* (NYC, 17 August): *Rockabye Your Baby with a Dixie Melody / Those Draftin' Blues* (NYC, 22 August): *Has Anybody seen my Corinne?* (NYC, 7 October): *Dallas Blues* (NYC, 5 December): *Ringtail Blues / Bluin' the Blues*
Fred Van Eps (June): *Key to Key Rag*

1919

The US Congress passes the Volstead Act, and National Prohibition begins in October.

Original Dixieland Jazz Band in London.

Kid Ory (29) moves to California, forms his own band in November.

Sidney Bechet (22) travels to Europe (June) with Will Marion Cook Orchestra. Stays on in London with a breakaway unit led by drummer Benny Peyton.

Brunswick Records is established.

BIRTHS

Al McKibbon (bass) 1 January
Herbie Nichols (piano) 3 January
Steve Jordan (guitar) 15 January
Israel Crosby (bass) 19 January
Snooky Young (trumpet) 3 February
Buddy Morrow (trombone/leader) 8 February
Bernie Privin (trumpet) 12 February
Harry Lim (record producer) 23 February
Fred Katz (cello) 25 February
Mercer Ellington (trumpet/leader) 11 March
George Avakian (record producer) 15 March
Leroy Lovett (piano) 17 March
Lennie Tristano (piano) 19 March
Benny Harris (trumpet) 23 April
Mary Ann McCall (vocal) 4 May
Georgie Auld (tenor sax) 19 May
Johnny Bothwell (alto sax) 23 May
Herbie Fields (saxes) 24 May
Calvin Jackson (piano) 26 May
Phil Bodner (saxes) 13 June
Al Viola (guitar) 16 June
Sadik Hakim (piano) 15 July
Joe Comfort (bass) 18 July
Arnold Fishkin (bass) 20 July
Jim Chapin (drums) 23 July
George Shearing (piano) 13 August
John Malachi (piano) 6 September
Peck Morrison (bass) 11 September
Shadow Wilson (drums) 25 September
Hal Singer (tenor sax) 8 October
Art Blakey (drums) 11 October
Babs Gonzales (vocal) 27 October
Joe Benjamin (bass) 4 November
Peter Schilperoort (clarinet/saxes) 4 November
Joe Carroll (vocal) 25 November
Sylvia Syms (vocal) 3 December
Al Williams (piano) 17 December
Barry Galbraith (guitar) 18 December
Anita O'Day (vocal) 18 December
George Treadwell (trumpet) 21 December
Henry Coker (trombone) 24 December
Mitchell 'Booty' Wood (trombone) 27 December

DEATHS

Henry Ragas (27) 18 February
James Reese Europe (38) 10 May

COMPOSITIONS

Felix Bernard / Johnny S Black / Fred Fisher: *Dardanella*
Euday L Bowman: *Twelfth Street Rag*
Victor Herbert: *Indian Summer*
Art Hickman / Harry Williams: *Rose Room*
Charles Warfield / Clarence Williams: *Baby, Won't You Please Come Home*
Clarence Williams / Spencer Williams: *I Ain't Gonna Give Nobody None o' This Jelly Roll*

RECORDINGS

Jim Europe's 369th Infantry Band (NYC, 3-7 March): *Broadway Hit Medley / St Louis Blues / How ya gonna keep 'em down on the farm? / Arabian Night / Indianola / Darktown Strutters Ball / Hesitatin' Blues / Plantation Echoes / That Moaning Trombone / Memphis Blues / Russian Rag / Ja Da* (NYC, 14 March): *Mirandy / On Patrol in No-Man's-Land / Jazz Baby / Jazzola / All of No-Man's-Land is ours / When the Bees Make Honey* (NYC, 7 May): *The Dancing Deacon / That's Got 'Em / Clarinet Marmalade / Missouri Blues / Dixie is Dixie Once More / My Choc'late Soldier Sammy Boy*
W.C. Handy's Memphis Blues Band (NYC, September): *Beale Street Blues / Joe Turner Blues / Hesitating Blues / Yellow Dog Blues*

Below: **The Original Dixieland Jazz Band in London. L to r: Eddie Edwards, J Russel Robinson, Larry Shields, Nick La Rocca, Tony Sbarbaro**
Bottom: **Fate Marable and his Orchestra with 18-year-old Louis Armstrong (cornet) and 21-year-old Baby Dodds (drums)**

Photograph Courtesy: Max Jones

Photograph Courtesy: *Max Jones*

19

CHICAGO

After the closure of Storyville in 1917, the big migration northwards was underway, via the Mississippi River and the railroads. The destination was Chicago, where the nightlife flourished after World War I. The recording industry was based in Chicago and in 1920, with the arrival of the phonograph and wax records, it really took off.

The great jazz era of the twenties centred on Chicago, and the main entertainment area was the South Side, the downtown section south of the Chicago River. A large proportion of the jazz spots were in this district, featuring musicians like King Oliver, Louis Armstrong, Kid Ory, Johnny Dodds, Jelly Roll Morton and Earl Hines.

CHICAGO NIGHTSPOTS

The Annex
2840 South State Street
2300 South State Street (October 1934–1939)
Apex Club
E35th Street between South Prairie Avenue and South Calumet Avenue (1926–1928).
Bacon's Casino
E49th Street & South Wabash Avenue (1927–1945)
Bee Hive Club
E55th Street & South Harper Avenue (1948–1956).
Blackhawk Restaurant
139 North Wabash Avenue, south of East Randolph (1920's–40's).
Blue Note Club
3 North Clark Street at West Randolph (1940's–50's).
Club Alabam
747 North Rush Street at West Chicago Avenue (1920's).
Club De Lisa
5516 South State Street (1933–41)
5521 South State Street (1941–?)
Colosimo Café
2126 South Wabash Avenue
Dave's Café
E51st Street & South Michigan Avenue (–1934)
343 E55th Street (1934–1936)
De Luxe Café
3503 South State Street (1920's)
Dreamland Ballroom
3518–20 South State Street (1912–)
Dreamland Café
3518–20 South State Street (–1928)
Harmon's Dreamland Ballroom
South Ashland Avenue & West Van Buren (1915–1930)
Elite Club
3030 South State Street
Entertainer's Club
E35th & Michigan Avenue
Fiume Café
South State Street, north of 35th Street (1919–)
Friar's Inn
South Wabash Avenue & East Van Buren Street (1920's)
Garrick Stage Bar
West Randolph Street & North Clark Street (1940's)
Grand Terrace
3955 South Parkway (1928–1937)
315–317 E35th Street at South Calumet (1937–)
Grand Theatre
3110–3112 South State Street at 31st Street
El Grotto
6412 South Cottage Grove Avenue at E64th Street (in the basement of the Pershing Hotel)
It Club
5450 South Michigan Boulevard (1930's)

Jazz Ltd
11 East Grand Avenue (1947–late 60's)
Joe Segal's Jazz Showcase
636 South Michigan Street (Blackstone Hotel) (from 1970's)
Kelly's Stables
431 North Rush Street at East Kinzie Street (1920's)
Lamb's Café
North Clark Street & West Randolph Street (1915–1930's)
Lincoln Gardens
459 E31st Street at South Cottage Grove Avenue (1921–1924)
Previously known as the Royal Gardens (1900–1921)
London House
360 North Michigan Avenue (1951–1970's)
McKee's Disc Jockey Lounge
E63rd Street & South Cottage Grove Avenue
Metropolitan Theatre
4644 South Grand Boulevard (1917–1930)
Midnite Club
3140 South Indiana Avenue (1930's)
Midway Gardens
South Cottage Grove between E55th & E63rd (1920's)
Pekin Theatre
2700 South State Street at 27th Street (1905–)
Pershing Hotel
E64th Street at South Cottage Grove
Plantation Café
338 E35th Street at Grand Boulevard (1924–1933)
Regal Theatre
4719 South Parkway (1928–)
Rick's Café Americain
910 North Lakeshore Drive *at the Holiday Inn* (1976–early 80's)
Savoy Ballroom
South Parkway Boulevard & E47th Street (1927–1948)
Schiller Café
318 E31st Street at South Calumet
Sherman Hotel
West Randolph Street & North Clark Street
Sunset Café
315–317 E35th Street at South Calumet (1921–1937)
Sutherland Show Lounge
South Drexel Boulevard & E47th Street 1950's)
Three Deuces
222 North State Street (1935–1940)
Trianon Ballroom
6201 South Cottage Grove Avenue (1930's–1954)
Vendome Theatre
3145 South State Street at 32nd Street (1909–1949)
White City Ballroom
E63rd Street at South Parkway Boulevard (1920's & 1930's)

CHICAGO

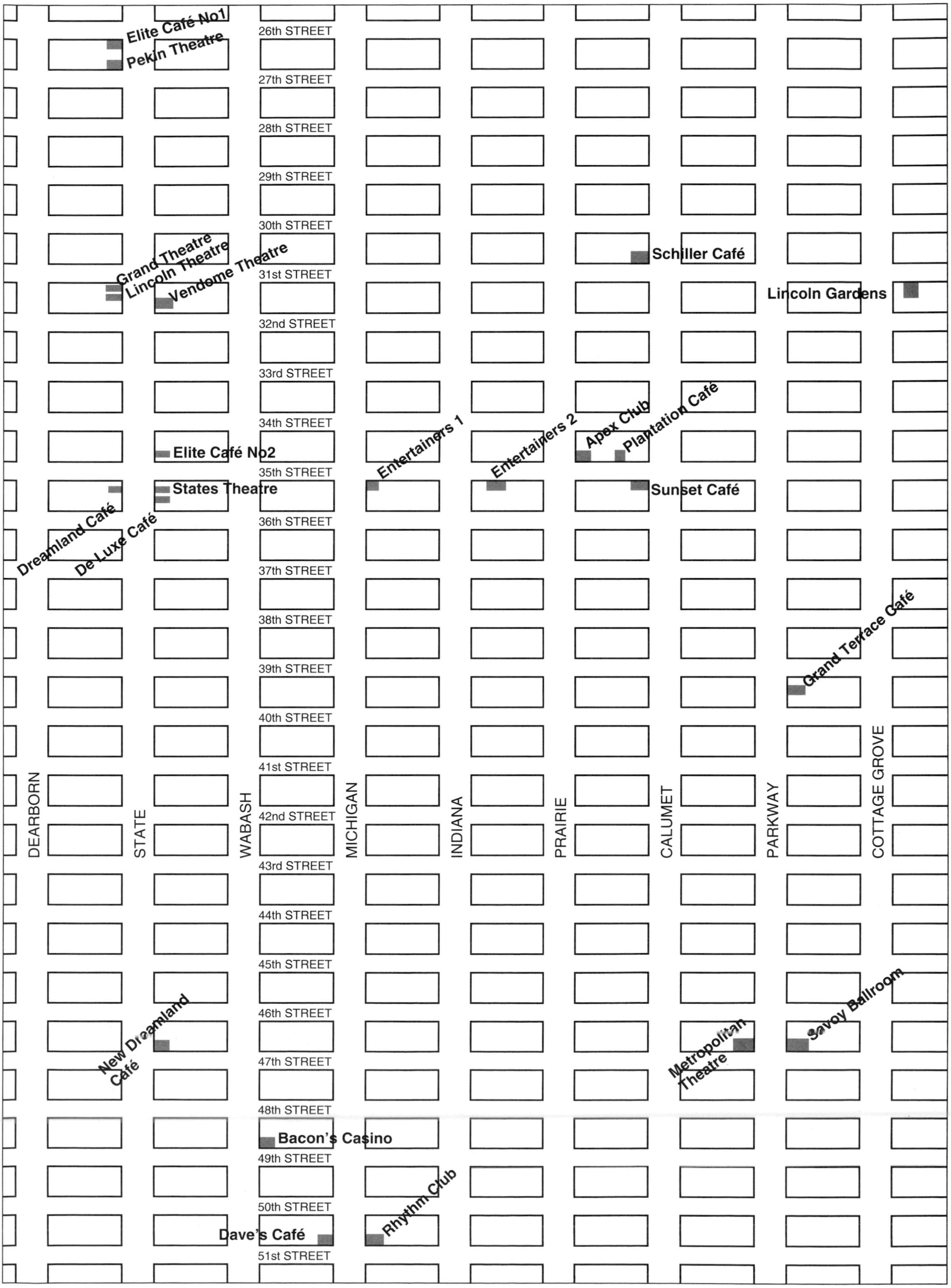

Elite Café No1
Pekin Theatre
26th STREET
27th STREET
28th STREET
29th STREET
30th STREET

Grand Theatre
Lincoln Theatre
Vendome Theatre
31st STREET

Schiller Café

Lincoln Gardens

32nd STREET
33rd STREET
34th STREET

Entertainers 1
Entertainers 2
Apex Club
Plantation Café

Elite Café No2
35th STREET

States Theatre
Sunset Café

Dreamland Café
De Luxe Café
36th STREET
37th STREET
38th STREET
39th STREET

Grand Terrace Café

40th STREET
41st STREET

DEARBORN
STATE
WABASH
MICHIGAN
INDIANA
PRAIRIE
CALUMET
PARKWAY
COTTAGE GROVE

42nd STREET
43rd STREET
44th STREET
45th STREET

New Dreamland Café
46th STREET

Metropolitan Theatre
Savoy Ballroom

47th STREET
48th STREET

Bacon's Casino
49th STREET

Rhythm Club
50th STREET

Dave's Café
51st STREET

King Oliver (35) takes over the leadership of the Creole Jazz Band to play a residency at the Dreamland Cafe in Chicago. The band comprises: King Oliver (cornet), Honore Dutrey (trombone), Ed Garland (bass), Lil Hardin (piano), Minor 'Ram' Hall (drums) and Jimmie Noone (clarinet), soon replaced by Johnny Dodds.

Mamie Smith (30) becomes the first blues singer to record. Her 10 August recording of 'Crazy Blues' becomes a hit for Okeh Records.

Radio broadcasting becomes a public service for the first time when Station KDKA in Pittsburgh broadcasts the results of the presidential election in November.

First electical recordings of phonograph discs.

BIRTHS

Betty Roche (vocal) 9 January
Bob Enevoldsen (trombone) 11 January
George Handy (piano/arranger) 17 January
Ray Abrams (tenor sax) 23 January
Jimmy Forrest (tenor sax) 24 January
Earl Watkins (drums) 29 January
Joe Mondragon (bass) 2 February
Jack Lesberg (bass) 14 February
Hall Overton (piano/composer) 23 February
Eddie Chamblee (tenor sax) 24 February
Abe Most (clarinet) 27 February
Ike Carpenter (piano/leader) 11 March
Marian McPartland (piano) 20 March
John La Porta (saxes) 1 April
Art Van Damme (accordion) 9 April
Walter 'Gil' Fuller (composer) 14 April
Buzzy Drootin (drums) 22 April
John Lewis (piano) 3 May
Al Hendrickson (guitar) 10 May
Joe Roland (vibes) 17 May
Bill Barber (tuba) 21 May
Peggy Lee (vocal) 26 May

Britt Woodman (trombone) 4 June
Kurt Edelhagen (piano/leader) 5 June
Shelly Manne (drums) 11 June
Hazel Scott (piano/vocal) 11 June
Herbie Harper (trombone) 2 July
Dick Kenney (trombone) 6 July
Paul Gonsalves (tenor sax) 12 July
Jerry Lloyd (trumpet) 17 July
Lennie Felix (piano) 16 August
George Duvivier (bass) 17 August
Don Lamond (drums) 18 August
Leonard Gaskin (bass) 25 August
Charlie Parker (alto sax) 29 August
Joe Guy (trumpet) 20 September
Yusef Lateef (saxes) 9 October
Ray Linn (trumpet) 20 October
Wendell Marshall (bass) 24 October
Dave Brubeck (piano) 6 December
Clark Terry (trumpet) 14 December
Marshall Brown (valve trombone) 21 December
Jerome Richardson (saxes) 25 December
Irving Ashby (guitar) 29 December
Albert McCarthy (writer)

COMPOSITIONS

Con Conrad / J Russel Robinson: *Margie / Palesteena / Singin' The Blues (Till My Daddy Comes Home)*
Lindsay McPhail / Walter Michels: *San*
Vincent Rose / Richard Coburn / John Schonburger: *Whispering*
Vincent Rose / Al Jolson / Buddy De Sylva: *Avalon*
Richard Whiting / Raymond B Egan: *The Japanese Sandman*

RECORDS

Eddie Edwards' Jazz Orchestra (NYC, 26 January): *Afghanistan / Irene-Medley*
Lucille Hegamin (NYC, November): *The Jazz Me Blues / Everybody's Blues*
Original Dixieland Jazz Band (London, 8 January): *My Baby's Arms / Tell Me / I've Got My Captain Working For Me Now* (London, 10 January): *I'm Forever Blowing Bubbles / Mammy O' Mine / I've Lost My Heart in Dixieland* (London, 14 May): *Sphinx / Alice Blue Gown / Soudan* (NYC, 1 December): *Margie* (NYC, 4 December): *Palesteena* (NYC, 30 December):*Broadway Rose / Sweet Mamma*
Noble Sissle/Eubie Blake (NYC, July): *Broadway Blues* (NYC, December): *Crazy Blues*
Mamie Smith (NYC, 10 August): *Crazy Blues / It's Right Here For You* (NYC, 12 September): *Fare Thee Honey Blues / The Road is Rocky* (NYC, 5 November): *Mem'ries of You, Mammy / If You Don't Want Me Blues* (NYC, 6 November): *Don't Care Blues / Lovin' Sam from Alabam*
Wilbur Sweatman's Original Jazz Band (NYC, 10 June): *But* (NYC, 23 June): *Think of Me Little Daddy*
Fred Van Eps (NYC, May): *Palm Beach Rag* (NYC, 22 September): *A Bunch of Rags* (NYC, 23 September): *St Louis Tickle*

Photograph courtesy: *Max Jones*

Photograph courtesy: *Duncan P Schiedt Collection*

Above: Mamie Smith and her Jazz Hounds publicise the first blues recording. The pianist is Willie 'The Lion' Smith.
Left: Louis Armstrong (19) poses with his mother and sister in New Orleans.

Opposite page: King Oliver and his Band in San Francisco. Minor Hall (drums), Honoré Dutrey (trombone), Lil Hardin (piano) and Johnny Dodds (clarinet) join in the hokum.

1921

King Oliver Creole Jazz Band at the Pergola Dancing Pavilion in San Francisco from June to December.

New Orleans Rhythm Kings, with Paul Mares, George Brunies and Leon Ropollo are resident at Friars Inn in Chicago.

In September, Louis Armstrong (20) leaves Fate Marable and returns to New Orleans. He works at Tom Anderson's Cabaret Club before joining Zutty Singleton's Trio at the Fernandez Club.

'Radio fever' grips the US providing work for thousands of musicians.

BIRTHS

Ray Sims (trombone) 18 January
André Hodeir (writer) 22 January
Arnold Ross (piano) 29 January
Bernie Leighton (piano) 30 January
Hans Koller (tenor sax) 12 February
Wardell Gray (tenor sax) 13 February
Tommy Gwaltney (clarinet) 28 February
Kenny Baker (trumpet) 1 March
Eddie 'Lockjaw' Davis (tenor sax) 2 March
Vinnie Burke (bass) 15 March
Harry Babasin (bass) 19 March
Steve Race (piano/broadcaster) 1 April
Boomie Richman (tenor sax) 2 April
Candido (conga) 22 April
Jimmy Giuffre (saxes) 26 April
Freddy Randall (trumpet) 6 May
Paul Quinichette (tenor sax) 7 May
Humphrey Lyttelton (trumpet) 23 May
Allen Tinney (piano) 28 May
Alan Clare (piano) 31 May
Marty Napoleon (piano) 2 June
Ernie Royal (trumpet) 2 June
Tal Farlow (guitar) 7 June
Erroll Garner (piano) 15 June
Tony Scott (clarinet) 17 June
Irv Kluger (drums) 9 July
George Barnes (guitar) 17 July
Mary Osborne (guitar) 17 July
Billy Taylor (piano) 24 July
Herb Ellis (guitar) 4 August
Buddy Collette (saxes) 6 August
Warren Covington (trombone) 7 August
Tony Aless (piano) 22 August
Norris Turney (saxes) 8 September
Gene Roland (composer) 15 September
Jon Hendricks (vocal) 16 September
Bill De Arango (guitar) 20 September
Chico Hamilton (drums) 21 September
Roy Kral (piano/vocal) 10 October
Monk Montgomery (electric bass) 10 October
Julius Watkins (french horn) 10 October
Betty Bennett (vocals) 23 October
Chico O'Farrell (composer) 28 October
Eddie Calhoun (bass) 13 November
Jack Marshall (guitar) 23 November
John Bunch (piano) 1 December

DEATHS

Tony Jackson (45) 20 April *syphilis*

COMPOSITIONS

Eubie Blake/Noble Sissle:*Bandana Days/I'm Just Wild About Harry/Love Will Find A Way/Shuffle Along*
Nacio Herb Brown / King Zany / Arthur Freed: *When Buddha Smiles*
Zez Confrey: *Kitten On The Keys*
W C Handy: *Loveless Love*
Turner Layton/Henry Creamer:*Dear Old Southland / Strut Miss Lizzie*
Fred Meinken / Dave Ringle: *Wabash Blues*
Gus Mueller / Buster Johnson / Henry Busse / Leo Wood: *Wang Wang Blues*
Ted Snyder / Harry B Smith / Francis Wheeler: *The Sheik Of Araby*
Maurice Yvain / Channing Pollock: *My Man*

RECORDS

Bailey's Lucky Seven (NYC, October): *How Many Times? / Wimmin* (NYC, December): *I've Got My Habits On / In My Heart, On My Mind, All Day Long*
Eubie Blake & his Shuffle Along Orchestra (NYC,

Photograph courtesy: Max Jones

Right: 18-year-old Bix Beiderbecke.

15 July): *Baltimore Buzz / Bandana Days*
Johnny Dunn & his Original Jazz Hounds (NYC, 21 December): *Bugle Blues / Birmingham Blues*
Lucille Hegamin (NYC, February): *Arkansas Blues / I'll Be Good But I'll Be Lonesome* (NYC, March): *He's My Man / Mama Whip – Mama Spank* (NYC, April): *I Wonder Where my Brownskin Daddy's Gone? / You'll Want My Love* (NYC, May): *I Like You Because You Have Such Loving Ways / Wang-Wang Blues / Strut, Miss Lizzie / Sweet Mama, Papa's Getting Mad* (NYC, May-June): *Lonesome Monday Morning Blues / Getting Old Blues* (NYC, October): *Mississippi Blues / Wabash Blues* (NYC, November): *Ain't Giving Nothin' Away / Can't Feel Jolly Blues*
Alberta Hunter (NYC, May): *He's a Darned Good Man / How Long, Sweet Daddy, How Long? / Bring Back the Joys / Someday, Sweetheart*
James P. Johnson (NYC, August): *The Harlem Strut* (NYC,18 October): *Keep Off The Grass/Carolina Shout*
Original Dixieland Jazz Band (NYC, 28 January): *Home Again Blues / Crazy Blues* (NYC, 3 May): *Jazz Me Blues* (NYC, 25 May): *St Louis Blues / Royal Garden Blues* (NYC, 7 June): *Dangerous Blues* (NYC, 1 December): *Bow Wow Blues*
Noble Sissle (NYC, 2 February): *Royal Garden Blues* (NYC, 2 March): *Boll Weevil Blues / Loveless Love* (NYC, 18 March): *Low Down Blues / Long Gone / My Mammy's Tears* (NYC, 3 May): *Baltimore Buzz / In Honeysuckle Time* (NYC, 9 June): *Love Will Find A Way / Oriental Blues* (NYC, 27 July): *I've Got The Blues, But I'm Just Too Mean To Cry / Arkansas Blues* (NYC, 10 October): *I've Got The Red, White And Blues / I'm A Doggone Struttin' Fool*
Mamie Smith (NYC, January): *Royal Garden Blues / Shim-me-King's Blues* (February): *Jazzbo Ball / What Have I Done? / Frankie's Blues / 'U' Need Some Lovin' Blues* (May): *Dangerous Blues* (5 August): *Daddy, Your Mama is Lonesome For You / I Want a Jazzy Kiss* (18 August): *Sax-O-Phoney Blues / Sweet Man O' Mine* (23 August): *Mama Whip! Mama Spank! / I'm Free, Single, Disengaged, Looking For Someone to Love* (29 August): *Weepin' / A-wearyin' Away the Blues* (30 August): *Down Home Blues / Get Hot* (31 August): *Oh! Joe / A Little Kind Treatment* (5 September): *Arkansas Blues / The Wang-Wang Blues* (10 September): *Stop! Rest a While / Sweet Cookie* (12 October): *Let's Agree to Disagree / Rambling Blues / Cubanita*
Trixie Smith (NYC, September): *Desperate Blues / Trixie's Blues* (November): *You Missed a Good Woman When You Picked All Over Me / Long Lost Weary Blues*
Ethel Waters (NYC, 21-22 March): *The New York Glide / At the New Jump Steady Ball* (April-May): *Oh Daddy / Down Home Blues* (August): *One Man Nan / There'll Be Some Changes Made* (September): *'Frisco Jazz Band Blues / Royal Garden Blues / Bugle Blues*
Clarence Williams (NYC, 11 October): *Roumania / The Dance They Call the Georgia Hunch / Pullman Porter Blues*

Photograph courtesy: Duncan P Schiedt Collection

1922

King Oliver (37) and the Creole Orchestra return to Chicago and open at the Lincoln Gardens Café in mid-June. Oliver sends to New Orleans for Louis Armstrong (21) who arrives in Chicago to join the band on 8 July.

Duke Ellington (23) makes his first, unsuccessful, trip to New York with Otto Hardwick (18) and Sonny Greer (19).

Coleman Hawkins (18) is with Mamie Smith (32) and her Jazz Hounds.

Kid Ory (36) records in Los Angeles with his Sunshine Orchestra.

Fats Waller (18) makes his recording debut in October.

Friars Society Orchestra record for Gennett.

BIRTHS

Harold Minerve (alto sax) 3 January
Frank Wess (tenor sax) 4 January
Ray Anthony (trumpet) 20 January
Jimmy Wyble (guitar) 25 January
Conrad Gozzo (trumpet) 6 February
Joe Dodge (drums) 9 February
Bob Carter (bass) 11 February
Clyde Lombardi (bass) 18 February
Joe Wilder (trumpet) 22 February
Johnny Carisi (trumpet/arranger) 23 February
Eddie 'Lockjaw' Davis (tenor sax) 2 March
Jackie Mills (drums) 11 March
Brian Rust (discographer) 19 March
King Pleasure (vocal) 24 March
Duke Jordan (piano) 1 April
Mongo Santamaria (conga/leader) 7 April
Carmen McRae (vocal) 8 April
Paul Smith (piano) 17 April
Mundell Lowe (guitar) 21 April
Charles Mingus (bass) 22 April
Lou Stein (piano) 22 April

Aaron Bell (bass) 24 April
Jean 'Toots' Thielemans (guitar/harmonica) 29 April
Floyd 'Candy' Johnson (tenor sax) 1 May
Gerald Wiggins (piano) 12 May
Eddie Bert (trombone) 16 May
Kai Winding (trombone) 18 May
Specs Powell (drums) 5 June
Beryl Booker (piano) 7 June
Gösta Theselius (tenor sax/piano) 9 June
Jaki Byard (piano) 15 June
Manny Albam (composer) 24 June
Johnny Smith (guitar) 25 June
Mousie Alexander (drums) 29 June
Ralph Burns (piano/arranger) 29 June
Bruce Turner (alto sax) 5 July
Danny Bank (baritone sax) 17 July
Joachim-Ernst Berendt (writer/producer) 20 July
Ernie Wilkins (saxes/composer) 20 July
Big Nick Nicholas (tenor sax) 2 August
Earl Swope (trombone) 4 August
Arv Garrison (bass) 17 August
Jack Sperling (drums) 17 August

Rolf Ericson (trumpet) 29 August
Joe Newman (trumpet) 7 September
Jack Costanzo (bongos) 24 September
Sammy Benskin (piano) 27 September
Nat Shapiro (writer/record producer) 27 September
Oscar Pettiford (bass) 30 September
Von Freeman (tenor sax) 3 October
Stan Hasselgard (clarinet) 4 October
Bernard Peiffer (piano) 23 October
Neal Hefti (trumpet/composer) 29 October
Illinois Jacquet (tenor sax) 31 October
Ted Nash (tenor sax) 31 October
Ralph Sutton (piano) 4 November
Al Hirt (trumpet) 7 November
Bobby Donaldson (drums) 29 November
Sol Yaged (clarinet) 8 December
Cecil Payne (baritone sax) 14 December
Lil Green (vocal)
Buddy Stewart (vocal)

COMPOSITIONS

Zez Confrey: *Stumbling*
Walter Donaldson / Gus Kahn: *My Buddy*
Edgar Dowell / Mamie Medina: *That Da Da Strain*
Cliff Friend / Irving Mills: *Lovesick Blues*
A Harrington Gibbs / Joe Grey / Leo Wood: *Runnin' Wild*
Turner Layton / Henry Creamer: *'Way Down Yonder in New Orleans*
Armand J Piron: *I Wish I Could Shimmy Like My Sister Kate*
Roy Turk / J Russel Robinson / Addy Britt: *Aggravatin' Papa*
Clarence Williams / Porter Grainger / Graham Prince: *'Tain't Nobody's Bizness If I Do*
Dick Winfree / Phil Boutelje: *China Boy*

Photograph courtesy: *Max Jones*

1922

RECORDS

Bailey's Lucky Seven (NYC, 1 February): *My Mammy Knows / On The 'Gin 'Gin 'Ginny Shore* (NYC, 18 March): *I Wonder Blues / Pick Me Up and Lay Me Down In Dear Old Dixieland* (NYC, 1 April): *Poor Little Me / Don't Leave Me, Mammy* (NYC, 13 April): *Hortense / Carolina Rolling Stone / California* (NYC, 19 April): *Do It Again / Some Sunny Day* (NYC, 23 May): *Kicky-Koo / Those Longing For You Blues* (NYC, 30 May): *Rock Me In My Swanee Cradle* (NYC, 6 June): *Dancing Fool / Those Longing For You Blues / Kicky-Koo* (NYC, 16 June): *Sweet Indiana Home / Nobody Lied* (NYC, 13 July): *Mary Dear / Who'll Take My Place? / 'Neath The South Sea Moon* (NYC, 17 August): *Truly / Hot Lips / Chicago* (NYC, 19 September): *No Wonder I'm Lonesome / Tomorrow / Homesick* (NYC, 6 October): *Stuttering / Toot-Toot-Tootsie / Carolina In The Morning* (NYC, 10 November): *Carolina Home / Gee, But I Hate To Go Home Alone / Tomorrow Morning* (NYC, 17 November): *Bees Knees / Lost / Where The Bamboo Babies Grow* (NYC, 8 December): *'Way Down Yonder In New Orleans / Open Your Arms, My Alabammy / Baby Blue Eyes*

Johnny Dunn & his Original Jazz Hounds (NYC, 24 February): *Put and Take / Moanful Blues* (NYC, 18 August): *Hawaiian Blues* (NYC, 21 September): *Four O'Clock Blues*

W.C. Handy's Memphis Blues Band (NYC, January): *St Louis Blues / Yellow Dog Blues* (NYC, March): *She's a Mean Job / Muscle Shoal Blues*

Lucille Hegamin (NYC, January): *He May Be Your Man, But He Comes to See Me Sometimes / You've Had Your Day* (NYC, 26 February): *I've Got The Wonder Where He Went Blues* (NYC, 30 April): *State Street Blues / High Brown Blues* (NYC, 16 July): *I've Got To Cool My Puppies Now / Send Back My Honey Man* (NYC, 23 July): *I've Got What It Takes / Can't Get Lovin' Blues* (NYC, August): *Voodoo Blues / You Can Have Him, I Don't Want Him Blues* (NYC, September): *Beale Street Mama / Aggravatin' Papa* (NYC, October): *Papa, Papa / He May Be Your Man* (NYC, December): *Syncopatin' Mama / Your Man – My Man*

Alberta Hunter (NYC, July): *Down Hearted Blues / Daddy Blues / Don't Pan Me / After All These Years* (NYC, July, with Eubie Blake): *I'm Going Away Just To Wear You Off My Mind / Jazzin' Baby Blues* (NYC, September): *You Can't Have It All / Lonesome Monday Morning Blues*

Sara Martin (NYC, 17 October): *Sugar Blues* (NYC, 3 November): *Achin' Hearted Blues* (NYC, 1 December): *Tain't Nobody's Bizness If I Do* (NYC, 14 December): *Mama's Got The Blues / Last Go Round Blues*

Lizzie Miles (NYC, 24 February): *Muscle Shoals Blues / She Walked Right Up and Took My Man Away* (NYC, 11 March): *Virginia Blues / State Street Blues* (NYC, 17 August): *Wicked Blues / He May Be Your Man* (NYC, 27 September): *Lonesome Monday Morning Blues / Please Don't Tickle Me, Babe* (NYC, 18 October): *Hot Lips / Take It, 'Cause It's All Yours*

New Orleans Rhythm Kings (Richmond, Indiana, 29 August): *Eccentric / Farewell Blues / Discontented Blues / Bugle Call Blues* (30 August): *Panama / Tiger Rag / Livery Stable Blues / Oriental*

Original Dixieland Jazz Band (NYC, 23 November): *Toddlin' Blues*

Original Memphis Five (NYC, April): *Gypsy Blues / My Honey's Lovin' Arms* (NYC, 10 May): *Lonesome Mama Blues / Those Longing For You Blues* (NYC, 11 May): *Cuddle Up Blues* (NYC, 14 June): *I Wish I Could Shimmy Like My Sister Kate / Pacific Coast Blues*

Kid Ory's Sunshine Orchestra (LA, June): *Ory's Creole Trombone / Society Blues*

Mamie Smith (NYC, 16 February): *Doo Dah Blues / There's Only One Man / Wabash Blues* (NYC, April-May): *Mean Daddy Blues / Dem Knock-out Blues / Lonesome Mama Blues / New Orleans* (NYC, 27 June): *Mamie Smith Blues / Alabama Blues* (NYC, 15 August): *Stuttering / Those Longing For You Blues* (NYC, 22 August): *Got To Cool My Doggies Now / You Can Have Him, I Don't Want Him, Didn't Love Him Anyway, Blues* (NYC, 6 September): *Sighin' Around With The Blues / That Da Da Strain* (NYC, 6 December): *I Ain't Gonna Give Nobody None O' This Jelly Roll / Don't Mess With Me* (NYC, 8 December): *Mean Man / The Darktown Flappers' Ball* (NYC, 20 December): *I'm Gonna Get You*

Trixie Smith (Long Island City, April): *He May Be Your Man / Pensacola Blues* (September): *Give Me That Old Slow Drag / My Man Rocks Me* (September): *I'm Through With You / Take It, Daddy, It's All Yours* (November, December): *I'm Gonna Get You / 2am Blues*

Fats Waller (21 October): *Muscle Shoals Blues / Birmingham Blues*

Ethel Waters (Long Island City, May): *Jazzin' Babies Blues / Kind Lovin' Blues / Georgia Blues / That Da Da Strain* (June-July): *Tiger Rag / Pacific Coast Blues / Spread Yo' Stuff*

Photograph courtesy: *Terry Dash*

Photograph courtesy: *Max Jones*

Above: Louis Armstrong (21) and King Oliver (37) soon after Louis' arrival in Chicago.

Left: Kid Ory's Original Creole Orchestra in Los Angeles. L to r: Baby Dodds (drums), Kid Ory (trombone), Mutt Carey (trumpet), Ed Garland (bass) and Wade Whaley (clarinet.

Right: Paul Mares (22), leader of The New Orleans Rhythm Kings, resident at Friars Inn in Chicago.

Louis Armstrong (22) is resident with the King Oliver (38) Creole Jazz Band at the Lincoln Gardens in Chicago; the band makes its first recordings for Gennett on 6 April.

Bessie Smith (29) makes her record debut on 16 February for Columbia in New York. *Downhearted Blues* is an immediate hit and Bessie embarks on a successful tour throughout the south.

Fletcher Henderson (24) organises a 10-piece band for the Club Alabam in New York; Coleman Hawkins (19) is a member of the band which makes its recording debut in October.

Ma Rainey (37) makes her recording debut for Paramount in Chicago (December).

Duke Ellington (24) settles in New York. His band are resident at Barron's Club in Harlem and then at the Kentucky Club on Broadway.

The Broadway musical *Runnin' Wild* popularises the Charleston dance craze.

BIRTHS
Milt Jackson (vibes) 1 January
Bobby Tucker (piano) 8 January
Osie Johnson (drums) 11 January
Wyatt Ruther (bass) 5 February
Art Mardigan (drums) 12 February
Mel Powell (piano) 12 February
Buddy de Franco (clarinet) 17 February
Dexter Gordon (tenor sax) 27 February
Chuck Wayne (guitar) 27 February
Bill Douglass (drums) 28 February
Orrin Keepnews (record producer) 2 March
Eddie Wasserman (tenor sax) 5 March
Wes Montgomery (guitar) 6 March
Don Abney (piano) 10 March
Percy Brice (drums) 25 March
Ike Isaacs (bass) 28 March
Thad Jones (trumpet) 28 March
Remo Palmieri (guitar) 29 March
Don Butterfield (tuba) 1 April
Bennie Green (trombone) 16 April
Tony Rizzi (guitar) 16 April
Percy Heath (bass) 30 April
Pat Smythe (piano) 2 May
Guy Warren (drums) 4 May
Red Garland (piano) 13 May
Ellis Larkins (piano) 15 May
Lloyd Trotman (bass) 25 May
Gene Wright (bass) 29 May
Al Harewood (drums) 3 June
Phil Nimmons (clarinet) 3 June
George Russell (composer) 23 June
Elmo Hope (piano) 27 June
Pete Candoli (trumpet) 28 June
Johnny Hartman (vocals) 3 July
Aaron Sachs (tenor sax) 4 July
Philly Joe Jones (drums) 15 July
Bola Sete (guitar) 16 July
Claude Luter (clarinet) 23 July
Roy Porter (drums) 30 July
Bjarne Nerem (tenor sax) 31 July
Jack Parnell (drums) 6 August
Idrees Sulieman (trumpet) 7 August
Jimmy Witherspoon (vocals) 8 August
Dill Jones (piano) 19 August
Wilbur Ware (bass) 8 September
Joe Shulman (bass) 12 September
Arvell Shaw (bass) 15 September
Ralph Sharon (piano/arranger) 17 September
Frank Socolow (tenor sax) 18 September
Fred Hunt (piano) 21 September
Fats Navarro (trumpet) 24 September
Sonny Igoe (drums) 8 October
Lenny Hambro (alto sax) 16 October
Barney Kessel (guitar) 17 October
Bob Graettinger (composer) 31 October
Sam Margolis (tenor sax) 1 November
Willie Cook (trumpet) 11 November
Charlie Mariano (alto sax) 12 November
Serge Chaloff (baritone sax) 24 November
Wes Ilcken (drums) 1 December
Marky Markowitz (trumpet) 11 December
Bob Dorough (piano/vocals) 12 December
Bill Reichenbach (drums) 18 December

COMPOSITIONS
Louis Armstrong: *Weather Bird Rag*
Zez Confrey: *Dizzy Fingers*
Jimmie Cox: *Nobody Knows You When You're Down And Out*
James P. Johnson: *After Hours / Charleston / Old Fashioned Love*
Jelly Roll Morton: *The Pearls / Grandpa's Spells / Kansas City Stomps / Wolverine Blues / London Blues / Mister Jelly Lord*
King Oliver: *Dippermouth Blues*
King Oliver & Alphonse Picou: *Snake Rag*
Jack Pettis / Billy Meyers / Elmer Schoebel: *Bugle Call Rag*
J Russel Robinson / Roy Turk: *Beale Street Mamma*
Vincent Rose /Harry Owens: *Linger Awhile*
Elmer Schoebel / Paul Mares / Leon Roppollo: *Farewell Blues*
Ted Snyder / Harry Ruby / Bert Kalmar: *Who's Sorry Now?*
Fats Waller: *Wildcat Blues*
Clarence Williams / Lucy Fletcher: *Sugar Blues*

RECORDS
Perry Bradford (NYC, May-June): *Fade Away Blues / Day Break Blues*
Ida Cox (Chicago, June): *Any Woman's Blues / 'Bama Bound Blues / Lovin' Is The Thing I'm Wild About / Graveyard Blues / Weary Way Blues* (Chicago, September): *Blue Monday Blues / I Love My Man Better Than I Love Myself / Ida Cox's Lawdy Lawdy Blues / Moanin' Groanin' Blues / Chattanooga Blue / Chicago Bound Blues / Come Right In / I've Got The Blues For Rampart Street* (Chicago, December): *Mama Doo Shee Blues / Worried Mama Blues / So Soon This Morning Blues / Mail Man Blues / Confidential Blues / Bear Mash Blues*
Johnny Dunn & His Original Jazz Hounds (NYC, 14 February): *Hallelujah Blues / Spanish Dreams* (NYC, 13 March): *Dixie Blues* (NYC, 11 April): *Sugar Blues* (NYC, 19 April): *Sweet Lovin' Mama / Vamping Sal* (NYC, 30 April): *Jazzin' Baby Blues / I Promised Not To Holler, But Hey! Hey!*
W.C. Handy's Orchestra (NYC, 5 January): *Aunt Hagar's Blues / Louisville Blues* (NYC, March): *Panama / St Louis Blues / Downhearted Blues / Mama's Got The Blues* (NYC, April): *Sundown Blues / My Pillow and Me* (NYC, May): *Gulf Coast Blues / Farewell Blues* (NYC, 4 June): *Memphis Blues / Florida Blues* (NYC, August): *Ole Miss Blues / Darktown Reveille*
Lucille Hegamin (NYC, March): *Waitin' For The Evenin' Mail / Now You've Got Him Can You Hold Him? / Two-time Dan / Wet Yo' Thumb* (NYC, June): *Bleeding Hearted Blues / Downhearted Blues / Wanna Go South Again Blues / Some Early Morning / Land of Cotton Blues / Sweet Papa Joe* (NYC, August): *Sam Jones Blues / St Louis Gal* (NYC, September): *Cold, Cold Winter Blues / Dina* (NYC, October): *Chattanooga Man / Rampart Street Blues* (NYC, November): *Reckless Daddy / Always Be Careful Mama* (NYC, 8 December): *If You Don't Give Me What I Want / You May Be Fast But Mama's Gonna Slow You Down*
Fletcher Henderson Orchestra (NYC, April): *Farewell Blues / Wet Yo' Thumb* (NYC, 1 May): *Beale Street Mama / Don't Think You'll Be Missed / Downhearted Blues / Gulf Coast Blues / When You Walked Out* (NYC, 13 September): *Dicty Blues / Do Doodle Oom* (NYC, 27 October): *You've Got To Get Hot* (NYC, 27 November): *Shake Your Feet / Linger Awhile* (NYC, 30 November): *Charleston Crazy*
Alberta Hunter (NYC, February): *Come On Home / You Shall Reap Just What You Sow / Tain't Nobody's Bizness / If You Want To Keep Your Daddy Home / Bleeding Hearted Blues / Chirping the Blues / Someone Else Will Take Your Place / Vamping Brown / You Can Have My Man / Aggravatin' Papa / Loveless Love / Bring It With You When You Come* (NYC, May): *Mistreated Blues / Michigan Water Blues / Down South Blues* (NYC, May/June, with Fats Waller): *Stingaree Blues / You Can't Do What My Last Man Did* (Chicago, October): *Experience Blues / Sad and Lonely Blues / Miss Anna Brown / Maybe, Someday*
James P. Johnson (NYC, 28 June): *Weeping Blues / Worried and Lonesome Blues* (Camden NJ, 25 July): *Why Can't You Do What My Last Man Did? / Bleeding Hearted Blues* (NYC, 8 August): *Scouting Around / Toddlin'*
Sara Martin (NYC, 6 April): *Keeps On-a-rainin' / Joe Turner Blues* (NYC, 9 April): *Michigan Water Blues* (NYC, 27 April): *Cruel Backbitin' Blues / Leave My Sweet Daddy Alone* (NYC, 30 April): *Monkey Man Blues* (NYC, 25 July): *Sympathizin' Blues* (NYC, 27 July): *Mistreated Mama Blues* (NYC, 1 August): *Blind Man Blues / Atlanta Blues* (NYC, 3 August): *My Good Man's Blues / Jelly's Blues / Troubled Blues / I'm Satisfied* (NYC, 6 August): *Blue Gum Blues*
Lizzie Miles (NYC, January): *The Yellow Dog Blues / The Black Bottom Blues / He Used To Be Your Man But He's My Man Now / Sweet Smellin' Mama / The Trixie Blues / Four O'clock Blues / Aggravatin' Papa / Tell Me Gypsy / You've Got To See Mama Every Night* (NYC, February): *Your Time Now / Haitian Blues* (NYC, 23 May): *You're Always Messin' Round With My Man* (NYC, 24 May): *Family Trouble Blues/ Triflin' Man* (NYC, 18 June): *My Pillow and Me / Black Man* (NYC, 19 July): *Keep Yourself Together Sweet Papa / Cotton Belt Blues*
Jelly Roll Morton (Richmond, Indiana, 17 July – piano solos): *King Porter Stomp / New Orleans Joys* (18 July): *Grandpa's Spells / Kansas City Stomp / Wolverine Blues / The Pearls*
New Orleans Rhythm Kings (Richmond, Indiana, 12 March): *Sweet Lovin' Man / That's A Plenty / Shimme Sha Wabble / Weary Blues* (13 March): *Da Da Strain / Wolverine Blues / Maple Leaf Rag / Tin Roof Blues* (17 July): *Sobbin' Blues / Marguerite / Angry / Clarinet Marmalade / Mr Jelly Lord* (18 July): *London Blues / Milenberg Joys*
King Oliver's Creole Jazz Band (Richmond, Indiana, 6 April): *Just Gone / Canal Street Blues / Mandy Lee Blues / I'm Going Away To Wear You Off My Mind / Chimes Blues / Weather Bird Rag / Dippermouth Blues / Froggie Moore / Snake Rag* (Chicago, 22 June): *Sweet Lovin' Man / High Society Rag / Sobbin' Blues* (Chicago, 23 June): *Where Did You Stay Last Night? / Jazzin' Babies Blues* (Richmond, 5 October): *Alligator Hop / Zulus Ball / Working Man's Blues / Krooked Blues* (Richmond, 15 October): *Chattanooga Stomp* (Richmond, 16 October): *London (Cafe) Blues / Camp Meeting Blues / New Orleans Stomp* (Richmond, 25 October): *Buddy's Habit / Tears / I Ain't Gonna Tell Nobody / Room Rent Blues* (Richmond, 26 October): *Riverside Blues / Sweet Baby Doll / Working Man Blues / Mabel's Dream* (Richmond, 24 December): *Mabel's Dream / The Southern Stomps / Riverside Blues*
Original Dixieland Jazz Band (NYC, 3 January): *Some Of These Days* (NYC, 20 April): *Tiger Rag / Barnyard Blues*
A J Piron Orchestra (NYC, 3 December): *Bouncing Around / Kiss Me Sweet* (NYC, 11 December): *New Orleans Wiggle / Mama's Gone Goodbye* (NYC, 21 December): *Sud Bustin' Blues / West Indies Blues*
Ollie Powers' Harmony Syncopators (Chicago, September): *Play That Thing* (Chicago, October): *Jazzbo Jenkins*
Ma Rainey (Chicago, December): *Bad Luck Blues / Bo Weavil Blues / Barrel House Blues / Those All Night Long Blues / Moonshine Blues / Last Minute Blues / Southern Blues / Walking Blues*
Bessie Smith (NYC, 16 February): *Downhearted Blues / Gulf Coast Blues* (NYC, 11 April): *Aggravatin' Papa / Beale Street Mama / Baby Won't You Please Come Home Blues / Oh Daddy Blues* (NYC, 26 April): *Tain't Nobody's Bizness If I Do / Keeps On-a-Rainin'* (NYC, 28 April): *Mama's Got The Blues / Outside Of That* (NYC, 14 June): *Sittin' On The Curbstone Blues / Bleeding Hearted Blues / Lady Luck Blues / Yodling Blues* (NYC, 15 June): *Midnight Blues* (NYC, 22 June): *If You Don't, I Know Who Will / Nobody In Town Can Bake A Sweet Jelly*

Roll Like Mine (NYC, 21 September): *Dot 'em Down Blues / Jail House Blues* (NYC, 24 September): *St Louis Gal / Sam Jones Blues* (NYC, 26 September): *Graveyard Dream Blues / Cemetery Blues* (NYC, 15 October): *Whoa, Tillie, Take Your Time / My Sweetie Went Away* (NYC, 16 October): *Any Woman's Blues* (NYC, 4 December): *Chicago Bound Blues / Mistreatin' Daddy*

Bessie & Clara Smith (NYC, 4 October): *Far Away Blues / I'm Going Back To My Used To Be*

Clara Smith (NYC, 28 June): *I Got Everything A Woman Needs / Every Woman's Blues* (NYC, 27 July): *Kind Lovin' Blues / Down South Blues / All Night Blues / Play It A Long Time Papa* (NYC, 31 August): *I Want To See My Sweet Daddy Now / Irresistible Blues* (NYC, 7 September): *I Never Miss The Sunshine* (NYC, 13 September): *Awful Moanin' Blues* (NYC, 1 October): *Don't Never Tell Nobody / Waitin' For The Evenin' Mail* (NYC, 2 October): *Kansas City Man Blues / Uncle Sam Blues*

Mamie Smith (NYC, 9 January): *You've Got To See Mamma Ev'ry Night* (NYC, 19 July): *You Can't Do What My Last Man Did* (NYC, 23 July): *Good Looking Papa* (NYC, 5 August): *Lady Luck Blues / Kansas City Man Bues* (NYC, 6 August): *Plain Old Blues* (NYC, 15 August): *Mistreatin' Daddy Blues / Do It, Mr So-and-So* (NYC, 16 August): *My Mammy's Blues*

Trixie Smith (Long Island City, March): *Log Cabin Blues / Voodoo Blues / Tired Of Waitin' Blues / Triflin' Blues*

Erskine Tate's Vendome Orchestra (Chicago, 23 June): *Cutie Blues / Chinaman Blues*

Sippie Wallace (Chicago, 26 October): *Up The Country Blues / Shorty George Blues*

Clarence Williams' Blue Five (NYC, 30 July): *Wild Cat Blues / Kansas City Man Blues* (NYC, 3 October): *Tain't Nobody's Bus'ness If I Do / New Orleans Hop Scop Blues / Oh Daddy Blues* (NYC, 10 November): *Shreveport / Old Fashioned Love* (NYC, 14 November): *House Rent Blues / Mean Blues*

Top right: **The New Orleans Rhythm Kings**
Right: **A J Piron Orchestra** *Below:* **King Oliver's Creole Jazz Band. L to r: Baby Dodds, Honoré Dutrey, King Oliver, Louis Armstrong, Bill Johnson, Johnny Dodds, Lil Hardin.**

Louis Armstrong (23) and Lil Hardin (22) marry on 5 February; Louis leaves King Oliver in June and works with Ollie Powers at Dreamland before joining Fletcher Henderson (25) in New York in September.

Bix Beiderbecke (21), with the Wolverines, makes his recording debut for Gennett on 18 February; he leaves the Wolverines in October to join the Jean Goldkette Orchestra.

Earl Hines (19) forms his first band which includes Benny Carter (17); later he moves to Chicago and opens as a single at the Elite No2 Club.

George Gershwin's *'Rhapsody in Blue'* is premiered by Paul Whiteman Orchestra at Aeolian Hall in New York on 12 February.

Bessie Smith (30) tours as 'Empress of Blues singers'.

Duke Ellington (25) writes the score for the revue *'Chocolate Kiddies'*.

BIRTHS

J. J. Johnson (trombone) 22 January
Joe Albany (piano) 24 January
Alice Babs (vocals) 26 January
Sonny Stitt (saxophones) 2 February
Sammy Nestico (arranger/composer) 6 February
Ray Crawford (guitar) 7 February
Buddy Jones (bass) 17 February
Dave Burns (trumpet) 5 March
Dick Katz (piano) 13 March
Brew Moore (tenor sax) 26 March
Sarah Vaughan (vocals) 27 March
Charlie Rouse (tenor sax) 6 April
Shorty Rogers (trumpet) 14 April
Henry Mancini (piano/composer) 16 April
Clara Ward (vocals) 21 April
Bobby Rosengarden (drums) 23 April
Teddy Edwards (tenor sax) 26 April
Oscar Valdambrini (trumpet) 11 May
Armando Peraza (percussion) 30 May
Herbie Lovelle (drums) 1 June
Hal McKusick (alto sax) 1 June
Lucky Thompson (tenor sax) 16 June
Mat Mathews (accordion) 18 June
Wally Fawkes (clarinet) 21 June
Major Holley (bass) 10 July
Kenny Graham (tenor sax/arranger) 19 July
Al Haig (piano) 22 July
Bill Perkins (tenor sax) 22 July
Louis Bellson (drums) 26 July
Corky Corcoran (tenor sax) 28 July
Martin Williams (writer) 9 August
Dinah Washington (vocals) 29 August
Kenny Dorham (trumpet) 30 August
Putte Wickman (clarinet) 10 September
Ella Mae Morse (vocals) 12 September
Ray Wetzel (trumpet) 22 September
Bud Powell (piano) 27 September
Marty Flax (saxes) 7 October
Terry Gibbs (vibes) 13 October
John Graas (french horn) 14 October
Earl Palmer (drums) 25 October
George Wallington (piano) 27 October
Dick Cathcart (piano) 6 November
Sam Jones (bass) 12 November
Paul Desmond (alto sax) 25 November
Bill Hood (baritone sax) 13 December
Arne Domnerus (alto sax) 20 December
Rita Reys (vocals) 21 December

COMPOSITIONS

Milton Ager / Jack Yellen / Bob Bigelow / Charles Bates: *Hard Hearted Hannah*
Philip Braham / Douglas Furber: *Limehouse Blues*
Ford Dabney / Cecil Mack / Lew Brown: *Shine*
George Gershwin: *Rhapsody in Blue*
George & Ira Gershwin: *Fascinating Rhythm / The Man I Love / Oh, Lady Be Good*
James P. Johnson: *Jungle Nymphs*
Isham Jones / Gus Kahn: *It Had To Be You*
Jelly Roll Morton: *King Porter Stomp*
W B Overstreet / Billy Higgins: *There'll Be Some Changes Made*
Jack Palmer / Spencer Williams: *Everybody Loves My Baby*
Elmer Schoebel / Ernie Erdman / Gus Kahn / Billy Meyers: *Nobody's Sweetheart*
Clarence Williams: *Cake-Walking Babies From Home*

RECORDS

Lovie Austin & her Blues Serenaders (Chicago, November): *Steppin' On The Blues / Traveling Blues*
Perry Bradford (NYC, February): *Charleston, South Carolina / Hoola Boola Dance*
Ida Cox (Chicago, February): *Mean Lovin' Man Blues / Down The Road Bound Blues / Last Time Blues / Worried Anyhow Blues / Chicago Monkey Man Blues / Mean Papa Turn Your Key / Blues Ain't Nothin' Else But* (Chicago, July): *Kentucky Man Blues / Cherry Picking Blues / Wild Women Don't Have The Blues / Worried In Mind Blues / Death Letter Blues / My Mean Man Blues*
Johnny Dunn (NYC, 11 April): *Dunn's Cornet Blues / You've Never Heard The Blues*
Duke Ellington & the Washingtonians (NYC, November): *Choo-Choo / Rainy Nights*
The Goofus Five (NYC, 11 August): *Tessie, Stop Teasin' Me / Them Ramblin' Blues* (NYC, 24 September): *Go Emaline / Hey Hey and Hee Hee* (NYC, 24 October): *Choo-Choo / Go 'Long Mule* (NYC, 25 November): *Everybody Loves My Baby / Oh, How I Love My Darling* (NYC, 16 December): *Oh, Mabel / I Ain't Got Nobody To Love*
Lucille Hegamin (NYC, April): *Mama's The Boss / If You'll Come Back* (NYC, August): *I Threw a Good Man Over For You / Sweet Temptation Man* (NYC, 6 October): *Hard Hearted Hannah / Easy-Goin' Mama*
Fletcher Henderson Orchestra (NYC, January): *Oh, Sister, Ain't That Hot? / Steppin' Out / Mamma's Gonna Slow You Down / House Rent Ball / Darktown Has a Gay White Way / Old Black Joe's Blues / Mistreatin' Daddy* (NYC, 29 January): *Cotton Picker's Ball / Lots O' Mama* (NYC, March): *Sud Bustin' Blues / War Horse Mama / Wish I Had You / Just Blues / I'm Crazy Over You / I Wish I Could Make You Cry / Say Say Sadie* (NYC, 16 April): *My Papa Doesn't Two-Time No Time / Somebody Stole My Gal / After The Storm / Driftwood* (NYC, 21 June): *Houston Blues / Muscle Shoals Blues* (NYC, 15 July): *Hard Hearted Hannah* (NYC, 8 September): *He's The Hottest Man In Town / I Never Care 'Bout Tomorrow* (NYC, 7 October, with Louis Armstrong): *Manda / Go 'Long Mule* (NYC, 13 October): *Tell Me, Dreamy Eyes / My Rose Marie / Don't Forget You'll Regret Day By Day / Shanghai Shuffle* (NYC, 30 October): *Words / Copenhagen* (NYC, 10 November): *One Of These Days / My Dream Man* (NYC, 24 November): *Everybody Loves My Baby* (NYC, November/December): *Prince Of Wails / Mandy Make Up Your Mind*

Alberta Hunter (NYC, February): *Old Fashioned Love / If The Rest of the World Don't Want You* (NYC, 6 November): *Everybody Loves My Baby* (NYC, 8 November): *Texas Moaner Blues* (NYC, 22 December): *Nobody Knows the Way I Feel Dis Mornin' / Early Every Morn / Cake-Walking Babies From Home*
Sara Martin (NYC, 16 September): *Jug Band Blues* (NYC, 19 September): *Don't You Quit Me Daddy / I Got the Cryin' Blues* (NYC, 26 September): *Old Fashioned Sara Blues / Sobbin' Hearted Blues / I'd Rather Be Blue Than Green / Cage of Apes* (NYC, 29 September): *Things Done Got Too Thick / Eagle Rock Me, Papa*
Red McKenzie's Candy Kids (NYC, 12 December): *When My Sugar Walks Down the Street / Panama*
Jelly Roll Morton – piano solos (Richmond, Indiana, 9 June): *Tia Juana / Shreveport Stomps / Froggie Moore / Mamamita / Jelly Roll Blues / Big Foot Ham / Bucktown Blues / Tom Cat Blues / Stratford Hunch / Perfect Rag*
Mound City Blue Blowers (Chicago, 23 February): *Arkansas Blues / Blue Blues* (Chicago, 14 March): *San / Red Hot* (NYC, 9 July): *Barb Wire Blues* (NYC, 10 July): *You Ain't Got Nothin' I Want* (NYC, 10 December): *Tiger Rag / Deep Second Street Blues*
King Oliver – cornet solos, accompanied by Jelly Roll Morton (Chicago, December): *King Porter / Tom Cat*
A J Piron Orchestra (NYC, 8 January): *Do-Doodle-Oom / West Indies Blues* (NYC, 7 February): *Purple Rose of Cairo / Day By Day* (NYC, 15 February): *Ghost of the Blues / Bright Star Blues* (NYC, 18 February): *Lou'siana Swing / Sittin' on the Curbstone Blues* (NYC, 21 February): *Day By Day / Kiss Me Sweet*
Ma Rainey (Chicago, March): *Lost Wandering Blues / Dream Blues / Honey, Where You Been So Long? / Ya-da-do / Those Dogs of Mine / Lucky Rock Blues* (Chicago, April): *South Bound Blues* (Chicago, May): *Lawd, Send Me a Man Blues / Ma Rainey's Mystery Record* (Chicago, August): *Shave 'Em Dry Blues / Farewell Daddy Blues* (NYC, 15 October): *Booze and Blues / Toad Frog Blues / Jealous Hearted Blues* (NYC, 16 October): *See See Rider Blues / Jelly Bean Blues / Countin' the Blues* (Chicago, November): *Cell Bound Blues*
Sioux City Six – Bix, Tram, Miff (NYC, 10 October): *Flock O' Blues / I'm Glad*
Bessie Smith (NYC, 8 January): *Frosty Mornin' Blues* (NYC, 9 January): *Haunted House Blues / Eavesdropper's Blues* (NYC, 10 January): *Easy Come, Easy Go Blues* (NYC, 4 April): *Sorrowful Blues / Pinchbacks, Take 'Em Away / Rockin' Chair Blues* (NYC, 5 April): *Ticket Agent, Ease Your Window Down* (NYC, 7 April): *Bo-Weavil Blues* (NYC, 8 April): *Hateful Blues / Frankie Blues* (NYC, 9 April): *Moonshine Blues* (NYC, 22 July): *Lou'siana Low Down Blues / Mountain Top Blues* (NYC, 23 July): *Work House Blues / House Rent Blues* (NYC, 31 July): *Salt Water Blues* (NYC, 8 August): *Rainy Weather Blues* (NYC, 26 September): *Weeping Willow Blues / The Bye Bye Blues* (NYC, 6 December): *Sing Sing Prison Blues* (NYC, 11 December): *Follow the Deal On Down / Sinful Blues* (NYC, 12 December): *Woman's Trouble Blues / Love Me Daddy Blues* (NYC, 13 December): *Dyin' Gambler's Blues*
Clara Smith (NYC, 11 January): *It Won't Be Long*

Now / Hot Papa (NYC, 18 January): I'm Gonna Tear Your Playhouse Down / I Don't Love Nobody (NYC, 29 January): Good Looking Papa Blues / You Don't Know My Mind (NYC, 31 January): My Doggone Lazy Man / Chicago Blues / 31st Street Blues (NYC, 10 April): War Horse Mama / Cold Weather Papa (NYC, 17 April): West Indies Blues / Mean Papa, Turn In Your Key / The Clearing House Blues (NYC, 23 April): Don't Advertise Your Man (NYC, 30 April): Back Woods Blues (NYC, 19 August): Deep Blue Sea Blues / Texas Moaner Blues (NYC, 20 September): Basement Blues / Mama's Gone, Goodbye (NYC, 30 September): Freight Train Blues / Done Sold My Soul To The Devil (NYC, 7 October): San Francisco Blues (NYC, 15 October): Death Letter Blues / Prescription for the Blues (NYC, 16 December): Steel Drivin' Sam / He's Mine, All Mine
Mamie Smith (NYC, September): My Sweet Man / What You Need Is Me / Just Like You Took My Man Away From Me / Remorseful Blues / Lost Opportunity Blues / Good Time Ball
Trixie Smith (NYC, May): I Don't Know and I Don't Care Blues / Freight Train Blues / Sorrowful Blues (NYC, June): Don't Shake It No More (NYC, September): Praying Blues / Ada Jane's Blues (NYC, December): Ride Jockey Ride / Choo Choo Blues
Sippie Wallace (NYC, 26 May): Mama's Gone, Goodbye / Caldonia Blues / Underworld Blues / Leavin' Me Daddy Is Hard To dDo (NYC, 27 May): Can Anybody Take Sweet Mama's Place? / Stranger's Blues (NYC, 13,14 June): Sud Bustin' Blues / Wicked Monday Mornin' Blues (NYC, 8 November): Baby, I Can't Use You No More / Trouble Everywhere I Roam (NYC, 1 December): I've Stopped My Man / Walkin' Talkin' Blues (NYC, 2 December): I'm So Glad I'm Brownskin / Off and On Blues (NYC, 3 December): He's The Cause of Me Being Blue / Let My Man Alone Blues
Ethel Waters (Chicago, March): Craving Blues
Clarence Williams Blue Five (NYC, 17 October): Texas Moaner Blues
Wolverines (Richmond, Indiana, 18 February): Fidgety Feet / Jazz Me Blues (6 May): Oh Baby / Copenhagen / Riverboat Shuffle / Susie (20 June): I Need Some Pettin' / Royal Garden Blues / Tiger Rag (16 September): Sensation / Lazy Daddy (7 October): Tia Juana / Big Boy (NYC, 5 December): When My Sugar Walks Down The Street (NYC, 12 December): Prince of Wails

Above right: Gertrude 'Ma' Rainey (35)

Photograph courtesy: Max Jones

The Wolverines. L to r: Vic Moore (drums), George Johnson (tenor sax), Jimmy Hartwell (clarinet), leader Dick Voynow (piano), Bix Beiderbecke (cornet), Al Gandee (trombone), Min Leibrook (tuba), Bob Gillette (banjo).

Photograph courtesy: Max Jones

Bessie Smith (31), now billed as 'the Greatest and Highest Salaried Race Star in the World', makes her first recording with Louis Armstrong on 14 January.

Louis Armstrong (24) leaves Fletcher Henderson in November and doubles with his wife's band, Lil Armstrong's Dreamland Syncopators, and the Erskine Tate Orchestra at the Vendome Theatre, Chicago.

The Louis Armstrong Hot Five makes its first recording in Chicago on 12 November.

Bubber Miley (22) joins the Duke Ellington Band.

BIRTHS

Lee Abrams (drums) 6 January
Dave Schildkraut (alto sax) 7 January
Sam Woodyard (drums) 7 January
Max Roach (drums) 10 January
Nat Peck (trombone) 13 January
Marty Paich (piano) 23 January
Barbara Carroll (piano) 25 January
Jutta Hipp (piano) 4 February
Elliot Lawrence (piano/arranger) 14 February
Frank Isola (drums) 20 February
Dave Pell (tenor sax) 26 February
Roy Haynes (drums) 13 March
Sonny Cohn (trumpet) 14 March
Doug Mettome (trumpet) 19 March
James Moody (saxes) 26 March
Harold Ashby (tenor sax) 27 March
Kathy Stobart (tenor sax) 1 April
Stan Levey (drums) 5 April
Gene Ammons (tenor sax) 14 April
Leo Parker (baritone sax) 18 April
Henri Renaud (piano) 20 April
Sonny Berman (trumpet) 21 April
Al Porcino (trumpet) 14 May
Eddie Thompson (piano) 31 May
Al Grey (trombone) 6 June
Nat Hentoff (writer) 10 June
Sahib Shihab (saxes) 23 June
Ken Moule (piano/composer/arranger) 26 June
Wallace Davenport (trumpet) 30 June
Mort Herbert (bass) 30 June
Nat Pierce (piano) 16 July
Cal Tjader (vibes) 16 July
Dom Um Romao (percussion) 3 August
Earl Coleman (vocals) 12 August

Benny Bailey (trumpet) 13 August
George Morrow (bass) 15 August
Oscar Peterson (piano) 15 August
Tony Crombie (drums) 27 August
Bill English (drums) 27 August
Art Pepper (alto sax) 1 September
Mel Torme (vocals) 13 September
Charlie Byrd (guitar) 16 September
Pia Beck (piano/vocals) 18 September
Phil Urso (tenor sax) 2 October
George Wein (piano/impresario) 3 October
Bill Dixon (trumpet) 5 October
Alvin Stoller (drums) 7 October
Zoot Sims (tenor sax) 29 October
Teo Macero (tenor sax/record producer) 30 October
Hubert Fol (alto sax) 11 November
Gunther Schuller (french horn/composer) 11 November
Michael Silva (drums) 12 November
Eddie Harvey (trombone/piano) 15 November
Nick Travis (trumpet) 16 November
June Christy (vocals) 20 November
Sal Salvador (guitar) 21 November
Johnny Mandel (trombone/composer) 23 November
Al Cohn (tenor sax) 24 November
Matthew Gee (trombone) 25 November
Dick Johnson (alto sax) 1 December
Bob Cooper (tenor sax) 6 December
Sammy Davis Jr (vocals) 8 December
Jimmy Smith (organ) 8 December
Dodo Marmarosa (piano) 12 December
Jimmy Nottingham (trumpet) 15 December
Walter Bolden (drums) 17 December
Esther Phillips (vocals) 23 December
Chris Woods (alto sax) 25 December

DEATHS

Emmett Hardy (22) 16 June *tuberculosis*

BOOKS

Alfred Frankenstein: *Syncopating Saxophones*

COMPOSITIONS

Harry Akst / Sam Lewis / Joe Young: *Dinah*
Ben Bernie / Maceo Pinkard / Kenneth Casey: *Sweet Georgia Brown*
Hoagy Carmichael / Mitchell Parish / Fred Callahan: *Washboard Blues*
Hoagy Carmichael / Dick Voynow / Irving Mills: *Riverboat Shuffle*
James P. Johnson: *Carolina Shout*
Jelly Roll Morton: *Milneberg Joys / Shreveport Stomps / Midnight Mama / New Orleans Blues*
Ted Fio Rito / Gus Kahn: *I Never Knew*
Richard Rodgers / Lorenz Hart: *Manhattan*
Fats Waller: *Squeeze me*
Vincent Youmans / Irving Caesar: *Tea For Two*

RECORDS

Louis Armstrong Hot Five (Chicago, 12 November): *My Heart / Yes, I'm In The Barrel / Gut Bucket Blues*
Lovie Austin & her Blues Serenaders (Chicago, April): *Charleston Mad / Charleston, South Carolina / Heebie Jeebies / Peepin' Blues / Mojo Blues* (Chicago, August): *Don't Shake It No More / Rampart Street Blues / Too Sweet For Words*
Bix Beiderbecke & his Rhythm Jugglers (Richmond, Indiana, 26 January): *Toddlin' Blues / Davenport Blues / Nobody Knows What It's All About*
Perry Bradford (NYC, 2 November): *Lucy Long / I Ain't Gonna Play No Second Fiddle*
Oscar Celestin & Original Tuxedo Jazz Orchestra (New Orleans, 23 January): *Original Tuxedo Rag / Careless Love / Black Rag*
Charleston Chasers (NYC, 28 August): *Red Hot Henry Brown / Loud Speakin' Papa*
Ida Cox (NYC, January): *Those Married Men Blues / Misery Blues / Graveyard Bound Blues / Mississippi River Blues / Georgia Hound Blues / Blue Kentucky Blues* (Chicago, April): *Black Crepe Blues / Fare Thee Well Poor Gal / Cold Black Ground Blues / Someday Blues / Mister Man*

Photograph courtesy: *Max Jones*

(Chicago, August): *Mistreatin' Daddy Blues / Long Distance Blues / Southern Woman's Blues / Lonesome Blues* (Chicago, September): *How Long, Daddy, How Long? / How Can I Miss You When I've Got Dead Aim? / I Ain't Got Nobody / Coffin Blues / Rambling Blues / One Time Woman Blues*

Duke Ellington's Washingtonians (NYC, September): *I'm Gonna Hang Around My Sugar / Trombone Blues*

The Goofus Five (NYC, 14 January): *Alabamy Bound / Deep Blue Sea Blues* (NYC, 12 June): *Yes Sir, That's My Baby* (NYC, 28 October): *Clap Hands, Here Comes Charley* (NYC, 21 December): *That Certain Party*

Lucille Hegamin (NYC, February): *Alabamy Bound / Hot Tamale Molly / Everytime / Pick A Sweetie* (NYC, 22 April): *My Sugar / I Had Someone Else Before I Had You*

Fletcher Henderson Orchestra (NYC, 12 January): *I'll See You In My Dreams / Why Couldn't It Be Poor Little Me?* (NYC, 30 January): *Alabamy Bound* (NYC, 18 April): *Memphis Bound / When You Do What You Do* (NYC, 29 May): *Sugar Foot Stomp / What-Cha-Call-Em Blues* (NYC, 23 November): *Spanish Shawl / Clap Hands, Here Comes Charley*

Bertha 'Chippie' Hill (Chicago, 9 November): *Low Land Blues / Kid Man Blues*

Alberta Hunter (NYC, 11 December): *Your Jelly Roll Is Good / Take That Thing Away*

Sara Martin (NYC, 16 November): *Down At The Razor Ball / Mournful Blues / Georgia Stockade Blues* (NYC, 23 November): *I'm Gonna Hoodoo You / What More Can a Monkey Woman Do?*

Red McKenzie's Candy Kids (NYC, 27 January): *Best Black / Stretch It, Boy* (NYC, 7 August): *The Morning After Blues / Happy Children Blues* (NYC, 29 October): *Hot Honey / If You Never Come Back*

Mound City Blue Blowers (NYC, 9 February): *Gettin' Told / Play Me Slow* (NYC, 24 March): *Wigwam Blues* (NYC, 25 March): *Blues in F*

New Orleans Rhythm Kings (New Orleans, 23 January): *Baby / I Never Knew What a Gal Could Do / She's Crying For Me Blues / Golden Leaf Strut* (New Orleans, 26 March): *She's Cryin' For Me / Everybody Loves Somebody Blues*

A J Piron Orchestra (New Orleans, 25 March): *Red Man Blues / Do Just as I Say*

Ma Rainey (Chicago, May): *Army Camp Harmony Blues / Explaining the Blues / Louisiana Hoo Doo Blues / Goodbye Daddy Blues* (Chicago, August): *Stormy Sea Blues / Rough and Tumble Blues / Night Time Blues / Levee Camp Moan / Four Day Honory Scat / Memphis Bound Blues*

Bessie Smith (NYC, 14 January): *The St Louis Blues / Reckless Blues / Sobbin' Hearted Blues / Cold in Hand Blues / You've Been a Good Old Wagon* (NYC, 5 May): *Cake Walkin' Babies* (NYC, 6 May): *The Yellow Dog Blues* (NYC, 14 May): *Soft Pedal Blues* (NYC, 15 May): *Dixie Flyer Blues* (NYC, 26 May): *Nashville Woman's Blues / Careless Love Blues* (NYC, 27 May): *J.C.Holmes Blues / I Ain't Gonna Play No Second Fiddle* (NYC, 23 June): *He's Gone Blues* (NYC, 19 August): *Nobody's Blues But Mine / I Ain't Got Nobody* (NYC, 17 November): *New Gulf Coast Blues / Florida Bound Blues* (NYC, 18 November): *At The Christmas Ball / I've Been Mistreated and I Don't Like It* (NYC, 20 November): *Red Mountain Blues / Golden Rule Blues* (NYC, 9 December): *Lonesome Desert Blues*

Clara Smith (NYC, 7 January): *Nobody Knows The Way I Feel Dis Mornin' / Broken Busted Blues* (NYC, 8 January): *If You Only Knowed / You Better Keep the Home Fires Burning* (NYC, 24 March): *My Good-for-nuthin' Man* (NYC, 27 March): *When I Steps Out / The L&N Blues* (NYC, 3 April): *Shipwrecked Blues / Courthouse Blues / My John Blues* (NYC, 6 July): *Different Way Blues / Down Home Bound Blues* (NYC, 20 August): *My Two-timing Papa / Kitchen Mechanic Blues* (NYC, 1 September): *My Man Blues* (NYC, 24 September): *Onery Blues / You Get Mad* (NYC, 25 September): *Alley Rat Blues / When My Sugar Walks Down The Street / Disappointed Blues* (NYC, 28 September): *I'm Tired of Being Good* (NYC, 10 November): *The Market Street Blues / It Takes The Lawd*

Trixie Smith (NYC, February): *You've Got To Beat Me To Keep Me / Mining Camp Blues* (NYC, March): *The World's Jazz Crazy And So Am I / Railroad Blues* (NYC, December): *Everybody's Doing That Charleston Now / He Likes It Slow / Black Bottom Hop / Love Me Like You Used To Do*

Hersal Thomas (Chicago, 22 February): *Suitcase Blues* (Chicago, June): *Hersal Blues / Wash Woman Blues / Morning Dove Blues*

Hociel Thomas (Richmond, 6 April): *I Can't Feel Frisky Without My Liquor / Worried Down With The Blues / I Must Have It* (Chicago, June): *Worried Down With The Blues / Fish Tail Dance* (Chicago, 11 November): *Gambler's Dream / Sunshine Baby / Adam And Eve Got The Blues / Put It Where I Can Get It / Wash Woman Blues / I've Stopped My Man*

Sippie Wallace (Chicago, 24 February): *Morning Dove Blues / Devil Dance Blues / Every Dog Has His Day* (Chicago, 19 August): *Section Hand Blues / Parlor Social De Luxe* (Chicago, 20 August): *Being Down Don't Worry Me / Advice Blues* (Chicago, 22 August): *Murder's Gonna Be My Crime / The Man I Love* (Chicago, 25 August): *I'm Leaving You / I'm Sorry For It Now / Suitcase Blues / Must Have It*

Ethel Waters (NYC, 12 September): *Pickaninny Blues* (NYC, 20 October): *Sweet Man / Dinah* (NYC, 23 December): *Shake That Thing*

Photograph courtesy: *Max Jones*

Above: Duke Ellington & the Washingtonians at the Kentucky Club in New York. L to r: Sonny Greer (drums), Charlie Irvis (trombone), Bubber Miley (trumpet), Elmer Snowden (banjo), Otto 'Toby' Hardwicke (saxes) and Duke Ellington (piano).

Left: Bix Beiderbecke & his Rhythm Jugglers recording for Gennett in January. L to r: Howdy Quicksell (banjo), Tommy Gargano (drums), Paul Mertz (piano), Don Murray (clarinet), Bix (cornet) and Tommy Dorsey (trombone).

Right: King Oliver's Dixie Syncopators, resident at the Plantation Café in Chicago from March. L to r: Bert Cobb (tuba), Bud Scott (banjo), Paul Barbarin (drums), Darnell Howard (reeds), King Oliver (cornet), Albert Nicholas (reeds), George Filhe (trombone), Bob Schoffner (trumpet), Barney Bigard (reeds), Luis Russell (piano).

Photograph courtesy: *Terry Dash*

1926

Louis Armstrong (25) joins Carroll Dickerson's Sunset Cafe Orchestra in April and continues to double with the Erskine Tate Orchestra at the Vendome Theatre.

Earl Hines (21) tours with the Carroll Dickerson Orchestra.

Red Nichols (21) & his Five Pennies make their recording debut in New York in December.

Ben Pollack (23) organises a band in California which includes Benny Goodman (17) and Glenn Miller (22).

Jelly Roll Morton (36) and his Red Hot Peppers make their first recordings in Chicago on 15 September.

Melody Maker is founded in London.

Bix Beiderbecke (23) rejoins the Jean Goldkette Orchestra.

Wellman Braud (35) and Tricky Sam Nanton (22) join the Duke Ellington Band.

US is divided into two major radio networks with the incorporation of the National Broadcasting System (September).

BIRTHS

Jack Brokensha (vibes/drums) 5 January
Roger Guerin (trumpet) 9 January
Bucky Pizzarelli (guitar) 9 January
Willie Dennis (trombone) 10 January
Melba Liston (trombone)13 January
Phil Guilbeau (trumpet) 16 January
Curtis Counce (bass) 23 January
Mimi Perrin (vocals/piano) 2 February
Bernie Glow (trumpet) 6 February
Pony Poindexter (alto sax) 8 February
Buddy Childers (trumpet) 12 February
Ron Jefferson (drums) 13 February
Bobby Jaspar (tenor sax) 20 February
Dave Bailey (drums) 22 February
Don Rendell (tenor sax) 4 March
Billy Mitchell (tenor sax) 11 March
Max Greger (tenor sax) 2 April
Randy Weston (piano) 6 April
Whitney Balliett (writer) 17 April
Jimmy Rowser (bass) 18 April
Blossom Dearie (piano/vocals) 28 April
Jimmy Cleveland (trombone) 3 May
Jymie Merritt (bass) 3 May
Sonny Payne (drums) 4 May
Herbie Steward (tenor sax) 7 May
Beryl Bryden (vocals) 11 May
Bonnie Wetzel (bass) 15 May
Lou Bennett (organ) 18 May
Elaine Leighton (drums) 22 May
Milt Bernhardt (trombone) 25 May
Miles Davis (trumpet) 25 May
Bud Shank (alto sax) 27 May
Russ Freeman (piano) 28 May
Chuck Thompson (drums) 4 June
Jimmy Gourley (guitar) 9 June
Hank Shaw (trumpet) 23 June
Bobby White (drums) 28 June
Billy Usselton (tenor sax) 2 July
Johnny Coles (trumpet) 3 July
Frank Rehak (trombone) 6 July
Ray Copeland (trumpet) 17 July
Arthur Edgehill (drums) 21 July
Tony Bennett (vocals) 3 August
Urbie Green (trombone) 8 August
Buddy Greco (vocals) 14 August
Mal Waldron (piano) 16 August
George Melly (vocal) 17 August
Frank Rosolino (trombone) 20 August
Med Flory (alto sax) 27 August
Phil Seamen (drums) 28 August
Ernie Henry (alto sax) 3 September
Sol Schlinger (baritone sax) 6 September
Bobby Short (piano/vocals) 15 September
Brother Jack McDuff (organ) 17 September
Jackie Paris (vocals) 20 September
Bill Smith (clarinet) 22 September
John Coltrane (tenor sax) 23 September
Oscar Brown Jr (vocals) 10 October
Sleepy Matsumoto (tenor sax) 12 October
Ray Brown (bass) 13 October
Tommy Whittle (tenor sax) 13 October
Don Elliott (vibes/mellophone) 21 October
Jesse Drakes (trumpet) 22 October
Jimmy Heath (tenor sax) 25 October
Lou Donaldson (alto sax) 1 November
Carlos 'Patato' Valdez (conga) 4 November
Johnny Windhurst (trumpet) 5 November
Irvin Stokes (trumpet) 11 November
George Masso (trombone) 17 November
Claude Williamson (piano) 18 November
Rob Swope (trombone) 2 December
Joe Harris (drums) 23 December
Stan Tracey (piano) 30 December

BOOKS

W.C. Handy & A. Niles: *Blues: an anthology*
Langston Hughes: *The Weary Blues* (poems)
Henry Osgood: *So this is jazz*
Carl Van Vechten: *Nigger Heaven*

COMPOSITIONS

Louis Armstrong / Percy Venable: *I Want a Big Butter and Egg Man*
Boyd Atkins & Richard M. Jones: *Heebie jeebies*
Duke Ellington: *East St Louis Toodle-oo / Birmingham Breakdown*
Ray Henderson / Mort Dixon: *Bye Bye Blackbird*
Ray Henderson / Buddy De Sylva / Lew Brown: *Birth Of The Blues / Black Bottom*
James P. Johnson: *If I could be with you one hour tonight*
Richard M Jones: *Trouble In Mind*
Jelly Roll Morton: *Chicago breakdown / Black bottom stomp / Sidewalk blues / Cannonball blues*
King Oliver: *Snag It*
Kid Ory: *Muskrat Ramble*
Jack Palmer / Spencer Williams: *I've Found a New Baby*
Richard Rodgers / Lorenz Hart: *The Blue Room / Mountain Greenery*
Clarence Williams / Spencer Williams: *What's The Matter Now?*

RECORDS

Lil Armstrong's Serenaders with Louis Armstrong (Chicago, 20 April): *After I Say I'm Sorry / Georgia Bo-Bo*
Lill's Hot Shots with Louis Armstrong (Chicago, 28 May): *Georgia Bo-Bo / Drop That Sack*
Louis Armstrong Hot Five (Chicago, 22 February): *Come Back, Sweet Papa* (Chicago, 26 February): *Georgia Grind / Heebie Jeebies / Cornet Chop Suey / Oriental Strut / You're Next / Muskrat Ramble* (Chicago, 16 June): *Don't Forget To Mess Around / I'm Gonna Gitcha / Dropping Shucks / Whosit* (Chicago, 23 June): *The King Of The Zulus / Big Fat Ma And Skinny Pa / Lonesome Blues / Sweet Little Papa* (Chicago, 16 November): *Jazz Lips / Skid-Dat-De-Dat / Big Butter And Egg Man / Sunset Café Stomp* (Chicago, 27 November): *You Made Me Love You / Irish Black Bottom / Leave Mine Alone*
Lovie Austin & her Serenaders (Chicago, April): *Jackass Blues / Frog Tongue Stomp* (Chicago, August): *Chicago Mess Around / Galion Stomp / In The Alley Blues / Merry Makers Twine*
Bailey's Lucky Seven (NYC, 15 January): *The Roses Brought Me You / Behind The Clouds* (NYC, 1 February): *Dinah / After I Say I'm Sorry* (NYC, 11 February): *Static / Let's Talk About My Sweetie*
Jimmy Bertrand's Washboard Wizards (Chicago, 29 May): *Little Bits / Struggling* (Chicago, 16 September): *Idle Hour Special / 47th Street Stomp*

Perry Bradford (NYC, 21 April): *Just Met A Friend From My Home Town / So's Your Old Man* (NYC, December): *Original Black Bottom Dance / Kansas City Blues*
Junie C Cobb (Chicago, August): *East Coast Trot / Chicago Buzz*
Ida Cox (Chicago, February): *Trouble Trouble Blues / Do Lawd Do / I'm Leaving Here Blues / Night And Day Blues* (Chicago, September): *Don't Blame Me / Scottle De Doo*
Duke Ellington's Washingtonians (NYC, March): *Georgia Grind / Parlor Social Stomp* (NYC, 21 June): *Animal Crackers / Li'l Farina*
Duke Ellington's Kentucky Club Orchestra (NYC, November): *East St Louis Toodle-o / Birmingham Breakdown* (NYC, 29 December): *Immigration Blues / The Creeper*
Jean Goldkette Orchestra with Bix Beiderbecke (NYC, 12 October): *Idolizing / Hush-a-Bye* (NYC, 15 October): *I'd Rather Be The Girl In Your Arms / Sunday / Cover Me Up With Sunshine / Just One More Kiss*
Lucille Hegamin (NYC, February): *No Man's Mama / Dinah / Poor Papa* (NYC, March): *Here Comes Malinda* (NYC, 28 September): *Nobody But My Baby Is Gettin' My Love / Senorita Mine*
Fletcher Henderson Orchestra (NYC, 6 January): *Dinah / I Want Somebody To Cheer Me Up / Let Me Introduce You To My Rosie* (NYC, 20 January): *I Found A New Baby / Nervous Charlie Stomp / Black Horse Stomp* (NYC, 14 May): *The Stampede / Jackass Blues* (NYC, 3 November): *The Henderson Stomp / The Chant* (NYC, 8 December): *Clarinet Marmalade / Hot Mustard*
Bertha 'Chippie' Hill (Chicago, 23 February): *Lonesome, All Alone And Blue / Trouble In Mind / Georgia Man* (Chicago, 14 June): *Leavenworth Blues* (Chicago, 15 June): *Panama Limited Blues / Streetwalker Blues* (Chicago, 23 November): *Pleadin' For The Blues / Pratts City Blues / Mess, Katie, Mess* (Chicago, 26 November): *Lovesick Blues / Lonesome Weary Blues*
Alberta Hunter (NYC, January): *Everybody Does It Now / A Master Man With A Master Mind / I Don't Want It All / I'm Hard To Satisfy / Empty Cellar Blues / Double Crossin' Papa* (NYC, 11 August): *If You Can't Hold The Man You Love / You For Me, Me For You* (NYC, September): *I'm Tired Blues / Wasn't It Nice? / I Didn't Come To Steal Nobody's Man / Everybody Mess Around / Don't Forget To Mess Around / Heebie Jeebies*
Freddie Keppard's Jazz Cardinals (Chicago, September): *Stock Yards Strut /Salty Dog*
Sara Martin (NYC, 24 March): *What's The Matter Now? / I Want Every Bit Of It, I Don't Like It Secondhand* (NYC, 25 March): *Brother Ben / Prisoner's Blues / Careless Man Blues / How Could I Be Blue?* (NYC, 5 September): *Look Out, Mr Jazz / Shipwrecked Blues*
Red McKenzie & Mound City Blue Blowers (NYC, 21 June): *There'll Be Some Changes Made / My Syncopated Melody Man*
Jelly Roll Morton's Red Hot Peppers (Chicago, 15 September): *Black Bottom Stomp / Smoke House Blues / The Chant* (Chicago, 21 September): *Sidewalk Blues / Dead Man Blues / Steamboat Stomp* (Chicago, 16 December): *Someday Sweetheart / Grandpa's Spells / Original Jelly Roll Blues / Doctor Jazz / Cannonball Blues*
New Orleans Wanderers – George Mitchell/Kid Ory/Johnny Dodds (Chicago, 13 July): *Perdido Street Blues / Gate Mouth / Too Tight / Papa Dip*
Red Nichols & his Five Pennies (NYC, 8 December): *Washboard Blues / That's No Bargain* (NYC, 20 December): *Buddy's Habits / Boneyard Shuffle*
King Oliver & his Dixie Syncopators (Chicago, 11 March): *Too Bad / Snag It* (Chicago, 21 April): *Deep Henderson* (Chicago, 21 April): *Jackass Blues* (Chicago, 29 May): *Sugar Foot Stomp / Wa Wa Wa* (Chicago, 23 July): *Tack Annie* (Chicago, 17 September): *Someday, Sweetheart / Dead Man Blues / New Wang-Wang Blues*
Ma Rainey (Chicago): *Slave To The Blues / Yonder Come The Blues / Titanic Man Blues / Chain Gang Blues / Bessemer Bound Blues / Oh My Babe Blues / Wringing and Twisting Blues / Stack O' Lee Blues* (Chicago, March): *Broken Hearted Blues / Jealousy Blues / Seeking Blues / Mountain Jack Blues*

(Chicago, August): *Down In The Basement / Sissy Blues / Broken Soul Blues / Trust No Man* (Chicago, December): *Little Low Mama Blues / Grievin' Hearted Blues / Don't Fish In My Sea*

Luis Russell's Hot Six (Chicago, 10 March): *29th and Dearborn / Sweet Mumtaz* (Chicago, 17 November): *Plantation Joys / Please Don't Turn Me Down / Dolly Mine*

Bessie Smith (NYC, 5 March): *Them 'Has Been' Blues / Squeeze Me / What's The Matter Now? / I Want Ev'ry Bit Of It* (NYC, 18 March): *Jazzbo Brown From Memphis Town / Gin House Blues* (NYC, 4 May): *Money Blues / Baby Doll / Hard Drivin' Papa / Lost Your Head Blues* (NYC, 25 October): *Hard Time Blues / Honey Man Blues* (NYC, 26 October): *One and Two Blues / Young Woman's Blues*

Clara Smith (NYC, 1 May): *Look Where The Sun Done Gone / Rock, Church, Rock* (NYC, 3 May): *Jelly Bean Blues* (NYC, 25 May): *How'm I Doin' / Whip It To A Jelly* (NYC, 26 May): *Salty Dog / My Brand New Papa* (NYC, 15 June): *Ain't Nothin' Cookin' What You're Smellin' / Separation Blues* (NYC, 23 November): *Percolatin' Blues / Ease It / Livin' Humble / Get On Board* (NYC, 29 November): *Cheatin' Daddy* (NYC, 30 December): *You Don't Know Who's Shakin' Your Tree / Race Track Blues*

Above: The Jean Goldkette Orchestra's September tour of New England. Bix Beiderbecke (23) is fourth from left.

Left: Jelly Roll Morton's Red Hot Peppers. L to r: Andrew Hilaire, Kid Ory, George Mitchell, John Lindsay, Jelly Roll, Johnny St Cyr and Omer Simeon.

Below: Louis Armstrong's Hot Five. Louis (cornet), Johnny St Cyr (banjo), Johnny Dodds (clarinet), Kid Ory (trombone) and Lil Hardin (piano).

Mamie Smith (NYC, 27 August): *Goin' Crazy With The Blues / Sweet Virginia Blues* (NYC, 31 August): *What Have You Done To Make Me Feel This Way? / I Once Was Yours, I'm Somebody Else's Now*

Victoria Spivey (St Louis, 11 May): *Black Snake Blues / Dirty Woman's Blues* (St Louis, 13 May): *Long Gone Blues / No More Jelly Bean Blues* (NYC, 12 August): *Hoodoo Man Blues / Spider Web Blues / It's Evil Hearted Me / Santa Fe Blues / Humored and Petted Blues* (NYC, 13 August): *Big Houston Blues / Got The Blues So Bad* (NYC, 16 August): *Blue Valley Blues*

Erskine Tate's Vendome Orchestra (Chicago, 28 May): *Static Strut / Stomp Off, Let's Go*

Hociel Thomas (Chicago, 24 February): *Deep Water Blues / G'wan I Told You / Listen To Ma / Lonesome Hours*

Joe Venuti/Eddie Lang (NYC, 29 September): *Black and Blue Bottom* (NYC, 8 November): *Stringing the Blues*

Sippie Wallace (Chicago, 1 March): *A Jealous Woman Like Me / Special Delivery Blues / Jack O' Diamond Blues* (Chicago, 3 March): *The Mail Train Blues / I Feel Good / A Man For Every Day In The Week* (Chicago, 20 November): *I'm A Mighty Tight Woman / Bedroom Blues*

Fats Waller – pipe organ solos (NYC, 17 November): *St Louis Blues / Lenox Avenue Blues*

Ethel Waters (NYC, 22 January): *I've Found A New Baby / Make Me A Pallet On Your Floor* (NYC, 29 July): *Heebie Jeebies*

Clarence Williams' Stompers (NYC, 4 January): *Spanish Shawl / Dinah* (NYC, 7 April): *Jackass Blues*

Louis Armstrong (26) leads his own big band in February at the Sunset Café, taking over the Carroll Dickerson Band. Louis doubles with Erskine Tate until April and then with Clarence Jones' Orchestra at the Metropolitan Theatre. In November Louis, Earl Hines (22) and Zutty Singleton (29) open their own night club at the Warwick Hall but it only lasts a few weeks.

Duke Ellington (28) enlarges his band and opens at the Cotton Club on 4 December. Harry Carney (17) and Barney Bigard (21) join the band.

Red McKenzie (20) and Eddie Condon (23) record the first classic Chicago jazz session on 8 December.

Jimmie Noone (32) plays at the Apex Club, Chicago and Don Redman (27) directs McKinney's Cotton Pickers.

Jack Teagarden (22) arrives in New York.

The Jean Goldkette Orchestra disbands on 18 September. Bix Beiderbecke (24) and Frankie Trumbauer play with the short-lived Adrian Rollini Band before joining Paul Whiteman on 27 October.

Charles Lindbergh flies the Atlantic (May). His tickertape parade up Broadway is watched by 4,000,000 people.

The first talking motion picture, *The Jazz Singer*, is released on 6 October.

A third radio network is created in US, the Columbia Broadcasting System (CBS).

BIRTHS

Lennie Hastings (drums) 5 January
Allen Eager (tenor sax) 10 January
Wilton 'Bogey' Gaynair (tenor sax) 11 January
Guy Lafitte (tenor sax) 11 January
J.R. Monterose (tenor sax) 19 January
Bill le Sage (vibes) 20 January
Antonio Carlos Jobim (piano/guitar) 25 January
Ronnie Scott (tenor sax) 28 January
Don Shirley (piano) 29 January
Ahmed Abdul-Malik (bass) 30 January
Stan Getz (tenor sax) 2 February
Don Fagerquist (trumpet) 6 February
Tom McIntosh (trombone) 6 February
Tony Fruscella (trumpet) 14 February
Ralph Pena (bass) 24 February
René Thomas (guitar) 25 February
Cy Touff (bass trumpet) 4 March
George Probert (clarinet) 5 March
Dick Hyman (piano) 8 March
Donn Trenner (piano) 10 March
Ruby Braff (cornet) 16 March
John R T Davies (alto sax) 20 March
Bill Barron (tenor sax) 27 March
Gerry Mulligan (baritone sax) 6 April
Charlie Smith (drums) 15 April
Fatty George (saxes) 24 April
Connie Kay (drums) 27 April
Sal Mosca (piano) 27 April
Billy Byers (trombone/composer) 1 May
Barbara Dane (vocals) 12 May
Bill Holman (tenor sax/composer) 21 May
Charles Greenlee (trombone) 24 May
Paul Oliver (writer) 25 May
Dick Hafer (tenor sax) 29 May
Thornel Schwartz Jr (guitar) 29 May
Shake Keane (trumpet) 30 May
Lennie Bush (bass) 6 June
Al Fairweather (trumpet) 12 June
Attila Zoller (guitar) 13 June
Charlie Kennedy (alto sax) 2 July
Karl Kiffe (drums) 6 July
Doc Severinson (trumpet) 7 July
Conte Candoli (trumpet) 12 July
Don Bagley (bass) 18 July
Benoit Quersin (bass) 24 July
Joe Puma (guitar) 13 August
Joe Castro (piano) 15 August
Danny Moss (tenor sax) 16 August
Jimmy Raney (guitar) 20 August
Joya Sherrill (vocals) 20 August
Martial Solal (piano) 23 August
Dickie Hawdon (trumpet) 27 August
Rolf Ericson (trumpet) 29 August
Red Kelly (bass) 29 August
Marion Williams (vocals) 29 August
Jorgen Grunnet-Jepsen (discographer) August
Specs Wright (drums) 8 September
Elvin Jones (drums) 9 September

Sam Butera (tenor sax) 17 September
Earl May (bass) 17 September
Johnny Dankworth (alto sax) 20 September
Red Mitchell (bass) 20 September
Ward Swingle (vocal/leader) 21 September
Romano Mussolini (piano) 26 September
Red Rodney (trumpet) 27 September
Lammar Wright Jr (trumpet) 28 September
Carmen Leggio (saxes) 30 September
Walter Bishop Jr (piano) 4 October
Tony Kinsey (drums) 11 October
Lee Konitz (alto sax) 13 October
Sonny Criss (alto sax) 23 October
Fats Sadi (vibes) 23 October
Warne Marsh (tenor sax) 26 October
Cleo Laine (vocals) 27 October
Chris Connor (vocals) 8 November
Mose Allison (piano/vocals) 11 November
Dolo Coker (piano) 16 November
Victor Sproles (bass) 18 November
André Persiany (piano) 19 November
Jimmy Knepper (trombone) 22 November
Dick Wellstood (piano) 25 November
Gigi Gryce (alto sax) 28 November
Benny Green (tenor sax/writer) 9 December
George Tucker (bass) 10 December
Micky Sheen (drums) 13 December
Gene Quill (alto sax) 15 December
Ronnie Ball (piano) 22 December
Bill Crow (bass) 27 December

DEATHS

Louis Cottrell Sr (48) 17 October

BOOKS

Isaac Goldberg: *Jazz Music, what it is and how to understand it*
R. Mendl: *The Appeal of Jazz*

FILMS

Noble Sissle and Eubie Blake: (9mins) music short

COMPOSITIONS

Bix Beiderbecke: *In A Mist*
Walter Donaldson: *At Sundown*
Duke Ellington: *Black and Tan Fantasy / Creole Love Call*
Byron Gay /Marco Hellman: *Four Or Five Times*
George & Ira Gershwin: *'S Wonderful*
Ray Henderson / Buddy De Sylva / Lew Brown: *Broadway*
Richard Rodgers / Lorenz Hart: *Thou Swell*
Fats Waller: *Alligator Crawl / St Louis Shuffle*
Harry Warren / Lew Brown / Sidney Clare: *One Sweet Letter From You*
Vincent Youmans / Irving Caesar: *Sometimes I'm Happy*

RECORDS

Louis Armstrong Hot Seven (Chicago, 7 May): *Willie the Weeper / Wild Man Blues* (Chicago, 10 May): *Alligator Crawl / Potato Head Blues* (Chicago, 11 May): *Melancholy Blues / Weary Blues / Twelfth Street Rag* (Chicago, 13 May): *Keyhole Blues / S.O.L. Blues* (Chicago, 14 May): *Gully Low Blues / That's When I'll Come Back To You*
Louis Armstrong Orchestra (Chicago, 9 May): *Chicago Breakdown*
Louis Armstrong Hot Five (Chicago, 6 September): *The Last Time* (Chicago, 9 December): *Struttin' With Some Barbecue / Got No Blues* (Chicago, 10 December): *Once In A While / I'm Not Rough* (Chicago, 13 December): *Hotter Than That / Savoy Blues*
Bix Beiderbecke – piano solo (NYC, 9 September): *Bixology (In A Mist)*
Bix & his Gang (NYC, 5 October): *At The Jazz Band Ball / Royal Garden Blues / Jazz Me Blues* (NYC, 25 October): *Goose Pimples / Sorry*
Jimmy Bertrand's Washboard Wizards (Chicago, 21 April): *Easy Come, Easy Go Blues / The Blues Stampede / I'm Goin' Huntin' / If You Want To Be My Sugar Papa*
Charleston Chasers (NYC, 27 January): *Someday, Sweetheart / After You've Gone* (NYC, 14 February): *One Sweet Letter From You / I'm Gonna Meet My Sweetie Now* (NYC, 25 February): *Farewell Blues / Davenport Blues / Wabash Blues* (NYC, 18 May): *My Gal Sal / Delirium* (NYC, 6 September): *Five Pennies / Sugar Foot Strut* (NYC, 8 September): *Imagination / Feelin' No Pain*
Ida Cox (Chicago, July): *'Fore Day Creep / Gypsy Glass Blues / Mojo Hand Blues / Alphonsia Blues / Pleading Blues / Lost Man Blues / Hard, O Lawd / Mercy Blues* (Chicago, September): *Seven Day Blues / Cold and Blue* (Chicago, October): *Midnight Hour Blues / Give Me A Break Blues*
Johnny Dodds' Black Bottom Stompers (Chicago, 22 April): *Weary Blues / New Orleans Stomp / Wild Man Blues / Melancholy* (Chicago, 8 October): *Come On and Stomp, Stomp, Stomp / After You've Gone / Joe Turner Blues / When Erastus Plays His Old Kazoo*
Johnny Dodds & His Chicago Footwarmers (Chicago, 3 December): *Ballin' The Jack / Grandma's Ball* (Chicago, 15 December): *My Baby / Oriental Man*
Duke Ellington Orchestra (NYC, 7 April): *Black and Tan Fantasy* (NYC, 6 October): *Black and Tan Fantasie / Washington Wobble* (Camden, NJ, 26 October): *Creole Love Call* (with Adelaide Hall) *The Blues I Love To Sing* (NYC, 3 November): *What Can A Poor Fellow Do? / Black And Tan Fantasy / Chicago Stomp Down*
Duke Ellington's Cotton Club Orchestra (NYC, 19 December): *Harlem River Quiver / East St Louis Toodle-oo / Blue Bubbles* (NYC, 29 December): *Red Hot Band / Doin' The Frog*
Jean Goldkette Orchestra with Bix Beiderbecke (NYC, 28 January): *Proud Of A Baby Like You / I'm Looking Over A Four Leaf Clover* (NYC, 31 January): *I'm Gonna Meet My Sweetie Now / Hoosier Sweetheart* (NYC, 1 February): *Look At The World And Smile / My Pretty Girl / Stampede* (NYC, 3 February): *Sunny Disposish / A Lane In Spain*
Goofus Five (NYC, 8 February): *Farewell Blues / I Wish I Could Shimmy Like My Sister Kate*
Fletcher Henderson & his Dixie Stompers (NYC, 20 January): *Have It Ready / Ain't She Sweet? / Snag It* (NYC, 24 October): *Black Maria / Goose Pimples / Baltimore*
Fletcher Henderson Orchestra (NYC, 19 March): *Fidgety Feet / Sensation* (NYC, April): *Swamp Blues / Off to Buffalo* (NYC, 28 April): *PDQ Blues / Livery Stable Blues* (NYC, 11 May): *Whiteman Stomp / I'm Coming, Virginia*
Bertha 'Chippie' Hill (Chicago, 14 May): *Do Dirty Blues / Sport Model Mama*
Alberta Hunter (Camden, NJ, 26 February): *I'll Forgive You Because I Love You / I'm Gonna Lose Myself 'Way Down In Louisville / My Daddy's Got A Brand New Way To Love / I'm Down Right Now But I Won't Be Down Always* (Camden, NJ, 20 May): *Sugar / Beale Street Blues / I'm Goin' To See My Ma*
Frankie 'Half Pint' Jaxon (Chicago, 12 July): *Can't You Wait Till You Get Home? / I'm Gonna Steal You*

A Million Dollars (Chicago, 22 July): *Willie The Weeper* (Chicago, 1 August): *She's Got It / I'm Gonna Dance Wit De Guy Wot Brung Me* (Chicago, 3 August): *Corinne*

Charlie Johnson's Original Paradise Ten (NYC, 25 February): *Paradise Wobble / Birmingham Black Bottom / Don't You Leave Me Here*

James P Johnson (NYC, 7 March): *All That I Had Is Gone / Snowy Morning Blues* (NYC, 2 September): *Skiddle-De-Skow / Can I Get It Now?*

Eddie Lang (NYC, 1 April): *Eddie's Twister*

Meade Lux Lewis (Chicago, December): *Honky Tonk Train Blues*

Wingy Manone's Harmony Kings (New Orleans, 11 April): *Cat's Head / Up The Country Blues / Ringside Stomp*

Red McKenzie/Eddie Condon Chicagoans (Chicago, 8 December): *Sugar / China Boy* (Chicago, 16 December): *Nobody's Sweetheart / Liza*

Lizzie Miles (NYC, 18 March): *Slow Up, Papa / Grievin' Mama Blues* (NYC, 12 October): *Mean Old Bed Bug Blues / You Can't Have It Unless I Give It To You* (NYC, 13 November): *When You Get Tired Of Your New Sweetie / Police Blues / Don't Let Your Love Come Down*

Miff Mole's Molers (NYC, 26 January): *Alexander's Ragtime Band / Some Sweet Day / Hurricane* (NYC, 7 March): *Davenport Blues / The Darktown Strutters Ball / A Hot Time In The Old Town Tonight* (NYC, 30 August): *Imagination / Feelin' No Pain / Original Dixieland One-Step* (NYC, 1 September): *My Gal Sal / Honolulu Blues / The new Twister*

Jelly Roll Morton's Red Hot Peppers (Chicago, 4 June): *Hyena Stomp / Billy Goat Stomp / Wild Man Blues / Jungle Blues* (Chicago, 10 June): *Beale Street Blues / The Pearls / Wolverine Blues / Mr Jelly Lord*

Red Nichol's Five Pennies (NYC, 12 January): *Alabama Stomp / Hurricane* (NYC, 3 March): *Bugle Call Rag / Back Beats* (NYC, 20 June): *Cornfed / Five Pennies* (NYC, 25 June): *Mean Dog Blues* (NYC, 15 August): *Riverboat Shuffle / Eccentric / Ida, Sweet As Apple Cider / Feelin' No Pain*

King Oliver & his Dixie Syncopators (Chicago, 22 April): *Doctor Jazz / Showboat Shuffle / Every Tub / Willie The Weeper* (Chicago, 27 April): *Black Snake Blues* (Chicago, 8 July): *Aunt Jemima* (NYC, 18 November): *Farewell Blues / Sobbin' Blues*

Ma Rainey (Chicago, February): *Morning Hour Blues / Weepin' Woman Blues / Soon This Morning* (Chicago, August): *Big Boy Blues / Blues, Oh Blues / Damper Down Blues / Gone Daddy Blues / Oh Papa Blues / Misery Blues / Dead Drunk Blues / Slow Driving Moan* (Chicago, December): *Blues The World Forgot / Ma Rainey's Black Bottom / Hellish*

Rag / Georgia Cake-Walk / New Bo-Weavil Blues / Moonshine Blues / Ice Bag Papa

Bessie Smith (NYC, 17 February): *Preachin' The Blues / Backwater Blues* (NYC, 2 March): *After You've Gone / Alexander's Ragtime Band / Muddy Water / There'll Be A Hot Time In The Old Town Tonight* (NYC, 3 March): *Trombone Cholly / Send Me To The 'Lectric Chair / Them's Graveyard Words / Hot Springs Blues* (NYC, 1 April): *Sweet Mistreater / Lock And Key* (NYC, 27 September): *Mean Old Bed Bug Blues / A Good Man Is Hard To Find* (NYC, 28 September): *Homeless Blues / Looking For My Man Blues* (NYC, 27 October): *Dyin' By The Hour / Foolish Man Blues*

Clara Smith (NYC, 7 April): *Troublesome Blues / You Can't Get It Now* (NYC, 1 June): *That's Why The Undertakers Are Busy Today / Black Woman's Blues* (NYC, 30 July): *Black Cat Moan / Strugglin' Woman's Blues*

Eddie South (Chicago, 2 December): *La Rosita / The Voice Of The Southland* (Chicago, 9 December): *By The Waters Of Minnetonka / My Ohio Home*

Victoria Spivey (St Louis, 27 April): *Steady Grind / Idle Hour Blues / Arkansas Road Blues / The Alligator Pond Went Dry / No.12 Let Me Roam / T.B. Blues* (NYC, 28 October): *Garter Snake Blues / Christmas Morning Blues / Dope Head Blues / Red Lantern Blues* (NYC, 31 October): *Bloodthirsty Blues / Nightmare Blues* (NYC, 1 November): *Murder In The First Degree / Jelly Look What You Done / Your Worries Ain't Like Mine / A Good Man Is Hard To Find*

Frank Trumbauer/Bix Beiderbecke (NYC, 4 February): *Trumbology / Clarinet Marmalade / Singin' The Blues* (NYC, 9 May): *Ostrich Walk / Riverboat Shuffle* (NYC, 13 May): *I'm Coming, Virginia / Way Down Yonder In New Orleans / For No Reason At All In C* (NYC, 17 September): *Wringin' and Twistin'* (NYC, 28 September): *Humpty Dumpty / Krazy Kat / Baltimore*

Joe Venuti/Eddie Lang (NYC, 24 January): *Wild Cat / Sunshine* (NYC, 4 May): *Doin' Things / Goin' Places* (NYC, 28 June): *Kickin' the Cat / Beatin' the Dog* (NYC, 13 September): *Cheese and Crackers / A Mug Of Ale* (NYC, 15 November): *Penn Beach Blues / Four String Joe*

Sippie Wallace (Chicago, 6 May): *Dead Drunk Blues / Have You Ever Been Down? / Lazy Man Blues / The Flood Blues*

Fats Waller (NYC, 20 May): *Fats Waller Stomp / Savannah Blues / Won't You Take Me Home?* (NYC, 1 December): *He's Gone Away / I Ain't Got Nobody / The Digah's Stomp / Red Hot Dan / Geechee / Please Take Me Out Of Jail*

Paul Whiteman Orchestra – with Bix Beiderbecke (Chicago, 18 November): *Washboard Blues* (Chicago, 23 November): *Changes* (Chicago, 25 November): *Mary*

Clarence Williams' Washboard Four (NYC, 29 January): *Nobody But My Baby Is Getting My Love / Candy Lips* (NYC, 13 April): *Cushion Foot Stomp / Take Your Black Bottom Outside* (NYC, 14 April): *Black Snake Blues / Old Folks Shuffle* (NYC, 25 November): *Yama Yama Blues*

Below: Fletcher Henderson and his Orchestra. Back row, l to r: Jimmy Harrison, Benny Morton (trombones), June Cole (tuba), Kaiser Marshall (drums). Front: Fletcher Henderson, Charlie Dixon (banjo), Don Pasquall, Buster Bailey, Coleman Hawkins (reeds), Tommy Ladnier, Joe Smith, Russell Smith (trumpets).

Bottom: Louis Armstrong and his Sunset Café Stompers. L to r: Earl Hines (piano), Peter Briggs (tuba), Honoré Dutrey (trombone), Louis Armstrong (trumpet), Billy Wilson (trumpet), Tubby Hall (drums), Arthur Bassett (banjo), Boyd Atkins, Joe Walker, Al Washington (saxes), Willard Hanby (piano).

Photograph courtesy: *Max Jones*

Louis Armstrong (27) rejoins Carroll Dickerson's Savoy Ballroom Orchestra in March.

Hot Chocolates opens at Connie's Inn with a score by Fats Waller(24) and Andy Razaf.

Benny Goodman (19) records his first session as leader on 23 January.

Sidney Bechet (31) joins Noble Sissle (39) in Paris.

Johnny Hodges (22) joins the Duke Ellington (29) Orchestra; Count Basie (24) joins Walter Page's Blue Devils; Bix Beiderbecke (25) is in the Paul Whiteman Band.

Luis Russell (26) and his Band are at the Savoy Ballroom in Harlem.

Earl Hines (23) and his Band make their debut at Chicago's Grand Terrace (December).

BIRTHS

Joe Muranyi (clarinet) 14 January
Dave Black (drums) 23 January
Dick Nash (trombone) 26 January
Ruth Brown (vocals) 30 January
Nelson Boyd (bass) 6 February
Gene Lees (writer) 8 February
Bruno Carr (drums) 9 February
Conrad Janis (trombone) 11 February
Frank Butler (drums) 18 February
Alun Morgan (writer) 24 February
Bill Green (alto sax) 25 February
Maxim Saury (clarinet) 27 February
Bob Hardaway (tenor sax) 1 March
Pierre Michelot (bass) 3 March
Lou Levy (piano) 5 March
Wilbur Little (bass) 5 March
Pee Wee Moore (baritone sax) 5 March
Willie Maiden (tenor sax) 12 March
Bob Wilber (clarinet/soprano sax) 15 March
Lem Winchester (vibes) 19 March
Archie Semple (clarinet) 31 March
Ed Hubble (trombone) 6 April
Monty Sunshine (clarinet) 8 April
Teddy Charles (vibes) 13 April
Ken Colyer (trumpet) 18 April
Alexis Korner (guitar/vocals) 19 April
Tommy Turrentine (trumpet) 22 April
Johnny Griffin (tenor sax) 24 April
Rick Henderson (saxes) 25 April
Herman Foster (piano) 26 April
Raymond Fol (piano) 28 April
Errol Buddle (saxes) 29 April
Maynard Ferguson (trumpet) 4 May
Lars Gullin (baritone sax) 4 May
Don De Michael (drums/writer) 12 May
Bert Dahlander (drums) 13 May
Joe Gordon (trumpet) 15 May
Lee Katzman (trumpet) 17 May
Jackie Cain (vocals) 22 May
Max Bennett (bass) 24 May
Gene di Novi (piano) 26 May
Freddie Redd (piano) 29 May
Teddy Kotick (bass) 4 June
Tony Ortega (saxes) 7 June
Bob Gordon (baritone sax) 11 June
Eric Dolphy (alto sax) 20 June
Bill Russo (trombone/composer) 25 June
Richard Wyands (piano) 2 July
Leroy Vinnegar (bass) 13 July
Joe Harriott (alto sax) 15 July
Vince Guaraldi (piano) 17 July
Joe Morello (drums) 17 July
Carl Fontana (trombone) 18 July
Peter Ind (bass) 20 July
Keter Betts (bass) 22 July
Bill Lee (bass) 23 July
Vernel Fournier (drums) 30 July
Eddie McFadden (guitar) 6 August
Carl Perkins (piano) 16 August
Addison Farmer (bass) 21 August
Art Farmer (trumpet) 21 August
Gil Coggins (piano) 23 August
Peter Appleyard (vibes) 26 August
Kenny Drew (piano) 28 August
Horace Silver (piano) 2 September
Albert Mangelsdorff (trombone) 5 September
Eddie Preston (trumpet) 5 September
Lorraine Geller (piano) 11 September
Jay Cameron (baritone sax) 14 September
Cannonball Adderley (alto sax) 15 September
Vi Redd (alto sax/vocals) 20 September
Frank Foster (tenor sax) 23 September
Michel Gaudry (bass) 23 September

Jimmy Woode (bass) 23 September
Jon Eardley (trumpet) 30 September
Junior Mance (piano) 10 October
Clare Fischer (piano) 22 October
Bobby Jones (tenor sax) 30 October
Herb Geller (alto sax) 2 November
Larry Bunker (drums/vibes) 4 November
Ernestine Anderson (vocals) 11 November
Hampton Hawes (piano) 13 November
Seldon Powell (tenor sax) 15 November
Chuck Andrus (bass) 17 November
John Sangster (drums/composer) 17 November
Sheila Jordan (vocals) 18 November
Etta Jones (vocals) 25 November
Frank Tiberi (tenor sax) 4 December
Frankie Dunlop (drums) 6 December
Ira Gitler (writer) 18 December
Harold Land (tenor sax) 18 December
Jimmy Campbell (drums) 24 December
Harry Klein (baritone sax) 25 December
Gene Mayl (bass) 30 December
Jack Montrose (tenor sax) 30 December

DEATHS

Ollie Powers (38) 14 April *diabetes mellitus*
Stump Evans (23) 29 August *tuberculosis*

COMPOSITIONS

Fred Ahlert / Roy Turk: *I'll Get By*
Harry Barris: *Mississippi Mud*
Harry Barris / Bing Crosby: *From Monday On*
Cliff Burwell / Mitchell Parish: *Sweet Lorraine*
Leroy Carr: *How Long Blues*
Walter Donaldson / Gus Kahn: *Love Me Or Leave Me / Makin' Whoopee*
Duke Ellington: *Black Beauty / The Mooche / Misty Mornin'*
George Gershwin: *An American in Paris*
George & Ira Gershwin / P G Wodehouse: *How Long Has This Been Going On?*
Earl Hines: *A Monday Date*
James P. Johnson: *Yamekraw*
J C Johnson / Bob Schafer / Andy Razaf: *Louisiana*
Roger Wolfe Kahn / Joseph Meyer / Irving Caesar: *Crazy Rhythm*
Carmen Lombardo / Charles Newman: *Sweethearts On Parade*
Jimmy McHugh / Dorothy Fields: *I Can't Give You Anything But Love / Diga Diga Doo / Doin' The New Low Down*
Jelly Roll Morton: *Ham and Eggs / Boogaboo*
Maceo Pinkard / Alexander Mitchell: *Sugar*
Don Redman: *Cherry*
Willard Robison: *Tain't So, Honey, Tain't So*
Fats Waller: *Handful of Keys / Honeysuckle Rose / Ain't Misbehavin' / What Did I Do To Be So Black and Blue / I've Got A Feeling I'm Falling*
Harry Warren / Mort Dixon: *Nagasaki*

RECORDS

Louis Armstrong Hot Five (Chicago, 27 June): *Fireworks / Skip The Gutter / A Monday Date* (Chicago, 28 June): *Don't Jive Me / West End Blues / Sugar Foot Strut* (Chicago, 29 June): *Two Deuces / Squeeze Me* (Chicago, 5 July): *Knee Drops*
Louis Armstrong Orchestra (Chicago, 5 December): *No, Papa, No / Basin Street Blues* (Chicago, 7 December): *Muggles* (Chicago, 12 December): *Heah Me Talkin' To Ya? / St James Infirmary / Tight Like That*
Louis Armstrong Savoy Ballroom Five (Chicago, 5 December): *No One Else But You / Beau Koo Jack / Save It, Pretty Mama*

Louis Armstrong/Earl Hines (Chicago, 5 December): *Weather Bird*
Bix Beiderbecke & his Gang (NYC, 17 April): *Somebody Stole My Gal / Thou Swell* (Chicago, 7 July): *Ol' Man River / Wa-Da-Da* (NYC, 21 September): *Rhythm King / Louisiana / Margie*
Charleston Chasers (NYC, 7 March): *My Melancholy Baby / Mississippi Mud*
Chocolate Dandies (NYC, 13 October): *Paducah / Star Dust / Birmingham Break-down / Four Or Five Times*
Junie C Cobb (Chicago, 21 August): *Endurance Stomp / Yearning And Blue*
Eddie Condon Quartet (NYC, 28 July): *Oh, Baby / Indiana*
Ida Cox (Chicago, July): *Bone Orchard Blues / Sobbin' Tears Blues / Booze Crazy Man Blues / Broadcasting Blues / Western Union Blues / Fogyism / Separated Blues / Tree Top Tall Papa* (Chicago, August): *Worn Down Daddy Blues / You Stole My Man*
Carroll Dickerson Orchestra – with Louis Armstrong & Earl Hines (Chicago, 5 July): *Symphonic Raps / Savoyagers' Stomp*
Johnny Dodds & His Chicago Footwarmers (Chicago, 2 July): *Get 'Em Again Blues / Brush Stomp / My Girl* (Chicago, 4 July): *Sweep 'Em Clean / Lady Love*
Johnny Dodds' Washboard Band (Chicago, 6 July): *Bucktown Stomp / Weary City / Bull Fiddle Blues*
Johnny Dunn (NYC, 13 March): *Sergeant Dunn's Bugle Call Blues / Ham And Eggs / Buffalo Blues / You Need Some Loving* (NYC, 26 March): *What's The Use Of Being Alone? / Original Bugle Blues*
Duke Ellington Orchestra (NYC, 9 January): *Sweet Mama / Stack O'Lee Blues / Bugle Call Rag* (NYC, 21 March): *Take It Easy / Jubilee Stomp / Black Beauty* (NYC, 5 June): *Yellow Dog Blues / Tishomingo Blues* (NYC, 10 July): *Diga Diga Doo / Doin' The New Low Down* (NYC, 1 October): *The Mooche / Move Over / Hot and Bothered* (NYC, 22 November): *The Blues With A Feelin' / Goin' To Town / Misty Mornin'*
Bud Freeman (Chicago, 3 December): *Craze-o-logy / Can't Help Lovin' Dat Man*
Benny Goodman's Boys (Chicago, 23 January): *A Jazz Holiday / Wolverine Blues* (NYC, 4 June): *Jungle Blues / Room 1411 / Blue / Shirt Tail Stomp*
Fletcher Henderson Orchestra (NYC, 14 March): *King Porter Stomp / D Natural Blues*
Bertha 'Chippie' Hill (Chicago, 12 October): *Some Cold Rainy Day / Weary Money Blues* (Chicago, 17 October): *Hard Time Blues / Christmas Man Blues* (Chicago, 1 November); *Trouble In Mind / Hangman Blues*
Earl Hines – piano solos (Long Island City, 8 December): *Blues In Thirds / Off Time Blues / Chicago High Life / A Monday Date / Stowaway / Chimes In Blues / Panther Rag / Just Too Soon* (Chicago, 12 December): *I Ain't Got Nobody / Fifty-Seven Varieties*
Frankie Jaxon (Chicago, 28 October): *Hit Ta Ditty Low Down / Down At Jasper's Bar-be-que / How Can I Get It?* (Chicago, 28 November): *Fan It*
James P. Johnson (NYC, 18 June): *Chicago Blues / Mournful Tho'ts*
Charlie Johnson's Paradise Ten (NYC, 24 January): *You Ain't The One / Charleston Is The Best Dance After All / Hot Tempered Blues*
Lonnie Johnson/Eddie Lang (NYC, 17 November): *Two Tone Stomp / Have To Change Key To Play These Blues*
Eddie Lang (NYC, 29 March): *Add A Little Wiggle* (NYC, 5 November): *Church Street Sobbin' Blues*
Louisiana Rhythm Kings (Chicago, 28 April): *Baby, Won't You Please Come Home? / Friars Point Shuffle*
McKinney's Cotton Pickers (Chicago, 11 July): *Four Or Five Times / Milenberg Joys* (Chicago, 12 July): *Cherry / Nobody's Sweetheart*
Lizzie Miles (NYC, 4 January): *Shootin' Star Blues / Lonesome Ghost Blues / If You Can't Control Your Man* (NYC, 29 February): *Nobody Shows What My Baby Shows / Second-hand Daddy / A Good Man Is Hard To Find* (NYC, 2 May): *Shake It Down / Banjo Papa / Your Worries Ain't Like Mine* (NYC, 30 June): *You're Such A Cruel Papa To Me / My Dif'rent Kind O' Man*
Miff Mole/Red Nichols (NYC, 6 July): *One Step To Heaven / Shimme-Sha-Wabble* (NYC, 27 July): *Crazy Rhythm / You Took Advantage Of Me*

Jelly Roll Morton's Red Hot Peppers (NYC, 11 June): *Georgia Swing / Kansas City Stomps / Shoe Shiner's Drag / Boogaboo / Shreveport / Mournful Serenade*

Red Nichols and his Five Pennies (NYC, 25 February): *Nobody's Sweetheart* (NYC, 27 February): *Avalon / Japanese Sandman* (NYC, 2 March): *Poor Butterfly / Can't Yo' Hear Me Calling, Caroline?* (NYC, 29 May): *Panama / There'll Come A Time* (NYC, 31 May): *Dear Old Southland / Limehouse Blues / Whispering / I Can't Give You Anything But Love* (NYC, 1 June): *Margie / Imagination / Original Dixieland One-Step* (NYC, 2 October): *A Pretty Girl Is Like A Melody / I Must Have That Man*

Jimmie Noone's Apex Club Orchestra (Chicago, 16 May): *I Know That You Know / Sweet Sue, Just You / Four Or Five Times / Every Evening* (Chicago, 14 June): *Ready For The River / Forevermore* (Chicago, 23 August): *Apex Blues / Blues My Naughty Sweetie Gives To Me / A Monday Date* (Chicago, 25 August): *King Joe / Oh Sister, Ain't That Hot? / Sweet Lorraine* (Chicago, 6 December): *Some Rainy Day* (Chicago, 27 December): *It's Tight Like That / Let's Sow A Wild Oat / She's Funny That Way*

King Oliver (NYC, 11 June): *Tin Roof Blues / West End Blues / Sweet Emmalina / Lazy Mama* (NYC, 13 August): *Got Everything / Four Or Five Times* (NYC, 10 September): *Speakeasy Blues / Aunt Hagar's Blues* (NYC, 14 November): *Slow and Steady*

Ma Rainey (Chicago, June): *Black Cat Hoot Owl Blues / Log Camp Blues / Hear Me Talking To You / Hustlin' Blues / Prove It On Me Blues / Victim Of The Blues / Traveling Blues / Deep Moaning Blues* (Chicago, September): *Daddy Goodbye Blues / Sleep Talking Blues / Tough Luck Blues / Blame It On The Blues / Sweet Rough Man / Runaway Blues / Screech Owl Blues / Black Dust Blues / Leaving This Morning / Black Eye Blues* (Chicago, October): *Ma and Pa Poorhouse Blues* (Chicago, December): *Big Feeling Blues*

Clarence 'Pinetop' Smith (Chicago, December): *Boogie Woogie*

Bessie Smith (NYC, 9 February): *Thinking Blues / Pickpocket Blues / I Used To Be Your Sweet Mama* (NYC, 16 February): *I'd Rather Be Dead And Buried In My Grave* (NYC, 21 February): *Standin' In The Rain Blues / It Won't Be You* (NYC, 19 March): *Spider Man Blues* (NYC, 20 March): *Empty Bed Blues / Put It Right Here* (NYC, 24 August): *Yes Indeed He Do / Devil's Gonna Get You / You Ought To Be Ashamed / Washwoman's Blues / Slow and Easy Man / Poor Man's Blues* (NYC, 25 August): *Please Help Me Get Him Off My Mind / Me And My Gin*

Clara Smith (NYC, 10 May): *Jelly, Look What You Done Done / It's All Coming Home To You* (NYC, 21 May): *Gin Mill Blues* (NYC, 23 May): *Steamboat Man Blues / Sobbin' Sister Blues* (NYC, 6 July): *Got My Mind On That Thing* (NYC, 13 July): *Wanna Go Home* (NYC, 9 August): *Ain't Got Nobody To Grind My Coffee*

Eddie South (NYC, 10 May): *That's What I Call Keen*

Victoria Spivey (NYC, 12 September): *My Handy Man / Organ Grinder Blues* (NYC, 13 October): *New Black Snake Blues* (NYC, 17 October): *No, Papa, No / Toothache Blues* (NYC, 18 October): *Furniture Man Blues / Mosquito, Fly and Flea*

Frank Teschmacher's Chicagoans (Chicago, 28 April): *Jazz Me Blues*

Frank Trumbauer/Bix Beiderbecke (NYC, 9 January): *There'll Come A Time / Jubilee* (NYC, 20 January): *Mississippi Mud*

Joe Venuti/Eddie Lang (NYC, 28 March): *Dinah / The Wild Dog* (NYC, 14 June): *The Man From The South / Pretty Trix* (NYC, 21 June): *Doin' Things / Wild Cat* (NYC, 27 September): *The Blue Room / Sensation* (NYC, 12 December): *My Honey's Lovin' Arms / Goin' Home*

Paul Whiteman Orchestra – with Bix Beiderbecke (NYC, 4 January): *Smile / Lonely Melody* (NYC, 11 January): *Ol' Man River* (NYC, 12 January): *San* (NYC, 24 January): *Smile / My Heart Stood Still* (NYC, 28 January): *Back In Your Own Backyard* (NYC, 8 February): *There Ain't No Sweet Man That's Worth The Salt Of My Tears* (NYC, 9 February): *Dardanella* (NYC, 10 February): *Love Nest* (NYC, 13 February): *From Monday On* (NYC, 18 February): *Mississippi Mud* (NYC, 28 February): *From Monday On / Sugar* (NYC, 29 February): *When You're With Somebody Else* (NYC, 1 March): *Selections From Showboat* (NYC, 2 March): *Coquette* (NYC, 2 March): *When* (NYC, 15 March): *Lovable* (NYC, 22 April): *My Pet / It Was The Dawn Of Love / Forget-Me-Not* (NYC, 23 April): *Louisiana* (NYC, 24 April): *Do I Hear You Saying I Love You* (NYC, 25 April): *You Took Advantage Of Me* (NYC, 15 May): *My Melancholy Baby* (NYC, 16 May): *The Man I Love* (NYC, 22 May): *Is It Gonna Be Long?* (NYC, 23 May): *Oh! You Have No Idea* (NYC, 25 May): *Felix The Cat* (NYC, 10 June): *'Tain't So Honey, 'Tain't So / I'd Rather Cry Over You* (NYC, 17 June): *That's My Weakness Now / Georgie Porgie* (NYC, 18 June): *Because My Baby Don't Mean Maybe Now / Out O' Town Gal* (NYC, 2 July): *Pickin' Cotton* (NYC, 18 September): *Sweet Sue* (NYC, 21 September): *I Can't Give You Anything But Love*

Clarence Williams (NYC, 23 May): *Shake It Down / Red River Blues* (NYC, 23 June): *Lazy Mama* (NYC, 2 July): *Organ Grinder Blues* (NYC, 20 July): *Farm Hand Papa*

Left: Bessie Smith on stage.

Below: The hit song from the Connie's Inn revue 'Hot Chocolates'.

Louis Armstrong (28) tours with the Carroll Dickerson Orchestra until it disbands in New York in June. Louis then appears in the show 'Hot Chocolates'.

Bix Beiderbecke (26) leaves Paul Whiteman's Orchestra in September through ill health.

Earl Hines (23) leads his orchestra at the Grand Terrace Ballroom in Chicago.

Cootie Williams (19) replaces Bubber Miley (26) in Duke Ellington's Band; Juan Tizol (29) also joins. The band appears simultaneously at the Cotton Club and in the Flo Ziegfeld Show 'Show Girl'.

The Stock Market crash on 29 October heralds the beginning of the Great Depression.

BIRTHS

Al Dreares (drums) 4 January
Joe Pass (guitar) 13 January
Granville T.Hogan (drums) 16 January
Jimmy Cobb (drums) 20 January
Harold Ousley (tenor sax) 23 January
Benny Golson (tenor sax) 25 January
Acker Bilk (clarinet/leader) 29 January
Ed Shaughnessy (drums) 29 January
Benny Barth (drums) 16 February
Sandy Brown (clarinet) 25 February
Eddie Jones (bass) 1 March
Cecil Taylor (piano) 15 March
Gene Taylor (bass) 19 March
Maurice Simon (saxes) 26 March
Buster Cooper (trombone) 4 April
Andre Previn (piano) 6 April
Art Taylor (drums) 6 April
Eiji Kitamura (clarinet) 8 April
Ray Barretto (conga) 29 April
Mel Lewis (drums/leader) 10 May
Lawrence Marable (drums) 21 May
Julian Euell (bass) 23 May
Sandy Mosse (tenor sax) 29 May
Lennie Niehaus (alto sax) 1 June
Gildo Mahones (piano) 2 June
Kenny Clare (drums) 8 June
Maurice Vander (piano) 11 June
Betty Smith (tenor sax) 6 July
Hal Gaylor (bass) 9 July
Alex Welsh (trumpet) 9 July
Buddy Clark (bass) 10 July
Alan Dawson (drums) 14 July
Dempsey Wright (guitar) 14 July
Danny Barcelona (drums) 23 July
Charlie Persip (drums) 26 July
Don Prell (bass) 4 August
Lorez Alexandria (vocals) 14 August
Bill Evans (piano) 16 August
Sonny Rollins (tenor sax) 7 September
Harry South (piano/arranger/composer) 7 September
Prince Lasha (alto sax) 10 September
Bert Courtley (trumpet) 11 September
Charles Moffett (drums) 11 September
Rod Levitt (trombone) 16 September
Teddi King (vocals) 18 September
Joe Temperley (baritone sax) 20 September
Shafi Hadi (tenor sax) 21 September
Dottie Dodgion (drums) 23 September
Rolf Kuhn (clarinet) 29 September
Howard Roberts (guitar) 2 October
Norman Simmons (piano) 6 October
Ed Blackwell (drums) 10 October
Curtis Amy (tenor sax) 11 October
Willie Jones (drums) 20 October
Dan Morgenstern (writer) 24 October
Elmon Wright (trumpet) 27 October
Gabe Baltazar (alto sax) 1 November
Terry Shannon (piano) 5 November
Francy Boland (piano) 6 November
Johnny Parker (piano) 6 November
Fred Assunto (trombone) 3 December
Toshiko Akiyoshi (piano) 12 December
Barry Harris (piano) 15 December
Nick Stabulas (drums) 18 December
Bob Brookmeyer (valve trombone) 19 December
Red Balaban (bass) 22 December
Chet Baker (trumpet) 23 December
Monty Budwig (bass) 26 December

DEATHS

Pinetop Smith (24) 14 March *accidentally shot during brawl*
Don Murray (24) 2 June *head injuries from a fall*
Chris Kelly (c.40) 19 August

COMPOSITIONS

Fred Ahlert / Roy Turk: *Mean To Me*
Harry Akst / Grant Clarke: *Am I Blue?*
Hoagy Carmichael: *Stardust*
Duke Ellington: *Saturday Night Function / Rent Party Blues / Wall Street Wail*
George & Ira Gershwin / Gus Kahn: *Liza*
Jesse Greer / Raymond Klagers: *Just You, Just Me*
Ralph Rainger / Howard Dietz: *Moanin' Low*
Arthur Schwartz / Howard Dietz: *I Guess I'll Have To Change My Plan*
Henry Sullivan / Harry Ruskin: *I May Be Wrong*
Kay Swift / Paul James: *Can't We Be Friends?*
Richard Whiting / Seymour Simons / Haven Gillespie: *Honey*
Vincent Youmans / Billy Rose / Edward Eliscu: *More Than You Know*

FILMS

After Seven (9mins): Chick Webb Band
Ben Pollack & his Park Central Orchestra (9mins): music short
Black and Tan (19mins): Duke Ellington & his Cotton Club Orchestra
Jailhouse Blues (9mins): Mamie Smith music short
St Louis Blues (16mins): Bessie Smith

Right: Bix Beiderbecke and Frank Trumbauer embarking on a Spring tour of the west coast with the Paul Whiteman Orchestra.
Below: Eddie Lang

RECORDS

Henry 'Red' Allen Orchestra (NYC, 16 July): *It Should Be You / Biff'ly Blues* (NYC, 17 July): *Feelin' Drowsy / Swing Out* (NYC, 24 September, with Victoria Spivey): *Make a Country Bird Fly Wild / Funny Feather Blues / How Do They Do It That Way? / Pleasin' Paul*
Louis Armstrong & Savoy Ballroom Five (NYC, 5 March): *I Can't Give You Anything But Love / Mahogany Hall Stomp*
Louis Armstrong Orchestra (NYC, 5 March): *I'm Gonna Stomp Mr Henry Lee / Knockin' a Jug* (NYC, 19 July): *Ain't Misbehavin'* (NYC, 22 July): *Black And Blue / That Rhythm Man / Sweet Savannah Sue* (NYC, 10 September): *Some Of These Days* (NYC, 11 September): *When You're Smiling* (NYC, 19 November): *Little By Little / Look What You've Done To Me* (NYC, 26 November): *After You've Gone* (NYC, 10 December): *I Ain't Got Nobody / Dallas Blues* (NYC, 13 December): *St Louis Blues / Rockin' Chair*
Jimmy Bertrand's Washboard Wizards (Chicago, 25 April): *Isabella / I Won't Give You None*
Charleston Chasers (NYC, 28 June): *Ain't Misbehavin' / Moanin' Low* (NYC, 24 July): *Red Hair and Freckles / Lovable and Sweet* (NYC, 28 September): *What Wouldn't I Do For That Man? / Turn On The Heat*
Junie C Cobb (Chicago, 7 February): *Shake That Jelly Roll / Don't Cry, Honey* (Chicago, 11 February): *Smoke Shop Drag / Boot That Thing* (Chicago, 24 October): *Once Or Twice*
Ida Cox (Chicago, October): *I'm So Glad / Jailhouse Blues*
Johnny Dodds Orchestra (Chicago, 30 January): *Sweet Lorraine / My Little Isabel* (Chicago, 7 February): *Pencil Papa / Heah Me Talkin' / Goober Dance / Too Tight / Indigo Stomp*

Photograph courtesy: *Max Jones*

Duke Ellington (NYC, 8 January): *Doin' The Voom Voom / Tiger Rag* (NYC, 16 January): *Flaming Youth / Saturday Night Function / High Life* (NYC, 18 February): *Japanese Dream / Harlemania* (NYC, 1 March): *Rent Party Blues / Paducah / Harlem Flat Blues* (NYC, 7 March): *The Dicty Glide / Hot Feet / Sloppy Joe / Stevedore Stomp* (NYC, 15 March): *Saratoga Swing / Who Said It's Tight Like That?* (NYC, 3 May): *Cotton Club Stomp / Misty Mornin' / Arabian Lover / Saratoga Swing* (NYC, 29 July): *Black And Blue / Jungle Jamboree* (NYC, 13 September): *Jolly Wog / Jazz Convulsions* (NYC, 16 September): *Mississippi / The Duke Steps Out / Haunted Nights / Swanee Shuffle* (NYC, 14 November): *Breakfast Dance / Jazz Lips / March Of The Hoodlums* (NYC, 20 November): *Lazy Duke / Blues Of The Vagabond / Syncopated Shuffle* (NYC, 10 December): *Sweet Mama / Wall Street Wail / Cincinnati Daddy*

Fletcher Henderson Orchestra (NYC, April): *Freeze And Melt / Raisin' The Roof* (NYC, 16 May): *Blazin' / The Wang-Wang Blues*

Bertha 'Chippie' Hill (Chicago, 18 March): *I Ain't Gonna Do It No More / Pratt City Blues*

Earl Hines Orchestra (Chicago, 13 February): *Sweet Ella May / Everybody Loves My Baby* (Chicago, 14 February): *Good Little, Bad Little You / Have You Ever Felt That Way?* (Chicago, 15 February): *Beau Koo Jack / Sister Kate* (Chicago, 25 October): *Grand Piano Blues / Blue Nights*

Alberta Hunter (NYC, 18 July): *Gimme All The Love You Got / My Particular Man*

Frankie Jaxon (Chicago, 13 February): *Let's Knock A Jug* (Chicago, 11 June): *It's Heated / Jive Man Blues* (Chicago, 22 July): *Corrine Blues* (Chicago, 27 August): *Take It Easy* (Chicago, 6 December): *You Got To Wet It / Down Home In Kentucky*

James P. Johnson (NYC, 29 January): *Riffs / Feelin' Blue* (NYC, 5 March): *Put Your Mind Right On It / Sorry* (NYC, 18 November): *You Don't Understand / You've Got To Be Modernistic*

Andy Kirk & his Twelve Clouds of Joy (Kansas City, 7 November): *Mess-a-Stomp / Blue Clarinet Stomp / Cloudy / Casey Jones Special*

Lonnie Johnson/Eddie Lang (NYC, 7 May): *Guitar Blues / Bull Frog Moan* (NYC, 8 May): *A Handful Of Riffs / Blue Guitars* (NYC, 9 October): *Deep Minor Rhythm / Midnight Call Blues / Hot Fingers / Blue Room Blues*

McKinney's Cotton Pickers (NYC, 8 April): *Save It, Pretty Mama* (NYC, 9 April): *Beedle-um-bum / Sellin' That Stuff* (NYC, 5 November): *Gee Baby, Ain't I Good To You?* (NYC, 6 November): *The Way I Feel Today / Miss Hannah* (NYC, 7 November): *Wherever There's A Will, Baby*

Lizzie Miles (NYC, 11 December): *I Hate A Man Like You / Don't Tell Me Nothin' 'Bout My Man*

Miff Mole's Molers (NYC, 19 April): *I've Got A Feelin' I'm Falling / That's A Plenty* (NYC, 12 July): *Birmingham Bertha / Moanin' Low* (NYC, 24 September): *You Made Me Love You / After You've Gone*

Jelly Roll Morton & his Red Hot Peppers (Camden NJ, 9 July): *Burnin' The Iceberg / Courthouse Bump / Pretty Lil* (Camden NJ, 10 July): *Sweet Aneta Mine /*

New Orleans Bump (Camden NJ, 12 July): *Down My Way / Try Me Out / Tank Town Bump* (NYC, 13 November): *Sweet Peter / Jersey Joe / Mississippi Mildred / Mint Julep*

Jelly Roll Morton Trio (NYC, 17 December): *Smilin' The Blues Away / Turtle Twist / My Little Dixie Home / That's Like It Ought To Be*

Bennie Moten's Orchestra (Chicago, 23 October): *Rumba Negro / The Jones Law Blues / Band Box Shuffle / Small Black / Every Day Blues* (Chicago, 24 October): *Boot It / Mary Lee / Rit Dit Rag / New Vine Street Blues / Sweetheart Of Yesterday*

Red Nichol's Five Pennies (NYC, 5 February): *Chinatown, My Chinatown / On The Alamo* (NYC, 16 February): *Alice Blue Gown / Allah's Holiday / Roses Of Picardy*

Jimmie Noone (Chicago, 26 February): *St Louis Blues / Chicago Rhythm* (Chicago, 2 March): *I Got A Misery* (Chicago, 27 April): *Wake Up, Chillun, Wake Up / Love Me Or Leave Me* (Chicago, 21 June): *Anything You Want* (NYC, 11 July): *Birmingham Bertha / Am I Blue? / My Daddy Rocks Me / Apex Blues* (Chicago, 24 September): *Sposin' / True Blue Lou* (Chicago, 26 September): *Through / Satisfied* (Chicago, 15 October): *I'm Doin' What I'm Doin' For Love*

King Oliver (NYC, 16 January): *West End Blues / I've Got That Thing* (NYC, 1 February): *Call Of The Freaks / The Trumpet's Prayer / Freakish Light Blues* (Chicago, 25 February): *Can I Tell You? / My Good Man Sam* (NYC, 8 October): *What Do You Want Me To Do? / Sweet Like This / Too Late* (NYC, 6 November): *I'm Lonesome, Sweetheart / I Want You Just Myself / I Can't Stop Loving You* (NYC, 30 December): *Everybody Does It In Hawaii / Frankie And Johnny / New Orleans Shout*

Walter Page's Blue Devils (Kansas City, 10 November): *Blue Devil Blues / Squabblin'*

Luis Russell Orchestra (NYC, 15 January): *Savoy Shout / The Call Of The Freaks* (NYC, 6 September): *The New Call Of The Freaks / Feelin' The Spirit / Jersey Lightning* (NYC, 13 September): *Broadway Rhythm / The Way He Loves Is Just Too Bad* (NYC, 17 December): *Doctor Blues*

Omer Simeon (Chicago, 21 August): *Smoke House Blues* (Chicago, 11 September): *Beau Koo Jack*

Bessie Smith (NYC, 8 May): *I'm Wild About That Thing / You've Got To Give Me Some / Kitchen Man* (NYC, 15 May): *I've Got What It Takes / Nobody Knows You When You're Down And Out* (NYC, 24 June): *St Louis Blues – film soundtrack* (NYC, 25 July): *Take It Right Back* (NYC, 20 August): *He's Got Me Goin' / It Makes My Love Come Down* (NYC, 1 October): *Wasted Life Blues / Dirty No-Gooder's*

Blues (NYC, 11 October): *Blue Spirit Blues / Worn Out Papa Blues / You Don't Understand / Don't Cry Baby*

Clara Smith (NYC, 17 January): *Tell Me When / Empty House Blues* (NYC, 26 January): *Daddy, Don't Put That Thing On Me Blues / It's Tight Like That* (NYC, 4 September): *Papa I Don't Need You Now / Tired Of The Way You Do* (NYC, 12 September): *Oh Mister Mitchell / Where Is My Man?* (NYC, 31 December): *You Can't Stay Here No More / Let's Get Loose*

Jabbo Smith (Chicago, 29 January): *Jazz Battle* (Chicago, 22 February): *Little Willie Blues / Sleepy Time Blues* (Chicago, 23 February): *Take Your Time / Sweet And Low Blues* (Chicago, 1 March): *Take Me To The River / Ace Of Rhythm / Let's Get Together / Sau Sha Stomp* (Chicago, 30 March): *Michigander Blues* (Chicago, 4 April): *Decatur Street Tutti / Till Times Get Better* (Chicago, 17 April): *Lina Blues* (Chicago, 9 June): *Croonin' The Blues / I Got The Stinger* (Chicago, 8 August): *Boston Shuffle / Tanguay Blues* (Chicago, 22 August): *Band Box Stomp / Moanful Blues*

Eddie South (Paris, 12 March): *Doin' The Raccoon / Two Guitars*

Victoria Spivey (NYC, 3 July): *You Done Lost Your Good Thing Now* (NYC, 10 July): *Funny Feathers / How Do You Do It That Way?* (NYC, 1 October): *Bloodhound Blues / Dirty TB Blues / Moaning The Blues / Telephoning The Blues*

Frankie Trumbauer/Bix Beiderbecke (NYC, 8 March): *Futuristic Rhythm / Raisin' The Roof* (NYC, 22 May): *Shivery Stomp*

Joe Venuti/Eddie Lang (NYC, 18 October): *Runnin' Ragged / Apple Blossoms*

Fats Waller (NYC, 1 March): *Handful Of Keys / The Minor Drag / Harlem Fuss / Numb Fumblin'* (Camden NJ, 2 August): *Ain't Misbehavin' / Sweet Savannah Sue / I've Got A Feeling I'm Falling / Love Me Or Leave Me / Gladyse / Valentine Stomp* (NYC, 24 September): *Smashing Thirds*

Ethel Waters (NYC, 14 May): *Am I Blue?*

Paul Whiteman Orchestra – with Bix Beiderbecke (NYC, 5 April): *I'm In Seventh Heaven* (NYC, 3 May): *When My Dreams Come True / Reaching For Someone And Not Finding Anyone There / China Boy* (NYC, 4 May): *Oh! Miss Hannah* (NYC, 13 September): *Waiting At The End Of The Road / When You're Counting The Stars Alone*

Clarence Williams Washboard Band (NYC, 2 July): *High Society / Whoop It Up*

Below: Louis Armstrong (28) with Luis Russell Orchestra
Below left: Jelly Roll Morton at a July recording session in Camden, New Jersey.

HARLEM

Harlem was originally a wealthy white suburb of Manhattan, but around the turn of the century over-speculation led to a collapse of the housing boom and thousands of black people flooded into Harlem to take advantage of the cheap rents.

By the early 1920's Harlem was the centre of a flourishing entertainment business with black theatres and black artists performing for black audiences. Soon Harlem was in vogue and white socialites filled the dance halls, theatres and nightclubs to see artists like Duke Ellington, Cab Calloway, Fats Waller, Chick Webb, Louis Armstrong and Bessie Smith.

The premier dance hall was the Savoy Ballroom – 'the home of happy feet', and the big four clubs were the Cotton Club, Connie's Inn, Small's Paradise and Barron Wilkins'. All four clubs catered exclusively to white audiences and first on the scene was Barron Wilkins' which opened in 1915 and featured performers like James P Johnson, Mamie Smith and Duke Ellington. In 1922 gangster Owney Madden took over Jack Johnson's De Luxe Club and reopened as the Cotton Club with lavishly staged shows featuring top stars like Bill 'Bojangles' Robinson and Ethel Waters with music by Duke Ellington and, later, Cab Calloway. The Cotton Club remained as the hub of Harlem nightlife until 1936 when it moved downtown, but for 10 years its greatest rival was Connie's Inn, opened in 1923 by George and Connie Immerman. Connie's Inn also featured spectacular shows like Andy Razaf and Fats Waller's 'Hot Chocolates' starring Louis Armstrong. The last of the big four clubs was Small's Paradise, run by Ed Smalls and featuring floor shows and big bands. It was also the most durable, opening in 1925 and eventually closing in 1986.

HARLEM CLUBS & THEATRES

Alhambra Theatre
W126th Street between 7th & 8th (1920's)
Apollo Theatre
253 W125th Street (1913–)
Bamboo Inn
Seventh Avenue between W139th & W140th (1926–29)
Bamville Club
65 W129th Street near Lenox (1942–?)
previously Rendezvous Cabaret
Band Box
161 W131st Streetbetween 7th & Lenox (late 20's)
Barron's Club
2259 Seventh Avenue at W134th Street (1915–25)
Brittwood
594 Lenox Avenue at W140th Street (1932–42)
Capitol Palace
575 Lenox Avenue between W139th & W140th (1922–29)
later the Saratoga Club
Club Basha
2493 Seventh Avenue at W145th Street (1925–26)
owned by Sidney Bechet
Connie's Inn
2221 Seventh Avenue at W131st Street (1923–33)
later the Ubangi Club
Cotton Club
644 Lenox Avenue at W142nd Street (1922–Feb 1936)
Count Basie's
2245 Seventh Avenue at W132nd (1955–60)
Dickie Wells Shim Sham Club
169 W133rd Street (1933–?)
previously the Nest Club
Garden of Joy
Seventh Avenue & W140th Street (1920–?)
Golden Gate Ballroom
46–48 W135th Street (1930's–1940's)
Harlem Club
W116th Street between Lenox & 7th (1930's)

Harlem Opera House
211 W125th Street (1889–1935)
Heat Wave
W145th Street (1930's & 1940's)
Lafayette Theatre
2227 Seventh Avenue at W131st Street (1915–1935)
Lenox Club
652 Lenox Avenue close to Cotton Club (1920's–30's)
Leroy's
135th Street & 5th Avenue (1910–?)
Lido Ballroom
160 W146th Street (1930's–?)
Lincoln Theatre
58 W135th Street (1915–?)
Luckey's Rendezvous
773 St Nicholas Avenue (1940–54)
Minton's Playhouse
210 W118th Street (1938–)
Monette's Supper Club
133rd Street (1930's)
Monroe's Uptown House
198 W134th Street (1930's & 40's)
Nest Club
169 W133rd Street (1920's–33)
later Dickie Wells Shim Sham Club
Pod's & Jerry's (Log Cabin)
168 W132nd Street (1933–?)
previously the Rhythm Club
Renaissance Ballroom
150 W138th Street (1920's–50's)
Rendezvous Cabaret
65 W129th Street near Lenox (Sept 1923–42)
later the Bamville Club
Rhythm Club
168 W132nd Street at Seventh Avenue (–1932)
169 W133rd Street (1932–)
Saratoga Club
575 Lenox Avenue between W139th & W140th (1929–33)
Savoy Ballroom
596 Lenox Avenue between W140 & W141 (March 1926–50's)
Smalls Paradise
2294½ Seventh Avenue at W135th Street (Oct 1925–1986)
Ubangi Club
2221 Seventh Avenue at 131st Street (1936–40's)
previously Connie's Inn
Yeah Man
Seventh Avenue & W137th Street (1925–33)
2350 Seventh Avenue (from 1933)

Photograph courtesy: *Max Jones*

HARLEM

EDGECOMBE AVENUE

ST NICHOLAS AVENUE

ST NICHOLAS PARK

EIGHTH AVENUE

SEVENTH AVENUE

LENOX AVENUE

FIFTH AVENUE

142nd STREET

Victoria Café

Cotton Club

141st STREET

Savoy Ballroom
Brittwood (under)

140th STREET

Capitol Palace

139th STREET

138th STREET

Yeah Man

Renaissance Ballroom

137th STREET

136th STREET

Tempo Club

HARLEM HOSPITAL

Leroy's

135th STREET

Small's Paradise

Lincoln Theatre

134th STREET

Monroe's Uptown House

Hotcha

Barron's

Pod & Jerry's

Dickie Wells' Shim Sham Club

133rd STREET

Tillie's Chicken Shack

Count Basie's

132nd STREET

Rhythm Club

Lafayette Theatre

Connie's Inn

131st STREET

Joe Well's

130th STREET

Bamville Club

129th STREET

128th STREET

127th STREET

Baby Grand

Apollo Theatre

Harlem Opera House

126th STREET

125th STREET

Theresa Hotel

1930

Louis Armstrong (29) appears as a cabaret artist at Frank Sebastian's Cotton Club in Culver City, California from July.

Duke Ellington (31) and his Orchestra go to Hollywood to appear in the film 'Check and Double Check'.

Jimmy Dorsey (26) and Muggsy Spanier (24) appear in Britain with the Ted Lewis Band.

The Chrysler Building is completed in New York and becomes the world's tallest building.

BIRTHS

Jack Nimitz (baritone sax) 11 January
Kenny Wheeler (trumpet) 14 January
Jimmie Johnson (drums) 20 January
Dick Meldonian (saxes) 27 January
Buddy Montgomery (vibes) 30 January
Don Goldie (trumpet) 5 February
Eddie Locke (drums) 8 February
Joe Maini (saxes) 8 February
Dwike Mitchell (piano) 14 February
Eddie Haas (bass) 21 February
Richard Boone (trombone/vocals) 23 February
Marty Grosz (guitar/vocals) 28 February
Benny Powell (trombone) 1 March
Vic Ash (tenor sax) 9 March
Ornette Coleman (alto sax) 9 March
Blue Mitchell (trumpet) 13 March
Tommy Flanagan (piano) 16 March
Paul Horn (saxes) 17 March
Grover Mitchell (trombone) 17 March
Bill Henderson (vocals) 19 March
Otis Spann (piano) 21 March
Eric Dixon (tenor sax) 28 March
Bill Hughes (trombone) 28 March
Knobby Totah (bass) 5 April
Claude Bolling (piano) 10 April
Richard Davis (bass) 15 April
Herbie Mann (flute) 16 April
Chris Barber (trombone) 17 April
Sam Noto (trumpet) 17 April
Frank Strazzeri (piano) 24 April
Claus Ogerman (composer/piano) 29 April
Bob Havens (trombone) 3 May
Papa Bue (trombone) 8 May
Betty Carter (vocals) 16 May
Friedrich Gulda (piano/composer) 16 May
Mike Zwerin (bass trumpet) 18 May
Tommy Bryant (bass) 21 May
Kenny Ball (trumpet) 22 May
Kenny Dennis (drums) 27 May
Tricky Lofton (trombone) 28 May
Dave McKenna (piano) 30 May
Morgana King (vocals) 4 June
Guy Pedersen (bass) 10 June
Jimmy Deuchar (trumpet) 26 June
Ahmad Jamal (piano) 2 July
Ronnell Bright (piano) 3 July
Pete Fountain (clarinet) 3 July
Hank Mobley (tenor sax) 7 July
Bill Trujillo (tenor sax) 7 July
Sabu Martinez (percussion) 14 July
Helen Merrill (vocals) 21 July
Richie Kamuca (tenor sax) 23 July
Annie Ross (vocals) 25 July
Jack Six (bass) 26 July
Abbey Lincoln (vocals) 6 August
Stan Greig (piano/drums) 12 August
Eddie Costa (vibes/piano) 14 August
Frank de Vito (drums) 14 August
Chuck Connors (trombone) 18 August
Walter Benton (tenor sax) 9 September
Bill Berry (trumpet) 14 September
Muhal Richard Abrams (piano) 19 September
Ray Charles (piano/vocal/leader) 23 September
Sam Rivers (tenor sax) 25 September
Pepper Adams (baritone sax) 8 October
Clifford Brown (trumpet) 30 October
Booker Ervin (tenor sax) 31 October
Les Tomkins (writer) 31 October
Mel Wanzo (trombone) 22 November
Jim Hall (guitar) 4 December
Ben Tucker (bass) 13 December
Sam Most (flute/alto sax) 16 December
Al Jones (drums) 18 December
Ed Thigpen (drums) 28 December
Jay Migliori (tenor sax)

DEATHS

Blind Lemon Jefferson (33)

FILMS

Check and double check (75mins): Duke Ellington Orchestra in Amos 'n' Andy feature.
King of Jazz (90mins): Paul Whiteman Orchestra musical feature.
Yamekraw (9mins): screen adaptation of James P. Johnson's symphonic tone poem.

COMPOSITIONS

Harold Arlen / Ted Koehler: *Get Happy*
Phil Baxter: *I'm a Ding Dong Daddy*
Irving Berlin: *Puttin' On The Ritz*
Eubie Blake / Andy Razaf: *Memories Of You*
Hoagy Carmichael: *Rockin' Chair*
Walter Donaldson: *You're Driving Me Crazy*
Duke Ellington: *Mood Indigo / Rockin' in Rhythm / Ring Dem Bells*
George & IraGershwin: *But Not For Me / Embraceable You / I Got Rhythm / I've Got A Crush On You*
Johnny Green / Ed Heyman / Robert Sauer / Frank Eyton: *Body And Soul*
James P. Johnson / Henry Creamer: *If I Could Be With You / You've Got to be Modernistic*
Bert Lown / Chauncey Gray / Fred Hamm / Dave Bennett: *Bye Bye Blues*
Jimmy McHugh / Dorothy Fields: *Exactly Like You / On The Sunny Side Of The Street*
Murray Mencher / Billy Moll: *I Want a Little Girl*
Maceo Pinkard / William Tracey / Doris Tauber: *Them There Eyes*
Cole Porter: *Love For Sale / What Is This Thing Called Love?*
Joe Primrose: *St James Infirmary*
Ralph Rainger / Billy Rose: *When A Woman Loves A Man*
Willard Robison / Larry Conley: *A Cottage For Sale*
Moises Simons / L Wolfe Gilbert / Marion Sunshine: *The Peanut Vendor*
Fats Waller / Andy Razaf: *Blue Turning Grey Over You*

RECORDS

Henry 'Red' Allen Orchestra (NYC, 18 February): *Sugar Hill Function / You Might Get Better, But You'll Never Get Well / Everybody Shout / Dancing Dave* (NYC, 15 July): *Roamin' / Singing Pretty Songs / Patrol Wagon Blues / I Fell In Love With You*
Louis Armstrong Orchestra (NYC, 24 January): *Song Of The Islands* (NYC, 1 February): *Bessie Couldn't Help It / Blue Turning Grey Over You* (NYC, 5 April): *Dear Old Southland / My Sweet / I Can't Believe That You're In Love With Me* (NYC, 4 May): *Indian Cradle Song / Exactly Like You / Dinah / Tiger Rag*
Louis Armstrong & New Cotton Club Orchestra (LA, 21 July): *I'm A Ding Dong Daddy / I'm In The Market For You* (LA, 19 August): *Confessin' / If I Could Be With You One Hour Tonight* (LA, 9 October): *Body And Soul* (LA, 16 October): *Memories Of You / You're Lucky To Me* (LA, 23 December): *Sweethearts On Parade / You're Driving Me Crazy / The Peanut Vendor*
Bix Beiderbecke & his Orchestra (NYC, 8 September): *Deep Down South / I Don't Mind Walkin' In The Rain / I'll Be A Friend With Pleasure*
Cab Calloway (NYC, 24 July): *Gotta Darn Good Reason Now / St Louis Blues* (NYC, 14 October): *Sweet Jennie Lee / Happy Feet* (NYC, 12 November): *Yaller / The Viper's Drag* (NYC, 23 December): *Is That Religion? / Some Of These Days / Nobody's Sweetheart / St James' Infirmary*
Charleston Chasers (NYC, 20 February): *Cinderella Brown / Sing, You Sinners* (NYC, 26 May): *Here Comes Emily Brown / Wasn't It Nice?* (NYC, 30 September): *Loving You The Way I Do / You're Lucky To Me*

The Chocolate Dandies – with Benny Carter, Coleman Hawkins (NYC, 3 December): *Goodbye Blues* (NYC, 31 December): *Cloudy Skies / Got Another Sweetie Now / Bugle Call Rag / Dee Blues*
Duke Ellington Orchestra (NYC, 29 January): *St James Infirmary / When You're Smiling / Rent Party Blues / Jungle Blues* (NYC, March): *Sing, You Sinners / St James Infirmary* (NYC, 20 March): *When You're Smiling / Maori / Admiration* (NYC, 3 April): *The Mooche / Ragamuffin Romeo / East St Louis Toodle-oo* (NYC, 22 April): *Double Check Stomp / My Gal Is Good For Nothing But Love / I Was Made To Love You* (NYC, 4 June): *Sweet Dreams Of Love / Jungle Nights In Harlem / Sweet Jazz O' Mine / Shout 'Em Aunt Tillie* (NYC, 12 June): *Sweet Mama / Hot And Bothered / Double Check Stomp / Black And Tan Fantasy* (LA, 20 August): *Ring Dem Bells / Old Man Blues* (NYC, 14 October): *Big House Blues / Rocky Mountain Blues* (NYC, 17 October): *Mood Indigo* (NYC, 27 October): *Home Again Blues / Wang-Wang Blues* (NYC, 30 October): *Ring Dem Bells / Three Little Words / Old Man Blues / Sweet Chariot / Mood Indigo* (NYC, 8 November): *Rockin' In Rhythm*
Fletcher Henderson Orchestra (NYC, 3 October): *Chinatown, My Chinatown / Somebody Loves Me* (NYC, 2 December): *Keep A Song In Your Soul / What Good Am I Without You?*
J.C. Higginbotham (NYC, 5 February): *Give Me Your Telephone Number / Higginbotham Blues*
Frankie Jaxon (Chicago, 28 October): *Scuddlin' / Chocolate To The Bone*
James P. Johnson (NYC, 21 January): *Crying For The Carolines / What Is This Thing Called Love? / You've Got To Be Modernistic / Jingles* (NYC, 31 January): *How Could I Be Blue? / I've Found A New Baby*
Wingy Manone (Richmond, Indiana, 28 August): *Shake That Thing / Tar Paper Stomp* (Richmond, 19 September): *Tin Roof Blues / Weary Blues / Big Butter And Egg Man*
Red McKenzie's Mound City Blue Blowers (NYC, 30 October): *Girls Like You Were Meant For Boys Like Me / Arkansas Blues*
McKinney's Cotton Pickers (NYC, 31 January): *If I Could Be With You One Hour Tonight* (Camden NJ, 29 July): *Blues Sure Have Got Me* (Camden NJ, 30 July): *Hullabaloo / I Want A Little Girl* (NYC, 3 November): *Talk To Me / Rocky Road*
Lizzie Miles (NYC, 27 January): *My Man O' War / Electrician Blues / Good Time Papa* (NYC, 27 February): *The Man I Got Ain't The Man I Want / Yellow Dog Gal Blues / Too Slow Blues / Done Throwed The Key Away*
Miff Mole's Molers (NYC, 6 February): *Navy Blues / Lucky Little Devil*
Jelly Roll Morton's Red Hot Peppers (NYC, 5 March): *Each Day / If Someone Would Only Love Me / That'll Never Do / I'm Looking For A Little Bluebird* (NYC, 19 March): *Little Lawrence / Harmony Blues* (NYC, 20 March): *Fussy Mabel / Ponchartrain* (NYC, 2 June): *Oil Well / Load Of Coal / Crazy Chords / Primrose Stomp* (NYC, 14 July): *Low Gravy / Strokin' Away / Blue Blood Blues / Mushmouth Shuffle* (NYC, 9 October): *Gambling Jack / Fickle Fay Creep*
Bennie Moten's Orchestra (Kansas City, 27 October): *Won't You Be My Baby?* (Kansas City, 28 October): *I Wish I Could Be Blue / Oh Eddie / That Too, Do / Mack's Rhythm / You Made Me Happy / Here Comes Marjorie / The Count* (Kansas City, 29 October): *Liza Lee* (Kansas City, 30 October): *Get Goin' / Professor Hot Stuff / When I'm Alone / New Moten Stomp / As Long As I Love You* (Kansas City, 31 October): *Somebody Stole My Gal / Now That I Need You / Bouncin' Around*
King Oliver (NYC, 28 January): *St James Infirmary / When You're Smiling* (NYC, 18 March): *I Must Have It / Rhythm Club Stomp / You're Just My Type* (NYC, 10 April): *Edna / Boogie Woogie / Mule Face Blues* (NYC, 22 May): *Struggle Buggy / Don't You Think I Love You / Olga* (NYC, 10 September): *Shake It And Break It / Stingaree Blues* (NYC, 19 September): *Nelson Stomp / Stealing Love*
Luis Russell Orchestra (NYC, 24 January): *Saratoga Shout / Song Of The Swanee* (NYC, 29 May): *Louisiana Swing* (NYC, 5 September): *Muggin' Lightly / Panama / High Tension* (NYC, 17 December): *Saratoga Drag / Ease On Down / Honey, That Reminds Me*

1930

Bessie Smith (NYC, 27 March): *Keep It To Yourself / New Orleans Hop Scop Blues* (NYC, 12 April): *See If I'll Care / Baby Have Pity On Me* (NYC, 9 June): *On Revival Day / Moan, You Mourners* (NYC, 22 July): *Hustlin' Dan / Black Mountain Blues*
Clara Smith (NYC, 21 July): *Don't Fool Around On Me / Down In The Mouf' Blues* (NYC, 9 September): *Lowland Moan / Woman To Woman* (NYC, 31

October): *You're Getting Old On Your Job / What Makes You Act Like That? / You Had Too Much / Don't Wear It Out*
Victoria Spivey (NYC, 4 February): *New York Blues / Lonesome With The Blues / Showered With The Blues / Haunted By The Blues*
Jack Teagarden Orchestra (NYC, 1 October): *Son Of The Sun / Just A Little Dance, Mam'selle*

Frank Trumbauer Orchestra (NYC, 8 May): *Happy Feet / I Like To Do Things For You* (NYC, 10 May): *Get Happy / Deep Harlem* (NYC, 22 July): *What's The Use / Hittin' The Bottle* (NYC, 8 September): *Bye Bye Blues*
Joe Venuti/Eddie Lang (NYC, 7 May): *Raggin' The Scale / Put And Take* (NYC, 7 October): *The Wild Dog / Really Blue / Dialogue on William Tell* (NYC, 12 November): *I've Found A New Baby / Sweet Sue, Just You*
Ethel Waters (NYC, 1 April): *Porgy* (NYC, 3 June): *You Brought A New Kind Of Love To Me* (NYC, 29 August): *Memories Of You* (NYC, 18 November): *I Got Rhythm*

Left: Louis Armstrong in California with the Les Hite Orchestra. L to r: Lawrence Brown (trombone), Jimmie Prince (piano), Louis Armstrong, Les Hite (alto sax), and Lionel Hampton (drums).
Below: The Duke Ellington Orchestra.

Don Redman (31) forms his own big band after leaving Earl Hines (26).

Mildred Bailey (24) makes her recording debut on 15 September.

Louis Armstrong (30) leaves California in March and returns to Chicago where he leads his own big band and tours for most of the year.

Bix Beiderbecke (28) dies on 6 August of lobar pneumonia.

Ivie Anderson (27) joins Duke Ellington Orchestra.

The Empire State Building becomes the tallest building in the world (1250 ft) when it opens on 1 May.

The hit musical on Broadway is 'Of Thee I Sing' with music and lyrics by George and Ira Gershwin.

Al Capone is indicted for tax evasion. He is convicted on 17 October and sentenced to 11 years in prison.

Legs Diamond is shot to death in Albany, NY, on 18 December.

BIRTHS

John Jenkins Jr (alto sax) 3 January
Dizzy Reece (trumpet) 5 January
Keith Christie (trombone) 6 January
Carson Smith (bass) 9 January
Horace Parlan (piano) 19 January
Bob Whitlock (bass) 21 January
Jerry Segal (drums) 16 February
Allan Ganley (drums) 11 March
Paul Motian (drums) 25 March
Burt Collins (trumpet) 27 March
Jake Hanna (drums) 4 April
Ira Sullivan (trumpet / sax) 1 May
Richard 'Groove' Holmes (organ) 2 May
Richard Williams (trumpet) 4 May
Dick Garcia (guitar) 11 May
Dewey Redman (tenor sax) 17 May
Tommy Gumina (accordion) 20 May
Louis Smith (trumpet) 20 May
Diz Disley (guitar) 27 May
Ronnie Bedford (drums) 2 June
John Pisano (guitar) 2 June
Grant Green (guitar) 6 June
Georges Arvanitas (piano) 13 June
Corky Hale (piano / harp) 3 July
Sonny Clark (piano) 21 July
Plas Johnson (tenor sax) 21 July

Patti Bown (piano) 26 July
Kenny Burrell (guitar) 31 July
Terry Pollard (piano / vibes) 15 August
Derek Smith (piano) 17 August
Frank Capp (drums) 20 August
Willie Ruff (bass) 1 September
Clifford Jordan (tenor sax) 2 September
Richie Powell (piano) 5 September
Ken McIntyre (alto sax) 7 September
John Gilmore (tenor sax) 28 September
Dusko Gojkovic (trumpet) 14 October
Phil Woods (alto sax) 2 November
Harold McNair (saxes/flute) 5 November
Wayne Andre (trombone) 17 November
Gloria Lynne (vocalist) 23 November
Nat Adderley (trumpet) 25 November
Jack Sheldon (trumpet) 30 November
Wynton Kelly (piano) 2 December
Phineas Newborn (piano) 14 December
Ray Bryant (piano) 24 December
Walter Norris (piano) 27 December
Gil Melle (sax) 31 December
Walt Dickerson (vibes)
Derek Humble (alto sax)
Dick Twardzik (piano)

DEATHS

Jimmy Blythe (30) 21 June
Buddy Petit (34) 4 July
Jimmie Harrison (30) 23 July
Bix Beiderbecke (28) 6 August
Buddy Bolden (54) 4 November

COMPOSITIONS

Harold Arlen / Ted Koehler: *Between The Devil And The Deep Blue Sea*
Cab Calloway / Barney Bigard / Irving Mills: *Minnie The Moocher*
Hoagy Carmichael / Sidney Arodin: *Lazy River*
Hoagy Carmichael / Stuart Gorrell: *Georgia On My Mind*
Hoagy Carmichael / Mitchell Parish: *Stardust*
Benny Carter / Irving Mills: *Blues In My Heart*
Duke Ellington: *Creole Rhapsody*
Herman Hupfield: *As Time Goes By*
John Klenner / Sam M Lewis: *Just Friends*
Jimmy McHugh / Dorothy Fields: *Singin' The Blues*
Matty Malneck / Fud Livingston / Gus Kahn: *I'm Through With Love*
Gerald Marks / Seymour Simon: *All Of Me*
Leon & Otis Rene / Clarence Muse: *When It's Sleepy Time Down South*
Fats Waller / Alex Hill: *I'm Crazy 'Bout My Baby*
Fats Waller / Andy Razaf: *Concentratin' (On You)*
Harry Warren / Billy Rose: *I Found A Million Dollar Baby*

RECORDS

Louis Armstrong (LA, 9 March): *Just A Gigolo / Shine* (Chicago, 20 April): *Walkin' My Baby Back Home / I Surrender Dear / When It's Sleepy Time Down South* (Chicago, 28 April): *Blue Again / Little Joe / I'll Be Glad When You're Dead, You Rascal You* (Chicago, 29 April): *Them There Eyes / When Your Lover Has Gone* (Chicago, 3 November): *Lazy River /*

Below: **The great Fletcher Henderson Orchestra on the boardwalk at Atlantic City. Back row, l to r: John Kirby, Coleman Hawkins, Russell Procope, Rex Stewart, Bobby Stark, Clarence Holiday. Front: Edgar Sampson, Sandy Williams, J.C.Higginbotham, Fletcher Henderson, Russell Smith and Walter Johnson.**

Photograph courtesy: *Rolf Dahlgren*

Chinatown, My Chinatown (Chicago, 4 November): Wrap Your Troubles In Dreams / Stardust (Chicago, 5 November): You Can Depend On Me / Georgia On My Mind (Chicago, 6 November): The Lonesome Road / I Got Rhythm

Mildred Bailey (NYC, 15 September): Blues In My Heart / You Call It Madness / Sleepy Time Down South / Wrap Your Troubles In Dreams (Chicago, 24 November): Too Late / Georgia On My Mind / Concentratin' (Chicago, 28 November): Home / Lies

Cab Calloway (NYC, 3 March): Dixie Vagabond / So Sweet / Minnie the Moocher / Doin' The Rumba (NYC, 9 March): Mood Indigo / Farewell Blues / I'm Crazy 'Bout My Baby (NYC, 6 May): Creole Love Song / The Levee Low-Down / Blues In My Heart (NYC, 11 June): Black Rhythm / Six Or Seven Times (NYC, 17 June): My Honey's Lovin' Arms / The Nightmare (NYC, 9 July): It Looks Like Susie / Sweet Georgia Brown / Basin Street Blues (NYC, 23 September): Bugle Call Rag / You Rascal, You (NYC, 12 October): Stardust / You Can't Stop Me From Lovin' You / You Dog / Somebody Stole My Gal (NYC, 21 October): Ain't Got No Gal In This Town / Between The Devil And The Deep Blue Sea / Trickeration / Kickin' The Gong Around (NYC, 18 November): You Dog / Downhearted Blues / Without Rhythm / Corrine Corrina / Stack O'Lee Blues

30-year-old Louis Armstrong poses proudly with his brand new Selmer trumpet.

Photograph courtesy: Max Jones

Charleston Chasers (NYC, 9 February): When Your Lover Has Gone / Walkin' My Baby Back Home / Basin Street Blues / Beale Street Blues

Duke Ellington (NYC, 10 January): Them There Eyes / Rockin' Chair / I'm So In Love With You (NYC, 16 January): Rockin' In Rhythm / The River And Me / Keep A Song In Your Soul / Sam And Delilah (NYC, 20 January): The Peanut Vendor / Creole Rhapsody Parts 1&2 (NYC, 16 June): Limehouse Blues / Echoes Of The Jungle (NYC, 17 June): It's Glory / The Mystery Song

Fletcher Henderson (NYC, 19 March): Clarinet Marmalade / Sugar Foot Stomp / Hot And Anxious / Comin' And Goin' (NYC, 10 April): Just Blues / Singin' The Blues (NYC, 17 July): Low Down On The Bayou / The House of David Blues / Radio Rhythm / You Rascal, You (NYC, October): Twelfth Street Rag / Milenberg Joys

James P. Johnson (NYC, 25 March): Go Harlem / A Porter's Love Song / Just A Crazy Song

McKinney's Cotton Pickers (NYC, 12 February): It's A Lonesome Old Town (NYC, 8 September): Wrap Your Troubles In Dreams

Mills Blue Rhythm Band (NYC, 30 March): Straddle The Fence / Levee Low Down / Moanin' (NYC, 28 April): Minnie The Moocher / Blue Rhythm / Blue Flame / Red Devil (NYC, 12 May): Low Down On The Bayou (NYC, 26 June): Heebie Jeebies / Minnie The Moocher (NYC, 30 July): Savage Rhythm / I'm Sorry I Made You Blue / Every Time I Look At You / Snake Hips

King Oliver (NYC, 9 January): Papa De Da Da / Who's Blue? / Stop Crying (NYC, 18 February): Sugar Blues / I'm Crazy 'Bout My Baby (NYC, 15 April): Loveless Love / One More Time / When I Take My Sugar To Tea

Don Redman (NYC, 24 September): Shakin' The African / Chant Of The Weed (NYC, 15 October): I Heard

Luis Russell (NYC, 28 August): You Rascal, You / Freakish Blues

Bessie Smith (NYC, 11 June): In The House Blues / Long Old Road / Blue Blue / Shipwreck Blues (NYC, 20 November): Need A Little Sugar In My Bowl / Safety Mama

Clara Smith (NYC, 7 March): I Wanna Two-Fisted, Double-Jointed Man / Good Times (NYC, 4 August): Ol' Sam Tages / Unemployed Papa – Charity Working Mama (NYC, 25 September): For Sale / You Dirty Dog

Mamie Smith (NYC, 19 February): Golfing Papa / Jenny's Ball / Keep A Song In Your Soul / Don't You Advertise Your Man

Eddie South (Chicago, 27 September): Marcheta / Hejre Kati / Mama, Yo Quiero Un Novio

Victoria Spivey (Chicago, 20 March): Nebraska Blues / He Wants Too Much / Low Down Man Blues / Don't Trust Nobody Blues

Jack Teagarden (NYC, January): Rockin' Chair / Loveless Love (NYC, 14 October): You Rascal, You / That's What I Like About You / Chances Are (NYC, 10 November): Tiger Rag

Frank Trumbauer (Chicago, 10 April): Bass Drum Dan (Chicago, 24 June): In The Merry Month Of Maybe / Crazy Quilt / Georgia On My Mind / Honeysuckle Rose

Venuti/ Lang (NYC, 10 June): Pardon Me, Pretty Baby / Little Girl / Little Buttercup / Tempo Di Modernage (NYC, 10 September): The Wolf Wobble / To To Blues (NYC, 22 October): Beale Street Blues/ After You've Gone / Farewell Blues / Someday, Sweetheart

Fats Waller (NYC, 13 March): I'm Crazy 'Bout My Baby / Draggin' My Heart Around

Ethel Waters (NYC, 10 February): When Your Lover Has Gone / Please Don't Talk About Me When I'm Gone

Chick Webb (NYC, 30 March): Heebie Jeebies / Blues In My Heart / Soft And Sweet

Garland Wilson (NYC, 18 May): Dear Old Southland / Limehouse Blues / St James Infirmary / When Your Lover Has Gone

1932

Louis Armstrong (31) visits Europe for the first time (July – November).

Art Tatum (22) arrives in New York with Adelaide Hall (23).

Duke Ellington (33) and his Orchestra play a concert in Columbia University at the request of Porter Grainger. Lawrence Brown (25) joins the band.

Franklin D. Roosevelt is elected President of the USA in a Democratic landslide (November).

One of the most popular songs of the year is 'Brother, can you spare a dime?'

BIRTHS

Grady Tate (drums) 14 January
Irene Kral (vocalist) 18 January
Teddy Smith (bass) 22 January
Frank Assunto (trumpet) 29 January
Derek Bailey (guitar) 29 January
Ottilie Patterson (vocals) 31 January
Roland Hanna (piano) 10 February
Walter Perkins (drums) 10 February
Eddie Higgins (piano) 21 February
Whitey Mitchell (bass) 22 February
Michel Legrand (piano/composer) 24 February
Aake Persson (trombone) 25 February
Donald Garrett (bass) 28 February
Bill Takas (bass) 5 March
Leroy Jenkins(violin) 11 March
Mark Murphy (vocalist) 14 March
Arif Mardin (composer) 15 March
Al Aarons (trumpet) 23 March
Kenny Baldock (bass) 5 April
Rusty Jones (drums) 13 April
Joe Romano (tenor sax) 17 April
Freddie Hill (trumpet) 18 April
Slide Hampton (trombone) 21 April
Willis 'Gator' Jackson (tenor sax) 25 April
Andrew Simpkins (bass) 29 April
Warren Smith Jr (percussion) 4 May
John Barnes (saxes) 15 May
Isaac 'Red' Holt (drums) 16 May
David Izenson (bass) 17 May
Jackie McLean (alto sax) 17 May
Bob Florence (arranger) 20 May
Les Spann (guitar/ flute) 23 May
Dakota Staton (vocalist) 3 June
Oliver Nelson (saxes/ composer) 4 June
Pete Jolly (piano/ accordion) 5 June
Tina Brooks (tenor sax) 7 June
George Joyner [Jamil Nasser] (bass) 21 June
Lalo Schifrin (piano) 21 June
George Gruntz (piano) 24 June
Della Reese (vocalist) 6 July
Joe Zawinul (piano) 7 July
John Chilton (trumpet/writer) 16 July
Ray Mosca (drums) 26 July
Dorothy Ashby (harp) 6 August
Duke Pearson (piano) 17 August
Jerry Dodgion (alto sax) 29 August
Walter Davis Jr (piano) 2 September
Emil Richards (vibes) 2 September
Mickey Roker (drums) 3 September
Bengt Hallberg (piano) 13 September
Michael James (writer) 13 September
Lol Coxhill (soprano sax) 19 September
Ray Charles (piano/ vocalist) 23 September
Johnny Lytle (vibes) 13 October
Paul Bley (piano) 10 November
Alan Levitt (drums) 11 November
Jerry Coker (tenor sax) 28 November
Ed Bickert (guitar) 29 November
Donald Byrd (trumpet) 9 December
Bob Cranshaw (bass) 10 December
Sonny Red (alto sax) 17 December

DEATHS

Frank Teschmacher (25) 29 February auto accident
Bubber Miley (26) 20 May tuberculosis

BOOKS

Stanley Turnbull: How to run a small dance band for profit

FILMS

The Big Broadcast (80mins): feature film with Cab Calloway, Benny Carter, Eddie Lang & the Mills Bros
Dancers in the Dark (76mins): feature film with Duke Ellington
Harlem is heaven (10mins): Tap dancing by Bill Robinson to the music of Eubie Blake Orchestra
I'll be glad when you're dead you rascal you (8mins): Betty Boop cartoon, Louis Armstrong appears live and animated
Pie, Pie, Blackbird : Eubie Blake and Nina Mae McKinney music short
Rhapsody in Black and Blue (9mins): Louis Armstrong music short

COMPOSITIONS

Harold Arlen / Ted Loehler: I Gotta Right To Sing The Blues
George Bassman / Ned Washington: I'm Getting Sentimental Over You
Irving Berlin: How Deep Is The Ocean?
Vernon Duke / E Y Harburg: April In Paris
Duke Ellington: It Don't Mean a Thing / Ducky Wucky / Sophisticated Lady
Earl Hines / Charles Carpenter / Louis Dunlop: You Can Depend On Me
Claude Hopkins / Alex Hill / Bob Williams: (I Would Do) Anything For You
Matty Malneck / Frank Signorelli / Gus Kahn: I'll Never Be The Same
Bernie Petkere / Joe Young: Lullaby Of The Leaves
Frank Perkins / Cab Calloway / Mitchell Parish: The Scat Song
Cole Porter: Night and Day
Don Redman: How'm I Doin'?
Richard Rodgers / Lorenz Hart: Lover
Ann Ronell: Willow Weep For Me
Fats Waller / Andy Razaf: Keepin' Out Of Mischief Now

RECORDS

Louis Armstrong (Chicago, 25 January): Between The Devil And The Deep Blue Sea / Kickin' The Gong Around (Chicago, 27 January): Home / All Of Me (Chicago, 2 March): Love, You Funny Thing (Chicago, 11 March): The New Tiger Rag / Keepin' Out Of Mischief Now / Lawd, You Made The Night Too Long (NYC, 8 December): That's My Home / Hobo, You Can't Ride This Train / I Hate To Leave You Now / You'll Wish You'd Never Been Born
Mildred Bailey (NYC, 1 March): Dear Old Mother Dixie (NYC, 3 March): Stop The Sun, Stop The Moon / Strangers (NYC, 18 August): Rockin' Chair / Love Me Tonight
Billy Banks & The Rhythmakers (NYC, 18 April): Bugle Call Rag / Oh Peter / Margie (NYC, 10 May): The Scat Song / Mighty Sweet / Minnie The Moocher's Weddin' Day (NYC, 23 May): Oh Peter / Spider Crawl / Who's Sorry Now? / Take It Slow And Easy / Bald-Headed Mama (NYC, 26 July): I Would Do Anything For You / Mean Old Bed Bug Blues / Yellow Dog Blues / Yes Suh! (NYC, 18 August): Oh! You Sweet Thing / It Don't Mean A Thing / You Wonderful Thing
Sidney Bechet (NYC, 15 September): Sweetie Dear / I Want You Tonight / I've Found A New Baby / Lay Your Racket / Maple Leaf Rag / Shag
Jack Bland & The Rhythmakers (NYC, 8 October): Who Stole The Lock On The Hen House Door? / A Shine On Your Shoes / It's Gonna Be You / Someone Stole Gabriel's Horn
Cab Calloway (Chicago, 29 February): The Scat Song / Cabin In The Cotton (Chicago, 14 March): Strictly Cullud Affair / Aw You Dawg (NYC, 20 April): Minnie The Moocher's Weddin' Day (NYC, 7 June): Dinah / How Come You Do Me Like You Do? / Old Yazoo / Angeline / I'm Now Prepared To Tell The World It's You / Swanee Lullaby (NYC, 9 June): Reefer Man / Old Man Of The Mountain / You Gotta Ho-de-Ho (NYC, 22 June): Strange As It Seems / This Time It's Love (NYC, 21 September): Git Along / Hot Toddy (NYC, 9 November): I've Got The World On A String / Harlem Holiday / Dixie Doorway (NYC, 15 November): Wah-Dee-Wah / Sweet Rhythm / Beale Street Mama (NYC, 30 November): That's What I Hate About Love / The Man From Harlem / I Gotta Right To Sing The Blues / My Sunday Gal (NYC, 7 December): Eadie Was A Lady / Gotta Go Places And Do Things / Hot Water
Benny Carter (NYC, 23 June): Tell All Your Daydreams To Me (NYC, 5 October): Hot Toddy / Jazz Cocktail / Black Jazz
Duke Ellington (NYC, 2 February): Moon Over Dixie / It Don't Mean A Thing If It Ain't Got That Swing / Lazy Rhapsody (NYC, 4 February): Blue Tune / Baby, When You Ain't There (NYC, 9 February): Dinah / Bugle Call Rag (NYC, 16 May): Blue Harlem / Sheik of Araby (NYC, 17 May): Swampy River / Fast And Furious / Best Wishes (NYC, 18 May): Slippery Horn / Blue Ramble / Clouds In My Heart (NYC, 19 September): Blue Mood / Ducky Wucky (NYC, 21 September): Jazz Cocktail / Lightnin' (NYC, 22 September): Swing Low (NYC, 21 December): Any Time, Any Day, Anywhere / Delta Bound
Adelaide Hall with Art Tatum (NYC, 5 August): Strange As It Seems / I'll Never Be The Same (NYC, 10 August): You Gave Me Everything But Love / This Time It's Love
Fletcher Henderson (NYC, 9 December): Honeysuckle Rose / New King Porter Stomp
Earl Hines (NYC, 28 June): Deep Forest (NYC, 14 July): Oh! You Sweet Thing / Blue Drag / I Love You Because I Love You / Sensational Mood / Love Me Tonight / Down Among The Sheltering Palms
Mills Blue Rhythm Band (NYC, 12 May): Rhythm Spasm / Swanee Lullaby / White Lightning / Wild Waves (NYC, 17 August): Sentimental Gentleman From Georgia / You Gave Me Everything But Love / Old Yazoo / Reefer Man (NYC, 23 September): Jazz Cocktail / Smoke Rings
Bennie Moten (NYC, 13 December): Toby / Moten Swing / The Blue Room / New Orleans / Milenberg Joys / Lafayette / Prince of Wails
Don Redman (NYC, 26 January): How'm I Doin'? / Try Getting a Good Night's Sleep (NYC, 28 June): It's a Great World After All (NYC, 30 June): Hot and Anxious / I Got Rhythm (NYC, 16 September): Two-Time Man (NYC, 6 October): Doin' What I Please / Nagasaki (NYC, 29 December): Doin' The New Low-Down
Clara Smith (NYC, 18 January): Street Department Papa / Pictures On The Wall (NYC, 25 March): So Long Jim / I'm Tired Of Fattenin' Frogs For Snakes
Ethel Waters with Duke Ellington (NYC, 22 December): I Can't Give You Anything But Love / Porgy
Garland Wilson (NYC, 2 February): Memories Of You / Rockin' Chair (Paris, November): Blues In C Flat / Get Up, Bessie

The Melody Maker (Dance Band News) July, 1932.

GROSVENOR HOUSE SENSATION—SEE PAGE 53!

Dance Band News

Vol. VII   JULY, 1932   No. 7

LOUIS ARMSTRONG COMING TO LONDON

Coloured Trumpet King to Appear at Palladium

Lyons All-Out

Top right: Cab Calloway fronts his band in the Hollywood movie The Big Broadcast.
Right: Fats Waller (3rd from right) at Bricktop's Restaurant in Paris. Bricktop herself is at far right with Spencer Williams next to her. Pianist Garland Wilson is at the extreme left.

Photograph courtesy: *Rolf Dahlgren*

Photograph courtesy: *Max Jones*

1933

Duke Ellington (34) and his Orchestra visit Europe.

Bunk Johnson (54) retires from music and settles in New Iberia.

Benny Carter (25) forms a band including Teddy Wilson (21).

Louis Armstrong (32) in London and Europe.

Bessie Smith (38) makes her final record date on 24 November.

Billie Holiday (18) makes her recording debut on 27 November.

President Roosevelt announces his 'New Deal' legislature.

Prohibition is repealed on 5 December.

BIRTHS
Jackie Williams (drums) 2 January
Don Payne (bass) 7 January
Jean-Louis Viale (drums) 22 January
Lennie McBrowne (drums) 24 January
Jimmy Bond (bass) 27 January
Sacha Distel (guitar) 29 January
Sadao Watanabe (alto sax) 1 February
John Handy (alto sax) 3 February
Spike Heatley (bass) 17 February
Nina Simone (piano/ vocalist) 21 February
David 'Fathead' Newman (saxes) 24 February
Quincy Jones (trumpet/arranger/leader) 14 March
Dave Frishberg (piano) 23 March
Donald Bailey (drums) 26 March
Tete Montoliu (piano) 28 March
Bill Hardman (trumpet) 6 April
Paul Jeffrey (tenor sax) 8 April
Ian Carr (trumpet) 21 April
Calvin Newborn (guitar) 27 April
Oliver Jackson (drums) 28 April
Stu Williamson (trumpet) 14 May
Charles Davis (baritone sax) 20 May
Michael White (violin/composer) 24 May
Michael Garrick (piano) 30 May
Nils Lindberg (piano) 11 June
Buddy Catlett (bass) 13 June
Kenny Napper (bass) 14 July
Wilfred Middlebrooks (bass) 17 July
Ben Riley (drums) 17 July
Sonny Simmons (alto sax) 4 August
Bill Dowdy (drums) 15 August
Wayne Shorter (tenor sax) 25 August
Gene Harris (piano) 1 September
Steve McCall (drums) 30 September
Ronnie Ross (baritone sax) 2 October
Gary McFarland (vibes/ composer) 23 October
Dennis Charles (drums) 4 December
John Lamb (bass) 4 December
Leo Wright (alto sax) 14 December
Johnny 'Hammond' Smith (organ) 16 December
Walter Booker (bass) 17 December
John Ore (bass) 17 December
Frank Morgan (alto sax) 23 December
Frank de la Rosa (bass) 26 December
Cal Collins (guitar)

DEATHS
Eddie Lang (29) 26 March *complications following tonsillectomy*
Freddie Keppard (44) 15 July *tuberculosis*
Lorenzo Tio Jr (40) 24 December

BOOKS
R.D. Darrell: *Black Beauty*

FILMS
Barber Shop Blues (9mins): Claude Hopkins Orchestra music short
Bundle of Blues (8mins): Duke Ellington Orchestra music short
Mills Blue Rhythm Band (9mins): music short
Rufus Jones for President (16mins): Black burlesque featuring Ethel Waters
Smash your baggage (9mins): Elmer Snowden Band music short
That's the spirit (9mins): Fictional short with the Noble Sissle Band including Wilbur de Paris and Buster Bailey

COMPOSITIONS
Harold Arlen / E Y Harburg: *It's Only A Paper Moon*
Harold Arlen / Ted Koehler: *Stormy Weather*
Hoagy Carmichael / Johnny Mercer: *Lazybones*
Benny Carter/Manny Kurtz/Irving Mills: *Blue Interlude*
Duke Ellington: *Drop Me Off At Harlem / Harlem Speaks / Daybreak Express*
Duke Ellington / Irving Mills / Mitchell Parish: *Sophisticated Lady*
Earl Hines / Reginald Foresythe / Andy Razaf: *Deep Forest*
Earl Hines / Henri Woode: *Rosetta*
Isham Jones / Charles Newman: *You've Got Me Crying Again*
Jerome Kern / Otto Harbach: *Smoke Gets In Your Eyes / Yesterdays*
Jimmy McHugh / Dorothy Fields: *Don't Blame Me*
Fats Waller / Andy Razaf: *Ain'tcha Glad?*

RECORDS
Henry Allen/ Coleman Hawkins (NYC, 27 March): *Someday Sweetheart / I Wish I Could Shimmy Like My Sister Kate* (NYC, 21 July): *The River's Takin' Care Of Me / Ain'tcha Got Music? / Stringing Along On A Shoestring / Shadows On The Swanee* (NYC, 9 November): *Hush My Mouth / You're Gonna Lose Your Gal / Dark Clouds / My Galveston Gal*
Louis Armstrong (Chicago, 26 January): *I've Got The World On A String / I Gotta Right To Sing The Blues / Hustlin' And Bustlin' For Baby / Sittin' In The Dark / High Society / He's A Son Of The South* (Chicago, 27 January): *Some Sweet Day / Basin Street Blues / Honey Do!* (Chicago, 28 January): *Snowball / Mahogany Hall Stomp / Swing, You Cats* (Chicago, 24 April): *Honey, Don't You Love Me Anymore? / Mississippi Basin /Laughin' Louie / Tomorrow Night / Dusky Stevedore* (Chicago, 26 April): *There's A Cabin In The Pines / Mighty River / Sweet Sue, Just You / I Wonder Who / St. Louis Blues / Don't Play Me Cheap*
Mildred Bailey (NYC, 8 April): *Is That Religion? / Harlem Lullaby* (NYC, 6 June): *There's A Cabin In The Pines / Lazy Bones* (NYC, 5 September): *Shouting In That Amen Corner / Snowball* (NYC, 17 October): *Give Me Liberty Or Give Me Love / Doin' The Uptown Lowdown*
Cab Calloway (NYC, 18 September): *Evenin'* (NYC, 21 September): *Little Town Gal / Harlem Hospitality* (NYC, 2 November): *The Lady With The Fan / Harlem Camp Meeting / Zaz Zuh Zaz / Father's Got His Glasses On* (NYC, 18 December): *Minnie The Moocher / The Scat Song / Kickin' The Gong Around / There's A Cabin In The Cotton* (NYC, 19 December): *I Learned About Love From Her / Little Town Gal*
Benny Carter (NYC, 14 March): *Swing It / Synthetic Love / Six Bells Stampede / Love, You're Not The One For Me* (NYC, 16 October): *Devil's Holiday / Lonesome Nights / Symphony In Riffs / Blue Lou*
Herman Chittison & Banjo Joe (NYC, 17 July): *Unlucky Blues / My Four Reasons*
The Chocolate Dandies with Benny Carter / Chu Berry / Teddy Wilson / Sid Catlett (NYC, 10 October): *Blue Interlude / I Never Knew / Once Upon A Time / Krazy Kapers*
Eddie Condon (NYC, 21 October): *The Eel / Tennessee Twilight / Madame Dynamite / Home Cooking*
Duke Ellington (NYC, 7 January): *Eerie Moan* (NYC, 15 February): *Sophisticated Lady / Merry-Go-Round / I've Got The World On A String* (NYC, 16 February): *Down A Carolina Lane* (NYC, 17 February): *Slippery Horn / Blackbirds Medley Parts 1&2 / Drop Me Off At Harlem* (NYC, 9 May): *Happy As The Day Is Long / Raisin' The Rent / Get Yourself A New Broom* (NYC, 16 May): *Bundle Of Blues / Sophisticated Lady / Stormy Weather* (London, 13 July): *Hyde Park / Harlem Speaks / Ain't Misbehavin' / Chicago* (NYC, 15 August): *I'm Satisfied / Jive Stomp / Harlem Speaks / In The Shade Of The Old Apple Tree* (Chicago, 26 September): *Rude Interlude / Dallas Doings* (Chicago, 4 December): *Dear Old Southland / Daybreak Express*
Benny Goodman (NYC, 18 October): *I Gotta Right To Sing The Blues / Ain'tcha Glad* (NYC, 27 October): *Dr Heckle and Mr Jibe / Texas Tea Party*
Coleman Hawkins (NYC, 29 September): *The Day You Came Along / Jamaica Shout / Heartbreak Blues*
Fletcher Henderson (NYC, 18 August): *Yeah Man! / King Porter's Stomp / Queer Notions / Can You Take It?* (NYC, 22 September): *It's The Talk Of The Town / Nightlife / Nagasaki*
Horace Henderson Orchestra (NYC, 3 October): *Happy Feet / Rhythm Crazy / Ol' Man River / Minnie The Moocher's Wedding Day / Ain't'Cha Glad?*
Billie Holiday (NYC, 27 November): *Your Mother's Son-in-Law* (NYC, 18 December): *Riffin' The Scotch*
Earl Hines (NYC, 13 February): *Rosetta / Why Must We Part? / Maybe I'm To Blame / Cavernism* (Chicago, 27 October): *Take It Easy / Harlem Lament / Bubbling Over / I Want A Lot Of Love*
Frankie Jaxon (Chicago, 29 July): *Mama Don't Allow It / My Baby's Hot / Fifteen Cents / Fan It*
Jimmy Lunceford (NYC, 15 May): *Flaming Reeds And Screaming Brass / While Love Lasts*
Mills Blue Rhythm Band (NYC, 1 March): *Ridin' In Rhythm / Weary Traveller / Buddy's Wednesday Outing* (NYC, 31 August): *Harlem After Midnight / Jazz Martini / Feelin' Gay / Out Of A Dream* (NYC, 5 October): *Break It Down / Kokey Joe / Love's Serenade / Harlem After Midnight*
Red Norvo (NYC, 8 April): *Knockin' On Wood / A Hole In The Wall* (NYC, 21 November): *In A Mist / Dance Of The Octopus*
Don Redman (NYC, February): *How Ya Feelin' / Mommy, I Don't Wanna Go To Bed / Shuffle Your Feet* (NYC, 26 April): *Sophisticated Lady / I Won't Tell* (NYC, 2 August): *Watching The Knife And Fork Spoon*
Adrian Rollini (NYC, 31 January): *Black And Blue / Clam House / Round House*
Bessie Smith (NYC, 24 November): *Do Your Duty / Gimme A Pigfoot / Take Me For A Buggy Ride / I'm Down In The Dumps*
Eddie South (Chicago, 3 May): *Old Man Harlem / No More Blues / Nagasaki* (Chicago, 12 June): *My! Oh My! /Mama Mocking-Bird / Gotta Go*
Spirits Of Rhythm (NYC, 24 October): *I Got Rhythm* (NYC, 20 November): *Rhythm / I've Got The World On A String* (NYC, 6 December): *I'll Be Ready When The Great Day Comes / My Old Man*
Joe Sullivan (NYC, 26 September): *Honeysuckle Rose / Gin Mill Blues / Little Rock Getaway / Onyx Bringdown*
Art Tatum (NYC, 21 March): *Tea For Two / St. Louis Blues / Tiger Rag / Sophisticated Lady*
Jack Teagarden (Chicago, 29 July): *I've Got It / Plantation Moods / Shake Your Hips / Somebody Stole Gabriel's Horn* (NYC, 11 November): *Love Me / Blue River / A Hundred Years From Today / I Just Couldn't Take It, Baby*
Venuti / Lang (NYC, 28 February): *Raggin' The Scale / Hey! Young Fella / Jig Saw Puzzle Blues / Pink Elephants*
Joe Venuti Blue Five (NYC, 8 May): *Hiawatha's Lullaby / Vibraphonia / Isn't It Heavenly? / My Gypsy Rhapsody*
Joe Venuti Blue Six (NYC, 2 October): *Sweet Lorraine / Doin' The Uptown Lowdown / The Jazz Me Blues / In De Ruff*
Ethel Waters (NYC, 3 May): *Stormy Weather* (NYC, 18 July): *Don't Blame Me* (NYC, 10 October): *Heat Wave* (NYC, 27 November): *I Just Couldn't Take It, Baby / A Hundred Years From Today*
Chick Webb (NYC, 20 December): *On The Sunny Side Of The Street / Darktown Strutters Ball*
Lee Wiley (NYC, 7 March): *You've Got Me Crying Again / I Gotta Right To Sing The Blues*
Clarence Williams (NYC, 14 July): *Black-Eyed Susan Brown / Mama Stayed Out All Night Long / High Society / I Like To Go Back In The Evening* (NYC, 7 August): *Shim Sham Shimmy Dance / Organ Grinder Blues / Chizzlin' Sam / High Society / Mister, Will You Serenade?* (NYC, 18 August): *Beer Garden Blues / The Right Key But The Wrong Keyhole / Dispossessin' Me / Breeze* (NYC, 1 September): *She's Just Got A Little Bit Left / After Tonight / Bimbo / Chocolate Avenue*

(NYC, 10 November): *Harlem Rhythm Dance / 'Way Down Home / For Sale* (NYC, 6 December): *Swaller-Tail Coat / Looka-There, Ain't She Pretty / St Louis Blues / How Can I Get It?*
Garland Wilson (Paris, December): *Mood Indigo / China Boy / The Way I Feel / You Rascal You*

Right: Ethel Waters and the Duke Ellington Orchestra in the lavish Cotton Club production number 'Stormy Weather'.
Below: The Duke Ellington Orchestra arrive in England at the start of their European tour in June. Back row, l to r: Bill Bailey (dancer), Sonny Greer (drums), Fred Guy (guitar), Harry Carney (saxes), Otto Hardwicke (saxes), Barney Bigard (saxes), Spike Hughes, Cootie Williams (trumpet), Wellman Braud (bass), Johnny Hodges (saxes), Tricky Sam Nanton (trombone), Lawrence Brown (trombone), Ivie Anderson (vocals). Front row, l to r: Bessie Dudley (dancer), Derby Wilson, Posey Jenkins (trumpet), Jack Hylton, Duke, Irving Mills, Juan Tizol (trombone) and Arthur Whetsol (trumpet).

Photograph courtesy: *Max Jones*

Photograph courtesy: *Max Jones*

Coleman Hawkins (30) tours Europe with Jack Hylton's Band. He is replaced by Lester Young (25) in the Fletcher Henderson Band.

Louis Armstrong (33) is still in Europe.

Buck Clayton (23) is in Shanghai with Teddy Weatherford.

Downbeat magazine is founded in July.

The Quintet of the Hot Club of Paris makes its debut.

Fats Waller (30) starts a series of combo records.

Chick Webb (32) and Jimmy Lunceford (32) record for Decca.

Ethel Waters (34) is in the stage hit 'As Thousands Cheer'.

Rex Stewart (27) joins Duke Ellington.

BIRTHS

Cedar Walton (piano) 17 January
Wade Legge (piano) 4 February
King Curtis (tenor sax/leader) 7 February
Richie Crabtree (piano) 23 February
Willie Bobo (percussion) 28 February
Doug Watkins (bass) 2 March
Jimmy Garrison (bass) 3 March
Billy Root (tenor sax/baritone sax) 6 March
Shirley Scott (organ) 14 March
Lanny Morgan (alto sax) 30 March
Horace Tapscott (piano/leader) 4 April
Stanley Turrentine (tenor sax) 5 April
Vic Feldman (vibes/ piano) 7 April
Warren Chiasson (vibes) 17 April
Shirley Horn (piano/vocals) 1 May
Bobby Bryant (trumpet) 19 May
Ray Mantilla (percussion) 22 June
Dave Grusin (composer/ piano) 26 June
Michel Ruppli (discographer) 3 July
Colin Bailey (drums) 9 July
René Urtreger (piano) 16 July
Bobby Bradford (trumpet) 19 July
Herman 'Junior' Cook (tenor sax) 22 July
Steve Lacy (soprano sax) 23 July
Tony Lee (piano) 23 July
Rudy Collins (drums) 24 July
Don Ellis (trumpet) 25 July
John Rae (drums) 11 August
Raul de Souza (trombone) 23 August
Oliver Jones (piano) 11 September
Dick Heckstall-Smith (tenor sax) 26 September
LeRoi Jones (writer) 7 October
Dollar Brand [Abdullah Ibrahim] (piano) 9 October
Alan Elsdon (trumpet) 15 October
Jacques Loussier (piano) 26 October
Barre Phillips (bass) 27 October
Pim Jacobs (piano) 29 October
George Riedel (bass) 8 November
Houston Person (tenor sax) 10 November
Marian Montgomery (vocals) 17 November
Vic Gaskin (bass) 23 November
Gato Barbieri (tenor sax) 28 November
Tony Coe (saxes) 29 November
Art Davis (bass) 5 December
Curtis Fuller (trombone) 15 December
Hank Crawford (alto sax) 21 December
Bob Cunningham (bass) 28 December
Candy Finch (drums)

DEATHS

Alcide 'Yellow' Nunez (50) 2 September

BOOKS

Martin Howe: *Blue Jazz*

FILMS

Belle of the nineties (70mins): Mae West feature film with Duke Ellington Orchestra
Ben Pollack & his Orchestra (9mins): music short
Bubbling over (20mins): Ethel Waters music short
Cab Calloway's Hi-de-ho (10mins): music short
Don Redman & his Orchestra (10mins): music short
Murder at the Vanities (87mins): comedy thriller with a production number 'Ebony Rhapsody' by Duke Ellington Orchestra
Nine o'clock folks (9mins): Mound City Blue Blowers music short
Symphony in black (9mins): Duke Ellington Orchestra/ Billie Holiday music short

COMPOSITIONS

Harold Arlen / Ted Koehler: *Ill Wind*
Hoagy Carmichael / Mitchell Parish: *One Morning In May*
Vernon Duke / E Y Harburg: *What Is There To Say?*
Duke Ellington: *Stompy Jones / Solitude*
Reginald Foresythe: *Serenade To A Wealthy Widow*
Benny Goodman / Arthur Schutt: *Georgia Jubilee*
Bernie Hanighen / Gordon Jenkins / Johnny Mercer: *When A Woman Loves A Man*
Will Hudson / Eddie De Lange / Irving Mills: *Moonglow*
Arthur Johnston / Sam Coslow: *My Old Flame*
Matty Malneck / Johnny Mercer: *If I Had A Million Dollars*
Sy Oliver / Jimmy Lunceford / Edward P Moran: *Dream Of You*
Frank Perkins / Mitchell Parish: *Stars Fell On Alabama*
Cole Porter: *I Get A Kick Out Of You*
Fats Waller / Andy Razaf: *How Can You Face Me?*
Victor Young / Ned Washington: *A Hundred Years From Today*

RECORDS

Henry 'Red' Allen (NYC,1 May):*I Wish I Were Twins / I Never Slept A Wink Last Night / Why Don't You Practice What You Preach? / Don't Let Your Love Go Wrong* (NYC, 28 July): *There's A House In Harlem For Sale / Pardon My Southern Accent / Rug Cutter Swing / How's About Tomorrow Night?*
Louis Armstrong (Paris, October): *St. Louis Blues / Tiger Rag / Will You, Won't You Be My Baby? / Sunny Side Of The Street / Song Of The Vipers*
Buster Bailey & his 7 Chocolate Dandies (NYC, 28 December): *Call of the Delta / Shanghai Shuffle*
Tiny Bradshaw & His Orchestra (NYC, 19 September): *Shout, Sister, Shout / Mister, Will You Serenade? / The Darktown Strutters' Ball / The Sheik Of Araby* (NYC, 3 October): *Ol' Man River / I Ain't Got Nobody / I'm A Ding Dong Daddy / She'll Be Coming 'Round The Mountain*
Cab Calloway (NYC, 22 January): *'Long About Midnight / Moon Glow / Jitter Bug* (NYC, 23 January): *Hotcha Razz-Ma-Tazz / Margie / Emaline* (Chicago, September): *Chinese Rhythm / Moonlight Rhapsody / Avalon / Weakness*
Benny Carter (NYC,13 December):*Shoot The Works / Dream Lullaby / Everybody Shuffle / Synthetic Love*
Herman Chittison (Paris, May–June): *Honeysuckle Rose / Harlem Rhythm Dance / Nagasaki / You Gave Me Everything But Love* (Paris, June): *Swingin' / Stormy Weather / St Louis Blues / You'll Be My Lover / Red Jill Rag / Bugle Call Rag*
Duke Ellington (Chicago, 9 January): *Delta Serenade / Stompy Jones* (Chicago, 10 January): *Solitude / Blue Feeling* (LA, 12 April): *Ebony Rhapsody / Cocktails For Two / Live And Love Tonight* (LA, 17 April): *I Met My Waterloo* (LA, 9 May): *Troubled Waters / My Old Flame* (NYC, 12 September): *Solitude / Saddest Tale / Moon Glow / Sump'n' 'Bout Rhythm*
Coleman Hawkins with Buck Washington (NYC, 8 March): *It Sends Me / I Ain't Got Nobody / Sunny Side Of The Street*
Fletcher Henderson (NYC, 6 March): *Hocus Pocus / Phantom Fantasie / Harlem Madness / Tidal Wave* (NYC, 11 September): *Limehouse Blues / Shanghai Shuffle / Big John's Special / Happy As The Day Is Long* (NYC, 12 September): *Down South Camp Meeting / Wrappin' It Up / Memphis Blues* (NYC, 25 September): *Wild Party / Rug Cutter's Swing /*

Hotter Than 'Ell / Liza
Earl Hines (NYC, 26 March): *Madhouse* (NYC, 27 March): *Darkness / Swingin' Down* (Chicago, 12 September): *That's A Plenty / Fat Babes / Maple Leaf Rag / Sweet Georgia Brown / Rosetta* (Chicago, 13 September): *Copenhagen / Angry / Wolverine Blues / Rock And Rye / Cavernism*
Jimmy Lunceford (NYC, 26 January): *White Heat / Jazznocracy / Chillen, Get Up / Leaving Me* (NYC, 20 March): *Swingin' Uptown / Breakfast Ball / Here Goes / Remember When* (NYC, 4 September): *Sophisticated Lady / Mood Indigo / Rose Room / Black And Tan Fantasy / Stratosphere* (NYC, 5 September): *Nana / Miss Otis Regrets / Unsophisticated Sue / Stardust* (NYC, 29 October): *Dream Of You / Shake Your Head / Stomp It Off / Call It Anything* (NYC, 7 November): *Because You're You / Chillen, Get Up / Solitude* (NYC, 17 December): *Rain / Since My Best Gal Turned Me Down / Jealousy* (NYC, 18 December): *Shake Your Head / Rhythm Is Our Business / I'm Walking Through Heaven With You*
Mezz Mezzrow (NYC, 7 May): *Old Fashioned Love / Apologies / Sendin' The Vipers / 35th and Calumet*
Mills Blue Rhythm Band (Chicago, 20 February): *The Stuff Is Here / The Growl* (NYC, 4 October): *Swingin' In E Flat / Let's Have A Jubilee / Out Of A Dream* (NYC, 5 December): *African Lullaby / Solitude / Dancing Dogs* (NYC, 11 December): *Love's Serenade / Keep The Rhythm Going / Like A Bolt From The Blue*
Jimmie Noone (Chicago, 23 November): *A Porter's Love Song / I'd Do Anything For You / Shine / Liza*
Red Norvo (NYC, 26 September): *Old Fashioned Love / I Surrender, Dear* (NYC, 4 October): *Tomboy / The Night Is Blue*
Quintette of the Hot Club of France (Paris,December): *Dinah / Tiger Rag / Lady Be Good / I Saw Stars*
Don Redman (NYC, 9 January): *Got The Jitters*
Adrian Rollini (NYC, 23 October): *It Had To Be You / Sugar / Davenport Blues / Somebody Loves Me / Riverboat Shuffle*
Spirits Of Rhythm (NYC, 14 September): *Junk Man / Dr Watson And Mr Holmes / That's What I Hate About Love / Shoutin' In That Amen Corner*
Art Tatum (NYC, 22 August): *Moonglow / Anything For You / When A Woman Loves A Man / Emaline / Love Me / Cocktails For Two* (NYC, 24 August): *After You've Gone / Stardust / Ill Wind / The Shout / Beautiful Love / Liza* (NYC, 9 October): *I Ain't Got Nobody*
Jack Teagarden (NYC, 18 September): *Junk Man / Stars Fell On Alabama / Your Guess Is Just As Good As Mine*
Frank Trumbauer (NYC, 12 January): *Break It Down / Juba Dance / How Am I To Know?* (NYC, 23 February): *China Boy / Emaline / In A Mist / 'Long About Midnight* (NYC, 20 November): *Blue Moon / Plantation Moods / Troubled*
Joe Venuti (London, 20 September): *Satan's Holiday / Tea Time / Romantic Joe / Hells Bells And Hallelujah* (NYC, 26 December): *Wild Party / Pardon Me, Pretty Baby / Satan's Holiday / My Monday Date / I Got Rhythm / Carmichael Medley / Rose Room / Smoke Rings / Wild Cat / I'm Confessin' / Hocus Pocus / Doin' Things / Fiddlesticks / Avalon*
Fats Waller (NYC, 16 May): *A Porter's Love Song To A Chambermaid / I Wish I Were Twins / Armful O' Sweetness / Do Me A Favour* (NYC, 17 August): *Georgia May / Then I'll Be Tired Of You / Don't Let It Bother You / Have A Little Dream On Me* (NYC, 28 September): *Serenade For A Wealthy Widow / How Can You Face Me? / Sweetie Pie / Mandy / Let's Pretend There's A Moon / You're Not The Only Oyster In The Stew* (NYC, 7 November): *Honeysuckle Rose / Believe It, Beloved / Dream Man / I'm Growing Fonder Of You / If It Isn't Love / Breakin' The Ice* (NYC, 16 November): *African Ripples / Clothes Line Ballet / Alligator Crawl / Viper's Drag*
Chick Webb (NYC, 15 January): *If Dreams Come True* (NYC, 18 May): *Stomping At The Savoy* (NYC, 19 November): *Don't Be That Way / Blue Lou*
Lee Wiley (NYC, 13 August): *Careless Love / Motherless Child* (NYC, 26 November): *Hands Across The Table / I'll Follow My Secret Heart*
Clarence Williams (NYC, 10 January): *On The Sunny Side Of The Street / Won't You Come Over And Say Hello / Old Street Sweeper / I'm Gonna Wash My Sins Away* (NYC, 17 January): *Jimmy*

Vocalion

Not Licensed for Radio Broadcast (152740)   Fox Trot
STOMPIN' AT THE SAVOY
Goodman-Webb-Sampson-
CHICK WEBB and
his ORCHESTRA
3246
US PAT 1,637,544 BRUNSWICK RECORD CORPORATION

Photograph courtesy: *Max Jones*

Photograph courtesy: *Max Jones*

Above: Fats Waller broadcasting for CBS.

Above right: Coleman Hawkins takes tea in London at the start of his five year stay in Europe.

Right: A rehearsal of the Dorsey Brothers Orchestra. Front: Bob Crosby, Kay Weber, Tommy Dorsey. Middle row: Skeets Herfurt, Jack Stacey, Jimmy Dorsey, Roc Hillman. Back: Don Matteson, Ray McKinley, George Thow, Glenn Miller, Bobby Van Eps, Delmar Kaplan.

Had A Nickel / He's A Colonel From Kentucky / Pretty Baby, Is It Yes Or No? / Mister, Will You Serenade? (NYC, 7 February): I Got Horses And Numbers On My Mind / New Orleans Hop Scop Blues / Let's Have A Showdown (NYC, 23 March): I Can't Dance, I Got Ants In My Pants / Christmas Night In Harlem / Ill Wind / As Long As I Live (NYC, 28 June): Tell The Truth / Sashay, Oh Boy! (NYC, 6 July): Jerry The Junker / Organ Grinder Blues / I'm Getting My Bonus In Love / Chizzlin' Sam (NYC, 14 August): Big Fat Mama / Ain't Gonna Give You None Of My Jelly Roll (NYC, 22 August): I Saw Stars / Crazy Blues / The Stuff Is Here And It's Mellow / Rhapsody In Love (NYC, 11 September): 'Tain't Nobody's Biz-ness If I Do / I Can't Think Of Anything But You / Sugar Blues / Jungle Crawl

Photograph courtesy: *Rolf Dahlgren*

Gene Krupa (26) joins Benny Goodman (26). The Goodman band has a big success at the Palomar Ballroom in California in the late summer.

The Savoy Ballroom in Harlem is at it's peak as a jazz centre. The bands of Chick Webb (33) and Teddy Hill (26) are the regular attractions.

Count Basie (31) leads his own band at the Reno Club in Kansas City.

Wellman Braud (44) leaves the Duke Ellington Orchestra and is replaced by two bassists, Billy Taylor (29) and Hayes Alvis (28).

Bob Crosby (22) forms his band, playing big band Dixieland.

The Dorsey Brothers Band split up. Tommy Dorsey (30) starts his own band.

Dizzy Gillespie (18) replaces Roy Eldridge (24) in the Teddy Hill Band.

Louis Armstrong returns to New York in late January and Joe Glaser becomes his manager.

Jazz clubs open on 52nd Street in New York – The Hickory House, Onyx, Famous Door and Adrian Rollini's Tap Room.

Wingy Manone (31) has a hit with his recording of 'Isle of Capri'.

BIRTHS
Chuck Flores (drums) 5 January
Kenny Davern (clarinet) 7 January
Tubby Hayes (tenor sax) 30 January
Rob McConnell (trombone) 14 February
Barry McRae (writer) 25 February
George Coleman (tenor sax) 8 March
Hugh Lawson (piano) 12 March
Carol Kaye (electric bass) 24 March
Karl Berger (vibes) 30 March
Gene Cherico (bass) 15 April
Dudley Moore (piano) 19 April
Ran Blake (piano) 20 April
Pat Rebillot (piano) 21 April
Paul Chambers (bass) 22 April
Don Friedman (piano) 4 May
Gary Peacock (bass) 12 May
Cecil McBee (bass) 19 May
Giuseppi Logan (saxes) 22 May
Ramsey Lewis (piano) 27 May
Harry Beckett (trumpet) 30 May
Albert Heath (drums) 31 May
Ted Curson (trumpet) 3 June
Julian Priester (trombone) 29 June
Rashied Ali (drums) 1 July
Frank Wright (tenor sax) 9 July
Big John Patton (organ) 12 July
Marion Brown (alto sax) 8 September
James Clay (tenor sax) 8 September
Fred Stone (trumpet) 9 September
Les McCann (piano) 23 September
Roland Alexander (tenor sax) 25 September
Ann Richards (vocalist) 1 October
Paul Humphrey (drums) 12 October
Don Rader (trumpet) 21 October
Henry Grimes (bass) 3 November
Roswell Rudd (trombone) 17 November
Peter Warren (bass) 21 November
Roy Burnes (drums) 30 November
Ronnie Mathews (piano) 2 December
Dannie Richmond (drums) 15 December
Bobby Timmons (piano) 19 December
Joe Lee Wilson (vocalist) 22 December
Peter Herbolzheimer (trombone) 31 December
Ronnie Boykins (bass)
Bill Chase (trumpet)

DEATHS
Edwin Swayze (28) 31 January *following operation*
Clara Smith (40) 2 February *heart trouble*
Bennie Moten (40) 2 April *complications following tonsillectomy*
Cecil Irwin (33) 3 May *killed when Earl Hines band coach crashed*
Leroy Carr (30) June
Honoré Dutrey (48) 21 July

BOOKS
W. Rundell: *Jazz Band*

FILMS
All colored vaudeville show (9mins): Adelaide Hall and Nicholas Brothers
By request (10mins): Claude Hopkins Orchestra music short
Cab Calloway's Jitterbug party (8mins): music short
King of burlesque (90mins): musical comedy featuring Fats Waller

COMPOSITIONS
Brooks Bowman: *East Of The Sun*
Nacio Herb Brown / Arthur Freed: *I've Got A Feelin' You're Foolin'*
Vernon Duke: *Autumn In New York*
Duke Ellington: *In A Sentimental Mood / Reminiscin' In Tempo*
George Gershwin / DuBose Heyward: *Summertime*
Will Grosz / Jimmy Kennedy: *Isle Of Capri*
Al Hoffman / Al Goodhart / Maurice Sigler: *Black Coffee*
Jimmy Lunceford / Saul Chaplin / Sammy Cahn: *Rhythm Is Our Business*
Jimmy McHugh / Dorothy Fields: *I'm In The Mood For Love*
Matty Malneck / Johnny Mercer: *If You Were Mine*
Ben Oakland / Mitchell Parish / Irving Mills: *I'm A Hundred Per Cent For You*
Cole Porter: *Begin The Beguine / Just One Of Those Things*
Ralph Rainger / Dorothy Parker: *I Wished On The Moon*
Ralph Rainger / Richard Whiting / Leo Robin: *Miss Brown To You*
Harry Warren / Al Dubin: *Lulu's Back In Town*
Harry Woods: *What A Little Moonlight Can Do*

RECORDS
Henry 'Red' Allen (NYC, 23 January): *Believe It, Beloved / It's Written All Over Your Face / Smooth Sailing / Whose Honey Are You?* (NYC, 29 April): *Rosetta / Body And Soul / I'll Never Say Never Again / Get Rhythm In Your Feet* (NYC, 19 July): *Dinah Lou / Roll Along, Prairie Moon / I Wished On The Moon / Truckin'* (NYC, 8 November): *I Found A Dream / On Treasure Island / Red Sails In The Sunset / Take Me Back To My Boots And Saddle*
Louis Armstrong (NYC, 3 October): *I'm In The Mood For Love / You Are My Lucky Star / La Cucaracha / Got A Bran' New Suit* (NYC, 21 November): *I've Got My Fingers Crossed / Old Man Mose / I'm Shooting High / Falling In Love With You* (NYC, 13 December): *Red Sails In The Sunset / On Treasure Island* (NYC, 19 December): *Thanks A Million / Shoe Shine Boy / Solitude / I Hope Gabriel Likes My Music*
Mildred Bailey (NYC, 20 September): *I'd Love To Take Orders From You / I'd Rather Listen To Your Eyes / Someday, Sweetheart / When Day Is Done* (NYC, 6 December): *Willow Tree / Honeysuckle Rose / Squeeze Me / Downhearted Blues*
Vic Berton Orchestra (NYC, 1 February): *Jealous / Dardanella / A Smile Will Go A Long, Long Way* (NYC, 25 March): *Taboo / Mary Lou / In Blinky Winky Chinky Chinatown / Blue / Lonesome And Sorry* (NYC, 14 June): *Devil's Kitchen / Imitations Of You / I've Been Waiting All Winter / Two Rivers Flow Through Harlem*
Cleo Brown (NYC, 12 March): *Lookie, Lookie, Here Comes Cookie / You're A Heavenly Thing / I'll Take The South / The Stuff Is Here And It's Mellow / Boogie Woogie* (NYC, 20 May): *Pelican Stomp* (NYC, 8 June): *Never Too Tired To Love / Give A Broken Heart A Break / Mama Don't Want No Peas An' Rice An' Coconut Oil / Me and My Wonderful One* (LA, 20 November): *When Hollywood Goes Black And Tan / When / You're My Fever / Breakin' In A Pair Of Shoes*
Willie Bryant Orchestra (NYC, 4 January): *Throwin' Stones At The Sun / It's Over Because We're Through / A Viper's Moon / Chimes At The Meeting* (NYC, 8 May): *Rigmarole / 'Long About Midnight / The Sheik / Jerry The Junker* (NYC, 1 August): *The Voice Of Old Man River / Steak And Potatoes / Long Gone / Liza*
Cab Calloway (NYC, 21 January): *Good Sauce From The Gravy Bowl / Devil In The Moon / Keep That Hi-De-Hi In Your Soul* (Chicago, 2 July): *Miss Otis Regrets / I Ain't Got Nobody / Nagasaki / Baby, Won't You Please Come Home?*
Duke Ellington (Chicago, 9 January): *Admiration / Farewell Blues / Let's Have A Jubilee / Porto Rican Chaos* (NYC, 30 April): *In A Sentimental Mood / Showboat Shuffle / Merry-Go-Round / Admiration* (NYC, 19 August): *Cotton / Truckin' / Accent On Youth* (NYC, 12 September): *Reminiscing In Tempo*
Bud Freeman (NYC, 4 December): *What Is There To Say? / The Buzzard / Tillie's Downtown Now / Keep Smilin' At Trouble*
Benny Goodman Orchestra (NYC, 15 January): *The Dixieland Band / Blue Moon / Throwing Stones At The Sun / Down Home Rag* (NYC, 19 April): *Japanese Sandman / Always* (NYC, 25 June): *Get Rhythm In Your Feet / Ballad In Blue / Blue Skies / Dear Old Southland* (NYC, 1 July): *Sometimes I'm Happy / King Porter / Jingle Bells* (Chicago, 22 November): *If I Could Be With You / When Buddha Smiles*
Benny Goodman Trio (NYC, 13 July): *After You've Gone / Body And Soul / Who? / Someday Sweetheart*
Stephane Grappelli with Django Reinhardt (Paris, 30 September): *St Louis Blues / Chinatown* (Paris, October): *Limehouse Blues / I Got Rhythm* (Paris, 21 October): *I've Found A New Baby / It Was So Beautiful / China Boy / Moon Glow / It Don't Mean A Thing*
Teddy Hill (NYC, 26 February): *Lookie, Lookie, Lookie, Here Comes Cookie / Got Me Doin' Things / When The Robin Sings His Song Again*
Earl Hines (NYC, 12 February): *Japanese Sandman / Bubbling Over / Blue / Julia*
Billie Holiday/ Teddy Wilson (NYC, 2 July): *I Wished On The Moon / What A Little Moonlight Can Do / Miss Brown To You / A Sunbonnet Blue* (NYC, 31 July): *What A Night, What A Moon, What A Girl / I'm Painting The Town Red / It's Too Hot For Words* (NYC, 25 October): *Twenty Four Hours A Day / Yankee Doodle Never Went To Town / Eeny Meeny Miney Mo / If You Were Mine* (NYC, 3 December): *These 'n That 'n Those / You Let Me Down / Spreadin' Rhythm Around*
Taft Jordan (NYC, 21 February): *Night Wind / If The Moon Turns Green* (NYC, 22 February): *Devil In The Moon / Louisiana Fairy Tale*
Gene Krupa & His Chicagoans (Chicago, 19 November): *The Last Round-Up / Jazz Me Blues / Three Little Words / Blues Of Israel*
Meade Lux Lewis (Chicago, 21 November): *Honky Tonk Train Blues*
Jimmie Lunceford (NYC, 29 May): *Sleepy Time Gal / Bird Of Paradise / Rhapsody Junior / Runnin' Wild / Four Or Five Times* (NYC, 23 September): *Babs / Swanee River / Thunder / Oh Boy* (NYC, 30 September): *I'll Take The South / Avalon / Charmaine / Hittin' The Bottle* (NYC, 23 December): *My Blue Heaven / I'm Nuts About Screwy Music / The Best Things In Life Are Free / The Melody Man*
Wingy Manone (NYC, 8 March): *The Isle Of Capri* (NYC, 8 October): *I've Got A Feelin' You're Foolin' / You Are My Lucky Star / I've Got A Note*
Paul Mares & Friars Society Orchestra (Chicago, 26 January): *Nagasaki / Reincarnation / Maple Leaf Rag / The Land Of Dreams*
Mills Blue Rhythm Band (NYC, 25 January): *Back Beats / Spitfire* (NYC, 2 July): *Ride, Red, Ride /*

Harlem Heat (NYC, 9 July): *Congo Caravan / There's Rhythm In Harlem / Tallahassee* (NYC, 20 December): *Blue Mood / E Flat Stride*

Red Norvo (NYC, 25 January): *Honeysuckle Rose / With All My Heart And Soul / Bughouse / Blues In E Flat*

Quintette of Hot Club of France (Paris, March): *Confessin' / The Continental* (Paris, April): *Blue Drag / Swanee River / The Sunshine Of Your Smile / Ultrafox* (Paris, July): *Avalon / Smoke Rings / Nuages / Believe It, Beloved* (Paris, September): *Chasing Shadows / I've Had My Moments / Some Of These Days / Djangology*

Adrian Rollini & his Tap Room gang (NYC, 14 June): *Bouncin' In Rhythm / Weather Man / Nagasaki / Honeysuckle Rose*

Willie 'The Lion' Smith (NYC, 23 April): *There's Gonna Be The Devil To Pay / Streamline Gal / What Can I Do With A Foolish Little Girl Like You? / Harlem Joys* (NYC, 22 May): *Echo Of Spring / Breeze / Swing, Brother, Swing / Sittin' At The Table*

Valaida Snow (London, 18 January): *I Wish I Were Twins* (London, 19 January): *I Can't Dance* (London, 20 February): *It Had To Be You / You Bring Out The Savage In Me* (London, 26 April): *Imagination / Sing, You Sinners / Whisper Sweet / Singin' In The Rain*

Jess Stacy (Chicago, 16 November): *In The Dark / Flashes / Barrelhouse / The World Is Waiting For The Sunrise / Go Back Where You Stayed Last Night*

Joe Sullivan (LA, 8 August): *My Little Pride And Joy / Little Rock Getaway / Just Strolling / Minor Mood*

Art Tatum (LA, September): *Tiger Rag / Stay As Sweet As You Are / Monday In Manhattan / I Would Do Anything For You / Theme For Piano / Take Me Back To My Boots And Saddle / After You've Gone / The Dixieland Band / The Shout / In The Middle Of A Kiss / Rosetta / I Wish I Were Twins / Devil In The Moon*

Joe Venuti (NYC, 20 March): *Mello As A Cello / Mystery / Send Me / Vibraphonia No2 / Nothing But Notes / Tap Room Blues*

Fats Waller (NYC, 5 January): *I'm A Hundred Per Cent For You / Baby Brown / Night Wind* (NYC, 6 March): *I Ain't Got Nobody / Whose Honey Are You? / Rosetta* (NYC, 8 May): *Lulu's Back In Town / I'm Gonna Sit Right Down And Write Myself A Letter* (NYC, 24 June): *Dinah / My Very Good Friend The Milkman* (NYC, 20 August): *Rhythm And Romance / Got A Bran' New Suit / I'm On A Seesaw* (NYC, 29 November): *When Somebody Thinks You're Wonderful / Spreadin' Rhythm Around / A Little Bit Independent* (NYC, 4 December): *Fat And Greasy / Functionizin' / I Got Rhythm*

Chick Webb (NYC, 12 June): *I'll Chase The Blues Away / Love And Kisses* (Ella Fitzgerald's first recording)

Clarence Williams (NYC, 9 February): *I Can See You All Over The Place / Savin' Up For Baby* (NYC, 7 March): *Milk Cow Blues / Black Gal / A Foolish Little Girl Like You / There's Gonna Be The Devil To Pay* (NYC, 14 May): *This Is My Sunday Off / Yama Yama Blues / Let Every Day Be Mother's Day / Lady Luck Blues*

Below: Earl Hines and his Grand Terrace Orchestra, with Trummy Young, Budd Johnson, Darnell Howard and Omer Simeon.
Middle: Billie Holiday (19) in *Symphony in Black*, her first film appearance.
Bottom: The Benny Goodman Orchestra just prior to its sensational success at the Palomar Ballroom.

Photograph courtesy: *Max Jones*

Photograph courtesy: *Max Jones*

Photograph courtesy: *Rolf Dahlgren*

52nd Street flourishes: Stuff Smith (27) and Jonah Jones (27) at the Onyx club and Wingy Manone (32) at the Famous Door.

Bunny Berigan (28) forms his big band and records '*I can't get started*'.

Mildred Bailey (29) teams up with Red Norvo (28) and his new band.

Woody Herman (23) forms a band.

Lionel Hampton (23) and Teddy Wilson (25) join Benny Goodman (27), and the famous Benny Goodman Trio & Quartet make their first appearances.

Lester Young (27), Jo Jones (25) and Buck Clayton (25) join Count Basie (32) and their broadcasts from the Reno Club in Kansas City are heard by John Hammond who raves about the band.

John Hammond (26) also rediscovers Meade Lux Lewis (31) and a boogie woogie vogue ensues.

BIRTHS

Eldee Young (bass) / January
Onzy Matthews (piano/ arranger) 15 January
Bobby Wellins (tenor sax) 24 January
Garnett Brown (trombone) 31 January
Buddy Deppenschmidt (drums) 16 February
Colin Purbrook (piano) 26 February
Buell Neidlinger (bass) 2 March
Gabor Szabo (guitar) 8 March
Harold Mabern (piano) 20 March
Mike Westbrook (piano/ composer) 21 March
Larry Gales (bass) 25 March
Scott la Faro (bass) 3 April
Jimmy McGriff (organ) 3 April
Harold Vick (tenor sax) 3 April
Manfred Schoof (trumpet) 6 April
Sonny Brown (drums) 20 April
Beaver Harris (drums) 20 April
Billy James (drums) 20 April
Don Menza (tenor sax) 22 April
John Tchicai (saxes) 28 April
Klaus Doldinger (tenor sax) 12 May
Peter Trunk (bass) 17 May
Rufus Harley (bagpipes) 20 May
Rufus Jones (drums) 27 May
Jim Hughart (bass) 28 July
Gary Foster (saxes) 25 May
Clea Bradford (vocalist) 2 June
Alan Branscombe (piano/vibes/alto sax) 4 June
Hermeto Pascoal (piano/flute/guitar) 22 June
Chris White (bass) 6 July
Albert Ayler (tenor sax) 13 July
Nick Brignola (saxes) 17 July
Carmell Jones (trumpet) 19 July
Don Patterson (organ) 22 July
Jim Galloway (saxes) 28 July
Jack Wilson (piano) 3 August
Roland Kirk (saxes) 7 August
Chuck Israels (bass) 10 August
Lex Humphries (drums) 22 August
Clifford Thornton (cornet) 6 September
Gordon Beck (piano) 16 September
Billy Higgins (drums) 11 October
JC Moses (drums) 18 October
Eddie Harris (tenor sax) 20 October
Don Cherry (trumpet) 18 November
Roy McCurdy (drums) 28 November
Bill Ashton (leader) 6 December
Chris McGregor (piano) 24 December
Mike Barone (trombone) 27 December

DEATHS

Charlie Green (36) February *froze to death on a Harlem doorstep*
Andrew Hilaire (36)

BOOKS

Louis Armstrong: *Swing that music*
Herbert Asbury: *The French Quarter*
Hugues Panassie: *Hot Jazz: the guide to swing music*
H.R.Schleman: *Rhythm on Record*

FILMS

The Big Broadcast of 1937 (99mins): variety show featuring Benny Goodman
Hit Parade of 1937 (78mins): musical revue featuring Duke Ellington Orchestra
Jimmie Lunceford & his Orchestra (10mins): music short
Pennies from heaven (80mins): feature film with Bing Crosby and Louis Armstrong
Red Nichols & his World Famous Pennies (9mins): music short
Swing it (17mins): Louis Prima, Pee Wee Russell music short

COMPOSITIONS

Fred Ahlert / Joe Young: *I'm Gonna Sit Right Down And Write Myself A Letter*
Saul Chaplin / `Sammy Cahn: *Shoe Shine Boy*
Vernon Duke / Ira Gershwin: *I Can't Get Started*
Duke Ellington: *Caravan / Clarinet Lament (Barney's Concerto) / Echoes of Harlem (Cootie's Concerto)*
Duke Ellington / Irving Mills / Manny Kurtz: *In A Sentimental Mood*
Ed Farley / Mike Riley / Red Hodgson: *The Music Goes 'Round And Around*
Will Hudson / Irving Mills / Mitchell Parish: *Organ Grinder's Swing*
Jerome Kern / Dorothy Fields: *A Fine Romance*
Matty Malneck / Johnny Mercer: *Goody Goody*
Billy Mayhew: *It's A Sin To Tell A Lie*
Cole Porter: *Easy To Love*
Louis Prima: *Sing, Sing, Sing*
Edgar Sampson / Benny Goodman / Chick Webb / Andy Razaf: *Stompin' At The Savoy*
Stuff Smith: *I'se A-Muggin'*
Fats Waller / Andy Razaf: *Stealin' Apples*

RECORDS

Henry 'Red' Allen (NYC, 1 April): *The Touch Of Your Lips / Lost / I'll Bet You Tell That To All The Girls / Every Minute Of The Hour* (NYC, 21 May): *You / Tormented / Nothing's Blue But The Sky / Would You?* (NYC, 19 June): *Take My Heart / Chloe / You're Not The Kind / On The Beach At Bali-Bali* (NYC, 5 August): *When Did You Leave Heaven? / Am I Asking Too Much? / Until Today / Algier's Stomp* (NYC, 31 August): *Darling, Not Without You / I'll Sing You A Thousand Love Songs / Picture Me Without You / (Trouble Ends) Out Where The Blue Begins* (NYC, 12 October): *Midnight Blue / Lost In My Dreams / Sitting On The Moon / Whatcha Gonna Do When There Ain't No Swing?* (NYC, 17 November): *Did You Mean It? / In The Chapel In The Moonlight / Here's Love In Your Eye / When My Dream Boat Comes Home* (NYC, 29 December): *I Adore You / He Ain't Got Rhythm / This Year's Kisses / Let's Put Our Heads Together*
Albert Ammons (Chicago, 13 February): *Nagasaki / Boogie Woogie Stomp* (Chicago, 14 February): *Early Mornin' Blues / Mile-Or-Mo Bird Rag*
Lillian Armstrong (Chicago, 27 October): *Or Leave Me Alone / My Hi-De-Ho Man / Brown Gal / Doin' The Suzie Q / Just For The Thrill / It's Murder*
Louis Armstrong (NYC, 18 January): *The Music Goes Round And Around / Rhythm Saved The World* (NYC, 4 February): *I'm Putting All My Eggs In One Basket / Yes! Yes! My! My!* (NYC, 28 April): *I Come From A Musical Family / Somebody Stole My Break* (NYC, 29 April): *If We Never Meet Again* (NYC, 18 May): *Lyin' To Myself / Eventide / Swing That Music / Thankful / Red Nose / Mahogany Hall Stomp*
Louis Armstrong with Jimmy Dorsey Orchestra (LA, 7 August): *The Skeleton In The Closet / When Ruben Swings The Cuban / Hurdy Gurdy Man / Dippermouth Blues / Swing That Music*
Louis Armstrong/Bing Crosby/Frances Langford (LA, 17 August): *Pennies From Heaven*

Mildred Bailey (NYC, 9 November): *For Sentimental Reasons / It's Love I'm After / 'Long About Midnight / More Than You Know*
Count Basie Quintet (Chicago, 9 October): *Shoe Shine Boy / Evenin' / Boogie Woogie / Lady Be Good*
Bunny Berigan (NYC, 24 February): *It's Been So Long / I'd Rather Lead A Band / Let Yourself Go / Swing, Mister Charlie* (NYC, 13 April): *A Melody From The Sky / I Can't Get Started / A Little Bit Later On / Rhythm Saved The World* (NYC, 9 June): *I Nearly Let Love Go Slipping Thru' My Fingers / But Definitely / If I Had My Way / When I'm With You* (NYC, 23 November): *That Foolish Feeling / Where Are You? / In A Little Spanish Town*
Barney Bigard & His Jazzopators (LA, 19 December): *Clouds In My Heart / Frolic Sam / Caravan / Stompy Jones*
Cleo Brown (LA, 4 April): *Latch On / Slow Poke / Love In The First Degree / My Gal Mezzanine*
Benny Carter (London, 15 April): *Swingin' At Maida Vale / Nightfall / Big Ben Blues / These Foolish Things* (London, late April): *When Day Is Done / I've Got Two Lips / Just A Mood / Swingin' The Blues* (London, mid June): *Scandal In A Flat / Accent On Swing / You Understand / If I Could Only Read Your Mind / I Gotta Go* (London, 20 June): *When Lights Are Low / Waltzing The Blues / Tiger Rag* (Copenhagen, 26 August): *Blue Interlude / Bugle Call Rag* (Copenhagen, 29 August): *Memphis Blues / When Lights Are Low* (Stockholm, 12 September): *Some Of These Days / Gloaming* (London, 19 October): *There'll Be Some Changes Made / Jingle Bells / Carry Me Back To Old Virginny*
Bill Coleman (Paris, 24 January): *What's The Reason? / Georgia On My Mind* (Paris, 31 January): *I'm In The Mood For Love / After You've Gone*
Duke Ellington (NYC, 27 February): *Clarinet Lament / Echoes Of Harlem* (NYC, 17 July): *Trumpet In Spades / Yearning For Love* (NYC, 29 July): *In A Jam / Exposition Swing / Uptown Downbeat* (LA, 21 December): *Scattin' At The Cotton Club / Black Butterfly*
Ella Fitzgerald & Savoy 8 (NYC, 18 November): *My Last Affair / Organ Grinder's Swing* (NYC, 19 November): *Shine / Darktown Strutter's Ball*
Benny Goodman Orchestra (Chicago, 24 January): *Stompin' At The Savoy / Goody Goody / Breakin' In A New Pair Of Shoes* (Chicago, 20 March): *Get Happy / Christopher Columbus / I Know That You Know* (Chicago, 23 April): *Stardust / Remember / Walk, Jennie, Walk* (NYC, 15 June): *Swingtime In The Rockies* (LA, 13 August): *Pick Yourself Up / Down South Camp Meeting*
Benny Goodman Trio (Chicago, 24 April): *China Boy / More Than You Know* (Chicago, 27 April): *Oh! Lady Be Good / Nobody's Sweetheart*
Benny Goodman Quartet (LA, 21 August): *Moonglow* (LA, 26 August): *Dinah / Exactly Like You / Vibraphone Blues* (NYC, 18 November): *Sweet Sue, Just You / My Melancholy Baby / Tiger Rag* (NYC, 2 December): *Stompin' At The Savoy / Whispering*
Fletcher Henderson (Chicago, 27 March): *Christopher Columbus / Grand Terrace Swing / Blue Lou / Stealin' Apples* (Chicago, 9 April): *I'm A Fool For Lovin' You / Moonrise On The Lowlands / I'll Always Be In Love With You / Jangled Nerves* (Chicago, 4 August): *Shoe Shine Boy / Sing, Sing, Sing / Until Today / Knock, Knock, Who's There? / Jim Town Blues*
Billie Holiday/Teddy Wilson (NYC, 30 January): *Life Begins When You're In Love* (NYC, 30 June): *It's Like Reaching For The Moon / These Foolish Things / I Cried For You / Guess Who* (NYC, 21 October): *Easy To Love / With Thee I Swing / The Way You Look Tonight* (NYC, 25 October): *Who Loves You?* (NYC, 19 November): *Pennies From Heaven / That's Life I Guess / I Can't Give You Anything But Love*
Billie Holiday (NYC, 10 July): *Did I Remember? / No Regrets / Summertime / Billie's Blues* (NYC, 29 September): *A Fine Romance / I Can't Pretend / One, Two, Button Your Shoe / Let's Call A Heart A Heart*
Andy Kirk & his 12 Clouds of Joy (NYC, 2 March): *Walkin' And Swingin' / Moten Swing / Lotta Sax Appeal* (NYC, 3 March): *Git / All The Jive Is Gone* (NYC, 4 March): *Froggy Bottom / Bearcat Shuffle /*

Steppin' Pretty (NYC, 7 March): *Christopher Columbus / Corky* (NYC, 11 March): *I'se A Muggin' / Until The Real Thing Comes Along* (NYC, 31 March): *Puddin' Head Serenade* (NYC, 3 April): *Blue Illusion / Cloudy* (NYC, 7 April): *Give Her A Pint*

Gene Krupa's Swing Band (Chicago, 29 February): *I Hope Gabriel Likes My Music / Mutiny In The Parlor / I'm Gonna Clap My Hands / Swing Is Here*

Meade Lux Lewis (Chicago, 11 January): *Yancey Special / Celeste Blues / I'm In The Mood For Love / Mr Freddie Blues*

Jimmie Lunceford (NYC, 31 August): *Organ Grinder's Swing* (NYC, 1 September): *On The Beach At Bali-Bali / Me And The Moon / Livin' From Day To Day / Tain't Good* (NYC, 14 October): *Muddy Water / Harlem Shout*

Wingy Manone (NYC, 28 January): *Old Man Mose* (NYC, 10 March): *Shoe Shine Boy / Goody Goody* (NYC, 8 May): *Basin Street Blues / Hesitation Blues / Panama*

Mills Blue Rhythm Band (NYC, 15 October): *Balloonacy / Barrel House / Showboat Shuffle* (NYC, 20 November): *Big John's Special / Mr Ghost Goes To Town / Callin' Your Bluff / Algiers Stomp*

Jimmie Noone (Chicago, 15 January): *He's The Different Type Of Guy / Way Down Yonder In New Orleans / The Blues Jumped A Rabbit / Sweet Georgia Brown*

Quintette of the Hot Club of France (Paris, 4 May): *I'se A Muggin' / I Can't Give You Anything But Love / Oriental Shuffle / After You've Gone / Are You In The Mood? / Limehouse Blues* (Paris, 15 October): *Nagasaki / Swing Guitars / Georgia On My Mind / Shine / In The Still Of The Night / Sweet Chorus*

Don Redman (NYC, 3 April): *Christopher Columbus* (NYC, 7 May): *Lazy Weather / I Gotcha* (NYC, 30 September): *Too Bad / We Don't Know From Nothin' / Bugle Call Rag*

Stuff Smith (NYC, 11 February): *I'se A Muggin' / I Hope Gabriel Likes My Music / I'm Putting All My Eggs In One Basket* (NYC, 13 March): *I Don't Want To Make History / Tain't No Use / After You've Gone / You'se A Viper* (NYC, 12 May): *Robins And Roses / I've Got A Heavy Date* (NYC, 1 July): *It Ain't Right / Old Joe's Hittin' The Jug / Serenade For A Wealthy Widow* (NYC, 21 August): *Knock, Knock, Who's There? / Bye Bye Baby / Here Comes The Man With The Jive*

Valaida Snow (London, 6 September): *Until The Real Thing Comes Along / High Hat, Trumpet And Rhythm* (London, 8 September): *I Want A Lot Of Love / Take Care Of You For Me* (London, 18 September): *Lovable And Sweet / I Must Have That Man / You're Not The Kind / You Let Me Down* (London, 25 September): *Mean To Me / Dixie Lee*

Jack Teagarden/Frank Trumbauer (NYC, 10 March): *I'se A Muggin'*

Frank Trumbauer (NYC, 29 January): *Flight Of A Haybag / Breakin' In A Pair Of Shoes / Announcer's Blues* (NYC, 5 February): *I Hope Gabriel Likes My Music* (NYC, 27 April): *Somebody Loves Me / The Mayor Of Alabam' / Ain't Misbehavin' / 'S Wonderful* (NYC, 15 June): *I'm An Old Cowhand / Diga Diga Doo*

Fats Waller (NYC, 1 February): *Moon Rose / Garbo Green* (NYC, 8 April): *Christopher Columbus / Cabin In The Sky / Us On A Bus* (NYC, 5 June): *It's A Sin To Tell A Lie / Big Chief De Sota* (NYC, 8 June): *Black Raspberry Jam / Fractious Fingering* (NYC, 1 August): *I'm Crazy 'Bout My Baby* (NYC, 9 September): *S'posin'* (Chicago, 29 November): *Swinging Them Jingle Bells / A Thousand Dreams Of You*

Chick Webb (NYC, 2 June): *Go Harlem / Sing Me A Swing Song* (NYC, 29 October): *If You Can't Sing It*

Mary Lou Williams (NYC, 7 March): *Corny Rhythm / Overhand / Isabelle* (NYC, 11 March): *Swingin' For Joy / Clean Pickin'* (NYC, 9 April): *Mary's Special*

Garland Wilson (London, 7 September): *Shim Sham Drag / Just A Mood / Just One Of Those Things / Your Heart And Mine*

Teddy Wilson (NYC, 17 March): *Christopher Columbus / I Know That You Know* (NYC, 14 May): *Too Good To Be True / Warmin' Up / Blues In C Sharp Minor* (NYC, 16 December): *Tea For Two*

Left: Bessie Smith. *Below:* The Benny Goodman Quartet. L to r: Benny Goodman, Teddy Wilson, Lionel Hampton, Gene Krupa. *Bottom:* Eddie Condon, Joe Bushkin, Joe Marsala, Mort Stuhlmaker and Red Allen.

Photograph: Carl van Vechten Courtesy: Max Jones

Photograph courtesy: Duncan P Schiedt Collection

Photograph courtesy: Hank O'Neal

Dizzy Gillespie (20) tours France and England with the Teddy Hill Band.

Benny Carter (30) leads an international band in Holland.

Mary Lou Williams (27) arrives in New York with Andy Kirk (39) and his band from Kansas City.

Charlie Parker (17) joins Jay McShann (28) Orchestra.

Harry James (21) joins Benny Goodman (28).

Grand Terrace Ballroom, Chicago, closes on 24 January ending an 8-year association with Earl Hines (32).

Maxine Sullivan (26) becomes a 52nd Street sensation with her version of '*Loch Lomond*'.

BIRTHS

Malcolm Cecil (bass) 9 January
Ted Dunbar (guitar) 17 January
Phil Wilson (trombone) 19 January
Bobby Scott (piano) 24 January
Jeff Clyne (bass) 29 January
Leroy Williams (drums) 3 February
Ed Polcer (cornet) 10 February
Brian Lemon (piano) 11 February
Nathan Davis (tenor sax) 15 February
Kirk Lightsey (piano) 15 February
Nancy Wilson (vocals) 20 February
Graham Collier (bass/keyboards/composer) 21 February
Don Randi (piano) 25 February
Barney Wilen (tenor sax) 4 March
Roy Williams (trombone) 7 March
Gene Bertoncini (guitar) 6 April
Spanky de Brest (bass) 24 April
Joe Henderson (tenor sax) 24 April
Ron Carter (bass) 4 May
Mike Melvoin (piano) 10 May
Karin Krog (vocals) 15 May
Archie Shepp (tenor sax) 24 May
Neil Ardley (composer) 26 May
Louis Hayes (drums) 31 May
Pierre Favre (drums) 2 June
Grachan Moncur III (trombone) 3 June
Frank Strozier (alto sax) 13 June
Burton Greene (piano) 14 June
Chuck Berghofer (bass) 19 June
Donald Dean (drums) 21 June
Reggie Workman (bass) 26 June
Andrew Hill (piano) 30 June
Charlie Shoemake (vibes) 27 July
Jimmy Spaulding (saxes/flute) 30 July
Charlie Haden (bass) 6 August
George Bohannon (trombone) 7 August
Jimmy Wormworth (drums) 14 August
Malachi Favors (bass) 22 August
Nathen Page (guitar) 23 August
Alice Coltrane (piano) 27 August
Larry Ridley (bass) 3 September
Joseph Jarman (saxes) 14 September
Sunny Murray (drums) 21 September
Mike Gibbs (composer/trombone) 25 September
Leon Thomas (vocalist) 4 October
Eddie Gladden (drums) 6 December
Mike Carr (piano/organ) 7 December
Don Sebesky (trombone/arranger) 10 December
Joe Farrell (tenor sax) 16 December
Milcho Leviev (piano) 19 December

DEATHS

Alex Hill (30) 1 February *tuberculosis*
Clarence Holiday (37) 1 March
Ward Pinkett (30) 15 March *alcoholism*
George Gershwin (38) 11 July
Johnny Dunn (40) 20 August
Bessie Smith (43) 26 September *auto accident*
Joe Smith (35) 2 December *tuberculosis*
Robert Johnson (23)

FILMS

Artists and Models (97mins): feature film with Louis Armstrong
Hi-de-ho (9mins): Cab Calloway Orchestra music short
Hollywood Hotel (110mins): musical feature with Benny Goodman Orchestra
March of Time – 3rd year, No7 (20mins): featuring the rediscovery of ODJB

COMPOSITIONS

Count Basie: *One O'Clock Jump*
Irving Berlin: *This Year's Kisses*
Joe Burke / Edgar Leslie: *Getting Some Fun Out Of Life*
Duke Ellington: *Azure / Diminuendo and Crescendo in Blue*
Duke Ellington / Juan Tizol / Irving Mills: *Caravan*
George & Ira Gershwin: *A Foggy Day / Nice Work If You Can Get It*
Ralph Rainger / Leo Robin: *Easy Living*
Richard Rodgers / Lorenz Hart: *Have You Met Miss Jones? / The Lady Is A Tramp / My Funny Valentine*
Fats Waller / Alex Hill / Joe Davis: *Our Love Was Meant To Be*
Chick Webb / Teddy McRae / Bud Green / Ella Fitzgerald: *You Showed Me The Way*
Richard Whiting / Johnny Mercer: *Too Marvellous For Words*
Allie Wrubel / Herb Magidson: *Gone With The Wind*

RECORDS

Henry 'Red' Allen (NYC, 4 March): *After Last Night With You / Goodnight, My Lucky Day / There's A Kitchen Up In Heaven / I Was Born To Swing* (NYC, 29 April): *Sticks And Stones / Meet Me In The Moonlight / Don't You Care What Anyone Says? / A Love Song Of Long Ago* (NYC, 19 June): *Till The Clock Strikes Three / The Merry-Go-Round Broke Down / You'll Never Go To Heaven / The Miller's Daughter, Marianne* (NYC, 7 September): *I Owe You / Have You Ever Been In Love? / Is It Love Or Infatuation? / Can I Forget You?*
Lil Armstrong & her Swing Band (NYC, 15 April): *Born To Swing / Sit-Down Strike For Rhythm / Bluer Than Blue / I'm Knockin' At The Cabin Door* (NYC, 23 July): *Lindy Hop / When I Went Back Home / Let's Call It Love / You Mean So Much To Me*
Louis Armstrong Orchestra (NYC, 2 July): *Public Melody Number One / Yours And Mine / Red Cap* (NYC, 7 July): *She's The Daughter Of A Planter From Havana / Alexander's Ragtime Band / Cuban Pete / I've Got A Heart Full Of Rhythm / Sun Showers* (LA, 15 November): *Once In A While / Sunny Side Of The Street*
Buster Bailey & his Rhythm Busters (NYC, 17 September): *Afternoon In Africa / Dizzy Debutante*
Mildred Bailey (Chicago, 19 January): *My Last Affair / Trust In Me / Where Are You? / You're Laughing At Me* (Chicago, 23 March): *Never In A Million Years / There's A Lull In My Life / Rockin' Chair / Little Joe* (NYC, 29 June): *If You Should Ever Leave / The Moon Got In My Eyes / Heaven Help This Heart Of Mine / It's The Natural Thing To Do* (LA, 27 September): *Bob White / Just A Stone's Throw From Heaven / Loving You / Right Or Wrong*
Count Basie Orchestra (NYC, 21 January): *Honeysuckle Rose / Pennies From Heaven / Swinging At The Daisy Chain / Roseland Shuffle* (NYC, 7 July): *Smarty / One O'Clock Jump / John's Idea*
Chu Berry & his Stompy Stevedores (NYC, 23 March): *Now You're Talkin' My Language / Indiana / Too Marvellous For Words / Limehouse Blues* (NYC, 10 September): *Chuberry Jam / Maelstrom / My Secret Love Affair / Ebb Tide*
Barney Bigard & His Jazzopators (NYC, 29 April): *Lament For A Lost Love / Four And One-Half Street / Demi-Tasse / Jazz à La Carte* (NYC, 16 June): *Get It Southern Style / Moonlight Fiesta / Sponge Cake And Spinach / If You're Ever In My Arms Again*
Benny Carter (London, 11–16 January): *Gin And Jive / Nagasaki / There's A Small Hotel / I'm In The

Mood For Swing (Laren, 24 March): *Black Bottom / Rambler's Rhythm / New Street Swing / I'll Never Give In* (The Hague, 17 August): *Skip It / Lazy Afternoon / I Ain't Got Nobody / Blues In My Heart* (The Hague, 18 August): *Somebody Loves Me / Mighty Like The Blues / Pardon Me, Pretty Baby / My Buddy*
Bill Coleman/Django Reinhardt (Paris, 12 November): *Indiana / Rose Room / Bill Street Blues / After You've Gone / The Merry-Go-Round Broke Down* (Paris, 19 November): *I Ain't Got Nobody / Baby, Won't You Please Come Home / Big Boy Blues / Swing Guitars / Bill Coleman Blues*
Bob Crosby's Bobcats (LA, 13 November): *Stumbling / Who's Sorry Now? / Coquette / Fidgety Feet*
Tommy Dorsey Orchestra (NYC, 29 January): *Song of India / Marie*
Roy Eldridge (Chicago, 23 January): *Wabash Stomp / Florida Stomp / Heckler's Hop* (Chicago, 28 January): *Where The Lazy River Goes By / That Thing / After You've Gone*
Duke Ellington Orchestra (NYC, 5 March): *The New Birmingham Breakdown / Scattin' At The Kit Kat / I've Got To Be A Rug Cutter / The New East St Louis Toodle-o* (NYC, 14 May): *Caravan / Azure* (NYC, 20 September): *Chatter Box / Jubilesta / Diminuendo In Blue / Crescendo In Blue / Harmony In Harlem / Dusk In The Desert*
Ella Fitzgerald & the Savoy Eight (NYC, 24 May): *All Over Nothing At All / If You Should Ever Leave / Everyone's Wrong But Me / Deep In The Heart Of The South* (NYC, 21 December): *Bei Mir Bist Du Schon / It's My Turn Now*
Benny Goodman Orchestra (NYC, 14 January): *I Want To Be Happy / Chloe / Rosetta* (NYC, 11 May): *Let's Dance* (LA, 6 July): *Can't We Be Friends / Sing, Sing, Sing* (LA, 13 July): *King Porter Stomp*
Benny Goodman Quartet (NYC, 3 February): *Ida, Sweet As Apple Cider / Tea For Two / Runnin' Wild* (NYC, 15 June): *The Sheik Of Araby* (LA, 30 July): *Avalon / Handful Of Keys / The Man I Love* (LA, 2 August): *Smiles / Liza* (LA, 10 August): *Shine*
Fletcher Henderson Orchestra (NYC, 2 March): *Slumming On Park Avenue / Rhythm Of The Tambourine* (NYC, 22 March): *Stampede / Back In Your Own Backyard / Blue Room / Great Caesar's Ghost*
Earl Hines Orchestra (Chicago, 10 February): *Flany Doodle Swing / Pianology / Rhythm Sundae / Inspiration / Honeysuckle Rose* (Chicago, 10 August): *Hines Rhythm / A Mellow Bit Of Rhythm / Ridin' A Riff*
Johnny Hodges Orchestra (NYC, 20 May): *Foolin' Myself / You'll Never Get To Heaven / Peckin'*
Billie Holiday (NYC, 12 January): *One Never Knows Does One? / I've Got My Love To Keep Me Warm / If My Heart Could Only Talk / Please Keep Me In Your Dreams* (NYC, 25 January): *He Ain't Got Rhythm / This Year's Kisses / Why Was I Born? / I Must Have That Man* (NYC, 18 February): *The Mood That I'm In / You Showed Me The Way / Sentimental And Melancholy / My Last Affair* (NYC, 21 March): *Carelessly / How Could You? / Moanin' Low* (NYC, 1 April): *Where Is The Sun? / Let's Call The Whole Thing Off / They Can't Take That Away From Me / Don't Know If I'm Comin' Or Goin'* (NYC, 11 May): *Sun Showers / Yours And Mine / I'll Get By / Mean To Me* (NYC, 1 June): *Foolin' Myself / Easy Living / I'll Never Be The Same* (NYC, 15 June): *Me, Myself And I / A Sailboat In The Moonlight / Born To Love / Without Your Love* (NYC, 13 September): *Getting Some Fun Out Of Life / Who Wants Love? / Travelin' All Alone / He's Funny That Way* (NYC, 1 November): *Nice Work If You Can Get It / Things Are Looking Up / My Man / Can't Help Lovin' Dat Man*
Jimmy Lunceford Orchestra (NYC, 26 January): *He Ain't Got Rhythm / Linger Awhile / Slumming On Park Avenue* (NYC, 15 June): *Coquette / The Merry-Go-Round Broke Down / Ragging The Scale / Hell's Bells / For Dancers Only* (LA, 5 November): *Pigeon Walk / Annie Laurie*
Wingy Manone (NYC, 4 February): *Sweet Lorraine* (NYC, 28 September): *I Ain't Got Nobody / Jazz Me Blues*
Joe Marsala's Chicagoans (NYC, 21 April): *Wolverine Blues / Chimes Blues / Jazz Me Blues*
Mills Blue Rhythm Band (NYC, 11 February): *Blue Rhythm Fantasy / Prelude To A Stomp / Rhythm

1937

Jam / *Jungle Madness* (NYC, 28 April): *The Lucky Swing* / *Let's Get Together* (NYC, 1 July): *Jammin' For The Jackpot*

Frankie Newton (NYC, 5 March): *Please Don't Talk About Me When I'm Gone* / *Who's Sorry Now?* (NYC, 15 April): *I Found A New Baby* / *The Brittwood Stomp* (NYC, 13 July): *The Onyx Hop*

Jimmie Noone (NYC, 1 December): *Sweet Lorraine* / *I Know That You Know* / *Bump It* / *Four Or Five Times* / *Hell In My Heart* / *Call Me Darling, Call Me Sweetheart, Call Me Dear* / *I'm Walkin' This Town* / *Japansy*

Quintette of the Hot Club of France (Paris, 21 April): *Exactly Like You* / *Charleston* / *You're Driving Me Crazy* / *Tears* / *Solitude* (Paris, 22 April): *Runnin' Wild* / *Chicago* / *Liebestraum No3* / *Miss Annabelle Lee* / *A Little Love, A Little Kiss* / *Mystery Pacific* / *In A Sentimental Mood* (Paris, 27 April): *The Sheik Of Araby* (Paris, 25 November): *Minor Swing* / *Viper's Dream* (Paris, 7 December): *Swinging With Django* / *Paramount Stomp*

Don Redman Orchestra (NYC, 28 May): *The Man On The Flying Trapeze* / *Swingin' With The Fat Man* / *Sweet Sue* / *That Naughty Waltz*

Stuff Smith & the Onyx Club Boys (NYC, 4 May): *Twilight in Turkey* / *Where Is The Sun?* / *Upstairs* / *Onyx Club Spree* / *Onyx Club Stomp*

Willie 'The Lion' Smith (NYC, 13 April): *The Swampland Is Calling Me* / *More Than That* / *I'm All Out Of Breath* / *I Can See You All Over The Place* (NYC, 14 July): *Get Acquainted With Yourself* / *Knock Wood* / *Peace, Brother, Peace* / *The Old Stamping Ground* (NYC, 15 September): *Blues, Why Don't You Let Me Alone?* / *I've Got To Think It Over* / *Achin' Hearted Blues* / *Honeymoonin' On A Dime*

Valaida Snow (London, 7 July): *The Mood That I'm In* / *Sweet Heartache* / *Don't Know If I'm Comin' Or Goin'* / *Where Is The Sun?* (London, 8 July): *Some Of These Days* / *Chloe* / *Swing Is The Thing* / *Nagasaki* (London, 9 July): *I Wonder Who Made Rhythm?* / *I Got Rhythm* (London, 14 July): *I Can't Believe That You're In Love With Me* / *Tiger Rag*

Eddie South/Django Reinhardt (Paris, 29 September): *Eddie's Blues* / *Sweet Georgia Brown* / *Lady Be Good* / *Dinah* / *Daphne* (Paris, 23 November): *Somebody Loves Me* / *I Can't Believe That You're In Love With Me* (paris, 25 November): *Fiddle Blues*

Maxine Sullivan (NYC, 6 August): *Loch Lomond* / *I'm Coming, Virginia* / *Annie Laurie* / *Blue Skies* (NYC, 22 October): *Easy To Love* / *The Folks Who Live On The Hill* / *Darling Nellie Gray* / *Nice Work If You Can Get It*

Art Tatum & his Swingsters (LA, 26 February): *Body And Soul* / *With Plenty Of Money And You* / *What Will I Tell My Heart?* / *I've Got My Love To Keep Me Warm*
(piano solos – NYC, 29 November): *Gone With The Wind* / *Stormy Weather* / *Chloe* / *Sheik Of Araby*

Fats Waller & Rhythm (NYC, 22 February): *You're Laughing At Me* (NYC, 9 April) *You Showed Me The Way* (NYC, 9 June): *Blue, Turning Grey Over You* (NYC, 11 June): *Keepin' Out Of Mischief Now* / *Stardust* / *Tea For Two* / *I Ain't Got Nobody* (NYC, 7 September): *You've Got Me Under My Thumb* (NYC, 7 October): *The Joint Is Jumpin'* (NYC, 16 December): *My First Impression Of You*

Chick Webb Orchestra (NYC, 24 March): *Clap Hands, Here Comes Charley* (NYC, 21 September): *I Got Rhythm* (NYC, 27 October): *Strictly Jive* / *Holiday In Harlem* (NYC, 1 November): *Rock It For Me*

Dicky Wells Orchestra (Paris, 7 July): *Bugle Call Rag* / *I Got Rhythm* (Paris, 12 July): *Lady Be Good* / *Dicky Wells Blues*

Cootie Williams & his Rugcutters (NYC, 8 March): *I Can't Believe That You're In Love With Me* / *Downtown Uproar* / *Diga Diga Doo* / *Blue Reverie* (NYC, 26 October): *Jubilesta* / *Watchin'* / *Pigeons And Peppers* / *I Can't Give You Anything But Love*

Teddy Wilson (NYC, 31 March): *Fine And Dandy* (NYC, 23 April): *I'm Coming, Virginia* (NYC, 1 June): *I've Found A New Baby* (LA, 5 September): *Ain't Misbehavin'* / *Just A Mood* / *Honeysuckle Rose*

Below: **Chick Webb (drums), Artie Shaw (clarinet) and Duke Ellington (piano) at a New York jam session.** *Bottom left:* **Stuff Smith and his Onyx Club Boys. Clyde Hart, Cozy Cole, Buster Bailey, Jonah Jones, Mack Walker and Stuff Smith.** *Bottom right:* **Bunny Berigan.**

Photograph courtesy: *Hank O'Neal*

1938

Benny Goodman (29) and his Orchestra feature in first ever jazz concert at Carnegie Hall on 16 January. Gene Krupa (29) and Harry James (22) leave Benny Goodman to form their own bands.

First of John Hammond's 'Spirituals to Swing' concerts at Carnegie Hall.

John Kirby (30) organises his famous sextet.

Artie Shaw (28) hires Billie Holiday (23).

Sid Catlett (28) joins Louis Armstrong (37).

Louis Jordan (30) forms his combo.

Fats Waller (34) and Art Tatum (28) both appear in London.

The Orson Welles radio play *War of the Worlds* causes panic when listeners believe reports of a invasion from Mars.

BIRTHS
Tony Inzalaco (drums) 14 January
Jimmie Smith (drums) 27 January
Charles Lloyd (saxes) 15 March
Dave Pike (vibes) 23 March
Steve Kuhn (keyboards) 24 March
Booker Little (trumpet) 2 April
Freddie Hubbard (trumpet) 7 April
Pete La Roca (drums) 7 April
Alex Schlippenbach (piano/composer) 7 April
Denny Zeitlin (piano) 10 April
Eddie Marshall (drums) 13 April
Hal Galper (piano) 18 April
Carla Bley (piano) 11 May
Ross Tompkins (piano) 13 May
Daniel Humair (drums) 23 May
Eje Thelin (trombone) 9 June
Tony Oxley (drums) 15 June
Al Dailey (piano) 16 June
Dennis Budimir (guitar) 20 June
Chris Hinze (flute) 30 June
John Heard (bass) 3 July
Arnie Lawrence (alto sax) 10 July
Lee Morgan (trumpet) 10 July
Tommy Vig (vibes) 14 July
Dudu Pukwana (alto sax) 18 July
Mike Mainieri (vibes) 24 July
Joanne Brackeen (piano) 26 July
Gap Mangione (piano) 31 July
Stix Hooper (drums) 15 August
Perry Robinson (clarinet) 17 August
Roy Brooks (drums) 3 September
Eric Gale (guitar) 20 September
Monica Zetterlund (vocals) 20 September
Ray Warleigh (alto sax) 28 September
Ronnie Greb (drums) 19 October
Odean Pope (trumpet) 24 October
Warren Bernhardt (piano) November
Carlos Garnett (tenor sax) 1 December
McCoy Tyner (piano) 11 December
Jimmie Noone Jr (clarinet)

DEATHS
King Oliver (52) 10 April
Dick McDonough (34) 25 May
Willie McWashington (30) 1 October

BOOKS
Dorothy Baker: *Young Man with a Horn* (novel)
Carl Gons & George Von Physter: *Destiny, a study of swing musicians*
W.C. Handy: *Negro Authors and Composers of the United States*
Frank Johnson & Ron Wills: *Jam, an annual of swing music*
Harlan Reed: *The Swing Music Murder* (novel)
Winthrop Sargeant: *Jazz, Hot and Hybrid*

FILMS
Woody Herman & his Orchestra (9mins): music short
Meet the Maestros (9mins): Cab Calloway/Isham Jones music short
Bob Crosby & his Orchestra (10mins): music short
Going Places (84mins): feature film with Louis Armstrong

COMPOSITIONS
Louis Armstrong / Zilmer Randolph: *Ol' Man Mose*
Hoagy Carmichael / Stanley Adams: *Jubilee*
Duke Ellington: *I Let a Song Go Out Of My Heart / Jeep's Blues / Prelude To a Kiss / The Jeep Is Jumpin' / Boy Meets Horn*
Al Foldman / Ella Fitzgerald: *A-Tisket A-Tasket*
Slim Gaillard / Slam Stewart / Bud Green: *Flat Foot Floogie*
Willard Robison / Dedette Hill: *Old Folks*
Edgar Sampson / Benny Goodman / Irving Mills: *If Dreams Come True*
Edgar Sampson / Benny Goodman / Mitchell Parish: *Don't Be That Way*
Edgar Sampson / Benny Goodman / Clarence Profit / Walter Hirsch: *Lullaby In Rhythm*
Artie Shaw: *Any Old Time*
Stuff Smith / Mitchell Parish: *It's Wonderful*
Alec Templeton: *Bach Goes To Town*

RECORDS
Albert Ammons (NYC, 24 December): *Boogie Woogie / Blues / Boogie Woogie No2 / Sweet Patootie Blues*
Lil Armstrong Orchestra (NYC, 2 February): *Let's Get Happy Together / Happy Today, Sad Tomorrow / You Shall Reap What You Sow / Oriental Swing* (NYC, 9 September): *Safely Locked Up In My Heart / Everything's Wrong, Ain't Nothing Right / Harlem On Saturday Night / Knock-Kneed Sal*
Louis Armstrong Orchestra (LA, 12 January): *Satchel Mouth Swing / Jubilee / Struttin' With Some Barbecue / The Trumpet Player's Lament / I Double Dare You / True Confession / Let That Be A Lesson To You / Sweet As A Song* (NYC, 13 May): *So Little Time / Mexican Swing / As Long As You Live, You'll Be Dead If You Die / When The Saints Go Marching In* (NYC, 18 May): *On The Sentimental Side / It's Wonderful / Something Tells Me / Love Walked In* (NYC, 24 June): *Naturally / I've Got A Pocketful Of Dreams / I Can't Give You Anything But Love / Ain't Misbehavin'*
Buster Bailey & his Rhythm Busters (NYC, 18 February): *Planter's Punch / Sloe Jam Fizz* (NYC, 7 December): *Chained To A Dream / Light Up / Man With A Horn Goes Berserk*
Mildred Bailey (NYC, 10 January): *I See Your Face Before Me / Thanks For The Memory / From The Land Of Sky Blue Water / Lover, Come Back To Me* (NYC, 14 March): *Bewildered / I Can't Face The Music / Don't Be That Way / At Your Beck And Call* (NYC, 19 April): *I Let A Song Go Out Of My Heart* (NYC, 21 April): *Moonshine Over Kentucky / Rock It For Me / After Dinner Speech / If You Were In My Place* (NYC, 9 May): *Washboard Blues / My Melancholy Baby / Round The Old Deserted Farm / The Lonesome Road* (NYC, 29 June): *So Help Me / Small Fry / Born To Swing / As Long As You Live, You'll Be Dead If You Die* (NYC, 28 July): *Now It Can Be Told / Jump, Jump's Here / I Haven't Changed A Thing / Love Is Where You Find It / I Used To Be Colour Blind* (NYC, 14 September): *With You On My Mind / My Reverie / What Have You Got That Gets Me? / Old Folks* (NYC, 29 September): *St Louis Blues* (NYC, 8 December): *They Say / Blame It On My Last Affair / I Go For That*
Count Basie Orchestra (NYC, 16 February): *Sent For You Yesterday And Here You Come Today / Every Tub / Swinging The Blues* (NYC, 6 June): *Blue And Sentimental / Doggin' Around* (NYC, 22 August): *Texas Shuffle / Jumpin' At The Woodside* (NYC, 16 November): *Shorty George / Panassie Stomp*
Sidney Bechet's New Orleans Feetwarmers (Carnegie Hall, 23 December): *Weary Blues / I Wish I Could Shimmy Like My Sister Kate*
Sidney Bechet Orchestra (NYC, 16 November): *What A Dream / Hold Tight / Jungle Drums / Chant In The Night*
Chu Berry/Roy Eldridge (NYC, 11 November): *Sittin' In / Stardust / Body And Soul / Forty-Six West Fifty-Two*
Al Cooper & the Savoy Sultans (NYC, 29 July): *Jump Steady / The Thing / Looney / Rhythm Doctor Man / Gettin' In The Groove*
Bob Crosby's Bobcats (NYC, 14 March): *March Of The Bobcats / The Big Crash From China*
Bob Haggart/Ray Bauduc (Chicago, 14 October): *The Big Noise From Winnetka*
Johnny Dodds (NYC, 21 January): *Wild Man Blues / Melancholy / 29th And Dearborn / Blues Galore / Stack O'Lee Blues / Shake Your Can*
Duke Ellington Orchestra (NYC, 13 January): *Steppin' Into Swing Society / The New Black And Tan Fantasy, Parts 1&2* (NYC, 2 February): *Riding On A Blue Note / Lost In Meditation / The Gal From Joe's* (NYC, 3 March): *I Let A Song Go Out Of My Heart / Braggin' In Brass* (NYC, 11 April): *I'm Slappin' Seventh Avenue / Dinah's In A Jam* (NYC, 9 August): *Lambeth Walk / Prelude To A Kiss / Hip Chic / Buffet Flat* (NYC, 19 December): *Jazz Potpourri / T.T. On Toast /Battle Of Swing* (NYC, 22 December): *Transblucency / Boy Meets Horn / Slap Happy*
Ella Fitzgerald & her Savoy Eight (NYC, 25 January): *It's Wonderful / I Was Doing All Right* (NYC, 3 May): *This Time It's Real / What Do You Know About Love? / You Can't Be Mine / We Can't Go On This Way / Saving Myself For You / If You Only Knew* (NYC, 18 August): *Strictly From Dixie / Woe Is Me*
Bud Freeman Trio (NYC, 17 January): *You Took Advantage Of Me / Three's No Crowd / I Got Rhythm* (NYC, 13 April): *Keep Smilin' At Trouble / At Sundown / My Honey's Lovin' Arms / I Don't Believe It* (NYC, 30 November): *Three Little Words / Swingin' Without Mezz / Blue Room / Exactly Like You*
Bud Freeman & his Gang (NYC, 12 July): *Tappin' The Commodore Till / Memories Of You / Life Spears A Jitterbug / What's The Use?*
Slim (Gaillard) & Slam (Stewart) (NYC, 17 February): *The Flat Foot Floogie / Chinatown, My Chinatown / That's What You Call Romance*
Benny Goodman Orchestra (NYC, 16 February): *Don't Be That Way / One O'Clock Jump*
Benny Goodman Trio/Quartet (NYC, 25 March): *Sweet Lorraine / The Blues In Your Flat / The Blues In My Flat / Sugar / Dizzy Spells* (Chicago, 13 September): *I Surrender, Dear / Some Of These Days* (Chicago, 12 October): *Opus 1/2 / I Must Have That Man / Sweet Georgia Brown / S' Wonderful*
Fletcher Henderson Orchestra (Chicago, 28 May): *Moten Stomp* (NYC, 24 April): *Let's Go Home / A Pixie From Dixie*
Woody Herman Orchestra (NYC, 22 December): *Indian Boogie Woogie*
Earl Hines Orchestra (NYC, 7 March): *Solid Mama / Goodnight, Sweet Dreams, Goodnight / Tippin' At The Terrace / Dominick Swing*

Below: Tommy Ladnier recording (December).

Photograph courtesy: *Terry Dash*

Johnny Hodges Orchestra (NYC, 28 March): *Jeep's Blues / Rendezvous With Rhythm* (NYC, 22 June): *Pyramid / Empty Ballroom Blues* (NYC, 1 August): *Swingin' In The Dell / Jitterbug's Lullaby* (NYC, 24 August): *The Jeep Is Jumpin' / Krum Elbow Blues* (NYC, 19 December): *I'm In Another World / Hodge Podge / Dancin' On The Stars / Wanderlust*

Billie Holiday (NYC, 6 January): *My First Impression Of You / When You're Smiling / I Can't Believe That You're In Love With Me / If Dreams Come True* (NYC, 11 May): *You Go To My Head / The Moon Looks Down And Laughs / If I Were You / Forget If You Can* (NYC, 12 June): *Now They Call It Swing / On The Sentimental Side / Back In Your Own Backyard / When A Woman Loves A Man* (NYC, 23 June): *Having Myself A Time / Says My Heart / I Wish I Had You / I'm Gonna Lock My Heart* (NYC, 15 September): *The Very Thought Of You / I Can't Get Started / I've Got A Date With A Dream / You Can't Be Mine* (NYC, 9 November): *You're So Desirable / You're Gonna See A Lot Of Me / Let's Dream In The Moonlight*

Pete Johnson (NYC, 24 December): *Dying Mother Blues / Fo' O'Clock Blues / Roll 'Em*

John Kirby Orchestra (NYC, 28 October): *Rehearsin' For A Nervous Breakdown / From A Flat To C / Pastel Blue / Undecided / By The Waters Of Minnetonka*

Andy Kirk & his 12 Clouds of Joy: *Twinklin' / Mess-a-Stomp / Jump, Jack, Jump / Dunkin' A Doughnut / Mary's Idea*

Tommy Ladnier (NYC, 28 November): *Ja-Da / Really The Blues / When You And I Were Young Maggie / Weary Blues*

Meade Lux Lewis/Pete Johnson/Albert Ammons (NYC, 23 December): *Cavalcade Of Boogie* (NYC, 30 December): *Boogie Woogie Prayer*

Jimmie Lunceford Orchestra (NYC, 6 January): *Margie / The Love Nest* (NYC, 12 April): *Down By The Old Mill Stream / My Melancholy Baby / Sweet Sue, Just You / By The River Sainte Marie*

Wingy Manone (NYC, 12 January): *Annie Laurie / Loch Lomond*

Joe Marsala's Chicagoans (NYC, 16 March): *Mighty Like The Blues / Woo Woo / Hot String Beans / Jim Jam Stomp*

Mezzrow/Ladnier Quintet (NYC, 19 December): *Royal Garden Blues / Everybody Loves My Baby / I Ain't Gonna Give Nobody None O' This Jelly-Roll / If You See Me Comin' / Gettin' Together*

Jelly Roll Morton (Washington, 21 May – July): Library of Congress recordings

Hot Lips Page (NYC, 10 March): *Good Old Bosom Bread / He's Pulling His Whiskers / Down On The Levee / Old Man Ben* (NYC, 27 April): *Jumpin' / Feelin' High And Happy / At Your Beck And Call / Rock It For Me / Skull Duggery / I Let A Song Go Out Of My Heart* (NYC, 24 June): *If I Were You / And So Forth / The Pied Piper / Small Fry / I'm Gonna Lock My Heart And Throw Away The Key / Will You Remember Tonight Tomorrow?*

Quintette of the Hot Club of France (London, 31 January): *Honeysuckle Rose / Sweet Georgia Brown / Night And Day / My Sweet / Souvenirs / Daphne / Black And White / Stompin' At Decca* (Paris, 14 June): *Billet Doux / Swing From Paris / Them There Eyes / Three Little Words / Appel Indirect* (London, 30 August): *The Flat Foot Floogie / Lambeth Walk / Why Shouldn't I Care?*

Artie Shaw Orchestra (NYC, 24 July): *Begin The Beguine / Indian Love Call / Comin' On / Back Bay Shuffle / Any Old Time* (Billie Holiday)

Trixie Smith (NYC, 26 May): *Freight Train Blues / Trixie Blues / My Daddy Rocks Me / He May Be Your Man, But He Comes To See Me Sometimes / Jack, I'm Mellow / My Unusual Man*

Willie 'The Lion' Smith (NYC, 10 January): *Passionette / Morning Air*

Joe Turner (NYC, 30 December): *Goin' Away Blues / Roll 'Em Pete*

Fats Waller (NYC, 11 March): *If You're A Viper* (NYC, 13 October): *Two Sleepy People*

Chick Webb Orchestra with Ella Fitzgerald (NYC, 2 May): *A-tisket, A-tasket* (NYC, 3 May): *Spinnin' The Webb / Liza* (NYC, 18 August): *Who Ya Hunchin'*

Cootie Williams & his Rugcutters (NYC, 19 January): *Have A Heart / Echoes Of Harlem* (NYC, 4 April): *Ol' Man River* (NYC, 2 August): *Chasin' Chippies / Swing Pan Alley* (NYC, 21 December): *Delta Mood / The Boys From Harlem / Mobile Blues / Gal-avantin'*

Garland Wilson (Paris, 9 March): *The Blues Got Me / You Showed Me The Way / The Blues I Love To Play / Sweet Lorraine / Bei Mir Bist Du Schon / Blue Morning*

Teddy Wilson (NYC, 13 May): *That Old Feeling / My Blue Heaven* (NYC, 11 August): *Loch Lomond / Tiger Rag / I'll See You In My Dreams / Alice Blue Gown*

Below left: Ella Fitzgerald with the Chick Webb Band.
Below: Count Basie
Bottom: Fats Waller recording in London (August). L to r: Ian Shepherd (tenor sax), Leonard Feather (producer), Len Harrison (bass), Fats, Edmundo Ros (drums), Alan Ferguson (guitar) and George Chisholm (trombone).

Photograph courtesy: *Max Jones*

Photograph courtesy: *Max Jones*

Photograph courtesy: *Max Jones*

1939

Jimmy Blanton (20), Billy Strayhorn (24) and Ben Webster (30) join the Duke Ellington (40) Orchestra.

Charlie Christian (20) joins Benny Goodman (30). Teddy Wilson (27) leaves to form his own band.

Sy Oliver (29) leaves Jimmie Lunceford (37) to join Tommy Dorsey (34).

The Glenn Miller (35) Band is nationally popular.

Charlie Parker (19) is in New York, playing at Monroe's Uptown House.

Billy Eckstine (25) joins Earl Hines (34) Band.

Jack Teagarden (34) forms a big band.

Outbreak of the Second World War in Europe (September).

BIRTHS
Brian Smith (saxes) 3 January
Alan Silva (bass) 22 January
Jeanne Lee (vocals) 29 January
Joe Sample (piano) 1 February
Chris Pyne (trombone) 14 February
Ronnie Zito (drums) 17 February
Freddy Robinson (guitar) 24 February
Trevor Watts (alto sax) 26 February
Mike Longo (piano) 19 March
Hugh Masakela (trumpet) 4 April
Ralf Hübner (drums) 3 May
Charles Owens (tenor sax) 4 May
Sonny Fortune (alto sax) 19 May
Richard Teitelbaum (composer) 19 May
Dick Berk (drums) 22 May
Marvin Stamm (trumpet) 23 May
Bill Watrous (trombone) 8 June
Mike Melillo (piano) 9 June
Bernard 'Pretty' Purdie (drums) 11 June
Tony Archer (bass) 14 July
Charles McPherson (alto sax) 24 July
Gilbert Rovère (bass) 29 August
Paul Winter (alto sax) 31 August
Butch Warren (bass) 8 September
Zbigniew Namyslowski (alto sax) 9 September
Steve Marcus (tenor sax) 18 September
Wayne Henderson (trombone) 24 September
Ed Xiques (saxes) 9 October
Joe Roccisano (alto sax) 15 October
John Guerin (drums) 31 October
Roger Kellaway (piano) 1 November
Andrew Cyrille (drums) 10 November
Hubert Laws (flute) 10 November
Idris Muhammad [Leo Morris] (drums) 13 November
Art Themen (tenor sax) 26 November
Nick Ceroli (drums) 22 December
Bob James (piano) 25 December

DEATHS
Herschel Evans (30) 9 February *heart ailment*
Tommy Ladnier (39) 4 June
Chick Webb (30) 16 June
Ma Rainey (53) 22 December
John Robichaux (73)
Charlie Irvis (40)

BOOKS
Benny Goodman: *The Kingdom of Swing*
Wilder Hobson: *American Jazz Music*
Frederic Ramsey: *Jazzmen*
Timme Rosenkrantz: *Swing Photo Album*

FILMS
Paradise in Harlem (70mins): gangster musical featuring Lucky Millinder Orchestra and Mamie Smith.
Readin', 'ritin' and rhythm (10mins): Don Byas, Lucky Millinder and Frankie Newton in a music short.
St Louis Blues (90mins): musical romance with Maxine Sullivan.
Artie Shaw & his Orchestra (10mins): music short.
Artie Shaw & his Orchestra in Symphony of Swing (10mins): music short.
Artie Shaw's Class in Swing (9mins): music short.
Hoagy Carmichael (10mins): music short with Jack Teagarden Orchestra.

COMPOSITIONS
Count Basie / Eddie Durham / Jimmy Rushing: *Sent For You Yesterday*
Rube Bloom / Ted Koehler: *Don't Worry 'Bout Me*
Rube Bloom / Johnny Mercer: *Day In, Day Out*
Cab Calloway / Frank Froeba / Jack Palmer: *The Jumpin' Jive*
Hoagy Carmichael: *I Get Along Without You Very Well*
Benny Carter / Ed Heyman: *Melancholy Lullaby*
Peter DeRose / Bert Shefter / Mitchell Parish: *The Lamp Is Low*
Duke Ellington: *Something To Live For*
Ziggy Elman / Johnny Mercer: *And The Angels Sing*
Joe Garland / Andy Razaf: *In The Mood*
Bob Haggart / Johnny Burke: *What's New?*
Irene Kitchings / Arthur Herzog Jr: *Some Other Spring*
Sy Oliver / Trummy Young: *'Tain't What You Do*
Charlie Shavers / Sid Robin: *Undecided*
Jimmy Van Heusen / Eddie DeLange: *Darn That Dream*
Trummy Young / Jimmy Mundy / Charles Carpenter: *A Lover Is Blue*

RECORDS
Albert Ammons (NYC, 1 January): *Shout For Joy* (NYC, 6 January): *Boogie Woogie Stomp / Boogie Woogie Blues* (NYC, 8 April): *St Louis Blues / Mecca Flat Blues / Bass Gone Crazy / Monday Struggle / Boogie Woogie* (NYC, 6 May): *Chicago In Mind* (Chicago, 9 October): *Pine Top Blues / Jesse James / Has Anyone Seen Corinne? / Woo Woo / Hersal Blues / Try Again / Mama's Blues / Shout For Joy* (Chicago, 17 October): *Monday Struggle*
Louis Armstrong Orchestra (NYC, 18 January): *Jeepers Creepers / What Is This Thing Called Swing?* (NYC, 5 April): *Hear Me Talkin' To Ya / Save It, Pretty Mama / West End Blues / Savoy Blues* (NYC, 25 April): *Confessin' / Our Monday Date / If Its Good Then I Want It / Me And Brother Bill* (NYC, 15 June): *Baby, Won't You Please Come Home / Poor Old Joe / You're A Lucky Guy / You're Just A No Account / Bye And Bye*
Mildred Bailey (NYC, 18 January): *I Cried For You / Begin The Beguine / What Shall I Say?* (NYC, 28 February): *Its Slumbertime Along The Swanee / 'Tain't What You Do / Love Is A Necessary Thing / Downhearted Blues / I Can Read Between The Lines* (NYC, 16 March): *There'll Be Some Changes Made / Barrelhouse Music / Arkansas Blues / Gulf Coast Blues / Prisoner Of Love* (NYC, 24 April): *That Sly Old Gentleman / Tit Willow / The Lamp Is Low / And The Angels Sing* (NYC, 14 June): *It Seems Like Old Times / Guess I'll Go Back Home / Moon Love / I'm Forever Blowing Bubbles* (NYC, 27 June): *The Little Man Who Wasn't There / The Ghost Of A Chance / You're The Moment In My Life / You And Your Love* (NYC, 21 September): *Don't Dally With The Devil / Ain't That Good News? / Sometimes I Feel Like A Motherless Child* (NYC, 3 November): *Blue Rain / I've Gone Off The Deep End / I Shoulda Stood In Bed* (NYC, 30 November): *Nobody Knows The Trouble I Seen / Swing Low, Sweet Chariot / All The Things You Are / Hold On*
Count Basie Orchestra (NYC, 4 February): *Jive At Five / Lady Be Good* (NYC, 13 February, with Jimmy Rushing): *Goin' To Chicago* (NYC, 19 March): *Rock-A-Bye Basie / If I Could Be With You / Taxi War Dance* (NYC, 20 March): *Jump For Me*
Count Basie's Kansas City Seven (NYC, 5 September): *Dickie's Dream / Lester Leaps In*
Sidney Bechet Quintet (NYC, 8 June): *Summertime*
Eddie Condon & his Chicagoans (NYC, 11 August): *There'll Be Some Changes Made / Nobody's Sweetheart / Friars Point Shuffle / Someday, Sweetheart* (NYC, 30 November): *I Ain't Gonna Give Nobody None Of My Jelly Roll / Strut, Miss Lizzie / It's All Right Here For You / Ballin' The Jack*
Al Cooper & his Savoy Sultans (NYC, 24 May): *Stitches / Jumpin' At The Savoy / We'd Rather Jump ThanSwing* (NYC, 16 October): *Little Sally Water / Jumpin' The Blues*
Duke Ellington Orchestra (NYC, 20 March): *Pussy Willow / Subtle Lament / Lady In Blue / Smorgasbord And Schnapps* (NYC, 21 March): *Portrait Of The Lion / Something To Live For* (NYC, 14 October): *Little Posey / I Never Felt This Way Before / Grievin' / Tootin' Through The Roof / Weely* (NYC, 22 November, duets with Jimmy Blanton): *Blues / Plucked Again / Smarty Pants*
Ella Fitzgerald & Savoy Eight (NYC, 2 March): *Once Is Enough For Me / I Had To Live And Learn* (NYC, 21 April): *Don't Worry 'Bout Me / If Anything Happened To You / If That's What You're Thinking / If You Ever Change Your Mind*
Ella Fitzgerald & Orchestra (NYC, 29 June): *Betcha Nickel / Stairway To The Stars / I Want The Waiter / That's All Brother / Out Of Nowhere* (NYC, 18 August): *My Last Goodbye / Billy / Please Tell Me The Truth / I'm Not Complainin'*
Bud Freeman & his Summa Cum Laude Orchestra (NYC, 19 July): *I've Found A New Baby / Easy To Get / China Boy / The Eel* (NYC, 18 September): *As Long As I Live / The Sail Fish / Sunday / Satanic Blues*
Benny Goodman Orchestra (NYC, 1 February): *And The Angels Sing* (with Martha Tilton)
Benny Goodman Sextet (NYC, 2 October): *Flying Home / Homeward Bound / Rose Room / Stardust* (NYC, 22 November): *Memories Of You / Soft Winds / Seven Come Eleven* (NYC, 27 November): *AC-DC Current*
Lionel Hampton Orchestra (NYC, 11 September): *When Lights Are Low / One Sweet Letter From You / Hot Mallets / Early Session Hop*
Coleman Hawkins Orchestra (NYC, 11 October): *Meet Doctor Foo / Fine Dinner / She's Funny That Way / Body And Soul*
Erskine Hawkins Orchestra (NYC, 18 July): *Tuxedo Junction*
Woody Herman Orchestra (NYC, 12 April): *Woodchopper's Ball / Big Wig In The Wigwam*
J.C.Higginbotham Quintet (NYC, 7 April): *Weary Land Blues* (NYC, 8 June): *Basin Street Blues*
Earl Hines Orchestra (NYC, 12 July): *Indiana / G.T. Stomp / Ridin' And Jivin' / Grand Terrace Shuffle / Father Steps In / Piano Man* (NYC, 6 October): *Riff Medley / XYZ / 'Gator Swing / Lightly And Politely / Rosetta*
Johnny Hodges Orchestra (NYC, 27 February): *Swingin' On The Campus / Dooji Wooji* (NYC, 21 March): *Savoy Strut / Rent Party Blues / Dance Of The Goon / Good Gal Blues / Finesse* (NYC, 2 June): *Kitchen Mechanic's Day / My Heart Jumped Over The Moon / You Can Count On Me / Home Town Blues* (NYC, 1 September): *The Rabbit's Jump / Moon Romance / Truly Wonderful / Dream Blues* (NYC, 14 October): *Skunk Hollow Blues / I Know What You Do / Your Love Has Faded / Tired Socks*
Billie Holiday (NYC, 20 January): *That's All I Ask Of You / Dream Of Life* (NYC, 30 January): *What Shall I Say? / It's Easy To Blame The Weather / More Than You Know / Sugar* (NYC, 21 March): *You're Too Lovely To Last / Under A Blue Jungle Moon / Everything Happens For The Best / Why Did I Always Depend On You? / Long Gone Blues* (NYC, 20 April): *Strange Fruit / Yesterdays / Fine And Mellow / I Gotta Right To Sing The Blues* (NYC, 5 July): *Some Other Spring / Our Love Is Different / Them There Eyes / Swing, Brother, Swing* (NYC, 13 December): *Night And Day / The Man I Love / You're Just A No Account / You're A Lucky Guy*
Harry James Orchestra (NYC, 20 February): *Ciribiribin* (NYC, 6 March): *Two O'Clock Jump* (LA, 30 November): *Concerto For Trumpet / Night Special / Back Beat Boogie*
Pete Johnson (NYC, 16 April): *Shuffle Boogie / Lone Star Blues / Buss Robinson Blues / B&O Blues / How Long, How Long? / Climbin' And Screamin' / Pete's Blues / Let 'Em Jump*
Pete Johnson & his Boogie Woogie Boys/Joe Turner (NYC, 30 June): *Cherry Red / Baby, Look At You / Lovin' Mama Blues / Cafe Society Rag*
Pete Johnson/Albert Ammons/Meade Lux Lewis (Chicago, September or October): *St Louis Blues*
Louis Jordan & his Tympany Five (NYC, 29 March): *Flat Face / Keep A' Knockin' / Sam Jones Done Snagged His Britches / Swingin' In The Cocoanut Trees / Doing The Jitterbug / At The Swing Cat's Ball*

(NYC, 14 November): *Jake, What A Snake / Honeysuckle Rose / 'Fore Day Blues / But I'll Be Back / You Ain't Nowhere / You're My Meat*
John Kirby Orchestra (NYC, 9 January): *It Feels Good / Effervescent Blues / The Turf / Down On The Desert* (NYC, 19 May): *Anitra's Dance / Sweet Georgia Brown / Drink To Me Only With Thine Eyes / Minute Waltz* (NYC, 28 July): *Front And Center / Royal Garden Blues / Opus 5* (NYC, 10 August): *Impromptu / Blue Skies / Rose Room / I May Be Wrong* (Chicago, 12 October): *Little Brown Jug / Nocturne / One Alone / Humoresque / Serenade*
Andy Kirk & his 12 Clouds of Joy (NYC, 16 March): *Close To Five / Floyd's Guitar Blues* (NYC, 15 November): *Big Jim Blues*
Gene Krupa Orchestra (Chicago, 2 November): *Drummin' Man*
Jimmy Lunceford Orchestra (NYC, 3 January): *Rainin' / 'Tain't What You Do / Cheatin' On Me / Le Jazz Hot / Times A' Wastin'* (NYC, 31 January): *Baby, Won't You Please Come Home? / The Lonesome Road* (NYC, 7 February): *What Is This Thing Called Swing? / Mixup / Shoemaker's Holiday / Blue Blazes* (NYC, 7 April): *Mandy / Easter Parade / Ain't She Sweet? / White Heat* (NYC, 14 December): *Put It Away / Wham / Uptown Blues / Lunceford Special*
Wingy Manone (NYC, 26 April): *Jumpy Nerves* (NYC, 19 June): *Royal Garden Blues / Farewell Blues / Limehouse Blues* (NYC, 6 September): *Blue Lou / Sudan / When The Saints Go Marchin' In / My Honey's Lovin' Arms*
Jelly Roll Morton's New Orleans Jazzmen (NYC, 14 September): *Oh Didn't He Ramble / High Society / I Thought I Heard Buddy Bolden Say / Winin' Boy Blues* (NYC, 28 September): *Climax Rag / Don't You Leave Me Here / West End Blues / Ballin' The Jack*
Jelly Roll Morton (NYC, 14 December): *Original Rags / The Crave / Mister Joe / King Porter Stomp / Winin' Boy Blues* (NYC, 16 December): *Buddy Bolden's Blues / The Naked Dance / Don't You Leave Me Here / Mamie's Blues* (NYC, 18 December): *Michigan Water Blues*
Frankie Newton (NYC, 13 January): *Rosetta / Minor Jive / The World Is Waitin' For The Sunrise / Who? / The Blues My Baby Gave To Me / Rompin'* (NYC, 7 April): *Daybreak Blues* (NYC, 12 April): *Tab's Blues / Jitters / Frankie's Jump / Jam Fever* (NYC, 8 June): *After Hour Blues* (NYC, 15 August): *Vamp / Parallel Fifths*
Quintette of the Hot Club of France (Paris, 21 March): *Hungaria / Jeepers Creepers / Swing 39 / Japanese Sandman / I Wonder Where My Baby Is Tonight?* (Paris, 22 March): *My Melancholy Baby / Time On My Hands / Twelfth Year* (Paris, 30 June): *Stockholm / Younger Generation* (London, 25 August): *HCQ Strut / The Man I Love*
Trixie Smith (NYC, 14 June): *No Good Man*
Willie 'The Lion' Smith (NYC, February): *Morning Air / Echoes Of Spring / Concentrating / Fading Star / Passionette / Rippling Waters / Sneakaway / What Is There To Say? / Between The Devil And The Deep Blue Sea / The Boy In The Boat / Tea For Two / I'll Follow You / Finger Buster / Stormy Weather*
Muggsy Spanier Ragtime Band (Chicago, 7 July): *Big Butter And Egg Man / Someday, Sweetheart / Eccentric / That Da Da Strain*

(NYC, 10 November): *At The Jazz Band Ball / I Wish I Could Shimmy Like My Sister Kate / Dippermouth Blues / Livery Stable Blues* (NYC, 22 November): *Riverboat Shuffle / Relaxin' At The Touro / At Sundown / Bluin' The Blues* (NYC, 12 December): *Lonesome Road / Dinah / Black And Blue / Mandy, Make Up Your Mind*
Art Tatum (LA, 12 April): *Tea For Two / Deep Purple* (LA, August): *All God's Chillun Got Rhythm / Sweet Emaline / Indiana / Day In, Day Out / Fine And Dandy / I've Got The World On A String / I've Got A Right To Sing The Blues / I'm Coming, Virginia*
Fats Waller (NYC, 19 January): *Hold Tight (want some seafood, mama)* (London, 13 June): *London Suite* (NYC, 28 June): *Honey Hush / Anita* (NYC, 10 August): *Squeeze Me* (NYC, 3 November): *Your Feet's Too Big / I Can't Give You Anything But Love*
Lee Wiley (NYC, 13 November): *Sweet And Low Down / Sam And Delilah / My One And Only / 'S Wonderful* (NYC, 15 November): *I've Got A Crush On You / Someone To Watch Over Me / How Long Has This Been Goin' On? / But Not For Me*
Cootie Williams & his Rugcutters (NYC, 28 February): *Beautiful Romance / Boudoir Benny / Ain't The Gravy Good? / She's Gone* (NYC, 22 June): *Night Song / Blues A-Poppin' / Top And Bottom / Black Beauty*
Teddy Wilson (NYC, 27 January): *Coquette / China Boy / Melody In F / When You And I Were Young, Maggie*

Left: Billie Holiday at Café Society Downtown.

Below left: Bud Freeman's Summa Cum Laude Orchestra at Nick's. L to r: Dave Bowman, Eddie Condon, Pee Wee Russell, Stan King, Max Kaminsky, Clyde Newcomb, Bud Freeman, Brad Gowans.

Below: Muggsy Spanier's Ragtime Band.

Photograph courtesy: *Max Jones*

Photograph courtesy: *Hank O'Neal*

Photograph courtesy: *Max Jones*

1940

First revivalist records made in New Orleans by Kid Rena (42).with Louis Nelson (60) and Alphonse Picou (62) on clarinets and Jim Robinson (48) on trombone.

Mintons Playhouse becomes the mecca of the new jazz.

Lionel Hampton (27) leaves Benny Goodman (31) and forms own band.

Cootie Williams (30) leaves Duke Ellington (41) and is replaced by Ray Nance (26).

Lester Young (31) leaves Count Basie (36).

Harry James (24) hires Frank Sinatra (24).

Charlie Parker (20) rejoins Jay McShann (31) and makes his first recordings.

The Grand Terrace closes, ending the 11-year run by Earl Hines (35).

BIRTHS
Waymon Reed (bass) 10 January
Ronald Shannon Jackson (drums) 12 January
Don Thompson (bass) 18 January
Eberhard Weber (bass) 22 January
Roberta Flack (vocals) 10 February
Harold Jones (drums) 27 February
Paul Rutherford (trombone) 29 February
Gene Perla (bass/composer) 1 March
Ralph Towner (guitar) 1 March
Louis Moholo (drums) 10 March
Keith Smith (trumpet) 19 March
Masabumi Kikuchi (piano) 23 March
Lonnie Hillyer (trumpet) 25 March
Sal Nistico (tenor sax) 2 April
Herbie Hancock (piano) 12 April
Jerry Hahn (guitar) 21 April
George Adams (tenor sax) 29 April
Carlos Ward (alto sax) 1 May
Dick Morrissey (tenor sax) 9 May
Oscar Castro-Neves (guitar) 15 May
Lew Tabackin (tenor sax) 26 May
Yolande Bavan (vocals) 1 June
Hank O'Neal (record producer/writer) 5 June
John Stevens (drums) 10 June
Chuck Rainey (bass) 17 June
Arthur Blythe (alto sax) 5 July
Roy Babbington (bass) 8 July
Ray Draper (tuba) 3 August
Roscoe Mitchell (saxes) 3 August
Peter King (alto sax) 11 August
Adam Makowicz (piano) 18 August
Ginger Baker (drums) 19 August
Alex Rodriguez (trumpet) 26 August
Sonny Sharrock (guitar) 27 August
Bennie Maupin (saxes) 29 August
Ray Neapolitan (bass) 30 August
Wilton Felder (tenor sax) 31 August
Herman Riley (tenor sax) 31 August
Mick Pyne (piano) 2 September
Roy Ayers (vibes) 10 September
Alex Riel (drums) 13 September
Eddie Moore (drums) 14 September
Hamiet Bluiett (saxes) 16 September
Dick Shearer (trombone) 21 September
Gary Bartz (saxes) 26 September
Michael Nock (piano) 27 September
'Sirone' Norris Jones (bass) 28 September
Steve Swallow (bass) 4 October
Larry Young (organ) 7 October
Pharaoh Sanders (tenor sax) 13 October
Eddie Henderson (trumpet) 26 October
Billy Hart (drums) 29 November
Chuck Mangione (trumpet) 29 November
Jay Leonhart (bass) 6 December
Reggie Johnson (bass) 13 December
Larry Willis (piano) 20 December
Lonnie Liston Smith (piano) 28 December
Jerry Granelli (drums) 30 December
Julius Hemphill (alto sax)

DEATHS
Guy Kelly (33) 24 February
Arthur Whetsol (35) 5 January *cancer*
Johnny Dodds (48) 8 August *stroke*
Hal Kemp (35) 21 December *car crash*
Blind Boy Fuller (37)

BOOKS
James Asman & Bill Kinnell (eds): *American Jazz*
D. Curran: *Piano in the band* (novel)
Sharon Pease: *Boogie-woogie Piano Styles*

George Simon: *Don Watson starts his band* (for children)
Ralph Williams: *How to build a dance band and make it pay*

FILMS
Beat me daddy, eight to the bar (17mins): Wingy Manone music short
Let's make music (80mins): musical featuring Bob Crosby Orchestra
Second Chorus (85mins): comedy romance starring Fred Astaire, featuring Artie Shaw

COMPOSITIONS
Hoagy Carmichael / Ned Washington: *The Nearness Of You*
Eddie Durham / Taps Miller: *Wham*
Duke Ellington: *Jack the Bear / Cottontail./ Koko / Harlem Airshaft / Day Dream / All Too Soon / Never No Lament /. In a Mellotone*
Earle Hagen: *Harlem Nocturne*
Erskine Hawkins / Julian Dash / William Johnson: *Tuxedo Junction*
Morgan Lewis / Nancy Hamilton: *How High The Moon*
Ruth Lowe: *I'll Never Smile Again*

RECORDS
Red Allen (NYC, 28 May): *Down In Jungle Town / Canal Street Blues*
Lil Armstrong & her Dixielanders (NYC, 18 March): *Sixth Street / Riffin' The Blues / Why Is A Good Man So Hard To Find? / My Secret Flame*
Louis Armstrong Orchestra (NYC, 14 March): *Hep Cat's Ball / You've Got Me Voodoo'd / Harlem Stomp / Wolverine Blues / Lazy 'Sippi Steamer* (NYC, 1 May): *Sweethearts On Parade / You Run Your Mouth, I'll Run My Business / Cut Off My Legs And Call Me Shorty / Cain And Abel*
Louis Armstrong/Sidney Bechet (NYC, 27 May): *Perdido Street Blues / 2.19 Blues / Down In Honky Tonk Town / Coal Cart Blues*
Buster Bailey Sextet (NYC, May): *Should I? / The Blue Room / April In Paris / Am I Blue?* (NYC, June): *Seems Like A Month Of Sundays / Fable Of A Rose / Pinetop's Boogie Woogie / Eccentric Rag*
Mildred Bailey (NYC, 15 January): *Wham / Little High Chairman / Easy To Love* (NYC, 25 January): *Give Me Time / They Can't Take That Away From Me / A Bee Gezindt / After All I've Been To You / Don't Take Your Love From Me* (NYC, 2 April): *Give Me Time / Fools Rush In / From Another World / I'm Nobody's Baby* (NYC, 15 May): *How Can I Ever Be Alone? / Tennessee Fish Fry / I'll Pray For You / Blue*
Count Basie Orchestra (NYC, 19 March): *Tickle Toe / I Never Knew* (NYC, 31 May): *Blow Top / Super Chief* (Chicago, 8 August): *Evenin'* (Jimmy Rushing) / *Moten Swing / I Want A Little Girl* (Jimmy Rushing)
Sidney Bechet & his New Orleans Feetwarmers (NYC, 5 February): *Indian Summer / One O'Clock Jump / Preachin' Blues / Sidney's Blues* (NYC, 4 June): *Shake It And Break It / Old Man Blues / Wild Man Blues / Nobody Knows The Way I Feel Dis Mornin' / Make Me A Pallet On The Floor* (Chicago, 6 September): *Blues In Thirds / Blue For You Johnny / Ain't Misbehavin' / Save It, Pretty Mama / Stompy Jones*
Sidney Bechet's Blue Note Quartet (NYC, 27 March): *Lonesome Blues / Dear Old Southland / Bechet's Steady Rider / Saturday Night Blues*
Bechet/Spanier Big Four (NYC, 28 March): *Four Or Five Times / Sweet Lorraine / Lazy River / China Boy* (NYC, 16 April): *If I Could Be With You One Hour Tonight / That's A Plenty / Squeeze Me / Sweet Sue*

Nat King Cole Trio (LA, 6 December): *Sweet Lorraine / Honeysuckle Rose / Gone With The Draft / This Side Up*
Johnny Dodds Orchestra (Chicago, 5 June): *Red Onion Blues / Gravier Street Blues*
Duke Ellington Orchestra (NYC, 14 February): *Solitude / Stormy Weather / Mood Indigo / Sophisticated Lady* (Chicago, 6 March): *Jack The Bear / Ko-Ko* (Chicago, 15 March): *Conga Brava / Concerto For Cootie (Do nothing till you hear from me)* (LA, 4 May): *Cottontail / Never No Lament (Don't get around much anymore)* (Chicago, 28 May): *Bojangles (Portrait of Bill Robinson) / A Portrait Of Bert Williams* (NYC, 22 July): *Harlem Air Shaft / All Too Soon* (Chicago, 5 September): *In A Mellotone* (Chicago, 17 October): *Warm Valley*
Duke Ellington/Jimmy Blanton (Chicago, 1 October): *Pitter Panther Patter / Body And Soul / Sophisticated Lady / Mr JB Blues*
Ella Fitzgerald Orchestra (NYC, March): *A Tisket, A-Tasket / Diga Diga Doo / Tain't Whatcha Do / Limehouse Blues / Blue Lou / I'm Confessin' / Swing Out*
Bud Freeman & his Summa Cum Laude Orchestra (NYC, 25 March): *Oh! Baby / I Need Some Pettin' / Susie / Big Boy* (NYC, 4 April): *Sensation / Fidgety Feet / Tia Juana / Copenhagen*
Bud Freeman & his Famous Chicagoans (NYC, 23 July): *Jack Hits The Road / 47th And State / Muskrat Ramble / That Da Da Strain / Shim-Me-Sha-Wabble / At The Jazz Band Ball / After Awhile / Prince Of Wails*
Benny Goodman Sextet with Charlie Christian (NYC, 7 February): *Till Tom Special / Gone With What Wind* (LA, 20 June): *Six Appeal / These Foolish Things / Good Enough To Keep* (NYC, 7 November): *Wholly Cats / Royal Garden Blues / As Long As I Live / Benny's Bugle* (NYC, 19 December): *I Can't Give You Anything But Love, Baby / Gilly*
Lionel Hampton Orchestra (Chicago, 26 February): *Shades Of Jade / Till Tom Special / Flying Home / Save It, Pretty Mama / Tempo And Swing*
Coleman Hawkins (NYC, 3 January): *When Day Is Done / The Sheik Of Araby / My Blue Heaven / Bouncing With Bean* (NYC, 25 May): *Dedication*
Earl Hines Orchestra (NYC, 13 February): *Boogie-Woogie On St Louis Blues / Deep Forest / Number 19* (NYC, 19 June): *Call Me Happy / Tantalizin' A Cuban* (LA, 2 December): *Easy Rhythm / In Swamp Lands / Comin' On Home*
Earl Hines (NYC, 26 February, piano solos): *Body And Soul / Child Of A Disordered Brain*
Art Hodes' Blue Three (NYC, May): *I've Found A New Baby / Four Or Five Times / Tin Roof Blues / Diga Diga Doo*
Johnny Hodges Orchestra (Chicago, 2 November): *Daydream / Good Queen Bess / That's The Blues, Old Man / Junior Hop*
Billie Holiday (NYC, 29 February): *Ghost Of Yesterday / Body And Soul / What Is This Going To Get Us? / Falling In Love Again* (NYC, 7 June): *I'm Pulling Through / Tell Me More / Laughing At Life / Time On My Hands* (NYC, 12 September): *I'm All For You / I Hear Music / It's The Same Old Story / Practice Makes Perfect* (NYC, 15 October): *St Louis Blues / Loveless Love*
Louis Jordan Tympany Five (NYC, 25 January): *June Tenth Jamboree / You Run Your Mouth And I'll Run My Business / I'm Alabama Bound* (NYC, 30 September): *Pompton Turnpike*
John Kirby Orchestra (NYC, 22 April): *Jumpin' In The Pump Room / Milumbu / You Go Your Way / 20th Century Closet* (NYC, 27 May): *Temptation / Blues Petite / On A Little Street In Singapore / Chloe* (NYC, 9 July): *Andiology / Can't We Be Friends? / Then I'll Be Happy / I Love You Truly / Frasquita Serenade / Sextet From 'Lucia' / Coquette / Zooming At The Zombie*
Andy Kirk (NYC, 25 June): *Scratching In The Gravel* (NYC, 8 July): *Little Miss* (NYC, 7 November): *The Count / Twelfth Street Rag*
Harlan Leonard & his Rockets (Chicago, 11 January): *Rockin' With The Rockets / Hairy Joe Jump / Contact / Skee* (NYC, 11 March): *Parade Of The Stompers* (Chicago, 15 July): *Rock And Ride / 400 Swing / A La Bridges* (Chicago, 13 November): *Decameron Stomp / Too Much / Keep Rockin' / Take 'em*
Jimmie Lunceford Orchestra (NYC, 5 January): *Bugs Parade / Blues In The Groove / I Wanna Hear Swing Songs / It's Time To Jump And Shout* (LA, 28

1940

February): *What's Your Story, Mornin' Glory?* / Dinah
Jay McShann (Wichita, 30 November): *I've Found A New Baby* (Wichita, 2 December): *Coquette / Moten Stomp*

Joe Marsala & his Delta Four (NYC, 4 April): *Wanderin' Man Blues / Salty Mama Blues / Three O'Clock Jump / Reunion In Harlem*

Jimmie Noone (Chicago, 5 June): *New Orleans Hop Scop Blues / Keystone Blues*

Hot Lips Page (NYC, 23 January): *I Would Do Anything For You / Gone With The Gin / Walk It To Me / I Won't Be Here Long* (NYC, 11 November): *Lafayette / South* (NYC, 10 December): *Thirsty Mama Blues / Just Another Woman / My Fightin' Gal / Evil Man's Blues / Do It If You Wanna*

Django Reinhardt (Paris, 13 December): *Swing 41 / Nuages / Exactly Like You / Fantaisie Sur Une Dance Norvegienne / Vendredi 13 / Liebesfreud / Mabel / Petits Monsonges / Les Yeux Noirs / Sweet Sue* (Paris, 17 December): *Swing De Paris / Oiseaux Des Iles / All Of Me*

Kid Rena (New Orleans, 21 August): *Panama / Gettysburg March / Milenberg Joys / Lowdown Blues / High Society / Clarinet Marmalade / Weary Blues / Get It Right*

Artie Shaw & his Gramercy Five (LA, 3 September): *Special Delivery Stomp / Summit Ridge Drive / Keepin' Myself For You / Cross Your Heart* (LA, 5 December): *Dr Livingstone, I Presume / When The Quail Comes Back To San Quentin / My Blue Heaven / Smoke Gets In Your Eyes*

Artie Shaw Orchestra (LA, 17 December): *Concerto For Clarinet*

Rex Stewart & the Ellingtonians (Chicago, 2 November): *Without A Song / My Sunday Gal / Mobile Bay / Linger Awhile*

Joe Sullivan Orchestra (NYC, 9 February): *Solitude / Oh, Lady Be Good / Low Down Dirty Shame / I Can't Give You Anything But Love* (NYC, 29 April): *Pom Pom / Coquette*

Art Tatum (LA, 22 February): *Elegie / Humoresque / Sweet Lorraine / Get Happy / Lullaby Of The Leaves / Tiger Rag / Emaline / Moonglow / Love Me / Cocktails For Two* (LA, 26 July): *St Louis Blues / Begin The Beguine / Rosetta / Indiana*

Jack Teagarden's Big Eight (NYC, 15 December): *St James Infirmary / The World Is Waiting For The Sunrise / The Big Eight Blues / Shine*

Joe Turner (NYC, 11 November): *Piney Brown Blues* (NYC, 26 November): *Doggin' The Dog / Careless Love / Jumpin' Down Blues / Rainy Day Blues*

Fats Waller (NYC, 11 April): *Too Tired / Send Me, Jackson* (NYC, 6 November): *Everybody Loves My Baby*

George Wettling's Chicago Rhythm Kings (NYC, 16 January): *I've Found A New Baby / Bugle Call Rag / I Wish I Could Shimmy Like My Sister Kate / Darktown Strutter's Ball*

Lee Wiley (NYC, February): *Baby's Awake Now / A Little Birdie Told Me So / I've Got Five Dollars / You Took Advantage Of Me / A Ship Without A Sail / As Though You Were There / Glad To Be Unhappy / Here In My Arms* (NYC, 10 April): *Let's Fly Away / Let's Do It / Hot House Rose / Find Me A Primitive Man* (NYC, 15 April): *Easy To Love / You Do Something To Me / Looking At You / Why Shouldn't I?* (NYC, 10 July): *Down To Steamboat Tennessee / Sugar*

Cootie Williams & his Rugcutters (NYC, 15 February): *Black Butterfly / Dry Long So / Toasted Pickles / Give It Up*

Above right: **The The Spirits of Rhythm at Kelly's Stables on 52nd Street. Teddy Bunn is the guitarist standing.**

Centre: **Charlie Christian (23) and Gene Krupa (31) at the Metronome All Stars recording session on 7 February.**

Bottom right: **More of the All Stars at the same session. L to r: Bob Haggart (bass), Eddie Miller (tenor sax), Benny Goodman (clarinet), and Benny Carter (alto sax) with Christian and Krupa in the background.**

Photograph courtesy: *Max Jones*

Duke Ellington Band in pit for new musical revue '*Jump for Joy*' in Los Angeles.

Stan Kenton(29) Band makes its debut at the Rendezvous Ballroom, Balboa, California.

Cootie Williams (31), Peggy Lee (21) and Big Sid Catlett (31) with Benny Goodman (32).

Gil Evans (29) joins Claude Thornhill Orchestra.

Charlie Parker (21) jams at Mintons Playhouse in Harlem with Dizzy Gillespie (24), Thelonious Monk (24), Charlie Christian (24), Bud Powell (17), Max Roach (16) and Kenny Clarke (27).

Dizzy Gillespie leaves the Cab Calloway Band after a fight with Cab over 'spitball' incident.

Roy Eldridge (30) and Anita O'Day (22) join Gene Krupa (32) Band.

Lu Watters & his Yerba Buena Band a big success at the Dawn Club in San Francisco.

Germany invades the USSR (22 June). On 7 December the Japanese attack the US base at Pearl Harbour, Hawaii and four days later Germany and Italy declare war on the US.

BIRTHS
David Lee Jr (drums) 4 January
Danny Moore (trumpet) 6 January
Aldo Romano (drums) 16 January
Bobby Hutcherson (vibes) 27 January
Rick Laird (bass) 5 February
Barry 'Kid' Martyn (drums) 23 February
John Williams (bass) 27 February
Bobby Shew (trumpet) 4 March
Peter Brötzmann (tenor sax) 6 March
Palle Mikkelborg (trumpet) 6 March
Franco D'Andrea (keyboards) 8 March
Meredith D'Ambrosio (vocals/piano) 20 March
Al Gafa (guitar) 9 April
Harry Miller (bass) 25 April
Mickey Tucker (piano) 28 April
Eddie Louiss (piano/organ) 2 May
Stanley Cowell (piano) 5 May
Trevor Tompkins (drums) 12 May
John von Ohlen (drums) 13 May
Charles Earland (organ) 24 May
Chick Corea (piano) 12 June
Alby Cullaz (bass) 25 June
Pete Yellin (alto sax) 18 July
Phil Upchurch (guitar) 19 July
Charles Tyler (baritone sax/alto sax) 20 July
Airto Moreira (percussion) 5 August
Howard Johnson (baritone sax) 7 August
Milford Graves (drums) 20 August
Clifford Jarvis (drums) 20 August
Carrie Smith (vocals) 25 August
John Marshall (drums) 28 August
Phillip Wilson (drums) 8 September
Norma Winstone (vocals) 23 September
Mike Osborne (alto sax) 28 September
Malcolm Griffiths (trombone) 29 September
Masahiko Sato (piano/composer) 6 October
Chucho Valdés (keyboards) 9 October
Lester Bowie (trumpet) 11 October
Eddie Daniels (saxes) 19 October
Glen Moore (bass) 28 October
Ron McClure (bass) 22 November
Jesper Thilo (tenor sax) 28 November
Valerie Wilmer (writer/photographer) 7 December
Franco Ambrosetti (trumpet) 10 December
Gary Barone (trumpet) 12 December
Leo Smith (trumpet) 18 December
Ronnie Cuber (baritone sax) 25 December
Don Pullen (piano) 25 December
John Hicks (piano)

DEATHS
Ken 'Snakehips' Johnson (23) 8 March *killed when a bomb fell on the Café de Paris in London*
Casper Reardon (33) 9 March
Jelly Roll Morton (50) 10 July
Frank Melrose (33) 1 September *murdered*
Chu Berry (31) 31 October *auto accident*
Dick Wilson (30) 24 November *tuberculosis*
Charlie Dixon (42) 6 December
Peetie Wheatstraw (36) December *killed*

BOOKS
R.English: *Strictly Ding-Dong and other Swing Stories*
Babs Gonzales & Paul Weston: *Boptionary: What is Bop?*
W.C. Handy: *Father of the Blues: an autobiography*
Edgar Jackson: *Swing Music*

Edgar Jackson & Leonard Hibbs: *Encyclopaedia of Swing*
Paul Specht: *How they became name bands*
Paul Whiteman & Leslie Lieber: *How to be a bandleader*

FILMS
Birth of the Blues (86mins): feature film with Bing Crosby and Jack Teagarden
Blues in the Night (88mins): feature film with Jimmie Lunceford
Boogie-woogie dream (13mins): music short featuring Lena Horne, Albert Ammons, Pete Johnson & Teddy Wilson
Harlem Hotshots (20mins):Teddy Wilson, Lena Horne
Hellzapoppin' (83mins): Olsen & Johnson comedy featuring Rex Stewart, Slim Gaillard & Slam Stewart
Gene Krupa, America's Ace drummer man & his Orchestra (10mins): music short
Las Vegas Nights (87mins): comedy musical featuring Tommy Dorsey Orchestra
Murder on Lenox Avenue : B-movie for black audiences starring Mamie Smith
Sunday Sinners : B-movie for black audiences starring Mamie Smith
Sun Valley Serenade (86mins): musical romance featuring Glenn Miller Orchestra
3-MINUTE SOUNDIES
Ain't misbehavin' : Fats Waller
Air mail special: Jimmy Rushing with Count Basie
*Boogie-woogie dream:*Albert Ammons & Pete Johnson
*Case of the blues:*Maxine Sullivan with Benny Carter
Cottontail: Duke Ellington
Honeysuckle Rose: Fats Waller

The joint is jumpin': Fats Waller
Lazybones: Hoagy Carmichael
The lonesome road: Sister Rosetta Tharpe
Shout, sister, shout: Sister Rosetta Tharpe with Lucky Millinder
Take me back, baby: Jimmy Rushing with Count Basie
Your feet's too big: Fats Waller

COMPOSITIONS
Harold Arlen / Johnny Mercer: *Blues In The Night*
Joe Bushkin / John DeVries: *Oh Look At Me Now*
Duke Ellington: *Jump For Joy / I Got It Bad / Just Squeeze Me*
Carl Fischer / Bill Carey: *You've Changed*
Jerry Gray / Eddie DeLange: *String Of Pearls*
Sy Oliver: *Yes Indeed*
Billy Strayhorn: *Passion Flower / Raincheck / Chelsea Bridge*
Mel Tormé: *Lament To Love*
Alec Wilder: *It's So Peaceful In The Country*

RECORDS
Red Allen (NYC, 17 April): *KK Boogie / Sometimes I'm Happy/Ol' Man River* (NYC,22 July): *A Sheridan 'Square'/ Siesta At The Fiesta / Indiana / Jack The Bellboy*
Louis Armstrong Orchestra (NYC, 10 March): *Everything's Been Done Before / I Cover The Waterfront / In The Gloaming / Long, Long Ago* (NYC, 11 April): *Hey Lawdy Mama / I'll Get Mine Bye And Bye / Do You Call That A Buddy / Yes Suh!* (Chicago, 16 November): *When Its Sleepy Time Down South / Leap Frog / I Used To Love You / You Rascal, You*
Mildred Bailey (NYC, 24 February): *When That Man Is Dead And Gone / Jenny* (NYC, 14 March): *Georgia On My Mind / Rockin' Chair / Sometimes I'm Happy* (NYC, 13 June): *Everything Depends On You / Lover, Come Back To Me / All Too Soon* (NYC, 24 June): *It's So Peaceful In The Country*
Count Basie Orchestra (NYC, 28 January): *Jump The Blues Away / Deep In The Blues / The Jitters / Tuesday At Ten / Undecided Blues* (Chicago, 10 April): *I Do Mean You / 9.20 Special / H And J / Feedin' The Bean / Goin' To Chicago Blues* (Jimmy Rushing) (NYC, 21 May): *Down, Down, Down / Tune Town Shuffle* (NYC, 2 July): *Basie Boogie / Fancy Meeting You / Diggin' For Dex* (NYC, 24 September): *Fiesta In Blue / Tom Thumb* (NYC, 3 November): *Platterbrains* (NYC, 17 November): *Feather Merchant / Down For Double*
Sidney Bechet & his New Orleans Feetwarmers (NYC, 8 January): *Coal Black Shine / Egyptian Fantasy / Baby, Won't You Please Come Home? / Slippin' And Slidin'* (NYC, 28 April): *Swing Parade /*

Photograph courtesy: *Duncan P Schiedt Collection*

I Know That You Know / When It's Sleepy Time Down South / I Ain't Gonna Give Nobody None O' This Jelly Roll (NYC, 13 September): *I'm Coming, Virginia / Limehouse Blues / Georgia Cabin / Texas Moaner / Strange Fruit / You're The Limit* (NYC, 14 October): *Rip Up The Joint / Suey / Blues In The Air / The Mooche / Laughin' In Rhythm* (NYC, 24 October): *Twelfth Street Rag / Mood Indigo / Rose Room / Lady Be Good / What Is This Thing Called Love?*

Sidney Bechet One Man Band (NYC, 18 April): *The Sheik Of Araby / Blues Of Bechet*

Chu Berry (NYC, September): *Blowing Up A Breeze / Sunny Side Of The Street / Monday At Minton's / Gee, Ain't I Good To You*

Duke Ellington Orchestra (LA, 15 February): *Take The A Train / Jumpin' Punkins / Blue Serge* (LA, 5 June): *Just-A-Settin' And A-Rockin'* (LA, 26 June): *I Got It Bad And That Ain't Good* (Ivie Anderson) (LA, 2 July): *The Brown Skin Gal / Jump For Joy* (LA, 26 September): *Rocks In My Bed* (LA, 2 December): *Chelsea Bridge / Raincheck*

Ella Fitzgerald Orchestra (NYC, 8 January): *Three Little Words / Hello Ma! I Done It Again / The One I Love / The Muffin Man* (NYC, 31 March): *Keep Cool, Fool / My Man* (LA, 31 July): *I Can't Believe That You're In Love With Me / I Must Have That Man / When My Sugar Walks Down The Street / I Got It Bad / Melinda The Mousie / Can't Help Lovin' Dat Man*

Benny Goodman Sextet with Charlie Christian (NYC, 15 January): *Breakfast Feud / On The Alamo / I Found A New Baby / Gone With What Draft* (NYC, 15 March): *Blues In B / Waitin' For Benny / A Smo-o-oth One / Air Mail Special*

Woody Herman Orchestra (NYC, 13 February): *Blue Flame / Fur Trapper's Ball*

Earl Hines Orchestra (NYC, 3 April): *Up Jumped The Devil / Jersey Bounce / South Side / Sunny Side Of The Street / My Melancholy Baby* (LA, 20 August): *Windy City Jive / Swingin' On C / Yellow Fire* (Chicago, 28 October). *The Father Jumps* (NYC, 17 November): *The Earl*

Johnny Hodges Orchestra (LA, 3 July): *Squatty Roo / Passion Flower / Things Ain't What They Used To Be / Goin' Out The Back Way*

Billie Holiday (NYC, 21 March): *Let's Do It / Georgia On My Mind / Romance In The Dark / All Of Me* (NYC, 9 May): *I'm In A Lowdown Groove / God Bless The Child / Am I Blue? / Solitude* (NYC, 7 August): *Jim / I Cover The Waterfront / Love Me Or Leave Me / Gloomy Sunday*

Pete Johnson/Albert Ammons (NYC, 7 May): *Boogie Woogie Man / Boogie Woogie Jump / Barrelhouse Boogie / Cuttin' The Boogie* (NYC, 17 June): *Foot Pedal Boogie / Walkin' The Boogie / Sixth Avenue Express / Pine Creek / Movin' The Boogie*

Louis Jordan Tympany Five (NYC, 24 January): *Pinetop's Boogie Woogie / The Two Little Squirrels / T-bone Blues / Pan-Pan* (NYC, 2 April): *St Vitus Dance / Saxa-Woogie / Brotherly Love* (NYC, 15 November): *How 'Bout That / Rusty Dusty Blues / Knock Me A Kiss* (Chicago, 2 November): *The Green Grass Grew All Around / I'm Gonna Move To The Outskirts Of Town*

John Kirby Orchestra (NYC, 15 January): *Bounce Of The Sugar Plum Fairy / Beethoven Riffs On / Double Talk / Cuttin' The Campus* (NYC, 25 July): *Close Shave / Bugler's Dilemma / It's Only A Paper Moon / Fifi's Rhapsody* (NYC, 7 October): *Night Whispers / Tweed Me / Move Over / Wondering Where*

Andy Kirk (NYC, 3 January): *Ring Dem Bells*

Gene Krupa Orchestra (Chicago, 17 November): *Drum Boogie* (NYC, 8 May): *Let Me Off Uptown* (NYC, 2 July): *Rockin' Chair*

Jimmie Lunceford Orchestra (NYC, 26 March): *Battle Axe* (LA, 23 June): *Siesta At The Fiesta*

(NYC, 26 August): *Hi Spook / Yard Dog Mazurka / Impromptu* (NYC, 22 December): *Blues In The Night*

Jay McShann Orchestra (Dallas, 30 April): *Swingmatism / Hootie Blues / Dexter Blues*

Django Reinhardt (Paris, 11 September): *Dinette / Crepuscule / Swing 42*

Rex Stewart & the Ellingtonians (LA, 3 July): *Some Saturday / Subtle Slough / Menelik – The Lion Of Judah / Poor Bubber*

Art Tatum Band with Joe Turner (NYC, 21 January): *Wee Baby Blues / Stompin' At The Savoy / Last Goodbye Blues / Battery Bounce* (NYC, 13 June): *Lucille / Rock Me, Mama / Corrine, Corrina / Lonesome Graveyard*

Joe Turner (NYC, 17 July): *Nobody In Mind / Somebody's Got To Go / Ice Man / Chewed Up Grass* (LA, 8 September): *Rocks In My Bed / Blues On Central Avenue / Goin' To Chicago / Sun Risin' Blues*

Fats Waller (NYC, 20 March): *All That Meat And No Potatoes* (NYC, 26 December): *Cash For Your Trash*

Photograph courtesy: *Rolf Dahlgren*

Above: The Benny Goodman Sextet with 24-year-old Charlie Christian on guitar. Standing l to r: Cootie Williams (trumpet), George Auld (tenor sax), Harry James (guesting on trumpet) and Benny Goodman (clarinet).

Left: The Cab Calloway Orchestra with Dizzy Gillespie (far left) in the trumpet section.

Opposite page: The Jay McShann Orchestra with the young Charlie Parker standing 3rd from left.

Photograph courtesy: *Duncan P Schiedt Collection*

1942

The United States' entry into World War II means that many musicians volunteer for service or are drafted. Ray McKinley (32), Bob Crosby (29) and Glenn Miller (38) disband and enter service. Dave Tough (34) and Claude Thornhill join Artie Shaw's (32) Navy Band. Other volunteers include Max Kaminsky and Buddy Rich.

Fats Waller (38) is featured in a Carnegie Hall concert (14 January).

The Duke Ellington Orchestra and Louis Armstrong are featured in the Hollywood film *Cabin in the Sky*. Barney Bigard (36) and Ivie Anderson (38) leave the band, Jimmy Hamilton (25) joins. Barney Bigard settles in Los Angeles where he persuades Kid Ory out of retirement.

Illinois Jacquet is the star tenor man with Lionel Hampton. Jess Stacy rejoins Benny Goodman's Band, while Cootie Williams leaves become a leader. Frank Sinatra leaves Tommy Dorsey for a solo career.

Max Roach (17) with Charlie Parker (22) at Monroe's.

RCA sprays the first gold disc – Glenn Miller's '*Chattanooga Choo choo*'.

Eddie Condon (38) and band appear on CBS Television – the first time a jazz band has been televised. Condon begins a series of Town Hall concerts.

Bunk Johnson (62) makes his first recording session on 11 June.

National U.S. recording ban from 1 August.

BIRTHS

John McLaughlin (guitar) 4 January
Bill Goodwin (drums) 8 January
Tony Mann (drums) 31 January
James 'Blood' Ulmer (guitar) 2 February
Keith Ingham (piano) 5 February
Barry Zweig (guitar) 7 February
Barbara Donald (trumpet) 9 February
Bob Neloms (piano) 2 March
Dave Green (bass) 5 March
Robin Kenyatta (alto sax) 6 March
Flora Purim (vocals/guitar) 6 March
Charles Tolliver (trumpet) 6 March
Adrian Macintosh (drums) 7 March
Buster Williams (bass) 1 April
Han Bennink (drums) 17 April
Alan Skidmore (tenor sax) 21 April
Sammy Rimington (clarinet/alto sax) 29 April
Pete Lemer (keyboards) 14 June
Eumir Deodato (piano) 22 June
Eddie Prévost (drums) 22 June
Joe Chambers (drums) 25 June
Mike Abene (piano) 2 July
Earl Grubbs (tenor sax) 13 July
David Horowitz (keyboards) 29 July
Marc Levin (flute/cornet) 6 August
Jack de Johnette (drums) 9 August
Andrew White (tenor sax) 6 September
John Taylor (piano) 25 September
Jean-Luc Ponty (violin) 29 September
Don Ayler (trumpet) 5 October
Cecil Bridgewater (trumpet) 10 October
Rein de Graaf (piano) 24 October
Terumasa Hino (trumpet) 25 October
Philip Catherine (guitar) 27 October
Aretha Franklin (vocals)

DEATHS

Willie Cornish (66) 12 January
Charlie Christian (25) 2 March
Joe Poston (47) May
Bunny Berigan (33) 2 June
Jimmy Blanton (23) 30 July

BOOKS

A. Fry, M.Kaplan & W.C.Love: *Who's who in jazz collecting*
G. Lee: *Beale Street Sundown*
Hugues Panassie: *The Real Jazz*
Frederic Ramsay & Charles E. Smith: *The Jazz Record Book*

FILMS

Cabin in the sky (99mins): feature film with Ethel Waters, Lena Horne, Louis Armstrong and Duke Ellington
Orchestra Wives (98mins): musical featuring Glenn Miller Orchestra
Syncopation (88mins): musical romance tracing the development of jazz, featuring Benny Goodman, Joe Venuti, Gene Krupa, Rex Stewart and many more

3 MINUTE SOUNDIES

Blues in the night: Cab Calloway
Caravan: Mills Brothers
C-Jam Blues: Duke Ellington
Down, down, down: Louis Jordan
Five guys named Moe: Louis Jordan
Flamingo: Duke Ellington
Fussy wuzzy: Louis Jordan
Harlem Serenade: Lucky Millinder
Hot in the groove: Erskine Hawkins
If you only knew: Valaida Snow
I'll be glad when you're dead, you rascal you: Louis Armstrong
I'm just a lucky so-and-so: Ray Bauduc
Jammin' in the panoram: Stan Kenton
Let me off uptown: Anita O'Day, Roy Eldridge & Gene Krupa Orchestra
Minnie the Moocher: Cab Calloway
Old Man Mose: Louis Jordan
St James Infirmary: Stan Kenton
Shine: Louis Armstrong
The Skunk song: Cab Calloway
Sleepytime down south: Louis Armstrong
Some of these days: Maxine Sullivan
Spirit of boogie woogie: Meade Lux Lewis
Swingin' on nothin': Velma Middleton with Louis Armstrong
Thanks for the boogie ride: Anita O'Day, Roy Eldridge & Gene Krupa Orchestra
This love of mine: Stan Kenton
Two guitars in jive: Stan Kenton
Virginia, Georgia and Caroline: Cab Calloway
The white cliffs of Dover: Stan Kenton

COMPOSITIONS

Harold Arlen / Johnny Mercer: *That Old Black Magic*
Hoagy Carmichael / Johnny Mercer: *Skylark*
Jimmy Davis / Ram Ramirez / Jimmy Sherman: *Lover Man*
Gene De Paul / Don Raye / Pat Johnston: *I'll Remember April*
Duke Ellington: *C Jam Blues*
Mercer Ellington: *Things Ain't What They Used To Be*
Bobby Plater / Tiny Bradshaw / Edward Johnson / Robert Wright: *Jersey Bounce*
Victor Schertzinger / Johnny Mercer: *Tangerine*
Billy Strayhorn: *Johnny Come Lately*
Juan Tizol: *Perdido*

RECORDS

Louis Armstrong (LA, 17 April): *Cash For Your Trash / Among My Souvenirs / Coquette / I Never Knew*
Mildred Bailey (NYC,12 February): *Sometimes / Wherever You Are / I Think Of You / More Than You Know*
Charlie Barnet Orchestra (NYC, 30 April): *I Like To Riff / Smiles / Shady Lady* (NYC, 17 July): *Things Ain't What They Used To Be / Washington Whirligig*
Count Basie (NYC, 21 January): *One O'Clock Jump / Blue Shadows And White Gardenias / 'Ay Now / For Good Of Your Country* (Chicago,3 April): *Basie Blues / I'm Gonna Move To The Outskirts Of Town / Time On*

My Hands (LA, 24 July): *How Long Blues / Royal Garden Blues / Bugle Blues / Sugar Blues / Farewell Blues / Cafe Society Blues / Way Back Blues / St Louis Blues* (LA,27 July): *Rusty Dusty Blues / Ride On / Lost The Blackout Blues / Time On My Hands / It's Sand, Man / Ain't It The Truth? / For The Good Of Your Country*
Pete Brown/Helen Humes (NYC, 9 February): *Mound Bayou / Unlucky Woman / Gonna Buy Me A Telephone*
Cab Calloway (Chicago, 2 February): *I Want To Rock / San Francisco Fan / I'll Be Around / Tain't No Good / Minnie The Moocher* (LA, 27 July): *Let's Go, Joe / Ogeechie River Lullaby / I Get The Neck Of A Chicken / Chant Of The Jungle*
Una Mae Carlisle (NYC, 13 February): *Don't Tetch It / So Long Shorty / I'm Tryin' / Sweet Talk*
Nat King Cole Quintet (NYC): *Heads / Pro-Sky / It Had To Be You / I Can't Give You Anything But Love*
Eddie Condon (NYC, 21 January): *Don't Leave Me Daddy / Fidgety Feet / Mammy O' Mine / Lonesome Tag Blues / Having A Ball At Carnegie Hall / Tortilla B Flat / More Tortilla B Flat*
Duke Ellington (Chicago, 21 January): *Perdido / C Jam Blues / Moon Mist* (NYC, 26 February): *What Am I Here For? / I Don't Mind / Someone* (LA, 26 June): *Main Stem / Johnny Come Lately* (Chicago, 28 July): *Hayfoot, Strawfoot / Sentimental Lady / A Slip Of The Lip / Sherman Shuffle*
Ella Fitzgerald (NYC, 11 March): *I'm Gettin' Mighty Lonesome / When I Come Back Crying* (NYC, 10 April): *All I Need Is You / Mama Come Home* (NYC, 31 July): *My Heart And I Decided / Four Leaf Clover In Your Pocket / He's My Guy*
Benny Goodman Orchestra (NYC, 15 January): *Jersey Bounce / The Lamp Of Memory / If You Built A Better Mousetrap / At The Darktown Strutters Ball* (NYC, 23 January): *Jersey Bounce / When The Roses Bloom Again / A Zoot Suit / Tangerine* (NYC, 5 February): *String Of Pearls / My Little Cousin / Ramona* (NYC, 12 March): *Before / I Threw A Kiss / We'll Meet Again / Full Moon* (NYC, 14 May): *All I Need Is You* (NYC, 17 June): *I've Got A Gal In Kalamazoo / Take Me / Serenade In Blue / Idaho* (NYC, 27 July): *Six Flats Unfinished / Why Don't You Do Right? / After You've Gone* (NYC, 30 July): *Dearly Beloved / I'm Old Fashioned / Mission To Moscow*
Benny Goodman Sextet/Quartet (NYC, 10 March): *The Wang Wang Blues / The World Is Waiting For The Sunrise / The Way You Look Tonight*
Lionel Hampton Sextet (NYC, 2 March): *Royal Family / I Can't Believe That You're In Love With Me / Blues In The News / Exactly Like You*
Lionel Hampton Orchestra (NYC, 26 May): *Now I Know / Half A Loaf Is Better Than None / Flying Home / In The Bag*
Woody Herman (LA, 24 July): *Down Under*
Billie Holiday (NYC, 10 February): *Wherever You Are / Mandy Is Two / It's A Sin To Tell A Lie / Until The Real Thing Comes Along* (LA, 12 June): *Trav'lin' Light*
Stan Kenton (NYC, 13 February): *Gambler's Blues / Reed Rapture / Concerto for Doghouse / Trumpet Symphonette / It Seems To Me / El Chocolo*
Joe Marsala's Chosen Seven (NYC, 6 July): *Chimes Blues / Sweet Mama / Walkin' The Dog / Lazy Daddy*
Jay McShann (NYC,2 July): *Lonely Boy Blues / Get You On My Mind / The Jumpin' Blues / Sepian Bounce*
Lucky Millinder (NYC, 18 February): *Fightin' Doug McArthur / I Want A Tall Skinny Papa / We're Gonna Have To Slap The Little Dirty Jap / Savoy* (NYC, 29 July): *Are You Ready? / Mason Flyer / When The Lights Go On Again / Little John Special*
Mel Powell (NYC, February): *When Did You Leave Heaven? / The World Is Waiting For The Sunrise / Blue Skies / Mood At Twilight*
Sammy Price and his Texas Bluesicians (NYC, 20 January): *It's All Right, Jack / Blow Katy Blow* (NYC, 25 July): *Teed Up / Frantic*
Fats Waller (NYC, 2 February): *Winter Weather / Cash For Your Trash* (NYC, 16 March): *We Need A Little Love / You Must Be Losing Your Mind / Really Fine / The Jitterbug Waltz*
Fats Waller and the Deep River Boys (NYC, 13 July): *By The Light Of The Silvery Moon / Swing Out To Victory / Up Jumped You With Love / Romance A La Mode*
Cootie Williams (NYC, March): *Marquita / When My Baby Left Me / Sleepy Valley / Flying High*
Lester Young / Nat King Cole (LA, 15 July): *Indiana / I Can't Get Started / Tea For Two / Body And Soul*

1942

Photograph courtesy: *Max Jones*

Photograph courtesy: *Hank O'Neal*

Eddie Condon Presents

Above right: The Duke Ellington Orchestra with newcomer Jimmy Hamilton (25). 'Tricky Sam' Nanton, Juan Tizol and Lawrence Brown (trombones). Ben Webster, Johnny Hodges and Jimmy Hamilton (saxes).

Bottom right: Eddie Condon begins a series of Saturday afternoon concerts at Town Hall in New York. Featured here is trumpeter Jonah Jones. The caricature of Eddie by Johnny de Vries was used on all the publicity for the concerts.

1943

Zoot suits and jive become popular. The dance rages of the year are the jitterbug and the Lindy Hop.

Dizzy Gillespie (26), Charlie Parker (23) and Sarah Vaughan (19) in the big band of Earl Hines (38).

Duke Ellington (44) presents 'Black, Brown & Beige' at his first Carnegie Hall concert on 23 January. His second Carnegie Hall concert in December features 'New World a'comin'.

Gene Krupa (34) disbands when he is convicted of marijuana possession (May) and sent to jail. He is released in August and joins Tommy Dorsey's Orchestra.

Kid Ory (56) with Bunk Johnson (63) in Los Angeles.

Art Tatum (33) forms trio with Tiny Grimes (26) and Slam Stewart (29).

Dinah Washington (19) joins Lionel Hampton (30) Band.

Ben Webster (34) leaves Ellington band.

Glenn Miller (39) forms an Air Force Dance Band featuring Mel Powell (20), Trigger Alpert (27) and Ray McKinley (33).

Artie Shaw (33) leads Navy Band in the South Pacific.

Fats Waller (39) dies aboard a trans-continental train on 15 December.

National U.S. recording ban ends.

BIRTHS
Barry Altschul (drums) 6 January
Billy Harper (tenor sax) 17 January
Ray Pizzi (saxes) 19 January
Valery Ponomarev (trumpet) 20 January
Steve Gilmore (bass) 21 January
Michal Urbaniak (violin/tenor sax) 22 January
Gary Burton (vibes) 23 January
Howard Riley (piano) 16 February
Amina Claudine Myers (piano/vocals) 21 March
George Benson (guitar) 22 March
Larry Coryell (guitar) 2 April
Noah Howard (alto sax) 6 April
Gerry Niewood (saxes) 6 April
Freddie Waits (drums) 27 April
Dom Minasi (guitar) 3 June
Kenny Barron (piano) 9 June
Frank Lowe (tenor sax) 24 June
Frank Tate (bass) 18 July
Mike Mantler (trumpet) 10 August
Enrico Rava (trumpet) 20 August
Jiggs Whigham (trombone) 20 August
Jeremy Steig (flute) 23 September
Michael Howell (guitar) 8 October
Urszula Dudziak (vocalist) 22 October
Ali Haurand (bass) 15 November
Richard Tee (keyboards) 24 November
Butch Thompson (piano/clarinet) 28 November
Jimmy Owens (flugelhorn) 9 December
Grover Washington Jr (tenor sax) 12 December

DEATHS
Armand J Piron (54) 17 February
Tiny Parham (43) 4 April
Min Leibrook (40) 8 June
Trixie Smith (48) 21 September
Leon Roppolo (41) 15 October
Fats Waller (39) 15 December
Zue Robertson (52)

BOOKS
R. Avery: Murder on the downbeat (novel)
Rudi Blesh: This is Jazz
Charles Delaunay: Hot Discography
Duke Ellington: Piano Method for Blues
I. Shurman: Death beats the band (novel)

FILMS
Band Parade (10mins): Count Basie music short
Cab Calloway Medley: music short
Choo choo swing (13mins): Count Basie music short
Duke Ellington & his Orchestra (9mins): music short
Funzapoppin' (80mins): Olsen & Johnson sequel to 'Hellzapoppin' with Count Basie Orchestra
Harry James & the Music Makers (14mins): music short
Hit Parade of 1943 (86mins): musical comedy featuring Count Basie
New Orleans Blues (15mins): Louis Prima music short
Reveille with Beverley (77mins): musical featuring

Duke Ellington Orchestra, Bob Crosby's Dixieland Band, Count Basie Orchestra, Ray McKinley Orchestra, Frank Sinatra and the Mills Brothers
Something to shout about (90mins): Backstage musical featuring Hazel Scott, Teddy Wilson Band
Stage Door Canteen (133mins): all-star variety show including Ethel Waters, Count Basie Orchestra, Benny Goodman Band
Stormy Weather (78mins): all-negro musical featuring Lena Horne, Fats Waller and Cab Calloway
The gang's all here (104mins): musical feature with Benny Goodman Orchestra
Top Man (83mins): comedy musical featuring three numbers by Count Basie Orchestra
3 MINUTE SOUNDIES
Because I love you : Mamie Smith
Errand boy for rhythm : Nat King Cole
Foo a little ballyhoo : Cab Calloway
Four or five times : Sister Rosetta Tharpe with Lucky Millinder Orchestra
G.I. Jive : Louis Jordan
Hello Bill : Lucky Millinder
Honey Chile : Louis Jordan
Hong Kong Blues : Hoagy Carmichael
House on 52nd Street : Red Allen/J.C.Higginbotham
If you can't smile and say yes : Louis Jordan
I got it bad and that ain't good : Ivie Anderson with Duke Ellington Orchestra
I was here when you left me : Cab Calloway
Man, that's groovy : Jimmy Dorsey

COMPOSITIONS
Harold Arlen / Johnny Mercer: One For My Baby
Gene De Paul / Don Raye: Star Eyes
Duke Ellington: Black, Brown & Beige
Phil Moore: Shoo Shoo, Baby
Jimmy Mundy / Trummy Young / Johnny Mercer: Trav'lin Light
Kurt Weill / Ogden Nash: Speak Low
Alec Wilder: I'll Be Around

RECORDS
Mildred Bailey (NYC, 9 November): Rockin' Chair / Sunday, Monday Or Always / Scrap Your Fat / More Than You Know
Charlie Barnet Orchestra (NYC, 20 October): Strollin' / The Moose / Pow Wow
Count Basie (LA, July): Dance Of The Gremlins / GI Stomp
Sidney Bechet's New Orleans Feetwarmers (NYC, 8 December): V-Disc Blues / After You've Gone / Bechet Parades The Blues
George Brunies Band (NYC, 29 November): Royal Garden Blues / Ugly Chile / Tin Roof Blues / That Da Da Strain
Nat King Cole Trio (LA, 1 March): Pitchin' Up A Boogie / I'm Lost / Beautiful Moons Ago / Let's Spring One (LA, 2 November): F.S.T. / Got A Penny / Let's Pretend / My Lips Remember Your Kisses

(LA,30 November): Straighten Up And Fly Right / Gee Baby Ain't I Good To You / Jumpin' At Capitol / If You Can Smile And Say Yes (LA, 15 December): Sweet Lorraine / Embraceable You / It's Only A Paper Moon / I Can't See For Lookin'
Eddie Condon (NYC, 20 November): Squeeze Me / That' A Plenty (NYC, 2 December): Rose Room / Basin Street Blues / Oh Katharina (NYC, 8 December): Pray For The Lights To Go Out / Tell 'Em About Me / Mandy Make Up Your Mind / Singin' The Blues (NYC, 11 December): Back In Your Own Backyard / Of All The Wrongs... / You Can't Cheat A Cheater / Save Your Sorrow
Wild Bill Davison (NYC, 27 November): That's A Plenty / Panama / Riverboat Shuffle /Muskrat Ramble (NYC, 30 November): Clarinet Marmalade / Original Dixieland One Step / At The Jazz Band Ball / Baby Won't You Please Come Home
Roy Eldridge (Chicago, 16 November): Minor Jive / The Gasser / Jump Through The Window / Stardust
Duke Ellington (Carnegie Hall, NYC, 23 January): The Star Spangled Banner / Black & Tan Fantasy / Rockin' In Rhythm / Moon Mist / Jumpin' Punkins / Portrait Of Bert Williams / Portrait Of Bojangles / Portrait Of Florence Mills / Mood Indigo / Koko / Dirge / Johnny Come Lately / Are You Sticking? / Bakhim / Jack The Bear / Cottontail / Daydream / Boy Meets Horn / Rose Of The Rio Grande / Don't Get Around Much Anymore / Goin' Up / Black Brown & Beige / Blue Belles Of Harlem (Carnegie Hall, NYC, 11 December): Star Spangled Banner / Take The A Train / Moon Mist / Tea For Two / Honeysuckle Rose / Excerpts from Black Brown & Beige / Ring Dem Bells / Medley / Jack The Bear / Do Nothing 'Till You Hear From Me / Black & Tan Fantasy / C-Jam Blues / Stardust / New World A-Comin' / Floor Show / Don't Get Around Much Anymore / Summertime / Cottontail / Rockin' In Rhythm / Sentimental Lady / Trumpet In Spades / Things Ain't What They Used To Be
Ella Fitzgerald (NYC, 3 November): Cow Cow Boogie
Dexter Gordon (LA): I've Found A New Baby / Rosetta / Sweet Lorraine / I Blowed And Gone
Coleman Hawkins (NYC, 8 December): Voodte / How Deep Is The Ocean / Hawkins' Barrel House / Stumpy (NYC, 23 December): Crazy Rhythm / Get Happy / The Man I Love / Sweet Lorraine
Woody Herman (LA, 22 February): Woodchopper's Ball (NYC, 17 November): Basie's Basement
Stan Kenton (LA, 19 November): Do Nothin' Till You Hear From Me / Eager Beaver / Harlem Folk Dance / Artistry in Rhythm
Jay McShann (NYC, 1 December): Say Forward, I'll March / Wrong Neighbourhood / Hometown Blues
Lucky Millinder (NYC, 19 October): Don't Cry Baby / Sweet Slumber / Shipyard Social Function (NYC, 22 November): Savoy
Fats Waller (LA, 23 January): Moppin' And Boppin' / Ain't Misbehavin' / That Ain't Right (LA, 23 September): Ain't Misbehavin' / Two Sleepy People / Slightly Less Than Wonderful / There's A Gal / This Is So Nice / Martinique / Jive / Waller Jive / Hallelujah / Reefer Song / That's What The Bird Said / Solitude / Bouncin' On A V-Disc / Sometimes I Feel Like A Motherless Child
Dinah Washington (NYC, 29 December): Evil Gal Blues / I Know How To Do It / Salty Papa Blues / Homeward Bound
Ben Webster (NYC, Autumn): Woke Up Clipped / The Horn
Dickie Wells (NYC, 21 December): I Got Rhythm / I'm Fer It Too / Linger Awhile / Hello Babe
Lee Wiley (NYC): Down With Love / Stormy Weather / Between The Devil And The Deep Blue Sea / I've Got The World On A String (NYC): Fun To Be Fooled / You Said It / Let's Fall In Love / Moanin' In The Morning
Lester Young (NYC, 28 December): Just You, Just Me / I Never Knew / Afternoon Of A Basie-ite / Sometimes I'm Happy

1943

Photograph courtesy: *Duncan P Schiedt Collection*

Photograph courtesy: *Max Jones*

Top: The Earl Hines Orchestra at the Apollo Theatre with Dizzy Gillespie (far left) on trumpet and Charlie Parker (far right) on tenor sax.

Above: Coleman Hawkins recording for Signature on 8 December. L to r: Coleman Hawkins (tenor sax), Bill Coleman (trumpet), Oscar Pettiford (bass), Andy Fitzgerald (clarinet), Bob Thiele (producer). Unseen members of the group are Ellis Larkins (piano), Al Casey (guitar) and Shelly Manne (drums).

Right: Fats Waller in the Hollywood movie *Stormy Weather*. Fats (39) died on 15 December en route from Hollywood to New York.

Photograph of Fat Waller courtesy: *Max Jones*

1944

Decca launch the first high-fidelity records.

Al Sears (34) and Cat Anderson (28) join Duke Ellington. Rex Stewart (37) and Juan Tizol (44) leave.

Lester Young (35) and Jo Jones (33) are drafted and replaced in the Basie Band by Lucky Thompson (20) and Shadow Wilson (25).

Orson Welles presents a radio programme on CBS in March including Jimmie Noone (48), Zutty Singleton (46), Kid Ory (57), Ed Garland (49), Buster Wilson (47), Bud Scott (54) and Mutt Carey (53).

Billy Eckstine (30) forms All-Star Bop Band including Bird and Diz (April).

Norman Granz (26) presents his first concert at the Philharmonic in Los Angeles (2 July).

Boyd Raeburn (30) leads a modern orchestra featuring Oscar Pettiford (22).

Stan Getz (17) and Anita O'Day (25) with Stan Kenton (32).

Dizzy Gillespie (27) and Oscar Pettiford lead a quintet with Don Byas (32) at the Onyx Club on 52nd Street. Erroll Garner (23) playing in 52nd Street clubs, but the highest paid band on the street is the Art Tatum (34) Trio.

Allied Forces land in Normandy (6 June) and move across France towards Germany.

BIRTHS
Louis Stewart (guitar) 5 January
Al Foster (drums) 18 January
Chuck Domanico (bass) 20 January
Roger Humphries (drums) 30 January
Bill Mays (piano) 5 February
Rufus Reid (bass) 10 February
Martin Drew (drums) 11 February
Marty Morell (drums) 15 February
Henry Threadgill (saxes) 15 February
Ron Mathewson (bass) 19 February
Lew Soloff (trumpet) 20 February
Quin Davis (alto sax) 12 March
Joachim Kuhn (piano) 15 March
Evan Parker (tenor sax) 5 April
Pat La Barbera (tenor sax) 7 April
Billy Cobham (drums) 16 May
Monty Alexander (piano) 6 June
Turk Mauro (baritone sax) 11 June
Jon Hiseman (drums) 21 June
Butch Miles (drums) 4 July
Didier Levallet (bass) 19 July
Carl Grubbs (alto sax) 27 July
Barbara Thompson (saxes) 27 July
Al Stinson (bass) 2 August
Nana Vasconcelos (percussion) 2 August
Oscar Brashear (trumpet) 18 August
Terry Clarke (drums) 20 August
Pat Martino (guitar) 25 August
John Surman (baritone sax) 30 August
George Mraz (bass) 9 September
Marlena Shaw (vocals) 22 September
Eddie Gomez (bass) 4 October
Willem Breuker (saxes) 4 November
Charles Sullivan (trumpet) 8 November
George Cables (piano) 14 November
Alex Acuña (percussion) 12 December
Michael Carvin (drums) 12 December
John Abercrombie (guitar) 16 December
Vyacheslav Ganelin (piano) 17 December
Bobby Colomby (drums) 20 December
Woody Shaw (trumpet) 24 December
Dwight Dickerson (piano) 26 December

DEATHS
Bob Zurke (33) 16 February pneumonia
Yank Porter (49) 22 March
Jimmie Noone (48) 19 April heart attack
Al Gandee (44) 3 June auto accident
Will Marion Cook (75) 19 July
O'Neil Spencer (34) 24 July tuberculosis
Dick Voynow (44) 15 September
Clarence Profit (32) 22 October
Rod Cless (37) 8 December fell over apartment railings
Glenn Miller (40) c.16 December aircraft disappeared

BOOKS
James Asman: Jazz
James Asman & Bill Kinnell: Jazz on Record
Dan Burley: Dan Burley's Original Handbook of Harlem Jive
Cab Calloway: The New Cab Calloway's Hepster's Dictionary: Language of Jive
David Ewen: Men of Popular Music
John Gee & Michael Wadsley (eds): Jazzography
Robert Goffin: Jazz from the Congo to the Metropolitan
Gordon Jacobs: A Study of Jazz
Cliff Jones: Hot Jazz / Jazz in New York / New Orleans and Chicago Jazz
Paul Miller (ed): Esquire's Jazz Book
Frederic Ramsay: Chicago Documentary: Portrait of a Jazz Era
John Rowe: Trombone Jazz
Frank Stacy: Harry James' Pin-up Life Story

FILMS
Artistry in Rhythm (20mins): Stan Kenton music short
Atlantic City (87mins): Paul Whiteman, Louis Armstrong feature
Broadway Rhythm (114mins): feature with Tommy Dorsey, Lena Horne & Hazel Scott
Cootie Williams & Orchestra (10mins): music short
Jammin' the blues (10mins): Gjon Mili film featuring Lester Young, Illinois Jacquet, Harry Edison, Sid Catlett, Jo Jones, Red Callender, Barney Kessell
Jam Session (74mins): musical with Louis Armstrong Orchestra & Charlie Barnet Band
Melody Parade (15mins): Charlie Barnet music short
Sweet and Low-down (76mins): feature with Benny Goodman Orchestra & Quartet playing a large part
Twilight on the Prairie (62mins): comedy about a cowboy band with Jack Teagarden playing a leading role
3-MINUTE SOUNDIES
Boogie Woogie: Meade Lux Lewis
Deacon Jones : Wingy Manone
Eager Beaver: Stan Kenton
I'm homesick, that's all: Stan Kenton
Jordan Jive: Louis Jordan
Jumpin' at the Jubilee: Louis Jordan
Lazy River: Mills Brothers
Low down dog: Meade Lux Lewis
My new gown: Lena Horne, with Albert Ammons, Pete Johnson & Teddy Wilson Orchestra
Ration Blues: Louis Jordan
Rhythm on the river: Wingy Manone
Roll 'em: Meade Lux Lewis
Sing, sing, sing: Wingy Manone
Unlucky Woman: Lena Horne with Teddy Wilson Orchestra

COMPOSITIONS
Hoagy Carmichael / Johnny Mercer: How Little We Know
Nat Cole / Irving Mills: Straighten Up And Fly Right
Duke Ellington: Blutopia / I'm Beginning To See The Light
Dizzy Gillespie: Woody 'N You
Louis Jordan / Billy Austin: Is You Is Or Is You Ain't My Baby?
Cole Porter: Everytime We Say Goodbye
Karl Suessedorf / John Blackburn: Moonlight In Vermont

RECORDS
Red Allen (NYC): Ride, Red, Ride / Dark Eyes / Dear Old Southland / Red Jump
Albert Ammons (NYC, 12 February): Albert's Special Boogie Woogie / The Boogie Rocks / The Blues In The Groove / The Breaks / Jammin' The Boogie / Bottom Blues
George Auld (NYC, 22 May): Sweet & Lovely / Concerto For Tenor / Taps Miller / I Can't Get Started
Auld/Hawkins/Webster Saxtet (NYC, 17 May): Pick Up Boys / Porgy / Uptown Lullaby / Salt Peanuts
Mildred Bailey (NYC, 24 May): Which Of The Great Forty Eight / Just You, Just Me / Bugle Call Rag (NYC, 20 October): Hold On / Summertime (NYC, 3 November): Right As Rain (NYC, 17 November): From The End Of The Sky / Blue Water / Accentuate The Positive (NYC, 8 December): Sometimes I Feel Like A Motherless Child / Rockin' Chair
Charlie Barnet Orchestra (LA, 3 August): Skyliner
Count Basie (NYC, 27 May): Kansas City Stride / Beaver Junction / Circus In Rhythm / Gee Baby, Ain't I Good To You / Basie Strides Again (NYC, 30 October): Harvard Blues (NYC, 6 December): Taps Miller / Jimmy's Blues / I Didn't Know About You / Red Bank Boogie
Sidney Bechet's New Orleans Feetwarmers (NYC, 20 December): St Louis Blues / Jazz Me Blues / Blue Horizon / Muskrat Ramble
Emmett Berry (NYC, 31 August): Sweet And Lovely / White Rose Kick / Deep Blue Dream / Byas'd Opinion
Barney Bigard (NYC, 22 January): Tea For Two / Step Steps Up / Step Steps Down / Moonglow (NYC, 27 November): Wrap Your Troubles In Dreams / A Lull At Dawn / Soft And Warm / A Portrait Of Louise (NYC, 29 December): Blues Before Dawn / Poon Tang / Nine O'Clock Beer / How Long Blues
Pete Brown Quartet (Chicago, 23 April): Jim's Idea / Eddie's Idea / Pete's Idea / Jim Daddy Blues
Pete Brown's Hot Five (NYC, 11 July): Ooh-Wee / Bellvue For You / Pete Brown's Boogie / Moppin' The Blues (19 July): All Depends On You / Talk Of The Town / That's My Weakness Now / I May Be Wrong (1 August): Sunshine Blues / Lazy Day / It's Great / Boot Zoot
Don Byas (NYC, 28 July): Riffin' And Jivin' / Free And Easy / Worried 'N' Blue / Don's Idea (17 August): What Do You Want With My Heart? / Bass C Jam / Savoy Jam Party 1 & 2
Sid Catlett (NYC, 18 April): Sleep / Linger Awhile / Memories Of You / Just A Riff / 1-2-3 Blues / I Found A New Baby (4 May): Blues In Room 920 / Blue Skies / Sweet Georgia Brown / Thermo-dynamics
Rod Cless (NYC, 1 September): Froggy Moore / Make Me A Pallet On The Floor / I Know That You Know / Have You Ever Felt That Way?
Cozy Cole All-Stars (NYC, 22 February): Blue Moon / Father Co-operates / Just One More Chance / Thru For The Night (13 March): Jericho / Talk To Me / Concerto For Cozy / Body And Soul / Nice And Cozy (1 May): Ol' Man River / Wrap Your Troubles In Dreams / Ridin' The Riff / Flat Rock (14 June): Jersey Jump Off / Stomping At The Savoy / On The Sunny Side / Jump Awhile (14 November): Willow Weep For Me / Look Here / Ghost Of A Chance / Take It On Back (21 November): Memories Of You / Comes The Don / When Day Is Done / The Beat
Nat King Cole Trio (LA, 17 January): The Man I Love / Body And Soul / Prelude In C-Sharp Minor / What Is This Thing Called Love? (6 March): Look What You Have Done To Me / Easy Listening Blues / I Realize Now (28 November): Bring Another Drink
Eddie Condon (Town Hall, NYC, 8 March): Uncle Sam's Blues / Tin Roof Blues (NYC, 1 July): Clarinet Chase (NYC, 8 July): Struttin' With Some Barbecue / Royal Garden Blues (NYC, 15 July): Wolverine Blues (NYC, 22 July): Fidgety Feet (NYC, 17 August): Clarinet Marmalade (NYC, 13 December): When Your Lover Has Gone / Whenever There's Love / Impromptu Ensemble No1 / The Man I Love / 'S Wonderful (NYC, 14 December): Someone To Watch Over Me / Sheik Of Araby / The Man I Love / Somebody Loves Me / Jam Session Jump / Jam Session Blues
Billy Eckstine Orchestra (NYC, 13 April): I Got A Date With Rhythm / I Stay In The Mood For You / Good Jelly Blues (NYC, 5 December): If That's The Way You Feel / I Want To Talk About You / Blowing The Blues Away / Opus X / I'll Wait And Pray / The Real Thing Happened To Me

1944

Roy Eldridge (NYC, 24 January): *Don't Be That Way / I Want To Be Happy / Fiesta In Brass / St Louis Blues* (NYC, 26 June): *I Can't Get Started / After You've Gone / Body And Soul* (NYC, 13 October): *Fish Market / Twilight Time / St Louis Blues*

Duke Ellington (NYC, 1 December): *I Ain't Got Nothin' But The Blues / I'm Beginning To See The Light / Don't You Know I Care / I Didn't Know About You* (NYC, 11,12 December): *Black, Brown & Beige Suite*

Erroll Garner (NYC, 16 November): *The Fighting Cocks* (NYC, 18 November): *Cloudburst* (NYC, 22 November): *Variations On Clair De Lune* (NYC, 24 November): *Sunny Side Of The Street* (NYC, 14 December): *All The Things You Are / I Hear A Rhapsody / You Were Born To Be Kissed* (NYC, 18 December): *Perdido / Soft And Warm / Everything Happens To Me / I'm In The Mood For Love / All The Things You Are / Rose Room / I Get A Kick Out Of You / Blues I Can't Forget / Boogie Woogie Boogie / Gliss In The Dark*

Benny Goodman Quartet (LA, 18 January): *Rachel's Dream*

Benny Goodman Quintet (NYC, October): *Sweet Georgia Brown / Sheik Of Araby / Rose Room* (NYC, 16 November): *Every Time We Say Goodbye* (NYC, 21 November): *Only Another Boy And Girl*

Clyde Hart (NYC, 19 December): *Smack That Mess / Dee Dee's Dance / Little Benny*

Coleman Hawkins (NYC, 29 May): *Make Believe / Don't Blame Me / Just One Of Those Things / Hallelujah* (NYC, 11 October): *In The Hush Of The Night / Out To Lunch / Look Out Jack / Every Man For Himself* (NYC, 19 October): *Drifting On A Reed / Recollections / Flying Hawk / On The Beam*

Woody Herman (NYC, 10 August): *Apple Honey / Jones Beachhead* (NYC, 16 August): *G.I.Jive*

Billie Holiday (NYC, 18 January): *Billie's Blues / Do Nothin' Till You Hear From Me / I'll Get By* (NYC, 25 March): *How Am I To Know? / My Old Flame / I'll Get By / I Cover The Waterfront* (NYC, 1 April): *I'll Be Seeing You / I'm Yours / Embraceable You / As Time Goes By* (NYC, 8 April): *He's Funny That Way / Lover Come Back To Me / Billie's Blues / On The Sunny Side Of The Street* (NYC, 4 October): *Lover Man / No More* (NYC, 8 November): *That Old Devil Called Love / Don't Explain / Big Stuff*

Wingy Manone (LA, 28 February): *Isle Of Capri / Memphis Blues* (LA, 7 March): *The Tailgate Ramble / Besame Mucho / Paper Doll / Sister Kate* (LA, 25 July): *The General Jumped At Dawn / Tin Roof Blues / If I Could Be With You / A-Card Blues* (NYC, 15 December): *O Sole Mio / Shake The Blues Away*

Mezz Mezzrow / Art Hodes Trio (NYC, 15 March): *Really The Blues / Milk For Mezz / Feather's Lament / Mezzin' Around*

Miff Mole (NYC, 8 March): *Ballin' The Jack / How Come You Do Me Like You Do / If I Had You* (NYC, 25 April): *St Louis Blues / Peg O' My Heart / Beale Street Blues / I Must Have That Man*

Benny Morton Trombone Choir (NYC, 30 May): *Where Or When / Liza / Once In A While / Sliphorn Outing*

Red Norvo (Chicago, 5 April): *Red Stuff / Rehearsin' / Confessin' / A Fawn Jumped At Dawn* (NYC, 27 July): *Subtle Sexology / Blues à la Red / The Man I Love / Seven Come Eleven* (NYC, 14 August): *Which Switch Which / Bass On The Bar Floor* (NYC, 10 October): *Russian Lullaby / I Got Rhythm*

Kid Ory's Creole Jazz Band (LA, 15, 29 March): *Panama Rag / Weary Blues / That's A Plenty / Muskrat Ramble / High Society / Mutt's Blues* (LA, 3 August): *Get Out Of Here / South / Blues For Jimmy / Creole Song*

Hot Lips Page (NYC, 8 March): *My Gal Is Gone / Rockin' At Ryan's / You'd Be Frantic / The Blues Jumped A Rabbit* (NYC, 14 June): *Dance Of The Tambourine / Uncle Sam's Blues / Pagin' Mr Page / I Keep Rollin' On* (NYC, 12 September): *I Got What It Takes / Double-Trouble Blues* (NYC, 29 September): *Six, Seven, Eight Or Nine / You Need Coachin' / These Foolish Things / Fish For Supper* (NYC, 30 November): *The Lady In Bed / Gee Baby, Ain't I Good To You / Big 'D' Blues / It Ain't Like That* (NYC, 7 December): *The Sheik Of Araby*

Oscar Pettiford (NYC, 27 July): *Dedicated To JB / Don't Blame Me*

Flip Phillips (NYC, 2 October): *Skyscraper / Pappiloma / A Melody From The Sky* (NYC, 9 October): *Bob's Belief / Sweet And Lovely / Lover Come Back To Me*

Sammy Price & his Texas Bluesicians (NYC, 1 March): *Pluckin' That Thing / Boogie Woogie Notion / Big Joe / Boogin' A Plenty / Honeysuckle Rose*

Ike Quebec (NYC, 18 July): *Tiny's Exercise / She's Funny That Way / Indiana / Blue Harlem* (NYC, 25 September): *Hard Tack / If I Had You / Mad About You / Facing The Face*

Lucky Thompson (NYC, 26 December): *Test Pilots 1&2*

Sarah Vaughan (NYC, 31 December): *Signing Off / Interlude / No Smokes / East Of The Sun*

Ben Webster (NYC, 25 March): *Perdido / I Surrender Dear* (NYC, 17 April): *Honeysuckle Rose / I Surrender Dear / Blue Skies / Kat's Fur*

Cootie Williams (NYC, 4 January): *You Talk A Little Trash / Floogie Boo / I Don't Know / Gotta Do Some War Work* (NYC, 6 January): *My Old Flame / Sweet Lorraine / Echoes Of Harlem / Honeysuckle Rose / Now I Know / Tee's Torch Song / Cherry Red Blues / Things Ain't What They Used To Be* (NYC, 22 August): *Is You Is Or Is You Ain't / Somebody's Gotta Go / 'Round Midnight / Blue Garden Blues*

Lester Young (NYC, 22 March): *After Theatre Jump / Six Cats And A Prince / Lester Leaps Again / Destination KC* (NYC, 28 March): *Three Little Words / Jo-jo / I Got Rhythm / Four O'Clock Drag* (NYC, 18 April): *These Foolish Things / Exercise In Swing / Salute To Fats / Basie English*

Trummy Young (Chicago, 7 February): *Talk Of The Town / The Man I Love* (NYC, 4 December): *Let Me Call You Sweetheart / Lame Brain / Please, Please, Please / Flogalapa*

Photograph courtesy: *Max Jones*

Top: **Sidney Bechet recording for Blue Note**
Photograph: *Chuck Peterson* Courtesy: *Max Jones*

Above: **The Coleman Hawkins Band during their summer engagement at the Downbeat Club on 52nd Street. Benny Harris is on trumpet and the other sidemen were Don Byas (tenor sax), Thelonious Monk (piano), Denzil Best (drums) and Eddie Robinson (bass).**

Right: **Billie Holiday and Art Tatum at the Esquire All Stars Concert in the Metropolitan Opera House, New York (17 January).**

Photograph courtesy: *Max Jones*

1945

Bop vogue at its height on 52nd Street.

Miles Davis (19) arrives in New York, studies at Juilliard.

Duke Ellington (46) premieres 'The Perfume Suite' at Carnegie Hall. Russell Procope (37) and Oscar Pettiford (23) join the band, Otto Hardwick (41) leaves.

Woody Herman (32) & his First Herd reach musical peak with Bill Harris (29), Flip Phillips (30), Ralph Burns (23), Neal Hefti (23), Dave Tough (36) & Chubby Jackson (27).

June Christy (20) joins Stan Kenton (33).

Dizzy Gillespie (28) tours with his first big band 'Hepsations of 1945'.

Charlie Shavers (28) joins Tommy Dorsey (39).

Bunk Johnson (65) brought to NYC to play at Stuyvesant Casino (September).

Eddie Condon Club opens in Greenwich Village (December).

Lester Young (36) released from Army on 15 December, works on West Coast.

Charlie Parker (25) and Dizzy Gillespie (28) open at Billy Berg's club in LA (December).

VE Day: Victory in Europe (8 May). Atomic bombs are dropped on Hiroshima (6 August) and Nagasaki (9 August) and Japan surrenders.

BIRTHS
Bob Maize (bass) 15 January
Fred Seldon (alto sax) 22 January
Bob Stewart (tuba) 3 February
John Stubblefield (tenor sax) 4 February
Keith Nichols (piano) 13 February
Pete Christlieb (tenor sax) 16 February
Ed Soph (drums) 21 March
Ole Kock Hansen (piano) 4 April
Steve Gadd (drums) 9 April
Keith Jarrett (piano) 8 May
Peter Donald (drums) 15 May
Michael Moore (bass) 16 May
Anthony Braxton (alto sax) 4 June
Joe Beck (guitar) 29 July
Dave Sanborn (alto sax) 30 July
Bryan Spring (drums) 24 August
Ernie Watts (saxes) 23 October
Arild Andersen (bass) 27 October
Elton Dean (alto sax) 28 October
David Parlato (bass) 31 October
Jim Mullen (guitar) 2 November
John La Barbera (trumpet) 10 November
Randy Brecker (trumpet) 27 November
Johnny Dyani (bass) 30 November
Tony Williams (drums) 12 December
Stanley Crouch (drums/critic) 14 December
Cameron Brown (bass) 21 December

DEATHS
Clyde Hart (35) 19 March *tuberculosis*
Teddy Weatherford (41) 25 April *cholera*
Nat Jaffe (27) 5 August
Pha Terrell (35) 14 October *kidney ailment*
Richard M Jones (56) 8 December
Jack Jenney (35) 16 December *complications following appendectomy*
Bobby Stark (39) 29 December
Jerome Kern

BOOKS
James Asman: *Jazz Today*
James Asman & Bill Kinnell: *Jazz Writings*
C. Cuthbert: *The Robbed Heart* (novel)
Stanley Dance: *Jazz Notebook*
Paul Miller (ed): *Esquire's 1945 Jazz Book*
Max Jones & Albert McCarthy (eds): *Jazz Review*
Max Jones & Albert McCarthy: *Piano Jazz*
Albert McCarthy: *The Trumpet in Jazz*
William Miller: *Three Brass (O'Brien / Kaminsky / Sherock)*
Sharon Pease: *Boogie Woogie Fundamentals*
Timme Rosencrantz: *Jazz Profiles*
John Rowe: *Recorded Information*
Lew Shelly: *Hepcats Jive Talk Dictionary*
Ken Williamson: *Jazz Quiz 1*

FILMS
Caldonia (18mins): Louis Jordan in all-black musical comedy
Stan Kenton & Orchestra – Artistry in Rhythm : music short
Make Mine Music (75mins): Disney revue featuring Benny Goodman Quartet

3 MINUTE SOUNDIES
Blow Top Blues: Cab Calloway
Buzz me: Louis Jordan
Caldonia: Louis Jordan
Contrast in Rhythm: Cecil Scott Orchestra
Don't be late: Cecil Scott Orchestra
Frim Fram Sauce: Nat King Cole
I'm gonna love that guy: June Christy with Stan Kenton Orchestra
It's been a long, long time: June Christy with Stan Kenton Orchestra
Mr X Blues: Cecil Scott Orchestra
Never too old to swing: Tiny Grimes Band
Tampico: June Christy with Stan Kenton Orchestra
Tillie: Louis Jordan
Walking with my honey: Cab Calloway
We the cats shall hep ya: Cab Calloway

COMPOSITIONS
Duke Ellington: *The Perfume Suite./ New World-a-comin'./ I'm Just A Lucky So-and-so*
Fleecie Moore: *Caldonia*
Mel Powell / Ray McKinley: *My Guy's Come Back*
David Raksin / Johnny Mercer: *Laura*

RECORDS
Louis Armstrong (NYC, 14 January): *Jodie Man / I Wonder*
Mildred Bailey (NYC, 19 December): *The Man I Love / The Gypsy In My Soul / I'm Glad There Is You / It's Never Too Late To Pray* (NYC, 30 December): *These Foolish Things / Got The World On A String / Can't Help Lovin' That Man / Summertime*
Count Basie (NYC, 11 January): *Taps Miller / Jimmy's Blues / Take Me Back Baby / Playhouse No2 Stomp / Just An Old Manuscript / On The Upbeat* (NYC, 26 February): *Avenue C / This Heart Of Mine / That Old Feeling* (NYC, 14 May): *High Tide / Sent For You Yesterday / Jimmy's Boogie Woogie / San Jose / B-flat Blues* (LA, 9 October): *Blue Skies / Jivin' Joe Jackson / High Tide / Queer Street*
Sidney Bechet Blue Note Jazzmen (NYC,21 January): *High Society / Salty Dog / Weary Blues / Jackass Blues*
Barney Bigard (NYC, 5 January): *Can't Help Lovin' That Man / Please Don't Talk About Me When I'm Gone / Sweet Marijuana Brown / Blues For Art's Sake* (NYC, 5 February): *Rose Room / Coquette*
Pete Brown (NYC, 20 February): *Fat Man's Boogie / That's The Curfew / Midnite Blues / That's It* (NYC, 6 March): *Just Plain Shuffle / Pushin' The Mop / Back Talk Boogie*
Don Byas All-Stars (NYC, 23 January): *Pennies From Heaven / Should I? / You Call It Madness / Jamboree Jump* (NYC, Spring): *Double Talk / Fruit Salad / Don Juan / Spots / Please Believe Me / Why Did You Do That? / You Got To Play Your Hand / Just A Dream* (NYC, 27 June): *Little White Lies / Deep Purple / Them There Eyes / Out Of Nowhere* (NYC, Autumn): *The Gypsy / Nancy / Poor Butterfly*
Don Byas Quartet (NYC, 30 August): *Three O'Clock In The Morning / One O'Clock Jump / Harvard Blues / Slammin' Around* (NYC, 6 September): *Laura / Stardust / Slam, Don't Shake Like That / Dark Eyes* (NYC, 12 September): *Embraceable you / The Sheik*

Of Araby / Super Session / Melody In Swing (NYC, 3 October): *Once In A While / Avalon / Blue And Sentimental / My Melancholy Baby*
Don Byas Quintet (NYC, Autumn): *Candy / How High The Moon / Donby / Byas-A-Drink*
Benny Carter (SF, 25 October): *Poinciana / Just A Baby's Prayer / Hurry Hurry / Love For Sale* (LA, 9 April): *Malibu* (NYC, 12 December): *Prelude To A Kiss*
Sid Catlett (LA, 19 January): *I Never Knew / Love For Sale / Just You, Just Me / Henderson Romp* (NYC): *Just A Riff / Before Long / What's Happenin' / Mop De Mop Mop*
Buck Clayton (NYC, 7 June): *Diga Diga Doo / Love Me Or Leave Me / We're In The Money / BC Blues*
Nat King Cole Trio (LA, 27 February): *If You Can't Smile And Say Yes / A Pile Of Cole / Any Old Time / Bring Another Drink / Candy / A Trio Grooves In Brooklyn* (LA, April): *I'm A Shy Guy* (LA, 19 May): *Don't Blame Me / I'm Thru With Love* (LA, 23 May): *Sweet Georgia Brown / I Tho't You Ought To Know / It Only Happens Once* (LA, May): *Satchel Mouth Baby / Solid Potato Salad* (LA, 11 October): *It's Better To Be By Yourself / Come To Baby Do / The Frim Fram Sauce* (LA, 1 November): *I'm An Errand Boy For Rhythm / This Way Out / I Know That You Know*
Eddie Condon (NYC, 17 May): *Stairway To Paradise / Lady Be Good 1&2 / My One And Only* (NYC, 14 June): *Lady Be Good / Swanee*
Wild Bill Davison (NYC, 18 January): *Little Girl / Jazz Me Blues / Ghost Of A Chance / Squeeze Me* (NYC, 22 January): *A Monday Date / Confessin' / Big Butter And Egg Man / Sister Kate* (NYC, September): *Sensation Rag / Who's Sorry Now? / On The Alamo / Someday Sweetheart*
Baby Dodds Four (NYC, 26 December): *Feelin' At Ease / Careless Love / High Society / Winin' Boy Blues*
Billy Eckstine Orchestra (NYC, 2 May): *Lonesome Lover Blues / A Cottage For Sale / Rhythm In A Riff / Last Night* (NYC, September): *My Deep Blue Dream / Prisoner Of Love / Memories Of You / It Ain't Like That* (NYC, October): *I'm In The Mood For Love / You Call It Madness / All I Sing Is Blues / Long Long Journey*
Harry Edison (LA, October): *Laura / I Blowed And Gone / Exit Virginia Blues / Ain't Cha Gonna Do It?*
Roy Eldridge (NYC, 5 March): *Little Jazz Boogie / Embraceable You* (NYC, 14 November): *Boy Meets Horn / Old Rob Roy / I've Found A New Baby*
Duke Ellington (NYC, 4 January): *Carnegie Blues / Blue Cellophane / The Mood To Be Wooed / My Heart Sings* (NYC, 1 May): *Kissing Bug / Ev'rything But You / Riff Staccato* (NYC, 10 May): *Prelude To A Kiss / Caravan / Black And Tan Fantasy / Mood Indigo* (NYC, 14 May): *In A Sentimental Mood / It Don't Mean A Thing If It Ain't Got That Swing / Tonight I Shall Sleep* (NYC, 24 July): *Perfume Suite*
Ella Fitzgerald (NYC, 26 February): *I'm Beginning To See / That's The Way It Is* (NYC, 27 March): *Paper Moon / Cry Out Of My Heart* (NYC, 29 August): *A Kiss Goodnight / Benny's Coming Home On Saturday* (NYC, 4 October): *Flying Home* (NYC, 8 October, with Louis Jordan): *Stone Cold Dead In De Market / Peetootie Pie* (NYC, 22 October): *That's Rich / I'll Always Be In Love With You / I'll See You In My Dreams*
Slim Gaillard (LA): *Voot Greene / Please Wait For Me / Sighing Boogie / Queen Boogie / Vout Boogie / Slim Gaillard's Boogie / Harlem Hunch / Tutti-Frutti / Travelin' Blues / Sightseeing Boogie / Central Avenue Boogie / Slim's Cement Boogie* (LA): *Laguna / Dunkin' Bagels / Boogin' At Bergs / Don't Blame Me / Chili and Beans / Millionaires Don't Whistle* (LA, 1 December): *Scotchin' With Soda / As Long As I Have Your Love / Cement Mixer* (LA, 15 December): *Novachord Boogie / Tee Say Malee / Atomic Cocktail / Yeproc Heresi* (LA, 20 December): *Baby Won't You Please Come Home / The Hop / Cuban Rhumbarini* (LA, 29 December): *Dizzy Boogie / Flat Foot Floogie / Popity Pop / Slim's Jam*
Erroll Garner (NYC, 10 January): *White Rose Bounce / Twistin' The Cat's Tail / Movin' Around / Night And Day* (NYC, 9 March): *Sweet Lorraine / Yesterdays / Loot To Boot / Gaslight* (NYC, 25 September): *Laura / Stardust / Somebody Loves Me / Indiana* (NYC, 14 October): *Man O' Mine / Lady Be Good / Don't Blame Me / How High The Moon* (NYC, 5 December): *Embraceable You / I've Got You Under My Skin / Always / High Octane / Sometimes I'm Happy / Lover Come Back To Me / I Can't Get*

Started / Symphony / Bouncing With Me
Dizzy Gillespie (NYC, 9 January): *I Can't Get Started / Good Bait / Salt Peanuts / Be-Bop* (NYC, 9 February): *Groovin' High / Blue 'n' Boogie*
Dizzy Gillespie/Charlie Parker (NYC, 29 February): *Groovin' High / All The Things You Are / Dizzy Atmosphere* (NYC, 11 May): *Salt Peanuts / Shaw 'Nuff / Lover Man / Hot House*
Benny Goodman Sextet (NYC, 4 February): *After You've Gone / Slipped Disc / Oomph Fah Fah / She's Funny That Way / Body And soul*
Dexter Gordon (NYC, 30 October): *Blow, Mr Dexter / Dexter's Deck / Dexter's Cuttin' Out / Dexter's Minor Mad*
George Handy (LA): *Perdido / Handy Man / Hop Scotch / I Surrender Dear / Where You At? / I've Got To Go, That's All / Tonsillectomy / These Foolish Things*
Bill Harris (Chicago, 5 April): *Cross Country / Characteristically BH / Mean To Me / She's Funny That Way*
Clyde Hart (NYC, January): *What's The Matter Now? / I Want Every Bit Of It / That's The Blues / 4-F Blues / Dream Of You / Seventh Avenue / Sorta Kinda / Ooh, Ooh, My, My, Ooh, Ooh*
Coleman Hawkins (LA, 23 February): *April In Paris / Rifftide / Stardust / Stuffy* (LA, 2 March): *Hollywood Stampede / I'm Through With Love / What Is There To Say? / Wrap Your Troubles In Dreams* (LA, 9 March): *Too Much Of A Good Thing / Bean Soup / Someone To Watch Over Me / It's The Talk Of The Town*
Woody Herman (NYC, 19 February): *Laura / Apple Honey* (NYC, 26 February): *Caldonia* (NYC, 1 March): *Goosey Gander / Northwest Passage* (NYC, 20 August): *The Good Earth / Bijou* (NYC, 5 September): *Your Father's Moustache* (NYC, 16 November): *Wild Root*
Billie Holiday (LA, 17 January): *I Cover The Waterfront* (NYC, 14 August): *Don't Explain / Big Stuff / You Better Go Now / What Is This Thing Called Love*
J.J. Johnson (NYC, 2 August): *Grand Slam / How Am I To Know? / Peek-A-Boo / Baby, It's Up To You*
Stan Kenton (Chicago, 4 May): *Tampico / Southern Scandal / Opus in Pastels* (LA, 30 October): *Artistry Jumps / Painted Rhythm*
Howard McGhee (LA, May): *Deep Meditation* (LA, 4 September): *Intersection / Lifestream / Mop-Mop / Stardust* (LA, September): *Cool Fantasy / McGhee Special*

Wingy Manone (NYC): *That Glory Day / Bread And Gravy / That's A Gasser / Georgia Girl / Mr Boogie Man / Where Can I Find A Cherry?* (LA): *Big Leg Mama / Last Call For Alcohol* (LA): *Hot Peanuts / Salt Pork, West Virginia / What Good Is You / My Blue Heaven / I Must Be Dreaming / Isle Of Capri*
Joe Marsala (NYC, 12 January): *My Melancholy Baby / Cherokee* (NYC, 4 May): *Southern Comfort / Lover / Don't Let It End / Gotta Be This Or That* (NYC, 30 November): *East Of The Sun / Slightly Dizzy / I Would Do Anything For You*
Mezz Mezzrow/Sidney Bechet (NYC, 30 July): *House Party / Perdido Street Stomp / Revolutionary Blues / Blood On The Moon* (NYC, 31 July): *Levee Blues / Layin' My Rules In Blues / Bad Baby Blues / Saw Mill Blues / Minor Swoon / The Sheik Of Araby* (NYC, 29 August): *Baby I'm Cuttin' Out / Ole Miss / Bowin' The Blues / Jelly Roll / Perdido Street Stomp* (NYC, 30 August): *Old School / Gone Away Blues / Out Of The Gallion*
Red Norvo (NYC, 13 November): *Dee Dee's Dance / Blue Skies / Seven Come Eleven / I Surrender Dear / Red Dust*
Kid Ory Creole Jazz Band (LA, 12 February): *Dippermouth Blues / Savoy Blues / High Society / Ballin' The Jack* (LA, 21 March): *High Society / Muskrat Ramble / The Girls Go Crazy / Blanche Touquatoux* (LA, 5 August): *Panama / Careless Love / Do What Ory Say / Under The Bamboo Tree* (LA, 8 September): *1919 Rag / Maryland, My Maryland / Down Home Rag / Didn't He Ramble* (LA, 3 November): *Original Dixieland One-Step / Maple Leaf Rag / Weary Blues / Ory's Creole Trombone*
Hot Lips Page (NYC, 7 September): *Happy Medium / Bloodhound / You Come In Here Woman / Got The World On A String / Love You Funny Thing* (NYC): *Corsicana / They Raided The Joint / Sunset Blues / Willie Mae Willow Foot / Florida Blues / The Lady In Debt / Race Horse Mama*
Charlie Parker (NYC, 26 November): *Billie's Bounce / Warming Up A Riff / Now's The Time / Thriving From A Riff / Koko / Meandering*
Oscar Pettiford (NYC, 9 January): *Something For You / Worried Life Blues / Empty Bed Blues 1&2*
Flip Phillips (NYC, June): *Why Shouldn't I? / Swingin' For Popsie / Stompin' At The Savoy*

Mel Powell (Paris, Spring): *Homage à Fats Waller / Homage à Debussy / For Miss Black / Don't Blame Me*
Sammy Price (NYC, 27 March): *In A Mezz / Those Mellow Blues / Gully Low Blues / Cow Cow Blues / 133rd Street Boogie / I Finally Gotcha / Boogin' With Mezz / Callin' 'Em Home / Step Down, Step Up / Shakin' Loose*
Ike Quebec (NYC, 10 April): *Dolores / Sweethearts On Parade* (NYC, 17 July): *I Surrender Dear / I Found A New Baby / Topsy / Cup-Mute Clayton* (NYC, 7 August): *Girl Of My Dreams / Jim Dawgs / Shufflin' / IQ Blues*
Sir Charles Thompson (NYC, 4 September): *Takin' Off / If I Had You / 20th Century Blues / The Street Beat*
Lucky Thompson (LA, September): *Short Day / You're In My Heart / Why Not? / No Good Man Blues / Irresistible You / Phace*
Sarah Vaughan (NYC, 25 May): *What More Can A Woman Do? / I'd Rather Have A Memory / Mean To Me*
Charlie Ventura (LA, 1 March): *I Don't Stand A Ghost Of A Chance With You / Tea For Two / CV Jump / I Surrender Dear* (NYC, 9 June): *Stomping At The Savoy / Body And Soul / Limehouse Blues* (NYC, 17 August): *Out You Go / CV Jam / Tammy's Dream / Let's Jump For Rita* (NYC, 28 August): *Charlie Comes On / Good Deal / Ever So Thoughtful / Jackpot / Dark Eyes*
Cootie Williams (NYC, 17 July): *Juice Head Baby / Salt Lake City Bounce* (NYC, 19 July): *House Of Joy / When My Baby Left Me / Everything But You*
Mary Lou Williams Trio (NYC, 29 June): *Taurus / Pisces / Gemini / Capricornus / Sagittarius / Aquarius / Libra / Virgo / Aries / Scorpio / Cancer / Leo / Stars / Moon / Sunset / Sunrise*
Kai Winding (NYC, 14 December): *Sweet Miss / Loaded / Grab Your Axe, Max / Always*
Lester Young (LA, October): *DB Blues / Lester Blows Again / These Foolish Things / Jumpin' At Messners*
Lester Young/Nat King Cole/ Buddy Rich (LA, December): *Back To The Land / I Cover The Waterfront / Somebody Loves Me / I Found A New Baby / The Man I Love / Peg O' My Heart / I Want To Be Happy / Mean To Me*
Trummy Young (NYC, 2 May): *Good And Groovy / Rattle And Roll / I'm Living For Today / Behind The Eight Bar* (NYC, 18 July): *Four Or Five Times / I Want A Little Girl*

Photograph courtesy: Terry Dash

Left and above: Bunk Johnson (65) is brought out of retirement and featured at the Stuyvesant Casino in NYC. He is shown here (second from right) with George Lewis, Tony Parenti and Alcide 'Slow Drag' Pavageau.

Right: 28-year-old Dizzy Gillespie.

1946

Kai Winding (24) and Shelly Manne (26) join Stan Kenton (34) Band.

Red Norvo (38) with Woody Herman (33) Band.

Fats Navarro (23), later Miles Davis (20), with Billy Eckstine Band.

Claude Thornhill (38) reorganises band with arrangements by Gil Evans (34).

Django Reinhardt (36) tours USA with Duke Ellington (47).

Stravinsky writes 'Ebony Concerto' for Woody Herman Band. Premiere at packed Carnegie Hall concert in March.

Charlie Parker (26) suffers breakdown in LA during 'Lover Man' session. Later taken to Camarillo State Hospital.

Billie Holiday (31) a success at her first solo concert at New York's Town Hall.

Duke Ellington premieres 'Deep South Suite' at Carnegie Hall.

BIRTHS
Isao Suzuki (bass) 2 January
Motohiko Hino (drums) 3 January
George Duke (keyboards) 12 January
Dill Katz (bass) 12 January
Spike Wells (drums) 16 January
Jeff Castleman (bass) 27 January
Stafford James (bass) 24 April
Digby Fairweather (trumpet) 25 April
Jack Walrath (trumpet) 5 May
Jimmy Ponder (guitar) 10 May
Don Moye (drums) 23 May
Niels-Henning Orsted Pederson (bass) 27 May
John Morell (guitar) 2 June
Zbigniew Seifert (violin) 6 June
Tom Harrell (trumpet) 16 June
Clint Houston (bass) 24 June
John Klemmer (tenor sax) 3 July
Brian Priestley (piano/writer) 10 July
Khan Jamal (vibes) 23 July
Allan Holdsworth (guitar) 6 August
Roland Prince (guitar) 27 August
Dave Liebman (tenor sax) 4 September
David Williams (bass) 17 September
Dave Holland (bass) 1 October
Palle Danielsson (bass) 15 October
Les de Merle (drums) 4 November
Bennie Wallace (tenor sax) 18 November
Bruce Ditmas (drums) 12 December

DEATHS
Fred Beckett (29) 30 January tuberculosis
Putney Dandridge (44) 15 February
Dave Nelson (41) 7 April heart attack
Tubby Hall (50) 13 May
Joe 'Tricky Sam' Nanton (42) 20 July
Mamie Smith (63) 30 October
Manuel Perez (74) stroke
Nick Rongetti, proprietor of 'Nicks'

BOOKS
Rudi Blesh: Shining Trumpets
Ernest Bornemann: A Critic looks at Jazz
Hoagy Carmichael: The Stardust Road
Dave Dexter Jr: Jazz Cavalcade
Max Jones & Albert McCarthy: Tribute to Huddie Ledbetter
Albert McCarthy: The PL Yearbook of Jazz
Mezz Mezzrow: Really the Blues
Paul Miller (ed): Esquire's 1946 Jazz Book
Adolph Niemoller: The Story of Jazz
Peter Noble: The Illustrated Yearbook of Jazz
G. Rosenthal (ed): Jazzways: a yearbook of hot music
Bill Treadwell: Big Book of Swing
Barry Ulanov: Duke Ellington
Stewart Williams: Jazz in Chicago
Stewart Williams & Brian Rust: Jazz in New Orleans
Ken Williamson: Jazz Quiz 2

FILMS
Beware (45mins): all-negro musical featuring Louis Jordan
Follow that music (18mins): Gene Krupa music short
3-MINUTE SOUNDIES
Come to baby do: Nat King Cole
Count me out: Red Allen / JC Higginbotham
Crawl, Red, Crawl: Red Allen / JC Higginbotham
Don't be a baby, baby: Joe Marsala
Drink hearty: Red Allen / JC Higginbotham
Got a penny, Benny: Nat King Cole

Millenium Jump: Joe Marsala
Mop: Red Allen / J C Higginbotham
Patience and fortitude: Valaida Snow
Solid Jive: Ray Bauduc
Southern Scandal: Stan Kenton

COMPOSITIONS
Harold Arlen/Johnny Mercer: Come Rain Or Come Shine
Duke Ellington: Esquire Swank
Slim Gaillard / Lee Ricks: Cement Mixer
Dizzy Gillespie: Things to Come
Billy Strayhorn: Midriff
Robert Troup: Route 66
Victor Young / Ned Washington: Stella By Starlight

RECORDS
Red Allen (NYC, 14 January): The Crawl / Buzz Me / Drink Hearty / Get The Mop (NYC, 16 July): Count Me Out / Check Up / If It's Love You Want / Let Me Miss You
Louis Armstrong & Ella Fitzgerald (NYC, 18 January): You Won't Be Satisfied / The Frim Fram Sauce
Louis Armstrong (NYC, 27 April): Linger In My Arms A Little Longer / Whatta Ya Gonna Do? / No Variety Blues / Joseph 'n' His Brothers / Back O' Town Blues (LA, 6 October): I Want A Little Girl / Sugar / Blues For Yesterday / Blues In The South (LA, 17 October): Endie / The Blues Are Brewin' / Do You Know What It Means To Miss New Orleans? / Where The Blues Were Born In New Orleans / Mahogany Hall Stomp
Mildred Bailey (NYC, 5 March): All That Glitters Is Not Gold / In Love In Vain / A Woman's Prerogative / Penthouse Serenade (NYC, 18 October): I'll Close My Eyes / Me And The Blues / At Sundown / Lover Come Back To Me
Charlie Barnet (NYC, 12 August): Bunny / New Redskin Rhumba / Cherokee / Atlantic Jump / Power Steering
Count Basie (NYC, 9 January): Patience And Fortitude / The Mad Boogie (NYC, 6 February): Lazy Lady Blues / Rambo / Stay Cool / The King (NYC, 31 July): Hob Nail Boogie / Danny Boy / Mutton Leg / Stay On It (NYC, 7 August): Wild Bill's Boogie / Fla-ga-la-pa / Don't Ever Let Me Be Yours / Goodbye Baby
Sidney Bechet/Albert Nicholas Blue Five (NYC, 11 February): Quincy Street Stomp / Old Stack O' Lee Blues / Bechet's Fantasy / Weary Way Blues
Sonny Berman (NYC, 23 January): Ciretose / Down With Up / Higgimus Hoggimus / Slumbering Giant (LA, 21 September): Curbstone Scuffle / Nocturne
Ray Brown All-Stars (NYC, 25 September): For Hecklers Only / Smoky Hollow Jump / Moody Speaks / Boppin' The Blues
Don Byas (NYC): You Go To My Head / Don't You Know I Care / Gloomy Sunday / More Than A Mood (NYC, 17 May): I Don't Know Why / London-Donnie / Old Folks / Cherokee / September In The Rain (NYC, 21 August): Living My Life / To Each His Own / They Say Its Wonderful / Cynthia's Love / September Song / St Louis Blues / I've Found A New Baby / Marie (Paris, 4 December): I'm Beginning To See The Light / Rosetta / Ain't Misbehavin' / Body And Soul / Blue And Sentimental
Harry Carney (NYC, 18 March): Minor Mirage / Jamaica Rhumble / Shadowy Sands / Candy Cane
Benny Carter (NYC, 5 January): Jump Call / Patience And Fortitude (NYC, 7 January): Diga Diga Doo / Who's Sorry Now / Some Of These Days (NYC, 8 January): I'm The Caring Kind / Looking For A Boy / Rose Room (NYC, August): Re-Bop

Boogie / Twelve O'Clock Jump / Your Conscience Tells Me So / Mexican Hat Dance
Benny Carter & his Chocolate Dandies (NYC, 23 August): Sweet Georgia Brown / Out Of My Way / What'll It Be / Cadillac Slim
Sid Catlett (NYC): Organ Boogie / Organ Blues / Sherry Wine Blues / Open The Door, Richard / Shirley's Boogie / Humoresque Boogie
Serge Chaloff/Ralph Burns Quintet (LA, 21 September): Dial-ogue / Blue Serge / Mad Monk
Kenny Clarke (NYC, 5 September): Epistrophy / 52nd Street Theme / Oop Bop Sh'bam / Rue Chaptal
Buck Clayton's Big Four (NYC, 26 June): Dawn Dance / Wells-a-Poppin' / On The Sunny Side Of The Street / It's Dizzy / Basie's Morning Bluesicale
Buck Clayton's Big Eight (NYC, 24 July): Saratoga Special / Sentimental Summer / Harlem Cradle Song / No Good Man Sam / I Want A Little Girl
Eddie Condon (NYC, 27 March): Farewell Blues / Improvisations For March Of Time / She's Funny That Way / Stars Fell On Alabama (NYC, 17 July): Some Sunny Day / Just You, Just Me / Atlanta Blues / The Way You Look Tonight
Eddie 'Lockjaw' Davis (NYC, May): Surgery / Lockjaw / Afternoon In A Doghouse / Athlete's Foot (NYC, October): Callin' Dr Jazz / Fracture / Maternity / Stealin' Trash / Just A Mystery / Red Pepper / Spinal / Hollerin' And Screamin'
Wild Bill Davison (NYC, January): High Society / Wrap Your Troubles In Dreams / I'm Coming Virginia / Wabash Blues
Baby Dodds Trio (NYC, 6 January): Wolverine Blues / Buddy Bolden's Blues / Albert's Blues / Drum Improvisations No1&2 (NYC, 10 January): Spooky Drums / Maryland / Rudiments With Drumstick / Tom Tom Workout
Kenny Dorham (NYC, 23 August): Bebop In Pastel / Fool's Fancy / Bombay / A Ray's Idea
Allen Eager (NYC, 22 March): Rampage / Vot's Dot / Booby Hatch / Symphony Sid's Idea
Billy Eckstine Orchestra (NYC, 3 January): I Only Have Eyes For You / You're My Everything / I've Got To Pass Your House / The Jitney Man (NYC, February): Blue / Second Balcony Jump /Gloomy Sunday / Tell Me Pretty Baby / Love Is The Thing / Without A Song / Cool Breeze / Don't Ever Take Your Love From Me (LA, September): Oo Bop Sh'bam / Love The Loveliness / In The Still Of The Night / Jelly Jelly / My Silent Love / Time On My Hands / All The Things You Are / In A Sentimental Mood (NYC): All Of Me / Blues For Sale / What's New / Serenade In Blue / Solitude / Sophisticated Lady
Roy Eldridge (NYC, 31 January): All The Cats Join In / Ain't That A Shame (NYC, 7 May): Hi Ho Trailus Boot Whip / Tippin' Out / Yard Dog / Les Bounce (NYC, 24 September): Lover Come Back To Me / Rockin' Chair / Talk Of The Town
Duke Ellington (LA, 9 July): Rockabye River / Suddenly It Jumped / Transblucency / Just Squeeze Me (LA, 10 July): A Gathering In The Clearing / You Don't Love Me No More / Pretty Woman / Hey Baby (LA, 26 August): Blue Is The Night / Love Man / Just You, Just Me / Beale Street Blues (LA, 3 September): My Honey's Loving Arms / Memphis Blues / A Ghost Of A Chance / St Louis Blues / Swamp Fire / Royal Garden Blues / Esquire Swank / Midriff (NYC, 23 October): Diminuendo In Blue / Magenta Haze (NYC, 25 November): Sultry Sunset / Happy-Go-Lucky Local / Trumpet No End / Beautiful Indians / Flippant Flurry (NYC, 5 December): Golden Feathers / Beautiful Indians (NYC, 18 December): Overture To A Jam Session / Jam-A-Ditty
Ella Fitzgerald (NYC, 21 February): I'm Just A Lucky So And So / I Didn't Mean A Word (NYC, 29 August): For Sentimental Reasons / It's A Pity To Say Goodnight
Slim Gaillard (LA, January): Early Mornin' Boogie / That Ain't Right Baby / Riff City / Mean Mama Blues (LA, March): Chicken Rhythm / Santa Monica Jump / Mean Pretty Mama / School Kids Hop (LA, 22 April): Introduzione-Pianissimo / Recitativo e Finale / Andante Cantabile In Modo De Blues / Presto Con Stomp
Erroll Garner (LA, Spring): Full Moon And Empty Arms / Frantonality / For You / If I Loved You (LA, 14 July): Memories Of You
Stan Getz (NYC, 31 July): Opus De Bop / And The Angels Swing / Running Water / Don't Worry 'Bout Me
Dizzy Gillespie (LA, 7 February): Confirmation /

Diggin' For Diz / Dynamo A / Dynamo B / When I Grow Too Old To Dream / 'Round About Midnight (NYC, 22 February): 52nd Street Theme / Night In Tunisia / Ol' Man Rebop / Anthropology (NYC, 15 May): One Bass Hit / Oop Bop Sh'bam / A Handfulla Gimme / That's Earl, Brother

Dizzy Gillespie Orchestra (NYC, 10 June): Our Delight / Good Dues Blues (NYC, 9 July): One Bass Hit / Ray's Idea / Things To Come / He Beeped When He Shoulda Bopped (NYC, 16 October): Ow (NYC, 12 November): I Waited For You / Emanon

Dexter Gordon (NYC, 29 January): Long Tall Dexter / Dexter Rides Again / I Can't Escape From You / Dexter Digs In

Wardell Gray (LA, 23 November): Dell's Bells / How High The Moon / The Man I Love / Steeplechase / The Great Lie

Bill Harris (Chicago, 6 May): Everything Happens To Me / Frustration (LA, 21 September): Woodchopper's Holiday / Curbstone Shuffle / Nocturne / Moon Burns / Flippin' The Wig / Somebody Loves Me / Harris Tweed

Woody Herman (LA, 19 August): Ebony Concerto (LA, 17 September): Sidewalks of Cuba (LA, 19 September): Summer Sequence Pts 1,2,3

Billie Holiday (NYC, 22 January): Good Morning Heartache / No Good Man (NYC, 13 March): Big Stuff (NYC, 9 April): Baby, I Don't Cry Over You / I'll Look Around (LA, 22 April): Strange Fruit / Travelin' Light / Body And Soul / He's Funny That Way / The Man I Love / Gee, Baby, Ain't I Good To You / All Of Me / Billie's Blues (LA, September, October): Farewell To Storyville / Do You Know What It Means To Miss New Orleans / The Blues Are Brewin' (NYC, 27 December): The Blues Are Brewin' / Guilty

JJ Johnson (NYC, 26 June): Jay Bird / Coppin' The Bop / Jay Jay / Mad Be Bop

Stan Kenton (LA, 14 January): Intermission Riff (LA, 4 June): Artistry in Boogie (LA, 12 July): Artistry in Percussion / Safranski / Artistry in Bolero (LA, 26 July): Concerto to end all Concertos

Howard McGhee (LA). 11.45 Swing / Playboy Blues / Around The Clock / Gee I'm Lonesome / Call It The Blues / The Jive I Like / I'm Drunk (LA): Sweet Potato / Hoggin' / Blues à la King / Night Mist (LA, 29 July):

Be-Bop / Trumpet At Tempo / Thermodynamics (LA, 18 October): High Wind In Hollywood / Dialated Pupils / Midnite At Minton's / Up In Dodo's Room

Dodo Marmarosa (LA, 11 January): Mellow Mood / How High The Moon / Dodo's Blues / I Surrender Dear (LA): Raindrops / I've Got News For You

Vido Musso (NYC, 25 February): Moose In A Caboose / Moose On The Loose / My Jo-Ann / Vido In A Jam (LA, December): Theme / Gone With Vido / You Keep Coming Back Like A Song / Connecticut / Cozy Blues / Theme / Blue Skies / So Would I / Moonglow / Dance To This / Theme

Kid Ory (LA, 15 October): Bill Bailey / Farewell To Storyville / Joshua Fit De Battle Of Jericho / Tiger Rag (LA, 21 October): Bucket's Got A Hole In It / Eh, La Bas / The World's Jazz Crazy / Creole Bo-Bo

Hot Lips Page (NYC, October): Birmingham Boogie / Gimme, Gimme, Gimme / Open The Door, Richard / Texas And The Pacific

Charlie Parker (LA, 28 March): Moose The Mooche / Yardbird Suite / Ornithology / Bird Lore / Night In Tunisia (LA, 29 July): Max Is Making Wax / The Gypsy / Lover Man

Mel Powell (NYC, June): Lover Man / Avalon / Sketches / Brahms Rhapsody

Ike Quebec (NYC, September): The Masquerade Is Over / Basically Blue / Someone To Watch Over Me / Zig billion

Red Rodney (NYC, 23 November): A Cent And A Half / Perdido / Charge Account / Gussie 'G'

Sonny Stitt (NYC, 23 August): Bebop In Pastel / Fools Fancy / Bombay / Ray's Idea (NYC, 4 September): Serenade To A Square / Good Kick / Seven Up / Blues In Bebop / Blues à la Bird / Diz-iz

Lucky Thompson (LA): Dodo's Bounce / Dodo's Lament / Slam's Mishap / Scuffle That Ruff / Smooth Sailing / Commercial Eyes

Lennie Tristano (NYC, 8 October): Out On A Limb / I Can't Get Started / I Surrender Dear / Interlude

Sarah Vaughan (NYC, 7 May): If You Could See Me Now / I Can Make You Love Me / You're Not The Kind / My Kinda Love (NYC, 18 July): I've Got A Crush On You / I'm Through With Love / Everything I Have Is Yours / Body And Soul

Charlie Ventura (LA, 27 January): The Man I Love / Stompin' At The Savoy (LA, March): Who's Sorry Now? / Nobody Knows The Trouble I've Seen / The Man I Love / 'S Wonderful (LA, 12 April): Charlie Boy / I Don't Know Why / I'm Through With Love / The Man In The Moon (LA, May): Chopin's Minute Waltz / Slow Joe / What Is This Thing Called Love? / I'm In The Mood For Love

Ben Webster (NYC, 15 May): Frog And Mule / Spang / Doctor Keets / Park And Tilford Blues

Dickie Wells (NYC, 21 March): We're Through / Bed Rock / Opera In Blue / Drag Nasty Walk

Cootie Williams (NYC, 29 January): Stingy Blues / Echoes Of Harlem (NYC, 5 July): Wrong Neighbourhood / I May Be Easy / Let's Do The Whole Thing (NYC, 11 September): Ain't Got No Blues Today / Bring 'Em Down Front

Mary Lou Williams (NYC, 16 February): How High The Moon / The Man I Love / Cloudy / Blue Skies / These Foolish Things / Lonely Moment (NYC, 7 October): Humoresque / Waltz Boogie / Hesitation Boogie

Mary Lou Williams Girl Stars (NYC, 24 July): Fifth Dimension / Harmony Grits / It Must Be True / Boogie Misterioso / Conversation / Humoresque

Teddy Wilson (NYC, 19 August): When We're Alone / Don't Worry 'Bout Me / I Want To Be Happy / Just One Of Those Things

Kai Winding (NYC, 7 January): Sweet Miss / Loaded / Grab Your Axe Max / Always

Lester Young (LA, January): Paper Moon / After You've Gone / Lover Come Back To Me / Jammin' With Lester (LA, March): These Foolish Things / Lester Leaps In (LA, April): DB Blues (LA, August): You're Driving Me Crazy / Lester Leaps In / Lester's Be-Bop / She's Funny That Way

Trummy Young (NYC, July): Fruitie Cutie / Blues Triste / Johnson Rock / Lucky Draw

Left: Louis Armstrong (45) in the feature film 'New Orleans' which also starred Billie Holiday. The film was shot in October and released in 1947.

Above right: Tony Parenti, Dave Tough, Wild Bill Davison and Jack Lesberg at Eddie Condon's Greenwich Village club.

Right: Django Reinhardt (36) is visited by Jimmy & Marian McPartland during his US tour.

All the photographs on this page are courtesy of: Hank O'Neal

Louis Armstrong's first Carnegie Hall concert (8 February). Louis (46) breaks up big band and forms All-Stars with Jack Teagarden (42), Barney Bigard (41) and Sid Catlett (37).

Woody Herman (34) organises Second Herd with 'Four Brothers' sax team.

Stan Kenton (35) breaks up first band and reforms.

Charlie Parker (27) is released from Camarillo in February, returns to NYC in April and forms quintet with Miles Davis (21) and Max Roach (22) to play on 52nd Street.

In May, Billie Holiday (32) is arrested for possession of heroin and sentenced to a year in prison.

Dizzy Gillespie (30) plays Carnegie Hall concert (September).

Dave Tough (37) leaves Eddie Condon Band in a huff.

Duke Ellington (48) premieres 'Liberian Suite' at Carnegie Hall. Tyree Glenn (35) joins the band.

BIRTHS

Baikida Carroll (trumpet) 15 January
Chris Biscoe (saxes) 5 February
Harvey Mason (drums) 22 February
Bob Magnusson (bass) 24 February
Norman Connors (drums) 1 March
Jan Garbarek (saxes) 4 March
Tommy Chase (drums) 22 March
Barry Miles (drums) 28 March
Frank Tusa (bass) 1 April
Barry Guy (bass) 22 April
Steve Khan (guitar) 28 April
Gregory Herbert (saxes) 19 May
Julie Tippetts (vocals) 8 June
Darius Brubeck (keyboards) 14 June
Tom Malone (trombone) 16 June
Carlos Santana (guitar) 20 July
Jasper Van't Hof (keyboards) 30 June
Terje Rypdal (guitar/flute) 23 August
Keith Tippett (piano) 25 August
Charles 'Bobo' Shaw (drums) 5 September
Bent Persson (cornet) 6 September
Billy Bang (violin) 20 September
Fred Hopkins (bass) 11 October
Egberto Gismonti (guitar) 5 December
Miroslav Vitous (bass) 6 December
Don Weller (tenor sax) 19 December
Steve Bohannon (drums)

DEATHS

Sonny Berman (22) 16 January *heart attack*
Fate Marable (56) 16 January *pneumonia*
Clifford 'Snags' Jones (46) 31 January
Michel Warlop (36) 20 March
Freddie Webster (30) 1 April *collapsed in hotel room*
Jimmie Lunceford (45) 13 July *collapsed during personal appearance*
John 'Bugs' Hamilton (36) 15 August *tuberculosis*
Crickett Smith (60)

BOOKS

S.S. Allen: *Stars of Swing*
Orin Blackstone: *Index to Jazz*
Eddie Condon & Thomas Sugrue: *We called it music*
A. Ewing: *Little Gate* (novel)
Vic Filmer: *Jive and Swing Dictionary*
Robert Goffin: *Horn of Plenty: The Story of Louis Armstrong*
Babs Gonzales: *Bebop Dictionary and History of its famous stars*
Max Jones: *Jazz Photo Album: A history of jazz in pictures*
Albert McCarthy: *Jazzbook 1947*
Paul Miller(ed): *Esquire's 1947 Jazz Book*
G. Sklar: *The Two Worlds of Johnny Truro* (novel)
Ralph de Toledano (ed): *Frontiers of Jazz*

FILMS

Beat the Band (67mins): feature with Gene Krupa
Boy! what a girl (70mins): Slam Stewart, Sid Catlett
Charlie Barnet & his Orchestra (14mins): music short
Drummer Man (15mins): Gene Krupa music short
Ee baba leba (10mins): Dizzy Gillespie Orchestra music short
The Fabulous Dorseys (87mins): feature with Dorsey Brothers, Art Tatum
Harlem after Midnight: 3 numbers by Billy Eckstine Orchestra
Harlem Dynamite: 3 numbers by Dizzy Gillespie Orchestra
Harlem Rhythm: 3 numbers by Dizzy Gillespie Orchestra
Hit Parade of 1947 (90mins): feature with Woody Herman Orchestra
Jivin' in Bebop (60mins): music short with Dizzy Gillespie, Helen Humes
Let's Make Rhythm (20mins): Stan Kenton Orchestra music short
New Orleans (90mins): feature film with Louis Armstrong, Billie Holiday
Night in Harlem (10mins): music short with Dizzy Gillespie & his Bebop Orchestra
Oop Bop Sh'Bam (10mins): music short with Dizzy Gillespie & his Bebop Orchestra
Reet, Petite and gone: all negro production featuring Louis Jordan
Sepia Cinderella (75mins): all negro musical comedy featuring John Kirby's Band
Tan and Terrific: music short with Helen Humes and Dizzy Gillespie

COMPOSITIONS

Louis Alter / Eddie DeLange: *Do You Know What It Means To Miss New Orleans?*
Sonny Burke / Lionel Hampton / Johnny Mercer: *Midnight Sun*
Duke Ellington: *Liberian Suite*
Bronislaw Kaper / Ned Washington: *On Green Dolphin Street*
Nellie Lutcher: *He's A Real Gone Guy / Hurry On Down*
Sir Charles Thompson / Illinois Jacquet: *Robbins' Nest*

RECORDS

Gene Ammons (Chicago, 17 June): *Concentration / Red Top / Idaho* (Chicago, 23 October): *McDougal's Sprout / Hold That Money / Shermansky / Harold The Fox* (Chicago, 1 December): *Jit-Jit / Odd-En-Dow / EAAK Blues / Going For The Okey Doak* (Chicago, 12 December): *Sugar Coated / Blowing The Family Jewels / Dues In The Blues / Jay Jay*
Louis Armstrong (Carnegie Hall, NYC, 8 February): *Black And Blue / Rockin' Chair / St Louis Blues / Oh, Didn't He Ramble* (NYC, 12 March): *I Wonder, I Wonder / I Believe / It Takes Time / You Don't Learn That In School* (Town Hall, NYC, 17 May): *Ain't Misbehavin' / Rockin' Chair / Back O' Town Blues / Pennies From Heaven / Save It, Pretty Mama / St James Infirmary* (NYC, 10 June): *Jack Armstrong Blues / Rockin' Chair / Someday / Fifty Fifty Blues* (NYC, 16 October): *A Song Was Born / Please Stop Playing Those Blues / Before Long / Lovely Weather We're Having* (Symphony Hall, Boston, 30 November): *Muskrat Ramble / Black And Blue / Royal Garden Blues / Lover / Stars Fell On Alabama / I Cried For You / Since I Fell For You / Tea For Two / Body And Soul / Steak Face / Mahogany Hall Stomp / Sunny Side Of The Street / High Society / Baby Won't You Please Come Home / That's My Desire / C-Jam Blues / How High The Moon / Boff Boff*
Mildred Bailey (NYC, 2 February): *That Ain't Right / I Don't Want To Miss Mississippi*
Count Basie (NYC, 13 March): *One O'Clock Boogie / Meet Me At No Special Place / Futile Frustration* (NYC, 20 May): *Swingin' The Blues / St Louis Boogie* (NYC, 21 May): *Shine On Harvest Moon / Sugar* (NYC, 23 May): *After You've Gone / South* (Chicago, 19 October): *Blue And Sentimental / Seventh*

Avenue Express (LA, 8,9 December): *Sophisticated Swing / Money Is Honey* (LA, 12 December): *Robbin's Nest / Bye Bye Baby*
Sidney Bechet/Mezz Mezzrow Feetwarmers (NYC, 15 February): *Royal Garden Blues / Slow Blues / Old Fashioned Love / Fast Blues / Bugle Blues*
Sidney Bechet/Bob Wilber Wildcats (NYC, 14 July): *Spreadin' Joy / It Is All Gone / Polka Dot Stomp / Kansas City Man*
Sidney Bechet Quartet (NYC, 23 July): *Buddy Bolden Stomp* (NYC, 31 July): *My Woman's Blues / Song Of Songs / Just One Of Those Things / Love For Sale / Laura / Shake 'Em Up*
Art Blakey (NYC, 22 December): *The Thin Man / Bop Alley / Groove Street / Musa's Vision*
Don Byas (Paris, 13 January): *Please Don't Talk About Me When I'm Gone / Walking Around / How High The Moon / Red Cross / Laura / Cement Mixer / Dynamo A* (Paris, 12 June): *These Foolish Things / Humoresque / Stormy Weather / Riffin' And Jivin' / I Can't Explain / Blues For Panassie*
Harry Carney: *Why Was I Born? / Triple Play*
Serge Chaloff (NYC, 5 March): *Pumpernickel / Gaberdine And Serge / Serge's Urge / A Bar A Second*
Arnett Cobb (NYC, 13 May): *Walkin' With Sid / Still Flying / Cobb's Idea / Top Flight* (NYC, August): *When I Grow Too Old To Dream / Cobb's Boogie / Dutch Kitchen Bounce / Go Red Go / Pay It No Mind / Chick She Ain't Nowhere / Arnett Blows For 3000 / Running With Ray / Flower Garden Blues / Big League Blues / Going Home*
Eddie Condon (NYC, 5 August): *My Melancholy Baby / Tulip Time In Hollywood / Nobody Knows / We Called It Music* (NYC, 6 August): *Aunt Hagar's Blues / Down Among The Sheltering Palms / Rose Of The Rio Grande / Ida, Sweet As Apple Cider*
Tadd Dameron (NYC, 26 September): *The Chase / The Squirrel / Our Delight / Dameronia* (NYC, 28 October): *A Bebop Carol / The Tadd Walk / Gone With The Wind / That Someone Must Be You*
Eddie 'Lockjaw' Davis (NYC, 12 April): *Lover / Licks A Plenty / Foxy / Sheila*
Miles Davis/Charlie Parker (NYC, 14 August): *Milestones / Little Willie Leaps / Half Nelson / Sippin' At Bells*
Wild Bill Davison (NYC, 27 December): *Just A Gigolo / She's Funny That Way / Ghost Of A Chance / Yesterdays / Why Was I Born / When Your Lover Has Gone*
Allen Eager (NYC, 15 July): *All Night, All Frantic / Donald Jay / Meeskite / And That's For Sure* (NYC, 6 November): *Nightmare Allen / Churchmouse / Jane's Bounce / Unmeditated*
Teddy Edwards (LA, 4 December): *Blues In Teddy's Flat*
Duke Ellington (LA, 14 August): *Hy'a Sue / Lady Of The Lavender Mist / Woman* (LA, 1 September): *It's Monday Every Day / Golden Cress / Put Yourself In My Place Baby* (LA, 29 September): *Cowboy Rhumba / The Wildest Gal In Town / I Fell And Broke My Heart* (LA, 30 September): *You're Just An Old Anti-disestablishmentarianismist / Don't Be So Mean Baby* (LA, 1 October): *It's Mad, Mad, Mad / You Gotta Crawl Before You Walk* (LA, 2 October): *Brown Penny / Kitty* (LA, 6 October): *Maybe I Should Change My Ways / Boogie Bop Blues / Sultry Serenade* (NYC, 10 November): *Stomp, Look And Listen / Air Conditioned Jungle / Three Cent Stomp* (NYC, 11 November): *Progressive Gavotte / He Makes Me Believe He's Mine* (NYC, 14 November): *Take Love Easy / I Can't Believe That You're In Love With Me / How High The Moon / Singin' In The Rain* (NYC, 18 November): *Do Nothin' Till You Hear From Me* (NYC, 20 November): *Don't Get Around Much Any More / Once Upon A Dream / It's Love I'm In* (NYC, 22 December): *I Could Get A Man / On A Turquoise Cloud* (NYC, 24 December): *Liberian Suite* (NYC, 30 December): *A Woman And A Man / The Clothed Woman / New York City Blues / Let's Go Blues*
Erroll Garner (LA, 17 February): *Pastel / Trio* (LA, 22 April): *Erroll's Bounce / Erroll's Blues / I Can't Escape From You / Stairway To The Stars*
Dizzy Gillespie Orchestra (NYC, 22 August): *Ow! / Oop-Pop-A-Da / Two Bass Hit / Stay On It* (Carnegie Hall, NYC, 29 September): *Toccata For Trumpet And Orchestra / Cubana Be-Cubana Bop / Salt Peanuts / One Bass Hit / Oop-Pop-A-Da / Stairway To The Stars / How High The Moon* (with Charlie Parker): *A Night In Tunisia / Dizzy Atmosphere / Groovin' High / Confirmation* (NYC, 22 December):

1947

Algo Bueno / Cool Breeze / Cubana Be-Cubana Bop (NYC, 30 December): *Manteca / Woody'n You / Good Bait / Ool-Ya-Koo / Minor Walk*

Dexter Gordon (LA, 5 June): *Mischievous Lady / Lullaby In Rhythm* (LA, 12 June): *Chromatic Aberration / Iridescence / On The Town / It's The Talk Of The Town / Bikini* (with Wardell Gray): *The Chase* (NYC, 4 December): *Ghost Of A Chance / Sweet And Lovely* (with Teddy Edwards): *The Duel* (NYC, 11 December): *Settin' The Pace / So Easy / Dexter's Riff* (NYC, 22 December): *Dexter's Mood / Dextrose / Index / Dextivity*

Wardell Gray (LA, 29 April): *Bebop / Grooving High / Hot House / Cherry Coke* (LA, 6 July): *Blow, Blow, Blow* (NYC, December): *How High The Moon / C-Jam Blues*

Stan Hasselgard (LA, 18 December): *Swedish Pastry / Sweet And Hot Mop / Who Sleeps / I'll Never Be The Same*

Woody Herman (LA, 24 December): *The Goof and I* (LA, 27 December): *Four Brothers / Summer Sequence Pt4*

Billie Holiday (NYC, Carnegie Hall, 8 February): *Do You Know What It Means To Miss New Orleans? / Don't Explain* (NYC, 13 February): *Deep Song / There Is No Greater Love / Easy Living / Solitude*

JJ Johnson (NYC, 24 December): *Bone-o-logy / Down Vernon's Alley / Yesterdays / Riffette*

Stan Kenton (LA, 6 December): *Cuban Carnival / The Peanut Vendor*

Howard McGhee (NYC, 3 December): *Dorothy / Night Mist / Coolie-rini / Night Music / Turnip Blood / Surrender / Sleepwalker Boogie / Stoptime Blues / You*

Dodo Marmarosa (LA, 3 December): *Bopmatism / Dodo's Dance / You Go To My Head / Trade Winds / Dary Departs / Cosmo Street / Lover*

Mezz Mezzrow/Sidney Bechet (NYC, 18 September): *Breathless Blues / Really The Blues / Evil Gal Blues / Fat Mama Blues / You Got To Give It To Me / Hey Daddy Blues / Whoop This Wolf Away From My Door / You Can't Do That To Me / Groovin' The Minor* (Chicago, 18 December): *Where Am I? / Tommy's Blues / Chicago Function / Revolutionary Blues* (Chicago, 19 December): *I Want Some / I'm Speaking My Mind / Never Will I Forget The Blues / The Blues And Freud / Kaiser's Last Break* (Chicago, 20 December): *I'm Goin' Away From Here / I Got You Some / I Must Have My Boogie / Funky Butt / Delta Mood / Blues Of The Roaring Twenties*

Thelonious Monk (NYC,15 October): *Humph / Evonce / Suburban Eyes / Thelonious* (NYC, 24 October): *Nice Work / Ruby My Dear / Well You Needn't / April In Paris / Introspection / Off Minor* (NYC, 21 November): *In Walked Bud / Monk's Mood / Who Knows? / Round About Midnight*

Vido Musso (LA, June): *Vido's Bop / On The Mercury / Gone With Vido / Vido In A Mist* (LA, August): *Trees / The Unfinished Boogie / The Day I Left Alsace-Lorrina / Checkerboard*

Fats Navarro (NYC, 16 January): *Fat Girl / Ice Freezes Red / Eb-Pob / Goin' To Minton* (NYC, 5 December): *Nostalgia / Barry's Bop / Rebop Romp / Fats Blows*

Red Norvo (LA, 14 October): *Hollyridge Drive / Under A Blanket Of Blue* (LA, 28 November): *I'll Follow You* (LA, 30 November): *Bop* (LA, 8 December): *Summer Nights / El Rojo* (LA, 10 December): *Twelve Street Rag / Take The Red Car / Ghost Of A Chance / Band In Boston*

Hot Lips Page (NYC, 28 October): *Take Your Shoes Off Baby / La Danse / St James Infirmary / Walkin' In A Daze*

Charlie Parker (LA, 19 February): *This Is Always / Dark Shadows / Bird's Nest / Hot Blues / Cool Blues* (LA, 26 February): *Relaxing At Camarillo / Cheers / Carvin' The Bird / Stupendous* (NYC, June): *Donna Lee / Chasin' The Bird / Cheryl / Buzzy* (NYC, 28 October): *Dexterity / Bongo Bop / Prezology / Dewey Square / The Hymn / Superman / Bird Of Paradise / Embraceable You* (NYC, 4 November): *Bird Feathers / Klactoveedsedstene / Scrapple From The Apple / My Old Flame / Out Of Nowhere / Don't Blame Me* (NYC,17 December): *Drifting On A Reed / Quasimodo / Charlie's Wig / Bongo Bop / Bird Feathers / Crazeology / How Deep Is The Ocean* (Detroit, December): *Another Hairdo / Blue Bird / Klaunstance / Bird Gets The Worm*

Leo Parker (Detroit, 4 October): *El Sino / Ineta / Wild Leo / Leapin' Leo* (NYC, 19 December): *Wee Dot / Solitude / Lion's Roar / Mad Lad Boogie*

Bud Powell (NYC, 10 January): *I'll Remember April / Indiana / Somebody Loves Me / I Should Care / Bud's Bubble / Off Minor / Nice Work / Everything Happens To Me*

Mel Powell (LA, 10 December): *Anything Goes / Way Down Yonder In New Orleans / Small Hotel / Hallelujah / You Go To My Head* (LA, 31 December): *Cuban Pete / Cookin' One Up / That Old Black Magic / When A Woman Loves A Man*

Red Rodney (NYC, 29 January): *All God's Children / Elevation / Fine And Dandy / The Goof And I*

George Shearing (NYC, 3 February): *So Rare / Have You Met Miss Jones? / George's Boogie Woogie* (NYC, 23 February): *Buccaneer's Bounce / When Darkness Falls* (NYC, 23 December): *Bop's Your Uncle / Sweet And Lovely / Cozy's Bop / Sophisticated Lady*

Lucky Thompson (LA, 22 April): *Just One More Chance / From Dixieland To Bop / Boulevard Bounce / Boppin' The Blues*

Lennie Tristano (NYC, 23 May): *Blue Boy / Atonement / Coolin' Off With Ulanov* (NYC, 27 August): *What Is This Thing Called Love? / A Knight In The Village / Just You, Just Me* (NYC, 23 September): *Ghost Of A Chance / Just Judy* (NYC, 23 October): *Supersonic / On A Planet / Air Pocket / Celestia* (NYC, 31 December): *Freedom / Parallel / Apellation / Abstraction / Palimpsest / Dissonance / Restoration / Through These Portals / Speculation / New Sound / Resemblance*

Sarah Vaughan (NYC, 2 July): *I Cover The Waterfront / Ghost Of A Chance / Tenderly / Don't Blame Me*

Charlie Ventura (NYC, March): *Synthesis / Soothe Me / Blue Champagne / Stop And Go* (NYC Carnegie Hall, 5 April): *Ghost Of A Chance / Characteristically BH / Ralph Burns Up / Just You, Just Me / Summertime / Sid Flips His Lid* (NYC, 11 September): *Pennies From Heaven / Eleven Sixty / East Of Suez / Baby, Baby All The Time*

Teddy Wilson (NYC, 3 December): *The Sheikh Of Araby / Limehouse Blues / Georgia On My Mind / After You've Gone*

Lester Young (Chicago, 18 February): *Sunday / SM Blues / Jumpin' With Symphony Sid / No Eyes Blues / Sax-o-re-bop / On The Sunny Side Of The Street* (NYC, 28, 30 December): *Movin' With Lester / One O'Clock Jump / Jumpin' At The Woodside / Easy Does It / Just Cooling / I'm Confessin' / Lester Smooths It Out*

Left: Charlie Parker recording in Los Angeles (February) following his release from Camarillo.

Below: Dizzy Gillespie and his Orchestra on stage during their record breaking concert at Carnegie Hall (September).

Photograph Courtesy: *Max Jones*

Photographs Courtesy: *Rolf Dahlgren*

77

52nd STREET

During the thirties many small nightclubs opened on the ground-floors of the brownstone houses on 52nd Street between Fifth and Sixth avenues. The majority of them featured jazz and the single block became the jazz centre of New York, known to everybody as Swing Street or simply 'The Street'.

Probably the first jazz club on the Street was the Onyx Club, which had been a speakeasy during Prohibition. On 4th February 1934, a few months after repeal, the Onyx opened as a legitimate club at 72 West 52nd Street featuring the music of The Spirits of Rhythm and Art Tatum.

With the success of the Onyx, there followed a number of other jazz-based clubs and by the late thirties there were half a dozen clubs on the Street featuring jazz, including the Famous Door (1935) and the Three Deuces (1937).

Swing was king on the Street, with stars like Billie Holiday, Red Allen, Wingy Manone, Stuff Smith, Coleman Hawkins, Ben Webster, John Kirby, Maxine Sullivan, Louis Prima, Tiny Grimes, Sid Catlett, Joe Marsala, Hot Lips Page, Jack Teagarden, Mildred Bailey and the Count Basie Orchestra.

Bop came to the Street in 1943 when Dizzy Gillespie took a small group into the Onyx. The new sounds flourished during the war years when the clubs were full of young servicemen, but by 1948 the boom was over and bop moved to Broadway, leaving the Street to the strippers and finally to the bulldozers.

The Street in 1948.

Photograph: *William P Gottlieb* Courtesy: *Redferns*

52nd STREET

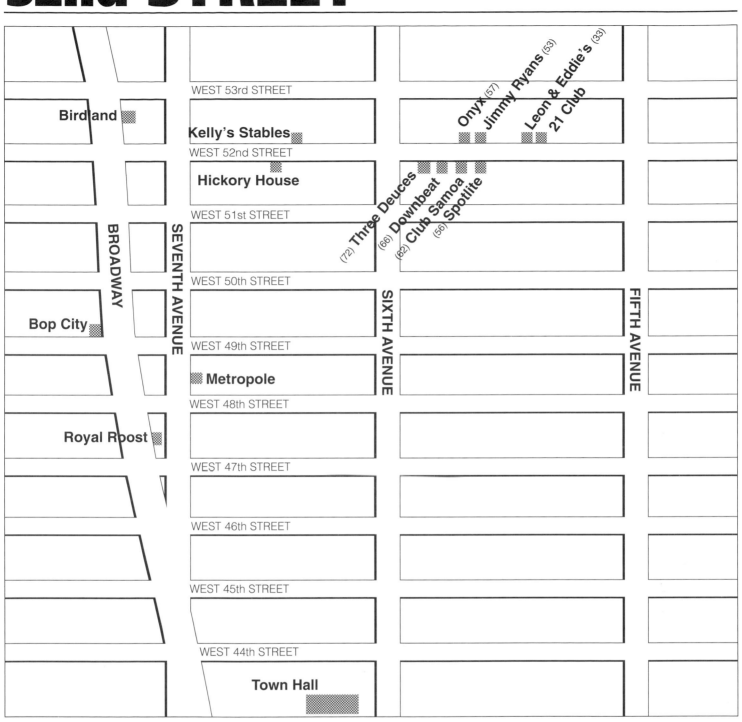

52nd STREET CLUBS

Onyx
35 W52nd Street (1927–34)
72 W52nd Street (4 Feb 1934–37)
62 W52nd Street (April 1937–Dec 1939)
57 W52nd Street (1942–49)

Famous Door
35 W52nd Street (March 1935–May 1936)
66 W52nd Street (Dec 1937–Nov 1943)
201 W52nd Street (Nov 1943–1944)
56 W52nd Street (1947–50)

Hickory House
144 W52nd Street (1933–1968)

Kelly's Stable
137 W52nd Street (1940–47)

Spotlite
56 W52nd Street (Dec 1944–46)

Three Deuces
72 W52nd Street (1937–1950)

Yacht Club
38 W52nd Street (1934–38
150 W52nd Street (1938–44
66 W52nd Street (Jan–May 1944)

Downbeat
66 W52nd Street (1944–48)

Club Samoa
62 W52nd Street (1940–43)
from 1943 it became a strip club

Jimmy Ryan's
53 W52nd Street (1940–62)

Flamingo
38 W52nd Street (1938–54) *non-jazz*

Leon & Eddie's
33 W52nd Street (1934–54) *non-jazz*

21 Club
21 W52nd Street (1932–) *non-jazz*

Tony's
57–59 W52nd Street (1934–c.50)

BOP CLUBS ON BROADWAY

Royal Roost
1574 Broadway (1948–53)

Bop City
1619 Broadway (1948–1950)

Birdland
1070 Broadway (Dec 1949–1967)

Bandbox
1680 Broadway (summer–autumn 1953)

OTHER MIDTOWN CLUBS

Cotton Club Downtown
200 W48th Street (Sept 1936–June 1940)

Ebony
1678 Broadway (1944–Dec 1948)

The Clique
1678 Broadway (Dec 1948–Dec 1949)

Metropole
Seventh Avenue (1953–1967)

Columbia introduce the first unbreakable vinyl plastic long-playing records.

US national recording ban (1 January–15 December).

Louis Armstrong All-Stars play festival at Nice (February).

Billie Holiday (33) returns to public performance with warmly received Carnegie Hall concert (27 March).

Eddie Condon (43) starts own TV series.

Duke Ellington (49) premieres 'The Tattooed Bride' at Carnegie Hall. Wendell Marshall (28) replaces Oscar Pettiford (26).

Earl Hines (43) breaks up band and joins Louis Armstrong All-Stars.

Stan Kenton (36) concert at Hollywood Bowl.

Dizzy Gillespie (31) and Band tour Scandinavia.

52nd Street era ends. The Royal Roost on Broadway ('the house that bop built') becomes the modern jazz centre.

BIRTHS

Thurman Barker (drums) 8 January
Bob Moses (drums) 28 January
Joe La Barbera (drums) 22 February
Maggie Nicols (vocal) 24 February
Mike Richmond (bass) 26 February
Richie Cole (alto sax) 29 February
David Schnitter (tenor sax) 19 March
Gary Giddins (writer) 21 March
Jan Hammer (keyboards) 17 April
Joe Bonner (piano) 20 April
Tania Maria (piano/vocals) 9 May
Tom Scott (tenor sax) 19 May
Paulinho da Costa (percussion) 31 May
Paquito D'Rivera (alto sax) 4 June
Chuck Wilson (alto sax) 31 July
Allan Holdsworth (guitar) 6 August
Steve Turré (trombone) 12 September
Billy Pierce (tenor sax) 25 September
Dave Samuels (vibes) 9 October
Hannibal Peterson (trumpet) 11 November
Alphonse Mouzon (drums) 21 November
Stan Sulzmann (saxes) 30 November
Harvie Schwartz (bass) 6 December
Mads Vinding (bass) 7 December

DEATHS

Kaiser Marshall (49) 3 January *pneumonia*
Sidney Arodin (46) 6 February
Red McKenzie (48) 7 February
Mutt Carey (56) 3 September
Kid 'Shots' Madison (49) September
Stan Hasselgard (26) 23 November *auto accident*
Chano Pozo (33) 2 December *shot to death in a Harlem bar*
Dave Tough (41) 9 December *fractured skull in a fall*

BOOKS

P. Arundel: *This Swing Business*
L.H.Bannister:*International Jazz Collector's Directory*
Ernest Bornemann: *Tremolo*
D. Curran: *Dupree Blues* (novel)
Gene Deitch: *The Cat*
Sidney W. Finkelstein: *Jazz: A People's Music*
Charles Graves (ed): *100 Facts on Swing Music*
Nard Griffin: *To Be or not to Bop*
C. Harvey (ed): *Jazz Parody: Anthology of Jazz*
Wingy Manone & Paul Vandervoort: *Trumpet on the Wing*
Roi Ottley: *Black Odyssey: The story of the negro in America*
S.G. Spaeth: *History of Popular Music in America*
Paul Whiteman: *Records for the Millions*

FILMS

Charlie Barnet & his Orchestra (11mins): music short
Featuring Gene Krupa & his Orchestra (10mins): music short
Woody Herman & his Orchestra (15mins): featurette with solos by Stan Getz, Shorty Rogers
Killer Diller (80mins): musical feature with Andy Kirk Band, Nat Cole Trio
Buddy Rich & his Orchestra (15mins): music short
Singin' the Blues (8mins): documentary story of the blues
A song is born (112mins): feature film with Benny Goodman in a leading role with Louis Armstrong, Tommy Dorsey, Lionel Hampton

COMPOSITIONS

Eden Ahbez: *Nature Boy*
Duke Ellington: *The Tattooed Bride*
Dizzy Gillespie: *Manteca / Cubana Be Cubana Bop / Tin Tin Deo*

RECORDS

Gene Ammons (Chicago): *Blowing Red's Top / Concentration / Chabootie* (Chicago, 10 December): *Swingin' For Christmas / It's The Talk Of The town / The Battle*
Louis Armstrong (Nice, 22 February): *My Monday Date / Royal Garden Blues / Black And Blue / Panama / That's My Desire* (NYC, 23 November – Condon TV show): *King Porter Stomp*
Count Basie (NYC, September): *The King / Spasmodic / X1 / Good Bait* (NYC): *It Serves Me Right / Little Dog*
Earl Bostic (NYC): *Bostic's Jump / Earl's Rhumboogie / Hot Sauce Boss / 8.45 Stomp / Disk Jockey Nightmare / Slightly Groovy / Bar Fly Bar / Artistry By Bostic / Apollo Theatre Jump / Serenade To Beauty / Tiger Rag / The Man I Love / Temptation / Bostic's Boogie Blues / Joy Dust / Liza / Scotch Jam*
Benny Carter (LA): *Baby You're Mine For Keeps / You'll Never Break My Heart Again/An Old Love Story / Chilpanicingo / Reina / Let Us Drink A Toast Together*
Kenny Clarke (Paris, 2 March): *Confirmation / A la Colette / Jumpin' There / Jay Mac* (Paris, 14 May): *Maggie's Draw / Anne / Out Of Nowhere / I'm In The Mood For Love*
Tadd Dameron (NYC, 13 September): *Jahbero / Lady Bird / Symphonette / 52nd Street Theme*

Photograph Courtesy: *Max Jones*

1948

Eddie 'Lockjaw' Davis (NYC): *Happy Birthday / Black Pepper / Jumpin' With Maxie-Waxie / Rudy's Boogie*
Duke Ellington (Carnegie Hall, NYC, 13 November): *The Tattooed Bride / How High The Moon / Cottontail / Manhattan Murals / Lush Life / Brown Betty / Humoresque / The Eighth Veil / Golden Feather / Flippant Flurry / Golden Cress / The Unbooted Character / Sultry Sunset / Magnolias Dripping With Molasses / Creole Love Call / Lady Of The Lavender Mist / She Wouldn't Be Moved / My Friend / Don't Be So Mean To Baby / Lover Come Back To Me / H'ya Sue / Fantasia / Trees / It's Monday Every Day / Medley / Limehouse Blues / Just A-Settin' And A-Rockin' / Trumpet No-End*
Ella Fitzgerald (NYC, 29 April): *Tea Leaves* (NYC, 30 April): *My Happiness* (NYC, 20 August): *It's Too Soon To Know / I Can't Go On Without You* (NYC, 10 November): *To Make A Mistake Is Human / In My Dreams*
Tony Fruscella (NYC, 10 December): *Foo's / Flues / Oh Yeah / Little Orgg / Out Of Nowhere*
Erroll Garner (Paris, 15 May): *Lover Man / What Is This Thing Called Love? / Early In Paris / These Foolish Things*
Stan Getz (NYC, October): *Pardon My Bop / As I Live And Bop / Interlude In Bebop / Pinhead*
Dizzy Gillespie Orchestra (Salle Pleyel, Paris, 28 February): *'Round Midnight / Algo Bueno / I Can't Get Started / Ool-Ya-Koo / Afro Cubano Suite / Things To Come / Oop-Pop-A-Da / Two Bass Hit / Good Bait* (NYC, December): *The Squirrel / Oo-Bop-A-Da / S'posin' / Tabu* (NYC, 29 December): *Guarachi Guaro / Duff Capers / Lover Come Back To Me / I'm Be Boppin' Too*

Benny Goodman Septet (LA, 9 September): *Stealin' Apples*
Wardell Gray (NYC, April): *Light Gray / Stoned / Matter And Mind / The Toupe*
Al Haig (NYC): *Haig'n'Haig / Always / Bopelbaby / Talk A Little Bop / In A Little Spanish Town*
Woody Herman (LA, 29 December): *That's Right / Lemon Drop* (LA, 30 December): *Early Autumn / Keeper of the Flame*
Billie Holiday (NYC, 10 December): *Weep No More / Girls Were Made To Take Care Of Boys / Porgy / My man*
Milt Jackson (Detroit, April): *Bobbin' With Robin / Autumn Breeze / Slits / Baggy Eyes / In A Beautiful Mood / Baggy's Blues*
Howard McGhee (Paris, 15 May): *How High The Moon / Al's Tune / Dimitar / Bop En Vogue / Swiss Vounce* (Paris, 18 May): *Denise / Nicole / Etoile / Punkins / Donna Lee / Big Will / Prelude To Nicole*
Howard McGhee/Fats Navarro (NYC, 11 October): *The Skunk / Boperation / Double Talk*
Howard McGhee/Milt Jackson (NYC, November): *Sweet And Lovely / I'm In The Mood For Love / The Man I Love / Merry Lee / Short Life / Talk Of The Town / Bass C Jam / Down Home*
Machito (NYC): *Cubop City 1&2* (NYC, 20 December): *No Noise 1&2 / Mango Mangue*
Billy Mitchell (Detroit): *Compulsory / Blue Room / The Zec / Alone Together*
Thelonious Monk (NYC, 2 July): *All The Things You Are / I Should Care / Evidence / Misterioso / Epistrophy / I Mean You*
James Moody (NYC, Summer): *The Fuller Bop Man / Workshop / Oh, Henry / Moodamorphosis* (NYC, December): *Tropicana / Cu-ba / Moody's All Frantic /*

Tin Tin Deo (NYC, 2 December): *A Choice Taste / A Lesson In Bopology / Loop-Plu-E-Du / Honeysuckle Bop*
Brew Moore (NYC, 22 October): *Brew Blew / Blue Brew / No More Brew / More Brew*
Fats Navarro (NYC, 29 November): *Move / Yardbird Suite / Guilty / A Stranger In Town / As Time Goes By*
Tony Parenti (NYC, 22 January): *Crawfish Crawl / The Entertainer's Rag / Lily Rag / Cataract Rag / Nonsense Rag / Redhead Rag*
Charlie Parker (NYC, 18 September): *Barbados / Ah-leu-cha / Constellation / Parker's Mood* (NYC, 24 September): *Perhaps / Marmaduke / Steeplechase / Merry-go-round*
Leo Parker (Detroit, 23 March): *On The House / Dinky / Senor Leo / Chase'n'lion / Leo's Bells / Sweet Talkin' Leo / Swingin' For Love / New Look Swing*
Sammy Price (Paris, February): *Eiffel Tower / Good Paree / Low Down Blues / Montparnasse / Sammy's Boogie / Frenchy's Blues*
Arnold Ross (LA, 23 February): *Please Don't Talk About Me When I'm Gone / Just You, Just Me / Jelly Jelly / Blues For Billy*
Sonny Stitt (NYC, June): *Stardust / Third Song / Body And Soul / Ratio And Proportion*
Buddy Tate (NYC): *Swingin' With Willie And Ray / Dear Mary*
Charlie Ventura (Chicago, October): *If I Had You / Euphoria / Lonely Woman / FYI / Oh, Lady Be Good / Deed I Do / Sweet Georgia Brown / Taking A Chance On Love / Pina Colada / I'm Forever Blowing Bubbles / Gone With The Wind / Once In A While*
Lester Young (NYC, 29 December): *Tea For Two / East Of Suez / Sheik Of Araby / Something To Remember You By*

Photograph: *William P Gottlieb* Courtesy: *Redferns*

Above: **Charlie Parker** (28) backstage at the Three Deuces.

Left: **Billie Holiday** (33) walks onto the stage of Carnegie Hall (27 March) for her first public performance following her release from prison. The pianist is Bobby Tucker.

Opposite page: **Louis Armstrong** and the All Stars relaxing backstage at the Nice Jazz Festival. L to r: Sidney Catlett, Louis, Barney Bigard and Earl Hines.

Photograph: *William P Gottlieb* Courtesy: *Redferns*

Miles Davis (23) and Nonet make 'Birth of the Cool' recordings.

Cool jazz trend develops. Lennie Tristano (30) and Lee Konitz (22) gain wide attention.

George Shearing (30) organises quintet.

Louis Armstrong (48) chosen as King of the Zulus for New Orleans Mardi Gras parade.

Cozy Cole (39) joins Louis Armstrong All-Stars (Spring).

Paris Jazz Festival (May) features Charlie Parker (29), Miles Davis (23), Max Roach (24), Hot Lips Page (41) and Sidney Bechet (52).

Howard Rumsey (31) inaugurates jazz policy at Lighthouse, Hermosa Beach.

Charlie Barnet (36) breaks up big band.

Dave Brubeck (29) records with a trio and octet.

Birdland opens on Broadway (15 December).

First jazz LP's issued. Battle between record companies over 33⅓ or 45rpm.

BIRTHS
Chris Laurence (bass) 6 January
Frank Ricotti (vibes) 31 January
Mike Brecker (tenor sax) 29 March
Gil Scott-Heron (singer/songwriter) 1 April
Eric Kloss (saxes) 3 April
Linda Sharrock (vocal) 3 April
Bill Bruford (drums) 17 May
Jim McNeely (piano) 18 May
Chico Freeman (tenor sax) 17 July
Lillian Boutté (vocals) 6 August
Danny Mixon (piano) 19 August
Onaje Allen Gumbs (piano/arranger) 3 September
Arturo Sandoval (trumpet) 6 November
David Ware (tenor sax) 7 November
Bill Reichenbach (trombone) 30 November
Lenny White (drums) 19 December

DEATHS
George Bacquet (66) 14 January
Irving Fazola (36) 20 March *heart attack*
Herbie Haymer (33) 11 April
Henry 'Kid' Rena (49) 25 May
Bud Scott (59) 2 July
Bunk Johnson (59) 7 July
Danny Polo (48) 11 July
Paul Mares (49) 18 August
'Big Eye' Louis Nelson (69) 20 August
Buster Wilson (52) 23 October
Stan King (49) 19 November
Bill 'Bojangles' Robinson (71) 25 November
Albert Ammons (42) 5 December
Huddie 'Leadbelly' Ledbetter (64) 6 December
Ivie Anderson (44) 28 December
John Trueheart (49)

BOOKS
Orin Blackstone: *The Jazz Finder '49*
Leonard Feather: *Inside Bebop*
A.P. Graham: *Strike up the Band: Bandleaders of Today*
W.C. Handy: *A Treasury of the Blues*
W.C. Love & Bill Rich: *Who's who in Jazz Collecting*

FILMS
Charlie Barnet & his Orchestra (11mins): music short
Begone Dull Care (8mins): abstract animated cartoon by Norman McLaren with 3 themes by Oscar Peterson
Deep Purple : Gene Krupa Orchestra music short
Lionel Hampton & his Orchestra (14mins): music short
Herman's Herd (15mins): Woody Herman music short
Gene Krupa & his Orchestra (15mins): music short
Make Believe Ballroom (78mins): musical featuring Jimmy Dorsey Orchestra, Pee Wee Hunt Band, Charlie Barnet Band, Gene Krupa Band and Nat King Cole Trio
Symphony in Swing (15mins): Duke Ellington music short
Young Man with a Horn (112mins): feature film inspired by the life of Bix Beiderbecke

COMPOSITIONS
Andy Gibson / Roy Alfred: *The Hucklebuck*
Joe Marsala: *Don't Cry, Joe*

RECORDS
Louis Armstrong (NYC, 1 September): *Maybe It's Because / I'll Keep The Lovelight Burning* (NYC, 6 September): *That Lucky Old Sun / Blueberry Hill* (NYC, 30 September, with Billie Holiday): *You Can't Lose A Broken Heart / My Sweet Hunk O' Trash*
Gene Ammons (Chicago, 5 February): *Daddy's Sauce Airlines / Little Irv / Abdullah's Fiesta / Brother Jug's Sermon* (Chicago, 28 February): *Do You Really Mean It? / Bless You / Tenor Eleven / Once In A While* (Chicago, 4 October): *Everything Depends On You / Hot Springs / When You're Gone / Little Slam*
Count Basie (LA, 11 April): *Cheek To Cheek / Just An Old Manuscript* (NYC, 29 June): *She's A Wine-O / Shoutin' Blues* (NYC, 13 July): *St Louis Baby* (NYC, 5 August): *The Slider / Normania*
Sidney Bechet's Blue Note Jazzmen (NYC, 21 January): *Sister Kate / Tiger Rag / Tin Roof Blues / I've Found A New Baby / Nobody Knows You When You're Down And Out / When The Saints Go Marchin' In* (NYC, 23 March): *Basin Street Blues / Cake Walking Babies / Fidgety Feet / At The Jazz Band Ball / Tailgate Ramble / Joshua Fit De Battle*
Sidney Bechet (NYC, 31 January): *I Got Rhythm / September Song / Who? / Cabash* (Chicago, February): *Maryland / Careless Love / Egyptian Fantasy* (Paris, 16 May): *Honeysuckle Rose / Coquette / High Society / Sunny Side Of The Street / Sugar / I Can't Believe That You're In Love With Me / Indiana / Festival Blues* (NYC, 8 June, with Bob Wilber): *I'm Through, Goodbye / Love Me With Feeling / Waste No Tears / Box Car Shorty / The Broken Windmill / Without A Home* (Paris, 14 October): *Ce Massieu / Buddy Bolden Story / Bechet's Creole Blues / Anita's Birthday / Les Oignons / Ridin' Easy Blues / Blues In Paris / Panther Dance* (Paris, 20 October): *Orphan Annie Blues / Happy Go Lucky Blues / Klook's Blues / American Rhythm / Out Of Nowhere / Mon Homme* (Paris, 5 November): *Wrap Your Troubles In Dreams / It Had To Be You / Baby Won't You Please Come Home / Please Don't Talk About Me When I'm Gone / Ooh Boogie / After You've Gone / Going Way Down Home / Margie* (London, 13 November, with Humphrey Lyttelton): *Some Of These Days / Black And Blue / Who's Sorry Now? / Sleepy Time Down South / I Told You Once / Georgia On My Mind*
Dave Brubeck Trio (SF, September): *Blue Moon / Tea For Two / Indiana / Laura*
Don Byas (Paris, 4 January): *Yesterday / All The Things You Are* (Paris, 4 July): *Summertime / Talk Of The Town / Stardust / A Pretty Girl / Old Man River / Flamingo*
Harry Carney (NYC): *Sono / Frustration*
Barbara Carroll (NYC): *Dancing On The Ceiling / Barbara's Carol / You Stepped Out Of A Dream / The Puppet That Dances Bop / Morocco 1&2*
Benny Carter (LA, May): *Time Out For The Blues / Cottontail / Surf Board / You're Too Beautiful*
Serge Chaloff & the Herdsmen (NYC, 10 March): *Chickasaw / Bop Scotch / The Most / Chasin' The Bass*
Serge Chaloff/Ralph Burns Septet (Boston, July): *Pat / King Edward The Flatted Fifth*
Kenny Clarke (NYC, 25 January): *Conglomerations / Bruz / You Go To My Head / Roll 'Em Bags / Don't Blame Me / French Licks*
Buck Clayton (Paris, 10 October): *High Tide /*

Swingin' At Sundown / Who's Sorry Now? / Sugar Blues / Blues In First / Blues In Second / Don's Blues (Paris, 21 November): *Uncle Buck / Buck Special / Night Life / Perdido / BC & BC / Sweet Georgia Brown*
Bill Coleman/Don Byas Quintet (Paris, 4 January): *Just You, Just Me / Bill Brother's Blues / Idaho / Bill Coleman Blues* (Paris, 5 January): *What Is This Thing Called Love / St Louis Blues / Lover Man / Liza / Blues At Noon*
Eddie Condon (NYC, 25 May): *Seems Like Old Times / Time Carries On* (NYC, 27 August): *Condon Floor Show*
Sonny Criss (LA, 22 September): *Calidad / Tornado / The First One / Blues For Boppers*
Tadd Dameron (NYC, 18 January): *Sid's Delight / Casbah* (NYC, 21 April): *John's Delight / What's New? / Heaven's Door Is Wide Open / Focus*
Eddie 'Lockjaw' Davis (NYC, 16 August): *Mountain Oysters / Huckle Boogie*
Miles Davis (NYC, 21 January): *Jeru / Move / Godchild / Budo* (NYC, 22 April): *Venus de Milo / Rouge / Boplicity / Israel*
Buddy de Franco (NYC, 23 April): *The Boy Next Door / A Bird In Igor's Yard / This Time The Dream's On Me* (NYC, 24 August): *Bud's Invention / Penthouse Serenade / Extrovert / Good For Nothin' Joe / Aishie*
Duke Ellington (NYC, 1 September): *You Of All People / Creole Love Call / The Greatest There Is / Snibor* (NYC, 22 December): *The World Is Waiting For The Sunrise / Joog, Joog / Good Woman Blues / On The Sunny Side Of The Street / B-sharp Boston*
Ella Fitzgerald (NYC, 14 January): *I Couldn't Stay Away / Old Mother Hubbard / Someone Like You* (NYC, 27 April): *My Baby Likes To Re-bop* (NYC, 28 April): *Happy Talk / I'm Gonna Wash That Man / Black Coffee / Lover's Gold* (NYC, 28 April, with Louis Jordan): *Baby It's Cold Outside / Don't Cry, Cry Baby* (LA, 20 July): *Crying / A New Shade Of Blue* (NYC, 20 September): *In The Evening / Talk Fast, My Heart, Talk Fast / I'm Waiting For The Junkman / Basin Street Blues* (NYC, 21 September): *I Hadn't Anyone Till You / Dream A Little Longer / Foolish Tears / A Man Wrote A Song* (LA, 7 November): *Fairy Tales / I Gotta Have My Baby Back*
Erroll Garner (LA, 29 March): *I Surrender Dear / I Only Have Eyes For You / I Cover The Waterfront / It's Easy To Remember / Penthouse Serenade / Love Walked In / September Song / Body And Soul / All The Things You Are / Ghost Of A Chance / Stompin' At The Savoy / Yesterdays / Goodbye / Cottage For Sale / Lady Be Good / I'm In The Mood For Love / I Can't Believe That You're In Love With Me / More Than You Know / Undecided / Red Sails In The Sunset / All Of Me / Over The Rainbow* (NYC, 20 August): *Reverie / Turquoise / Blue And Sentimental / Pavanne Mood / Flamingo / Skylark / I Can't Give You Anything But Love / Impression / Twilight / The Way You Look Tonight*
Stan Getz (NYC, 8 April): *Battleground / Four And One Moore / Five Brothers / Battle Of The Saxes* (NYC, 2 May): *Stan Gets Along / Stan's Mood / Slow / Fast* (NYC, 21 June): *Indian Summer / Long Island Sound / Mar-cia / Prezervation / Crazy Chords*
Dizzy Gillespie Orchestra (NYC, 14 April): *Swedish Suite / St Louis Blues / I Should Care / That Old Black Magic* (NYC, 6 May): *Dizzier And Dizzier / Jump Di-Le-Ba* (NYC, 6 July): *Hey Pete, Let's Eat Mo' Meat / Jumpin' With Symphony Sid / If Love Is Trouble / In The Land Of Oo-bla-dee* (NYC, 21 November): *Say When / Tally-Ho / You Stole My Wife You Horsethief / I Can't Remember*
Benny Goodman Sextet/Quartet (LA, 14 April): *Bedlam / Small Hotel / Oo-bla-dee / Blue Lou*
Wardell Gray (NYC, 11 November): *Twisted / Southside / Easy Living / Sweet Lorraine*
Al Haig (NYC, April): *Five Star / Sugar Hill Bop / In A Pinch / Talk Of The Town* (NYC, 12 May): *Skull Buster / Ante Room / Poop Deck / Pennies From Heaven* (NYC, 28 July): *Pinch Bottle / Earless Engineering / Be Still TV / Short P, Not LP*
Coleman Hawkins (NYC, 18 September): *Body And Soul / Riff-tide / Sophisticated Lady*
Earl Hines (Paris, 4 November): *Chicago / Night Life In Pompeii / Japanese Sandman / Rhythm Business / Air France Stomp*
Billie Holiday (LA, 2 June): *My Man / Miss Brown To You / Lover Man* (NYC, 17 August): *'Tain't Nobody's*

1949

Business If I Do / Baby, Get Lost (NYC, 27 August):
*Keeps On A' Rainin' / Lover Man / All Of Me / I Cover
The Waterfront / Billie's Blues* (NYC, 29 August):
Keeps On A' Rainin' / Them There Eyes (NYC, 8
September): *Do Your Duty / Gimme A Pigfoot* (NYC,
30 September): *You Can't Lose A Broken Heart / My
Sweet Hunk O' Trash / Now Or Never* (NYC, 19
October): *You're My Thrill / Crazy He Calls Me /
Please Tell Me Now / Somebody's On My Mind*
Milt Jackson (NYC, 23 February): *Hearing Bells /
Junior / Bluesology / Bubu*
JJ Johnson (NYC, 11 May): *Audobahn / Don't Blame
Me / Goof Square / Bee Jay* (NYC, 26 May): *Elysees /
Opus V / Hi-lo / Fox Hunt* (NYC, 17 October):
Afternoon In Paris / Elora / Teapot / Blue Mode
Howard McGhee (NYC, 23 August): *Lo-flame /
Fugue / Fluid Drive / Meciendo / Donello Square /
I'll Remember April*
Machito (NYC, January): *Caravan / Okiedoke /
Tanga / Flying Home / Bucabu*
Wingy Manone (LA, 25 March): *Face On Bass / Can't
Get You Off My Mind / Trumpet On The Wing / 13th
Street Rag* (LA, 9 May): *Riders In The Sky / The
Round Square Dance / North Hollywood Blues /
Flamingo* (LA, 8 October): *Japanese Sandman / Dixie*
James Moody (Lausanne, 30 April): *Monday Blues /
Just Moody / Stardust / Curley Top Blues / Moody
And Soul* (Zurich, 1 May): *Hot House / Lover Man*
(Paris, 7 July): *Convulsions / Oh Well / Verso / Redo*
(Stockholm, 7 October): *Out Of Nowhere / These
Foolish Things* (Stockholm, 12 October): *I'm In The
Mood For Bop / The Flight Of The Bopple Bee / Body
And Soul / I'm In The Mood For Love / Lester Leaps
In / Indiana / Good Bait / Dexterious* (Stockholm, 18
October): *Over The Rainbow / Blue And Moody*
Brew Moore (NYC, 21 May): *The Mud Bug / Gold
Rush / Lestorian Mode / Kai's Kid* (NYC): *Brew
Blew / Moore Brew / No More Brew / Blue Brew*

Fats Navarro/Don Lanphere (NYC, 20 September):
Wailing Wall / Go / Infatuation / Stop
Red Norvo (LA): *Swedish Pastry / Cheek To Cheek /
Night And Day / Time And Tide*
Kid Ory (LA, Shrine Auditorium, 7 October): *12th
Street Rag / Tiger Rag / Savoy Blues / Eh, La Bas*
Hot Lips Page (NYC, 15 March): *The Egg Or The
Hen / I Got An Uncle In Harlem / Jeeter Road Joad /
Don't Tell A Man* (NYC, 16 September): *That Lucky
Old Sun / I Never See Maggie Alone*
Charlie Parker (NYC, April): *Cardboard / Visa*
(NYC, 5 May): *Segment / Passport / Diverse* (Paris,
9/14 May): *Salt Peanuts / Barbados / 52nd Street
Theme / Out Of Nowhere / Scrapple From The
Apple / Hot House* (NYC, 30 November, with
strings): *Just Friends / Everything Happens To Me /
April In Paris / Summertime / I Didn't Know What
Time It Was / If I Should Lose You*
Leo Parker (NYC): *Woody / Rolling With Parker*
Cecil Payne (NYC, 21 June): *Egg Head / No Chops /
Big Joe / Hippy Dippy* (NYC, 23 November): *The
Worst Is Yet To Come / Angel Child / Block Buster*
Flip Phillips/Howard McGhee (LA, January): *Cake /
Znarg Blues / My Old Flame / Cool*
Flip Phillips (NYC, 24 September): *This Can't Be
Love / Cookie* (NYC, 26 September): *Swingin' For
Julie And Brownie / Put That Back / Lazy River*
(NYC, 5 December): *Drowsy / Vortex / Milano / But
Beautiful* (NYC, 9 December): *Lover / Don't Take
Your Love / Flip's Boogie / Feeling The Blues / Lover
Come Back To Me / Blue Room*
Bud Powell Trio (NYC, May): *Tempus Fugit / Celia /
Cherokee / I'll Keep Loving You / Strictly
Confidential / All God's Chillun*
Bud Powell Modernists (NYC, 8 August): *Bouncing
With Bud / Wail / Dance Of The Infidels / 52nd
Street Theme / You Go To My Head / Ornithology /
Parisian Thoroughfare* (NYC, 19 December):

*Jumping With Symphony Sid / I'll Be Seeing You /
52nd Street Theme / Ornithology*
George Shearing (NYC, 31 January): *Cherokee /
Four Bar's Short / Bebop's Fables / Midnight On
Cloud 69 / Sorry, Wrong Rhumba / Cotton Top /
Moon Over Miami / Life With Feather* (NYC, 17
February): *September In The Rain / Good To The
Last Bop / Bop, Look And Listen / You Are Too
Beautiful* (NYC, 28 June): *I Didn't Know What Time
It Was / The Continental / Nothing But D Best /
Summertime* (NYC, 27 July): *East Of The Sun / In A
Chinese Garden / Conception* (NYC, 12 December):
*I'll Remember April / Little White Lies / Carnegie
Horizons / Jumpin' With Symphony Sid*
Sonny Stitt (NYC, 11 December): *All God's Chillun
Got Rhythm / Sonny Side / Bud's Blues / Sunset*
Lennie Tristano (NYC, 11 January): *Tautology /
Subconscious-Lee / Progression / Retrospection /
Judy* (NYC, 4 March): *Wow / Crosscurrent* (NYC,
14 March): *Yesterdays* (NYC, 16 May): *Marionette /
Sax Of A Kind / Intuition / Digression*
Sarah Vaughan (NYC, 20 January): *Bianca / As You
Desire Me / Black Coffee* (NYC, 25 January): *While
You Are Gone* (LA, 6 May): *Tonight I Shall Sleep /
That Lucky Old Sun* (NYC, 7 July): *Give Me A Song
With A Beautiful Melody / Make Believe / You
Taught Me To Love Again / Just Friends* (NYC, 25
September): *Lonely Girl* (NYC, 28 September): *You
Say You Care / Fool's Paradise / I Cried For You*
(NYC, 21 December): *You're Mine You / I'm Crazy
To Love You / Summertime / The Nearness Of You*
Sarah Vaughan/Billy Eckstine (NYC, 21 December):
*Dedicated To You / You're All I Need / I Love You /
Every Day*
Charlie Ventura (NYC, 6 January): *Whatta You Say
We Go / Body And Soul / Birdland / Lullaby In
Rhythm* (NYC, 5 February): *Fine And Dandy* (NYC,
12 March): *Boptura / Barney Google / Smoke Gets
In Your Eyes* (NYC, 7 April): *For Bopper's Only /
Flamingo / Deed I Do* (NYC, 11 April): *Barney
Google / Smoke Gets In Your Eyes*
Charlie Ventura Orchestra (NYC, 12 August):
Boptura / Feather's Den / Yankee Clipper / Lotus Blue
(NYC, 30 September): *High On An Open Mike / Too
Marvellous For Words / Lullaby Of The Leaves / Ha!*
(NYC, 28 December): *Take The A Train / Prelude To A
Kiss / Solitude / Mood Indigo / It Don't Mean A Thing /
Sophisticated Lady / Caravan*
Kai Winding (NYC, February): *Bop City /
Wallington's Godchild / Crossing The Channel /
Sleepy Bop* (NYC, 23 August): *Sid's Bounce /
Broadway / Water-works / A Night On Bop Mountain*
Lester Young (NYC, 28 June): *Crazy Over Jazz /
Ding Dong / Blues'n'Bells*

Left: Max Roach, Charlie Parker, Miles Davis
(hidden) and Kenny Clarke in Paris for the
International Jazz Festival (May).
Below left: Miles Davis and his Nonet at a Birth of
the Cool recording session. Saxists Gerry Mulligan
and Lee Konitz are visible in the foreground.
Below right: The George Shearing Quintet with
John Levy (bass), George Shearing (piano), Margie
Hyams (vibes), Chuck Wayne (guitar) and Denzil
Best (drums).

Photographs Courtesy: *Max Jones*

1950

Count Basie (46) breaks up big band, leads septet featuring Clark Terry (30), Buddy de Franco (27) and Wardell Gray (29).

Dizzy Gillespie (33) breaks up big band.

Woody Herman (37) organises Third Herd after a spell with a septet.

First Mahalia Jackson (39) concert at Carnegie Hall.

Stan Kenton (38) tours with 'Innovations in Modern Music' 40-piece orchestra.

Horace Silver (22) joins Stan Getz (23) group.

Red Norvo (42) Trio features Charlie Mingus (28) and Tal Farlow (29).

Charlie Parker (30) in Sweden in November. Plays Birdland regularly and records with strings.

Paul Desmond (26) joins Dave Brubeck (30).

Benny Goodman (41) tours Europe with small group including Zoot Sims (25) and Roy Eldridge (39).

JATP tours Europe.

Artie Shaw (40) breaks up big band and works with a combo.

Paul Gonsalves (30) joins Duke Ellington Band. Third European tour for Ellington band.

BIRTHS

Pete Robinson (keyboards) 3 March
Bobby McFerrin (vocals) 11 March
Bobbi Humphrey (flute) 25 April
Harold Land Jr (piano) 25 April
Chip Jackson (bass) 15 May
Pete Jacobsen (piano) 16 May
Dee Dee Bridgewater (vocals) 27 May
Glenn Ferris (trombone) 27 June
Niles Weston (conga) 12 August
Alvin Queen (drums) 16 August
Will Lee (bass) 8 September
Mark Helias (bass) 1 October
Ronnie Laws (tenor sax) 3 October
Paolo Nonnis (drums)

DEATHS

Buddy Stewart (27) 1 February *auto accident*
Leo Watson (52) 2 May *pneumonia*
Chelsea Quealey (45) 6 May
Bertha 'Chippie' Hill (45) 7 May *hit and run victim*
John Lindsay (55) 3 July
Fats Navarro (26) 7 July *tuberculosis*
Alvin Burroughs (38) 1 August
Al Killian (33) 5 September *murdered by psychopathic landlord*
Ray Perry (35) Autumn

BOOKS

Rudi Blesh & Harriet Janis: *They all played ragtime*
Dave Carey & Albert McCarthy: *The Directory of Recorded Jazz & Swing Music – Volume 1*
Lena Horne: *In Person, Lena Horne*
Alan Lomax: *Mister Jelly Roll*
B. Spicer: *Blues for the Prince*

FILMS

Cab Calloway & his Cabaliers (19mins): music short
I'll get by (83mins): musical feature with Harry James Orchestra
King Cole & his Trio (15mins): music short
Red Nichols & his Five Pennies (15mins): music short
Salute to Duke Ellington (15mins): music short
Sarah Vaughan & Herb Jeffries/ Kid Ory & his Creole Jazz Band (15mins): featurette
Sugar Chile Robinson/Billie Holiday/Count Basie Sextet (15mins): music short
That's my desire (10mins): French film record of Louis Armstrong All-Stars
3-MINUTE SOUNDIES
Andy's Boogie: Charlie Barnet
Basie's Boogie: Count Basie Sextet
Basie's Conversation: Count Basie Sextet
One O'Clock Jump: Count Basie Sextet
I can't give you anything but love: Cab Calloway
One for my baby: Cab Calloway
St James Infirmary: Cab Calloway

COMPOSITIONS

Duke Ellington: *Love You Madly*
Jimmy Mundy / Illinois Jacquet / Al Stillman: *Don'cha Go 'Way Mad*

RECORDS

Gene Ammons (Chicago, 8 January): *Pennies From Heaven / The Last Chance / The Last Mile / Full Moon / More Moon* (NYC, 5 March): *Keep Your Head From Ammons / Bye Bye / Let It Be / Blues Up And Down / You Can Depend On Me / Touch Of The Blues / Dumb Woman Blues* (NYC, 26 April): *Chabootie / Who Put The Sleeping Pills In Rip van Winkle's Coffee? / Gravy / Easy Glide* (Chicago, 2 May): *Tenor Eleven / Goodbye / It's You Or No One / My Foolish Heart* (NYC, 28 June): *I Wanna Be Loved / I Can't Give You Anything But Love* (NYC, 27 July): *Back In Your Own Backyard / Sweet Jennie Lou / La Vie En Rose / Seven Eleven* (Chicago, August): *Jug Head Ramble / Can Anyone Explain / Don't Do Me Wrong / Prelude To A Kiss* (NYC, 28 October): *Stringin' The Jug / When I Dream Of You / A Lover Is Blue*

Louis Armstrong (NYC, 24–27 April): *Panama / New Orleans Function / Twelfth Street Rag / That's For Me / Bugle Call Rag / I Surrender Dear / Russian Lullaby / Baby Won't You Please Come Home / Fine And Dandy / Bucket's Got A Hole* (NYC, 26 June): *La Vie En Rose /C'est Si Bon* (NYC, 25 August, with Ella Fitzgerald): *Dream A Little Dream Of Me / Can Anyone Explain?* (NYC, 31 August): *Sit Down You're Rockin' The Boat / That's What The Man Said*

Count Basie Octet (NYC, 6 February): *If You See My Baby / Rat Race / Sweets* (NYC, 16 May): *Neal's Deal / Bluebeard Blues / Golden Bullet / You're My Baby, You* (NYC, 2 November): *Song Of The Islands / These Foolish Things / I'm Confessin' / One O'Clock Jump* (NYC, 3 November): *I Ain't Got Nobody / Little White Lies / I'll Remember April / Tootie*

Sidney Bechet's Blue Note Jazzmen (NYC, 19 April): *Copenhagen / China Boy / Ain't Gonna Give You None O' My Jelly Roll / Runnin' Wild / Mandy / Shimme-Sha-Wabble*

Sidney Bechet's New Orleans Feetwarmers (NYC, Spring): *Jelly Roll Blues / Georgia Camp Meeting / National Emblem March / Hindustan*

Ray Brown Trio (NYC, 1 July): *Blue Lou / Song Of The Volga Boatmen*

Kenny Clarke (Paris, 9 October): *Paris Be-bop Sessions* (LP)

Arnett Cobb (NYC, 12 September): *Smooth Sailing / Your Wonderful Love / That's All Brother / Bee-Bee*

Al Cohn (NYC, 29 July): *Groovin' With Gus / Infinity / How Long Has This Been Going On? / Let's Get Away From It All*

Eddie Condon (NYC, 20 March): *Maple Leaf Rag / Dill Pickles / Sweet Cider* (NYC, 22 March): *At The Jazz Band Ball / Jazz Me Blues* (NYC, 9 June): *Black Bottom / Original Charleston / Yellow Dog Blues* (NYC, 2 October): *Raggin' The Scale / Grace And Beauty / Everybody Loves My Baby / 100 Years From Today*

Miles Davis (NYC, 13 March): *Deception / Rocker / Moon Dreams / Darn That Dream*

Roy Eldridge (Paris, 9,14 June): *King David and his Little Jazz* (album)

Duke Ellington (NYC, 20 November): *Build That Railroad / Love You Madly / Great Times* (NYC, 18 December): *Mood Indigo / Sophisticated Lady* (NYC, 19 December): *The Tattooed Bride / Solitude*

Ella Fitzgerald (NYC, 2 February): *Baby, Won't You Say You Love Me / Doncha Go 'Way Mad* (NYC, 6 March): *Solid As A Rock / I've Got The World On A String / Sugarfoot Rag / Peas And Rice* (LA, May): *M-i-s-s-i-s-s-i-p-p-i / I Don't Want The World* (NYC, 15 August, with Louis Jordan): *Ain't Nobody's Business / I'll Never Be Free* (NYC, 11,12 September): *Ella with Ellis Larkins* (album)

Stan Getz (NYC, 6 January): *Stardust / Goodnight My Love / There's A Small Hotel / Too Marvellous For Words / I've Got You Under My Skin / What's New / Into It* (NYC, 14 April): *You Stepped Out Of A Dream / My Old Flame / The Lady In Red / Wrap Your Troubles In Dreams* (NYC, 17 May): *On The Alamo / Gone With The Wind / Yesterdays / Sweetie Pie / You Go To My Head / Hershey Bar* (NYC, 10 December): *Tootsie Roll / Strike Up The Band / Imagination / For Stompers Only / Navy Blue / Out Of Nowhere / 'S Wonderful / Penny / Split Kick / It Might As Well Be Spring / The Best Thing For You*

Dizzy Gillespie Orchestra (NYC, 9 January): *Coast To Coast / Carambola / Oo-la-la / Honeysuckle Rose*

Dizzy Gillespie Sextet (NYC, 16 September): *She's Gone Again / Nice Work If You Can Get It / Thinking Of You / Too Much Weight*

Dizzy Gillespie with strings (LA, 31 October): *Swing Low Sweet Chariot / Lullaby Of The Leaves / Million Dollar Baby / What Is There To Say* (LA, 1 November): *Alone Together / These Are The Things I Love / On The Alamo / Interlude In C*

Benny Goodman Sextet (NYC, 10 May): *Oh, Babe / You're Gonna Lose Your Gal / Walkin' With The Blues* (NYC, 24 November): *Lullaby Of The Leaves / Then You've Never Been In Love / Walkin' / Temptation Rag*

Wardell Gray (Detroit, 25 April): *A Sinner Kissed An Angel / Blue Gray / Grayhound / Treadin' With Treadwell* (LA, 27 August): *Scrapple From The Apple / Move*

Benny Green (NYC, 13 August): *La Vie En Rose / Our Very Own / Lowland Shuffle / The Blues Is Green*

Al Haig (NYC, 27 February): *Liza / Stars Fell On Alabama / Stairway To The Stars / Opus Caprice*

Coleman Hawkins (NYC, 16 September): *Yesterdays / Hawk's Tune / Stuffy*

Billie Holiday (LA, 8 March): *God Bless The Child / This Is Heaven To Me*

Willis 'Gator' Jackson (NYC): *On My Own / Chuck's Chuckles / Can't Help Lovin' Dat Man / Dance Of The Lady Bug / Later For The Gator / The Call Of The Gators / Pee Wee*

Al Killian (Stockholm, 4 June): *St Louis Blues / Big Al / Body And Soul / Y'oughta*

John Lewis (Paris, 13 April): *Period Suite / Perdido*

Machito (NYC, 21 December): *Cancion / Mambo / Mambo II / 6-8 / Jazz / Rhumba Abierta*

Dodo Marmarosa (Pittsburgh, 21 July): *My Foolish Heart / Blue Room / Why Was I Born / The Night Was Young*

Lucky Millinder (Cincinnati, 23 February): *Who Said Shorty Wasn't Coming Back? / Mr Trumpet Man* (NYC, May): *Let It Roll Again / My Little Baby / The Jumping Jack / Clap Your Hands* (NYC, 18 October): *Please Open Your Heart / Silent George*

James Moody (Europe, 16 April): *That's It / Mean To Me / A Date With Kate / Embraceable You / Big And Little E / 'S Wonderful* (Paris, 3 July): *Delooney / Real Cool / In The Anna* (Paris, 9 October): *I Can't Get Started / In A Rush / Embraceable You*

Red Norvo Trio (LA): *September Song / Move / I've Got You Under My Skin / I Get A Kick Out Of You / I'll Remember April / I Can't Believe That You're In Love With Me / Little White Lies / Have You Met Miss Jones? / Zing Went The Strings Of My Heart*

Kid Ory (LA, 27 June): *Glory Of Love / Savoy Blues / Georgia Camp Meeting / Mahogany Hall Stomp* (LA, 6 July): *Blues For Jimmy / Go Back Where You Stayed Last Night / Creole Song / Yaaka Hula Hickey Dula*

Hot Lips Page (NYC, 1 February): *Where Are You Blue Eyes? / Ain't No Flies On Me / Miss Larceny Blues / You Stole My Wife* (Chicago, 15 June): *Blow, Mr Low-Blow / Sharecropper's Boogie /Chi / Lyin' Gal Blues* (NYC, 13 July): *I Was Under The Impression / Chocolate Candy Blues / Pacifying Blues / Sharp Little Sister*

1950

Charlie Parker (NYC, March/April): *Star Eyes / Blues / I'm In The Mood For Love* (NYC, 6 June): *Bloomdido / An Oscar For Treadwell / Mohawk / Melancholy Baby / Leap Frog / Relaxin' With Lee* (NYC, 5 July, with strings): *Dancing In The Dark / Out Of Nowhere / Laura / East Of The Sun / They Can't Take That Away From Me / Easy To Love / I'm In The Mood For Love / I'll Remember April* (NYC Carnegie Hall, 16 September): *Easy To Love / Repetition / Rocker / April In Paris / What Is This Thing Called Love?* (NYC, October): *Celebrity / Ballade / Anthropology / Cheers / Lover Man / Cool Blues* (Halsingborg, Sweden, 24 November): *Anthropology / Scrapple From The Apple / Embraceable You / Cool Blues / Star Eyes / All The Things You Are / Strike Up The Band*

Leo Parker (NYC, 20 July): *Mona Lisa / Who's Mad? / Darn That Dream / I Cross My Finger / Mad Lad Returns* (NYC, 28 December): *Woody / Rolling With Parker / On The House / Solitude / Symphony Sid / Rollin' With Leo*

Oscar Peterson (NYC, March): *Debut / They Didn't Believe Me / Lover Come Back To Me / Where Or When / Three O'Clock In The Morning / All The Things You Are / Oscar's Blues / Tenderly* (NYC, May): *Little White Lies / Nameless / I Get Happy / Jumpin' With Symphony Sid / Robbins Nest / Lover / Exactly Like You / In The Middle Of A Kiss / Tico Tico / Smoke Gets In Your Eyes* (NYC, August):

Squatty Roo / Salute To Garner / I Get A Kick Out Of You / Dark Eyes / What's New? (Carnegie Hall, 16 September): *Padovani / Ray's Blues / Gai / Carnegie Blues / Fine And Dandy / I Only Have Eyes For You*

Oscar Pettiford (NYC, 13 September): *Perdido / Take The A Train / Oscalypso / Blues For Blanton / 12 O'Clock Bump*

Flip Phillips (NYC, 1 July): *Be Be / Dream A Little Dream / Bright Blues*

Bud Powell (NYC, January/February): *So Sorry Please / Get Happy / Sometimes I'm Happy / Sweet Georgia Brown / Yesterdays / April In Paris / Body And Soul* (NYC, July): *Hallelujah / Tea For Two*

George Shearing (NYC, 3 April): *November Seascape / How's Trix? / Changing With The Times / Strollin'* (NYC, 4 April): *When Your Lover Has Gone / As Long As There's Been Music / Cynthia / Tenderly* (NYC, 5 July): *Roses Of Picardy / For You / Move / Pick Yourself Up*

Zoot Sims (Stockholm, 23 April): *All The Things You Are / You Go To My Head / Tickle Toe* (Stockholm, 24 April): *Yellow Duck / Americans In Sweden* (Paris, 26 June): *Night And Day / Slingin' Hash / Tenderly / I Understand / Don't Worry 'Bout Me / Crystals / Zoot And Zoot / The Big Shot* (NYC, 16 September): *My Silent Love / Jane-O / Dancing In The Dark / Memories Of You*

Herb Steward (NYC, 17 January): *Medicine Man / Passport To Pimlico / T'ain't No Use / Sinbad The Sailor*

Sonny Stitt (NYC, 26 January): *Strike Up The Band / I Want To Be Happy / Taking A Chance On Love / Fine And Dandy* (NYC, 17 February): *Avalon / Later / Ain't Misbehavin' / Mean To Me / Stairway To The Stars* (NYC, 18 February): *The Way You Look Tonight* (NYC, 28 June): *Count Every Star / Nice Work If You Can Get It / There'll Never Be Another You / Blazin'* (NYC, 8 October): *To Think You've Chosen Me / After You've Gone / Our Very Own / 'S Wonderful* (NYC, 15 December): *Nevertheless / Jeepers Creepers / Imagination / Cherokee*

Sarah Vaughan (NYC, 18 May): *Ain't Misbehavin' / Goodnight My Love / Can't Get Out Of This Mood / It Might As Well Be Spring* (NYC, 19 May): *Mean To Me / Come Rain Or Shine / Nice Work If You Can Get It / East Of The Sun*

Charlie Ventura (NYC, 6 April): *You've Got A Date With The Blues / Dark Eyes* (NYC, 20 July): *Lonesome Darling / It's Me Again / Tea For Two*

Mary Lou Williams (NYC, 3 January): *Bye Bye Blues / Moonglow / Willow Weep For Me / I'm In The Mood For Love*

Teddy Wilson (NYC, 29 June/25 August): *CL 6153* (album)

Lester Young (NYC, March): *Too Marvellous For Words / Deed I Do / Encore / Polka Dots And Moonbeams / Up 'n' Adam* (NYC, July): *Three Little Words / Neenah / Jeepers Creepers*

Right: The Red Norvo Trio with Tal Farlow (guitar), Charlie Mingus (bass) and Red Norvo (vibes).
Below: Louis Armstrong and the All-Stars. Jack Teagarden (trombone), Cozy Cole (drums), Louis and Barney Bigard (clarinet).
Bottom right: Wild Bill Davison and Sidney Bechet in the WOR Studios, New York City, at a Blue Note Jazzmen recording session (19 April).

Photograph Courtesy: *Terry Dash*

Photograph: *Francis Wolff* Courtesy: *Mosaic Images*

1951

Count Basie (47) reorganises big band.

Duke Ellington (52) presents 'Harlem' at the Metropolitan Opera House in January.

Louis Bellson (27), Juan Tizol (51) and Willie Smith (43) join Duke Ellington replacing Sonny Greer (47), Lawrence Brown (43) and Johnny Hodges (44).

Wild Bill Davis (33) starts organ trio trend.

Earl Hines (46) leaves Louis Armstrong All-Stars. Jack Teagarden (46) also leaves to form his own band.

Miles Davis (25) returns to NYC after several months on the West Coast and makes his first records for Prestige with Sonny Rollins (21) and John Lewis (31).

Buddy Rich (34) and Chubby Jackson (33) join Charlie Ventura (35) and Marty Napoleon (30) in the 'world's greatest quartet'.

BIRTHS
Mark Egan (electric bass) 14 January
Steven Grossman (saxes) 18 January
Alphonso Johnson (bass) 2 February
Anthony Davis (piano) 20 February
Warren Vaché Jr (cornet) 21 March
James Williams (piano) 8 March
Bill Frisell (guitar) 18 March
Bob Berg (tenor sax) 7 April
Dick Pearce (trumpet) 19 April
Stanley Clarke (bass) 30 June
Sue Evans (percussion) 7 July
Michael Henderson (electric bass) 7 July
Trilok Gurtu (percussion) 30 October
Gerry Brown (drums) 9 November
Jaco Pastorius (bass) 1 December
Barry Finnerty (guitar) 3 December
Robben Ford (guitar) 16 December
Brooks Kerr (piano) 26 December
John Scofield (guitar) 26 December
Rebecca Parris (vocals) 28 December
Dennis Irwin (bass)
Janice Robinson (trombone)

DEATHS
Shirley Clay (48) 7 February
Big Sid Catlett (41) 25 March *heart attack*
Harold 'Doc' West (35) 4 May
Ray Wetzel (27) 17 August *auto crash*
Jimmy Yancey (57) 17 September
Charlie Creath (60) 23 October
Mildred Bailey (44) 2 December *liver & heart failure*
Vic Berton (55) 26 December

BOOKS
Ethel Waters: *His Eye is on the Sparrow: an autobiography*

FILMS
Count Basie Orchestra (19mins): music short
Eddie Condon's (10mins): film visit to the club
George Shearing Quintet Telescriptions (18mins)
Stage Entrance (7 mins): Leonard Feather presents Downbeat Award to Bird & Diz who play 'Hot House'
The Strip (86mins): Mickey Rooney as jazz drummer with Louis Armstrong, Jack Teagarden, Earl Hines, Barney Bigard
Tommy Dorsey & his Orchestra (15mins): music short
3 MINUTE SOUNDIES
Cherokee: Charlie Barnet Orchestra
Skyliner: Charlie Barnet Orchestra
TV Special: Lionel Hampton
Vibes Boogie: Lionel Hampton
Who Cares?: Lionel Hampton
Conception: George Shearing
Move: George Shearing
Swedish Pastry: George Shearing
Jack Armstrong Blues: Jack Teagarden

RECORDS
Gene Ammons (NYC, 16 January): *Around About 1am / Jug / Wow! / Blue And Sentimental* (NYC, 31 January): *New Blues Up And Down / The Thrill Of Your Kiss / If The Moon Turns Green* (Chicago, 3 May): *You Go To My Head / Baby Won't You Please Come Home / Happiness Is Just A Thing Called Joe / It's You Or No One / I'm Not The Kind Of Guy* (NYC, 29 June): *Ammons Boogie / Echo Chamber Blues / Sirocco / Fine And Foxy* (NYC, 14 August): *Hot Stuff / Them There Eyes / When The Saints Go Marching In / Archie* (NYC, 14 November): *Undecided / Until The Real Thing Comes Along / Because Of Rain / Charmaine*

Louis Armstrong All-Stars (Concert, Pasadena, 30 January): *Indiana / Baby It's Cold Outside / Just You, Just Me / The Hucklebuck / Honeysuckle Rose / My Monday Date / Way Down Yonder In New Orleans / You Can Depend On Me / That's A Plenty / Stardust / Big Daddy Blues* (LA, 23 April): *Unless / A Kiss To Build A Dream On / You're The Apple Of My Eye*

Count Basie (NYC, 10 April): *Howzit / Nails / Little Pony / Beaver Junction*

Sidney Bechet Hot Six (NYC, 5 November): *That's A Plenty / Blues My Naughty Sweetie / Ballin' The Jack / Avalon / Original Dixieland One-Step / There'll Be Some Changes Made*

Earl Bostic (NYC, 10 January): *Rocking And Reelin' / September Song / I Can't Give You Anything But Love / Flamingo* (NYC, 23 January): *Sleep / How Could I / Always / I'm Getting Sentimental Over You* (Cincinnatti, 4 October): *The Moon Is Low / Lover Come Back To Me / Chains Of Love / I Got Loaded*

Teddy Charles Trio (NYC, 10 November): *Teddy Cohen Trio (LP)*

Kenny Clarke (Paris, 6 April): *I'll Get You Yet / Lady Be Good / All The Things You Are / Klook Returns*

Arnett Cobb (NYC, 19 January): *Holy Smoke / Willow Weep For Me / Run For The Hills / Lunar Moon* (NYC, 7 August): *Cocktails For Two / Walkin' Home / Jumpin' The Blues / I'm In The Mood For Love* (NYC, 20 November): *Without A Word Of Warning / Whispering / Charmaine / Open House*

Miles Davis (NYC, 17 January): *Morpheus / Down / Blue Room* (NYC, 5 October): *Conception / Out Of The Blues / Denial / Bluing / Dig / My Old Flame / It's Only A Paper Moon*

Buddy de Franco (NYC, 19 February): *Out Of Nowhere / Dancing On The Ceiling / Rumpus Room* (NYC, 26 March): *Body And Soul / King Phillip Stomp / Polka Dots And Moonbeams* (NYC, 22 July): *Make Believe / Why Do I Love You? / Tiny's Blues* (NYC, 14 October): *The Closer You Are / Too Many Dreams / Swing Low, Sweet Chariot / Will You Still Be Mine?*

Sidney de Paris (NYC, 15 June): *Blue Note Stompers (LP)*

Duke Ellington (NYC, 10 May): *Fancy Dan / The Hawk Talks / VIP's Boogie / Jam With Sam / Monologue (Pretty and the Wolf)* (NYC, 24 May): *Ting-a-ling / Eighth Veil / Brown Betty* (NYC,8 August): *Deep Night / Please Be Kind / Smada / Rock skippin' At The Blue Note* (NYC, 7 December): *Bensonality / A Tone Parallel To Harlem* (NYC, 11 December): *Blues At Sundown / Duet / Controversial Suite / Azalea / Vagabonds / Something To Live For*

Ella Fitzgerald (NYC, 12 January): *Lonesome Gal / The Bean Bag Song* (NYC, 27 March): *Chesapeake And Ohio / Little Man In A Flying Saucer / Because Of Rain / The Hot Canary* (NYC, 24 May): *Even As You And I / If You Really Love Me / Love You Madly* (NYC, 26 June): *Mixed Emotions / Smooth Sailing / Come On-a My House* (NYC, 18 July): *It's My Own Darn Fault / I Don't Want To Take The Change / There Never Was A Baby / Give A Little, Get A Little* (LA, 26 December): *Baby Doll / What Does It Take / Lady Bug / Lazy Day*

Stan Getz (Stockholm, 23 March): *S'cool Boys / Ack Varmeland Du Skona / I'm Getting Sentimental Over You / Prelude To A Kiss / Night And Day* (Stockholm, 24 March): *Don't Be Afraid / Flamingo* (NYC, 15 August): *Melody Express / Yvette / Potter's Luck / The Song Is You / Wild Wood* (Boston, 28 October): *Stan Getz at Storyville Vols 1 & 2*

Terry Gibbs (NYC, February): *Loot To Boot / Out Of Nowhere / Between The Devil And The Deep Blue Sea / Somebody Loves Me / Mean To Me / Serenade In Blue / Tea For Two / You Go To My Head* (NYC, 28 August): *Swing's The Thing / Begin The Beguine / Serenade In Blue / I've Got You Under My Skin*

Dizzy Gillespie Sextet (Detroit, 1 March): *Love Me / We Love To Boogie / Tin Tin Deo / Birk's Works* (NYC, 16 April): *Lady Be Good / Love Me Pretty Baby / The Champ* (NYC, 9 August): *In A Mess / Schooldays / Swing Low Sweet Cadillac / The Bluest Blues* (NYC, 16 August): *Bopsie's Blues / I Couldn't Beat The Rag / They Can't Take That Away From Me* (NYC, 25 October): *Caravan / Nobody Knows The Trouble I've Seen / The Bluest Blues / Sunny Side Of The Street / Stardust / Time On My Hands*

Bennie Green (NYC, 27 June): *Groovin' At Birdland* (NYC, 5 October): *Green Junction / Flowing River / Whirl-a-licks / Bennie's Pennies / Tenor Sax Shuffle / Sugar Syrup*

Hampton Hawes (LA, 22 September): *Another Hairdo / Hamp's Paws / Hamp's Claws / Buzzy / What Is This Thing Called Love? / Bud's Blues / All The Things You Are / Blue Bird*

Billie Holiday (NYC, 29 April): *Be Fair To Me / Rocky Mountain Blues / Blue Turning Grey Over You / Detour Ahead* (Boston, 29 October): *Ain't Nobody's Bizness If I Do / You're Driving Me Crazy / Lover Come Back To Me / Miss Brown To You / Crazy He Calls Me / Billie's Blues / Lover Man / I Cover The Waterfront / Strange Fruit / All Of Me / He's Funny That Way*

Milt Jackson (NYC, 18 August): *Milt Meets Sid / D And E / Yesterdays / Between The Devil And The Deep Blue Sea* (NYC, 18 September): *Autumn Breeze / Bluesology / Round About Midnight / Moving Nicely*

Willis 'Gator' Jackson (NYC, 9 July): *Harlem Nocturne / Street Scene / Wine-o*

Ahmad Jamal (Chicago, 25 October): *The Surrey With The Fringe On Top / Will You Still Be Mine / Rica Pulpa / Perfidia*

Wynton Kelly (NYC, 28 July): *New Faces, New Sounds (LP)*

Shelly Manne (Chicago, 12 November): *Pooch McGooch / The Count On Rush Street / Back In Your Own Backyard / All Of Me*

Charlie Mariano (Boston, December): *Charlie Mariano Septet (LP)*

Mezz Mezzrow (Paris, 15 November): *Boogie Parisien / Clarinet Marmalade / Struttin' With Some Barbecue / The Sheik / Blues Jam / Revolutionary Blues No2 / Blues No One Dug / Mezzerola Blues / Drum Face / Blues Des Années*

James Moody (Stockholm, 23 January): *The Man I Love / Again / Embraceable You / How Deep Is The Ocean?* (Stockholm, 24 January): *Am I Blue? / I'll Get By / Love Walked In / Andrew Got Married / Moody's Bounce / Two Feathers* (Stockholm, 25 January): *Pennies From Heaven / Cherokee* (Paris, 13 July): *Aimer Comme Je T'aime / Bedelia / Les Feuilles Mortes / Si Jolie / Chanter Pour Moi / Une Boucle Blonde / Jackie My Little Cat / September Serenade* (Paris, 27 July): *More Than You Know / Deep Purple / I Cover The Waterfront / Moody's Mode / That's My Desire / Bootsie / Lover Come Back To Me / This Is Always* (NYC, September, October): *Serenade In Blue / Margie / Moody's Home / Wiggle Wag*

Thelonious Monk (NYC, 23 July): *Four In One / Criss Cross / Eronel / Straight No Chaser / Ask Me Now / Willow Weep For Me*

Gerry Mulligan (NYC, 21 September): *Mulligan plays Mulligan (LP)*

Red Norvo Trio (LA): *If I Had You / This Can't Be Love / Godchild / I'm Yours*

Kid Ory (Pomona, 5 May): *St Louis Blues / Ory's Boogie / Blues For Home*

Hot Lips Page (NYC, 7 March): *That's The One For Me / Let Me In* (NYC, 3 May): *I Want To Ride Like The Cowboy Do / Strike While The Iron's Hot / You're My Baby, You*

Charlie Parker (NYC, 17 January): *Au Privave / She Rote / KC Blues / Star Eyes* (NYC, 12 March): *My Little Suede Shoes / Un Poquito De Tu Amor / Tico Tico / Fiesta / Why Do I Love You?* (Boston, 12 April): *Happy Bird / Scrapple From The Apple / Lullaby In Rhythm / I Remember April* (NYC, 8 August): *Blues For Alice / Si Si / Swedish Schnapps / Back Home Blues / Lover Man*

1951

Leo Parker (Chicago, 7 July): *Candlelight Serenade / Hornet / Reed Rock / Leo's Blues*
Art Pepper/Shorty Rogers (LA,27 December):*Popo (LP)*
Oscar Peterson Trio (LA, 25 November): *It's Easy To Remember / Pooper / Love For Sale / Until The Real Thing Comes Along / Turtle Neck*
Oscar Peterson Quartet (LA, December): *Stompin' At The Savoy / Astaire Blues / Lady Be Good / Body And Soul / Second Astaire Blues / I Cover The Waterfront / Tea For Two*
Oscar Pettiford Octet (NYC, 28 April): *Swingin' Till The Girls Come Home / Bei Mir Bist Du Schoen*
Flip Phillips (NYC, 8 March): *Cheek To Cheek / Sorjordo / I've Got My Love To Keep Me Warm / Funky Blues / Indiana* (LA, 9 August): *Broadway / Wrap Your Troubles In Dreams / Apple Honey / Long Island Boogie / Stardust*
Bud Powell (NYC, February, solo): *Parisian Thoroughfare / Oblivion / Dusk In Sandi / Hallucinations / The Fruit / A Nightingale Sang / Just One Of Those Things / The Last Time I Saw Paris* (NYC, 1 May, trio): *Un Poco Loco / Over The Rainbow / Night In Tunisia / It Could Happen To You / Parisian Thoroughfare*
Red Rodney (NYC,9 September):*The New Sounds (LP)*
Shorty Rogers (LA, 8 October): *Modern Sounds (LP)*
Sonny Rollins (NYC, 17 January): *I Know* (NYC, 17 December): *Time On My Hands / Mambo Bounce / This Love Of Mine / Shadrack / Slow Boat To China / With A Song In My Heart / Scoops / Newk's Fadeaway*
George Shearing (NYC, 5 February): *I'll Never Smile Again / I'll Be Around / I Remember You / My Silent Love / If You Were The Only Girl In The World / Indian Summer / Quintessence / The Breeze And I* (NYC, 7 February): *They All Laughed / For Evans Sake / Loose Leaf / Minoration* (LA, 10 May): *To A Wild Rose / Midnight Mood / Brain Wave / Five O'Clock Whistle* (LA, 16 May): *Simplicity / We'll Be Together Again / So This Is Cuba* (NYC, 2 October): *Appreciation / Over The Rainbow / Thine Alone / Easy Livin' / Don't Blame Me* (NYC, 18 December): *I Hear Music / Ghost Of A Chance / Wait Till You See Her / Swedish Pastry / Lonely Moments / How High The Moon*
Zoot Sims (NYC, 14 August): *Trotting / It Had To Be You / Zoot Swings The Blues / Swingin' / East Of The Sun / I Wonder Who*
Sonny Stitt (NYC, 31 January): *Liza / Can't We Be*

Right: Jack Teagarden and Louis Armstrong visit Pee Wee Russell in a San Francisco hospital.
Below: Duke Ellington and his Orchestra with newcomer Louis Bellson on the drums.

Friends / The Thrill Of Your Kiss / If The Moon Turns Green (NYC, 1 February): *P.S. I Love You / This Can't Be Love* (Chicago, 3 May): *I Cover The Waterfront / Don't Worry 'Bout Me* (NYC, 14 August): *Down With It / For The Fat Man / Splinter / Confessin'*
Lennie Tristano (NYC, 30 October): *Ju-Ju / Passtime*
Charlie Ventura (NYC, 7 March): *Avalon / Confessin' / Bugle Call Rag / Rose Room / That Old Feeling* (NYC, 6 August): *There's No You / Perdido / Can't Get You Off My Mind / Lover / Yesterdays*
Charlie Ventura Big Four (NYC, 8 August): *After You've Gone / Love Is Just Around The Corner / Ol' Man River / Big Four Blues*

George Wallington (NYC, 21 November): *George Wallington Trio (LP)*
Ben Webster (LA, 27 December): *Randle's Island / Old Folks / King's Riff / You're My Thrill*
Kai Winding (NYC, 27 April): *Deep Purple / I'm Shooting High / You're Blasé / Moonshower* (NYC, 31 May): *Honey / Someone To Watch Over Me / Cheek To Cheek / Harlem Buffet* (NYC, 3 September): *Donna Lee / East Of The Sun*
Lester Young (NYC, 16 January): *Thou Swell / Undercover Girl Blues / Frenesi / Little Pee's Blues* (NYC, 8 March): *A Foggy Day / In A Little Spanish Town / Let's Fall In Love / Down 'n' Adam*

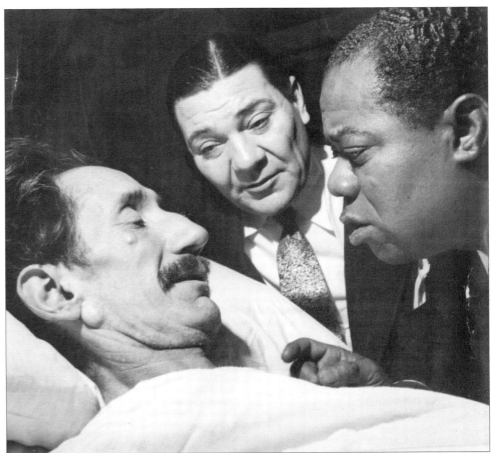

Photograph Courtesy: Hank O'Neal

Photograph Courtesy: *Rolf Dahlgren*

Gerry Mulligan (25) organises his piano-less quartet featuring Chet Baker (23).

Sauter-Finegan Band is formed.

Jazz at the Philharmonic (JATP) tours Europe for the first time (March/April)..

Charlie Ventura (36) and Gene Krupa (43) tour Japan.

John Lewis (32) forms Modern Jazz Quartet with Milt Jackson (29), Percy Heath (29) and Kenny Clarke (38).

Charlie Parker (32) plays in Los Angeles and San Francisco.

Louis Armstrong (51) enjoys a very successful European tour.

West Coast jazz thrives around Shorty Rogers (28).

Art Pepper (27) forms a quartet featuring Hampton Hawes (23).

Charlie Mingus (30) forms his own record label, Debut.

BIRTHS
Chris Brubeck (trombone/bass) 19 March
Bob Mover (alto sax) 22 March
Narada Michael Walden (drums) 23 April
Hilton Ruiz (piano) 29 May
John Lee (bass) 28 June
Ndugu Leon Chancler (drums) 1 July
George Lewis (trombone) 14 July
Dennis Wilson (trombone/arranger) 22 July
Mike Wolff (piano) 31 July
Frank Szabo (trumpet) 16 September
Ray Anderson (trombone) 16 October
Lee Ritenour (guitar) 1 November
Rocky White (drums) 3 November
Mark Dresser (bass) 26 November
Joe Lovano (tenor sax) 29 December

DEATHS
Henry Allen Sr (85) 11 January
Herb Morand (46) 23 February
Joe Eldridge (44) 5 March
Cassino Simpson (42) 27 March
John Kirby (43) 14 June *diabetes complications*
Fletcher Henderson (54) 29 December
Mel Stitzel (50) 31 December

BOOKS
B Bird: *Downbeat for a dirge*
C Brossard: *Who walk in darkness*
Thomas Cusack: *Jelly Roll Morton: An Essay in Discography*
J Hanley: *Hot Lips* (novel)
Rex Harris: *Jazz*
John Clellan Holmes: *Go* (novel)
Artie Shaw: *The Trouble with Cinderella*
H Sinclair: *Music out of Dixie*

FILMS
Symphonie sous le ciel (21mins): film record of Sidney Bechet's wedding
3-MINUTE SOUNDIES
I cried for you: Count Basie
Little girl: Nat King Cole
Route 66: Nat King Cole
Caravan: Duke Ellington
The Hawk Talks: Duke Ellington
The mooche: Duke Ellington
Mood Indigo: Duke Ellington
Sophisticated Lady: Duke Ellington
VIP's Boogie: Duke Ellington
Solitude: Duke Ellington with Jimmy Grissom
Hoboken Bounce: Slim Gaillard
Spanish melody swing: Slim Gaillard
If I could be with you: Helen Humes & Count Basie
American Patrol: Red Nichols
Battle Hymn of the Republic: Red Nichols
Basin Street Blues: Jack Teagarden
Dark Eyes: Jack Teagarden
Georgia: Jack Teagarden
Lover: Jack Teagarden
Nobody knows the trouble: Jack Teagarden
Rockin' Chair: Jack Teagarden
Stars fell on Alabama: Jack Teagarden
That's a plenty: Jack Teagarden
That's what makes the world: Jack Teagarden
Way down yonder in New Orleans: Jack Teagarden
Wheel of Fortune: Jack Teagarden
Wolverine Blues: Jack Teagarden
Perdido: Sarah Vaughan
These things I offer you: Sarah Vaughan

RECORDS
Gene Ammons (NYC, 24 March): *I'll Walk Alone / Old Folks / Beezy / Somewhere Along The Way* (Chicago, 18 November): *Just Chips / Street Of Dreams / The Beat / Travellin' Light*
Count Basie (NYC, 19 January): *New Basie Blues / Sure Thing / Why Not? / Fawncy Meeting You* (NYC, 25 January): *Jive At Five / No Name / Redhead / Every Tub* (NYC, 22-26 July): *Jack And Jill / Bread / There's A Small Hotel / Hob Nail Boogie / Basie Talks / Paradise Squat / Bunny / Tippin' On The QT / Blee Blop Blues / Be My Guest / Blues For Count And Oscar / Sent For You Yesterday / Goin' To Chicago*
Sidney Bechet/Lil Armstrong/Zutty Singleton (Paris, 7 October): *Limehouse Blues / Milenberg Joys / Rockin' Chair / Big Butter And Egg Man / My Melancholy Baby / Black Bottom / I've Got A Right To Sing The Blues / Blue Room / Stars Fell On Alabama / Lazy River*
Louis Bellson (LA, February): *Just Jazz All Stars* (LP)
Eddie Bert (NYC, 19 March): *Malshaja / First Day Of Spring / All The Things You Are / The Ming Tree*
Earl Bostic (Cincinnati, 7 April): *Velvet Sunset / Moonglow / Linger Awhile / Ain't Misbehavin'* (LA, 15 August): *You Go To My Head / The Hour Of Parting / Smoke Gets In Your Eyes / For You* (NYC, 17 December): *Sheik Of Araby / Cherokee / Steamwhistle Jump / The Song Is Ended*
Dave Brubeck Trio/Quintet (Boston, 22 October): *Jazz at Storyville* (LP)
Joe Carroll (NYC, 30 December): *I Was In The Mood / Pennies From Heaven / Got A Penny, Benny / Make It Right*
Benny Carter (LA, August): *The Formidable Benny Carter* (LP)
Teddy Charles (NYC, 23 December): *Teddy Charles Quartet* (LP)
Arnett Cobb (NYC, August): *Li'l Sonny / The Shy One / Someone To Watch Over Me / Linger Awhile*
Miles Davis (NYC, 9 May): *Dear Old Stockholm / Change It / Donna / Woodyn' You / Yesterdays / How Deep Is The Ocean?*
Buddy de Franco (NYC, 27 February): *Lady Be Good / Buddy's Blues / Gone With The Wind / Sweet Georgia Brown* (NYC, 3 March): *Get Happy / Cario / Pennywhistle Blues / Samai Shuffle* (SF, 30 June): *Just One Of Those Things / Street Of Dreams / Carioca / Easy Living* (SF, 23 July): *The Way You Look Tonight / Sophisticated Lady / Lover Come Back To Me / I Got It Bad*
Wilbur de Paris (NYC, 11 September): *And his Rampart Street Ramblers* (LP)
Lou Donaldson (NYC, 20 June / 19 November): *New Faces, New Sounds* (LP)
Roy Eldridge (NYC, 13 December): *Roy Eldridge with the Oscar Peterson Trio* (LP)
Duke Ellington (Seattle, 25 March): *Seattle Concert* (LP) (NYC, 30 June, 1 July, 10 August): *Ellington Uptown* (LP)
Tony Fruscella (NYC, 16 February): *PU Stomp / Darn That Dream / Tangerine / Loopadoo*
Stan Getz (Birdland, NYC, 5 April, 31 May, 16 August): *Stan Getz Quintet* (LP)
Terry Gibbs (NYC, 11 July): *T And S / You Don't Know What Love Is / Flying Home*
Dizzy Gillespie (Paris, 25 March): *Cocktails For Two / Cognac Blues / Moon Nocturne / Sabla-y-blu / Blue And Sentimental / Just One More Chance* (Paris, 27 March): *Hurry Home / Afro-Paris / Say Eh! / I Cover The Waterfront* (Paris, 6 April): *Sleepy Time*

Down South / Lullaby In Rhythm / Just Blues / Blues Marine / Blues Chante / Mama Blues / Ain't Misbehavin' / Summertime / Blue Moon (Paris, 11 April): *Cripple Crapple Crutch / Dizzy Song / Somebody Loves My Baby / She's Funny That Way / Wrap Your Troubles In Dreams / Sweet Lorraine / Everything Happens To Me / I Don't Know Why* (Chicago, 18 July): *Blue Skies / Umbrella Man / Pop's Confessin' / Oo-shoo-be-doo-be*
Benny Goodman (NYC, 29,30 July/22 October): *The New Benny Goodman Sextet* (LP)
Dexter Gordon/Wardell Gray (Pasadena, 2 February): *The Chase / Steeplechase* (LA, June): *The Rubyiat / I Hear You Knockin' / My Kinda Love / Jingle, Jangle, Jump / Citizen's Bop / Man With A Horn*
Wardell Gray (LA, 21 January): *April Skies / Bright Boy / Jackie / Farmer's Market / Sweet And Lovely / Lover Man* (LA, 9 September): *Live in Hollywood* (LP) (LA, 9 September): *Out of Nowhere* (LP)
Al Haig (LA, 6 September): *Taking A Chance On Love*
Bill Harris (NYC, 15 January): *You're Blasé / Bill Not Phil / D'Anjou / Imagination* (NYC, 10 March): *Gloomy Sunday / Bijou / Poggerini / Blackstrap*
Hampton Hawes (LA, December): *Hampton Hawes Quartet* (LP)
Billie Holiday (LA, 26 March): *East Of The Sun / Blue Moon / You Go To My Head / You Turned The Tables On Me / Easy To Love / These Foolish Things / I Only Have Eyes For You / Solitude* (LA, April): *Everything I Have Is Yours / Love For Sale / Moonglow / Tenderly / If The Moon Turns Green / Remember? / Autumn In New York* (NYC, 27 July): *My Man / Lover Come Back To Me / Stormy Weather / Yesterdays / He's Funny That Way / I Can't Face The Music*
Milt Jackson (NYC, April): *Softly As In A Morning Sunrise / Love Me Pretty Baby / Heart And Soul / True Blues* (NYC, 7 April): *Tahiti / Lillie / Bag's Groove / What's New? / Don't Get Around Much Anymore / On The Scene*
Ahmad Jamal (Chicago, 5 May): *Aki And Ukthay / Billy Boy / Ahmad's Blues / A Gal In Calico*
Howard McGhee (Guam, 17 January): *Howard McGhee Korean All-stars* (LP)
Shelly Manne (LA, 7 January): *It Don't Mean A Thing / Deep Purple / Princess Of Evil / Slightly Brightly*
Wingy Manone (LA, 5 March): *Awful Waffle Man / At Last* (LA, May): *Hello Out There, Hello / Just A Gigolo*
Warne Marsh (The Haig, LA, 23 December): *Live in Hollywood* (LP)
Gil Melle (NYC, February): *The Gears / Four Moons / Sunset Concerto / Mars*
Charlie Mingus (NYC, 12 April): *Precognition / Portrait / Extrasensory Perception* (NYC, 16 September): *Paris In Blue / Make Believe / Montage* (NYC, April): *Strings and Keys* (LP)
Modern Jazz Quartet (NYC, 22 December): *All The Things You Are / La Ronde / Vendome / Rose Of The Rio Grande*
Thelonious Monk Sextet (NYC, 30 May): *Skippy / Hornin' In / Carolina Moon / Let's Cool One / Sixteen / I'll Follow You*
Thelonious Monk Trio (NYC, 15 October): *Little Rootie Tootie / Sweet And Lovely / Bye Ya / Monk's Dream* (NYC, 18 October): *Trinkle Tinkle / These Foolish Things / Bemsha Swing / Reflections*
James Moody (NYC, 21 May): *Until The Real Thing Comes Along / Hey Jim / Moody's Theme / My Ideal* (NYC, 6 June): *The Bite / Poor Butterfly / St Louis Blues*
Gerry Mulligan Quartet (LA, 9 July): *Haig And Haig / She Didn't Say Yes* (LA, 16 August): *Bernie's Tune / Mullenium / Utter Chaos / Lullaby Of The Leaves* (LA, 2 September): *Line For Lyons / Carioca / My Funny Valentine / Bark For Barksdale / Utter Chaos* (LA, 15 October): *Nights At The Turntable / Frenesi / Aren't You Glad You're You / Walkin' Shoes / Soft Shoe / Freeway*
Vido Musso (LA, 6 January): *Cutting The Nut / Come Back To Sorrento / Grunions A-Running*
Herbie Nichols (NYC, 6 March): *Who's Blues? / 'S Wonderful / Nichols And Dimes / Walkin' Wig / My Lady Gingersnap / Blues Too Much / Cherokee*
Red Norvo Trio (LA, 1 July): *Tenderly* (LA, 16 October): *Skylark / I Remember You*

1952

Hot Lips Page (NYC, 21 March): *I Tin Whistle You / Tin Whistle Blues* (NYC, 26 June): *The Devil's Kiss / Casanova Cricket* (Paris, 29 October): *Last Call For Alcohol / Ruby / Old Paree / I Bongo You*

Charlie Parker (NYC, 22 January, with strings): *Temptation / Lover / Autumn In New York / Stella By Starlight* (NYC, 23 January): *Mama Inez / La Cucuracha / Estrellita / Begin The Beguine / La Paloma* (NYC, 30 December): *The Song Is You / Laird Baird / Kim / Cosmic Rays*

Leo Parker (Chicago, 15 November): *Leo's Boogie / Cool Leo / Hey Good Lookin'*

Art Pepper (LA, 12 February): *The Late Show (LP) / The Early Show (LP)* (LA, 4 March): *Brown Gold / These Foolish Things / Surf Ride / Holiday Flight* (LA, 8 October): *Chili Pepper / Suzy The Poodle / Everything Happens To Me / Tickle-Toe*

Oscar Peterson Trio (LA, 26 January): *Pastel Moods (LP)* (LA, October/November): *Oscar Peterson plays Duke Ellington (LP) / Oscar Peterson plays Cole Porter (LP)*

Oscar Peterson Quartet (LA, March): *Willow Weep For Me / Rough Ridin' / Just One Of Those Things / But Not For Me / Too Marvellous For Words / These Foolish Things / From This Moment On*

Oscar Pettiford Quartet (NYC, October): *Cello Again / Ah-Dee-Dong Blues / Sonny Boy / I'm Beginning To See The Light*

King Pleasure (NYC, 19 February): *Moody's Mood For Love / Exclamation Blues* (NYC, 12 December): *Red Top / Jumpin' With Symphony Sid*

Paul Quinichette (NYC, January): *Cross Fire* (NYC, February): *Sandstone / Prevue / No Time* (NYC, March): *Shad Roe / Paul's Bunion / Crew Cut / The Hook / Samie / I'll Always Be In Love With You / Sequel* (NYC, July): *Bustin' Suds / Let's Make It / PQ Blues / Bot, Bot* (NYC, December): *Green's Blues / You Belong To Me / Birdland Jump / Sleepy Time Gal*

Red Rodney (NYC, 22 May): *Dig This Menu Please / Red's Mambo / Honeysuckle Rose / Buckle My Shoe*

Frank Rosolino (Detroit, September): *Rubberneck / Mean To Me / Sweet And Lovely / Take Me Out To The Ball Game*

Annie Ross (NYC, 1 April): *Everytime / The Way You Look Tonight / I'm Beginning To Think You Care / Between The Devil And The Deep Blue Sea* (NYC, 9 October): *Twisted / Farmer's Market / The Time Was Right / Annie's Lament*

Howard Rumsey (LA, June): *Whispering / You Know I'm In Love With You / I Get A Kick Out Of You / Big Boy / More Big Boy* (LA, 22 July): *Out Of Somewhere / Big Girl / Swing Shift / Viva Zapata*

George Shearing (NYC, 10 July): *Love / It's Easy To Remember / I Wished On The Moon / Midnight*

Belongs To You (NYC, 17 July): *Night Flight / There's A Lull In My Life / When Lights Are Low / Lullaby Of Birdland* (LA, 12 September): *Moonlight In Vermont / The Love Nest / Basic English*

Horace Silver Trio (NYC, 9 October): *Safari / Thou Swell / Yeah / Horacescope* (NYC, 29 October): *Prelude To A Kiss / Ecaroh / Quicksilver / Knowledge Box*

Zoot Sims (NYC, 8 September): *Tangerine / Zoot Case / The Red Door / Morning Fun*

Johnny Smith (NYC, 11 March/April): *Johnny Smith Quintet (LP)*

Sonny Stitt (NYC, 25 February): *Cool Mambo / Sonny Sounds / Blue Mambo / Stitt's It* (NYC, May): *Why Do I Love You / Symphony Hall Swing*

Billy Taylor (NYC, 18 April): *To Be Or Not To Bop / Lonesome And Blue / Paradise* (NYC, 2 May): *Cuban Nightingale / Titoro / Makin' Whoopee / Moonlight Saving Time* (NYC, 11 July): *Three Little Words / Oscar Rides Again* (NYC, 18 November/ 10 December): *Billy Taylor Trio (LP)*

Lennie Tristano (Toronto, 17 July): *Live in Toronto (LP)*

Charlie Ventura (NYC, 22 December): *Charlie Ventura Quartet (LP)*

Kai Winding (NYC, 4 March): *I Could Write A Book / Speak Low / Carioca / The Boy Next Door*

Lester Young (NYC, 4 August): *Lester Young with the Oscar Peterson Trio (LP)*

Left: Gerry Mulligan's pianoless Quartet recording in Los Angeles. Gerry Mulligan (baritone sax), Bob Whitlock (bass), Chico Hamilton (drums) and Chet Baker (trumpet).

Above: Ben Webster, Charlie Parker and Johnny Hodges confer during a Los Angeles recording session for Verve in June.

Left: JATP concert in Stockholm in March. Lester Young solos, backed by Irving Ashby (guitar), Hank Jones (piano), Ray Brown (bass), Roy Eldridge (trumpet), Flip Phillips (tenor sax) and Max Roach (drums).

Lionel Hampton (40) tours Europe with big band featuring Clifford Brown (23), Jimmy Cleveland (27), Art Farmer (25), Quincy Jones (20) and Gigi Gryce (26).

Johnny Dankworth (26) forms big band.

The Dorsey Brothers, Tommy (48) and Jimmy (50) are reunited.

JATP in London for benefit show – first British visit by US jazz group for 16 years.

Gerry Mulligan (26) Quartet very popular, especially Chet Baker (24).

Charlie Parker (34) appears regularly at the Open Door in Greenwich Village.

Sam Woodyard (28) joins Duke Ellington Band.

BIRTHS
Bob Mintzer (saxes) 27 January
Ralph Penland (drums) 15 February
Danny Gottlieb (drums) 18 April
James Newton (flute) 1 May
Michael di Pasqua (drums) 4 May
Jon Burr (bass) 22 May
Gray Sargent (guitar) 10 June
Duffy Jackson (drums) 3 July
Jon Faddis (trumpet) 24 July
Jeff Hamilton (drums) 4 August
Bobby Watson (alto sax) 23 August
Azar Lawrence (tenor sax) 3 November
Chris Flory (guitar) 13 November
Earl McIntyre (trombone) 21 November
Lyle Mays (keyboards) 27 November
Chucho Merchan (bass) 25 December

DEATHS
Django Reinhardt (43) 16 May
Tiny Kahn (29) 19 August
Howdy Quicksell (52) 30 October
Larry Shields (60) 21 November

BOOKS
John R T Davies: *The Music of Thomas 'Fats' Waller*
E Gilbert: *The Hot and the Cool* (novel)

FILMS
The Dorsey Brothers Encore (16mins): music short
The Glenn Miller Story (116mins): bio featuring
Louis Armstrong and Gene Krupa

COMPOSITIONS
Duke Ellington: *Satin Doll*

RECORDS
Gene Ammons (Chicago, 15 April): *Red Top / Fuzzy / Stairway To The Stars / Jim Dawgs / Big Slam*
Chet Baker (LA,14,22 December): *Chet Baker Ensemble* (LA, 30,31 December): *Chet Baker and Strings*
Count Basie (NYC, 12 December): *Dance Session (LP)*
Sidney Bechet (Paris, 28 May): *Avec André Reweliotty Orchestre* (NYC, 25 August): *Blue Note Jazzmen* (LA, 30 October): *With Bob Scobey's Jazzmen* (Boston, 25 October): *Jazz at Storyville*
Eddie Bert (NYC, 10 June): *Little Train / Conversation Piece / Love Me Or Leave Me / Prelude To A Kiss* (NYC, 29 July): *Around Town / Broadway / Inter Woven / Kaleidoscope / Ripples / He Ain't Got Rhythm / Melting Pot / Cherokee*
Clifford Brown (NYC, 28 August): *Easy Livin' / Hymn To The Orient / Cherokee / Wail Bait / Minor Mood / Brownie Eyes* (Paris, 29 September): *Conception / All The Things You Are / I Cover The Waterfront / Goofin' With Me* (Paris, 8 October): *Minority / Salute To The Bandbox / Strictly Romantic / Baby* (Paris, 15 October): *Vogue LD179 (LP)*
Clifford Brown/Art Farmer Swedish All-Stars (Stockholm, 15 September): *Stockholm Sweetnin' / 'Cuse These Blues / Lover Come Back To Me / Falling In Love With Love*
Dave Brubeck Quartet (Oberlin College, 2 March): *Jazz at Oberlin (LP)* (College of Pacific, 14 December): *Jazz at College of the Pacific*
Teddy Charles (NYC, 19 January): *Teddy Charles Trio (LP)* (LA, 20 February): *Teddy Charles West Coasters (LP)* (LA, 21 August): *Collaboration/West (LP)*
Buck Clayton (NYC, 14,16 December): *Buck Clayton Jam Session*
Arnett Cobb (NYC, 14 June): *Congratulations To Someone / Poor Butterfly* (NYC, September): *Apple Wine / The Traveller*
Eddie Condon (NYC, 24 November): *Beale Street Blues / Riverboat Shuffle / Medley / Jam Session Blues*

Tadd Dameron (Atlantic City, 11 June): *Philly Joe Jones / Choose Now / Dial B For Beauty / Theme Of No Repeat*
Miles Davis (NYC,30 January): *Collector's Items (LP)* (NYC,19 February): *Miles and Horns (LP)* (NYC,20 April): *Miles Davis Vol 2* (NYC,19 May): *Blue Haze (LP)*
Lou Donaldson (NYC, 9 June): *Lou Donaldson with Clifford Brown*
Kenny Dorham (NYC, 15 December): *Kenny Dorham Quintet (LP)*
Harry Edison (LA): *The Inventive Mr Edison (LP)* (LA, 1 July): *Sweets at the Haig (LP)*
Roy Eldridge (June): *Dale's Wail (LP)*
Duke Ellington Trio (LA, 13,14 April): *Duke meets Ellington (LP)*
Tal Farlow (NYC, 8 June): *Early Tal (LP)* (NYC, 4 November): *Tal Farlow Quartet (LP)*
Art Farmer (NYC, 2 July): *Work Of Art / The Little Bandmaster / Mau Mau / Up In Quincy's Room* (Paris, 28 September): *Strike Up The Band* (Paris, 10 October): *Serenade To Sonny*
Frank Foster: *Jazz Studio One (LP)*
Stan Getz (NYC, 4 May): *Cool Mix / Rustic Hop / Have You Met Miss Jones? / Erudition* (LA, 30 July, 22 August): *Interpretations of Stan Getz (LP)*
Dizzy Gillespie (Paris, 9 February): *Concert at the Salle Pleyel (LP)* (LA, 9 December): *Diz & Getz (LP)*
Wardell Gray (LA, 20 February): *The Man I Love / Lavonne / So Long, Broadway / Paul's Cause* (Chicago, 19 January): *Sweetmouth / Oscar's Blues / Dat's It / Hey There*
Bennie Green (NYC, 23 July): *Blues In Lament / Blow Your Horn / Expense Account / Takin' My Time*
Ted Heath (London, 12 April): *At the London Palladium (LP)*
Elmo Hope (NYC, May, June): *Elmo Hope Trio (LP)*
JJ Johnson (NYC, 22 June): *The Eminent Jay Jay Johnson (LP)*
Barney Kessel (LA, 14 November, 19 December): *Easy Like (LP)*

Lee Konitz (LA, 25, 30 January, 1 February): *Lee Konitz plays with the Gerry Mulligan Quartet (LP)*
Peggy Lee (NYC, 30 April, 1,4 May): *Black Coffee (LP)*
Shelly Manne (LA, 6 April, 20 July): *West Coast Sound (LP)*
Wingy Manone (NYC, 5 August): *Vaya Con Dios / Where Is Your Heart?*
Charlie Mariano (NYC, 27 January): *Charlie Mariano Boston All-Stars (LP)*
Gil Melle (NYC, March): *Gil Melle Quintet (LP)*
Charlie Mingus (NYC, 27 October): *Pink Topsy / Miss Bliss / Eclipse / Blue Tide*
Modern Jazz Quartet (NYC, 25 June): *Queen's Fancy / Delaunay's Dilemma / Autumn In New York / But Not For Me*
Thelonious Monk (NYC, 13 November): *Let's Call This / Think Of One / Friday The 13th*
James Moody (NYC, 15 June): *James Moody Story / And Now Moody Speaks / Feeling Low / Wail Bait*
Oscar Moore (LA, September): *Sonny Boy / Beautiful Moons Ago / A Foggy Day / Oscar's Blues*
Gerry Mulligan Tentette (LA, 29,31 January): *Walkin' Shoes (LP)* (LA, 7 May): *The Tentette*
Gerry Mulligan Quartet (LA, 24 February): *Lee Konitz with Gerry Mulligan Quartet* (LA, 27,29,30 April): *The Gerry Mulligan Quartet*
Red Norvo Trio (NYC, 21 April): *Spider's Webb / Lover Come Back To Me / Dancing On The Ceiling* (NYC, 23 April): *Strike Up The Band / Good Bait*
Hot Lips Page (NYC, 4 February): *What Shall I Do? / The Cadillac Song / Jungle King / Ain't Nothing Wrong Baby* (Port Monmouth, 24 May, with Marian McPartland Trio): *St Louis Blues / Sunny Side Of The Street / St James Infirmary / The Sheik Of Araby*
Charlie Parker (NYC, 22 May): *In The Still Of The Night / Old Folks / If I Love Again* (NYC, 4 August): *Chi Chi / I Remember You / Now's The Time / Confirmation*
Leo Parker (Chicago, 10 August): *Anything Can Happen / Tippin' Lightly / Blue Sails / Smoke Gets In Your Eyes*
Dave Pell (LA, 25,29 April): *The Dave Pell Octet plays Irving Berlin* (LA): *The Dave Pell Octet plays Burke & Van Heusen*
Art Pepper (LA,30 March, 1 April): *Deep Purple / Bluebird / 'S Wonderful / Pennies From heaven* (LA, 31 May): *Art Pepper with the Sonny Clark Trio (LP)*
Oscar Peterson Trio (NYC, February): *Tenderly* (LA, 21 May): *Oscar Peterson Sings*
Oscar Pettiford (LA, June): *Words / Monti Cello / In A Cello Mood / Blues In The Closet* (NYC, 29 December): *The new Oscar Pettiford Sextet (LP)*
King Pleasure (NYC, 19 September): *Sometimes I'm*

Photograph Courtesy: Max Jones

1953

Happy / This Is Always (NYC, 24 December): Parker's Mood / What Can I Say Dear?

Bud Powell Trio (Washington, 5 April): Inner Fires (NYC,14 August): The Amazing Bud Powell Vol 2 (LP)

Mel Powell (NYC, 30 December): It's Been So Long / I Must Have That Man / You're Lucky To Me / 'S Wonderful

Andre Previn (LA, 24 June): Andre Previn plays Fats Waller (LP)

Jimmy Raney (NYC, 23 April): Signal / Lee / Round Midnight / Motion

Max Roach (NYC, 10 April): Orientation / Mobleyzation / Glow Worm / Sfax (NYC, 21 April): Just One Of Those Things / Cou Manchi-Cou / Kismet / Drum Conversation / Chi Chi / I'm A Fool To Want You

Shorty Rogers (LA, 26 March, 2 April): Cool and Crazy

Sonny Rollins with MJQ (NYC, 7 October): In A Sentimental Mood / The Stopper / Almost Like Being In Love / No Moe

Frank Rosolino (Stockholm, 23 August): Monotones / Don't Blame Me

Annie Ross (Stockholm, 14 September): The Song Is You / Jackie

Howard Rumsey (LA, 21 February, 15 May): Sunday Jazz à la Lighthouse (LA, 13 September): At Last! Miles Davis and the Lighthouse All-Stars (LP)

Sal Salvador (NYC, 24 December): Sal Salvador Quartet/Quintet (LP)

Tony Scott (NYC, 5 February): Katz Meow / After After Hours / I Never Knew / Away We Go (NYC, 13 April): Bob's Blob / Cupcake (NYC, 20 June): The Blues Have Got Me / Time To Go / Opus No One

George Shearing (LA, 12 March): I Hear A Rhapsody / Spring Is Here / The Lady Is A Tramp / Body And Soul (LA, 13 March): Hallelujah / Undecided / Mood For Milt / Wrap Your Troubles In Drums (LA, 15 April): Love Is Here To Stay / Easy To Love / Love Is Just Around The Corner / Point And counterpoint (NYC, 2 September). Tempi-di Concerto / Ill Wind / A Sinner Kissed An Angel

Horace Silver (NYC, 23 October): Horace Silver Trio/Spotlight on Drums (LP)

Zoot Sims (NYC, 23 June): There I've Said It Again /

Jaguar / Dream / Baby Please Come On Home (Paris, 18 November): Zoot Sims Sextet (LP)

Johnny Smith (NYC, 5 June): Ramona / Limelight (NYC, 6 June): My Funny Valentine (NYC, July): Cavu / I'll Be Around (NYC, August): Yesterdays / Cherokee

Sonny Stitt (NYC): SOS / I Can't Get Started / Jaws / Marchin'

Billy Taylor (NYC, 7 May): Cross Section (LP) (NYC, 2 November, 29 December): Billy Taylor Trio Volume 2 (LP)

Phil Urso (NYC, 14 April): Little Pres / Three Little Words / Don't Take Your Love From Me / She's Funny That Way

George Wallington (Paris, 24 September): A Day in Paris (LP)

Chuck Wayne (NYC, 13 April): Chuck Wayne Quintet (LP)

Ben Webster (NYC, 21 May): Cottontail / Danny Boy / Bounce blues (LA, 8 December): That's All / Pennies From Heaven / Tenderly / Jive At Six / Don't Get Around Much Anymore

Mary Lou Williams (Paris, 2 December): Mary Lou Williams & Don Byas

Kai Winding (NYC, June): Hot Blues / Perdido / That's A Plenty / Get Happy

Lester Young (NYC, 11 December): Lester Young Quintet (LP)

Photograph: Francis Wolff Courtesy: Moseic Images

Right: Miles Davis recording for Blue Note with (l to r) Jimmy Heath, Percy Heath and Gil Coggins.
Left: Louis Armstrong & the Allstars on the set of *The Glenn Miller Story* with James Stewart.
Below: Dizzy Gillespie and Charlie Parker on stage at Massey Hall, Toronto, with Bud Powell, Charlie Mingus and Max Roach (**May**).

Photograph Courtesy: Duncan P Schiedt

Count Basie (50) and Woody Herman (41) make first European tours.

Jazz Club USA tours Europe with Billie Holiday (39), Buddy de Franco (31), Red Norvo (46) and Beryl Booker (32).

JJ Johnson (30) and Kai Winding (32) form quintet.

First Newport Jazz Festival (17 July).

Joe Williams (36) joins Count Basie Orchestra on Christmas Day.

Sonny Rollins (25) records *Oleo* and *Airegin*.

Charlie Parker (34) swallows iodine in suicide attempt, is admitted to Bellevue Hospital.

Norman Granz records Art Tatum (44) in a marathon session, later issuing 5 albums from the date.

Gerry Mulligan (27) and Quartet (including Bob Brookmeyer), Thelonious Monk (33) and Jonah Jones (44) star at the Paris Jazz Festival.

Charlie Mingus (32) begins his famous Jazz Workshop.

BIRTHS
Ricky Ford (tenor sax) 4 March
Brian Torff (bass) 16 March
Peter Erskine (drums) 5 June
Al Di Meola (guitar) 22 July
Pat Metheny (guitar) 12 August
Scott Hamilton (tenor sax) 12 September
Earl Klugh (guitar) 16 September
Jay Hoggard (vibes) 24 September
Patrice Rushen (piano) 30 September

DEATHS
Frankie Newton (48) 11 March
Garland Wilson (44) 31 May
Elmer James (44) 25 July
Brad Gowans (50) 8 September *cancer*
Rudy Williams (45) September *fishing boat accident*
Hot Lips Page (46) 5 November *heart attack*
Dink Johnson (62) 29 November
Oscar Celestin (70) 15 December
Lil Green (32)

BOOKS
B H Aaslund: *The Wax Works of Duke Ellington*
Louis Armstrong: *Satchmo: my life in New Orleans*
William Claxton: *Jazz West Coast*
W Gwinn: *Jazz Bum* (novel)
Adrian Heerkens: *Jazz: Picture Encyclopaedia*
Langston Hughes: *The First Book of Jazz*
J Lucas: *Basic Jazz on Long Play*
Humphrey Lyttelton: *I play as I please*
Alan P Merriam & Robert J Brenford: *A Bibliography of Jazz*
Frederic Ramsey: *A guide to Long Play Jazz Records*
Robert Reisner: *The Literature of Jazz*
T Rieman: *Vamp till ready*

FILMS
Carmen Jones (103mins): feature film with Pearl Bailey, Max Roach
Jazz Dance (22mins): filmed jazz session with Jimmy McPartland group

RECORDS
Toshiko Akiyoshi (Tokyo): *Amazing Toshiko Akiyoshi* (Boston): *The Toshiko Trio (LP)*
Laurindo Almeida (LA, 15,22 April): *Laurindo Almeida Quartet with Bud Shank*
Gene Ammons (NYC, 26 November): *Sock / What I Say / Count Your Blessings / Cara Mia*
Louis Armstrong (Chicago, 12-14 July): *Plays WC Handy*
Chet Baker (Ann Arbor, 9 May): *Jazz at Ann Arbor*
Count Basie (NYC, 16,17 August): *The Band of Distinction (LP) / Dance Session No2 (LP)*
Sidney Bechet (Paris, 8 December): *At Olympia*
Louis Bellson (NYC, March): *The Amazing Artistry of Louis Bellson (LP)*
Art Blakey (NYC, 21,22 February): *A night at Birdland Vols 1&2 (LPs)*
Ruby Braff (Boston, 9 June): *Ruby Braff All-Stars (LP)* (NYC, October): *Ruby Braff Quartet (LP)*
Clifford Brown/Max Roach (LA, 2 August): *Delilah / Darn That Dream / Parisian Thoroughfare* (LA, 3 August): *Jordu / Clifford's Fantasy / Sweet Clifford /*

Ghost Of A Chance (LA, 6 August): *Joy Spring / Mildama / These Foolish Things / Daahoud* (LA, 10 August): *Stompin' At The Savoy / I Get A Kick Out Of You / I'll String Along*
Clifford Brown All-Stars (LA, 11 August): *Coronado / You Go To My Head / Caravan / The Boss Man / Autumn in New York* (LA, 13 August): *Blueberry Hill / Bones For Jones / Gone With The Wind / Tiny Capers / Bones For Zoot*
Dave Brubeck Quartet (Universities of Michigan & Ohio, March, April): *Jazz goes to College (LP)* (NYC, 12, 13, 14 October): *At Basin Street (LP)*
Conte Candoli (LA, 20 November): *Sincerely Conte (LP)*
Benny Carter (NYC, 14 September): *New Jazz Sounds (LP)*
Serge Chaloff (Boston, September): *The Fable of Mabel (LP)*
Teddy Charles/Bob Brookmeyer (NYC, 6 January): *The dual role of Bob Brookmeyer (LP)*
Kenny Clarke (LA, 1 November): *Kenny Clarke All-Stars (LP)*
Buck Clayton (NYC, 31 March): *Buck Clayton Band (LP)* (NYC, 1 July): *Buck meets Ruby (LP)* (NYC, 31 March, 13 August): *Jumpin' at the Woodside (LP)*
Al Cohn (NYC, 29 July): *Broadway 1954 (LP)* (NYC, 26 October, 22, 23 December): *Mr Music (LP)*
Chris Connor (NYC, 9,11 August): *Lullaby of Birdland (LP)*
Bob Cooper (LA, 7,14 May/30 July): *Quintet/Sextet*
Miles Davis (NYC, 6 March): *Miles Davis Volume 2* (NYC, 15 March, 3, 29 April): *Walkin'* (NYC, 29 June, 24 December): *Bags' Groove (LP)*
Bill de Arango (NYC, March): *Bill de Arango*
Buddy de Franco (LA, September): *Buddy de Franco & Oscar Peterson play George Gershwin (LP)*
Paul Desmond (SF, October/November): *Desmond*
Vic Dickenson (NYC, 29 November): *Vic Dickenson Septet (LP)*
Lou Donaldson (NYC, 21 August): *Lou Donaldson Sextet (LP)*
Tal Farlow (NYC, 11 April): *The Tal Farlow Album (LP)* (NYC, 15 November): *Autumn in New York (LP)*
Art Farmer (NYC, 20 January): *Art Farmer Quintet (LP)* (NYC, 19 May): *When Farmer met Gryce (LP)* (NYC, 7 June): *Art Farmer Septet (LP)* (NYC, 9 November): *Early Art (LP)*
Frank Foster (NYC, 5 May): *New Faces, New Sounds (LP)*
Stan Getz (LA, 8,9 November): *Getz at the Shrine (LP)*
Dizzy Gillespie (NYC, 24 May, 3 June): *Manteca (LP)*
Dizzy Gillespie/Roy Eldridge (NYC, 29 October): *Roy and Diz (LP)*
Bennie Green (NYC, 13 April): *I Wanna Blow / People Will Say We're In Love / I May Be Wrong / Rhumblues*
Al Haig (NYC, 13 March): *The Al Haig Trio & Quintet*
Lionel Hampton (NYC, September): *The High and the Mighty*
Coleman Hawkins (NYC, 8 November): *Jazz Tones (LP)*
Johnny Hodges (NYC, 5 August): *Used to be Duke*
Billie Holiday (NYC, 14 April): *I Cried For You / How Deep Is The Ocean / What A Little Moonlight Can Do* (LA, 3 September): *Too Marvellous For Words / I Thought About You / Love Me Or Leave Me / Willow Weep For Me / Stormy Blues*
Elmo Hope (NYC, 9 May): *Elmo Hope Quintet (LP)*

Milt Jackson (NYC, 16 June): *Milt Jackson Quintet*
JJ Johnson/Kai Winding (NYC, 24,26 August): *Jay & Kai (LP)* (NYC, 17 October): *At Birdland (LP)*
Barney Kessel (LA, 4 June, 1 July): *Plays Standards*
Gene Krupa (NYC, January): *The Rocking Mr Krupa*
Gene Krupa/Buddy Rich (NYC): *Krupa and Rich*
Mundell Lowe (NYC, 12 February, 8,29 March): *Mundell Lowe Septet (LP)*
Shelly Manne (LA, 18 December 1953, 17 May): *West Coast Sound Vol 1* (LA, 10,14 September): *The Three and the Two (LP)*
Gil Melle (NYC): *New Faces, New Sounds (LP)*
Charlie Mingus (NYC, 31 October): *Jazz Composers Workshop (LP)* (NYC, December): *The Jazz Experiments of Charlie Mingus (LP)*
Modern Jazz Quartet (NYC, 23 December): *Django / One Bass Hit / Milano*
Thelonious Monk (NYC, 11 May): *Wee See / Smoke Gets In Your Eyes / Locomotive / Hackensack* (Paris, 7 June): *Portrait of an Ermite (LP)* (NYC, 22 September): *Work (LP)*
James Moody (NYC, 8 January, 12 April): *Moody's Workshop (LP)*
Frank Morgan (LA): *Gene Norman presents Frank Morgan (LP)*
Sam Most (NYC, 3 December): *Sam Most Sextet (LP)*
Gerry Mulligan (Paris, Salle Pleyel, 1-4 June): *The Fabulous Gerry Mulligan Quartet (LP)* (California, 12 November, 14 December): *California Concerts*
Boots Mussulli (Boston, 9 June): *The Fable of Mabel (LP)* (Boston, 14 June / NYC, 7 November): *Little Man (LP)*
Joe Newman (NYC, 9 March): *Joe Newman and his Band (LP)* (Boston, September): *Joe Newman and the Boys in the Band (LP)* (NYC): *Joe Newman Sextet (LP)*
Lennie Niehaus (LA, 2,9 July): *Lennie Niehaus Quintet (LP)* (LA, 23 August): *Zounds! The Octet (LP)*
Charlie Parker (NYC, 31 March): *I Get A Kick Out Of You / Just One Of Those Things / My Heart Belongs To Daddy / I've Got You Under My Skin* (NYC, 10 December): *Love For Sale / I Love Paris*
Art Pepper (LA, 25 August): *Art Pepper Quintet (LP)*
Oscar Peterson (August, September): *Plays Harold Arlen (LP) / Plays Jimmy McHugh (LP)*
Flip Phillips (LA, August): *Rock with Flip (LP)*
King Pleasure (NYC, 7 December): *Don't Get Scared / I'm Gone / You're Crying / Funk Junction*
Bud Powell (NYC, June): *Bud Powell's Moods (LP)*
Mel Powell (NYC, 17 August): *Border Line (LP)* (NYC, 24 August): *Thingamajig (LP)* (NYC, 1 December): *Bandstand (LP)*
Paul Quinichette *Moods (LP)*
Jimmy Raney (Paris, February): *Jimmy Raney Quartet (LP)* (Paris, 10 February): *Visits Paris (LP)*
Shorty Rogers (LA, 2,9 February, 3 March): *Shorty courts the Count (LP)*
Sonny Rollins (NYC, 18 August, 25 October): *Moving Out (LP)*
Frank Rosolino (LA, 12,16 March, 6 November): *Frank Rosolino Quintet (LP)*
Jimmy Rowles (LA, September): *Jimmy Rowles Trio (LP)*
Jimmy Rushing (NYC): *Goin' to Chicago (LP)*
Sal Salvador (NYC, 21 July, 8,9 October): *Boo Boo de Doop (LP)*
Bud Shank (LA, March): *Bud Shank/Shorty Rogers Quintet (LP)* (LA, 3 April, 22 June): *Bud Shank and Three Trombones (LP)*
George Shearing (LA, 25,26,28 March): *Get Off My Bach / Stranger In Paradise / I've Never Been In Love Before / Minor Trouble / Basso Profundo / Mambo Inn / Drums Negrita / Cool Mambo*
Horace Silver (NYC, 13 November): *Horace Silver Quintet Volume 1 (LP)*
Zoot Sims (LA, 16 June): *Howdy Podner / Toot No2 / Indian Summer / What's New?*
Sonny Stitt (Boston, 11 February): *Super Stitt! Volumes 1&2 (LPs)*
Art Tatum/Benny Carter (LA, July): *Makin' Whoopee (LP)*
Billy Taylor (NYC, 7 September): *Billy Taylor Trio with Candido (LP)* (NYC, 17 December): *Billy Taylor at Town Hall (LP)*
Sir Charles Thompson (NYC, 22 January): *Sir Charles Thompson Quartet (LP)*
Cal Tjader (NYC, 6,25 March): *Ritmo Caliente (LP)* (SF, August, September): *Tjader plays Mambo (LP)*

1954

Sarah Vaughan (NYC, 2 April): *Swingin' Easy*
(NYC, 18 December): *Sarah Vaughan*
Dinah Washington (LA, 14 August): *Dinah Jams*
Julius Watkins (NYC, August): *Julius Watkins Sextet (LP)*
Frank Wess (NYC, 8 May): *Wess Point (LP)* (NYC, 12 August): *Frank Wess Sextet (LP)*
Randy Weston (NYC, 27 April): *Cole Porter – in a modern mood (LP)*
Claude Williamson (LA, 26,29 June): *Salute to Bud (LP)*
Phil Woods (NYC, 12 October): *Pot Pie / Open Door / Robin's Bobbin' / Mad About The Girl*
Lester Young (NYC, 10 December): *It don't mean a thing if it ain't got that swing*

Above right: The Count Basie Orchestra with Gus Johnson (drums), Thad Jones (trumpet) and Frank Wess (tenor sax).
Right: Illinois Jacquet, Coleman Hawkins and Sarah Vaughan performing at a USAAF base in England
Below: Billie Holiday in London

Photograph Courtesy: Max Jones

Photograph Courtesy: Max Jones

Photograph Courtesy: Max Jones

Photograph Courtesy: Max Jones

Above: Clifford Brown recording in Los Angeles.
Right: Clifford Brown drops in on the Miles Davis recording session for Blue Note on 6 March. Horace Silver is on piano.

Photograph: *Francis Wolff* Courtesy: *Mosaic Images*

1955

Duke Ellington (56) and his Orchestra and Symphony of the Air play '*Night Creature*' at Carnegie Hall. Johnny Hodges (49) rejoins the band.

Cannonball Adderley (26) makes his record debut in New York.

The Dorsey Brothers star in their own weekly TV show.

Stan Kenton (43) in 'Music 55' TV show.

Art Blakey (36) leads the Jazz Messengers including Horace Silver (27) and Kenny Dorham (31).

Miles Davis (29) is a big hit at the 2nd Newport Jazz Festival in July and forms a quintet including Sonny Rollins (26).

Connie Kay (28) replaces Kenny Clarke (41) in the Modern Jazz Quartet.

Clifford Brown (24) records '*Joy Spring*'.

Teo Macero (30) incorporates electronic music techniques in his Third Stream work '*Sounds of May*'.

Charlie Parker (34) plays his last engagement at Birdland on 4 & 5 March. Dies on 12 March of lobar pneumonia. Memorial Concert is held at Carnegie Hall.

BIRTHS
Marilyn Mazur (percussion) 8 January
David Murray (tenor sax) 19 February
Bheki Mseleku (piano/saxes) 10 March
Danny Brubeck (drums) 4 May
Nat Adderley Jr (piano) 22 May
Brian Grice (drums) 13 August
Mulgrew Miller (piano) 13 August
Kenny Kirkland (piano) 28 September
Tony Dumas (bass) 1 October
Adam Nussbaum (drums) 29 November
Dan Barrett (trombone) 14 December
Pheeroan AkLaff (drums)

DEATHS
Buck Washington (51) 31 January
Charlie Parker (34) 12 March
Sara Martin (70) 24 May
Wardell Gray (34) 25 May
Bob Gordon (26) 28 August *auto accident*
Dick Twardzik (24) 21 October *heroin overdose*
Junior Raglin (38) 10 November
James P Johnson (64) 17 November
Charles 'Cow Cow' Davenport (61) 2 December
Cyrus St Clair (65)

BOOKS
S. Allen: *Bop Fables*
Walter Allen & Brian Rust: *King Joe Oliver*
Stephen Bedwell: *A Glenn Miller Discography and Biography*
Arna Bontemps: *Lonesome Boy* (novel)
William Broonzy & Yannick Bruynoghe: *Big Bill Blues*
Leonard Feather: *The Encyclopaedia of Jazz*
Langston Hughes: *Famous Negro Music Makers*
Orrin Keepnews & B. Grauer: *Pictorial History of Jazz*
Albert McCarthy: *Jazzbook 1955*
Nat Shapiro & Nat Hentoff: *Hear me talkin' to ya*
S. Whitmore: *Solo* (novel)

FILMS
The Benny Goodman Story (116mins): feature bio
Lionel Hampton & Herb Jeffries (15mins): music short
Harlem Jazz Festival (51mins): musical revue with Lionel Hampton, Sarah Vaughan, Count Basie, Dinah Washington
The Man with a Golden Arm (118mins): Frank Sinatra as jazz drummer with a habit. Shorty Rogers and Shelly Manne appear.
Momma don't allow (22mins): an evening at Wood Green Jazz Club featuring Chris Barber's Band
The Nat 'King' Cole musical story (18mins): featurette
Pete Kelly's Blues (95mins): jazz feature movie with appearance by Ella Fitzgerald
Rock'n'roll revue (65mins): revue of jazz items by Lionel Hampton, Duke Ellington, Nat 'King' Cole, Joe Turner, Dinah Washington

RECORDS
Cannonball Adderley (NYC, 14 July): *The Cannonball Adderley Quintet* (NYC, 21,29 July, 5 August): *Julian 'Cannonball' Adderley*
Nat Adderley (NYC, 26 July): *That's Nat* (NYC, 6 September): *Introducing Nat Adderley*
Tony Aless (NYC, July): *Long Island Suite*
Gene Ammons (NYC, 15 June): *Gene Ammons All-Stars*
Louis Armstrong All-Stars (LA, 21 January): *At the Crescendo Volumes 1&2* (NYC, 26,27 April/3 May): *Plays Fats Waller* (Holland & Italy): *Ambassador Satch*
Chet Baker (LA, 28 February/7 March): *Sings & Plays with Strings*
Count Basie (NYC, 8 May, August): *Count Basie Swings, Joe Williams Sings* (LP)
Eddie Bert (NYC, 31 May): *Eddie Bert with the Hank Jones Trio* (NYC, 22 June, 1 September): *Encore*
Art Blakey (NYC, 11,23 November): *The Jazz Messengers at the Cafe Bohemia Volumes 1 &2*
Ruby Braff/Ellis Larkins (NYC, 17 February): *Ruby Braff and Ellis Larkins* (NYC, 14 October): *Two by Two*
Ruby Braff (NYC, 17,18 March): *Holiday in Braff* (NYC, 25 April): *The Ruby Braff All-Stars* (NYC, 17 October): *The Ruby Braff Special: Hey Ruby!*
Bob Brookmeyer (NYC, 30 June): *The Dual Role of Bob Brookmeyer*
Clifford Brown (NYC, 18,19,20 January): *Clifford Brown with Strings*
Clifford Brown/Max Roach (NYC, 23,24,25 February): *Study in Brown*
Lawrence Brown *Slide Trombone*
Ralph Burns (NYC, 29 September, 6 October): *Jazz Studio No5*
Donald Byrd (Detroit, 23 August): *Donald Byrd* (NYC, 29 September): *Long Green* (NYC, 3 November): *And then some* (Massachusetts, 2 December): *Byrd's Eye View*
Billy Byers (NYC, 9,23,30 December): *Jazz Workshop*
Conte Candoli (LA, 16,17 August): *West Coast Wailers*
Serge Chaloff (Boston, 4,5 April): *Boston Blow Up*
Teddy Charles (NYC, 6 January): *Evolution*
Kenny Clarke (NYC, August): *Bohemia After Dark*
Buck Clayton (NYC, 18,19,23 August): *Cat meets Chick* (NYC, 15 March): *Buck Clayton Jam Session*
Jimmy Cleveland (NYC, 4,12 August, 19 November): *Hear ye!*
Al Cohn (NYC, 9,14,16 May): *Jazz Workshop* (NYC, 24,25 June): *The Brothers*
Bob Cooper (LA, 26 April/13,14 June): *Bob Cooper Septet*
Sonny Criss (LA): *Criss Cross*
Miles Davis (NYC, 7 June): *The Musings of Miles* (NYC, 9 July): *Blue Moods* (NYC, 5 August): *Milt & Miles* (NYC, 16 November): *Miles*
Buddy de Franco: *Sweet and Lovely* (LA): *Cooking the Blues*
Lou Donaldson (NYC, 27 January): *Wailing with Lou*
Kenny Dorham (NYC, 30 January, 29 March): *Afro-Cuban*
Roy Eldridge/Benny Carter (LA, 9 January): *The Urbane Jazz of Roy Eldridge & Benny Carter*
Duke Ellington (Chicago, 17,18 May): *Ellington Showcase*
Don Elliott (LA): *Doubles in Jazz*
Tal Farlow (NYC): *Fascinatin' Rhythm* (NYC): *A Recital by Tal Farlow* (NYC): *The Tal Farlow Album* (NYC): *Interpretations by Tal Farlow*

Art Farmer (NYC, 21 October): *Evening in Casablanca*
Bud Freeman (NYC, July): *Bud Freeman*
Four Freshmen (LA): *Four Freshmen and Five Trombones*
Tony Fruscella (NYC, March, April): *Tony Fruscella*
Erroll Garner (Carmel, 19 September): *Concert by the Sea*
Herb Geller (LA, 19,22 August): *Herb Geller Sextet*
Stan Getz (LA, 15,19 August): *West Coast Jazz*
Terry Gibbs (NYC, 19,31 October): *Vibes on Velvet*
Dizzy Gillespie (Washington, 13 March): *One Night in Washington* (NYC, 2 November): *Tour de Force*
Jimmy Giuffre (LA, May): *Finger Snapper*
Benny Goodman (LA, August): *The Benny Goodman Story*
Dexter Gordon (LA, 18 September): *Daddy plays the Horn* (LA, 11,22 November): *Dexter plays Hot and Cool*
Joe Gordon (NYC, 3,8 September): *Introducing Joe Gordon*
Bennie Green (NYC, 10 June, 22 September): *Bennie Green blows his Horn*
Chico Hamilton (California, 4,5 August): *Spectacular* (4,23 August): *Chico Hamilton Quintet*
Lionel Hampton (LA, 1 August): *Hamp & Getz* (LA, 2 August): *Hampton-Tatum-Rich Trio* (LA, 2 August): *Lionel Hampton and his Giants*
Hampton Hawes (LA, 28 June): *The Trio Volume 1* (LA, 5 December): *This is Hampton Hawes Volume 2*
Coleman Hawkins (NYC): *Jazz Giant*
Johnny Hodges (NYC): *Ellingtonia '56*
Billie Holiday (LA, 14 February): *Stay With Me* (LA, 22,23,24,25 August): *Music for Torching* (LA, same dates): *Velvet Mood*
Elmo Hope (NYC, 28 June): *Meditations* (NYC, 4 October): *Wail, Frank, Wail*
Milt Jackson (NYC, 28 October): *Meet Milt Jackson*
Illinois Jacquet (August, September): *Groovin' with Jacquet*
Ahmad Jamal (Chicago, 23 May): *Chamber Music of the New Jazz*
JJ Johnson (NYC, 6 June): *The Eminent Jay Jay Johnson*
JJ Johnson/Kai Winding (NYC, 25,27 January): *Jai & Kai*
Hank Jones (NYC, 4 August): *The Trio*
Duke Jordan (NYC, 7 March): *Do it yourself Jazz* (NYC, 10 October): *The Street Swingers* (NYC, 10 October, 20 November): *Trio and Quintet*
Stan Kenton (LA): *Contemporary Concepts*
Barney Kessel (LA, 28 March, 26 June, 12 September): *To swing or not to swing*
Lee Konitz: *Konitz in Hi-Fi / The Real Lee Konitz*
Stan Levey (LA, 27,28 September): *Stan Levey Sextet: Stanley the Steamer*
Mundell Lowe (NYC, 27 August, 4 October): *The Mundell Lowe Quartet*
Meade Lux Lewis (LA, 16 January, July): *Yancey's Last Ride*
Teo Macero (NYC, 19 September): *What's New?*
Howard McGhee (NYC, 22 October): *That Bop Thing*
Dave McKenna (NYC, 31 October): *Solo Piano*
Ray McKinley (NYC): *Ray McKinley's Dixie Six*
Hal McKusick (NYC, 13,14,29 September): *In a Twentieth Century Drawing Room*
Jackie McLean (NYC, 21 October): *Jackie McLean Quintet*
Herbie Mann (NYC, 12,17 October): *Herbie Mann/Sam Most*
Shelly Manne (LA, 13 September): *The West Coast Sound Vol 2*
Charlie Mariano (NYC, 11 July): *Alto Sax for Young Musicians*
John Mehegan (NYC): *Reflections*
Gil Melle (NYC): *Gil Melle Quintet Volume 4*
Charlie Mingus (NYC, 30 January): *Charlie Mingus - Wally Cirillo Quartet* (NYC, 23 December): *Mingus at the Bohemia*
Red Mitchell (LA, 27 February): *Red Mitchell*
Mitchell-Ruff (NYC, 18 November, 5,6 December): *The Mitchell-Ruff Duo*
Hank Mobley (NYC, 27 March): *Hank Mobley Quartet*
Modern Jazz Quartet (NYC, 9 January): *La Ronde Suite* (NYC, 2 July): *Concorde*
Thelonious Monk (NYC, 21,27 July): *Plays Duke Ellington*
Jack Montrose (LA, May): *Arranged / Played / Composed by Jack Montrose* (LA, 24 June, 6 July):

1955

Jack Montrose Sextet
James Moody (NYC, 28 January): *Moody's Moods*
(NYC, 23,24 August): *Hi-Fi Party*
(NYC, 12 December): *Wail Moody*
Sal Mosca (NYC, August): *Sal Mosca and Peter Ind at the Den*
Gerry Mulligan (NYC, 21 September, 31 October): *Presenting the Gerry Mulligan Sextet*
Joe Newman (NYC, 8 February): *All I wanna do is swing* (NYC, September): *The Count's Men* (NYC, 3 October): *I'm still swinging*
Herbie Nichols (NYC, 4,13 May): *The Third World* (NYC, 29 July, 7 August): *Herbie Nichols Trio*
Lennie Niehaus (LA, 11,26 January, 15 February): *Lennie Niehaus Volume 3* (LA, 16,30 March): *Lennie Niehaus Quintet with Strings*
Marty Paich Octet (LA, 9,10 November): *Tenors West*
Tony Parenti (NYC, 29 August): *Happy Jazz*
Oscar Peterson (NYC, 2 October): *Stage right*
Oscar Pettiford (NYC, 12 August): *Bohemia After Dark*
Nat Pierce (NYC, 10 February): *Bandstand*
Bud Powell (NYC, 16 December 1954, 11,12 January): *Ups'n'downs* (NYC, 13 January): *The Lonely one*
Mel Powell (NYC, 19 October): *Out on a Limb*
Andre Previn (LA, 11,13,18 April): *Let's get away from it all*
Sammy Price (NYC, 20 March): *Sammy Price & his Kaycee Stompers* (Paris, 29 December): *Sammy Price & his Bluesicians*
Buddy Rich (NYC, 16 May): *The Wailing Buddy Rich* (LA, 27 October): *Buddy & Sweets*
Red Rodney (Chicago, 20 June): *Modern Music from Chicago*
Sonny Rollins (NYC, 2 December): *Worktime*
Frank Rosolino (NYC, 4,5 May): *Frankly Speaking*
Howard Rumsey (LA, 22 February, 1 March): *Lighthouse All Stars Vol 6* (LA, 20 June): *Lighthouse at Laguna*
Jimmy Rushing (NYC): *Listen to the Blues*
Bud Shank (LA, 7 January, 29 March): *Bud Shank & Strings* (LA, 2 May): *Bud Shank/Bill Perkins*
Charlie Shavers: *Most Intimate*
Horace Silver (NYC, 6 February):

Horace Silver Quintet Volume 2
Sonny Stitt (NYC, 30 September, 17 October): *Sonny Stitt with Quincy Jones Orchestra*
Art Tatum (LA, February): *Art Tatum-Buddy de Franco Quartet / Art Tatum-Benny Carter-Louis Bellson* (LA, 7 September): *Art Tatum Sextet with Lionel Hampton & Harry Edison*
Billy Taylor (NYC, 10 April): *A Touch of Taylor*
Jack Teagarden (NYC): *T for Trombone*
Sir Charles Thompson (NYC, 16 February): *Sir Charles Thompson Trio*
Cal Tjader (SF, December 1954, 6 June 1955): *Tjader plays Jazz*
Cy Touff (LA, 4,5 December): *Having a Ball*
Lennie Tristano (NYC, Summer): *Lines*

Dick Twardzik: *The Last Set*
Sarah Vaughan (NYC, 25-27 October): *In the Land of Hi-Fi*
George Wallington (NYC, 9 September): *Live! At the Cafe Bohemia!*
Dinah Washington (LA, 11,12 November): *Dinah*
Julius Watkins (NYC, 19 March): *Julius Watkins Sextet Volume 2*
Ben Webster (February): *Music for Loving*
Randy Weston (NYC, 25 January): *The Randy Weston Trio with Art Blakey* (NYC, 29,31 August): *Get Happy*
Claude Williamson (LA, 2,19 May): *Keys West*
Stu Williamson (LA, 18 January): *Stu Williamson Plays*
Phil Woods (NYC, 25 November): *Woodlore*

Photograph Courtesy: Max Jones

Right: The Benny Goodman Trio are reunited for the soundtrack of *The Benny Goodman Story.*
Below: The Gerry Mulligan Sextet with Gerry (baritone sax), Bob Brookmeyer (valve trombone), Bill Crow (bass), Zoot Sims (tenor sax), Dave Bailey (drums) and Jon Eardley (trumpet).

Photograph Courtesy: Hank O'Neal

First US/British band exchange. Ted Heath (56) tours US, Stan Kenton (44) tours England and the Continent.

First US Government sponsored jazz: Dizzy Gillespie (39) forms new big band to tour Near & Middle East and Latin America under State Department auspices.

Louis Armstrong (55) and the All-Stars tour Britain.

Nat 'King' Cole begins his own TV series.

Benny Goodman (47) tours Far East.

Horace Silver (28) forms quintet including Louis Hayes.

Duke Ellington (57) triumphs at Newport Jazz Festival in July. Paul Gonsalves (35) plays 27 choruses on 'Diminuendo and Crescendo in Blue'.

Gerry Mulligan (29) and JATP tour Europe.

Sonny Rollins (27) joins Max Roach/Clifford Brown Quintet. His replacement in the Miles Davis Quintet is John Coltrane (29).

BIRTHS
Didier Lockwood (violin) 11 February
J.J. Wiggins (bass) 15 April
Jamaaladeen Tacuma (bass guitar) 11 June
Phil Flanigan (bass) 28 June
Rodney Jones (guitar) 30 August
Steve Coleman (saxes) 20 September
Joe Cohn (guitar) 28 December
Ted Nash (tenor sax) 28 December
Martin Taylor (guitar)

DEATHS
Cripple Clarence Lofton (59) 28 January
Don Kirkpatrick (50) 13 May
Adrian Rollini (51) 15 May
Valaida Snow (55) 30 May cerebral haemorrhage
Frankie Trumbauer (56) 11 June
Clifford Brown (25) 26 June auto accident
Richie Powell (24) 26 June auto accident
Isham Jones (62) 19 October
Art Tatum (47) 5 November
Una Mae Carlisle (40) 7 November
Achille Bacquet (71) 20 November
Tommy Dorsey (51) 26 November
Tommy Fulford (44) 16 December
Dave Peyton (71)

BOOKS
J. Baird: Hot, Sweet and Blue (novel)
Eddie Condon & Richard Gehman: Eddie Condon's Treasury of Jazz
O. Duke: Sideman (novel)
Leonard Feather: Encyclopaedia Yearbook of Jazz
William Grossman & Jack Farrell: Jazz and Western Culture
William Grossman & Jack Farrell: The Heart of Jazz
Andre Hodeir: Jazz: Its Evolution and Essence
Billie Holiday with William Dufty: Lady Sings the Blues
E. Hunter: Second Ending (novel)
Stephen Longstreet: The Real Jazz: Old and New
Ida Martucci: Jive Jungle (novel)
Alun Morgan & Raymond Horricks: Modern Jazz: a survey of developments since 1939
Hugues Panassie: Guide to Jazz
Hugues Panassie & Madeleine Gautier: Dictionary of Jazz
Marshall Stearns: The Story of Jazz
Sinclair Traill: Play That Music
J. Updyke: It's always Four O'clock
W. Woodward: Jazz Americana

FILMS
Big Bill Blues (18mins): Big Bill Broonzy music short
Chris Barber Jazz Band (16mins): music short
Cool and Groovy (15mins): Chico Hamilton Quintet, Buddy de Franco Quartet, Anita O'Day – music short
Date with Dizzy (10mins): Dizzy Gillespie Quintet
High Society (107mins): feature film with Louis Armstrong All-Stars
Satchmo the Great (64mins): documentary of Louis Armstrong All-Stars on tour in Europe and Africa
Tailgate Man from New Orleans (12mins): French documentary about Kid Ory

COMPOSITIONS
Billy Strayhorn: Snibor / U.M.M.G.

RECORDS
Cannonball Adderley (NYC, 8,18 June): In the Land of Hi-Fi (NYC, 17 December): Sessions, Live
Nat Adderley (NYC, 13 July): To the Ivy League
Manny Albam (NYC, 5,6,7 March): Drum Suite
Gene Ammons (NYC, 13 July): Jammin' with Gene Ammons All-Stars
Louis Armstrong (NYC, 11–13 December): Satchmo: a musical autobiography
Louis Armstrong/Eddie Condon (Newport, 6,7 July): Louis Armstrong & Eddie Condon at Newport
Louis Armstrong/Ella Fitzgerald (LA, 16 August): Ella & Louis
Chet Baker (LA, 21-31 July): Chet Baker & his Crew (LA, 18 October): Chet Baker Big Band (LA, 31 October): Chet Baker-Art Pepper Sextet (LA, 6 November): Chet Baker-Russ Freeman Quartet (LA, 8 November): Chet Baker-Bud Shank Orchestra
Chet Baker/Art Pepper (LA, 26,28 July): Playboys
Count Basie : Hall of Fame
Sidney Bechet (Paris, 16 May): Sidney Bechet with Sammy Price's Bluesicians
Art Blakey (NYC, 12,13 December): Hard Bop
Clifford Brown/Max Roach Quintet (NYC, 4 January, 16,17 February): At Basin Street
Lawrence Brown (NYC, March): Slide Trombone
Dave Brubeck (NYC, 12 March, 18,19 April): Brubeck plays Brubeck (Newport, 6 July): Dave Brubeck and Jay & Kai at Newport
Kenny Burrell (NYC, 29 May): Introducing Kenny Burrell (NYC, 29,31 May, 10 November, 3 December): Kenny Burrell Volume 2 (NYC, 28 December): All Night Long
Hoagy Carmichael (LA, 10,11,13 September): with the Pacific Jazzmen
Serge Chaloff (LA, 4 March): Blue Serge
Paul Chambers (LA, March): Chamber's Music (NYC, 21 September): Whims of Chambers
Teddy Charles (NYC, 6,17 January): Tentet (NYC, 23 October, 12 November): Word from Bird
Kenny Clarke (NYC, 6 February): Klook's Clique (NYC, 30 April, 9 May): Kenny Clarke meets the Detroit Jazzmen
Al Cohn/Zoot Sims (NYC, 24 January): From A to Z
Al Cohn (NYC, 29 September): Cohn on Saxophone
Buddy Collette (LA, 13,24 February, 17 April): Man of Many Parts (LA, 6,29 November): Nice Day with Buddy Collette
Chris Connor (NYC, 23 January/8 February): Songs (NYC, 17,19 December): A Jazz Date with Chris Connor
Eddie Costa (NYC, February): Eddie Costa with the Vinnie Burke Trio
Curtis Counce (LA, 8,15 October): Landslide
Sonny Criss (LA): Plays Cole Porter
Tadd Dameron (NYC, 9 March): Fontainbleu (NYC, 30 November): Mating Call
Eddie 'Lockjaw' Davis (NYC): Jazz with a Horn
Miles Davis (NYC, 11 May, 18 October): Workin' / Relaxin' / Cookin' / Steamin' with the Miles Davis Quintet
Blossom Dearie (NYC): Blossom Dearie
Wilbur de Paris (Boston, 26 October): At Symphony Hall
Kenny Dorham (NYC, 4 April): And his Jazz Prophets (NYC, 31 May): 'Round about Midnight at the Cafe Bohemia
Kenny Drew (NYC, 20,26 September): The Kenny Drew Trio
Jon Eardley (NYC, 13 January): Jon Eardley Seven

Harry Edison (LA, 4 September): Sweets
Don Elliott (NYC, 29,30 June): A musical offering by Don Elliott (NYC, 16 August): At the Modern Jazz Room
Duke Ellington (Chicago, 7,8 February): Historically Speaking (Newport, 6,7 July): Ellington at Newport (NYC, 17,24,25,28 September, 22,23 October, 6 December): A Drum is a Woman
Herb Ellis (LA, February): Ellis in Wonderland
Bill Evans (NYC, 18,27 September): New Jazz Conceptions
Tal Farlow (NYC, March): Tal (NYC, June): The Swinging Guitar (NYC, 18 December): First set / Second set
Art Farmer (NYC, 23 November): Farmer's Market
Maynard Ferguson (NYC, 7,11 September): The Birdland Dreamband
Ella Fitzgerald (LA, February/March): Sings the Cole Porter Songbook (LA, August): Rodgers & Hart Songbook (LA, September): Duke Ellington Songbook
Russ Freeman/Chet Baker (LA, 6 November): Freeman/Baker Quartet
Frank Foster (NYC, 5 March): No Count
Red Garland (NYC, 17 August): A Garland of Red
Stan Getz (LA, 24 November): The Steamer
Bennie Green/Art Farmer (NYC, 13 April): Bennie Green & Art Farmer
Bennie Green (NYC, 29 June): Walkin' Down
Terry Gibbs (NYC, 1,2,8 October): Swingin' with Terry Gibbs
Jimmy Giuffre (LA, March): The Jimmy Giuffre Clarinet (NYC, 2,3,4 December): The Jimmy Giuffre Three
Dizzy Gillespie (NYC, 18,19 May, 6 June): World Statesman
Dizzy Gillespie/Stan Getz/Sonny Stitt (LA, 16 October): For Musicians Only
Johnny Griffin (NYC, 17 April): Introducing Johnny Griffin
Hampton Hawes (LA, 25 January): Everybody Likes Hampton Hawes (LA, 12,13 November): All Night Sessions, Volumes 1,2,3
Tubby Hayes (London, 17 July): After Lights Out
Ernie Henry (NYC, 23,30 August, 5 October): Presenting Ernie Henry
Billie Holiday (LA, 6 June): Lady Sings The Blues (LA, August): All Or Nothing At All (NYC, Carnegie Hall, 10 November): The Essential Billie Holiday
Elmo Hope (NYC, 7 May): Informal Jazz
Milt Jackson (NYC, 19 January): Jacksonsville
Ahmad Jamal (Chicago, 27 September, 4 October): Count 'em
JJ Johnson/Bobby Jaspar (NYC, 24 July): J is for Jazz
JJ Johnson/Kai Winding (NYC, 2 April): Jay & Kai Trombone Octet (Newport, 6 July): Jay & Kai at Newport
Hank Jones (NYC, 9 July, 8,20 August): Have you met Hank Jones? (NYC, 21 August): Relaxin' at Camarillo
Thad Jones (NYC, 13 March): Detroit/New York Junction
Barney Kessel (LA, 6 August/15 October/4 December): Music to Listen to
Lee Konitz (NYC, 26 September, 5,21,22 October): Inside Hi-Fi
Gene Krupa (NYC, April): Drummer Man
Stan Levey (LA, November): Grand Stan
John Lewis (LA, 10 February): 2 degrees East, 3 degrees West (NYC, 30 July): The John Lewis Piano
John Lewis/Sacha Distel (Paris, 4,7 December): Afternoon in Paris
Ramsey Lewis (Chicago): Ramsey Lewis & his Gentle Men of Swing
Mundell Lowe (NYC, 20 February, 2 March): Guitar Moods
Jackie Mc Lean (NYC, 27 January): Lights Out (NYC, 13,20 July): 4,5 and 6 (NYC, 31 August): Jackie's Pal
Herbie Mann (Stockholm, 10,12,16 October): Mann in the Morning (Hilversum, 8 November): Salute to the Flute
Shelly Manne (LA, 19,26 January, 2 February): Swinging Sounds (LA, 11 February): Shelly Manne & his Friends (LA, 19 July, 15,16 August): More Swinging Sounds (LA, 17 August): My Fair Lady
Warne Marsh (LA, September): Jazz of the Two Cities
Gil Melle (NYC, 1 April): Patterns in Jazz (NYC, 20 April, 1 July): Primitive Modern (NYC, 10,24 August): Gil's Guests

1956

Charlie Mingus (NYC, 30 January): *Pithecanthropus Erectus*

Hank Mobley (NYC, 30 January, 8 February): *The Jazz Message* (NYC, 20 July): *Mobley's Message* (NYC, 27 July): *Mobley's Second Message* (NYC, 25 November): *Hank Mobley with Donald Byrd & Lee Morgan*

Modern Jazz Quartet (NYC, 22 January, 14 February): *Fontessa* (Lenox, 28 August): *MJQ at Music Inn with Jimmy Giuffre*

Thelonious Monk (NYC, 17 March, 3 April): *The Unique Thelonious Monk* (NYC, 17,23 December): *Brilliant Corners*

JR Monterose (NYC, 21 October): *J.R.Monterose*

Jack Montrose (LA, 24,26 December): *Blues and Vanilla*

James Moody (Chicago, November): *Flute 'n' the Blues*

Lee Morgan (NYC, 4 November): *Indeed!* (NYC, 2 December): *Lee Morgan Sextet Volume 2*

Gerry Mulligan (Boston, 1-6 December): *Gerry Mulligan Quartet at Storyville*

Phineas Newborn (NYC, 3,4 May): *The Piano Artistry of Phineas Newborn* (NYC, 16,19,22 October): *Phineas Rainbow*

Joe Newman (NYC, 4,11,14 March): *Salute to Satch*

Joe Newman/Frank Wess (NYC, 8,10,13 July): *Joe Newman/Frank Wess Septet* (NYC, 26 December): *Jazz for Playboys*

Lennie Niehaus (LA, 20 January): *Vol 1: The Quintets* (LA, 10 December): *The Octet*

Red Norvo (LA, 18,27 December): *Ad Lib*

Anita O'Day (LA, February): *Anita* (LA, May): *Anita sings the most* (LA, 17 December): *Pick Yourself up*

Kid Ory (Paris, 5 December): *Kid Ory in Europe*

Cecil Payne (NYC): *Cecil Payne Quintet at the Five Spot Cafe*

Art Pepper (LA, 26 November): *The Way it Was*

Carl Perkins (LA): *Introducing Carl Perkins*

Oscar Peterson (LA, February): *Plays Count Basie* (Canada, 8 August): *At the Stratford Festival*

Bud Powell (NYC, 5 October): *Strictly Powell*

Prestige All-Stars (NYC, 3 August): *Two Trumpets* (NYC, 7 September): *Tenor Conclave*

Andre Previn (LA): *But Beautiful*

Paul Quinichette (NYC, 16 July): *The Kid from Denver*

Jimmy Raney (NYC, 4,14,23 May, 15 June): *In Three Attitudes*

Max Roach (NYC, 12 October): *Max Roach + 4*

Shorty Rogers (LA, 2 July): *Wherever the Five Winds Blow*

Sonny Rollins (NYC, 22 March): *Sonny Rollins Plus Four* (NYC, 24 May): *Tenor Madness* (NYC, 22 June): *Saxophone Colossus* (NYC, 7 December): *Tour de Force* (NYC, 16 December): *Sonny Rollins Quintet* (NYC, 5 October, 7 December): *Sonny Boy*

Frank Rosolino (LA, May): *Frank Rosolino Quartet*

Pete Rugolo (LA, 9-11 July): *Music for Hi-Fi Bugs*

Howard Rumsey (LA, 2,9,16 October): *Music for Lighthouse Keeping*

Jimmy Rushing (NYC, 6,7,8 November): *The Jazz Odyssey of James Rushing Esq*

George Russell (NYC, 31 March, 17 October, 21 December): *The Jazz Workshop*

Bud Shank (LA, 25 January): *The Bud Shank Quartet* (LA, January): *Live at the Haig*

Bud Shank/Bob Cooper (LA, 29 November, 25 December): *Bud Shank/Bob Cooper Quintet*

Horace Silver (NYC, 2,17 July): *Silver Blue* (NYC, 10 November): *Six Pieces of Silver*

Zoot Sims (NYC, 31 January): *Tonight's Music Today* (NYC, September): *The Big Stampede* (NYC, 2,9 November): *Plays Alto, Tenor and Baritone* (NYC, 13, 18 December): *Zoot!*

Jimmy Smith (NYC, 13,18 February): *A New Sound – A New Star* (NYC, 11 March): *The Champ* (NYC, 12 June): *The Incredible Jimmy Smith at the Organ* (Wilmington, 1 August): *The Incredible Jimmy Smith at Club Baby Grand*

Rex Stewart/Cootie Williams (NYC): *The Big Challenge*

Art Tatum (LA, January): *The Art Tatum Trio* (LA, February): *Art Tatum/Buddy de Franco Quartet* (LA, 15 August): *At the Hollywood Bowl* (LA, September): *Art Tatum/Ben Webster Quartet*

Cal Tjader (SF): *Latin Kick*

Mel Torme (LA, 20 January): *Lulu's Back in Town* (LA, November): *Sings Fred Astaire*

George Wallington (NYC, 20 January): *Jazz for the Carriage Trade* (NYC, 4,5 September): *Knight Music*

Dinah Washington (NYC, 24,25 April): *In The Land Of Hi-Fi*

Doug Watkins (Detroit, 8 December): *Doug at large*

Frank Wess (NYC, 7 March): *North, South, East... Wess* (NYC, 7 March): *No Count* (NYC, 20 June): *Opus in Swing*

Randy Weston (NYC, 14,21 March): *With these Hands* (NYC, 10 September): *Trio and Solo* (NYC, 14 October): *Jazz à la Bohemia*

Joe Wilder (NYC, 19 January): *Wilder 'n' Wilder*

Claude Williamson (LA, 19 January): *Claude Williamson Trio*

Phil Woods/Gene Quill (NYC, 15 March): *Phil and Quill* (NYC, 15 June): *Pairing Off*

Phil Woods (NYC, 2 November): *The Young Bloods*

Lester Young/Teddy Wilson (NYC, 12,13 January): *Pres & Teddy*

Lester Young (Washington, December): *In Washington DC / Laughin' to keep from Cryin' / Lester Young at Olivia Davis' Patio Lounge*

Left: Teddy Wilson, Billy Strayhorn and Duke Ellington reflecting on Duke's triumphant appearance at the Newport Jazz Festival (July).
Bottom left: Louis Armstrong's All Stars arrive in Africa.
Below: Max Roach at the Blue Note recording session for *Introducing Johnny Griffin* (April).

Photo Courtesy: *Max Jones*

Photo: *Francis Wolff* Courtesy: *Mosaic Images*

Sonny Rollins (28) forms his own combo.

Cannonball Adderley (29) joins Miles Davis (31) Sextet.

Miles Davis and Gil Evans (45) begin a series of LP collaborations with 'Miles Ahead'.

Duke Ellington (58) premiéres a TV special 'A drum is a woman'.

Benny Goodman (48) makes a State Department tour of Cambodia.

Wilbur de Paris (57) makes a State Department tour of Africa with a combo including Doc Cheatham (52).

Earl Hines (52), Jack Teagarden (52), George Lewis (57), Gerry Mulligan (30) and Eddie Condon (53) all tour Britain.

BIRTHS
Chris Hunter (alto sax) 21 February
Mino Cinélu (percussion) 10 March
Geri Allen (piano) 12 June
Jean Toussaint (tenor sax) 27 July
Chuck Riggs (drums) 5 August
Emily Remler (guitar) 18 September
Kevin Eubanks (guitar) 15 November
Doug Raney (guitar)

DEATHS
Jimmy Wade (61) February
Alfred 'Baby' Laine (61) 1 March
Bob Graettinger (33) 12 March
Fud Livingston (50) 25 March
Jimmy Dorsey (53) 12 June
Wes Ilcken (33) 13 July
Serge Chaloff (34) 16 July
Joe Shulman (33) 2 August
Carroll Dickerson (62) October
'Wooden Joe' Nicholas (74) 17 November
Dick McPartland (52) 30 November
Walter Page (57) 20 December
Ernie Henry (31) 29 December

BOOKS
A. Anderson: Helpful Hints to Jazz Collectors
Leonard Feather: The Book of Jazz
Harold Flender: Paris Blues (novel)
Raymond Horricks: Count Basie and his Orchestra, its music and its musicians
Jack Kerouac: On the Road (novel)
J. Lucas: The Great Revival on Long Play
Nat Shapiro and Nat Hentoff: The Jazz Makers
Studs Terkel: Giants of Jazz
Sinclair Traill: Concerning Jazz
Sinclair Traill and Gerald Lascelles: Just Jazz, Vol 1
Barry Ulanov: A Handbook of Jazz
Michael Wyler: A glimpse at the Past

FILMS
The Big Beat (82mins) Charlie Barnet, George Shearing, Cal Tjader
Lift to the Scaffold (89mins): feature film with music by Miles Davis
No Sun in Venice : feature film with score by John Lewis, played by MJQ
The Sound of Jazz (60mins): from TV show featuring Red Allen, Billie Holiday, Count Basie All-Stars, Jimmy Giuffre and Thelonious Monk
The Sweet Smell of Success (93mins): feature film with Chico Hamilton Quintet

COMPOSITIONS
Duke Ellington: Such Sweet Thunder

RECORDS
Pepper Adams (LA, 12 July): Pepper Adams Quintet (LA, 23 August): Critics' Choice (NYC, 19 November): Cool Sound of Pepper Adams
Cannonball Adderley (NYC, 8 February): Sophisticated Swing (same date): Cannonball en route
Toshiko Akiyoshi (NYC, 28 September): The many sides of Toshiko
Manny Albam (LA, 14,15 August): The Jazz Greats of our Time, Vol 2
Joe Albany / Warne Marsh (California, September): The Right Combination
Mose Allison (Hackensack, 7 March): Back Country Suite (Hackensack, 8 November): Local Color
Gene Ammons (Hackensack, 11 January): Funky (Hackensack,12 April): Jammin' in Hi-Fi
Louis Armstrong (Chicago, 14 October): Louis Armstrong with Oscar Peterson Trio

Louis Armstrong / Ella Fitzgerald (LA, July, August):Ella & Louis
Chet Baker / Art Pepper (LA): Playboys
Count Basie (Newport, 7 July): Count Basie at Newport (same date): Joe Williams with Count Basie (NYC, 21,22 October): The Atomic Mr Basie
Sidney Bechet (Paris, 12 March/17 June): Sidney Bechet-Martial Solal Quartet
Louis Bellson (Las Vegas, 3 November): At the Flamingo
Art Blakey (NYC,22 February): Drum Suite (NYC, 7 March): Orgy in Rhythm, Vols 1&2 (NYC,8,9 March): Reflections of Buhaina (NYC, 8 April): A Night in Tunisia (NYC, 13 May): Cu-Bop (NYC, 14,15 May): with Thelonious Monk (NYC, 9,11 October): The Jazz Messengers (NYC, December): Art Blakey's Big Band
Paul Bley (LA): Solemn Meditation
Ruby Braff (NYC, 26 March, 5,12 April): Hi-Fi Salute to Bunny (Newport, 5 July): Ruby Braff at Newport
Bob Brookmeyer (LA, 13,16 July): Traditionalism Revisited (NYC, 13,16 December): The Street Swingers
Dave Brubeck (California, 8 February): Dave Brubeck Plays (February): Dave Brubeck Quintet (NYC, 29,30 June): Dave digs Disney
Ray Bryant (NYC, 5 April): Django
Kenny Burrell (NYC, 4 January): All Day Long (NYC,1 February): Blue Moods (NYC, 10 February): KB Blues (NYC, 5 March): Kenny Burrell & Jimmy Raney (NYC, 10 May): Guitar Soul
Billy Butterfield (NYC, 30 July, 1,2 August): Thank you for a lovely evening
Charlie Byrd (NYC, 4 February): Jazz Recital / the Spanish Guitar of Charlie Byrd (NYC,4 August): Blues for Night People
Donald Byrd / Gigi Gryce (NYC, August): X-tasy (NYC, 30 August, 3,5 September): The Jazz Lab Quintet
Donald Byrd (NYC, 10 September): Jazz Eyes
Paul Chambers (LA, 22,23 January): The East / West Controversy (NYC, 19 May): Paul Chambers Quintet (NYC, 14 July): Bass on top
Ray Charles / Milt Jackson (NYC, 12 September): Soul Brothers
Teddy Charles (NYC, 1 April): Teddy Charles' Vibe-rant Quintet (NYC, 29 May): Three for Duke
Sonny Clark (NYC, 21 July): Dial S for Sonny (NYC, 9 October): Sonny's Crib (NYC, 13 November): Sonny Clark Trio
Jimmy Cleveland (NYC, 12,13 December): Cleveland Style
Al Cohn / Zoot Sims (NYC, 27 March): Al & Zoot
John Coltrane (NYC, 20 April): Dakar (NYC, 31 May): Coltrane (NYC,23 August): Trane-ing in (NYC, 15 September): Blue Train
John Coltrane / Paul Quinichette (NYC, 17 April):John Coltrane / Paul Quinichette Quintet
Eddie Condon (NYC, 28 June, 19 August, 24 September): Eddie Condon & his All-Stars
Bob Cooper (LA,26,27 August): Coop! (LA): Jazz Rolls Royce
Curtis Counce (LA, 22,27 April, 31 May): Carl's Blues
Eddie 'Lockjaw' Davis (NYC, 22 January, 5 February): Jazz with a beat (NYC, 17,18,19 December): Count Basie presents the Eddie Davis Trio plus Joe Newman
Miles Davis (NYC, 6,10,23,27 May): Miles Ahead (Paris, 4 December): Lift to the Scaffold
Buddy de Franco (LA, 29-31 October, 1 November): Plays Benny Goodman (same date): Plays Artie Shaw
Lou Donaldson (NYC, 9 June): Swing and Soul (NYC,15 December): Lou takes off
Kenny Dorham (NYC, 21,27 May): Jazz Contrasts (NYC,13 November & 2 December): 2 Horns / 2 Rhythm

Ray Draper (NYC, 15 March): Ray Draper Quintet (NYC,12 July): Strange Blues (NYC,20 December): Ray Draper Quintet featuring John Coltrane
Kenny Drew (NYC, 15 October): Pal Joey (NYC, 28 March, 3 April): This is new
Harry Edison (LA,5 March):Gee baby, ain't I good to you
Duke Ellington (NYC, 15,24 April/3 May): Such Sweet Thunder (NYC, 13 March, 9 September, 1,10,14 October): Ellington Indigos
Herb Ellis (NYC, 7 October): Nothing but the blues
Gil Evans (NYC, 6,27 September / 10 October): Gil Evans Ten
Vic Feldman (LA, September): Mallets a forethought
Maynard Ferguson (NYC, July): Boy with lots of brass
Ella Fitzgerald (LA, September): Porgy and Bess (Chicago, 19 October): At the Opera House (LA, October): Like Someone in Love
Tommy Flanagan (Stockholm, 15 August): Trio Overseas (NYC, 5 September): Jazz...it's magic
Bud Freeman (NYC, 7 March, 3 April, 8 July): Bud Freeman's Summa Cum Laude Orchestra
Curtis Fuller (NYC, 11 May): New Trombone (NYC, 14 May): Curtis Fuller with Red Garland (NYC, 16 June): The Opener (NYC, 21 August): Bone and Bari (NYC, 1 December): Curtis Fuller and Art Farmer
Red Garland (NYC, March): Red Garland's Piano (NYC, 24 May): Groovy (NYC, 15 November/ 13 December): All Morning Long / Soul Junction / High Pressure / Dig It
Erroll Garner (NYC, 6 February): Soliloquy
Herb Geller (LA, March): Fire in the West
Stan Getz (NYC, 12 July/ LA, 2 August): The Soft Swing (LA, August): Getz meets Mulligan (LA, 2 August): Award Winner (Chicago, 19 October): Stan Getz & JJ Johnson at the Opera House (Chicago, 19 October): Stan Getz & the Oscar Peterson Trio
Terry Gibbs (LA, September): Jazzband Ball (LA, 4 December): Plays the Duke
Dizzy Gillespie (NYC, 23 March/ 17,18 April): Birk's Works (NYC, 17 April): Dizzy Gillespie/ Stuff Smith (Newport, 6 July): Dizzy Gillespie at Newport (NYC, 11,19 December): Dizzy Gillespie with Sonny Rollins and Sonny Stitt (NYC, 17 December): The Greatest Trumpet of them all
Benny Golson (NYC, 14,17 October): Benny Golson's New York Scene (NYC, 19,23 December): The Modern Touch
Johnny Griffin (NYC, 6 April): A Blowing Session (NYC,23 October): The Congregation
Gigi Gryce (NYC, 27 February/ 7 March): Gigi Gryce & the Jazz Lab Quintet
Bobby Hackett/ Jack Teagarden (NYC, September): Jazz Ultimate
Jim Hall (LA, 10,24 January): Jazz Guitar
John Handy (NYC, 13 May): Messages
Bill Harris (NYC): The Harris Touch (LA, 23 September): Bill Harris & Friends
Coleman Hawkins (NYC, 12,15 March): The Hawk flies high (NYC, 24 October): The Genius of Coleman Hawkins
Coleman Hawkins/ Roy Eldridge (Newport, 5 July): Hawkins/Eldridge All-Stars at Newport (Chicago, 19 October): At the Opera House
Coleman Hawkins/ Ben Webster (LA, 16 October): Blue Saxophones
Ernie Henry (NYC, 30 September): Seven standards and a blues (NYC, September): Last Chorus
Woody Herman (NYC,2,3 July): Woody Herman '58
Billie Holiday (LA, 7,9 January): Songs For Distingué Lovers / Body And Soul
Paul Horn (LA, September): House of Horn
Milt Jackson (NYC,5,7 January): Plenty, plenty soul (NYC,21 May/ 10,17 June): Bags and flutes
Milt Jackson/ Ray Charles (NYC, September): Soul Brothers
Jo Jones (NYC): The Jo Jones Special
Clifford Jordan/ John Gilmore (NYC,3 March): Blowing in from Chicago
Clifford Jordan (NYC,2 June): Cliff Jordan (NYC,10 November): Cliff Craft
Wynton Kelly (NYC): Wynton Kelly
Stan Kenton (Balboa,8-11 October): Rendezvous with Kenton
Barney Kessel (LA, 6 August/ 11 November): Let's cook
Jimmy Knepper (NYC): A swinging introduction to Jimmy Knepper

Lee Konitz (Pittsburgh, 15 February): *The real Lee Konitz* (NYC, August): *Very Cool*

Lambert, Hendricks & Ross (NYC, 26 August/ 16,27 September/ 11 October/ 26November): *Sing a Song of Basie*

Yusef Lateef (NYC, September): *Before Dawn* (NYC,9 October): *Jazz and the sounds of nature* (NYC,10 October): *Prayer to the East* (NYC, 11 October): *The Sounds of Yusef / Other Sounds / Cry! Tender*

Herbie Mann (NYC, 18,29 April): *Salute to the Flute* (NYC, 9 May): *Mann Alone* (NYC, 14 May): *Yardbird Suite* (LA, July): *Great Ideas of Western Mann* (LA, July/ September): *The Magic Flute of Herbie Mann* (LA, August): *Flute Fraternity*

Shelly Manne (LA, 4 January): *The Gambit* (LA, 6,7,25 February): *Lil' Abner* (LA, 24,25 July): *Concerto for Clarinet & Combo*

Jackie McLean (NYC, 8 February): *Jackie McLean & Co* (NYC, 15 February): *Makin' the Changes* (NYC, 3 May): *Alto Madness* (NYC, 30 August): *A long drink of the blues* (NYC, 27 December): *Tune up*

Gil Melle (NYC, 26 April): *Quadrama*

Charlie Mingus (NYC, 12 February/ 13 March): *Reincarnation of a lovebird* (NYC, 9 July): *Trio* (NYC, 18 July/ 6 August): *Tijuana Moods* (NYC, 6 August): *East Coasting* (NYC, October): *Duke's Choice*

Red Mitchell (LA, 26 March): *Presenting Red Mitchell*

Hank Mobley (NYC, 13 January): *Hank Mobley All-Stars* (NYC, 9 March): *Hank Mobley with Art Farmer* (NYC, 21 April): *Hank Mobley Sextet* (NYC, 23 June): *Hank Mobley* (NYC, 20 October): *Poppin'*

MJQ (NYC, 4,5 April): *One Never Knows* (Donaueschingen, 27 October): *The historic Donaueschingen Concert*

Thelonious Monk (NYC,12 April): *Thelonious Himself* (NYC, 12,16 April): *Thelonious Monk with John Coltrane* (NYC, 19 May): *Thelonious Monk with Art Blakey's Jazz Messengers* (NYC, 26 June): *Monk's Music*

Jack Montrose (LA, 22,23 January): *West Coast Conference* (LA, 10,11 September): *The Horn's Full*

Below: Johnny Griffin, John Coltrane and Hank Mobley at Blue Note's *A Blowin' Session.*
Far right: Sonny Rollins recording *Sonny Rollins Volume 2.* Photographs: *Francis Wolff* Courtesy: *Mosaic Images*

Lee Morgan (NYC, 24 March): *Lee Morgan Volume 3* (NYC, 25 August): *City Lights* (NYC, 29 September): *The Cooker*

Gerry Mulligan (NYC, 19,20 April): *Gerry Mulligan, the Arranger* (Stockholm, May): *Quartet live in Stockholm* (NYC, 1,27 August): *Gerry Mulligan meets Paul Desmond* (NYC, 12,13 August): *Mulligan meets Monk* (LA, 22 October): *Gerry Mulligan meets Stan Getz* (NYC, 4,5 December): *Gerry Mulligan & the Sax Section* (NYC, 3,11,17 December): *Gerry Mulligan Quartet – Reunion*

Phineas Newborn (NYC, 7,8,9 September): *Jamaica*

Joe Newman (NYC, 7,8 January): *The happy cats* (NYC, 10 April): *Joe Newman/ Zoot Sims Quartet*

Lennie Niehaus (LA, October): *I swing for you*

Herbie Nichols (NYC, November): *Out of the shadow*

Anita O'Day (January): *Anita swings the most*

Kid Ory (San Francisco, September): *Song of the Wanderer*

Cecil Payne (NYC, 12 August): *Bird's Night*

Art Pepper (LA, 19 January): *Meets the Rhythm Section* (1 April): *Omega Man*

Oscar Peterson (Newport, 7 July): *Oscar Peterson Trio with Eldridge, Stitt & Jo Jones at Newport* (NYC, July): *Soft Sands* (Chicago, 19 October): *The Oscar Peterson Trio at the Opera House*

Oscar Pettiford (NYC,23 August): *The Oscar Pettiford Orchestra in Hi-Fi*

Bud Powell (NYC): *Piano Interpretations* (NYC, January): *Blues in the Closet* (NYC,11 February): *Swingin' with Bud* (NYC, 3 August): *Bud! The amazing Bud Powell Volume 3*

The Pollwinners (LA,18,19 March): *The Pollwinners*

Andre Previn (LA, 6,7,25 February): *Li'l Abner* (LA, 30 April/ 11 May): *Double Play* (LA, 28,29 October): *Pal Joey*

Paul Quinichette/ Charlie Rouse (NYC,29 August): *The Chase is on*

Paul Quinichette (NYC, 18 October): *For Basie*

Max Roach/ Stan Levey (LA, March): *Drummin' the Blues*

Max Roach (NYC, 18-21 March): *Jazz in 3/4 Time* (NYC, 23 December): *Max plays Charlie Parker*

Shorty Rogers (LA, 15 July/ 11 August): *Portrait of Shorty*

Sonny Rollins (LA, 7 March): *Way Out West* (NYC, 14 April): *Sonny Rollins Volume 2*

(NYC,11,12,19 June): *The Sound of Sonny* (NYC,22 September): *Newk's Time* (NYC, 3 November): *A Night at the Village Vanguard*

Jimmy Rushing (NYC, 5 March): *If this ain't the blues*

Horace Silver (NYC, 8 May): *The stylings of Silver*

Jimmy Smith (NYC, 11 February): *A date with Jimmy Smith, Volumes 1 & 2* (NYC, 8 May): *Plays pretty just for you* (NYC, 4 July): *Jimmy Smith Trio with Lou Donaldson* (NYC, 14 November): *Groovin' at Small's Paradise, Volumes 1 & 2*

Rex Stewart (NYC): *The Big Reunion*

Sonny Stitt (NYC, August): *Personal Appearance* (NYC, 11 October): *Only the Blues* (NYC, November): *Sonny Stitt with the New Yorkers*

Art Taylor (NYC, 25 February / 22 March): *Taylor's Wailers*

Clark Terry (NYC, 29 July/ 6 September): *Duke with a difference* (Chicago, September): *Out on a Limb*

Cal Tjader (San Francisco, 20 January): *Jazz at the Blackhawk* (San Francisco, 10,11,15 April): *Cal Tjader* (SF, 10 September/Chicago, 11 October/NYC, 20 November): *Mas Ritmo Caliente*

Leroy Vinnegar (LA, 15 July/16,23 September): *Leroy Walks* (LA, 21 October/15 December): *Sessions, Live*

Mal Waldron (NYC, 19 April/17 May): *Mal Waldron Sextet*

George Wallington (NYC, 1 March): *The New York Scene* (NYC, 4,5 March): *The Prestidigitator* (NYC, 14 November): *Jazz at Hotchkiss*

Ben Webster (LA, 15 October): *Soulville*

Frank Wess (NYC, 5 January): *Jazz for Playboys*

Frank Wess/Kenny Burrell (NYC, 21 June): *After Hours*

Randy Weston (NYC): *Piano à la Mode*

Lee Wiley (NYC, 23,24,25 July): *A Touch of the Blues*

Cootie Williams (NYC, 30 April/ 7 May): *Cootie and Rex in the Big Challenge*

Claude Williamson (LA): *'Round Midnight*

Teddy Wilson (Newport, 6 July): *Teddy Wilson Trio at Newport* (NYC): *The Impeccable Mr Wilson* (NYC): *I Got Rhythm*

Jimmy Witherspoon (NYC, 4,5 December): *A Spoonful of Blues*

Phil Woods (NYC, 9 February): *Four Altos* (NYC, 29 March): *Phil and Quill* (NYC, 19 July): *Sugan* (NYC, 12 August): *Bird's Night* (NYC, 17 November): *Bird Calls*

First stereo records issued.

Eddie Condon (54) opens new club on New York's East Side.

First Monterey Jazz Festival (September).

Lambert, Hendricks & Ross trio organised.

Ella Fitzgerald (40) and Duke Ellington (59) appear in concert at Carnegie Hall.

Woody Herman (45) tours Latin America for the US State Department.

Bill Evans (28) joins Miles Davis (32) group which also features John Coltrane and Cannonball Adderley.

The Savoy Ballroom closes.

Jack Teagarden (53) tours Far East for US State Department.

Dave Brubeck (38) tours Middle East and India for US State Department.

Duke Ellington Orchestra tours England for the first time since 1933.

Guitarist Herb Ellis (36) leaves the Oscar Peterson Trio to be replaced by drummer Ed Thigpen (27).

BIRTHS
Bill Evans (tenor sax) 9 February
Michael Formanek (bass) 7 May
Kenny Washington (drums) 29 May
Howard Alden (guitar) 17 October

DEATHS
Carl Perkins (29) 17 March
Tom Brown (68) 25 March
W.C.Handy (84) 28 March
Ted Donnelly (45) 8 May
Albert Glenny (88) 11 June
Sterling Bose (52) June
Big Bill Broonzy (65) 14 August
Herbie Fields (39) 17 September *suicide (sleeping pills)*
Lorraine Geller (30) 13 October
George E Lee (62) October
Tiny Bradshaw (53) 26 November
Danny Alvin (56) 6 December
Julia Lee (56) 8 December
Doc Cook (67) 25 December

BOOKS
Walter Allen: *King Joe Oliver*
David Boulton: *Jazz in Britain*
P. Bunyan: *The Big Blues* (novel)
Samuel Charters: *Jazz: New Orleans 1885 – 1957*
W. Clapham: *Come Blow Your Horn*
Donald Connor: *B.G. Off the Record*, a bio-discography of Benny Goodman
Art Dedrick & Al Polhamus: *How the Dance Band Swings*
Leonard Feather: *New Yearbook of Jazz*
Peter Gammond: *Duke Ellington: His Life and Music*
Peter Gammond (ed): *The Decca Book of Jazz*
Ralph J. Gleason: *Jam Session: An Anthology of Jazz*
Rex Harris & Brian Rust: *Recorded Jazz: A Critical Guide*
John Clellan Holmes: *The Horn* (novel)
Langston Hughes: *Tambourines to Glory* (novel)
Jack Kerouac: *The Subterraneans* (novel)
G. Lea: *Somewhere There's Music* (novel)
Martin Lindsay: *Teach Yourself Jazz*
Humphrey Lyttelton: *Second Chorus*
Albert McCarthy: *Jazz Discography, Part 1*
Sinclair Traill & Gerald Lascelles (eds): *Just Jazz, Vol 2*
Jake Trussell: *After Hours Poetry*
Charles Wareing & George Garlick: *Bugles for Beiderbecke*
J. Wilson: *Collector's Jazz: Traditional and Swing*

FILMS
Django Reinhardt (21mins): documentary
I Want to Live (120mins): feature film with Gerry Mulligan
Jack Teagarden in Thailand (15mins): documentary
St Louis Blues (93mins): feature film bio of WC Handy played by Nat King Cole

RECORDS
Ahmed Abdul-Malik (NYC, October): *Jazz Samba*
Pepper Adams/Jimmy Knepper (NYC, 25 March): *The Pepper-Knepper Quintet*
Pepper Adams (NYC, 1 April): *10 to 4 at the Five Spot*
Cannonball Adderley (NYC, 9 March): *Somethin' Else* (NYC, 1 July): *Portrait of Cannonball* (NYC, 20 August): *Jump for Joy* (NYC, 28 October): *Things are getting better*
Cannonball & Nat Adderley (NYC, 4,6 March): *Sharpshooters*
Nat Adderley (NYC, September): *Branching Out*
Toshiko Akiyoshi (NYC, 13 June): *United Nations*
Mose Allison (NYC, 24 January): *Young Man Mose* (NYC, 18 April): *Ramblin' with Mose* (NYC, 15 August): *Creek Bank*
Gene Ammons (NYC, 3 January): *The Big Sound* (NYC, 3 January): *Groove Blues* (NYC, 3 May): *Blue Gene*
Gene Ammons/Benny Green (NYC): *Juggin' Around*
Chet Baker (NYC, August): *It could happen to you – Chet Baker Sings* (NYC, September): *Chet Baker in New York*
Count Basie (NYC, 3,4,14 April): *Basie Plays Hefti*
Sidney Bechet (Paris, 4 July): *Sidney Bechet & Teddy Buckner* (Knokke,7,10 July): *Festival de Jazz 1958* (Brussels, 29 July/3 August, with Buck Clayton & Vic Dickenson): *Concert à Bruxelles*
Art Blakey (NYC, 30 October): *Moanin'* (NYC, 9 November): *Holiday for Skins* (Paris, 22 November): *Olympia Concert*
Ruby Braff (NYC, 11,19 August): *Ruby Braff & His Men* (NYC, 4,5 December): *Ruby Braff & his Schubert Alley Cats*
Bob Brookmeyer (NYC, 23 October): *Kansas City Revisited*
Dave Brubeck (Copenhagen, 5 March): *The Dave Brubeck Quartet in Europe* (Newport, 3 July): *Newport 1958* (NYC, 28,30 July): *Jazz Impressions of Eurasia*
Ray Bryant (NYC, 19 December): *Alone with the Blues*
Kenny Burrell (NYC, 7 March): *Kenny Burrell & John Coltrane* (NYC, 15 May): *Blue Lights*
Billy Butterfield (NYC, 23,24,27 January): *A lovely way to spend an evening*
Charlie Byrd (Washington): *Jazz at the Showboat*
Donald Byrd (NYC, 2 December): *Off to the Races*
Benny Carter (LA): *Jazz Giant* (LA, 2 November): *Swingin' the 20's*
Ray Charles (Newport, 5 July): *At Newport*
Ray Charles/Milt Jackson (NYC, 10 April): *Soul Meeting*
Sonny Clark (NYC, 5 February): *Cool Struttin'*
Buck Clayton (NYC, 25 November): *Songs for Swingers*
Jimmy Cleveland (NYC, 16,17,18 December): *A map of Jimmy Cleveland*
Ornette Coleman (LA, 10,22 February, 24 March): *Somethin' Else*
John Coltrane (NYC, 10 January): *Lush Life* (NYC, 7 February): *Soultrane* (NYC, 26 March): *Settin' the Pace* (NYC, 23 May): *Black Pearls* (NYC, 11 July): *Standard Coltrane* (NYC, 10 January, 26 March, 16 August): *The Last Trane* (NYC, 13 October): *Coltrane Time*
Eddie Condon (NYC): *Eddie Condon & his Boys*
Chris Connor (NYC, 13 March, 8 April, 23 May): *Chris Craft*
Curtis Counce (NYC, April): *Exploring the Future*
Eddie 'Lockjaw' Davis (NYC, 20 June): *The Eddie 'Lockjaw' Davis Cookbook*
Miles Davis (NYC, 2,3 April): *Milestones* (NYC, 22,29 July, 4,18 August): *Porgy and Bess*
Lou Donaldson (NYC, 28 July): *Blues Walk* (NYC, 14 December): *Light Foot*

Kenny Dorham (NYC, 7 July, 15 August): *This is the Moment*
Ray Draper (NYC, November): *A Tuba Jazz*
Harry Edison (NYC, October): *The Swinger* (NYC, 12-14 November): *Roulette S2023*
Duke Ellington (LA, 5,11,12 February): *Black, Brown & Beige* (NYC, 20,24,26,31 March, 1 April): *At the Bal Masque* (Newport, 3 July, NYC, 21 July): *Newport 1958*
Duke Ellington's Spacemen (NYC, 2,3 April): *The Cosmic Scene*
Bill Evans (NYC, 15 December): *Everybody Digs Bill Evans*
Gil Evans (NYC, 9 April, 2,21,26 May): *New Bottle, Old Wine*
Tal Farlow (NYC, June): *This is Tal Farlow*
Art Farmer (NYC, 19 April, 1 May): *Portrait of Art Farmer* (NYC, 10,11,14 September): *Modern Art*
Victor Feldman (LA, 21,22 January): *The Arrival of Victor Feldman*
Maynard Ferguson (NYC, 6,7,8 May): *A Message from Newport*
Ella Fitzgerald (LA, March): *Sings the Irving Berlin Songbook Volumes 1&2*
Red Garland (NYC, 7 February): *It's a Blue World* (NYC, 11 April): *Manteca* (NYC, 22 August): *Rojo* (NYC, 21 November): *The Red Garland Trio* (NYC, 27 November): *All Kinds of Weather*
Erroll Garner (NYC, 27 March, 11 May): *Paris Impressions*
Stan Getz (Chicago, 16 February): *Stan meets Chet*
Dizzy Gillespie/Sonny Stitt/Sonny Rollins (NYC): *Sonny Side Up*
Jimmy Giuffre (NYC, 2,3,6 January): *The Music Man* (NYC, 20,21,23 January): *Trav'lin' Light* (NYC, 3 December): *The Western Suite*
Benny Golson (NYC, 12 November): *The Other Side of Benny Golson* (NYC, 17 November): *Benny Golson's Philadelphians*
Paul Gonsalves (Chicago): *Cookin'*
Benny Goodman (Brussels, 25 May): *Benny in Brussels* (Brussels, May, June): *Plays World Favourites in High Fidelity*
Bennie Green (NYC, 23 March): *Back on the Scene* (NYC, 28 April): *Soul Stirrin'*
Johnny Griffin (NYC, 25 February): *The Johnny Griffin Sextet* (NYC, 26,27 February): *Way Out!*
Tiny Grimes/Coleman Hawkins (NYC, 28 February): *Blues Groove*
Tiny Grimes (NYC, 18 July): *Callin' the Blues*
Bobby Hackett (NYC): *Don't Take Your Love From Me* (NYC): *At the Embers*
Chico Hamilton (LA, 29,30 January): *Plays South Pacific in Hi-Fi* (LA, 25 March): *Introducing Freddy Gambrell* (LA, 29,30 December): *Gongs East*
Wilbur Harden/Tommy Flanagan (NYC, 13 March): *Mainstream 1958*
Wilbur Harden (NYC, 18 August): *Jazz Way Out* (NYC, 26 August): *Tanganyika Strut* (NYC, 23,30 September): *The King and I*
Barry Harris (Chicago, 31 July): *Breakin' it up*
Hampton Hawes (LA, 27 January): *Four* (LA, 17 March): *For Real*
Roy Haynes (NYC, 14 November): *We Three*
Woody Herman (NYC, July): *The Herd rides again... in stereo* (NYC): *Herman's Heat and Puente's Beat*
Johnny Hodges (NYC, Summer): *Blues-a-plenty*
Billie Holiday (NYC, 18,19,20 February): *Lady in Satin*
Paul Horn (LA): *Plenty of Horn*
Mahalia Jackson (Newport, 7 July, NYC, 11 August): *Newport 1958*
Milt Jackson (Paris, 13,14 February): *Paris Session* (NYC, 28,29 December): *Bags Opus*
Milt Jackson/Coleman Hawkins (NYC, 12 September): *Bean Bags*
Ahmad Jamal (Chicago, 16 January): *At the Pershing Volumes 1&2 – But Not For Me* (Washington, 5,6 September): *Ahmad Jamal Trio*
Jazz Couriers (London, 16 February): *In Concert*
JJ Johnson (NYC, 19 February): *JJ in Person*
Hank Jones (NYC): *The Talented Touch* (NYC, 31 January): *Swings Songs from Gigi*
Philly Joe Jones (NYC, 17 September): *Blues for Dracula*
Wynton Kelly (NYC, 31 January): *Wynton Kelly*
Stan Kenton (Balboa, 20,21 January): *Back to Balboa* (LA, 22,29 April, 15,19 May): *The Ballad Style of Stan Kenton*

Barney Kessel (LA, 19,21 August): *The Pollwinners ride again!* (LA, 19,22 December): *Plays Carmen*
Lee Konitz (Pittsburgh, March): *The Real Lee Konitz*
Gene Krupa (NYC): *Krupa Rocks*
Lambert, Hendricks & Ross (NYC, 26,27 May, 2,3 September): *Sing Along with Basie*
Harold Land (LA, 13,14 January): *Harold in the Land of Jazz*
Yusef Lateef (Detroit,8 April): *At Cranbrook*
Ramsey Lewis (Chicago, 9 February): *Ramsey Lewis and the Gentle Men of Swing Volume 2*
Abbey Lincoln (NYC): *That's Him* (NYC, April): *It's Magic*
Herbie Mann (NYC, 14 February): *Just Wailin'*
Shelly Manne (LA, 15 April, 22 July): *The Bells are Ringing*
Blue Mitchell (NYC, 2,3 July): *Big Six*
Hank Mobley/Lee Morgan (NYC, 9 February): *Peckin' Time*
Hank Mobley (NYC, 21 April): *Monday Night at Birdland*
Modern Jazz Quartet (Stuttgart, 20,21 February): *European Windows* (Lenox, 3 August): *The Modern Jazz Quartet at Music Inn*
Thelonious Monk/Clark Terry (NYC, 7-12 May): *Globetrotters*
Thelonious Monk (Five Spot, NYC, August): *Thelonious in Action / Misterioso*
Montgomery Brothers (Indianapolis, January): *The Montgomery Brothers and Five Others*
Wes Montgomery/Harold Land (LA, April): *Wes Montomery/Harold Land Quintet*
James Moody (Chicago, 13,14,16 September): *Last Train from Overbrook*
Lee Morgan (NYC, 2 February): *Candy*
Gerry Mulligan (LA, 24 May): *The Jazz Combo from 'I Want to Live'* (NYC, 17,18,23 December): *The New Gerry Mulligan Quartet*
Phineas Newborn (NYC, 28 March, 3 April): *Phineas Newborn Trio*
David 'Fathead' Newman (NYC, 5 November): *Ray Charles presents David Newman*
Joe Newman (NYC, 13,15,17 January): *Soft Swinging Jazz* (Scandinavia, 2,13 October): *Joe Newman and Count Basie's All Stars*

Lennie Niehaus (LA): *I Swing for you*
Red Norvo (LA, 3,4 June): *Windjammer City Style*
Anita O'Day (Chicago, 16 April): *At the London House* (LA, September): *Sings the Winners*
Kid Ory (SF): *Kid Ory Plays WC Handy*
Oscar Peterson (Amsterdam, March): *At the Concertgebouw* (Toronto, July): *A Night on the Town* (NYC, 18 November): *Plays 'My Fair Lady'*
Bud Powell (NYC, 25 May): *The Amazing Bud Powell – Time Waits* (NYC, 29 December): *The Scene Changes – The Amazing Bud Powell*
Andre Previn (LA, 7,8 April): *Gigi* (LA, 10 August): *Sessions, Live* (LA, 12,13,20,30 August): *Plays Songs by Vernon Duke* (LA, 26 November): *King Size*
Gene Quill (NYC): *Three Bones and a Quill*
Paul Quinichette (NYC, July): *Kid from Denver*
Dizzy Reece (London, 24 August, 2 October): *Blues in Trinity*
Jerome Richardson (NYC, 10 November): *Midnight Oil*
Max Roach (Chicago, 4 January): *Max* (Chicago): *Max Roach, Plus Four, On the Chicago Scene* (NYC, April): *Max Plays Charlie Parker* (NYC, 4 September): *Deeds not Words*
Luckey Roberts/Willie 'The Lion' Smith (NYC, 18 March): *Luckey & The Lion: Harlem Piano*
Shorty Rogers (LA, 27,30 January): *Gigi in Jazz* (LA, 19,26 June): *Afro-Cuban Influence*
Sonny Rollins (NYC, February): *Freedom Suite* (NYC, 10,11 July): *Sonny Rollins & The Big Brass* (NYC, 28 September): *Newk's Time* (LA, 20-22 October): *Sonny Rollins and the Contemporary Leaders*
Jimmy Rushing (NYC, 20,26,27 February): *Little Jimmy Rushing and the Big Brass*
George Russell (NYC, 12 September): *New York, NY*
Pee Wee Russell (NYC): *A Portrait of Pee Wee*
Shirley Scott (NYC, 27 May): *Shirley's Sounds / Great Scott* (NYC, 23 November): *Scottie / Shirley Scott Trio*
Bud Shank/Laurindo Almeida (LA, March): *Latin Contrasts*
Bud Shank (Johannesburg, April): *Bud Shank in Africa*
Horace Silver (NYC, 13 January): *Further Explorations*
Zoot Sims/Bob Brookmeyer (NYC, 27 December): *Zoot Sims/Bob Brookmeyer Quintet*

Jimmy Smith (NYC, 25 February): *The Sermon* (NYC, 26 February): *Softly as a Summer Breeze* (NYC, 25 February, 25 August): *Houseparty* (NYC, 7 April): *Cool Blues* (NYC, 15 July): *On the Sunny Side* (NYC, 17 July): *Home Cookin'*
Willie 'The Lion' Smith (NYC): *The Lion Roars* (NYC): *The Legend of Willie 'The Lion' Smith*
Rex Stewart (Long Island, 1 August): *Henderson Homecoming*
Sonny Stitt (Chicago, 1 August): *Burnin'*
Buddy Tate (NYC, 12,26 February): *Swinging Like Tate!*
Cecil Taylor (NYC, 9 June): *Looking Ahead*
Jack Teagarden (Chicago, April): *Big T's Dixieland Band*
The Three Sounds (NYC, 16,18 September): *Introducing the Three Sounds / The Three Sounds Volume 2*
Cal Tjader/Stan Getz (SF, 8 February): *Cal Tjader/Stan Getz Sextet*
Cal Tjader (SF): *San Francisco Moods* (SF, September): *Latin Concept* (SF): *Latin for Lovers with Strings*
Cy Touff (Chicago, 28,29 August): *Touff Assignment*
Sarah Vaughan (Chicago, 7 March): *After Hours at the London House* (Chicago, March): *At Mister Kelly's*
Mal Waldron (NYC, 31 January): *Mal 3 / Sounds*
Dinah Washington (NYC): *Sings Fats Waller* (NYC): *Sings Bessie Smith*
Dickie Wells (NYC, 3,4 February/21 April): *Bones for the King*
Randy Weston (Newport, 5 July): *New Faces at Newport* (NYC, October): *Little Niles*
Cootie Williams (NYC, 5,25 March, 8 April): *Cootie Williams in Hi-Fi*
Claude Williamson (LA): *Mulls the Mulligan Scene* (Milan, 1 April): *In Italy*
Kai Winding (NYC, 22,26,29 August): *The Swingin' States*
Lem Winchester (Chicago, 8 October): *Lem Winchester and the Ramsey Lewis Trio*
Lester Young (NYC, 8 February): *Laughin' To Keep From Cryin'*

Top left: Count Basie and his Orchestra.
Bottom left: Leonard Feather presents Horace Silver with a silver record awarded by Blue Note Records. Looking on are Five Spot owner Joe Termini and Francis Wolff and Alfred Lion of Blue Note.
Above: Woody Herman conducts his swinging Herd at a dance session.

Photograph Courtesy: Max Jones

1959

Dwike Mitchell (29) and Willie Ruff (28) take jazz to USSR.

Thelonious Monk (42) and his Band appear at Town Hall Concert in New York.

Ornette Coleman (29) and Don Cherry (23) arrive in New York.

Ronnie Scott (32) opens his club in Gerrard Street, London.

Kid Ory (72) and his Band, featuring Red Allen (51), tour Europe.

Buddy Rich (42) suffers a heart attack in December.

Wes Montgomery (34) is featured with the Mastersounds.

BIRTHS
Ken Peplowski (reeds) 23 May
Marcus Miller (bass guitar) 14 June
Stanley Jordan (guitar) 31 July
Tony Reedus (drums) 22 September
Omar Hakim (drums)

DEATHS
Ed Cuffee (56) 3 January
Boyce Brown (48) 30 January
Baby Dodds (60) 14 February
Lester Young (49) 15 March
Hal McIntyre (44) 5 May
Sidney Bechet (68) 14 May
Lawrence Marrero (58) 5 June
Shadow Wilson (39) 11 July
Billie Holiday (44) 17 July
Omer Simeon (57) 17 September
Alphonso Trent (54) 14 October
Minor 'Ram' Hall (62) 23 October
Leslie 'Jiver' Hutchinson (52) 22 November *auto crash*
Sidney Desvignes (66) 2 December
Avery Parrish (42) 10 December
Charlie Johnson (68) 13 December
Willie Hightower (70) December
Sheldon Hemphill (53) December

BOOKS
Samuel Charters: *The Country Blues*
Larry Gara: *The Baby Dodds Story*
Nat Hentoff: *Jazz: New Perspectives on the History of Jazz*
Raymond Horricks: *These Jazzmen of our Time*
Grady Johnson: *The Five Pennies: The Biography of Red Nichols*
Albert McCarthy: *Louis Armstrong*
Robert Reisner: *The Literature of Jazz: a selective bibliography*
Martin Williams: *The Art of Jazz: essays on the nature and development of jazz*

FILMS
Anatomy of a Murder (160mins): feature film with music and an appearance by Duke Ellington
The Beat Generation (93mins): feature film with appearance by Louis Armstrong Band
Drum Crazy (99mins): feature film biography of Gene Krupa
The Five Pennies (117mins): feature film biography of Red Nichols with Louis Armstrong, Shelly Manne
Tteater for a Story (30mins): Miles Davis Quintet in show made for TV

RECORDS
Cannonball Adderley (Chicago, 3 February): *In Chicago* (NYC, 12 April, 12 May): *Cannonball Takes Charge* (SF, 18,20 October): *In San Francisco*
Nat Adderley (NYC, 23 March): *Much Brass*
Mose Allison (NYC, 13 February): *Autumn Song*
Louis Armstrong All-Stars (NYC, 29,30 September/1 October): *AFLP 1930*
Chet Baker (NYC, March): *New Blue Horns* (Milan, 25 September): *In Milano* (Milan, 28,29 September, 5,6 October): *With Strings*
Count Basie (NYC, 23,24 January): *One More Time* (NYC, 28,29 April): *Chairman of the Board*
Louis Bellson (LA): *Drummer's Holiday*
Art Blakey (NYC, 15 April): *At the Jazz Corner of the World* (NYC, 10 November): *Africaine* (Paris, 15 November): *Paris Concert* (Paris, 18 December): *Paris Jam Session*
Ruby Braff (NYC): *Blowing Around the World*
Bob Brookmeyer/Bill Evans (NYC, 12 March): *The Ivory Hunters*
Bob Brookmeyer (NYC, 9 March, 6,9 April): *The Blues – Hot and Cold*

Pete Brown (NYC): *Pete Brown Quintet*
Dave Brubeck (LA, 22 April): *Gone With the Wind* (NYC, 25 June, 1 July): *Time Out* (NYC, 12,13 August): *The Riddle*
Ray Bryant (NYC, 21 September): *Little Susie* (hit single)
Kenny Burrell (NYC, 26 August): *At the Five Spot Cafe* (NYC, 17 September): *A Night at the Vanguard*
Charlie Byrd (Washington): *Byrd in the Wind* (Washington): *Jazz at the Showboat*
Donald Byrd (NYC, 31 May): *Byrd in Hand* (NYC, 4 October): *Fuego*
Candoli Brothers (LA): *Two For the Money*
Benny Carter (LA): *The Benny Carter Jazz Calendar*
Ray Charles (NYC, 6 May, 23 June): *The Genius*
June Christy (LA): *The Cool School*
Sonny Clark (NYC, 29 March): *My Conception*
Arnett Cobb (NYC, 9 January): *Blow, Arnett, Blow* (NYC, 27 February): *Smooth Sailing* (NYC, 14 May): *Party Time*
Ornette Coleman (LA, 16 January, 23 February, 9,10 March): *Tomorrow is the Question* (NYC, 22 May, 8 October): *The Shape of Jazz to Come* (NYC, 8,9 October): *Change of the Century*
John Coltrane/Milt Jackson (NYC, 15 January): *Bags and Trane*
John Coltrane (NYC, 4,5 May): *Giant Steps* (NYC, 24 November, 2 December): *Coltrane Jazz*
Chris Connor (NYC, 13 September): *Chris in Person* (NYC, 14,21 September/5 October): *Witchcraft*
Eddie Davis/Coleman Hawkins/Arnett Cobb/Buddy Tate (NYC): *Very Saxy*
Eddie Davis (NYC, 1 May): *Eddie 'Lockjaw' Davis Quintet with Shirley Scott* (NYC, 20 December): *Bacalao*
Miles Davis (NYC, 2 March, 22 April): *Kind of Blue*
Walter Davis Jr (NYC, 2 August): *Davis Cup*
Paul Desmond (NYC, 5-7 September): *And Friends*
Lou Donaldson (NYC, 12,18 February): *Lou Donaldson with the Three Sounds* (NYC, 31 October): *The Time is Right*
Kenny Dorham (NYC, 20 January, 18 February): *Blue Spring* (NYC, 13 November): *Quiet Kenny*
Teddy Edwards (LA, 16 August): *Teddy Edwards Quartet*
Duke Ellington (LA, 29 May/1,2 June): *Anatomy of a Murder* (NYC, 2 December): *Blues in Orbit*
Mercer Ellington (NYC, 16,18,20 March): *Colours in Rhythm*
Herb Ellis/Jimmy Giuffre (LA, 26 March): *Herb Ellis meets Jimmy Giuffre*
Bill Evans (NYC, 19 January): *Peace Piece and other pieces* (NYC, 15 May): *Undercurrent* (NYC, 28 December): *Portrait in Jazz*
Gil Evans (NYC, January/February): *Great Jazz Standards*
Art Farmer (NYC, May): *Brass Shout* (NYC): *Aztec Suite*
Vic Feldman (LA, 2,3,20 March, 4 May): *Latinville*
Ella Fitzgerald (LA, July): *Ella Sings Gershwin Vol 2*
Tommy Flanagan (NYC, 10 March): *Lonely Town*
Curtis Fuller (NYC, 21 May): *Blues-ette* (NYC, 25 August): *Arabia* (NYC, 17 December): *Imagination* (NYC, December): *Sliding Easy*
Red Garland (NYC, 17 April): *Red in Bluesville* (NYC, 11 December): *Red Garland Trio with Eddie 'Lockjaw' Davis*
Erroll Garner (NYC, 18 December): *Dreamstreet*
Terry Gibbs (LA,17,18 February): *Launching a new band*
Dizzy Gillespie (NYC, 17,18,19 February): *Have Trumpet, Will Excite*
Jimmy Giuffre (LA, January): *Seven Pieces* (LA, January): *Ad Lib* (NYC, 6,7 August): *The Easy Way*
Benny Golson (NYC, 30 June): *Gone with Golson* (NYC, 28 August): *Groovin' with Golson* (NYC, 23 December): *Gettin' with it*

Bennie Green (NYC, 25 January): *Walkin' and Talkin'*
Al Grey (NYC): *The Last of the Big Plungers*
Johnny Griffin (NYC, 4,5 August): *The Little Giant*
Chico Hamilton (LA, 9,12 January): *Ellington Suite* (LA, 19,20 May): *That Hamilton Man*
John Handy (NYC): *In the Vernacular*
Coleman Hawkins (NYC, 3 May): *Hawk Eyes*
Tubby Hayes (London, 26 June, 3 July): *Message from Britain* (London, December): *Tubby's Groove*
Jimmy Heath (NYC, 27,30 November, 7 December): *The Thumper*
Woody Herman (NYC, 31 July, 1 August): *The Fourth Herd*
Billie Holiday (NYC, 3,4,11 March): *Last Recording*
Elmo Hope (LA, 8 February): *Elmo Hope Trio*
Milt Jackson (NYC, 1 May, 9,10 September): *The Ballad Artistry of Milt Jackson*
Ahmad Jamal (Chicago, 22,28 February): *Jamal at the Penthouse*
Jazz Couriers (London, 27 May): *The Couriers of Jazz* (London, 26 June, 3 July): *The Last Word*
Jonah Jones (NYC): *I Dig Chicks*
Philly Joe Jones (NYC, 4,11,28 May): *Drums Around the World* (NYC, 17,18 November): *Showcase*
Quincy Jones (NYC, 26,27,28 May): *Birth of a Band*
Wynton Kelly (NYC, 19 February): *Kelly Blue* (NYC, 12 August): *Kelly Great*
Barney Kessel (LA, 30,31 March): *Some Like it Hot*
Harold Land (LA, August): *The Fox*
Yusef Lateef (NYC, 16 October): *Cry! Tender*
George Lewis (LA, October): *Doctor Jazz*
John Lewis (NYC, 7,8 May): *Improvised Meditations and Excursions* (NYC, 16,17,20 July): *Odds Against Tomorrow*
Ramsey Lewis (Chicago, April): *An Hour with the Ramsey Lewis Trio*
Teo Macero/Teddy Charles (NYC, 30 April, 15 May): *Something New, Something Blue*
Lennie McBrowne (LA): *Lennie McBrowne & the Jazz Souls*
Jackie McLean (NYC, 18 January): *Jackie's Bag* (NYC, 2 May): *New Soil* (NYC, 2 October): *Swing Swang Swingin'*
Shelly Manne (LA, 19,20 January): *Shelly Manne & his Men play Peter Gunn* (LA, 21-26 May): *Son of Gunn* (SF, 22,23,24 September): *At the Blackhawk, 4 Vols*
Warne Marsh (NYC): *The Art of Improvising*
The Mastersounds (Pasadena, 11 April): *In Concert*
Charlie Mingus (NYC, 16 January): *Jazz Portraits* (NYC, 4 February): *Blues and Roots* (NYC, 5,12 May): *Mingus Ah Um* (NYC, 1,13 November): *Mingus Dynasty*
Blue Mitchell (NYC, 5 January): *Out of the Blue* (NYC, 28 September): *Blue Soul*
Mitchell/Ruff Duo (NYC, 11 September): *Jazz Mission to Moscow*
Modern Jazz Quartet (NYC, 9,10 October): *Odds Against Tomorrow* (NYC, 21 December): *Pyramid*
Thelonious Monk (NYC, 28 February): *The Thelonious Monk Orchestra at Town Hall* (NYC, 1,2 June): *Five by Monk by Five* (SF, 21,22 October): *Thelonious Monk Alone in San Francisco*
J.R. Monterose (NYC, 24 November): *Straight Ahead*
Wes Montgomery (NYC, 5,6 October): *The Wes Montgomery Trio*
James Moody (Chicago, August): *James Moody* (Chicago, 29 December): *Hey! It's James Moody*
Sal Mosca (NYC, October): *On Piano*
Gerry Mulligan (LA, 3 November, 2 December): *Mulligan Meets Ben Webster*
Oliver Nelson (NYC, 30 October): *Meet Oliver Nelson*
Phineas Newborn (Rome, 28 May): *Phineas Newborn Plays Again* (NYC, 26,29 October): *I Love A Piano*
Albert Nicholas (Chicago, 19,27 July): *The Albert Nicholas Quartet*
Anita O'Day (LA, May): *Swings Cole Porter* (LA, July): *Cool Heat*
Marty Paich (LA): *The New York Scene* (LA, 14 September, 6 October): *Marty Paich Piano Quartet*
Duke Pearson (NYC, 29 October): *Profile* (NYC, 6 December): *Tender Feelin's*
Art Pepper (LA, 28 March, 13 May): *Art Pepper Plus Eleven*
Oscar Peterson (Paris, 18 May): *Jazz Portrait of Frank Sinatra* (Chicago, 14 July, 9 August): *The Cole Porter Songbook / The George Gershwin Songbook / The Duke Ellington Songbook / The Jerome Kern Songbook / The Richard Rodgers Songbook / The Harry Warren &*

Vincent Youmans Songbook / The Harold Arlen Songbook / The Jimmy McHugh Songbook (Chicago, August): *The Jazz Soul* (LA, October): *Porgy and Bess* (SF, October): *Swingin' Brass*

Oscar Pettiford (Vienna, 10,11 January): *The Legendary Oscar Pettiford* (Baden-Baden, 19 February / Copenhagen, 22 August): *Oscar Pettiford/Hans Koller Quintet*

The Pollwinners (LA, 2 November): *Pollwinners Three*

Andre Previn (LA, 26 February): *Plays Songs by Jerome Kern* (LA, 24,25 August): *West Side Story*

Dizzy Reece (NYC, 9 November): *Star Bright*

Jerome Richardson (NYC, 21 October): *Roamin' with Jerome Richardson*

Max Roach (NYC, Autumn): *The Many Sides of Max Roach* (NYC, 25 November): *Award-winning Drummer*

Sonny Rollins (Stockholm, 4 March): *In Sweden, 1959*

Ronnie Ross/Allan Ganley (NYC, 23 September): *The Jazzmakers*

Shirley Scott (NYC, 24 April): *Shirley Scott Plays the*

Duke (NYC, 4 December): *Soul Searchin'*

Tony Scott (NYC, 1,9 August): *Golden Moments / I'll Remember*

Wayne Shorter (NYC, 10 November): *Wayne Shorter Quintet*

Horace Silver (NYC, 1 February): *Finger Poppin'* (NYC, 10 August): *Blowin' the Blues Away*

Jimmy Smith (NYC, 24 May, 16 June): *Home Cookin'*

Johnny 'Hammond' Smith (NYC, 11 September): *All Soul* (NYC, 4 November): *That Good Feeling*

Sonny Stitt (NYC): *The Hard Swing* (Paris, 18 May): *Sits in with the Oscar Peterson Trio* (LA, December): *Saxophone Supremacy*

Ira Sullivan (Chicago, 26 July): *Ira Sullivan Quintet*

Art Taylor (NYC, 3 June): *Taylor's Tenors*

Billy Taylor (NYC, 24 June): *One For Fun* (NYC, 20,24 July): *Billy Taylor and Four Flutes*

Clark Terry (NYC, 24,26 February): *Top and Bottom Brass*

The Three Sounds (NYC, 11 February): *Bottoms Up*

(NYC, 20 May): *Good Deal*

Cal Tjader (SF): *A Night at the Blackhawk* (SF): *Goes Latin* (Carmel, 20 April): *Cal Tjader's Concert by the Sea*

Stan Tracey (London, 22,26 May): *Little Klunk*

Ben Webster (NYC, 9 April): *Ben Webster and Associates* (NYC, 6 November): *Ben Webster with the Oscar Peterson Trio*

Dickie Wells (NYC): *Trombone Four in hand*

Frank Wess (NYC, 8 December): *Opus de Blues*

Randy Weston (NYC, May): *Destry Rides Again* (NYC, 26 October): *Live at the Five Spot*

Tommy Whittle (London, May): *New Horizons*

Lem Winchester (NYC, 25 September): *Winchester Special*

Lester Young (Paris, 4 March): *Lester Young In Paris*

Left: Ornette Coleman and Don Cherry recording for Atlantic.
Below: Billie Holiday photographed in London in February, just five month prior to her death, with accompanist Mal Waldron.

Photograph Courtesy: *Max Jones*

GREENWICH VILLAGE

By the middle fifties, many of New York's jazz clubs were in the Village; the Village Gate, Half Note, Five Spot, Café Bohemia and the Village Vanguard featuring musicians like Miles Davis, John Coltrane, Thelonious Monk, Charlie Mingus, Zoot Sims, Bill Evans, Art Blakey etc. The oldest of these clubs was Max Gordon's Village Vanguard which opened in 1935 and remains, into the 90's, a mecca for jazz lovers from all over the world, even surviving Max Gordon's death in 1989.

In the late thirties and throughout the forties, Dixielanders held sway, first at Nick's with Bobby Hackett, Pee Wee Russell, Eddie Condon et al, and later, for more than a decade, at Eddie Condon's club on West 3rd Street.

Another successful club was Barney Josephson's Café Society at Sheridan Square which opened in 1939 with Billie Holiday, Frankie Newton and the Boogie Woogie Boys (Meade Lux Lewis, Albert Ammons and Pete Johnson).

In 1953 Charlie Parker was briefly featured at the short-lived Open Door, and through the 60's and 70's many clubs opened and closed in quick succession. The 80's saw the emergence of Sweet Basil, the Blue Note and Carlos 1 to rank alongside the long running Village Gate and Village Vanguard.

Another popular feature of the Village nightlife is the piano bar, typified by the Cookery, Bradley's and the Knickerbocker Saloon.

1930's
Café Society Downtown
2 Sheridan Square (Jan 1939–50's)
Nick's
W 10th Street & Seventh Avenue (1937–63)
Village Vanguard
178 Seventh Avenue (1935–)
1940's
Eddie Condon's
47 W 3rd Street (20 Dec 1945–1957)
Pied Piper
15 Barrow Street
1950's
Arthur's Tavern
57 Grove Street (1950's–)
Café Bohemia
15 Barrow Street (1955–?)
Five Spot
5 Cooper Square (1950's–1962)
Half Note
289 Hudson Street, near Spring Street (1957–72)
Jazz Gallery
80 St Mark's Place at 1st Avenue (Dec 1959–?)
Open Door
55 W 3rd Street (1953)
Village Gate
160 Bleecker Street at Thompson (1958–)

1960's
Slugs
242 E 3rd Street (1966–72)
1970's
Ali's Alley
North Greene Street between Spring & Broome (1973–79)
Boomer's
340 Bleecker Street at Christopher Street (1971–77)
Bottom Line
15 W4th Street at Mercer Street (1974–?)
Bradley's
70 University Place at E11th (1970's–)
Cookery
21 University Place at E8th Street (1970–80's)
Fat Tuesday's
190 Third Avenue at E 17th Street (1979–)
Knickerbocker Saloon
33 University Place at E9th Street (1978–)
One Fifth Avenue
Fifth Avenue at 8th Street (1970's & 80's)
Seventh Avenue South
21 Seventh Avenue South at Leroy Street (1978–85)
Sweet Basil
88 Seventh Avenue South at Bleecker Street (Jan 1975–)
1980's
Blue Note
131 W3rd Street (1981–)
Carlos 1
432 Sixth Avenue at W10th Street (1980's–)
Condon's
117 E 15th Street
Greene Street
101 Greene Street near Prince Street (1980–)
Knitting Factory
47 E Houston Street
Lush Life
184 Thompson Street at Bleecker (1982–84)
Village West
577 Hudson Street near Bank Street (1982–84)
Visiones
125 Macdougal Street
Whippoorwill
18 E18th Street (1986)
Zinno's
126 W13th Street (1982–)

GREENWICH VILLAGE

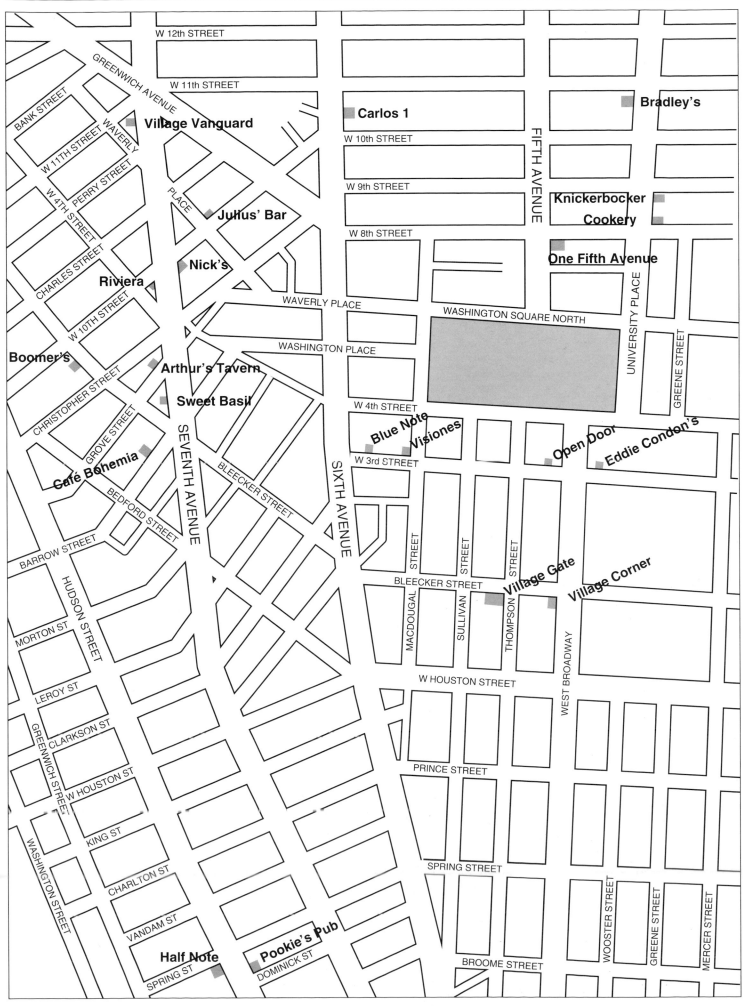

W 12th STREET

W 11th STREET

GREENWICH AVENUE

BANK STREET

WAVERLY

Village Vanguard

Carlos 1

W 10th STREET

Bradley's

FIFTH AVENUE

W 11TH STREET

PERRY STREET

W 4TH STREET

PLACE

W 9th STREET

Julius' Bar

Knickerbocker

Cookery

CHARLES STREET

Nick's

W 8th STREET

One Fifth Avenue

Riviera

UNIVERSITY PLACE

W 10th STREET

WAVERLY PLACE

WASHINGTON SQUARE NORTH

Boomer's

WASHINGTON PLACE

Arthur's Tavern

CHRISTOPHER STREET

GREENE STREET

Sweet Basil

W 4th STREET

Blue Note

Visiones

Open Door

Eddie Condon's

GROVE STREET

W 3rd STREET

Café Bohemia

SEVENTH AVENUE

BLEECKER STREET

BEDFORD STREET

BARROW STREET

SIXTH AVENUE

HUDSON STREET

MACDOUGAL STREET

SULLIVAN STREET

THOMPSON STREET

Village Gate

Village Corner

MORTON ST

BLEECKER STREET

WEST BROADWAY

LEROY ST

W HOUSTON STREET

CLARKSON ST

GREENWICH STREET

W HOUSTON ST

PRINCE STREET

KING ST

CHARLTON ST

SPRING STREET

WASHINGTON STREET

VANDAM ST

WOOSTER STREET

GREENE STREET

MERCER STREET

Pookie's Pub

Half Note

SPRING ST

DOMINICK ST

BROOME STREET

1960

Art Farmer (32) and Benny Golson (31) co-lead the Jazztet.

Quincy Jones (27) tours Europe with a big band.

Herbie Mann (30) tours Africa for the US State Department.

Gerry Mulligan (33) organises a 13-piece Concert Jazz Band.

Cannonball Adderley (31) and his Quintet are a commercial hit following their recording of 'This Here'.

George Russell (37) forms a sextet.

Riot at Newport curtails the jazz festival. A rival festival is held several blocks away at Cliff Walk Manor, organised by Charlie Mingus (38).

Art Pepper (34) is jailed on a narcotics charge.

Shelly Manne (40) opens a jazz club, Shelly's Manne-Hole, in Los Angeles (2 November).

John Coltrane (33) leaves Miles Davis (34) Quintet and later forms a quartet featuring Elvin Jones (32) on drums.

Stan Getz (33) is living in Copenhagen.

Gene Krupa (51) is ordered to take a complete rest following a heart attack.

BIRTHS
Eliane Elias (piano) 19 March
John Pizzarelli (guitar) 6 April
Donald Harrison (alto sax) 23 June
Greg Osby (saxophones) 3 August
Branford Marsalis (tenor sax) 26 August
Lonnie Plaxico (bass) 4 September
Django Bates (piano) 2 October
Kenny Garrett (alto sax) 9 October

DEATHS
Lee Collins (58) 3 July
Prince Robinson (58) 23 July
Arv Garrison (37) 30 July
Jimmy Bertrand (60) August
Oscar Pettiford (37) 8 September
Lawrence Duhé (83)

BOOKS
Edward Albee: *The Death of Bessie Smith* (play)
Sidney Bechet: *Treat it Gentle*
H.O. Brunn: *The Story of the Original Dixieland Jazz Band*
Dom Cerulli, Burt Korall & Mort Nasatir: *The Jazz Word*
Leonard Feather: *The New Edition of the Encyclopaedia of Jazz*
Charles Fox: *Fats Waller*
Charles Fox, Peter Gammond & Alun Morgan: *Jazz on Record: a critical guide*
Andre Francis: *Jazz*
J. Gelber: *The Connection* (play)
Rex Harris: *Enjoying Jazz*
Max Harrison: *Charlie Parker*
Michael James: *Ten Modern Jazzmen*
Albert McCarthy: *Louis Armstrong*
Paul Oliver: *Blues fell this morning*
Leroy Ostransky: *The Anatomy of Jazz*
Frederic Ramsey Jr: *Been here and gone*
Jay D. Smith & Len Gutteridge: *Jack Teagarden – the story of a jazz maverick*
D. Stock: *Jazz Street*
Sinclair Traill & Gerald Lascelles (eds): *Just Jazz, Vol 4*
Howard J. Waters Jr: *Jack Teagarden's Music*
Martin Williams: *King Oliver*
K. Williamson (ed): *This is Jazz*

FILMS
Jazz on a Summer's Day (86mins): filmed at 1958 Newport Jazz Festival
Let no man write my epitaph (106mins): feature film with Ella Fitzgerald in an acting role
Mann with a flute (14mins): Herbie Mann music short
Memphis Slim (35mins): music short
The Subterraneans (89mins): feature film with Gerry Mulligan in an acting role

COMPOSITIONS
Duke Ellington: *Suite Thursday / Paris Blues*

RECORDS
Cannonball Adderley (NYC, 1 February / Chicago, 29 March): *Them dirty blues* (SF, 21 May / LA, 5 June): *Cannonball and the Poll Winners* (LA, 16 October): *Live at the Lighthouse*

Nat Adderley (NYC, 25,27 January): *Work Song* (NYC, 9 August / 15 September): *That's Right!*
Henry 'Red' Allen (NYC): *Plays King Oliver*
Gene Ammons (NYC, 16 June): *Boss tenor* (NYC, 17 June): *Angel eyes*
Curtis Amy (LA, August): *The Blues Message*
Curtis Amy/Frank Butler (LA): *Groovin' Blue*
Louis Armstrong (NYC, 24,25 May): *Louis Armstrong with the Dukes of Dixieland*
Benny Bailey (NYC, 25 November): *Big Brass*
Dave Bailey (NYC, 19,20 July): *One foot in the gutter* (NYC, 26,27 October): *Gettin' into somethin'*
Count Basie (NYC, June/July): *The Count Basie Story* (NYC, 15 July): *Not now, I'll tell you when* (NYC, 17 November): *Kansas City Suite*
Art Blakey (NYC, 6 March): *The Big Beat* (NYC, 7 August): *Like someone in love* (NYC, 14 August): *A night in Tunisia* (NYC, 14 September): *Meet you at the jazz corner of the world, vols 1&2*
Bob Brookmeyer (NYC, 6,9 April): *Portrait of the artist* (NYC, June): *Jazz is a kick* (LA, 28 July): *The blues hot and cold*
Tina Brooks (NYC, 25 June): *True Blue* (NYC, 1 September / 20 October): *Back To The Tracks*
Oscar Brown Jr (NYC): *Sin and Soul*
Ray Brown (LA): *Jazz Cello*
Dave Brubeck (NYC, 30 January / 14 February): *Bernstein Plays Brubeck Plays Bernstein* (NYC, May/June): *Brubeck à la mode* (NYC): *Dave Brubeck Quartet featuring Jimmy Rushing* (NYC, September/December): *Tonight Only!*
Ray Bryant (NYC, 19 January): *Little Susie* (NYC, March): *Madison time*
Charlie Byrd (Washington): *Charlie's choice* (NYC, December): *At the Village Vanguard*
Donald Byrd (NYC, 10 July): *Byrd in flight* (Chicago, 28 October): *Two sides of Donald Byrd* (NYC, 11 November): *At the Half Note Cafe*
Harry Carney (Boston, 16,17 September): *Harry Carney and the Duke's men*
Paul Chambers (NYC, 12 May): *First Bassman*
Ray Charles (NYC, 25,29 March): *Genius hits the road* (NYC, 26,27 December): *Genius + soul = jazz*
Sonny Clark (NYC, 23 March): *Sonny Clark Trio*
Buck Clayton/Buddy Tate (NYC, 20 December): *Kansas City nights*
Arnett Cobb (NYC, 16 February): *More Party Time* (NYC, 16,17 February): *Movin' right along* (NYC, 1 November): *Ballads by Cobb* (NYC, 30 November): *Sizzlin'*
Al Cohn/Zoot Sims (NYC, 1,3 June): *You'n'me*
Ornette Coleman (NYC, 19,26 July / 2 August): *This is our music* (NYC, 21 December): *Free jazz*
John Coltrane (NYC, July): *John Coltrane & Don Cherry, the avant garde* (NYC, 21-24, 26 October): *My favourite things* (NYC, 24 October): *Coltrane plays the blues* (NYC, 24,26 October): *Coltrane's sound*
Chris Connors (NYC, 27 October / 16 November): *Portrait of Chris*
Eddie 'Lockjaw' Davis (NYC, 20 September): *Trane whistle*
Miles Davis (NYC, 10,11 March): *Sketches of Spain*
Wilbur de Paris (NYC, 9.10 May): *The Wild Jazz Age* (Antibes, 9 July): *On the Riviera*

Eric Dolphy (NYC, 1 April): *Outward bound* (NYC, 15 August): *Out there* (NYC, 21 December): *Far cry!*
Lou Donaldson (NYC, 5,29 February): *Sunny side up* (NYC, 22 July): *Midnight sun*
Kenny Dorham (NYC, 11,12 February): *Jazz contemporary* (NYC, 9 December): *Showboat*
Kenny Drew (NYC, 11 February): *Undercurrent*
Harry Edison (NYC, 12 February): *Patented by Edison*
Teddy Edwards (LA, 17 August): *Teddy's ready*
Duke Ellington (LA, June): *Asphalt Jungle*
Don Ellis (NYC, 4,5 October): *How time passes*
Herb Ellis (LA): *Thank you, Charlie Christian*
Booker Ervin (NYC, June): *The Book cooks* (NYC, 26 November): *Cookin'*
Gil Evans (NYC, 18,30 November / 10,15 December): *Out of the cool*
Al Fairweather/Sandy Brown (London, 6,8 July / 10,11 October): *Doctor McJazz*
Art Farmer (NYC): *Nature boy* (NYC, 6,9,10 February): *Meet the Jazztet* (NYC, 16,19 September): *Big city sounds* (NYC, September): *Art*
Ella Fitzgerald (Berlin, 13 February): *Ella in Berlin*
Tommy Flanagan (NYC, 18 May): *The Tommy Flanagan Trio*
Jimmy Forrest (NYC, 9 August): *Forrest fire!*
Curtis Fuller (NYC, 6,7 June): *Images*
Hank Garland (NYC): *Jazz winds from a new direction*
Red Garland (NYC, 15 July): *Hallelo-y'all*
Stan Getz (Copenhagen): *At large*
Dizzy Gillespie (NYC, 27,28 April): *Portrait of Duke Ellington* (NYC, 14,15,16 November): *Gillespiana*
Jimmy Giuffre (NYC, August): *Jimmy Giuffre Quartet in person*
Paul Gonsalves (NYC, 20 December): *Getting Together*
Dexter Gordon (LA, 13 October): *The resurgence of Dexter Gordon*
Bennie Green (NYC, December): *Hornful of soul*
Johnny Griffin (NYC, 24 May): *Johnny Griffin and the big soul band* (NYC, 27 September): *Studio jazz party*
Johnny Griffin/Lockjaw Davis (NYC): *The Tenor Scene*
Tiny Grimes (NJ): *Tiny in Swingville*
Gigi Gryce (NYC, 11 March): *Sayin' something* (NYC, 3 May): *The hap'nin's* (NYC, 7 June): *The rat race blues*
Slide Hampton (NYC): *Sister Salvation* (NYC, 15 February / 17 October): *Somethin' sanctified*
John Handy: *In the vernacular*
Joe Harriott (London, November): *Free form*
Barry Harris (LA, 15,16 May): *At the Jazz Workshop*
Coleman Hawkins (NYC): *The Hawk swings* (NYC, 29 January): *At ease with Coleman Hawkins*
Coleman Hawkins/Lockjaw Davis (NYC, 30 December): *Night Hawk*
Roy Haynes (NYC, 5 July): *Just us*
Jimmy Heath (NYC, 24,28 June): *Really big*
Woody Herman (Chicago, 22 March): *The new swinging Herman herd*
Earl Hines (NYC, January): *Earl's pearls*
Elmo Hope (LA, February): *Elmo Hope with Frank Butler and James Bond*
Lightnin' Hopkins (NYC, October): *Lightnin' in New York*
Freddie Hubbard (NYC, 19 June): *Open sesame* (NYC, 6 November): *Goin' up*
Helen Humes (LA, 6,7,8 September): *Songs I like to sing*
Milt Jackson (NYC, 23,24 February): *Vibrations*
Ahmad Jamal (Chicago, 15,16 August): *Listen to the Ahmad Jamal Quintet*
JJ Johnson/Kai Winding (NYC, 3 October / 2,4,9 November): *The great Jay & Kai*
Etta Jones (NYC, 21 June): *Don't go to strangers*
Hank Jones (NYC): *Porgy & Bess – Swinging impressions*
Philly Joe Jones (NYC, 20 May): *Philly Joe's beat*
Quincy Jones (Paris, 27,29 February / 21 April): *I dig dancers*
Sam Jones (NYC, 8,10 March): *The Soul Society*
Clifford Jordan (NYC, 10 August): *Spellbound*
Duke Jordan (NYC, 4 August): *Flight to Jordan*
Stan Kenton (Las Vegas): *At the Tropicana*
Wynton Kelly (NYC, 27 April): *Kelly at midnight*
Barney Kessel (LA, 19 July): *Swingin' party at Contemporary*
Roland Kirk (Chicago, 7 June): *Introducing Roland Kirk*
Steve Lacy (NYC, Autumn): *The straight horn*
Harold Land (SF, 17,18 May): *West Coast blues*

(NYC, 5,8 July): *Eastward ho! Harold Land in New York* (LA, 25 July): *Take aim*

Yusef Lateef (NYC, 30 April): *Contemplation* (NYC, 9 May): *Three faces of Yusef Lateef* (NYC, 4,6 October): *The centaur and the phoenix* (NYC, 22 October): *Lost in sound*

Latin Jazz Quintet featuring Eric Dolphy (NYC, 19 August): *Caribe*

John Lewis (NYC, 12,15,16 February): *The golden striker* (NYC, 29 July / 8 September): *The wonderful world of jazz*

John Lewis/Gunther Schuller (NYC, 20 December): *Jazz abstractions*

Ramsey Lewis (Chicago): *Stretching out* (Chicago, April): *The Ramsey Lewis Trio in Chicago* (Chicago): *The sound of Christmas*

Booker Little (NYC): *The Legendary Quartet Album*

Johnny Lytle (NYC, 16 June): *Blue vibes*

Les McCann (LA, February): *The truth* (LA, June): *The shout* (SF, December): *Les McCann in San Francisco*

Jack McDuff (NYC, 25 January): *Brother Jack* (NYC, 12 July): *Tough Duff*

Howard McGhee (NYC, 13 June): *Dusty blue* (NYC, Spring): *Music from the Connection*

Ken McIntyre (NYC, 31 May): *Stone blues*

Ken McIntyre/Eric Dolphy (NYC, 28 June): *Looking ahead*

Jackie McLean (NYC, 17 April): *Capuchin swing* (NYC, 1 September): *Jackie's bag*

Junior Mance (NYC, 25 October): *The soulful piano of Junior Mance*

Mangione Brothers (NYC, 8 August): *The Jazz brothers*

Herbie Mann (NYC, 2,3,4 August): *The common ground*

Shelly Manne (LA, 28 January): *The proper time* (London, March): *West coast jazz in England*

Barry Miles (NYC): *Miles of genius*

Charlie Mingus (NYC, 24,25 May): *Pre-Bird / Mingus revisited* (Antibes, 13 July): *At Antibes* (NYC, 20 October): *Charles Mingus presents Charles Mingus* (NYC, 20 October / 11 November): *Stormy weather*

Blue Mitchell (NYC, 24,25 August): *Blue's moods*

Red Mitchell (LA, November): *Rejoice*

Hank Mobley (NYC, 7 February): *Soul Station* (NYC, 13 November): *Roll Call*

Modern Jazz Quartet (Scandinavia, April): *European Concerts, Vols 1&2* (NYC, 3,4 June): *MJQ with symphony orchestra*

Thelonious Monk (SF, 29 April): *Quartet plus two at the Blackhawk*

J.R. Monterose (NYC, October): *The message*

Wes Montgomery (NYC, 26,28 January): *The incredible jazz guitar of Wes Montgomery* (LA, 11 October): *Movin' along*

James Moody (NYC, July): *James Moody with strings*

Lee Morgan (NYC, 3 February): *Here's Lee Morgan* (NYC, 28 April): *Lee-way* (Chicago, 13 October): *Expoobident*

Gerry Mulligan (NYC, 28,29 May): *The Concert Jazz Band* (LA, July): *Meets Johnny Hodges* (Milan, Berlin, California, November): *On tour* (NYC, December): *New York, December 1960*

Oliver Nelson (NYC, 22 March): *Taking care of business* (NYC, 27 May): *Screamin' the blues* (NYC, 23 August): *Nocturne* (NYC, 9 September): *Soul battle*

David Newman (NYC, 21 December): *Straight ahead*

Joe Newman (NYC, 4 May): *Jive at five*

Anita O'Day (LA): *Waiter, make mine blues*

Horace Parlan (NYC, 29 February): *Movin' and groovin'* (NYC, 20 April): *Us three* (NYC, 14 July): *Speakin' my piece* (NYC, 4 December): *Headin' south*

Art Pepper (LA, 29 February): *Gettin' together* (LA, 24,25 October): *Smack up* (LA, 23,25 November): *Intensity*

Charles Persip (NYC, 2 April): *Charles Persip and the Jazz Statesmen*

Oscar Peterson (Chicago): *The Trio*

King Pleasure (LA, 14 April): *Golden days*

The Pollwinners (LA, 30,31 August / 1 September): *Exploring the scene*

Bud Powell (Paris, 14 February / 12 March / 15 June): *Bud in Paris* (Essen, 2 April): *Bud Powell in Concert*

Andre Previn (LA, 20 February / 1 March): *Like Previn* (LA, 4,5 May): *Plays Harold Arlen* (LA): *Give my regards to Broadway* (LA): *Camelot*

Julian Priester (NYC, 12 July): *Spiritsville*

Freddie Redd (NYC, 15 February): *The Connection* (NYC, 13 August): *Shades of Redd*

Dizzy Reece (NYC, 12 May): *Soundin' off*

Buddy Rich (Chicago, 3,4 October): *Playtime*

Max Roach (NYC, January): *Quiet as it's kept* (Paris, 1 March): *Parisian sketches* (NYC, 31 August/ 6 September): *We insist! Freedom now* (NYC, November): *Moon faced and starry eyed*

Shorty Rogers (LA, 3,17,24 May): *The swingin' Nutcracker Suite*

Charlie Rouse (NYC, 11 May): *Takin' care of business* (NYC, 20,21 December): *Yeah!*

Jimmy Rushing (NYC, 7,13 July): *Jimmy Rushing and the Smith girls*

George Russell (NYC): *Jazz in the Space Age* (NYC, 20 September): *At the Five Spot* (NYC, September/October): *George Russell Sextet in KC* (NYC, 18 October): *Stratusphunk*

Pee Wee Russell/Buck Clayton (NYC, 29 March): *Swingin' with Pee Wee*

Shirley Scott (NYC, 8 April): *Shirley Scott Trio* (NYC, 23 June): *Soul Sisters* (NYC, 8 July): *Mucho mucho* (NYC, 27 September): *Like Cozy*

Bud Shank (LA): *New Groove*

Horace Silver (NYC, 9 July): *Horace-scope*

Zoot Sims (NYC, July): *Down Home*

Jimmy Smith (NYC, 4 January): *Crazy baby* (NYC, 22 March): *Open House* (NYC, 25 April): *The Midnight Special* (NYC, 25 April): *Back at the Chicken Shack*

Johnny 'Hammond' Smith (NYC, 22 April): *Talk that talk* (NYC, 14 October): *Gettin' the message*

Les Spann (NYC, 8,16 December): *Gemini*

Sonny Stitt (NYC): *Stittsville / Sonny Side Up*

Buddy Tate (NYC, 18 October): *Tate-a-Tate*

Art Taylor (NYC, 6 August): *AT's Delight*

Cecil Taylor (NYC, 12,13 October): *The world of Cecil Taylor*

Clark Terry (NYC, 10 November): *Colour changes*

The Three Sounds (NYC, 28 June): *Moods / Feelin' good* (NYC, 13,14 December): *Here we come / It just got to be*

Bobby Timmons (NYC, 13,14 January): *This Here is Bobby Timmons* (NYC, 12,17 August): *Soul time*

Cal Tjader (LA): *Demasiado caliente* (SF): *Concert on the campus* (LA, November): *West Side Story*

Stanley Turrentine (NYC, 18 June): *Look out!* (NYC, 16 December): *Blue Hour*

Doug Watkins (NYC, 17 May): *Soulnik*

Ben Webster (NYC, 18,19 January): *The Warm Moods*

Frank Wess (NYC, 9 May): *The Frank Wess Quartet*

Randy Weston (NYC, November/December): *Uhuru Africa*

Bob Wilber (NYC, 22 July): *Blowing the blues away*

Don Wilkerson (SF, 19,20 May): *The Twister*

Lem Winchester (NYC, 19 April): *Lem's Beat* (NYC, 4 June): *Another Opus* (NYC, 7 October): *With Feeling*

Mitchell 'Booty' Wood (NYC, December): *Booty*

Left: Art Blakey and Hank Mobley at the Soul Station session for Blue Note.
Below: Allan Ganley and Shelly Manne.

Photograph: *Francis Wolff* Courtesy: *Mosaic Images*

1961

Stan Getz (34) returns to US in January.

Miles Davis (35) and Gil Evans (38) feature in Carnegie Hall concert.

Eric Dolphy (33) and John Coltrane (34) collaborate.

Sonny Rollins (31) opens at a New York club with a quartet after a 2 year sabbatical.

Art Blakey (42), Ella Fitzgerald (43), Oscar Peterson (36), Nat King Cole (44), Toshiko (31) & Charlie Mariano (37) and MJQ all tour Japan.

Eddie Harris (25) has a hit with his recording of the 'Exodus Theme'.

BIRTHS

Clark Tracey (drums) 5 February
Makoto Ozone (piano) 25 March
Gary Thomas (tenor sax/flute) 10 June
Marvin 'Smitty' Smith (drums) 24 June
Wynton Marsalis (trumpet) 18 October
Dave Catney (piano) 7 November

DEATHS

Lem Winchester (32) 13 January *accident while playing Russian roulette*
Alphonse Picou (82) 4 February
Andy Gibson (47) 10 February
Velma Middleton (43) 10 February *stroke*
Nick La Rocca (71) 22 February
Wilbur Sweatman (79) 9 March
Miff Mole (63) 29 April
Scott La Faro (25) 6 July *auto crash*
Booker Little (23) 5 October *uremia*
Joe Guy (41)
Don Barbour *auto crash*

BOOKS

Stanley Dance: *Jazz Era: The Forties*
Charles Delaunay: *Django Reinhardt*
Nat Hentoff: *The Jazz Life*
Langston Hughes: *Ask your mama: 12 moods for jazz* (poems)
Burnett James: *Essays on Jazz*
Michael James: *Miles Davis*
J.G. Jepsen & Kurt Mohr: *Hot Lips Page*
G.E. Lambert: *Johnny Dodds*
P. Leslie & P. Gwynne-Jones: *Book of Bilk*
Henry Pleasants: *Death of a Music*
Ross Russell: *The Sound* (novel based on the life of Charlie Parker)
Brian Rust: *Jazz Records A-Z*
George T. Simon: *The Feeling of Jazz*
Jay Stuart: *Call him George* (Lewis)
John A. Williams: *Night Song* (novel)

FILMS

After Hours (27mins): Coleman Hawkins, Roy Eldridge, Cozy Cole
All Night Long (95mins): jazz version of Othello with Brubeck, Mingus, Dankworth & Tubby Hayes
Bill Coleman from boogie to funk (9mins): impressions of a Paris jazz club
Bobby Hackett (25mins): music short
Buck Clayton & his All-Stars (54mins): film record of studio performances
Chick Corea (32mins): study of Chick
Coleman Hawkins Quartet (30mins): music short
The Connection (110mins): feature film with Freddie Redd Quartet
Eddie Condon (26mins): music short
Living Jazz (43mins): documentary of Bruce Turner Jump Band
Louis Armstrong and the All-Stars (25mins): music short
Paris Blues (98mins): feature film starring Paul Newman and Sidney Poitier as jazz musicians; Duke and Louis appear
The Tony Kinsey Quartet (9mins): music short
Too Late Blues (103mins): feature film about a jazz combo

RECORDS

Pepper Adams (NYC): *Out of this World* (NYC): *Jammin' with Herbie Hancock*
Cannonball Adderley (NYC, 27 January): *Know what I mean* (NYC, 8 February/9,15 May): *African Waltz* (NYC, 11 May): *Quintet Plus*
Nat Adderley (NYC, 20 June/19 July): *Naturally*
Gene Ammons (NYC, 26 January): *Nice an' Cool* (NYC,27 January): *Jug* (LA, 15 August): *Groovin' with Jug* (Chicago, 26 August): *Dig him* (Chicago, 29 August): *Just Jug* (NYC, 17,18 October): *Up Tight* (NYC, 28 November): *Twisting the Jug*
Curtis Amy/Paul Bryant (LA): *Meetin' here*
Louis Armstrong/Duke Ellington (NYC, 3,4 April): *Together for the first time*
Harold Ashby/Paul Gonsalves (NYC, January/February): *Two from Duke*
Dave Bailey (NYC, 15 March): *Our Miss Brooks* (NYC, 6 October): *Two feet in the gutter*
Count Basie (NYC, 28 July): *At Birdland* (NYC, 30,31 October/1,2 November): *The Legend*
Count Basie/Duke Ellington (NYC): *The First Time*
Walter Bishop Jr (NYC, 14 March): *Speak Low*
Art Blakey (Tokyo, 2 January): *A day with Art Blakey* (NYC, 18 February): *Roots and Herbs* (NYC, 14 March): *The Witchdoctor* (NYC, 27 May): *The Freedom Rider* (NYC, 2 October): *Mosaic* (NYC, 28 November / 18 December): *Buhaina's Delight*
Ruby Braff/Marshall Brown (NYC): *Ruby Braff/Marshall Brown Sextet*
Bob Brookmeyer (NYC, 29 June): *7 X Wilder* (NYC, 6,7,8 November): *Gloomy Sunday and other bright moments*
Oscar Brown Jr (NYC): *Between Heaven and Hell*
Dave Brubeck (LA, 20 March): *Near Myth* (NYC, May/June): *Time Further Out / Countdown – Time in Outer Space* (NYC, 6,12 September, with Carmen McRae & Louis Armstrong): *The Real Ambassadors*
Ray Bryant (NYC, 26 January): *Con Alma* (NYC, 23,26 October): *Dancing the Big Twist*
Gary Burton (NYC, 6,7 July): *New Vibe Man in Town*
Jaki Byard (NYC, 14 March): *Here's Jaki*
Donald Byrd (NYC, 17 April): *Chant* (NYC, 2 May): *The Cat Walk* (NYC, 21 September): *Royal Flush* (NYC, 11 November): *Free Form*
Benny Carter (NYC, 13,15 November): *Further Definitions*
Ray Charles/Betty Carter (LA, 13,14 June): *Ray Charles & Betty Carter*
Sonny Clark (NYC, 13 November): *Leapin' and Lopin'*
Kenny Clarke/Francy Boland (Cologne, 18,19 May): *The Golden Eight* (Cologne, 13 December): *Jazz is Universal*
Buck Clayton (NYC, 10 April): *One for Buck* (Paris, 22 May): *All-Star Performance* (Paris, 15,16 May): *Passport to Paradise* (NYC, 15 September): *Buck & Buddy blow the blues*
Al Cohn/Zoot Sims (NYC, February): *Either Way*
Ornette Coleman (NYC, 31 January): *Ornette!* (NYC, 22,27 March): *Ornette on Tenor*
Johnny Coles (NYC, 10,13 April): *The Warm Sound*
John Coltrane (NYC, 23 May / 7 June): *Africa/Brass* (NYC, 25 May): *Olé Coltrane* (NYC, 2,3 November): *Live at the Village Vanguard* (NYC, 21 December): *Coltrane*
Junior Cook (LA, 10 April / NYC, 4 December): *Junior's Cookin'*
Chris Connor/Maynard Ferguson (NYC): *Double Exposure* (NYC): *Two's Company*
Eddie 'Lockjaw' Davis (NYC, 4,12 May): *Afro-Jaws*
Eddie 'Lockjaw' Davis/Johnny Griffin (NYC, 6 January): *The First Set*
Miles Davis (NYC, 20,21 March): *Someday my prince will come* (SF, 14,21 April): *Friday Night at the Blackhawk* (SF, 15,22 April): *Saturday Night at the Blackhawk*
Walt Dickerson (NYC, 7 March): *This is Walt Dickerson* (NYC, 5 May): *A sense of direction*
Eric Dolphy (NYC, 16 July): *At the Five Spot* (Copenhagen, 8 September): *In Europe*
Lou Donaldson (NYC, 23 January): *Here 'tis* (NYC, 28 April): *Gravy Train*
Kenny Dorham (NYC, 15 January): *Whistle Stop* (NYC, 1 February): *Ease it!* (SF, November): *Inta somethin'*

Teddy Edwards/Howard McGhee (LA, 15,17 May): *Together Again*
Teddy Edwards (LA, 23,24,25 August): *Good Gravy*
Booker Ervin (NYC, 6 January): *That's it!*
Bill Evans (NYC, 2 February): *Explorations* (NYC, 25 June): *Sunday at the Village Vanguard / Waltz for Debbie*
Gil Evans (NYC): *Out of the Cool*
Art Farmer/Benny Golson (NYC, 9 January): *The Jazztet & John Lewis* (Chicago, 15 May): *The Jazztet at Birdhouse*
Art Farmer (NYC, 25,26,27 October): *Perception*
Vic Feldman (LA, 6,11 January): *Merry Old Soul*
Ella Fitzgerald (LA): *The Harold Arlen Songbook*
Jimmy Forrest (NYC, 18 April): *Out of the Forrest* (NYC, 1 September): *Sit down and relax* (NYC, 19 October): *Most much*
Red Garland (NYC, 19 July): *Bright and Breezy* (NYC, 30 December): *The nearness of you*
Erroll Garner (NYC, July/August): *Dream Street* (NYC): *Close-up in swing*
Stan Getz (NYC): *Focus*
Stan Getz/Bob Brookmeyer (SF, 12,13 September): *Fall '61*
Terry Gibbs (LA, 21,22 January): *Live at the Summit: the exciting big band of Terry Gibbs*
Dizzy Gillespie (NYC, 9 February): *An Electrifying evening with the Dizzy Gillespie Quintet* (NYC, 4 March): *Carnegie Hall Concert* (NYC, June): *Perceptions* (Monterey, 23 September): *A Musical Safari*
Jimmy Giuffre (NYC, 27 January / 1 March): *Fusion* (NYC, 7,8 August): *Thesis*
Benny Golson (NYC, December 1960/11 April): *Take a number from 1 to 10*
Paul Gonsalves/Harold Ashby (NYC, January): *Tenor Stuff*
Dexter Gordon (NYC, 6 May): *Doin' Allright* (NYC, 9 May): *Dexter Calling*
Joe Gordon (LA, 11,12,18 July): *Lookin' good*
Bennie Green (NYC, 9,22 March): *Gliding along*
Grant Green (NYC, 28 January): *Grant's First Stand* (NYC, 1 April): *Green Street* (NYC, 4 June): *Sunday mornin'* (NYC, 1 August): *Grant Stand* (NYC, 23 December): *Gooden's Corner*
Al Grey/Billy Mitchell: *Al Grey/Billy Mitchell Sextet*
Johnny Griffin (NYC, 7,16 February): *Change of Pace* (NYC, 13,14,17 July): *White Gardenia*
Gigi Gryce (NYC, January): *Reminiscin'*
Barry Harris (NYC, 19 January): *Preminado* (NYC, 4 July): *Listen to Barry Harris* (NYC, 28 September): *Newer than new*
Eddie Harris (Chicago, 17 January): *Exodus to Jazz* (Chicago): *Breakfast at Tiffany's*
Coleman Hawkins (NYC): *Stasch*
Tubby Hayes (London, 21,22,23 March): *Tubbs* (NYC, 3,4 October): *Tubby the tenor*
Jimmy Heath (NYC, 14,20 March): *The Quota*
Richard Holmes (LA): *Tell it like it is*
Richard Holmes/Gene Ammons (LA, 15 August): *Groovin' with Jug*
Richard Holmes/Ben Webster (LA, March): *Groove*
Freddie Hubbard (NYC, 9 April): *Hub Cap* (NYC, 21 August): *Ready for Freddie*
Helen Humes (LA, 27–29 July): *Swingin' with Humes*
Elmo Hope (NYC, 22,29 June): *Homecoming* (NYC, 9,14 November): *Hope-full*
Milt Jackson (NYC, 14,15 March): *Statements*
Milt Jackson/Wes Montgomery (NYC, 18,19 December): *Bags meets Wes*
Ahmad Jamal (Chicago, June): *Ahmad Jamal's Alhambra* (SF): *Ahmad Jamal at the Blackhawk*
Carmell Jones (LA, June): *The Remarkable Carmell Jones*
Elvin Jones (NYC, 2 February): *Together*
Clifford Jordan (NYC, 14 February): *A story tale* (NYC, 14,15 June): *Starting Time*
Wynton Kelly (NYC, 20,21 July): *Wynton Kelly*
Barney Kessel (LA, 9,10 January): *Workin' Out*
Roland Kirk (NYC, 11 July): *Kirk's Work*
Lee Konitz (NYC, 20 April): *Motion*
Yusef Lateef (NYC, 5 September): *Eastern Sounds* (NYC, 29 December): *Into something*
Ramsey Lewis (Chicago, February): *More music from the soil* (Chicago, 10,11 August): *Never on Sunday*
Abbey Lincoln (NYC, 22 February): *Straight Ahead*
Booker Little (NYC, 17 March / 4 April): *Out Front* (NYC, August/September): *Victory and Sorrow*

Johnny Lytle (NYC, 23 March): *Happy Ground*
Les McCann (LA, August): *Pretty Lady* (LA, August): *Les McCann Sings* (NYC): *New from the Big City* (Village Vanguard, NYC, December): *In New York* (Village Gate, NYC, 28 December): *Plays the Shampoo*
Jack McDuff (NYC, 3 February): *The Honeydripper* (NYC, 14 July): *Goodnight, it's time to go* (NYC, 1 December): *On with it*
Howard McGhee (LA, 26 June): *Maggie's Back in Town* (NYC, 8 December): *The Sharp Edge*
Jackie McLean (NYC, 8 January): *Bluesnik* (NYC, 26 October): *A Fickle Sonance*
Junior Mance (NYC, 22,23 February): *At the Village Vanguard* (NYC, 1 August): *Big Chief!* (NYC): *The Soul of Hollywood*
Herbie Mann (NYC, 24,25,26 April): *The Family of Man* (NYC, 10,11 November): *At the Village Gate*
Herbie Mann/Bill Evans (NYC, 8 December): *Nirvana*
Shelly Manne (LA, 3,4,5 March): *Live! Shelly Manne & his Men at the Manne-Hole* (LA, 17,24 October): *Checkmate*
Dodo Marmarosa (Chicago, 9,10 May): *Dodo's Back*
Charles Mingus (NYC, 6 November): *Oh Yeah*
Red Mitchell/Harold Land (LA, 14 October / 13 December): *Hear Ye!*
Hank Mobley (NYC, 26 March): *Work Out* (NYC, 5 December): *Another Workout (released in 1985)*
Thelonious Monk (Paris): *In Europe* (Bern, 10 May): *1961 European Tour Vols 1&2* (Stockholm, 16 May): *In Stockholm*
Montgomery Brothers (NYC, 3 January): *Groove Yard* (Toronto, December): *Montgomery Brothers in Canada*
Wes Montgomery (NYC, 4 August): *So much guitar* (St Louis, 19 August): *Live at Jorgies Jazz Club / Live at Jorgies and more*
James Moody (Jazz Workshop, SF): *Cookin' the Blues*
Joe Morello (NYC): *It's About Time*
Gerry Mulligan (NYC, 10-17 April): *Holliday with Mulligan* (NYC, 10,11 July): *A Concert in Jazz*
Oliver Nelson (NYC, 23 February): *Blues and the Abstract Truth* (NYC, 1 March): *Straight Ahead* (NYC, 25 August): *Main Stem* (NYC, 29 September / 10 November): *Afro/American Sketches*
Phineas Newborn (LA, 16 October / 21 November): *A World of Piano*

Joe Newman (NYC, 17 March): *Good'n'Groovy* (NYC, 9 May): *Joe's Hapnin's* (NYC): *At Count Basie's*
Anita O'Day (LA, January): *Travelin' Light* (NYC): *All the Sad Young Men*
Leo Parker (NYC, 9 September): *Let me tell you 'bout it* (NYC, 12,20 October): *Rollin' with Leo*
Horace Parlan (NYC, 18 March): *On the spur of the moment* (NYC, 18 June): *Up and down*
Duke Pearson (NYC, 1 August): *Hush!* (NYC, 2 August): *Dedication*
Oscar Peterson (Chicago, September/October): *Live from Chicago / The Sound of the Trio*
Oscar Peterson/Milt Jackson (NYC, Autumn): *Very Tall*
The Pollwinners (LA, 30,31 August / 1 September): *Exploring the scene!*
Bud Powell (Essen, 14 March): *In Europe* (Paris, April): *At the Blue Note Cafe* (Paris, 17 December): *A portrait of Thelonious*
Ike Quebec (NYC, 26 November): *Heavy Soul* (NYC, 9 December): *It might as well be spring* (NYC, 16,23 December): *Blue and Sentimental*
Max Roach (NYC, 1,3,8,9 August): *Percussion Bittersweet*
Shorty Rogers (LA, 10,22,24 November): *The Fourth Dimension in Sound*
George Russell (NYC, 8 May): *Ezz-thetics*
Pee Wee Russell/Coleman Hawkins (NYC, 23 February): *Jazz Reunion*
Shirley Scott (NYC, 7 March): *Satin Doll* (NYC, 24 March): *Stompin'* (NYC, 2 June): *Hip Soul* (NYC, 22 August): *Blue Seven* (NYC, 17 November): *Shirley Scott plays Horace Silver* (NYC, 17 November): *Hip Twist*
Bud Shank (LA, May): *New Groove*
Horace Silver (Village Gate, NYC, 19,20 May): *Doin' the thing*
Zoot Sims (London, 13,14,15 November): *Zoot Sims at Ronnie Scott's*
Johnny 'Hammond' Smith (NYC, 14 February): *Stimulation* (NYC, 12 May): *Opus de Funk*
Sonny Stitt (Chicago, June): *Sonny Stitt at the DJ Lounge*
Billy Strayhorn (Paris, May): *The peaceful side of jazz*
Frank Strozier (NYC, 12 September): *Long Night*
Clark Terry (NYC, 12 November): *Everything's Mellow*
The Three Sounds (NYC, 13 August): *Hey There*

Bobby Timmons (NYC, 13 March): *Easy does it* (NYC, 1 October): *The Bobby Timmons Trio in person at the Village Vanguard*
Cal Tjader (LA): *The Harold Arlen Songbook* (LA, 28,29 August): *In a Latin bag*
Stanley Turrentine (NYC, 23 February): *Up at Minton's Vols 1&2* (NYC, 8 June): *Dearly Beloved* (NYC, 13 September): *ZT's Blues*
Sarah Vaughan (NYC): *The Divine One* (NYC, June): *After Hours*
Mal Waldron (NYC, 27 June): *Fire Waltz*
Ben Webster (LA): *Warm Moods*
Baby Face Willette (NYC, 30 January): *Face to Face* (NYC, 22 May): *Stop and Listen*
Joe Williams/Harry Edison (NYC): *Together*
Kai Winding/JJ Johnson (NYC): *The Great Kai & J*
Phil Woods (NYC, 26 January / 10 February): *Rights of Swing*

Top: Thelonious Monk in London.
Above: Sonny Clark recording *Leapin' and Lopin'* for Blue Note in November.
Left: Ike Quebec and Philly Joe Jones at the *Blue and Sentimental* session in December.

1962

Annie Ross (32) leaves Lambert-Hendricks-Ross and is replaced by Yolande Bavan.

Charlie Mingus (40) assembles a big band for a NYC Town Hall Concert.

Archie Shepp (25) leaves Cecil Taylor (30) to form the Shepp-Dixon Quartet.

Oscar Brown Jr hosts a series of 26 TV shows 'Jazz Scene USA'.

Benny Goodman (53) organises a big band to tour Russia for the US State Department (July).

Bossa Nova fad follows the hit recording of 'Desafinado' by Stan Getz and Charlie Byrd.

Duke Ellington (63) makes another European tour; Buster Cooper joins the band and Cootie Williams (52) returns.

BIRTHS
Terence Blanchard (trumpet) 13 March
Renee Rosnes (piano) 24 March
Ralph Peterson (drums) 20 May
Michel Petrucciani (piano) 28 December

DEATHS
Claude Jones (60) 17 January *aboard SS United States*
Doug Watkins (27) 5 February *auto crash*
Les Hite (58) 6 February
Leo Parker (37) 11 February
Jean Goldkette (63) 24 March
Jack Purvis (55) 30 March
John Graas (37) 13 April
Eddie South (57) 25 April
Eddie Costa (31) 28 July *auto crash*
Israel Crosby (43) 11 August *heart attack*
Johnny Stein (67-70) 30 September
Rubberlegs Williams (55) 17 October
Monette Moore (60) 21 October
Paul Lingle (59) 30 October
Scrapper Blackwell

BOOKS
Whitney Balliett: *Dinosaurs in the Morning*
Joachim Berendt: *The New Jazz Book*
I. Berg & I. Yeomans: *Trad: an A-z Who's Who of the British Trad Jazz Scene*
Samuel B. Charters & Leonard Kunstadt: *Jazz; a history of the New York scene*
Lillian Ehrlich: *What jazz is all about*
Lewis Gilkenson (ed): *Esquire's World of Jazz*
Benny Green: *The Reluctant Art*
Andre Hodeir: *Toward Jazz*
Neil Leonard: *Jazz and the White American*
Adrian Mitchell: *If you see me comin'* (poems)
J. Oliver (ed): *Jazz Classic: an album of personalities from the World of Jazz*
Rosey Pool: *Beyond the Blues* (poems)
Robert G. Reisner: *Bird: the legend of Charlie Parker*
Herbert Simmons: *Man Walking on Eggshells* (novel)
Martin Williams (ed): *Jazz Panorama*
Martin Williams: *Jelly Roll Morton*

FILMS
Duke Ellington & his Orchestra (25mins): music short
Flash: Zoot Sims at work in the Blue Note, Paris
It's Trad, Dad! (73mins): comedy feature with Kenny Ball, Terry Lightfoot, Chris Barber, Acker Bilk & Bob Wallis
New Orleans Funeral (6mins): film record
TV series *Jazz Scene USA* including:
Pete Fountain Sextet (23mins)
Shelly Manne & his Men (20mins)
Shorty Rogers & his Giants (20mins)
Stan Kenton & his Orchestra (24mins)
Barney Kessel Trio (23mins)

COMPOSITIONS
Duke Ellington: *Money Jungle*

RECORDS
Cannonball Adderley (Village Vanguard, NYC, 12,14 January): *Cannonball Adderley Sextet in New York* (Belgium, 4,5 August): *Cannonball at Comblain-La-Tour* (SF, 21 September): *Jazz Workshop Revisited* (NYC, December): *Cannonball's Bossa Nova*
Nat Adderley (New Orleans, June): *In the Bag*
Henry 'Red' Allen (NYC, 5 June): *Mr Allen*
Gene Ammons/Sonny Stitt (NYC, February): *Boss Tenors in Orbit* (NYC, 19 February): *Soul Summit*
Gene Ammons/Dodo Marmarosa (Chicago, 4 May): *Jug & Dodo*
Gene Ammons (Chicago, 27 April): *Blue Groove*

(Chicago, 3 May): *Preachin'* (NYC, 9 September): *Bad! Bossa Nova*
Curtis Amy (LA): *Way Down* (LA, June): *Tippin' on through*
Earl Anderza (LA, March): *Outa Sight*
Chet Baker (Rome, 5 January): *Chet is back*
Count Basie (NYC, 21,22 March): *Kansas City Seven* (Stockholm, 11,12 August): *In Sweden* (NYC, 2,3,5 November): *On my way and shoutin' again*
Louis Bellson (LA, 22-24 January): *At the Summit*
Art Blakey (NYC, 24 January): *The African Beat* (LA, 9-18 March): *Three Blind Mice* (NYC, 23,24 October): *Caravan*
Bob Brookmeyer (NYC, 21,23 August / 14 September): *Trombone Jazz Samba*
Ray Brown (NYC, 22,23 February): *All Star Big Band*
Dave Brubeck (Amsterdam, 3 December): *Brubeck in Amsterdam*
Ray Bryant (NYC, 27,30 March/10 April): *Hollywood Jazz Beat*
Kenny Burrell (NYC, 6 March / 30 April): *Bluesin' around* (NYC, 14 September): *Bluesy Burrell*
Gary Burton (NYC, 14,15 September): *Who is Gary Burton?*
Jaki Byard (NYC, 30 January): *Hi-Fly*
Don Byas (Paris, 2-4 May): *Ballads for Swingers*
Charlie Byrd (NYC, 18 April): *Latin Impressions* (NYC, 28 September / 1 October): *Bossa Nova Pelos Passaros*
Benny Carter/Barney Bigard/Ben Webster (LA, 10 April): *BBB & Co*
Tony Coe (London, 10 July): *Swingin' till the girls come home*
Ornette Coleman (NYC, 21 December): *Town Hall*
John Coltrane (NYC, 18 September / 13 November): *Ballads*
Tadd Dameron (NYC, 27 February/9 March/16 April): *The Magic Touch*
Eddie 'Lockjaw' Davis (NYC): *Trackin'*
Eddie 'Lockjaw' Davis/Johnny Griffin (NYC, 5 February): *Tough Tenor Favourites*
Paul Desmond/Gerry Mulligan (NYC, 26 June / 3 July / 13 August): *Two of a mind*
Walt Dickerson (NYC, 16 January): *Relativity* (NYC, 21 September): *To my Queen*
Lou Donaldson (NYC, 9 May): *The Natural Soul*
Kenny Dorham (NYC, 15 April): *Matador*
Harry Edison/Lockjaw Davis (NYC, 18 April): *Jawbreakers*
Harry Edison/Ben Webster (NYC, 6,7 June): *Ben & Sweets*
Teddy Edwards (LA, 24 April): *Heart and Soul*
Roy Eldridge/Bud Freeman (NYC, 12 February): *Saturday Night Fish Fry*
Duke Ellington/Coleman Hawkins (NYC, 18 August): *Duke Ellington & Coleman Hawkins*
Duke Ellington/John Coltrane (NYC, 26 September): *Duke Ellington & John Coltrane*
Duke Ellington/Charlie Mingus/Max Roach (NYC, 17 September): *Money Jungle*
Herb Ellis (NYC, 12,13,14 June): *The Midnight Roll*
Bill Evans (NYC, 17 May / 5 June): *Moonbeams* (NYC, 17,29 May / 5 June): *How my heart sings* (NYC, 16 July): *Interplay* (NYC, 14 August): *Empathy*
Art Farmer/Benny Golson (NYC, 28 February / 2 March): *Here and Now*
Art Farmer (NYC, 10 August / 5,20 September): *Listen to Art Farmer*
Vic Feldman (LA, September): *Stop the world, I want to get off* (LA, 26 October / 12 November): *Soviet Jazz Themes*
Clare Fischer (LA, April): *First Time Out* (LA): *Surging Ahead*
Ella Fitzgerald (NYC, May): *Rough Ridin'*

Don Friedman (NYC, 14 May): *Circle Waltz*
Curtis Fuller (NYC, 24,25 April): *Cabin in the Sky*
Red Garland (NYC, 30 January): *Solar* (NYC, 22 March): *Red's good groove* (NYC, 9 October): *When there are grey skies*
Stan Getz/Charlie Byrd (Washington, 13 February): *Brazilian Mood*
Dizzy Gillespie (Juan-les-Pins, 24 July): *New Wave* (LA, September): *The New Continent*
Jimmy Giuffre (NYC, 10 July / 7,10 October / 1 November): *Free Fall*
Benny Golson (NYC, 30,31 October / 1 November): *Turning Point* (NYC, 26 December): *Free*
Benny Goodman (Moscow, 1-8 July): *Benny Goodman in Moscow*
Dexter Gordon (NYC, 5 May / 25 June): *Landslide* (NYC, 27 August): *Go!* (NYC, 29 August): *A Swingin' Affair*
Grant Green (NYC, 13 January): *Nigeria* (NYC, 31 January): *Oleo* (NYC, 26 April): *The Latin bit* (NYC, 30 November): *Goin' West* (NYC, 21 December): *Feelin' the spirit*
Al Grey: *Night Song*
Al Grey/Billy Mitchell: *Snap your fingers*
Johnny Griffin (NYC, 5,29 January): *The Kerry Dancers* (LA, 28 July): *Grab this*
Vince Guaraldi (SF): *Cast your fate to the wind*
Chico Hamilton (NYC, 18,20 September): *Passin' Thru*
Herbie Hancock (NYC, 28 May): *Takin' Off*
Barry Harris (NYC, 31 May / 23 August): *Chasin' the Bird*
Tubby Hayes (NYC, 23 June): *Tubby's back in town*
Roy Haynes (NYC, 16,23 May): *Out of the afternoon*
Jimmy Heath (NYC, 4,17 January): *Triple Threat*
Woody Herman (NYC, January): *Swing Low, Sweet Clarinet* (NYC, October): *Woody Herman 1963*
Freddie Hubbard (NYC,2 July): *The Artistry of Freddie Hubbard* (NYC, 10 October): *Hub-tones* (NYC, 27 December): *Here to stay*
Milt Jackson (NYC, 19 June, 5 July): *Big Bags* (NYC, 30 August, 31 October, 7 November): *Invitation*
Willis Jackson (NYC, 31 March): *Thunderbird* (NYC, 30 October): *Shuckin'* (NYC, 19 December): *Neapolitan Nights*
Ahmad Jamal (NYC, 20,21 December): *Macanudo*
Jazz Crusaders (LA, 5,6 August): *At the Lighthouse*
Carmell Jones (LA): *Brass Bag* (LA): *Business Meetin'*
Elvin Jones (NYC, 3 January): *Elvin!*
Sam Jones (NYC, 15,16 August): *Down Home*
Duke Jordan (NYC, 12 January): *Les Liaisons Dangereuses*
Sheila Jordan (NYC, 19 September/12 October): *Portrait of Sheila*
John Lewis (Milan, 17 January, NYC, 25 January): *A Milanese Story*
John Lewis/Svend Asmussen (Stockholm, 2,3 July): *European Encounter*
Ramsey Lewis (Chicago, 14,15 February): *Sound of Spring* (NYC, 2,3 August): *Country meets the Blues* (Chicago, 22,25 September): *Bossa Nova* (Chicago): *Pot Luck*
Johnny Lytle (NYC, 29 January): *Nice and easy* (NYC, 5 July): *Moonchild*
Les McCann (LA, July/August): *On time*
Jack McDuff/Gene Ammons (NYC, 23 January): *Mellow Gravy*
Jack McDuff (NYC, 23 October): *Screamin'*
Howard McGhee (NYC): *Nobody knows you when you're down and out*
Jackie McLean (NYC, 19 March): *Let Freedom Ring* (NYC, 14 June): *Hipnosis* (NYC, 28 September): *Tippin' the scales*
Junior Mance (NYC, 14 February): *Junior Blues* (NYC, 18 July): *Happy Time*
Herbie Mann (NYC, 12,28 March/19 April): *Right Now*
Shelly Manne (NYC, 5,6 February): *2-3-4* (LA): *Sounds unheard of* (LA, 17,18,20 December): *My son, the jazz drummer*
Mike Mainieri (NYC, 5 September): *Blues on the other side*
Charlie Mingus (NYC, 12 October): *Town Hall Concert*
Blue Mitchell (NYC, 7,28 March): *A sure thing*
MJQ (NYC, 25,29 January, 2 February): *Lonely Woman*
Thelonious Monk (NYC, 31 October, 1,2,6 November): *Monk's Dream*

Wes Montgomery (California, 25 June): *Full House*
James Moody (Chicago, 30 January): *Another Bag*
Lee Morgan (NYC, 24 January): *Take Twelve*
Gerry Mulligan (NYC, 11,12 December): *Spring is Sprung*
Phineas Newborn (LA, 12 September): *The great jazz piano of Phineas Newborn*
Joe Newman (NYC): *In a mellow mood*
Sal Nistico (NYC, 17 October): *Comin' on up*
Jackie Paris (NYC, 22,24,26 January, 8 May): *The Song is Paris*
Cecil Payne (NYC, 14,15,16 March): *The Connection*
Duke Pearson (NYC, 12 January): *Hush*
Oscar Peterson (NYC, 24,25 January): *West Side Story* (NYC, 13,14,15,26,28 June): *Oscar Peterson Trio with the All-Star Big Band* (Chicago): *Something Warm* (Chicago, 25,26,27 September): *Affinity* (Chicago, 15,16 December): *Night Train*
Dave Pike (NYC, 6,7 September): *Bossa Nova Carnival* (NYC, 12 December): *Limbo Carnival* (NYC, 28 December): *Dave Pike plays the jazz version of Oliver!*
Pony Poindexter (NYC, 16 February, 18 April, 10 May): *Pony's Express*
Bud Powell (Stockholm, 23 April): *At the Golden Circle* (Copenhagen, 26 April): *Bouncing with Bud* (Paris): *Bud Powell '62*
Ike Quebec (NYC, February): *With a song in my heart* (NYC, 5 November): *Soul Samba*
Dizzy Reece (NYC, 13 March): *Asia Minor*
Buddy Rich/Gene Krupa (NYC, 18,19 January): *Burnin' Beat*
Jerome Richardson (NYC, Spring): *Going to the Movies*
Freddie Roach (NYC, 23 August): *Down to Earth*
Max Roach (NYC): *It's Time* (SF, 4 October): *Speak, brother, speak*

Shorty Rogers (LA): *Bossa Nova* (LA, December): *Jazz Waltz*
Sonny Rollins (NYC, 30 January, 13,14 February): *The Bridge* (NYC, 5,25,26 April, 14 May): *What's New?* (NYC, 29,30 July): *Our Man in Jazz*
Charlie Rouse (NYC, 11 November): *Bossa Nova Bacchanal*
George Russell (NYC): *The Stratus Seekers*
Pee Wee Russell/Marshall Brown (NYC): *New Groove*
Shirley Scott (NYC, 5 December): *Happy Talk*
Charlie Shavers (Chicago, May): *Live at the London House*
George Shearing (NYC, 20,21 June): *Live at Basin Street East*
Archie Shepp (NYC, October): *Bill Dixon/Archie Shepp Quartet*
Horace Silver (NYC, 13,14 July): *The Tokyo Blues*
Jimmy Smith (NYC, 23 January): *Plays Fats Waller* (NYC, 26,28 March): *Bashin'*
Johnny 'Hammond' Smith (NYC, 22 January): *Look out* (NYC, 12 June): *Cooks with Willis Jackson* (NYC, 8 November): *Black Coffee*
Sonny Stitt/Jack McDuff (NYC, 16 February): *Stitt meets Brother Jack*
Sonny Stitt (NYC, 4 April): *Low Flame* (NYC, 16,17 July): *Blues Brass Groove* (Chicago, 24 September): *Rearin' Back*
Frank Strozier (NYC, 28 March): *March of the Siamese*
Cecil Taylor (Copenhagen, 23 November): *Live at the Cafe Montmartre*
The Three Sounds (NYC, 4 February, 7,8 March): *Out of this world* (NYC, 7,8 March): *Black Orchid* (NYC, 13 October): *Blue genes*
Bobby Timmons (NYC, 18,19 June): *Sweet and soulful sounds*
Cal Tjader (LA, 5,6,7 March): *Plays the Contemporary Music of Mexico and Brasil*

Lennie Tristano (NYC, July, August): *The New Tristano*
Stanley Turrentine (NYC, 2 January): *That's where it's at* (NYC, 18 October): *Jubilee Shouts*
McCoy Tyner (NYC, 10 January): *Inception* (NYC, 14 November): *Reaching Fourth*
Sarah Vaughan (NYC): *You're mine you*
Dinah Washington (NYC): *Drinking Again*
Frank Wess (NYC): *Wheelin' & Dealin'* (NYC, 22 March): *Southern Comfort*
Don Wilkerson (NYC, 3 May): *Elder Don* (NYC, 18 June): *Preach Brother!*
Gerald Wilson (LA, September): *Moment of Truth*
Jimmy Witherspoon/Ben Webster: *Roots*
Leo Wright (NYC, 23 April): *Suddenly the Blues*
Larry Young (NYC, 27,28 February): *Groove Street*

Photo: Brian Foskett

Photo: Francis Wolff Courtesy: Mosaic Images

Above: Ella Fitzgerald and Roy Eldridge in London for another JATP concert.
Left: Dexter Gordon recording *A Swingin' Affair* for Blue Note in August.

Duke Ellington (64) creates and directs a stage show 'My People' for the Negro Century of Progress exposition in Chicago. In November the Ellington State Department tour to the Near & Middle East is cut short by the assassination of President Kennedy.

Several US jazzmen settle in Europe, including Donald Byrd (30), Art Taylor (34), Ron Jefferson (37), Dexter Gordon (40), Johnny Griffin (35), Leroy Vinnegar (35) and Leo Wright (29).

Charlie (39) and Toshiko Mariano (33) settle in Japan.

Bud Powell (39) is hospitalised in Paris with TB.

BIRTHS
John Colianni (piano) 7 January
Benny Green (piano) 4 April
Marty Richards (drums) 2 October
Marcus Roberts (piano)

DEATHS
John Casimir (64) 12 January
Sonny Clark (31) 13 January
Ike Quebec (44) 16 January lung cancer
Nat Towles (57) January
Specs Wright (35) 6 February
Addison Farmer (34) 20 February
June Clark (62) 23 February
Bobby Jaspar (37) 28 February
Lizzie Miles (67) 17 March
Gene Sedric (55) 3 April
Eddie Edwards (71) 9 April
Herbie Nichols (44) 12 April leukemia
Bob Scobey (46) 12 June cancer
Curtis Counce (37) 31 July
Wade Legge (29) 15 August
Glen Gray (57) 23 August
Clyde Hurley (47) September
Pete Brown (56) 20 September
J Russel Robinson (71) 30 September
Joe Gordon (35) 4 November fire burns
Luis Russell (61) 11 December cancer
Dinah Washington (39) 14 December overdose
Roy Palmer (71) 22 December
Dan Grissom
Terry Snyder

BOOKS
Samuel B. Charters: Jazz: New Orleans 1885-1963 (revised edition)
Samuel B. Charters: The Poetry of the Blues
Harold Courlander: Negro Folk Music USA
Leonard Feather (with Jack Tracy): Laughter from the Hip
Peter Gammond & Peter Clayton: Know about Jazz
Jorgen Jepsen: Jazz Records: a discography Vols 3,5 &6
LeRoi Jones: Blues People
R.P. Jones: Jazz
Max Kaminsky (with V.E. Hughes): My Life in Jazz
Shirley Kay (ed): The Book of the Blues
Albert McCarthy: Coleman Hawkins
Paul Oliver: The Meaning of the Blues

FILMS
Future One (8mins): impressions of Copenhagen jazz club, Jazzhus Montmartre, with New York Contemporary Five
Patterns in Jazz (10mins): educational short
Playback: series of promotional telerecordings featuring Andre Previn (4mins), Dave Brubeck Quartet (5mins), Duke Ellington (4mins), Mahalia Jackson (4mins), Teddy Wilson (4mins)
Stop for Bud (12mins): Danish film portrait of Bud Powell at leisure and at work in Copenhagen
Woody Herman & the Swingin' Herd (30mins): music programme from TV 'Jazz Casual' series

COMPOSITIONS
Duke Ellington: Afro-Bossa

RECORDS
Pepper Adams (NYC, September): Plays the compositions of Charlie Mingus
Cannonball Adderley (Tokyo, 15 June): A day with Cannonball Adderley (Tokyo, 9,14,15,19 July): The Japanese Concerts (Nippon Soul)
Nat Adderley (NYC, 23 September, 4 October): Natural Soul

Curtis Amy (LA, March): Katanga
Roy Ayers (LA, July): West Coast Vibes
Count Basie (NYC, 21,22,23 April): Li'l old groovemaker (NYC, April): Basie-land
Louis Bellson (Las Vegas): Thunderbird
Louis Bellson/Gene Krupa (NYC): The Mighty Two
Art Blakey (NYC, 16 June): Ugetsu (NYC, 10 July): A Jazz Message
Dave Brubeck (NYC, 22 February): At Carnegie Hall
Kenny Burrell (NYC, 7 January): Midnight Blue (NYC, 8,26 January): Crash (NYC, 27 March, 2 April): Freedom (NYC, 16,25,29 July): Blue Bash!
Charlie Byrd (Washington, 21 February): Once More! Bossa Nova (NYC, 9,10 May): Byrd at the Gate
Donald Byrd (NYC, 12 January): A new perspective
Johnny Coles (NYC, 18 July/9 August): Little Johnny C
John Coltrane (NYC, 6,7 March): John Coltrane with Johnny Hartman (NYC, 8 October, 18 November): Coltrane 'Live' at Birdland
Miles Davis (LA, 16,17 April, 14 May): Seven steps to heaven (St Louis, June): Miles in St Louis (Antibes, 26-31 July): Miles Davis in Europe
Eric Dolphy (NYC, May/June): Iron Man
Lou Donaldson (NYC, 24 January): Good Gracious (NYC, 17 July): Signifyin'
Kenny Dorham (NYC, 1 April): Una mas (Copenhagen, 5 December): Scandia skies (Copenhagen, 19 December): Short story
Duke Ellington (Paris, 2 January): The Art of Duke Ellington (Paris, 27 January): The Symphonic Ellington (Chicago, 20,21,28 August): My People
Herb Ellis (LA, 16 January): Three guitars in Bossa Nova time (LA, 18 January): Herb Ellis & Stuff Smith together!
Booker Ervin (NYC, 19 June): Exultation (NYC, 3 December): The Freedom Book
Bill Evans (NYC, January, February): Conversations with myself (LA, 30,31 May): At Shelly's Manne-Hole (NYC, 18 December): Trio '64
Art Farmer (NYC, 25,29 July, 1 August): Interaction (NYC, 6,7 December): Live at the Half Note
Clare Fischer (LA): Extension
Ella Fitzgerald/Count Basie (NYC, 16,17 July): Shiny Stockings
Frank Foster (Chicago, 18,20 February): Basie is our boss
Don Friedman (NYC): Flashback
Jimmy Garrison (NYC, 8 August): Illumination
Stan Getz (NYC, 8,9 February): Stan Getz & Luis Bonfa (NYC, 18,19 March): Getz & Gilberto (NYC, March): Getz & Laurindo Almeida at Webster Hall (NYC, 21,22 October): Getz with Strings
Terry Gibbs (NYC, 19 February): The Family Album
Dizzy Gillespie (NYC, 23,24,25 April): Something Old, Something New (Paris, 8 July): Dizzy Gillespie et Les Double Six
Paul Gonsalves (NYC, 21 May): Cleopatra (NYC, 4 September): Duke's Place
Paul Gonsalves/Sonny Stitt (NYC, 5 September): Salt and Pepper
Benny Goodman (NYC, 13,14 February/27 August): Together Again
Dexter Gordon (Paris, 23 May): Our man in Paris
Grant Green (NYC, 16 May): Am I Blue? (NYC, 4 November): Idle Moments
Johnny Griffin (NYC): Do nothin' til you hear from me
Herbie Hancock (NYC, 19 March): My point of view (NYC, 30 August): Inventions and Dimensions
Roy Haynes (NYC, 10 April): Cracklin' (NYC, 10 September): Cymbalism
Jimmy Heath (NYC, 11 March/28 May): Swamp seed
Joe Henderson (NYC, 3 June): Page One (NYC, 9 September): Our thing

Andrew Hill (NYC, 8 November): Black Fire (NYC, 13 December): Smoke Stack
Red Holloway (NYC, 10 October): The Burner
Elmo Hope (NYC, 19 August): Sounds from Rikers Island
Milt Jackson (NYC, December): Live at the Village Gate
Willis Jackson (NYC, 26 March): Loose (NYC, 23,24 May): Grease and Gravy (NYC, 24 October): More Gravy
JJ Johnson (NYC, 12 March/6 April): JJ's Broadway
Elvin Jones/Jimmy Garrison (NYC, 8 August): Illumination
Hank Jones (NYC, 19 October): Here's Love
Hans Koller (Villingen, 26 November): Exclusiv
Lou Levy (LA, April): The Hymn
Ramsey Lewis (NYC, 10,12 July): Barefoot Sunday Blues
Johnny Lytle (NYC): Got that feeling
Les McCann (LA): The Gospel Truth (LA): Soul Hit (LA): Jazz Waltz
Jack McDuff (NYC, 8 January): Something Slick (NYC, 26 February): Crash (NYC, 5 June): Live! (SF, 3 October): Brother Jack alive! at the Jazz Workshop
Jackie McLean (NYC, 11 February): Vertigo (NYC, 30 April): One Step Beyond (NYC, 20 September): Destination Out
Charlie Mariano (NYC, summer): Portrait in Jazz
Ronnie Mathews (NYC, 17 December): Doin' the thang
Charlie Mingus (NYC, 20 January): The Black Saint and the Sinner Lady (NYC, 30 July): Mingus plays piano (NYC, 20 September): Mingus, Mingus, Mingus, Mingus
Blue Mitchell (NYC, 11 April): The Cup Bearers (NYC, 13 August): Step Lightly
Hank Mobley (NYC, 2 October): No room for squares
MJQ (NYC, 16 May): The Sheriff
Thelonious Monk (NYC, 26,27,28 February, 29 March): Criss Cross (Tokyo, 21 May): Tokyo Concerts (Newport, 4 July): At Newport (NYC, 12 November): Live at the Village Gate (NYC, 30 December): Big Band & Quartet
Wes Montgomery (NYC, 18 April): Fusion (NYC, 22 April): Boss Guitar (NYC, 10 October): Portrait of Wes (NYC, 10 October, 27 November): Guitar on the go
James Moody (NYC, 17,18 June): Great Day (NYC, 16 September): Comin' on strong
Lee Morgan (NYC, 21 December): The Sidewinder
Horace Parlan (NYC, 15 February): Back from the gig
Joe Pass (LA, summer): The complete 'Catch me' sessions
Don Patterson (Chicago, 22 January): Goin' down home
Big John Patton (NYC, 5 April): Along came John (NYC, 11 July, 2 August): Blue John
Oscar Peterson (NYC): We get requests
Pony Poindexter (NYC, 31 January): Plays the big ones (NYC, 27 June): Gumbo
Bud Powell (Paris, February): Bud Powell in Paris
Andre Previn (LA, 18 December): 4 to go!
Freddie Roach (NYC, 21 January, 11 March): Mo' greens please (NYC, 29 November): Good move
Sonny Rollins (NYC, 15,18 July): Sonny meets Hawk (Stuttgart, Autumn): Stuttgart 1963
Lalo Schifrin (LA): Between Broadway and Hollywood
Shirley Scott (NYC, 10 January): The soul is willing (NYC, 27 May): Drag 'em out (NYC, 15 October): Soul shoutin'
Archie Shepp (Copenhagen, 11 November): New York Contemporary Five, Vol 1
Horace Silver (NYC, 11,12 April): Silver's Serenade
Jimmy Smith (NYC, 31 January): I'm movin' on (NYC, 1 February): Bucket! (NYC, 2 February): Rockin' the boat (NYC, 8 February): Prayer meetin' (NYC, 15,20 March): Hobo flats (NYC, 31 May): Live at the Village Gate (NYC, 10,17,25,29 July): Any Number can win / Blue Bash
Johnny 'Hammond' Smith (NYC): Mr Wonderful (NYC): Open House (NYC): A little taste
Martial Solal (Paris, 3 May): Piano Jazz (NYC, 11,15,16 July): Martial Solal at Newport 1963
Sonny Stitt (NYC, 29 January): Sonny Stitt plays Bird (NYC, 18 June): Now! (Chicago): Move on over (NYC, 5 September): Salt and Pepper (NYC, 31 December): Primitivo Soul
Sonny Stitt/Jack McDuff (NYC, 17 September): Soul shack

1963

Bobby Timmons (NYC, 12 August, 10 September): *Born to be blue*
Cal Tjader (NYC, 23,24,25 April): *Several Shades of Blue* (NYC, 26,27 November, 2 December): *Breeze from the East*
Stanley Turrentine (NYC, 13 February): *Never let me go* (NYC, 21 October): *A chip off the old block*
McCoy Tyner (Newport, 5 July): *At Newport*
Harold Vick (NYC, 21 May): *Steppin' out*
Leroy Vinnegar (LA, 5 March): *Leroy walks again*
Chuck Wayne (NYC): *Tapestry*
Frank Wess (NYC, 24 January): *Yo ho!*
Randy Weston (NYC, August): *Music from the African Nations*
Jack Wilson (NYC, 6 February): *Corcovado*
Paul Winter (NYC, 5 December): *The Winter Consort*
Jimmy Witherspoon (NYC/LA): *Baby, Baby, Baby*

Top right: Herbie Hancock recording *Inventions and Dimensions* for Blue Note in August.
Bottom right: Andrew Hill at the *Smoke Stack* session in December.
Below: Alex Welsh and Bud Freeman in London.
Charlie Mingus recording *Black Saint and the Sinner Lady* for Impulse Records. Left to right: producer Bob Thiele, Quentin Jackson, Jaki Byard and Mingus.

Photo: *Francis Wolff* Courtesy: *Mosaic Images*

Photo: *Brian Foskett*

Photo: *Impulse Records* Courtesy: *Max Jones*

THE SIDEWINDER
JOE HENDERSON   BARRY HARRIS   BOB CRENSHAW   BILLY HIGGINS
LEE MORGAN

Photo: *Francis Wolff* Courtesy: *Mosaic Images*

Wayne Shorter (31) joins Miles Davis (38) group.

Duke Ellington (65) & Orchestra tour Japan for the first time (June – July). Mercer Ellington joins the band.

Charles Mingus (42) performs his extended work '*Meditations on Integration*' at the Monterey Jazz Festival (September).

BIRTHS
Iain Ballamy (saxes) 20 February
Courtney Pine (tenor sax) 18 March
Barbara Dennerlein (organ)

DEATHS
Artie Bernstein (54) 4 January
Cecil Scott (58) 5 January
Frank 'Big Boy' Goudie (64) 9 January
Jack Teagarden (58) 15 January
Willie Bryant (55) 9 February
Doug Mettome (38) 17 February
Joe Rushton (56) 2 March
Joe Maini (34) 8 May *shooting accident*
Meade Lux Lewis (59) 7 June *auto crash*
Eric Dolphy (36) 29 June *heart attack (diabetic)*
Teddy Napoleon (50) 5 July *cancer*
Babe Russin (53) 4 August
Ernest 'Bass' Hill (64) 16 September
Nick Travis (38) 7 October
Conrad Gozzo (42) 8 October
Jasper Taylor (70) 7 November
Jack Washington (52) 28 November
Don Redman (64) 30 November
Dave Bowman (50) 28 December *auto crash*

BOOKS
Jerry Coker: *Improvising Jazz*
Dave Dexter: *The Jazz Story, from the 90's to the 60's*
John Godrich & R.M.W. Dixon: *Blues and Gospel Records 1902-1942*
Robert S. Gold: *A Jazz Lexicon*
P. Heaton: *Jazz*
Jorgen Jepsen: *Jazz Records: a discography Vol 7*
Wilfred Mellers: *Music in a New Found Land*
D. Myrus: *I like jazz*
Winthrop Sargent: *Jazz: a history*
Willie 'The Lion' Smith & George Hoefer: *Music on my Mind*
Paul Tanner & Maurice Gerow: *A Study of Jazz*
Leo Walker: *The Wonderful Era of the Great Jazz Bands*
C. Wilson: *Brandy of the Damned*

FILMS
Ballad in Blue (88mins): Ray Charles feature
Dizzy Gillespie: musical documentary
Dizzy Gillespie Quintet (29mins): music short
Earl 'Fatha' Hines (30mins): documentary
The John Coltrane Quartet (30mins): film record
The Modern Jazz Quartet (28mins): documentary
Tubby Hayes (25mins): performance at the Marquee Club by Tubby Hayes Quintet with vocalist Betty Bennett

COMPOSITIONS
Duke Ellington: *Far East Suite*

RECORDS
Ahmed Abdul-Malik (NYC, 12 March): *Spellbound*
Cannonball Adderley (LA, 31 July, 1,2 August): *Live!* (LA, 4 October): *Live Session!* (NYC, 19,21 October): *Fiddler on the Roof*
Albert Ayler (NYC, 10 July): *Spiritual Unity* (Copenhagen, 9 September): *Ghosts*
Art Blakey (NYC, 10 February): *Free for all* (NYC, 20 February): *Kyoto* (NYC, 24 April, 15 May): *Indestructible*
Walter Bishop Jr (NYC): *Summertime*
Bob Brookmeyer (NYC, 25,26,27 May): *Bob Brookmeyer & his Friends*
Bob Brookmeyer/Clark Terry (NYC, March): *The Power of Positive Swinging*
Ray Brown/Milt Jackson (NYC, January): *Much in Common*
Dave Brubeck (NYC, 16,17 June): *Impressions of Japan*
Ray Bryant (NYC): *At Basin Street* (NYC): *Cold Turkey*
Kenny Burrell (NYC, 7 April): *Soul Call*
Jaki Byard (NYC, 21,28 May): *Out Front*

Don Byas (Copenhagen, 14,15 January): *At the Montmartre*
Donald Byrd (NYC, 17,18 December): *I'm trying to get home*
John Coltrane (NYC, 27 April, 1 June): *Crescent* (NYC, 9 December): *A Love Supreme*
John Dankworth/Cleo Laine (London): *Shakespeare & all that jazz*
Miles Davis (NYC, 12 February): *My Funny Valentine / Four and More* (Tokyo, 14 July): *Miles in Tokyo* (Berlin, 25 September): *Miles in Berlin*
Buddy de Franco (NYC). *Blues Bag*
Paul Desmond (NYC, July-September): *Glad to be unhappy*
Walt Dickerson (NYC, 5 March): *Unity*
Eric Dolphy (NYC, 25 February): *Out to Lunch* (Hilversum, 2 June): *Last Date*
Lou Donaldson (Chicago): *Possum Head* (NYC, 19 June): *Cole Slaw* (NYC, December): *Rough house blues*
Kenny Dorham (NYC, 4 September): *Trumpeta Toccata*
Duke Ellington (Chicago, 4,8,9 September): *Mary Poppins*
Booker Ervin (NYC, 27 February): *The Song Book* (NYC, 30 June): *The Blues Book* (NYC, 2 October): *The Space Book*
Bill Evans (Sausalito): *The Bill Evans Trio Live*
Art Farmer (NYC): *The Many Faces of Art Farmer*
Clare Fischer (LA, December): *So Danso Samba*
Ella Fitzgerald (Juan-les-Pins, July): *Ella at Juan-les-Pins*
Don Friedman (NYC): *Dream & Explorations*
Erroll Garner (Amsterdam, 7 November): *Live at the Concertgebouw*
Stan Getz (NYC, 19 August): *Getz au go go*
Terry Gibbs (NYC, 16 January): *Take it from me*
Benny Golson (Stockholm, 14 July): *Stockholm Sojourn*
Dexter Gordon (Paris, 2 June): *One Flight Up* (Copenhagen, 11 June): *Cheesecake* (Copenhagen, 25 June): *King Neptune* (Copenhagen, 9 July): *I want more* (Copenhagen, 23 July): *Love for Sale* (Copenhagen, 6 August): *It's you or no one* (Copenhagen, 20 August): *Billie's Bounce*
Grant Green (NYC, May): *Matador* (NYC, 12 June): *Solid* (NYC, 11 September): *Talkin' about* (NYC, 16 November): *Street of Dreams*
Herbie Hancock (NYC, 17 June): *Empyrean Isles*
Hampton Hawes (LA, 17 February): *The Green Leaves of Summer*
Tubby Hayes (London, 20 April, 26 June): *Tubb's Tours*
Roy Haynes (LA, May): *People*
Jimmy Heath (NYC, Spring): *On the Trail*
Joe Henderson (NYC, 10 April): *In'n'out* (NYC, 30 November): *Inner Urge*
Andrew Hill (NYC, 8 January): *Judgement* (NYC, 31 March): *Point of Departure* (NYC, 25 June): *Andrew!*
Red Holloway/Jack McDuff (LA, 2 February): *Cookin' Together*
Red Holloway (Stockholm, August): *Sax, Strings & Soul*
Freddie Hubbard (NYC, 7 May): *Breaking Point*
Milt Jackson (NYC, 6,7 August): *Jazz'n'Samba*
Willis Jackson (NYC, 9 January): *Boss Shoutin'* (NYC, 21 March): *Live! Jackson's action / Live action / Soul night – live / Tell it*
Jazz Crusaders (July): *Stretchin' Out*
JJ Johnson (NYC, 1 May): *Proof Positive* (Newport, 4 July): *Tribute to Charlie Parker* (NYC, 7 December): *The Dynamic Sound of JJ with Big Band*
Yusef Lateef (Pep's, Philadelphia, 26 June): *The Live Sessions* (Philadelphia, 29 June): *Live at Pep's*
Ramsey Lewis (Chicago): *Bach to the Blues* (Washington, 4-6 June): *The Ramsey Lewis Trio at the Bohemian Caverns*
Jack McDuff (LA, 6,7 February / NYC, 23 April): *Dynamic!* (Stockholm, July): *The Concert McDuff* (Stockholm, July): *Silk and Soul*

Jackie McLean (NYC, 5 August): *It's Time* (NYC, 16 September): *Action*
Charles McPherson (NYC, 20 November): *Bebop Revisited*
Charlie Mingus (NYC, 4 April): *Town Hall Concert 1964* (Amsterdam, 10 April): *Concertgebouw Amsterdam* (Paris, 17,19 April): *The Great Concert of Charlie Mingus* (Wuppertal, 26 April): *Mingus in Europe* (Stuttgart, 28 April): *Mingus in Stuttgart* (SF, 2,3 June): *Right Now* (Monterey, 20 September): *Mingus at Monterey*
Blue Mitchell (NYC, 30 July): *The Thing to do*
Thelonious Monk (LA, 31 October): *Live at the It Club* (SF, 3 November): *Live at the Jazz Workshop*
J.R. Monterose (Cedar Rapids, Iowa): *In action*
Wes Montgomery (NYC, 11,16 November): *Movin' Wes*
James Moody (NYC, 1,4 August): *Group Therapy*
Lee Morgan (NYC, 15 February): *Search for the New Land* (NYC, 11 August): *Tom Cat*
Oliver Nelson (Chicago, 17 March): *Fantabulous* (NYC, 10,11 November): *More Blues and the Abstract Truth*
Phineas Newborn (LA, 1 April): *The Newborn Touch*
Joe Pass (LA, 6 February): *Joy Spring* (LA, October): *For Django*
Don Patterson (NYC, 12 May): *The Exciting New Organ of Don Patterson* (NYC, 10 July): *Don Patterson/Booker Ervin* (NYC, 25 November): *Holiday Soul*
Big John Patton (NYC, 19 June): *The way I feel*
Duke Pearson (NYC, 24 November): *Wahoo*
Oscar Peterson (NYC, 17 August): *Oscar Peterson + One* (NYC, 9 September): *Canadian Suite*
Bud Powell (Paris, 31 July): *Blues for Bouffemont*
Andre Previn (LA, 14 April): *My Fair Lady*
Jimmy Raney (NYC, May): *Two Jims and Zoot*
Freddie Roach (NYC, 18,19 March): *Brown Sugar* (NYC, 16 October): *All that's good*
Sonny Rollins (NYC, January, February): *Now's the Time* (NYC, June): *The Standard Sonny Rollins*
Shirley Scott (NYC, 17 February): *Travelin' Light* (NYC, 31 March): *Blue Flames* (NYC, 23 September): *Everybody Loves a Lover* (New Jersey, 23 September): *The Great Live Session*
Tony Scott (Tokyo, February): *Music for Zen Meditation*
Wayne Shorter (NYC, 29 April): *Night Dreamer* (NYC, 3 August): *Juju* (NYC, 24 December): *Speak no evil*
Horace Silver (Westbury, NY, 6 June): *Live 1964* (NYC, 26,31 October): *Song for my Father*
Jimmy Smith (NYC, 20,21,27 January): *Who's Afraid of Virginia Woolf* (NYC, 20 April, 29 September): *Christmas Cookin'* (NYC, 27-29 April): *The Cat*
Sonny Stitt/Benny Green (Chicago, 10,11 March): *My Main Man*
Sonny Stitt (NYC, 19 March): *Shangri-la* (NYC, 25 August): *Soul People*
Bobby Timmons (NYC): *From the Bottom* (NYC, 18 June): *Little Barefoot Soul* (NYC, 12 August): *Chungking* (NYC, 21 October): *Workin' Out* (NYC, 24 November): *Holiday Soul*
Cal Tjader: *Warm Wave* (NYC, 20 November): *Soul Sauce*
Stanley Turrentine (NYC, 24 January): *Hustlin'* (NYC, 3 June): *In Memory of* (NYC, 4 September): *Mr Natural*
Leroy Vinnegar (LA): *Walker*
Chuck Wayne (NYC, 8 December): *Morning Mist*
Ben Webster (NYC) with Joe Zawinul: *Soulmates*
Baby Face Willette (Chicago, 27 March, 2 April): *Mo-roz* (Chicago, 30 November): *Behind the 8-ball*
Jack Wilson (LA, 13 May): *The Two Sides of Jack Wilson*
Larry Young (NYC, 12 October): *Into something*

ERIC DOLPHY
FREDDIE HUBBARD | BOBBY HUTCHERSON | RICHARD DAVIS | ANTHONY WILLIAMS
'OUT TO LUNCH!'
WILL BE BACK

Left: Stan Kenton in London.
Below left: Stan Getz at the Marquee Club in London.
Below right: Eric Dolphy recording *Out to Lunch* for Blue Note Records in February. Dolphy died of a heart attack in June during a European tour with the Charles Mingus Band.

Stan Kenton (53) presents his first concerts by his Los Angeles Neophonic Orchestra.

Ornette Coleman (35) returns to club playing at the Village Vanguard, NYC, after a 2-year absence.

Ronnie Scott (38) opens a new club in Frith Street, London.

Definite emergence of Albert Ayler (29), Paul Bley (32), Archie Shepp (28) and John Tchicai (29).

Lee Morgan (27) has a hit with 'Sidewinder'.

Duke Ellington (66) presents his first Sacred Concert at Grace Cathedral, San Francisco and makes another European tour.

Miles Davis (39) undergoes a hip operation.

Liberty Records buys the Blue Note label from Alfred Lion and Francis Wolff.

BIRTHS
Javon Jackson (tenor sax) 16 June
Delfeayo Marsalis (trombone) 28 July

DEATHS
Joe Robichaux (64) 17 January
Benny Peyton (74) 24 January
Arthur Schutt (62) 28 January
Bonnie Wetzel (38) 12 February
Nat King Cole (47) 15 February *lung cancer*
Tadd Dameron (48) 8 March *cancer*
Joe Sanders (68) 14 May
Denzil Best (48) 24 May *fell down subway steps*
Carl Kress (57) 10 June *heart attack*
William 'Keg' Purnell (50) 25 June
Red Nichols (60) 28 June *heart attack*
Claude Thornhill (55) 1 July *heart attack*
Willie Dennis (39) 8 July *auto crash*
Spencer Williams (75) 14 July
Freddie Slack (55) 10 August
Bass Edwards (67) 22 August
Steve Brown (75) 15 September
George Tucker (37) 10 October
Earl Bostic (52) 28 October
Clarence Williams (72) 6 November
Buster Harding (48) 14 November
Ernie Shepard (49) 23 November
Cuban Bennett (63) 28 November
Hank d'Amico (50) 3 December *cancer*
Dave Barbour (53) 11 December
Dorothy Dandridge

BOOKS
Perry Bradford: *Born with the Blues*
Owen Bryce & A. McLaren: *Let's Play Jazz: a beginner's guide to jazz*
Hoagy Carmichael with Stephen Longstreet: *Sometimes I wonder*
Samuel Charters: *The Poetry of the Blues*
Sammy Davis Jr with Jane & Burt Boyar: *Yes I Can*
Leonard Feather: *The Book of Jazz from then till now*
Joe Goldberg: *Jazz Masters of the 50's*
Richard Hadlock: *Jazz Masters of the 20's*
Nat Hentoff: *Jazz Country*
Lena Horne & R. Shickel: *Lena*
Jorgen Jepsen: *Jazz Records: a discography Vol 8*
W.M. Kelly: *A drop of patience* (novel)
Stephen Longstreet: *Sportin' House: a history of the New Orleans Sinners and the Birth of Jazz*
Hans J. Maurerer (ed): *The Pete Johnson Story*
George Melly: *Owning Up*
Paul Oliver: *Conversation with the Blues*
Brian Rust: *Jazz Records A-Z, 1932-1942*
George Schaun: *The Story of Music in America*
Artie Shaw: *I love you, I hate you, drop dead*
John Sinclair: *This is our music* (poems)
Leo Walker: *The wonderful era of the great dance bands*

FILMS
John Handy at the Blue Horn (26mins): music short
Notes for a film on jazz (35mins): Bologna jazz festival
Solo: Louis Armstrong All-Stars music short

COMPOSITIONS
Duke Ellington: *Virgin Island Suite*

RECORDS
Cannonball Adderley (NYC, 26 April): *Domination*
Mose Allison (Hermosa Beach, 22-31 October): *Mose Alive!*
Dorothy Ashby (NYC, 3,4 May): *The fantastic jazz harp of Dorothy Ashby*
Albert Ayler (NYC, September): *Spirits Rejoice*
Chet Baker (NYC, May): *Sings & Plays Billie Holiday* (NYC, 23,25,29 August): *Boppin' / Groovin' / Smokin' / Comin' on / Cool burnin'*
Art Blakey (NYC, 12,13 May): *Soul Finger*
Paul Bley (NYC, October): *Closer*
Dollar Brand (Copenhagen, 30 January): *Anatomy of a South African Village* (London, 16 March): *This is Dollar Brand*
Bob Brookmeyer (NYC, 26 November): *Suitably Zoot*
Dave Brubeck (NYC, 8 December): *Dave Brubeck plays Cole Porter*
Kenny Burrell (NYC, 4,5,12 April): *Guitar Forms*
Jaki Byard (Massachusetts, 15 April): *Live at Lennie's*
Charlie Byrd: *Solo Flight*
Don Cherry (NYC, 24 December): *Complete Communion*
John Coltrane (NYC, 17,18 February): *The John Coltrane Quartet Plays* (28 June, October): *Kulu se Mama* (28 June): *Ascension* (May,June): *Transition* (26 August): *Sun Ship* (Seattle, 30 September): *Live in Seattle* (23 November): *Meditations*
Miles Davis (LA, 20,21,22 January): *E.S.P.* (Chicago, 22,23 December): *Live at the Plugged Nickel*
Lou Donaldson (NYC, 3 June): *Musty Rusty*
Duke Ellington (NYC, 26 December): *Concert of Sacred Music*
Duke Ellington/Ella Fitzgerald (LA, October/November): *Ella at Duke's Place*
Booker Ervin (Munich, 27 October): *Setting the Pace / The Trance*
Bill Evans (NYC, January): *Trio '65* (Paris): *Quiet Now*
Art Farmer (NYC, 12 March): *Sing me softly of the blues*
Ella Fitzgerald (LA): *Whisper Not*
Frank Foster (NYC, 2 December): *Fearless Frank Foster*
Stan Getz (Vancouver, March): *The Canadian Concert of Stan Getz* (NYC, April, May, June): *Mickey One*
Dizzy Gillespie (LA, September): *with Gil Fuller & the Monterey Jazz Festival Orchestra*
Dexter Gordon (NYC, 27 May): *Clubhouse* (NYC, 28,29 May): *Gettin' Around*
Grant Green (NYC, 31 March): *I want to hold your hand* (NYC, 26 May): *His Majesty, King Funk*
Herbie Hancock (NYC, 17 March): *Maiden Voyage*
Hampton Hawes (LA, 12 May): *Here and now*
Andrew Hill (NYC, 10 February): *One for one* (NYC, 8 October): *Compulsion*
Red Holloway (NYC, December): *Red Soul*
Richard 'Groove' Holmes (NYC, 3 August): *Soul Message*
Freddie Hubbard (NYC, 19,26 February): *Blue Spirits*
Freddie Hubbard/Lee Morgan (NYC, 9,10 April): *The Night of the Cookers, Vols 1&2*
Bobby Hutcherson (NYC, 3 April): *Dialogue* (NYC, 10 June): *Components*
Milt Jackson (NYC, 12 August): *Milt Jackson at the Museum of Modern Art*
Willis Jackson (NYC, 15 November): *Smokin' with Willis*

Ahmad Jamal (NYC, 24,25 February): *The roar of the greasepaint* (NYC, 18,19,20 May): *Extensions*
Carmell Jones (NYC, 8 May): *Jay Hawk Talk*
Elvin Jones (NYC, 16 February, 18 March): *And then again* (NYC, 23,25 February): *Dear John C*
Clifford Jordan (NYC, 1,17 February): *These are my roots*
Roger Kellaway (NYC, 11,12,13 May): *The Roger Kellaway Trio*
Wynton Kelly (NYC, 5 February): *Undiluted* (Half Note, NYC, 25 June, 17 August): *Blues on purpose*
Wynton Kelly/Wes Montgomery (NYC, 22 September): *Smokin' at the Half Note*
Barney Kessell (LA, Summer): *On Fire*
Eric Kloss (NYC, 1 September): *Introducing Eric Kloss*
Hans Koller (Villingen, 16 January): *Koller/Zoller/Solal*
Pete La Roca (NYC, 19 May): *Basra*
Yusef Lateef (Philadelphia, 24 February): *Live at Pep's Musical Lounge*
Ramsey Lewis (Washington, 13,14 May): *The In Crowd* (Hermosa Beach, 14,15,16 October): *Hang on, Ramsey*
Les McCann (LA, 31 December): *Live at Shelly's Manne-Hole*
Jack McDuff (NYC, 19 October): *Hot Barbecue*
Jackie McLean (NYC, 29 January): *Right now!* (NYC, 3 December): *Consequence*
Charles McPherson (NYC, 6 August): *Con Alma*
Herbie Mann (NYC, 18,19 November): *Herbie Mann today*
Shelly Manne (LA, 24,25,26 February): *Manne – that's Gershwin!*
Warne Marsh (Copenhagen, 27 December): *Live at the Montmartre Club*
Charlie Mingus (Minneapolis, 13 May): *My Favourite Quintet* (LA, 25 September): *Music written for Monterey, 1965*
Blue Mitchell (NYC, 14 July): *Down with it*
Hank Mobley (NYC, 5 February): *The Turnaround* (NYC, 18 June): *Dippin'* (NYC, 18 December): *A Caddy for Daddy*
Thelonious Monk (Montreal, 21 August): *Canadian Concert*
Wes Montgomery (NYC, May): *Shadow of your smile* (Half Note, NYC, May, June): *Smokin' at the Half Note*
Lee Morgan (NYC, 21 April): *The Rumproller* (NYC, 25 June/1 July): *The Gigolo* (NYC, 8 September): *Cornbread* (NYC, 16 November): *Infinity*
Don Patterson (NYC, 19 July): *Satisfaction*
Don Patterson/Sonny Stitt (NYC, 28 December): *The Boss-men*
Big John Patton (NYC, 8 March): *Oh Baby* (NYC, 11 December): *Let 'em roll*
Oscar Peterson (Copenhagen, 29 May): *Eloquence* (Montreal, 25 August): *The Extraordinary Canadian Concert* (LA, 28 October/13 November): *With Respect to Nat*
Dave Pike (NYC, 26 October, 2 November): *Jazz for the Jet Set*
Bud Powell (NYC): *Ups 'n' downs*
Sonny Rollins (MOMA, NYC, 17 June): *There will never be another you* (NYC, 8 July): *Sonny Rollins on Impulse!*
Bud Shank (LA): *Brazil '65*
Wayne Shorter (NYC, 4 March): *The Soothsayer* (NYC, 14 June): *Etcetera* (NYC, 15 October): *The All-seeing Eye*
Horace Silver (NYC, 1,22 October): *The Cape Verdean Blues*
Zoot Sims (NYC, 29 October, 26 November): *Suitably Zoot*
Jimmy Smith (NYC, 19,20 January): *Monster* (Hamburg, 27 May): *In Hamburg Live* (Paris, 28 May): *Live in Concert/Paris* (NYC, 14,15 June): *Organ Grinder Swing* (NYC, 16,17 December): *Got my Mojo workin'*
Johnny 'Hammond' Smith (NYC, 7 May): *The Stinger*
Sonny Stitt (Chicago, 25 January): *Interaction* (NYC, 10 September): *Pow!* (NYC, 21 September): *Night Crawler*
Sun Ra (NYC, April): *The Heliocentric Worlds of Sun Ra*
Bobby Timmons (NYC, 12 July): *Chicken and Dumplin's*
Cal Tjader (NYC, 1,2 June, 21,22 July): *Soul Bird*
Stan Tracey (London, 25 March): *Under Milk Wood*

1965

Photo: *Francis Wolff* Courtesy: *Mosaic Images*

Stanley Turrentine (NYC, 14 April): *Joyride*
Ben Webster (Copenhagen, 30,31 January):
*Saturday Night at the Montmartre / Midnight at the
Montmartre / Sunday Morning at the Montmartre*
Randy Weston (NYC, 18 August, 14 October):
Randy Weston...alone...and together
Anthony Williams (NYC, 12 August): *Spring*
Larry Young (NYC, 10 November): *Unity*

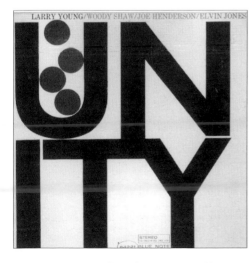

Top: Lee Morgan and Jackie McLean at a Blue
Note recording session.
Right: John Coltrane (39) on soprano saxophone
with Elvin Jones (38) at the drums.

Photo Courtesy: *Rolf Dahlgren*

Buddy Rich (49) forms his Big Band.

The Thad Jones (43) – Mel Lewis (37) Orchestra begins playing Monday nights at the Village Vanguard (February).

The Duke Ellington Band tours Europe with Ella Fitzgerald and plays 4 concerts at the first World Festival of Negro Arts in Senegal under UNESCO auspices (April). Duke Ellington (67) receives the President's Gold Medal.

Earl Hines (62) and his Band make 6-week tour of Russia for US State Department from 8 July.

BIRTHS
Birelli Lagrene (guitar) 4 September
Sebastian Whitaker (drums) 12 September
Harry Allen (tenor sax) 12 October

DEATHS
Charlie Smith (38) 15 January
Osie Johnson (43) 10 February
Billy Kyle (52) 23 February
Russell Smith (76) 27 March
Kid Howard (57) 28 March
Fred Assunto (36) 21 April
Paul Webster (56) 6 May
'Papa' Jack Laine (92) 2 June
Johnny St Cyr (76) 17 June *leukaemia*
Bud Powell (41) 31 July
Boyd Raeburn (52) 2 August
Darnell Howard (74) 2 September *brain tumour*
Lucky Millinder (66) 28 September
Dave Lambert (49) 3 October
Wellman Braud (75) 29 October
Harold 'Shorty' Baker (52) 8 November *cancer*
Marshall Stearns (58) 18 December *heart attack*
Jazz Gillum (62)
Washboard Sam (60)

BOOKS
Whitney Balliett: *Such Sweet Thunder*
Gene Fernett: *A Thousand Golden Horns: the exciting age of America's Greatest Dance Bands*
Peter Gammond & Peter Clayton: *Fourteen Miles on a Clear Night*
Ira Gitler: *Jazz Masters of the 40's*
Tony Glover: *Blues Harp*
Mahalia Jackson & Evan Wylie: *Movin' on up*
Jorgen Jepsen: *Jazz Records: a discography Vols 1&2*
Charles Keil: *Urban Blues*
Ed Kirkeby: *Ain't Misbehavin': the story of Fats Waller*
A.B. Spellman: *Four LIves in the Bebop Business*
Mary Hays Weik: *The Jazz Man* (children's fable)
Martin Williams: *Where's the Melody?*
John S. Wilson: *Jazz: theTransition Years 1940-1960*

FILMS
Assault on a Queen (106mins): feature film with score by Duke Ellington
Duke Ellington – Love You Madly (59mins): documentary
A Man Called Adam (103mins): feature film with Louis Armstrong & Sammy Davis Jr
Pete's Place (17mins): Pete Fountain in action during Mardi Gras
Sweet Love, Bitter (92mins): adaptation of novel 'Night Song' inspired by Charlie Parker

COMPOSITIONS
Duke Ellington: *La Plus Belle Africaine / Swamp Goo*

RECORDS
Pepper Adams (NYC, 26 April, 4,9 May): *Mean what you say*
Cannonball Adderley (Chicago, July): *Mercy, Mercy, Mercy* (Tokyo, 26 August): *Live in Japan*
Nat Adderley (NYC, 16 February): *Sayin' Somethin'* (LA, 3 October): *Live at Memory Lane*
Albert Ayler (Germany, 7 November, Paris, 13 November): *Lorrach/Paris 1966*
George Benson (NYC): *It's Uptown*
Art Blakey (Hermosa Beach, January): *Buttercorn Lady* (NYC, 27 May): *Hold on, I'm coming*
Paul Bley (NYC): *Touching*
Dave Brubeck: *Time in*
Ray Bryant (NYC, 17,18 February): *Gotta Travel On* (NYC, December): *Slow Freight*
Kenny Burrell (NYC, 4,5 April): *The Tender Gender*

(Chicago, October): *Have yourself a soulful little Christmas*
Gary Burton (Nashville, Autumn): *Tennessee Firebird*
Jaki Byard (NYC, 11 January): *Freedom Together*
Donald Byrd (NYC, 24 June): *Mustang*
Benny Carter (LA, 2,4 March): *Additions to Further Definitions*
Don Cherry (NYC, 11 November): *Where is Brooklyn?*
Don Cherry/Gato Barbieri (Paris): *Togetherness*
Buck Clayton (Paris, 2 May): *And Friends*
Ornette Coleman (NYC, July): *The Empty Foxhole* (Paris): *Who's Crazy?*
John Coltrane (NYC, 2 February): *Cosmic Music* (NYC, 28 May): *Live at the Village Vanguard Again* (Japan, 22 July): *Concert in Japan*
Sonny Criss (NYC, 21 October): *This is Criss*
Ted Curson (Holland, 13 May): *Urge*
Eddie 'Lockjaw' Davis (NYC, 13 July): *Lock the Fox*
Miles Davis (NYC, 24,25 October): *Miles Smiles*
Blossom Dearie (London, Summer): *Sweet Blossom Dearie*
Lou Donaldson (NYC, 30 August): *Blowin' in the Wind*
Teddy Edwards (NYC, 13 December): *Nothin' but the truth*
Duke Ellington (Antibes, Summer): *At the Cote d'Azur* (NYC, December): *Far East Suite*

Booker Ervin (LA, December): *Structurally Sound* (NYC, 9 September): *Heavy!*
Bill Evans (NYC, 21 February): *Town Hall Concert* (NYC, 11 October): *A Simple Matter of Conviction*
Bill Evans/Jim Hall (NYC, 7 April, 10 May): *Intermodulation*
Art Farmer (NYC, 13,15 September): *Baroque Sketches*
Ella Fitzgerald/Duke Ellington (Antibes, Summer): *Ella & Duke at the Cote d'Azur*
Clare Fischer (LA): *Manteca!*
Frank Foster (NYC, 27 June, 11 July): *Soul Outing*
Bud Freeman (London, June): *Bud Freeman, Esq* (London, 2 November): *Freeman & Co*
Stan Getz (NYC): *Didn't We* (Paris): *Stan Getz Quartet in Paris*
Dizzy Gillespie (Newport, 4 July): *Trumpet Workshop*
Stephane Grappelli/Stuff Smith/Svend Asmussen/Jean-Luc Ponty: *Violin Summit*
Milford Graves/Don Pullen (Yale, 30 April): *Nommo – in concert at Yale University*
Chico Hamilton (NYC, 2,5 May): *The Further Adventures of El Chico* (NYC, 9 September): *The Dealer*
John Handy (August): *The Second John Handy Album* (Monterey, September): *Live at Monterey*
Hampton Hawes (LA, 30 April, 1 May): *The Seance / I'm all smiles*
Tubby Hayes (London, 10,12,13 May): *100% Proof*
Joe Henderson (NYC, 27 January): *Mode for Joe*
Andrew Hill (NYC, 7 March): *Involution*
Earl Hines (NYC, 10,11 January): *Once Upon a Time* (London, 31 May): *Jazz means Hines*
Johnny Hodges/Earl Hines (NYC, 14 January): *Stride Right*
Richard 'Groove' Holmes (NYC, 22 April): *Living Soul* (NYC, 28 November): *Spicey*

Below: Ornette Coleman at the *Empty Foxhole* recording session.

Photo: *Francis Wolff* Courtesy: *Mosaic Images*

Elmo Hope (NYC, 8,9 March): *Last Sessions*
Freddie Hubbard (NYC, 19,24 October): *Backlash*
Bobby Hutcherson (NYC, 8 February): *Happenings*
(NYC, 14 July): *Stick Up!*
Illinois Jacquet (Lennie's on the Turnpike, March):
Go Power
Ahmad Jamal (Washington, 17,18 February): *Heat Wave*
JJ Johnson: *The Total JJ Johnson*
Elvin Jones (NYC, 24,25 March): *Midnight Walk*
Thad Jones/Mel Lewis (NYC, Summer): *The Jazz Orchestra* (NYC, Summer): *Presenting Joe Williams*
Eric Kloss (NYC, 14 March, 11 April): *Love and all that jazz* (NYC, 21,22 December): *Grits and Gravy*
Yusef Lateef (NYC, 15,16 June): *The Golden Flute*
Ramsey Lewis (Chicago, 26 May, 7,29 June, 1 July):
Wade in the Water (Chicago, 27,28 July): *The Movie Album*
Charles Lloyd (NYC, April): *Dream Weaver*
(Monterey, 18 September): *Forest Flower* (Oslo,
October): *The Flowering*
Howard McGhee (NYC, 22 September): *Cookin' Time*
Jackie McLean (NYC, 12 April): *Jacknife* (Baltimore,
18 December): *Dr Jackle*
Charles McPherson (NYC, 13 October): *The Quintet – Live!*
Jay McShann: *McShann's Piano*
Herbie Mann: *Impressions of the Middle East* (NJF,
4 July): *New Mann at Newport*
Blue Mitchell (NYC, 6 January): *Bring it home to me* (NYC, 17 November): *Boss Horn*
Hank Mobley (NYC, 18 March): *A slice of the top*
(NYC, 17 June): *Straight No Filter*
MJQ (NYC, 27 April): *Blues at Carnegie Hall*
Wes Montgomery (NYC, 17,18,21 March): *Tequila*
(NJ, 14,15,16 September): *California Dreaming*
Wes Montgomery/Jimmy Smith (NYC, 21,28
September): *The Dynamic Duo / Further Adventures of Jimmy & Wes*
Lee Morgan (NYC, 8 April, 27 May): *Delightful-Lee*
(NYC, 29 September): *Charisma* (NYC, 29
November): *The Rajah*
Dick Morrissey (London, 23-25 September): *Here and now and sounding good*
Gerry Mulligan: *Something borrowed, something blue*
Sonny Murray (NYC): *Sonny Murray*
Oliver Nelson (NYC, 13,14 April): *Plays Michelle*
Albert Nicholas (Brussels,5 September): *Albert's Blues*
Anthony Ortega (LA, 15 October): *New Dance*
Don Patterson (NYC, 5 August): *Soul Happening*
Big John Patton (NYC,29 April): *Got a good thing goin'*

Cecil Payne (Manchester, 5 November): *Brookfield andante*
Duke Pearson (NYC, 13 September): *The Right Touch*
Bill Perkins (LA, 23,28,30 November): *Quietly There*
Oscar Peterson (NYC, 5 April): *Blues Etude*
(Chicago, December): *Soul Espanol*
Don Rendell/Ian Carr (London, 16,17 March): *Dusk Fire*
Buddy Rich (LA): *Swinging New Big Band* (LA):
Big Swing Face
Freddie Roach (NYC, 13,28 June): *The Soul Book*
Max Roach (NYC): *Drums Unlimited*
Sonny Rollins (NYC, 26 February): *Sonny Plays Alfie*
(NYC, 9 May): *East Broadway Run Down*
Archie Shepp (SF, 9 February): *Live in San Francisco / Three for a quarter, one for a dime*
Wayne Shorter (NYC, 24 February): *Adam's Apple*
Horace Silver (NYC, 2,23 November): *The Jody Grind*
Jimmy Smith (NYC, 11,12 May): *Peter and the Wolf*
(NJ, 14 June): *Hoochie Coochie Man*
Johnny 'Hammond' Smith (NYC, 4 January): *The Stinger meets the Golden Thrush* (NYC, 28 September):
Love Potion No9
Harry South (London, 25,26 January): *Presenting the Harry South Big Band*
Spontaneous Music Ensemble (March): *Challenge*
Rex Stewart (Switzerland,12 June):*Meets Henri Chaix*

Sonny Stitt (NYC, March): *Sonny* (Chicago, 15 April):
Soul in the Night (NYC, 28 July): *What's New?*
Gabor Szabo (NYC, 6 May): *Spellbinder*
(NYC, 4,17 August): *Jazz Raga*
Cecil Taylor (NYC, 19 May): *Unit Structures*
(Paris, 30 November): *Student Studies*
Ed Thigpen (NYC, 18,19,20 April): *Out of the Storm*
Bobby Timmons (NYC, 20 January): *The Soul Man*
(NYC, 30 September, 14 October): *Soul Food*
Cal Tjader (NYC, 9,10,11 February): *Soul Burst*
(LA, 24,25,26 May): *El Sonido Nuevo*
Stan Tracey (London, 8,9,23 March): *Alice in Jazzland* (London): *Stan Tracey...In Person*
Stanley Turrentine (NYC, 1 July): *Rough 'n' Tumble*
(NYC, July): *Let it go* (NYC, 8 July): *Easy Walker*
(NYC, 22 September): *The Spoiler*
Harold Vick (NYC, June): *Commitment* (NYC, 15,16
June): *The Caribbean Suite* (NYC, 3,4 October):
Straighten Up
Ben Webster (Copenhagen): *Blue Light*
Gerald Wilson (LA): *The Golden Sword*
Jack Wilson (LA): *Ramblin'*
Larry Young (NYC): *Of Love and Peace*
Joe Zawinul (NYC, 7 February): *Money in the Pocket*

Below: Joe Henderson at the *Mode for Joe* session.

Above: Thelonious Monk recording for BBCTV's *Jazz Goes to College* in Cambridge, England.

Photo: Brian Foskett

Photo: Francis Wolff Courtesy: Mosaic Images

1967

Eddie Condon (62) and his Band tour Britain.

Eddie Condon Club closes.

Charles Lloyd (29) tours the Soviet Union, the first jazzman to be invited by Russian People's Group.

European tour by 'Jazz from a Swinging Era' package (March/April). The package includes Earl Hines (61), Buck Clayton (55), Vic Dickenson (60), Roy Eldridge (56), Earle Warren (52), Budd Johnson (56), Sir Charles Thompson (49), Oliver Jackson (33) and Bill Pemberton (49).

Dave Brubeck (46) breaks up the Quartet after 26 years (26 December).

BIRTHS
Tommy Smith (tenor sax) 27 April

DEATHS
Rob Swope (40) 9 January
Edmond Hall (65) 11 February *heart attack*
Muggsy Spanier (60) 12 February *heart attack*
Walter 'Fats' Pichon (60) 25 February
Willie Smith (56) 7 March
Herman Chittison (58) 8 March
Pete Johnson (62) 23 March
Buster Bailey (64) 12 April
Henry 'Red' Allen (59) 17 April *cancer*
Charlie Margulis (63) 24 April
Wayman Carver (62) 6 May
George Treadwell (47) 14 May
Elmo Hope (43) 19 May
Billy Strayhorn (51) 31 May *cancer*
John Coltrane (41) 17 July
Rex Stewart (60) 7 September *brain haemorrhage*
Sidney de Paris (62) 14 September
Boots Mussulli (49) 23 September *cancer*
Stuff Smith (58) 26 September
Billy Banks (59) 19 October *heart attack*
Henderson Chambers (59) 19 October *heart attack*
Keg Johnson (58) 8 November *heart attack*
Ida Cox (71) 10 November *cancer*
Jimmy Archey (65) 16 November
George Hoefer () 19 November
Floyd Casey (67) 7 December
Louis Bacon (63) 8 December
Paul Whiteman (77) 29 December
Peter Bocage (80) 3 December
Wilbert Hogan

BOOKS
Samuel Charters: *The Bluesmen: The Story and the Music of the Men who made the Blues*
Leonard Feather: *Encyclopaedia of Jazz in the Sixties*
Babs Gonzales: *I Paid My Dues*
Benny Green: *Blame it on my Youth*
Jorgen Jepsen: *Jazz Records: a discography Vol 3*
LeRoi Jones: *Black Music*
Barry McRae: *The Jazz Cataclysm*
Reese Markewich: *Jazz Publicity*
Charlemae Rollins: *Famous Negro Entertainers*
Al Rose & Edmond Souchon: *New Orleans Jazz: a family album*
George Simon: *The Big Bands*
Roy Wilbraham: *Charles Mingus – a biography and discography*
Martin Williams: *Jazz Masters of New Orleans*

FILMS
Ambitas (16mins): Cecil Taylor
Big Ben (31mins): documentary on Ben Webster
The New Orleans Jazz Museum (14mins): documentary
Reverend Gary Davis (26mins): film portrait

COMPOSITIONS
Billy Strayhorn: *The Intimacy of the Blues / Blood Count*

RECORDS
Monty Alexander (NYC, 11,14 December): *Zing*
Roy Ayers (NYC, 6 March): *Virgo Vibes*
Count Basie (NYC, 15 February): *Basie's Beat*
Lester Bowie (August): *Number 1 / Number 2*
Ruby Braff (London, 28 October/8 November): *Hear me talkin'*
Ray Bryant (LA, 19,20 May): *The Ray Bryant Touch*
Kenny Burrell (NYC, December): *Ode to 52nd Street*
Gary Burton (NYC, 15 June): *Lofty Fake Anagram*
Jaki Byard (NYC, 15 February): *On the spot!* (NYC, 31 October): *The Sunshine of my Soul*
Donald Byrd (NYC, 9 January): *Blackjack* (NYC, 12 May): *Slow Drag* (NYC, 5 October): *The Creeper*
Tony Coe (London, June): *Tony's Basement*
Bill Coleman/Ben Webster (London, 27 April): *Swingin' in London*
John Coltrane (NYC, 15 February, 7 March): *Expression* (NYC, 22 February): *Interstellar Space*
Sonny Criss (NYC, 12 March): *Portrait of Sonny Criss* (NYC, 18 August): *Up, up and away*
Eddie 'Lockjaw' Davis: *The Fox and the Hounds*
Eddie 'Lockjaw' Davis/Paul Gonsalves: *Love Calls*
Miles Davis (NYC, 16,17,24 May): *Sorcerer* (NYC, 7,19,22,23 May): *Nefertiti* (NYC, 4,28 December): *Circle in the Round*
Nathan Davis (Paris, December): *Rules of Freedom*
Lou Donaldson (NYC, 20 January): *Sweet Slumber* (Buffalo): *Fried Buzzard* (NYC, 7 April): *Alligator Boogaloo* (NYC, 27 October): *Mr Shing-a-ling*
Teddy Edwards (NYC, 24,27 May): *It's Alright*
Duke Ellington (LA): *The Popular Duke Ellington* (NYC, 28,30 August, 1 September): *And his mother called him Bill*
Don Ellis: *Electric Bath*
Booker Ervin (LA, October): *Booker and Brass*

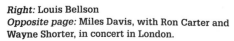

Duke Ellington's Concert of Sacred Music

Great St Mary's Church Cambridge Monday 20 February 1967 at 8.30 pm Admission by programme only

Right: Louis Bellson
Opposite page: **Miles Davis, with Ron Carter and Wayne Shorter, in concert in London.**

Photo: *Brian Foskett*

1967

Bill Evans (NYC, 9 August): *Further Conversations with Myself*
Art Farmer (NYC, 8 February): *The time and the place* (NYC, 16,23,25 May, 7 June): *Art Farmer Quintet plays Great Jazz Hits*
Stan Getz (NYC, 3,30 March): *Sweet Rain*
Dizzy Gillespie (LA, 25,26 May): *Swing Low, Sweet Cadillac* (Village Vanguard, NYC, 10 October): *Jazz on a Sunday Afternoon*
Dexter Gordon (Copenhagen, 20,21 July): *The Montmartre Collection, Vols 1,2,3*
Grant Green (NYC): *Iron City*
Johnny Griffin (Copenhagen, 30,31 March): *Hush-a-bye / A Night in Tunisia / You Leave me Breathless*
Chico Hamilton: *The Gamut*
Barry Harris (NYC, 20 April): *Luminescence!*
Eddie Harris (NYC): *The Electrifyin' Eddie Harris*
Hampton Hawes (Villingen, 8 November): *Hampton Hawes in Europe*
Tubby Hayes (London, 2 February, 7 March): *Mexican Green*
Joe Henderson (NYC, 16 May/27 September): *Tetragon* (NYC, 10 August): *The Kicker*
Woody Herman (Monterey Jazz Festival, September): *Concerto for Herd*
Earl Hines/Jimmy Rushing (NYC, 19 July): *Blues & Things*
Johnny Hodges/Earl Hines (SF, 13,14 November): *Swing's our Thing*
Richard 'Groove' Holmes (Chicago, 26,27 April): *Super Soul* (NYC, 29 May): *Get up and get it* (NYC, 19 December): *Soul Power*
Freddie Hubbard (NYC, November): *High Blues Pressure*
Bobby Hutcherson (NYC, 12 July): *Total Eclipse*
Ahmad Jamal (Chicago): *Cry Young*
Thad Jones/Mel Lewis (NYC): *Live at the Village Vanguard*
Barney Kessel/Jim Hall (Berlin, 5 November): *Guitar Workshop/Berlin Festival*

Roland Kirk (NYC, April): *Now don't you cry, beautiful Edith*
John Klemmer (Chicago, May): *Involvement*
Eric Kloss (NYC, 14 July): *First Class Kloss* (NYC, 18 September): *Life Force* (NYC, 22 December): *We're going up*
Lee Konitz (NYC, 25 September): *Duets*
Pete La Roca (NYC, 25 May): *Bliss!*
Ramsey Lewis (Chicago): *Goin' Latin* (SF, July): *Dancing in the Street*
Charles Lloyd (Tallinn, 14 May): *In the Soviet Union: Journey Within / Charles Lloyd in Europe*
Jackie McLean (NYC, 3 February): *Hipnosis* (NYC, 24 March): *New and Old Gospel* (NYC, 8 September): *'Bout Soul* (NYC, 22 December): *Demon's Dance*
Herbie Mann (NYC, 26,27 July): *Glory of Love*
Shelly Manne (LA, 19,20 June): *Perk up*
Pat Martino (NYC, 1 May): *El Hombre* (NYC, 2 October): *Strings*
Blue Mitchell (NYC, 17 November): *Heads up!*
Hank Mobley (NYC, 24 February): *Third Season* (NYC, 24 February): *Hi Voltage* (NYC, 26 May): *Far Away Lands*
MJQ (Bristol, 12 December): *Under the Jasmin Tree*
Thelonious Monk (Paris, 14 November): *Epistrophy / Sphere*
Wes Montgomery (NYC, 6,7,8 June): *A day in the life* (NYC): *Down here on the ground*
Lee Morgan (NYC, 14,28 April): *Sonic Boom* (NYC, 14 July): *The Procrastinator* (NYC, 10 November): *The Sixth Sense*
Mark Murphy (Cologne, 18 December): *Midnight Mood*
Oliver Nelson (NYC, 16,17 February): *The Kennedy Story* (LA, 2,3,4 June): *Live at Marty's on the Hill*
Jimmy Owens/Kenny Barron (NYC, 16,18 January, 19 April): *You had better listen*
Don Patterson/David Newman (NYC, 10 May): *Mellow Soul*
Don Patterson/Houston Person (NYC, 25 August): *Four Dimensions*

Duke Pearson (NYC, December): *Introducing*
Houston Person (NJ, 14 June): *Chocomotive* (NJ, 13 October): *Trust in me*
Oscar Peterson (Villingen, November): *Girl Talk*
King Pleasure (NYC): *Mr Jazz*
Jerome Richardson (NYC, 13,17 October): *Groove Merchant*
Freddie Roach (NYC, 5 January): *Mocha Motion* (NYC, 22,29 June): *My People (soul people)*
Archie Shepp: *Mama Too Tight* (NYC, 26 April): *The Magic of Ju Ju* (Germany, 21 October): *One for the Trane*
Wayne Shorter (NYC, 20 March): *Schizophrenia*
Jimmy Smith (NYC, 2,14 June): *Respect*
Johnny 'Hammond' Smith (NYC, 3 March): *Ebb Tide* (NYC, 27 September): *Soul Flowers*
Sonny Stitt (Chicago, 13 July): *Made for each other* (NYC, 18 October): *Night Work*
The Three Sounds (Hermosa Beach, July): *Live at the Lighthouse*
Bobby Timmons (NYC): *Got to get it*
Cal Tjader (NYC, 28,29 March): *Along comes Cal* (NYC): *Hip Vibrations*
Stan Tracey (London, 8,14 October): *With Love from Jazz*
Stanley Turrentine (NYC, 17 February, 23 June): *New Time Shuffle*
McCoy Tyner (NYC, 1 December): *Tender Moments*
Harold Vick (NYC, 21,22 August): *The Melody is Here*
Cedar Walton (NYC, 10 July): *Cedar!*
Mike Westbrook (London): *Celebration*
Jack Wilson (LA, July, August): *Something Personal* (NYC, October): *Easterly Winds*
Teddy Wilson (London, 18 June): *Moonglow*
Mike Wofford (LA, 12 October, 27 November): *Summer Night*
Phil Woods (NYC, 31 January, 1 February): *Greek Cooking*
Joe Zawinul (NYC, 16,21 October, 12 December): *The rise and fall of the Third Stream*

Photo: Brian Foskett

1968

'Jazz Expo 68' festival of concerts in London, part of an 18 city 'Newport Jazz Festival in Europe' tour featuring Dizzy Gillespie (51), Gerry Mulligan (41), Dave Brubeck (47), Gary Burton (25), Earl Hines (62) and the Newport All-Stars – Benny Carter (61), Ruby Braff (41), Barney Kessel (45).

Formation of 'The World's Greatest Jazzband' by Yank Lawson (57) and Bob Haggart (54).

Duke Ellington (69) & his Orchestra make their first tour of Latin America in September. Second Sacred Concert at St John the Divine in New York.

The Jazz Composers' Orchestra is formed, and recorded.

BIRTHS
Larry Goldings (organ) 28 August

DEATHS
Earl Swope (45) 3 January
Luckey Roberts (80) 5 February
Leo McConville (68) 26 February
Monk Hazel (64) 5 March
Bumps Myers (56) 8 April
George Wettling (60) 6 June *lung cancer*
Hank Duncan (71) 7 June
Bobby Pratt 12 June
Wes Montgomery (43) 15 June *heart attack*
Ziggy Elman (54) 26 June *liver ailment*
Cutty Cutshall (56) 16 August *heart attack*
Bill Stegmeyer (51) 19 August
Edmond Souchon (70) 24 August
Ed Wilcox (60) 29 September
Johnny Richards (56) 7 October
Steve Bohannon (21) 21 October
Alcide 'Slow Drag' Pavageau (80) 8 November *mugging victim*
Hilton Jefferson (65) 14 November
Floyd O'Brien (64) 18 November
George Lewis (68) 31 December
Rudy Jackson (67)

BOOKS
Pearl Bailey: *The Raw Pearl*
Whitney Balliett: *Super Drummer: a profile of Buddy Rich*
Charles Boeckman: *Cool, Hot and Blue: a history of jazz for young people*
Larry Borenstein & Bill Russell: *Preservation Hall Portraits*
Avril Dankworth: *Jazz: an introduction to its musical basis*
Sidney Fox: *The Origins and Development of Jazz*
Nat Hentoff: *Journey into Jazz*
Jorgen Jepsen: *Jazz Records: a discography Vol 4*
LeRoi Jones & Larry Neal: *Black Fire: an anthology of Afro-American Writing*
Mike Leadbitter & Neil Slaven: *Blues Records, Jan 1943 to Dec 1966*
Albert McCarthy, Paul Oliver, Alun Morgan & Max Harrison: *Jazz on Record: a critical guide to the first 50 years*
Elizabeth Montgomery: *William C. Handy, Father of the Blues*
Paul Oliver: *Screening the Blues*
Kenneth Richards: *Louis Armstrong*
Gunther Schuller: *Early Jazz*
Arnold Shaw: *Sinatra*
Marshall & Jean Stearns: *Jazz Dance*
Pete Venudor & Michael Sparke: *The Standard Stan Kenton Directory*
Roy Wilbraham: *Milt Jackson: a discography and biography*

FILMS
Bill Evans (17mins): documentary feature on Bill Evans Trio
Blues accordin' to Lightnin' Hopkins (31mins): documentary
Jazz the intimate art (53mins): documentary with Louis Armstrong, Dizzy Gillespie, Dave Brubeck, Charles Lloyd
Mingus (56mins): documentary/interview with Charlie Mingus
Monterey Jazz (120mins): film of 1967 Monterey Jazz Festival with Carmen McRae, Woody Herman Orchestra, Illinois Jacquet, Don Ellis Band, Dizzy Gillespie etc.
Sonny Rollins, musician (30mins): documentary

COMPOSITIONS
Duke Ellington: *The Latin American Suite*

RECORDS
Pepper Adams (NYC, 11,12 December): *Encounter*
Cannonball Adderley (NYC): *Accent on Africa*
Nat Adderley (NYC, 18,19 January): *The Scavenger* (NYC, 26,27,28 March): *You, baby* (NYC, 19,21 November, 4 December): *Comin' out of the shadows*
Toshiko Akiyoshi (NYC, 30 July): *Toshiko at the Top of the Gate*
Mose Allison (NYC, 9,10,12 July): *I've been doin' some thinkin'*
Dorothy Ashby (Chicago, April): *Soul Vibrations*
Albert Ayler (NYC, 5,6 September): *New Grass*
Gato Barbieri/Dollar Brand (Milan, 16 March): *Confluence*
Count Basie (USA, 23 July): *The Great Concert* (LA, 31 August, 3,4 September): *Straight Ahead*
Gordon Beck (London): *Gyroscope*
Louis Bellson (NYC): *Dynamic Drums*
Art Blakey (NYC, August): *Art Blakey Live!*
Carla Bley/Gary Burton (NYC): *A genuine Tong funeral*
Paul Bley (Seattle, 10-12 May): *Mr Joy*
Anthony Braxton (Chicago): *Three Compositions of New Jazz*
Dave Brubeck/Gerry Mulligan (Mexico, Summer): *Compadres* (NYC, 4 October, 13 December): *Blues Roots*
Ray Bryant (NYC, September): *Up above the Rock*
Kenny Burrell (NYC, February): *The Common Ground* (NYC, Summer): *Night Song*
Gary Burton (Carnegie Hall, NYC, 23 February): *In Concert*
Jaki Byard (NYC, 2 April): *Jaki Byard with Strings* (NYC, 17 September): *The Jaki Byard Experience*
Kenny Clarke/Francy Boland (Cologne, 13,14 May): *All Smiles* (Cologne, 28,29 June): *Faces*
Bill Coleman/Buddy Tate (Paris, 5 December): *Together at last*
Ornette Coleman (NYC, January): *New York is now* (NYC, 29 April): *Love Call*
Alice Coltrane (NYC, 29 January/6 June): *A Monastic Trio*
Chick Corea: *Bliss!*
Sonny Criss (NYC, 12 January): *The beat goes on* (LA, 8 May): *Sonny's Dream* (NYC, 2 July): *Rockin' in Rhythm*
Miles Davis (NYC, 16 January, 15,16,17 May): *Miles in the Sky* (NYC, 19,20,21 June, 24 September): *Filles de Kilimanjaro* (NYC, November): *Water Babies*
Paul Desmond (NYC, 10,16,24 October, 5 November, 20 December): *Summertime*
Klaus Doldinger (Munich, 19 August): *Blues happening*
Lou Donaldson (NYC, 15 March): *Midnight Creeper* (NYC, 8 November): *Say it Loud*
Duke Ellington (NYC, January/February): *Second Sacred Concert*
Booker Ervin (LA, 12 January): *The 'In' between* (NYC, 24 June): *Booker Ervin*
Bill Evans (Montreux, 15 June): *Bill Evans at Montreux Jazz Festival* (NYC, September, October): *Bill Evans Alone*
Art Farmer/Phil Woods (Rome, 12 October): *Art Farmer & Phil Woods*
Clare Fischer (LA, Autumn): *Thesaurus*
Ella Fitzgerald : *Sunshine of your love*
Frank Foster (NYC, 21 March): *Manhattan Fever*
Dizzy Gillespie (Germany, 7 November): *The Dizzy Gillespie Reunion Big Band*
Johnny Griffin (Cologne, 27 August): *Foot-patting*
Herbie Hancock (NYC, 9,11 March): *Speak like a child*

John Handy (15 April): *Projections*
Joe Harriott/John Mayer (London): *Indo-Jazz Fusions*
Barry Harris (NYC, 4 June): *Bull's Eye*
Hampton Hawes (Paris, 11 March): *Spanish Steps* (Tokyo, 7,9,12 May): *The Challenge* (Tokyo, 15 May): *Jam Session*
Woody Herman (Chicago, October): *Light my fire*
Andrew Hill (NYC, 5 August): *Grass Roots* (NYC, 11 October): *Dance with Death*
Earl Hines (NYC, 8,11 March): *Fatha blows best*
Richard 'Groove' Holmes (NYC, 14 February): *The Groover* (NYC, 26 August): *That healin' feelin'*
Bobby Hutcherson (NYC, 14 March): *Patterns* (NYC, 11 November): *Spiral*
Bobby Hutcherson/Harold Land (NYC, 12 July): *Total Eclipse*
Willis Jackson (NYC, 9 September): *Swivel Hips* (NYC, 11 November): *Gator's Groove*
Keith Jarrett (LA, 30,31 August): *Somewhere before*
Eddie Jefferson (27 September): *Body and Soul*
Elvin Jones (NYC): *Heavy Sounds* (NYC, 8 April): *Puttin' it together* (NYC, 6 September): *The Ultimate*
Philly Joe Jones (London, 1,31 October): *Trailways Express*
Thad Jones/Mel Lewis (NYC, October): *Monday Night at the Village Vanguard*
Wynton Kelly/George Coleman (Baltimore, 22 September): *Live in Baltimore*
Stan Kenton (LA): *The Jazz Compositions of Dee Barton*
Barney Kessel (London, 29,30,31 October): *Swinging easy* (London, 2 November): *Hair is beautiful*
Roland Kirk: *Now please don't you cry, beautiful Edith* (July): *Volunteered Slavery*
Eric Kloss (NYC, 13 August): *Sky Shadows*
Hans Koller (Villingen, 18 January): *New York City*
Lee Konitz (Rome, October): *Stereokonitz*
Charles Kynard (LA, 6 August): *Professor Soul*
Johnny Lytle (NYC): *The sound of Velvet Soul*
Harold Mabern (NYC, 11 March): *A few miles from Memphis* (NYC, 23 December): *Rockin' and Scrapin'*
Jack McDuff (Chicago, April): *The Natural Thing* (Chicago, September, October): *Gettin' our thing together*
Jimmy McGriff (NYC, Autumn): *The Worm*
Charles McPherson (NYC, 31 January): *From this moment on* (NYC, 27 August): *Horizons*
Junior Mance (NYC, September): *Live at the Top of the Gate*
Albert Mangelsdorff: *Zo-Ko-Ma*
Herbie Mann (NYC, 21 August): *Memphis Underground*
Pat Martino (NYC, 8 January): *East* (NYC, 11 June): *Baiyina*
Helen Merrill (NYC, July): *A shade of difference*
Blue Mitchell (LA, 11,12 September): *Collision in Black*
Roscoe Mitchell (March): *Congliptious*
Hank Mobley (NYC, January): *Reach Out*
Thelonious Monk (LA, 19 November): *Monk's Blues*
Wes Montgomery (NYC, 7,8,9 May): *Road Song*
Lee Morgan (NYC, 15 February): *Taru* (NYC, 3 May): *Caramba*
Gerry Mulligan/Dave Brubeck (New Orleans, May): *Live in New Orleans 1968*
Don Patterson (NYC, 22 February): *Boppin' and Burnin'* (NYC, 5 June): *Opus de Don* (NYC, 24 September): *Funk you*
Big John Patton (NYC, 8 March): *That certain feeling* (NYC, 25 October): *Understanding*
Duke Pearson (NYC, 11 September): *The Phantom* (NYC, 2,3 December): *Now Hear This!*
Art Pepper (LA, 24 November): *Live at Donte's*
Houston Person (NJ, 12 March): *Blue Odyssey*
Oscar Peterson (Villingen, April): *The way I really play / My favourite instrument / Mellow Mood*
Don Rendell/Ian Carr (London, 18 March): *Live*
Max Roach (Oslo, May): *Sounds as a Roach* (NYC, 25 June, July): *Members don't git weary*
Ronnie Ross (London, June): *Cleopatra's Needle*
Ronnie Scott (London, 25,26 October): *Live at Ronnie Scotts*
Archie Shepp (NYC, 29 January): *The way ahead*
Sahib Shihab (Cologne, 9 June): *Seeds*
Don Shirley (NYC Carnegie Hall, 22 March): *In Concert*
Horace Silver (NYC, 25,29 March): *Serenade to a Soul Sister*

1968

Jimmy Smith (NYC, January): *Stay Loose*
(LA, 13,14 May): *Livin' it up*
Johnny 'Hammond' Smith (NYC, 31 January): *Dirty Grape* (NYC, 18 June): *Nasty*
Lonnie Smith (NYC, 23 July): *Think!*
Martial Solal (Paris): *Falasifa* (Paris, January): *Martial Solal & Hampton Hawes*
Spontaneous Music Ensemble (18 February): *Karyobin*
Sonny Stitt (NYC, 23 September): *Soul Electricity*
Sun Ra (NYC): *Pictures of infinity*
Cecil Taylor (Italy, July): *Praxis*
John Tchicai (Denmark, 27 October): *Cadentia Nova Danica*
The Three Sounds (LA, 11 April): *Coldwater Flat* (LA, 19,20 September): *Elegant Soul*
Bobby Timmons: *Do you know the way?*
Cal Tjader (NYC, 15 January): *Solar heat* (NYC, August): *Sounds out Burt Bacharach*
Stan Tracey (London, 16,17 July): *The Latin American Caper* (London, August): *We love you madly*
Stanley Turrentine (NYC, 30 August): *Common Touch* (NYC, 29 September, 5,6 October): *Look of Love* (NYC, 14,28 October): *Always something there*
McCoy Tyner (NYC, 17 May): *Time for Tyner* (NYC, 23 August): *Expansions* (NYC): *Tender Moments*
Cedar Walton (NYC, 24 May): *Spectrum*
Ray Warleigh (London, 26 November, 13 December): *First Album*
Jack Wilson (LA, September): *Song for my daughter*
Phil Wilson (Providence, RI): *The Prodigal Son*
Phil Woods (Ljubljana, 6 June): *Jazz Festival Ljubljana 1968* (Paris, 14,15 November): *Alive and well in Paris*
Larry Young (NYC, 9 February): *Heaven on Earth* (NYC): *Contrasts*

Right: Elvin Jones at Jazz Expo, London.
Below: Art Farmer, James Moody and Illinois Jacquet.

Photo: *Brian Foskett*

1969

The Art Ensemble of Chicago moves to Paris.

Don Cherry (32) is also in Paris, where he records 'Mu'.

Duke Ellington is honoured at the White House on his 70th birthday (29 April). The Orchestra tours Europe, making their first visit to Eastern Europe.

BIRTHS
Joshua Redman (tenor sax) 1 February

DEATHS
Paul Chambers (33) 4 January *tuberculosis*
Alcide 'Slow Drag' Pavageau (80) 19 January
Paul Barbarin (69) 10 February *heart attack*
Pee Wee Russell (62) 15 February *liver complaint*
Charles Clark (24) 15 April *cerebral haemorrhage*
Coleman Hawkins (65) 19 May *broncopneumonia*
Ralph Pena (42) 20 May *road accident*
Al Stinson (24) 2 June
Ernie Farrow (41) 14 July
Russ Morgan (65) 7 August
Timme Rosencrantz (58) 11 August
Tony Fruscella (42) 14 August
Dave Goldberg (47) 21 August
Josh White (61) 5 September
Cedric Haywood (54) 9 September
Bert Courtley (40) 13 September
Joe Watkins (69) 13 September
Manuel Manetta (80) 10 October
Bill McKinney (74) 14 October
Nate Kazebier (57) 22 October
Pops Foster (77) 30 October
Tony Spargo (Sbarbaro) (72) 30 October *stroke*
Tony Pastor (62) 31 October
Wilmore 'Slick' Jones (62) 2 November
Ted Heath (69) 18 November
Joy Marshall (26) 21 November
Cub Teagarden (54)

BOOKS
Mickey Baker: *Jazz and Rhythm 'n' Blues Guitar*
Rap Brown: *Die Nigger, Die*
Walter Bruyninckx: *Fifty Years of Recorded Jazz 1917 – 1967*
Donald Connor & Warren Hicks: *B.G. on the Record*
Charles Fox: *Jaxx in Perspective*
Phyl Garland: *The Sound of Soul*
Benny Green: *Jazz Decade: Ten Years at Ronnie Scott's*
Carl Herzog zu Mecklenburg: *International Jazz Bibliography: Jazz Books from 1918 to 1968*
Jorgen Jepsen: *A Discography of Miles Davis*
Jorgen Jepsen: *A Discography of Dizzy Gillespie*
Jorgen Jepsen: *A Discography of Billie Holiday*
Paul Oliver: *The Story of the Blues*
Henry Pleasants: *Serious Music & All That Jazz*
Arrigo Polillo: *Jazz: A Guide to its History*
Frank Surge: *Singers of the Blues*
Peter Williams: *Bluff your way in Folk and Jazz*

FILMS
Discovering Jazz (22mins): documentary
Duke Ellington at the White House (18mins): film record
Whooping the Blues (14mins): portrait of Sonny Terry

RECORDS
Cannonball Adderley (Milam): *Alto Giant* (Chicago, October): *Country Preacher*
Amalgam (London, 20 May): *Prayer for Peace*
Gene Ammons (Chicago, 10 November): *The Boss is back* (Chicago, 11 November): *Brother Jug*
Art Ensemble of Chicago (Paris, 12 August): *Message to our folks / Reese and the Smooth Ones* (Paris, 5 September): *Live*
Dorothy Ashby (Chicago, March): *Dorothy's Harp*
Roy Ayers (NYC, 11 March, 12 May): *Daddy Bug*
Albert Ayler (NYC, 26-29 August): *Music is the Healing Force of the Universe*
Count Basie (Las Vegas, March): *Standing Ovation* (Chicago, 20 October): *Basic Basie*
Louis Bellson (London, 21,23 May): *Louie in London*
Marion Brown (Holland): *Porto Novo*
Ray Bryant (Chicago, 26,27 June): *Cadet LPS 830*
Dave Burrell (Paris, 13 August): *Echo*
Kenny Burrell (NYC, February): *Night Song* (NYC, Autumn): *Asphalt Canyon Suite*

Gary Burton (NYC, June): *Throb* (NYC): *Country Roads & Other Places*
Jaki Byard (NYC, 31 July): *Solo*
Donald Byrd (NYC, 9 May, 6 June): *Fancy Free*
Ron Carter: *Uptown Conversation*
Don Cherry (Paris): *Mu*
Kenny Clarke/Francy Boland (Ronnie Scott's, London, 28 February): *Nobody slept here*
Stanley Cowell (London, September): *Blues for the Viet-cong*
Kenny Cox (Detroit, 26 November): *Multidirection*
Sonny Criss (LA, 20 January): *I'll catch the sun*
Miles Davis (NYC, 18 February). *In a Silent Way* (NYC, 19,20,21 August): *Bitches Brew*
Richard Davis (Villingen, December): *Muses for Richard Davis*
Paul Desmond (NYC, 24,25 June, 13,14 August): *Crystal Illusions* (NYC): *Bridge over troubled waters*
Klaus Doldinger (Munich, 18,19 June): *The Ambassador*
Lou Donaldson (NYC, 25 April): *Hot Dog*
Charles Earland (NYC, 15 December): *Black Talk*
Duke Ellington (Bristol & Manchester, 25,26 November): *70th Birthday Concert*
Herb Ellis (NYC, 5,6 November): *Hello Herbie*
Bill Evans (NYC, 30 January, 3,4,5 February, 11 March): *What's New?* (Pescara, 18,20 July): *Pescara Live* (Amsterdam, 28 November): *Quiet Now*
Tal Farlow (NYC, 23 September): *Tal Farlow Returns*
Clare Fischer (LA): *Duality*
Bud Freeman (10,12 December): *The Compleat Bud Freeman*
Jan Garbarek (Oslo): *Esoteric Circle*
Stan Getz (London): *Marrakesh Express*
Benny Goodman (London, 28 October, 27 November): *London Date*
Dexter Gordon (Amsterdam, 5 February): *Live at the Amsterdam Paradiso* (Copenhagen, 10 March): *A day in Copenhagen* (NYC, 2,4 April): *Tower of Power*
Stephane Grappelli/Barney Kessel (Paris, 23,24 June): *I remember Django*
Grant Green (NYC, 3 October): *Carryin' on*
Charlie Haden (NYC): *Liberation Suite*
Jim Hall (Berlin, 27,28 June): *It's nice to be with you*
Slide Hampton (Paris, 6 January): *The Fabulous Slide Hampton Quartet*
Herbie Hancock (NYC, 18,21,23 April): *The Prisoner* (NYC): *Fat Albert Rotunda*
Barry Harris (NYC, 25 November): *Magnificent!*
Hampton Hawes (Paris, January): *Key for two*
Al Heath: *Kawaida*
Bobby Henderson (NYC, March): *A Home in the Clouds*
Joe Henderson (NYC, 23,29 May): *Power to the People*
Andrew Hill (NYC, 16 May): *Lift every voice*
Freddie Hubbard (Villingen, 9 December): *The Hub of Hubbard*
Bobby Hutcherson (NYC): *Now* (NYC, 11 August): *Medina*
Milt Jackson (LA, 1,2 August): *That's the way it is / Just the way it had to be* (LA, 9,10 October): *Memphis Jackson*
Ahmad Jamal (NYC Village Gate): *Jamal at the Top*
Elvin Jones (NYC, 14 March): *The Prime Element* (NYC, 26 September): *Poly-currents* (NYC, 26 September): *Mr Jones*
Philly Joe Jones (Italy, 18 July): *Round Midnight*
Clifford Jordan (NYC, Spring): *In the World*
Barney Kessel (LA, 12 March): *Feeling Free* (Rome, 7 May): *Reflections in Rome* (Rome, 7,8,9 May): *Kessel's Kit* (Paris, 16,18,23 June): *What's New...* *Barney Kessel* (Paris, 24 June): *Limehouse Blues*
Eric Kloss (NYC, 2 January): *In the land of the giants* (NYC, 22 July): *To hear is to see*
Lee Konitz (NYC, 20,21 March): *Peacemeal*
Joachim Kuhn (Germany, 25 January): *Sounds of Feelings* (Villingen, 2,3 June): *Bold Music*
Steve Kuhn (Paris, 13 October): *Childhood is Forever*

Charles Kynard (NYC, 10 March): *The Soul Brotherhood* (NYC, 11 August): *Reelin' with the Feelin'*
Steve Lacy (Rome, September): *Moon* (Paris, 23 September): *Epistrophy*
Ramsey Lewis (Chicago, 12-14 May): *Another Voyage*
Harold Mabern (NYC, 30 June): *Workin' and Wailin'*
Les McCann/Eddie Harris (Montreux, 22 June): *Swiss movement*
John McLaughlin (London, 18 January): *Extrapolation*
Harold McNair (London): *Flute and Nut*
Charles McPherson (NYC, 23 December): *McPherson's Mood*
Jay McShann: *Confessin' the Blues*
Herbie Mann (NYC): *Memphis Underground* (NYC): *Concerto Grosso in D Blues*
Shelly Manne (LA, 11,12 December): *Outside*
Warne Marsh (LA, 14 September, 25 October): *Nec Plus Ultra*
Blue Mitchell (LA, 22,23 May): *Bantu Village*
Red Mitchell (Paris, February): *One Long String*
Mitchell/Ruff Duo (NYC, Summer): *Strayhorn*
Hank Mobley (Paris, 12 July): *The Flip*
MJQ (NYC): *Space*
Grachan Moncur III (Paris, 11 August): *New Africa*
James Moody (NYC, 14 February): *Don't look away now*
Oliver Nelson (LA): *Black, Brown and Beautiful*
Phineas Newborn (LA, 12,13 February): *Please send me someone to love / Harlem Blues*
Don Patterson (NYC, 2 June): *Oh happy day!*
Big John Patton (NYC, 15 August): *Accent on the Blues*
Duke Pearson (NYC, 20 February, 20 August): *Merry Ole Soul* (NYC, 11,14 April, 5 May): *How Insensitive*
Oscar Peterson (NYC, late March): *Motions & Emotions* (Villingen, 5,6 November): *Hello Herbie*
Pony Poindexter (Munich, September): *The Happy Life of Pony*
Sammy Price (London, 4 December): *Blues on my mind*
Dewey Redman (Paris, 1 October): *Tarik*
Buddy Rich (LA, 3 January): *Buddy and Soul*
Joe Sample (Stockholm, 20 April): *Try us*
Pharoah Sanders (NYC, 20 October): *Jewels of Thought*
Archie Shepp (Paris, 14 August): *Poem for Malcolm* (Paris, November): *Black Gipsy*
Wayne Shorter (NYC, 29 August, 2 September): *Super Nova*
Horace Silver (NYC, 10,17 January): *You gotta take a little love*
Sonny Simmons California, 10 February): *Manhattan Egos*
Jimmy Smith (Atlanta): *The Boss* (NYC): *Groove Drops*
Johnny 'Hammond' Smith (NYC, 19 May): *Soul Talk* (NYC, 22 December): *Black Feeling*
Lonnie Smith (NYC, 3 January): *Turning Point* (Atlantic City, 9 August): *Move Your Hand*
Sonny Stitt (NYC, 27 October): *Night Letter*
Maxine Sullivan/Bob Wilber (NYC, 11,13 June): *Close as the pages in a book*
Billy Taylor (NYC, April): *Billy Taylor Today*
Clark Terry (Montreux, 22 June): *At the Montreux Jazz Festival*
Leon Thomas (21,22 October): *Spirits Known and Unknown*
The Three Sounds (LA, September): *Soul Symphony*
Charles Tolliver (London, 2 June): *The Ringer*
Stan Tracey (London): *Free an' One*
Stanley Turrentine (NYC, 3 March): *Another Story* (NYC, 23 June): *Ain't no way*
McCoy Tyner (NYC, 4 April): *Cosmos*
Miroslav Vitous (NYC, 8 October): *Infinite Search*
Mal Waldron (Paris, 12 June): *Ursula* (Paris, October): *Set me free* (Ludwigsburg, 24 November): *Free at Last*
Cedar Walton (NYC, 14 January): *The electric boogaloo song* (NYC, 25 July): *Soul Cycle*
Sadao Watanabe (Tokyo, 15 March): *Dedicated to Charlie Parker* (Tokyo, 24 June): *Pastoral*
Ben Webster (Amsterdam, 24 January): *Live in Amsterdam* (26 May, 29 October): *For the Guvnor* (Copenhagen, 29 October): *Blow, Ben, blow*
Randy Weston (Paris, June): *Randy Weston's African Rhythms* (Paris, June): *Niles Little Bag*
Tony Williams (26,28 May): *Emergency*
Phil Woods (Montreux, June): *At the Montreux Jazz Festival* (NYC, 9,10 July): *Round Trip*
Frank Wright (Paris, 5 December): *One for John*
Larry Young (NYC, 7 February): *Mother Ship*

Left: Don Ellis in London.
Below: The JPJ Quartet with (l to r) Bill Pemberton (bass), Dill Jones (piano), Oliver Jackson (drums) and Budd Johnson (tenor sax).

Photograph Courtesy: *Hank O'Neal*

Dave Holland (24) and Chick Corea (29) leave Miles Davis (44) at the end of the band's European tour. They form a trio with Barry Altschul called Circle. Later Anthony Braxton (25) joins to make it a quartet.

London Jazz Composers Orchestra forms.

Max Roach (45) forms M'Boom, a percussion ensemble.

Duke Ellington Orchestra tours Europe, Australasia and the Far East.

BIRTHS
Dwayne Burno (bass) 10 June

DEATHS
Lem Davis (55) 16 January
Lucille Hegamin (75) 1 March
Emile Barnes (78) 2 March
Ralph Escudero (71) 10 April
Perry Bradford (77) 22 April
Otis Spann (40) 25 April
Johnny Hodges (64) 11 May
Cliff Jackson (67) 23 May *heart failure*
Lonnie Johnson (81) 16 June
Booker Ervin (39) 31 July *kidney disease*
Scoops Carry (55) 4 August
Otto Hardwicke (66) 5 August
Gene Gifford (62) 12 November
Don Stovall (56) 20 November
Albert Ayler (34) 25 November *drowned*
Elmer Schoebel (74) 14 December
Charles Edward Smith (66) 16 December
Willie 'The Lion' Smith (73)

BOOKS
Ernest Bellocq: *Storyville Portraits*
John Chilton: *Who's Who of Jazz*
Stanley Dance: *The World of Duke Ellington*
Robert Dixon & John Godrich: *Recording the Blues*
John Fahey: *Charley Patton*
Gene Fernett: *Swing Out: Great Negro Dance Bands*
Karl GertzurHeide: *Deep South Piano*
Michael Harper: *Dear John, Dear Coltrane* (poems)
Donald Kennington: *The Literature of Jazz*
Derek Langridge: *Your Jazz Collection*
Philip Larkin: *All What Jazz: A Record Diary 1961-68*
Carmen Moor: *Somebody's Angel Child: the story of Bessie Smith*
Paul Oliver: *Savannah Syncopators: African Retentions in the Blues*
Pauline Rivelli & Robert Levin (eds): *The Black Giants*
Tony Russell: *Blacks, Whites and Blues*
Derrick Stewart-Baxter: *Ma Rainey and the Classic Blues Singers*
Martin Williams: *The Jazz Tradition*
Martin Williams: *Jazz Masters in Transition 1957-69*
Valerie Wilmer: *Jazz People*

FILMS
Anatomy of a Performance: Louis Armstrong documentary
L'Aventure du Jazz: Buck Clayton, Willie 'The Lion' Smith
Blues like showers of rain (30mins): documentary
Dave Brubeck (32mins): music short
The Legacy of a Drum: documentary featuring Dizzy Gillespie
Music Power: documentary on Amougies Festival 1969 featuring Joachim Kuhn, Anthony Braxton, John Surman
The Super Show (93mins): film record of group appearances in London featuring MJQ, Roland Kirk Quartet, Buddy Guy
Zachariah (93mins): feature film with Elvin Jones in an acting role

RECORDS
Muhal Richard Abrams (Chicago): *Things to come from those gone now*
Cannonball Adderley (LA): *The price you got to pay to be free*
Nat Adderley (LA): *Love, Sex and the Zodiac*
Gene Ammons (Chicago, 11 November): *The Black Cat*
Louis Armstrong (NYC, 26,27,29 May): *And His Friends*
Art Ensemble of Chicago (Paris, February): *Certain Blacks* (Paris, March): *Go Home* (Paris, May/June): *Chi Congo* (Festival of Chateauvallon, 13 August): *Live, Pts 1&2*

Albert Ayler (St Paul de Vence, France, 25-27 July): *Nuits de la Fondation Maeght, Vols 1&2*
Gary Bartz (NYC, 19,23 November): *Harlem Bush Music: Taifa*
Count Basie (NYC, 22,23 December): *Afrique*
Harry Beckett (London): *Flare-up*
Paul Bley (NYC, 9 December): *The Paul Bley Synthesizer Show*
Anthony Braxton (Paris, January): *This Time*
Roy Brooks (NYC, 26 April): *The Free Slave*
Marion Brown (NYC, 10 August): *Afternoon of a Georgia Faun*
Donald Byrd (NYC, 15 May): *Electric Byrd*
Ian Carr (London, 14,15 December): *Solar Plexus*
Ornette Coleman (NYC, 14 February): *Friends and Neighbours*
Graham Collier (London, 8 December): *Mosaics*
Chick Corea (NC, 7 April): *The Song of Singing* (NYC, 21 August): *Circulus* (NYC, 13 October): *Circling In*
Ted Curson (Helsinki, 3 September): *Ode to Booker Ervin*
Eddie 'Lockjaw' Davis/Johnny Griffin (Cologne, 24 April): *Tough Tenors Again*
Miles Davis (NYC, 16,17,27 February): *Live-Evil* (NYC, 17,18,19,20 June): *Miles Davis at Fillmore* (NYC, 7 April, 11 November): *A Tribute to Jack Johnson* (SF, 10 April): *Black Beauty*
Jack De Johnette (Tokyo, 4 July): *Have You Heard?*
Neville Dickie (London, 16 July/4 August): *A Salute to Fats Waller*
Klaus Doldinger: *Passport*
Lou Donaldson (NYC, 9 January): *Everything I play is funky* (NYC, 9 January, 12 June): *Pretty Things*
Charles Earland (NYC, 1 June): *Black Drops* (Newark, 17 September): *Living Black!*
Duke Ellington (NYC, 27 April): *New Orleans Suite* (Bristol/Manchester, 25,26 November): *70th Birthday Concert*
Bill Evans (Montreux, 19 June): *Montreux 2*
Don Ewell (NYC, September): *A Jazz Portrait of the Artist*
Art Farmer (Villingen, 7 September): *From Vienna with Art*
Joe Farrell (1,2 July): *Joe Farrell Quartet*
Clare Fischer (LA, 2 January): *Great White Hope!*
Jan Garbarek (Oslo, 22,23 September): *Afric Pepperbird*
Michael Garrick (London, 20,22 January): *The Heart is a Lotus*
Michael Gibbs (London, 10,12 November/2,23 December): *Tanglewood '63*
Dizzy Gillespie (NYC): *Souled Out*
Paul Gonsalves (Paris, 6 July): *And his All Stars*
Paul Gonsalves/Ray Nance (NYC, 28 August/3 September): *Just a-sittin' and a-rockin'*
Benny Goodman (Stockholm): *Benny Goodman Today*
Dexter Gordon (NYC, 7 July): *The Panther* (Chicago, 26 July): *The Chase* (NYC, 27 August): *The Jumpin' Blues*

Photograph Courtesy: *Rolf Dahlgren*

1970

Stephane Grappelli (London, 29 June): *Stephane Grappelli and friends*
Grant Green (NYC, 20 January): *Green is beautiful* (NYC, 15 August): *Grant Green Alive!*
Bobby Hackett (NYC, April/May): *Live at the Roosevelt Grill*
Herbie Hancock: *Mwandishi*
Joe Henderson (Hermosa Beach, 24,25,26 September): *If you're not part of the solution, you're part of the problem*
Earl Hines/Maxine Sullivan (NYC, November): *Live at the Overseas Press Club*
Johnny Hodges (NYC, 17,19 March): *Three Shades of Blue*
Freddie Hubbard (NYC, 27,28,29 January): *Red Clay* (NYC, 16 November): *Straight Life*
Ahmad Jamal (NYC, 2,3 February): *The Awakening*
Elvin Jones (NYC, 17 July): *Coalition*
Quincy Jones (NYC, 25,26 March/12 May): *Gula Matari*
Thad Jones/Mel Lewis (LA, 20,21,28 January/25 May): *Consummation*
Roland Kirk (NYC, 11,12 May): *Rashaan/Rahsaan*
John Klemmer (LA, 25 August): *Eruptions*
Eric Kloss (NYC, 6 January): *Consciousness*
Lee Konitz (NYC, August): *Charlie Parker Memorial Concert*
Karin Krog/Dexter Gordon (Stockholm, 10 May): *Some Other Spring*
Charles Kynard (NYC, 6 April): *Afro-disiac* (NYC, 14 December): *Wa-tu-wa-zui*
Steve Lacy (Paris, August): *Stations*
Brian Lemon (London, 30 June): *Our Kind of Music*
Ramsey Lewis (Minneapolis, May): *Them Changes*
David Liebman (NYC, February): *Night Scrapes*

Harold Mabern (NYC, 26 January): *Greasy Kid Stuff*
Chris McGregor (London): *Brotherhood of Breath*
John McLaughlin (NYC): *Devotion* (NYC): *My Goals Beyond*
Junior Mance (NYC, 16,18,19 March): *With a lotta help from my friends*
Herbie Mann (NYC): *Stone Flute*
Shelly Manne (Ronnie Scott's, London, 30,31 July): *Alive in London*
Pat Martino (NYC, 9 March): *Desperado*
Gil Melle: *Waterbirds*
Charlie Mingus (Paris, 30,31 October): *Blue Bird* (Berlin, November): *In Berlin*
Hank Mobley (NYC, 31 July): *Thinking of home*
Thelonious Monk (Tokyo, October): *Thelonious Monk in Tokyo*
Lee Morgan (Hermosa Beach, 10,11,12 July): *Live at the Lighthouse / All That Jazz*
Oliver Nelson (Berlin, 5 November): *Berlin dialogue for Orchestra*
Nucleus (London, 12,13,15,21 January): *Elastic Rock* (London, 21,22 September): *We'll talk about it later*
Jimmy Owens (NYC, 6,13 March): *The Quartet Plus, no escaping it!*
Tony Oxley (London, 7 February): *Four Compositions for Sextet*
Joe Pass (Villingen, June): *Intercontinental*
Duke Pearson (NYC, 13 March, 10 April): *It could only happen with you*
Houston Person (NYC, 22 February): *The Truth!* (NYC, 12 October): *Person to Person*
Oscar Peterson (NYC, January): *Tristeza on Piano* (Villingen, November): *Tracks* (Villingen, 10 November): *Another Day* (Villingen, 12,13 November): *Walkin' the Line*

Dizzy Reece (Paris, 28 October): *From In to Out*
Buddy Rich (Las Vegas): *Keep the Customer Satisfied*
Howard Riley (London, 1 March/17 April): *The Day Will Come*
Woody Shaw (NYC,8,9 December): *Blackstone Legacy*
Archie Shepp (Antibes, 20 July): *Live in Antibes*
Wayne Shorter (NYC, 26 August): *Odyssey of Iska* (NYC, 26 August): *Moto Grosso Feio*
Horace Silver (NYC, 8 April, 18 June): *That Healin' Feelin'*
Johnny 'Hammond' Smith (NYC, 21 September): *Here it is*
Lonnie Smith (NYC, 2 January): *Drives*
Willie 'The Lion' Smith (Washington, 11 June): *Live at Blues Alley / Relaxing*
Melvin Sparks (NYC, 14 September): *Sparks!*
Spontaneous Music Ensemble (London, 18 November): *The Source*
Sun Ra (Berlin, 7 November): *It's after the end of the world*
John Surman (London, March): *The Trio*
Buddy Tate (Villingen, 30 June/1 July): *Unbroken – the Buddy Tate Celebrity Club Orchestra*
John Tchicai (Rotterdam, 3 March): *Fragments*
Eddie Thompson (Villingen,December): *Out of Sight*
Keith Tippett (London): *Dedicated To You, But You Weren't Listening*
Charles Tolliver (NYC, 1 May/11 November): *Music Inc – Live at Slugs*
McCoy Tyner (NYC, 9 February): *Extensions*
Miroslav Vitous (NYC, 25 August): *Purple*
Mal Waldron (Tokyo, 7 February): *Tokyo Reverie* (Tokyo, 7,12 February): *Tokyo Bound* (Tokyo, 13 February): *One for Lady* (Paris, 12 May): *Blood and Guts* (Paris, 19 November): *The Opening*
Sadao Watanabe (Montreux, 18 June): *Live at the Montreux Jazz Festival* (Hamburg, 26 June): *Around the time* (NYC, 15 July): *Round Trip*
Mike Westbrook (London, 13 March/15 April): *Love Songs*
Tony Williams (NYC, 17 January): *Turn it over* (NYC): *Ego*
Teddy Wilson (Stockholm, 14-16 April): *Swedish Jazz My Way*
Jimmy Witherspoon (LA, 19,20 February): *Handbags and Gladrags*
Phil Woods (Paris, 5 July): *Chromatic Banana*
World's Greatest Jazzband (NYC, 17,18 April): *The World's Greatest Jazzband*
Joe Zawinul (NYC, 6,10,12 August): *Concerto retitled*

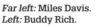

Far left: Miles Davis.
Left: Buddy Rich.

Photograph Courtesy: *Hank O'Neal*

127

1971

Joe Zawinul (38) and Wayne Shorter (37) form Weather Report with Alphonse Mouzon and Miroslav Vitous.

Duke Ellington Orchestra premiere 'The Goutelas Suite' at Lincoln Centre, and 'Togo Brava' at the Newport Jazz Festival. The band tours Russia, Europe, South America and Mexico. Cat Anderson (55) leaves the band. New members include Harold Minerve, Money Johnson, Joe Benjamin and Rufus Jones.

Richie Cole (23) forms Alto Madness.

The first quadraphonic discs are released.

BIRTHS
Joey DeFrancesco (organ) 10 April
Geoff Keezer (piano) 20 November

DEATHS
Ernie Caceres (59) 10 January
Captain John Handy (70) 12 January
Harry Roy (71) 1 February
Derek Humble (40) 22 February after-effects of street violence
Harold McNair (39) 7 March
Morey Feld (55) 28 March died in a fire
Manzie Johnson (64) 9 April
Wynton Kelly (39) 12 April
Lenny Hayton (63) 24 April
Sonny White (53) 29 April
Ben Pollack (67) 7 June suicide by hanging
Bobby Donaldson (48) 2 July
Louis Armstrong (71) 6 July
Charlie Shavers (53) 8 July throat cancer
Lil Hardin (69) 27 July heart attack
King Curtis (36) 14 August stabbed outside home
Tab Smith (62) 17 August
Lou McGarity (54) 24 August
Ben Thigpen (62) 5 October
Joe Sullivan (64) 13 October
Jerome Don Pasquall (69) 18 October
Gary McFarland (38) 3 November
Fred Guy (72) 22 November
Punch Miller (77) 4 December

BOOKS
Walter Allen (ed): Studies in Jazz Discography
Louis Armstrong: Louis Armstrong: a self-portrait
Whitney Balliett: Ecstasy at the Onion
Rudi Blesh: Combo USA: Eight Lives in Jazz
Maria Cole & Louie Robinson: Nat King Cole: an intimate biography
Dicky Wells & Stanley Dance: The Night People
George Foster & Tom Stoddard: The Autobiography of Pops Foster, New Orleans Jazzman
Paul Garon: The Devil's Son-in-law: The story of Peetie Wheatstraw
Richard Garvin & Edmond Addeo: The Midnight Special (novel)
Leonard Huber: New Orleans, a pictorial history
Ted Joans: A Black Manifesto in Jazz Poetry & Prose
Max Jones & John Chilton: Louis: The Louis Armstrong Story
W.B. McGhee: Guitar Styles of Brownie McGhee
Albert McCarthy: The Dance Band Era: the dancing decades from ragtime to swing
Raymond Martinez: Portraits of New Orleans Jazz
Charles Mingus: Beneath the Underdog
Hugues Panassie: Louis Armstrong
A. Robertson: Artie Shaw '36 -'55
James Rooney: Bossmen:Bill Moore & Muddy Waters
Ross Russell:Jazz Style in Kansas City & the Southwest
Jack Schiffman: Uptown: The Story of Harlem's Apollo Theatre
Arnold Shaw: The Street that never slept: New York's fabled 52nd Street
Ben Sidran: Black Talk
George Simon: Simon Says: the sights and sounds of the Swing Era 1935-55
Mel Torme: The Other Side of the Rainbow

FILMS
Louis Armstrong (9mins): bio of Satchmo
Marion Brown (23mins): study of the reed player
Dexter Gordon (26mins): music short
Archie Shepp chez les Tourages (17mins)
'Til the butcher cuts him down (53mins): documentary about Punch Miller with appearances by Dizzy Gillespie and Kid Ory
Mal Waldron (17mins): documentary

RECORDS
Toshiko Akiyoshi (Tokyo, 27 March): Solo piano
Joe Albany (LA, 31 August, 5 September): At Home
Monty Alexander (NYC, 6 June): Here comes the sun (Rochester, NY, 1 December): We've only just begun
Mose Allison (NYC, 2,3,11 February, 3,4 March): Western Man
Gene Ammons/Sonny Stitt (NYC, 8 February): You talk that talk
Art Ensemble of Chicago (Paris, February):Phase One
Gato Barbieri (NYC, 27,28 April): Fenix (NYC): Under Fire (Montreux, 18 June): El Pampero
Gary Bartz (NYC, November 1970/January 1971): Harlem Bush Music: Uhuru
Count Basie (LA, July, August): Have a nice day
Walter Bishop Jr (LA): Coral Keys
Paul Bley (Rotterdam, 26 March / Paris, 16 November): Improvise
Bobby Bradford (London, 9 July): And The Spontaneous Music Ensemble
Anthony Braxton (London, 4,5 February): The Complete Braxton
Dave Brubeck/Gerry Mulligan (Newport, 3 July): The last set at Newport
Kenny Burrell (NYC, 4 May): God bless the child
Gary Burton (Tokyo, 12 June): Live in Tokyo (Montreux, 19 June): Alone at Last
Gary Burton/Keith Jarrett (NYC): Gary Burton & Keith Jarrett
Jaki Byard (Paris, 26 July): Live at the Jazz Inn (Paris, 29 July): Parisian Solos
Donald Byrd (NYC, 25,26 August): Ethiopian Night
Don Cherry (Paris, 22 April): Don Cherry (Stockholm, 4 July): The Creator Has A Master Plan (Donaueschingen, 17 October): Don Cherry and the New Eternal Rhythm Orchestra
Circle (Paris, 21 February): Paris Concert
Tony Coe (London, January): Tony Coe with the Brian Lemon Trio
Ornette Coleman (NYC, 9,10,13 September): Science Fiction (Paris): Paris Concert
Johnny Coles: Katumbo
Chick Corea (Oslo, 21,22 April): Piano Improvisations, Vols 1&2
Chick Corea/Anthony Braxton (Paris, February): Paris Concert
Larry Coryell (NYC, 20,21 January): At The Village Gate (NYC): Barefoot Boy (Montreux, June): Fairyland
Ted Curson (Paris, 18 June): Pop Wine
Richard Davis (NYC, January): The Philosophy of the Spiritual
Paul Desmond/MJQ (NYC, 25 December): Concert at Town Hall
Lou Donaldson (NYC, 16 July): Cosmos
Charles Earland (NYC, 3 May): Soul Story
Duke Ellington (Bristol, 22 October / Birmingham, 24 October): The English Concert
Bill Evans (NYC, 11,12,17,19,20 May): The Bill Evans Album

Photo Courtesy: Hank O'Neal

1971

Art Farmer (NYC, Summer): *Homecoming*
Joe Farrell (NYC, November): *Outback*
Jan Garbarek (Oslo, 14,15 April): *Sart*
Red Garland (NYC, May): *Auf Weidersehn* (NYC, 3 May): *The Quota*
Stan Getz (London, 11 January, 15,16,17 March): *Dynasty* (Paris, November): *Communications*
Dizzy Gillespie/Bobby Hackett (NYC, 31 January): *Giants*
Dizzy Gillespie (New Hampshire): *Dizzy Gillespie and the Mitchell-Ruff Duo*
Dexter Gordon (Stockholm, 21 April): *The Shadow of your Smile*
Stephane Grappelli (Villingen, March): *Afternoon in Paris*
Grant Green (NYC): *Visions* (LA, 23,24 November / NYC, 16,17 December): *Shades of Green*
Jim Hall (NYC, July): *Where would I be?*
Herbie Hancock (NYC, December): *Crossings*
Roland Hanna (Villingen, 11,12 February): *Child of Gemini*
Hampton Hawes (London, August): *Anglo-American Jazz Phase* (Copenhagen, 2 September): *This guy's in love with me / A little Copenhagen night music*
Joe Henderson (Tokyo, 4 August): *In Japan*
Earl Hines (): *My Tribute to Louis / Hines comes in Handy / Hines does Hoagy / Hines Plays Ellington*
Dave Holland/Barre Phillips (Germany, 15 February): *Music from Two Basses*
Willis Jackson (NYC, August): *Gatorade*
Ahmad Jamal (Montreux,17 June):*Free Flight Vol 1*
Keith Jarrett (Oslo): *Facing You*
Elvin Jones (NYC): *Genesis* (NYC, 15 December): *Merry-go-round*
JPJ Quartet (Montreux, July): *Montreux 71*

Roland Kirk (NYC, 26,28 January): *Natural Black Inventions* (NYC,31 August/8 September): *Blacknuss*
John Klemmer (Chicago,12,19 May):*Constant Throb*
Lee Konitz (NYC, February/March): *Spirits*
Joachim Kuhn (Villingen, December): *Interchange* (Villingen, December): *Piano* (Paris, 15,19 March): *Solos*
Steve Lacy (Paris, 4 January): *Wordless* (Paris, 9,10 September): *Lapis* (Paris, 30 November): *Journey Without End*
Johnny Lytle (NYC, 15 July): *The Soulful Rebel*
Jimmy McGriff (NYC): *Moonglow*
John McLaughlin Mahavishnu Orchestra (NYC, 14 August): *The Inner Mountain Flame*
Charlie Mingus (NYC, 23 September, 1,18 October): *Let my children hear music*
Blue Mitchell (NYC, 26,27 June): *Vital Blue*
MJQ (NYC): *Plastic Dreams*
Thelonious Monk (London, 15 November): *Blue Sphere / The Man I Love*
Tete Montoliu (Munich, 25 September): *Lush Life*
James Moody (NYC): *Heritage Hum* (NYC, 12 August): *Too heavy for words*
Lee Morgan (NYC, 17,18 September): *Capra Black*
Gerry Mulligan (LA, February-July): *The Age of Steam*
Oliver Nelson (Montreux, 18 June): *Swiss Suite*
Houston Person (NYC, 8,9 April): *Houston Express*
Oscar Peterson/Milt Jackson (Villingen, July): *Reunion Blues*
Oscar Peterson (Villingen, October): *Great Connection*
Jean-Luc Ponty (Villingen, December): *Open Strings*
Freddie Redd (Paris, 26-29 July): *Under Paris Skies*
Buddy Rich (NYC): *A Different Drummer*
Howard Riley (London, 20 March): *Flight*

George Russell (Oslo, 26 May): *Listen to the Silence*
Pharaoh Sanders (NYC, 8 December): *Black Unity* (NYC): *Live at the East*
Phil Seamen (London, 17 December): *Phil on drums*
Archie Shepp (NYC, 17 May): *Things have got to change*
Singers Unlimited (Villingen, July): *In Tune*
Johnny 'Hammond' Smith (NYC, 12 April): *What's goin' on?*
Martial Solal (Paris, 20 November): *Martial Solal en solo*
Melvin Sparks (NYC, 1,8 March): *Sparkplug* (NYC): *Akilah*
Spontaneous Music Ensemble (London,7 May): *Live*
Sonny Stitt (NYC, 4 January): *Turn it on!* (NYC): *Black Vibrations*
Sun Ra (Cairo, 12,16 December): *Nature's God* (Cairo, 17 December): *Horizon*
Stanley Turrentine (NYC, February/March): *The Sugar Man* (NYC, July/September): *Salt Song*
Mal Waldron (Stuttgart, 1 February): *The Call* (Tokyo, 3 March): *Mal: Live 4 to 1* (Tokyo, 8 March): *First Encounter* (Paris, 11 March): *Skippin'* (Holland, 30 May): *Number Nineteen* (Munich, 29 June): *Plays The Blues* (Holland, 14 August): *Signals* (Paris, 30 November): *Journey Without End*
Sadao Watanabe (Tokyo, June): *Paysages*
Weather Report (NYC,16,17 February): *Orange Lady*
Dick Wellstood (NYC, December): *From Ragtime on*
Mike Westbrook (London, 3-5 August): *Metropolis*
Mary Lou Williams (NYC, May/June): *From the Heart*

Left: The World's Greatest Jazz Band. Bob Wilber, Ralph Sutton, Billy Butterfield, Ed Hubble, Bud Freeman, Gus Johnson, Vic Dickenson and co-leaders Yank Lawson and Bob Haggart.
Below: Eddie Condon (65) at Alice Tully Hall in New York at the end of his last tour.

Photo: *Rollo Phlecks* Courtesy: *Hank O'Neal*

The complete works of Scott Joplin are published.

Charles Mingus New York Concert at Philharmonic Hall (4 February).

Duke Ellington Orchestra make their longest tour of the Far East.

John McLaughlin's Mahavishnu are the most sensational new band.

Shelly's Manne-Hole closes on 4 September.

Miles Davis (46) breaks both legs in a car crash (October).

Debut of Supersax group at Donte's club in LA (November).

BIRTHS
Christian McBride (bass) 31 May

DEATHS
Mahalia Jackson (60) 27 January
Lee Morgan (33) 19 February *shot by mistress*
Clancy Hayes (63) 13 March
Sharkey Bonano (67) 27 March
Tony Parenti (71) 17 April
Marty Flax (48) 3 May
Reverend Gary Davis (76) 5 May
George Mitchell (73) 27 May
Jimmy Rushing (68) 8 June *leukemia*
Bob McCracken (67) 4 July
Lovie Austin (84) 10 July
Mezz Mezzrow (72) 5 August
André Ekyan (64) 9 August
Don Byas (59) 24 August *lung cancer*
Phil Seamen (46) 13 October
Hall Overton (52) 25 November
Jimmy Lytell (68) 26 November
Bill Johnson (98) 3 December
Kenny Dorham (48) 5 December *kidney failure*
Eli Robinson (61) 24 December
Dud Bascomb (56) 25 December
Hayes Alvis (65) 30 December

BOOKS
Chris Albertson: *Bessie*
Ken Barnes: *Sinatra and the Great Song Stylists*
John Chilton: *Who's Who of Jazz: Storyville to Swing Street*
James Cone: *The Spirituals and the Blues*
Jean Gay Cornell: *Louis Armstrong: Ambassador Satchmo*
Leonard Feather: *From Satchmo to Miles*
John Flower: *Moonlight Serenade: a bio-discography of the Glenn Miller Civilian Band*
Pete Fountain with Bill Neely: *A Closer Walk*
Charles Fox: *The Jazz Scene*
Hampton Hawes with Don Asher: *Raise up off me*
Andre Hodeir: *The Worlds of Jazz*
Edward Lee: *Jazz: an Introduction*
Elizabeth Montgomery: *Duke Ellington: King of Jazz*
Ann Quin: *Tripticks*
Michel Ruppli: *A discography Prestige Jazz Records 1949-1971*
Brian Rust: *The Dance Bands*
Herb Sanford: *Tommy & Jimmy: The Dorsey Years*
Rex Stewart: *Jazz Masters of the 30's*

FILMS
Band of Thieves (69mins): Acker Bilk feature
Jazz is our Religion (50mins): Johnny Griffin Quintet, Clarke-Boland Band, Art Blakey
Lady Sings the Blues (144mins): bio of Billie Holiday starring Diana Ross
The Mexican Suite: Duke Ellington Orchestra filmed in concert

RECORDS
Cannonball Adderley (LA): *Music, you all*
Nat Adderley (LA): *Soul of the Bible*
Mose Allison (Palo Alto): *Mose in your ear*
Art Ensemble of Chicago (Chicago, 15 January): *Live at Mandel Hall* (Ann Arbor, 9 September): *Bap-Tizum*
Gato Barbieri (Rome, 20-25 November): *Last Tango in Paris*
Gary Bartz (Berkeley, October): *Juju Street Songs* (Berkeley, October): *Follow the Medicine Man*
Karl Berger (Munich, 24 June): *With Silence*
Art Blakey (NYC, 23 May, 28 July): *Child's Dance*
Paul Bley (Oslo, 11 September): *Open, to Love* (NYC, 22 October/24 November): *Scorpio*

Ruby Braff (NYC, 27 September, 9 October): *The Music of Ruby Braff & his International Jazz Quartet*
Ruby Braff/Ellis Larkins (NYC, 4 November): *The Grand Reunion*
Dollar Brand (Copenhagen, June): *Ancient Africa*
Anthony Braxton (Paris, 18 February): *Dona Lee* (Paris, 25 February): *Saxophone Improvisations, Series F* (NYC, 22 May): *Town Hall 1972*
Ray Bryant (Montreux, July): *Alone at Montreux*
Jaki Byard (Tokyo, 31 July): *The Entertainer* (NYC, 27 December): *There'll be some changes made*
Don Cherry (Sweden, 3 August): *Organic Music*
Eddie Condon et al (NYC, 2 April): *Jazz at the New School*
Chick Corea (NYC, 2,3 February): *Return to Forever* (London, Autumn): *Light as a Feather*
Chick Corea/Gary Burton: *Crystal Silence*
Larry Coryell (NYC, 17,18,20 January): *Offering* (NYC): *Introducing the Eleventh House*

Stanley Cowell (NYC, 29 November): *Illusion Suite*
Miles Davis (NYC, 1,6 June): *On the Corner*
Richard Davis (NYC): *With Understanding*
Lou Donaldson (NYC, 8,11,18 December): *Sophisticated Lou*
Dutch Swing College Band (Munich, 15 November): *With Teddy Wilson*
Charles Earland (NJ, 16,17 February): *Charles III / Intensity* (Hermosa Beach): *Live at the Lighthouse*
Art Farmer (Vienna): *Gentle Eyes*
Joe Farrell (NYC, 21 November): *Moongerms*
Clare Fischer (LA, December): *Soon*
Jan Garbarek (Oslo, 8 November): *Triptykon*
Stan Getz (NYC, 3 March): *Captain Marvel* (Montreux, 23 July): *At Montreux* (Montreux, 23 July): *Portrait*
Jimmy Giuffre (NYC, December): *Music for people, birds, butterflies & mosquitoes*
Dexter Gordon (NYC, 22 June, 28 July): *Tangerine* (NYC): *Ca' Putange* (NYC, 22 July): *Generation* (Amsterdam, 2 November): *All Souls*
Grant Green (Hermosa Beach, 21 April): *Live at the Lighthouse*
Jim Hall/Ron Carter (NYC, 4 August): *Alone Together*
Gene Harris (LA, 29,30 June): *Gene Harris of the Three Sounds*
Jimmy Heath (NYC, 1 March): *The Gap Sealer*
Joe Henderson (March/April): *Black is the Colour*
Earl Hines (NYC, October): *An Evening with Earl Hines and his Quartet*
Dave Holland (NYC, 30 November): *Conference of the Birds*

Photo courtesy: *Gladys Dobell*

1972

Claude Hopkins (NYC, April/August): *Crazy Fingers*
Ahmad Jamal (Montreux, 17 June): *Outer Time, Inner Space*
Keith Jarrett (NYC): *Expectations* (NYC, March): *Ruta & Daytya* (Hamburg): *NDR Jazz Workshop*
Dill Jones (NYC, April'): *The Music of Bix Beiderbecke*
Elvin Jones (LA, 9 September):*Live at the Lighthouse*
Jonah Jones/Earl Hines (NYC, 22 March): *Back on the Street*
Roland Kirk (NYC): *A Meeting of the Times*
John Klemmer (LA, 17,22 June): *Waterfalls* (LA, 22 June): *Magic and Movement*
Eric Kloss (NYC, 28 August): *One, Two, Free*
Hans Koller (25,26 September): *Phoenix*
Steve Kuhn (NYC, November): *Raindrops, Raindrops*

Steve Lacy (Lisbon, 29 February): *Live in Lisboa* (Paris, May): *The Gap* (Avignon, 7,8 August): *In Concert at Theatre du Chene Noir*
Ramsey Lewis: *Funky Serenity*
Dave Liebman (NYC, 1May/10 June): *Open Sky*
Johnny Lytle (NYC, August): *People & Love*
Humphrey Lyttelton (Hamburg, 12 March): *Doggin' Around*
Les McCann (Montreux, 24 June): *Live at Montreux*
Jimmy McGriff (NYC): *Fly Dude*
John McLaughlin Mahavishnu Orchestra (NYC): *Birds of Fire* (NYC): *Love Devotion Surrender*
Jackie McLean (Copenhagen, 5 August): *Live at Montmartre*
Jay McShann (Toronto, 4 June): *The Man from Muskogee*

Shelly Manne (LA): *Mannekind*
Warne Marsh (LA, 9 May): *Relaxed Improvisation*
Pat Martino (NYC, 24 March): *Footprints* (NYC, 7 September): *Live!*
Charlie Mingus (NYC, 4 February): *Charlie Mingus and Friends* (France, 22 August): *Live in Chateauvallon 1972* (Berlin, 5 November): *Mingus meets Cat Anderson*
Blue Mitchell (NYC): *Blue's blue*
MJQ (NYC): *The Legendary Profile*
James Moody (NYC, 8 June): *Never Again* (NYC): *Feelin' it together*
Paul Motian (NYC, 25,26 November): *Conception Vessel*
Harold Ousley (NYC, 28 March): *Sweet Double Hipness*
Houston Person (NYC, 11 September, 7 November): *Sweet Buns & Barbecue*
Oscar Peterson (Villingen): *Walkin' the line* (LA, 27 December): *History of an Artist*
Bucky Pizzarelli (NYC, 3,12,19 May/30 June): *Green Guitar Blues*
Jean-Luc Ponty (Montreux, July): *Sonata Erotica*
Howard Roberts (LA, 19 January): *Equinox, Express Elevator*
Sonny Rollins (NYC, July): *Next Album*
Pharaoh Sanders (NYC): *Wisdom Through Music*
Bola Sete (9,10 March): *Ocean*
Woody Shaw (LA, 15,18 September): *Song of Songs*
Archie Shepp (NYC, 24-26 January): *Attica Blues* (NYC, 25-27 September): *The Cry of my People*
Jimmy Smith (LA, 8 February): *Root Down* (LA): *Bluesmith* (Yankee Stadium, NYC, 7 July): *The Jimmy Smith Jam*
Sonny Stitt (NYC, 15 February): *Goin' down slow* (NYC, 27 June): *Constellation* (Berkeley, 13,14 September):*So doggone good* (NYC,12 December): *12!*
Sun Ra (Chicago, 7 May): *Astro Black* (Ann Arbor, 8-10 September): *Ann Arbor Blues & Jazz Festival 1972* (Chicago, 19 October): *Space is the Place*
Buddy Tate/Wild Bill Davis (Paris, 10 May): *Buddy Tate & Wild Bill Davis*
Charles Tolliver (Munich, 23 March): *Impact*
Stan Tracey/Mike Osborne (April): *Original*
Stanley Turrentine (NYC, May): *Cherry*
McCoy Tyner (NYC, January): *Sahara* (Tokyo, 11 November): *Echoes for a Friend* (NYC, 27 November): *Song for my Lady*
Mal Waldron (Holland, 5 February): *Blues for Lady Day* (Nuremburg, 6 May): *A Touch of the Blues* (Paris, 11 May): *Mal Waldron on Steinway* (Tokyo, 12 July): *Meditations*
Cedar Walton/Hank Mobley (NYC, 22 February): *Breakthrough*
Sadao Watanabe (Tokyo, 24 February): *Sadao Watanabe*
Weather Report (NYC, November 1971/January 1972): *I Sing The Body Electric*
Ben Webster (Barcelona,28 November):*Did you call?*
Mike Westbrook (Tavistock, 15 January / London, 23 February): *Live*
Teddy Wilson (NYC, May): *With Billie in Mind*

Opposite page: Duke Ellington with tenor saxist Harold Ashby.

Left: John McLaughlin.

1973

Eubie Blake (90) releases three new albums.

Benny Goodman (64), Lionel Hampton (60), Gene Krupa (64) and Teddy Wilson (60) feature at the Newport Jazz Festival in New York (30 June).

Mahavishnu Orchestra disbands (31 December).

DEATHS

Joe Harriott (44) 2 January *cancer*
Wilbur de Paris (72) 3 January
Clara Ward (48) 16 January
Edgar Sampson (65) 17 January
Kid Ory (83) 23 January
Andy Razaf (77) 3 February
Nick Stabulas (43) 6 February *auto accident*
AG Godley (73) February
Spanky de Brest (35) 2 March
Lammar Wright Sr (65) 13 April
Willie 'The Lion' Smith (75) 18 April
Elmer Snowden (72) 14 May
J.C. Higginbotham (67) 26 May
Sid Phillips (70) 26 May
Volly de Faut (69) 29 May
Al Wynn (65) May
Tubby Hayes (38) 8 June *undergoing heart surgery*
Eddie Condon (67) 4 August
Brew Moore (49) 19 August
Jack Marshall (51) 2 September
Albert Nicholas (73) 3 September
Bill Harris (57) 19 September
Ben Webster (64) 20 September
Sister Rosetta Tharpe (52) 9 October
Gene Krupa (64) 16 October
Dede Pierce (69) 23 November *cancer*
Emile Christian (78) 3 December
Peter Trunk (37) 31 December *auto crash*

BOOKS

Max Abrams: *The Book of Django*
Walter Allen: *Hendersonia: The Music of Fletcher Henderson & his Musicians*
Jack Buerkle & Danny Barker: *Bourbon Street Black*
Ian Carr: *Music Outside: Contemporary Jazz in Britain*
Samuel Charters: *Robert Johnson*
Graham Collier: *Inside Jazz*
Eddie Condon & Hank O'Neal: *The Eddie Condon Scrapbook of Jazz*
Bruce Cook: *Listen to the Blues*
Carol Easton: *Kenton Straight Ahead*
Duke Ellington: *Music is my Mistress*
Benny Green: *Drums in my Ears*
Edward Greenfield: *Andre Previn*
Jorgen Jepsen: *A discography of Louis Armstrong*
Robert Kimball & William Bolcom: *Reminiscin' with Sissle & Blake*
Woody Mann: *Six Black Blues Guitarists*
Dan Morgenstern: *The Jazz Story*
John Postgate: *A Plain Man's Guide to Jazz*
Mike Rowe: *Chicago Breakdown*
Ross Russell: *Bird Lives*
Ruby Sanders: *Jazz Ambassador: Louis Armstrong*
William Schafer & Johannes Riedel: *The Art of Ragtime*
Allen Scott: *Jazz Educated Man*
Joe Scotti: *Jazz*
Bennett Wayne: *Three Jazz Greats*

FILMS

Bienvenue a...Duke Ellington (75mins): music documentary
Born to Swing (50mins): Buddy Tate, Joe Newman etc in tribute to the Swing Era
Monterey Jazz (81mins): film of 1970 Monterey Jazz Festival with Duke Ellington, MJQ, Big Joe Turner, Eddie 'Cleanhead' Vinson, Jimmy Rushing, Woody Herman
Sonny Rollins Live at Laren (37mins): film record of Sonny Rollins Quintet at the Laren Jazz Festival, August 1973
That's Jazz (28mins): Freddy Randall-Dave Shepherd All-Stars music short

RECORDS

Pepper Adams (London, 10 September): *Ephemera*
Cannonball Adderley (Berkeley, 4 June): *Inside Straight*
Joe Albany (Copenhagen, 25,30 April): *Birdtown Birds*
Monty Alexander (NYC, 18 June): *Perception!*
Gene Ammons (Montreux, 7 July): *Gene Ammons & Friends at Montreux*
Gene Ammons/Sonny Stitt (NYC, 20,21 November, 10 December): *Together Again for the Last Time*
Art Ensemble of Chicago (Chicago, 6-8 September): *Fanfare for the Warriors*
Chet Baker (NYC, 16,21,22 February, 13 May): *You can't go home again*
Gato Barbieri (Buenos Aires, April): *Gato – Chapter One: Latin America*
Kenny Barron (NYC, 2 April): *Sunset at Dawn*
Gary Bartz (Montreux, 7 July): *I've known rivers and other bodies*
Count Basie (LA, 10 December): *Basie Jam*
Count Basie/Joe Turner (LA, 11 December): *The Bosses*
George Benson (NYC): *The electrifyin' George Benson* (NYC, July): *Body talk*
Walter Bishop Jr (LA): *Keeper of my Soul*
Art Blakey (Berkeley, March): *Buhaina / Anthenagin*
Paul Bley (Copenhagen, 24 June): *Bley–NHOP*
Ruby Braff/George Barnes (NYC, July): *The Ruby Braff/George Barnes Quartet*
Dollar Brand (Toronto, 18 February): *Sangoma* (Berne): *African Sketchbook* (NYC, 7 November): *African Space Program* (Ludwigsburg, 12 December): *Ode to Duke Ellington*
Anthony Braxton (Tokyo, 11 January): *Four Compositions 1973*
Marion Brown (NYC, 4,5 June): *Geechee Recollections*
Dave Brubeck (NYC, August): *Two Generations of Brubeck*
Kenny Burrell (LA): *'Round Midnight* (Berkeley, 15,16,19 February): *Both Feet on the Ground*
Gary Burton (Massachusetts, March): *The new Quartet*
Charlie Byrd (NYC, April): *Crystal Silence*
Donald Byrd (LA, 13,15 June): *Street Lady*
Conte Candoli (Milan, 25 May): *Conversation*
Ron Carter (NYC, 24 October): *All Blues*
Doc Cheatham (NYC, December): *Doc Cheatham prescribes...*
Don Cherry (NYC, 14 February): *Relativity Suite* (Stockholm, 30 April/1 May): *Eternal Now*
Al Cohn/Zoot Sims (NYC, 23 March): *Body and Soul*
Bill Coleman/Guy Lafitte (July): *Mainstream at Montreux*
Buddy Collette (LA): *Now and Then* (San Diego, 17 September): *Blockbuster*
Stanley Cowell (NYC, 10,11 December): *Musa: Ancestral Streams*
Ted Curson (Stockholm, 31 August): *Jazz Meeting One* (Paris, 26 October): *Cattin' Curson*
Eddie Daniels (NYC, February): *A Flower for all Seasons*
Miles Davis (NYC): *Big Fun*
Wild Bill Davison (NYC, 8-25 June): *Live at the Rainbow Room*
Paul Desmond (NYC, November, December): *Skylark*
Klaus Doldinger (October): *Passport / Looking Thru*
Lou Donaldson (NYC, 17,18 April): *Sassy Soul Strut*
Kenny Drew (Copenhagen, 2 April): *Duo* (Copenhagen, 1 October, 14 November, 31 December): *Everything I Love*
Charles Earland (NYC, November): *The Dynamite Brothers* (Berkeley, 11,12,13 December): *Leaving this Planet*
Duke Ellington (NYC, 8 January): *Duke's Big Four* (London, 24 October): *Third Sacred Concert* (NYC, 5 December): *This One's for Blanton*
Herb Ellis/Joe Pass (Concord, 29 July): *Jazz/Concord / Seven Come Eleven*
Bill Evans (Tokyo, 20 January): *Live in Tokyo*
Gil Evans (NYC, Summer): *Svengali*

Don Ewell (NYC, 20-23 August): *Take it in Stride* (NYC, 28,29 September): *With Buddy Tate*
Joe Farrell (NYC, October): *Penny Arcade*
Maynard Ferguson (NYC, 10 July): *Live at Jimmy's*
Clare Fischer (LA, May): *The State of hisArt* (LA, 9 May): *Jazz Song*
Ella Fitzgerald (NYC, 5 July): *Live at Carnegie Hall/Newport Jazz Festival*
Ella Fitzgerald/Joe Pass: *Take love easy*
Jan Garbarek (Oslo, 19,20 November): *Red Lanta* (Oslo, 27,28 November): *Witchi-Tai-To*
Michael Garrick (London, 13,25,26 October): *Troppo*
Dizzy Gillespie (Paris, April): *The Source*
Dexter Gordon (Montreux, 7 July): *Blues a la Suisse*
Stephane Grappelli (Montreux, 4 July): *Just one of those things* (London, 5,7 September): *Meets the Rhythm Section* (London, 5 November): *I got rhythm*
Johnny Griffin (Copenhagen, 4,5 July): *Blues for Harvey*
Herbie Hancock (SF): *Headhunters*
Roland Hanna (April, May): *Sir Elf*
Billy Harper (NYC): *Capra Black*
Gene Harris (Detroit, 14,15 June): *Yesterday, Today & Tomorrow*
Hampton Hawes (Berkeley, 16,17,18 January): *Blues for Walls* (Chicago, June): *Live at the Jazz Showcase in Chicago* (Montreux, 7 July): *Playin' in the Yard*
Roy Haynes (NYC, 21 October): *Togyu*
Al Heath (NYC, 4 June): *Kwanza (The First)*
Jimmy Heath (NYC, 11 June): *Love and Understanding*
Joe Henderson (NYC, 30,31 January): *Multiple* (LA, 15,17 October): *The Elements* (Berkeley, October): *Canyon Lady*
Woody Herman (NYC, 9,11,12 May): *Giant Steps*
Earl Hines (NYC, 27 March): *Live at the New School* (NYC, November): *Quintessential Recording Session*
Terumasa Hino (Munich, 29 June): *Taro's Mood*
Freddie Hubbard (Chicago, 3 March, Detroit, 4 March): *In Concert Vols 1&2* (NYC, October): *Keep Your Soul Together*
Bobby Hutcherson (Montreux, 5 July): *Live at Montreux*
Milt Jackson (NYC, December): *Goodbye*
Willis Jackson (NYC, 22 October): *West Africa*
Illinois Jacquet (Paris, 15,16 January): *With Wild Bill Davis*
Keith Jarrett (NYC, 24 February): *Fort Yawuh* (Lausanne, 20 March / Bremen, 12 July): *Solo Concerts*
Elvin Jones (NYC, 24,25,26 July): *The Prime Element* (NYC): *Live at the Village Vanguard*
Clifford Jordan (NYC, 29 October): *Glass Bead Games*
Duke Jordan/Cecil Payne (NYC, 16 March): *Brooklyn Brothers*
Duke Jordan (NYC, 7 April): *The Murray Hill Caper* (Copenhagen, 25 November, 2 December): *Flight to Denmark*
JPJ Quartet (NYC, 9 July): *JPJ Quartet*
Barney Kessel/Red Mitchell (Stockholm, 5 June): *Two-Way Conversation*
Barney Kessel (Montreux, 4 July): *Summertime in Montreux* (Stockholm, 27 September): *Just Friends*
Rahsaan Roland Kirk (SF, June): *Bright Moments*
Eric Kloss (NYC, 14 December): *Essence*
Lee Konitz (Copenhagen, 15 July): *Altissimo*
Joachim Kuhn (Paris, 18 January): *This Way Out*
Steve Lacy (Vienna, 26 April): *Flaps* (London, 30 July): *The Crust*
Dave Liebman (Tokyo, 20,21 July): *First Visit* (NYC, 10,11 October): *Lookout Farm*
Humphrey Lyttelton (London, 5 November): *South Bank Swing Session*
Dave McKenna (NYC, 24 February): *Dave McKenna*
John McLaughlin (NYC, August): *Between Nothingness and Eternity*
Jackie McLean (Copenhagen, 17 July): *Ode to Super* (Copenhagen, 18,19 July): *A Ghetto Lullaby*
Jackie McLean/Dexter Gordon (Copenhagen, 20,21 July): *The Meeting / The Source*
Charlie Mingus (NYC, 29,30,31 October): *Mingus Moves*
Sy Oliver (Paris, 19,21 May): *Yes Indeed*
Horace Parlan (Copenhagen, 21,22 December): *Arrival*
Joe Pass (LA, December): *Virtuoso*

1973

Don Patterson (NYC, 17 September): *These are Soulful Days*
Oscar Peterson (Chicago, 16,19 May): *The Trio*
Oscar Peterson/Stephane Grappelli (Paris, 22,23 February): *Oscar Peterson/Stephane Grappelli Quartet, Vols 1&2*
Julian Priester (SF,28 June/12 September): *Love, Love*
Dewey Redman (NYC, 8,9 June): *The Ear of the Behearer*
Return to Forever (August): *Hymn of the Seventh Galaxy*
Buddy Rich (NYC, October): *The Roar of 74*
Sam Rivers (Montreux, 6 July): *Streams*
Red Rodney (NYC, 9 July): *Bird Lives!*
Sonny Rollins (NYC, June, July): *Horn Culture* (Tokyo, 30 September): *Sonny Rollins in Japan*
Roswell Rudd (NYC, 6 July): *Numatik Swing Band*
Terje Rypdal (Oslo, 7,8 August): *What comes after*
Pharaoh Sanders (LA, 7,9,13 September): *Elevation*
Ronnie Scott (London, 3,4 August): *At Ronnie's*
Zoot Sims (NYC, 30 May, 9 August): *Zoot at Ease*
Jimmy Smith (NYC, 8,9 February): *Portuguese Soul*
Spear (London, 25 August/10 November): *In the townships*
Sonny Stitt (NYC, 18 April): *The Champ* (NYC): *Mr Bojangles*
Frank Strazzeri (LA, 6 January): *View from Within*
Sun Ra (Paris, October): *Live at the Gibus*
Supersax (LA): *Supersax plays Bird*
Gabor Szabo (NYC, September): *Rambler*
Buddy Tate (NYC,1 June): *Buddy Tate & his Buddies*
Cecil Taylor (Tokyo, 29 May): *Solos*
Charles Tolliver (Tokyo, 7 December): *Live in Tokyo*
Stanley Turrentine (NYC, June): *Don't Mess with Mr T*
McCoy Tyner (NYC, 6,9 April): *Song of the New World* (Montreux, 7 July): *Enlightenment*
Sarah Vaughan (Tokyo,24 September): *Live in Japan*

Joe Venuti/Zoot Sims (NYC,27 September): *Joe & Zoot*
Mal Waldron (NYC,28 December): *Up popped the devil*
Cedar Walton/Clifford Jordan (NYC, 4 January): *A Night at Boomer's Vols 1&2*
Bill Watrous (NYC, 4 January): *Bone Straight Ahead*
Chuck Wayne/Joe Puma (LA,November): *Interactions*
Eberhard Weber (Ludwigsburg, December): *The Colours of Chloe*
Ben Webster (Copenhagen): *Live at Montmartre* (Leiden, Holland, 6 September): *Last Concert*
Dick Wellstood (NYC, 12 December): *Featuring Kenny Davern*

Randy Weston (NYC, 21,22 May): *Randy*
Kenny Wheeler (London, 10,11 January): *Song for Someone*
Bob Wilber/Kenny Davern (NYC,17,21,22 December): *Soprano Summit*
Joe Williams (Berkeley, Calif. 7 August): *Live*
Phil Wilson (Chicago,16 August): *Thursday Night Dues*
Teddy Wilson (Montreux, 4 July); *Runnin' Wild*
Chris Woods (Paris, 24 October): *Chris meets Paris meets Chris*
World's Greatest Jazz Band (NYC, January): *At Carnegie Hall*

Photo courtesy: Duncan P Schiedt

Right: The Benny Goodman Quartet is reunited.
L to r: Benny Goodman, Teddy Wilson, Lionel Hampton and Gene Krupa.
Below: The roarin' Buddy Rich and his big band.

Photo: David Redfern

Duke Ellington (75) collapses in January, dies on 24 May.

The year of jazz-rock, starring Miles Davis (48), John McLaughlin (32), Chick Corea (33) and Herbie Hancock (34).

MJQ disbands in July after 22 years.

Oscar Peterson (49) has own TV series in Canada 'Oscar Peterson Presents'.

DEATHS

Eddie Safranski (56) 10 January
Don Fagerquist (46) 24 January
Joe Benjamin (54) 26 January car accident
Archie Semple (45) 26 January alcoholism
Ed Allen (76) 28 January pneumonia
Frank Assunto (42) 25 February
Julian Dash (57) 25 February
Bobby Timmons (38) 1 March cirrhosis of liver
Floyd Bean (69) 9 March
Arthur 'Big Boy' Crudup (69) March
Baby Laurence ( ) March
Sam Donahue (55) 22 March
Al Morgan (65) 14 April
Jesse Price (64) 19 April
Jesse Crump (68) 21 April
Paul Gonsalves (54) 14 May
Tyree Glenn (62) 18 May
Duke Ellington (75) 24 May
Graham Bond (36) May
Gil Rodin (67) 10 June
Gene Ammons (49) 23 July cancer
Bill Chase (39) 9 August air crash
Tina Brooks (42) 13 August
Marvin Ash (59) 21 August
Billie Pierce (67) 29 September
Kenneth Hollon (64) 30 September
Harry Carney (64) 8 October
Georg Brunis (72) 19 November
Hugues Panassie (62) 8 December

BOOKS

David Baker & Austin Caswell: Black Music Now
Whitney Balliett: Alec Wilder and his Friends
Joachim Berendt: The Jazz Book
Ralph Berton: Remembering Bix
Edmund Blandford: Artie Shaw
Bill Cole: Miles Davis: a musical biography
Graham Collier: Compositional Devices based on Songs for my Father
Mary Collins: Oh Didn't He Ramble
Jean Cornell: Mahalia Jackson: Queen of Gospel Song
Stanley Dance: The World of Swing
Bud Freeman: You don't look like a musician
Michael Haralambos: Right On: from Blues to Soul in Black America
Ekkehard Jost: Free Jazz
Roger Kinkle: The Complete Encyclopaedia of Popular Music 1900-50
Eric Kriss: Barrelhouse and Boogie Piano
Albert McCarthy: Big Band Jazz
Jim Marks: Jazz, Women, Soul (poems)
Henry Pleasants:The Great American Popular Singers
Al Rose: Storyville, New Orleans
Brian Rust: The Dance Bands
Richard Seidel: Basic Record Library of Jazz
Arnold Shaw: The Rockin' 50's
George Simon: Glenn Miller and his Orchestra
Vladimir Simosko & Barry Tapperman: Eric Dolphy
Dick Sudhalter & Philip R Evans: Bix: Man & Legend

FILMS

Got to Tell it (35mins): a tribute to Mahalia Jackson
Jazz in Piazza (80mins): Umbria Jazz Festival in Italy with Horace Silver Quintet, Gerry Mulligan Quartet, Marian McPartland, Mingus Group, Thad Jones/Mel Lewis Band, Sonny Stitt etc.
Last of the Blue Devils
On the Road with Duke Ellington (58mins): documentary filmed originally in 1967

RECORDS

John Abercrombie (NYC, 21,22 June): Timeless
Cannonball Adderley: Pyramid
Nat Adderley: Double Exposure
Toshiko Akiyoshi/Lew Tabackin Big Band (LA, 3,4 April): Kogun
Joe Albany (Copenhagen, 17 February): Two's Company (Rome, June): The Legendary Joe Albany

Monty Alexander (Jamaica): Rass (Villingen, October): Unlimited Love / Love and Sunshine
Amalgam (Oxfordshire, November/December): Innovation
Gene Ammons (NYC, 18,19,20 March): Goodbye
Art Ensemble of Chicago (Montreux, 4 July): Kabalaba
Derek Bailey/Anthony Braxton (Luton, 2 July): Royal, Vol 1
Chet Baker (NYC, July,October, November): She was too good to me (Woodstock): In Concert
Gato Barbieri (NYC, 25,26 June): Chapter Three
Kenny Barron (NYC, 14 March): Peruvian Blue
Count Basie Trio (LA, 22 May): For the First Time
Walter Bishop Jr (NYC, 30 December): Valley Land
Carla Bley (NYC & London, September): Tropic Appetites
Paul Bley (NYC, 16 June): Paul Bley (Oslo, 8,9 August): Alone Again
Lester Bowie (NYC, September): Fast Last
Dollar Brand (Tokyo, 21 February): African Breeze
Anthony Braxton (Copenhagen, 29 May): In The Tradition (Moers, 1 June): Solo at Moers New Jazz Festival (Moers, 2 June): Quartet Live at Moers New Jazz Festival (London, 30 June): Duo, Vols 1&2 (Toronto, 15 September): Trio and Duet (NYC, 27 September): New York Fall 1974
Dee Dee Bridgewater (Tokyo, 10,12,14 March): Afro-Blue
Roy Brooks (NYC, 26 May): Live at Town Hall
Marion Brown (Boston,6,7 May): Sweet Earth Flying
Dave Brubeck (NYC, 3 October): All the things we are
Kenny Burrell (Berkeley, January, February): Up the Street, Round the Corner, Down the Block (Berkeley, 18,20 June): Stormy Monday
Gary Burton (Massachusetts, 13,14 May): Hotel Hello (Ludwigsburg, 23,24 July): Ring (Ludwigsburg, 26,27 July): Matchbook
Charlie Byrd (NYC, 1,3 March): Byrd by the sea
Donald Byrd (LA, November, December): Stepping into Tomorrow (LA): Black Byrd
Baikida Carroll (Paris, 3-5 June): Orange Fish Tears
Ron Carter (NYC, November): Spanish Blue
Buck Clayton (NYC, 25,26 March): Jam Session
Arnett Cobb (France, 21 May): Jumpin' at the Woodside
Al Cohn/Zoot Sims (Stockholm, 25 November): Motoring Along
Graham Collier (13 March): Darius
Chick Corea (NYC, July/August): Where have I known you before?
Larry Coryell (Montreux, 4 July): The Eleventh House at Montreux (NYC): Level One
Miles Davis (NYC, 30 March): Dark Magus
Buddy de Franco (LA, July): Free Sail
Jack De Johnette (NYC, March): Sorcery
Paul Desmond (NYC, September): Pure Desmond
Vic Dickenson (NYC, February): Vic Dickenson in Session
Eric Dixon (NYC, 25 January, 3 May): Eric's Edge
Lou Donaldson (NYC, 14,19,22 March): Sweet Lou
Kenny Drew (Copenhagen, 11,12 February): Duo 2 (Copenhagen, 21,22 May): If you could see me now (Utrecht, 8 June): Duo live in concert
Charles Earland (Montreux, 6 July): Kharma
Teddy Edwards (LA, 25 March): Feelin's
Herb Ellis/Ray Brown (SF): Soft Shoe
Herb Ellis/Joe Pass (LA, 30 January, 13,20 February): Two for the Road
Herb Ellis (Concord Jazz Festival, August): After You've Gone
Bill Evans (Village Vanguard, NYC, 11,12 January): Since we met (Berkeley, 7,8 November): Intuition
Art Farmer (Stockholm, 4,6 January): A Sleeping Bee (Vienna, December): Talk to me
Joe Farrell (NYC,November/December): Canned Funk
Frank Foster (NYC): The Loud Minority
Jan Garbarek/Keith Jarrett (Oslo, 24,25 April): Belonging (Ludwigsburg,29,30 April): Luminessence

Dizzy Gillespie (NYC, 19 September): Dizzy Gillespie's Big Four
Jimmy Giuffre (NYC): Quiet Song
Dexter Gordon (Copenhagen, 8 September): The Apartment
Stephane Grappelli/Earl Hines (London, 4 July): The Giants
Johnny Griffin (Rome, 7 April): Live at Music Inn
Al Haig (London, 7 January): Invitation (NYC, 27 November): Special Brew
Slide Hampton (Munich, January): Give me a double
Herbie Hancock (Japan, 29 July): Dedication (SF, 26 August): Thrust / Death Wish
Roland Hanna (Montreux, 2 July): Perugia – Live at Montreux
Billy Harper/Jon Faddis (Tokyo,13 March):Jon & Billy
Hampton Hawes (18,19 July): Northern Windows
Louis Hayes (NYC,2 February, 26 July): Breath of Life
Joe Henderson (Paris, 1,3,6 October): Black Narcissus
Woody Herman (Berkeley, 2-4 January): Thundering Herd
Andrew Hill (NYC, 17 October): Invitation
Earl Hines (NYC, 26 March): Quintessential 1974 (16 July): At Sundown (NYC, 6 August): Piano Portraits of Australia
Bobby Hutcherson (LA, 17,18 April): Cirrus
Milt Jackson (NYC, January): Olinga
Willis Jackson (NYC, 16 May): Headed and Gutted
Keith Jarrett (NYC, 27,28 February): Treasure Island (NYC, 9,10 October): Death and the Flower
Keith Jarrett/Jan Garbarek (Ludwigsburg, 20,30 April): Luminessence
Elvin Jones (Warsaw, September): Mr Thunder
Sam Jones (Tokyo, 21 December): Seven Minds
Thad Jones/Mel Lewis (Tokyo, 12,13 March): Live in Tokyo
Louis Jordan (California): Jump'n'Jive
Tony Kinsey (London, 17 February, 17 March): Thames Suite
Lee Konitz (Juan-les-Pins, 26 July): Lee Konitz Jazz à Juan (Copenhagen, 29 July): Lee Konitz/Red Mitchell (Copenhagen, 30 July): I Concentrate On You (NYC, 30 September): Satori
Karin Krog (Copenhagen, 20-22 May): You Must Believe In Spring (Oslo, 19 December 1973 / 19 June 1974): Gershwin With Karin Krog
Joachim Kuhn (May): Cinemascope/Piano
Steve Kuhn (NYC, 11,12 November): Trance (Oslo, November): Ecstasy
Steve Lacy (Paris, 18,21 February): Scraps (Rome, 12 May): Flakes (Holland, 23,24,29 September): Lumps (19 December): Saxophone Special
LA4 (Concord Festival, 27 July): The LA Four Scores
Dave Liebman (NYC, May): Drum Ode
Mundell Lowe (LA): California Guitar
Ken McIntyre/Kenny Drew (Copenhagen, 13 January): Hindsight
Dave McKenna (NYC, October): Dave McKenna Quartet featuring Zoot Sims
Jackie McLean (NYC,30 October):New York Calling
Charlie Mariano (Helsinki, 14,15 March): Reflections
Pat Martino (NYC, 7 October): Consciousness
Charlie Mingus (NYC, 19 January): Mingus at Carnegie Hall (NYC, 27,28,30 December): Changes One/Changes Two
Blue Mitchell (NYC): Many Shades of Blue
Red Mitchell (Stockholm, 14,17 January): Communications (Stockholm, 24 October): Red Mitchell meets Guido Manusardi
MJQ (Lincoln Centre, NYC, 25 November): The Last Concert
Paul Motian (NYC, May): Tribute
Gerry Mulligan/Chet Baker (NYC, 24 November): Carnegie Hall Concert
Oliver Nelson (London): Oliver Nelson with Oily Rags
Joe Pass (LA, 21 June): Portraits of Duke Ellington
Oscar Peterson (Tokyo, 15 January): Terry's Tune (Tallinn, 17 November): Oscar Peterson in Russia
Oscar Peterson/Dizzy Gillespie (London, 28,29 November): Oscar Peterson & Dizzy Gillespie
Oscar Peterson/Count Basie (LA, 2 December): Satch & Josh
Oscar Peterson/Roy Eldridge (LA, 8 December): Oscar Peterson & Roy Eldridge
Oscar Peterson/Harry Edison (LA, 21 December): Oscar Peterson & Harry Edison
Jimmy Raney (Germany, 21 July): Momentum
Dewey Redman: (NYC, 9,10 September): Coincide

1974

Red Rodney (LA, 26 March): *Superbop*
Sonny Rollins (Montreux, 6 July): *The Cutting Edge*
Charlie Rouse (NYC): *Two is One*
Jimmy Rowles (NYC, 7 April): *The Special Magic of Jimmy Rowles*
Roswell Rudd (NYC, March): *Flexible Flyer*
Shirley Scott (NYC, November): *One for me*
Woody Shaw (NYC, 11,18 December): *The Moontrane*
George Shearing (Villingen, 25 June): *My Ship* (SF, 23,24 July): *Light, airy and swinging* (Villingen): *The way we are*

Wayne Shorter (LA): *Native Dancer*
Zoot Sims (NYC, April): *Zoot Sims' Party*
Martial Solal (Paris, September): *Himself*
Jess Stacy (NYC, 5 July): *Stacy still swings*
Sonny Stitt (NYC): *Satan*
Sun Ra (NYC, 16 June): *Discipline 99* (NYC, 17 August): *The Antique Blacks* (Philadelphia, 20 September): *Sub Underground*
Supersax (LA): *Salt Peanuts* (LA, Autumn): *Supersax plays Bird with Strings*
Lew Tabackin (Tokyo, 19 December): *Tabackin*

Cecil Taylor (Montreux, 2 July): *Silent Tongues*
Ed Thigpen (Stockholm, 21,22,23 August): *Ed Thigpen's Action-Reaction*
The Three Sounds (LA, July, August): *Gene Harris/The Three Sounds*
Stanley Turrentine (LA): *Yester me, yester you*
McCoy Tyner (NYC, 26-28 March): *Sam Layuca* (SF, 31 August): *Atlantis*
Joe Venuti (NYC, 20 May): *Blue Fours*
Joe Venuti/Joe Albany (Rome, 14 April): *Joe Venuti &Joe Albany*
Harold Vick (NYC, November): *Don't Look Back*
Mal Waldron (Stuttgart, 4 May): *Hard Talk*
Cedar Walton (Rochester, NY, April): *Firm Roots* (Tokyo, 23 December): *Pit Inn*
Sadao Watanabe (Tokyo, 20 September): *Mubali Africa* (Tokyo, September): *Echo*
Bill Watrous (NYC, 1,2,3 May): *Manhattan Wildlife Refugee*
Weather Report (NYC): *Tale Spinnin'*
Dick Wellstood (London, 23 January): *Walkin' with Wellstood* (NYC, November): *Live at the Cookery*
Randy Weston (Montreux, 5 July): *Carnival* (France, 11 July): *Informal Solo Piano* (Zurich, 14 August): *Blues to Africa*
Kai Winding (LA): *Kai Winding Caravan* (Phoenix): *Danish Blue*
Chris Woods (Paris, 7 November): *Together in Paris*
Phil Woods (NYC, 14 January): *Musique de bois*

Left: Gerry Mulligan.
Below: Joe Venuti, Zoot Sims and George Duvivier recording for Chiaroscuro in New York City.

Photo: *David Redfern*

Photo: *Rollo Phlecks* Courtesy: *Hank O'Neal*

1975

Dave Brubeck (54) and Paul Desmond (50) are reunited in June on the Jazz Cruise aboard *SS Rotterdam*, recorded by BBC TV.

Milt Jackson (52) signs with Pablo Records – triumphs at Montreux (July).

Cecil Taylor (42) attracts overflow audiences at New York's Five Spot.

Mercer Ellington (56) leads the Duke Ellington Orchestra on tour of England.

Don Ellis (41) is hospitalized and forced to give up trumpet.

Charlie Mingus (53) and his band tour Europe, playing festivals in Bergamo, Antibes and Montreux.

Miles Davis (49) gives up playing.

DEATHS

Rene Thomas (47) 3 January *heart attack*
Louis Jordan (66) 4 February
Aake Persson (42) 4 February *auto accident*
Benny Harris (55) 11 February
Gene Schroeder (60) 16 February
T-Bone Walker (66) 17 March
Sandy Brown (46) 15 March
Marty Marsala (66) 27 April
Joe Mooney (64) 12 May
Arthur Trappier (64) 17 May
Ralph Gleason (58) 3 June
Zutty Singleton (77) 14 July
Cannonball Adderley (47) 8 August
Warren Smith (67) 28 August
Reuben Reeves (69) September
Oliver Nelson (43) 28 October *heart attack*
Frank Signorelli (74) 9 December
Lee Wiley (60) 11 December
Noble Sissle (86) 17 December
Fess Williams (81) 17 December
Stan Wrightsman (65) 17 December

BOOKS

Chris Albertson & Gunther Schuller: *Bessie Smith: Empress of the Blues*
Samuel B. Charters: *The Legacy of the Blues*
John Chilton: *Billie's Blues*
Jerry Coker: *The Jazz Idiom*
Graham Collier: *Jazz: a student's and teacher's guide*
Peter Gammond: *Scott Joplin and the Ragtime Era*
Paul Garon: *Blues and the Poetic Spirit*
Ralph J. Gleason: *Celebrating the Duke, and Louis, Bessie, Billie, Bird, Carmen, Miles, Dizzy and other heroes*
Robert S. Gold: *Jazz Talk*
Babs Gonzales: *Movin' on down de line*
Laurraine Goreau: *Just Mahalia, Baby*
Max Harrison et al: *Modern Jazz: The Essential Records*
Humphrey Lyttelton: *Take it from the top*
Brian Rust: *The American Dance Band Discography 1917-42*
C.O. Simpkins: *Coltrane: a biography*
James Shacter: *Piano Man, the story of Ralph Sutton*
J.C. Thomas: *Chasin' the Trane*

RECORDS

John Abercrombie (Ludwigsburg, March): *Gateway*
Muhal Richard Abrams (Chicago, 9 September): *Afrisong* (NYC, 13,14 October): *Sightsong*
Pepper Adams (Munich, 13 August): *Julian / Twelfth and Pingree*
Cannonball Adderley (Berkeley, February-April): *Phenix* (Berkeley, 24,25 June): *Lovers*
Air (Chicago, 10 September): *Air Song*
Toshiko Akiyoshi/Lew Tabackin (LA, 1,2,3 December): *Tales of a Courtesan*
Gato Barbieri (NYC, 20,23 February): *Chapter Four / Alive in New York*
Kenny Barron (NYC, 28 April): *Lucifer*
Kenny Barron/Ted Dunbar (NJ, 15 February): *In Tandem*
Count Basie/Zoot Sims (NYC, 9 April): *Basie & Zoot*
Count Basie (LA, 26,27 August): *Basie Big Band*
Count Basie Trio (LA, 28 August): *For the Second Time*
Lester Bowie (NYC, 17 June): *Rope-a-dope*
Joanne Brackeen (NYC, March): *Snooze*
Dollar Brand (Johannesburg, November): *Blues for a Hip King*
Anthony Braxton (NYC, 1 July): *Five Pieces 1975*

Brecker Brothers (NYC, January): *The Brecker Brothers* (NYC): *Back to Back*
Ray Brown (LA, December): *Brown's Bag*
Dave Brubeck/Paul Desmond (NYC, 10 June, 15,16 September): *The Duets*
Ray Bryant (NYC, 15 October): *Hot Turkey*
John Bunch (NYC, Spring/Summer): *Plays Kurt Weill*
Kenny Burrell (Berkeley, 29,30 January): *Sky Street* (Berkeley, 4,5 February): *Ellington is Forever*
Gary Burton (Ludwigsburg, December): *Dreams so real*
Charlie Byrd (NYC, February): *Top Hat*
Donald Byrd (LA, August, September): *Places and Spaces*
Ron Carter (NYC, June/July): *Anything Goes*
Don Cherry (NYC & Woodstock): *Brown Rice*
Al Cohn (NYC, 19 June): *Play it now*
Richie Cole (Trenton, 5 May): *Trenton makes – the world takes*
Chick Corea (NYC, January): *No Mystery* (NYC): *The Leprechaun*
Stanley Cowell (White Plains, 27 April): *Regeneration*
Sonny Criss (LA, 24 February): *Criss Craft* (LA, 1 March): *Saturday Morning* (LA, 20 October): *Out of Nowhere*
Harold Danko (NYC, 5 April): *Harold Danko Quartet featuring Gregory Herbert*
Miles Davis (Osaka, 1 February): *Agharta / Panagea*
Richard Davis (NYC, 19,26 October): *As One*
Buddy de Franco (Buffalo/Boston): *Boronquin*
Jack De Johnette (NYC, 24-26 April): *Cosmic Chicken*
Paul Desmond (Toronto, 25,27,30,31 October, 1 November): *The Paul Desmond Quartet Live*
Walt Dickerson (NYC, 14 November): *Peace*
Klaus Doldinger (Hamburg, 28,29 August): *Doldinger Jubilee 75*
Kenny Drew (Copenhagen, 8 September): *Morning*
John Eaton (NYC, January/February): *Solo Piano*
Harry Edison: *Just Friends*
Herb Ellis (Concord Jazz Festival): *Hot Tracks*
Bill Evans (Montreux, 20 July): *Montreux 3* (California, 16,18 December): *Alone (again)*
Art Farmer (NYC, 5 March): *To Duke with Love* (NYC, 16,17 July): *Yesterday's Thoughts*
Clare Fischer (Villingen, October): *Alone together* (Meersburg, October): *Clare declares*
Tommy Flanagan (Tokyo, 15 February): *The Tokyo Festival*
Frank Foster (Tokyo, 13,17 November): *Giant Steps*
Chico Freeman (NYC): *Streetdancer Rising*
Don Friedman (NYC, 8,9 July): *Hope for Tomorrow*
Jan Garbarek (Oslo, November): *Dansere*
Herb Geller (Hamburg, January): *Rhyme and Reason*
Stan Getz (NYC, 21 May): *The Best of Two Worlds* (NYC, 24 June, 18 July): *This is my love* (NYC, 1 October): *The Master* (NYC, October): *The Peacocks*
Dizzy Gillespie (NYC, 3 June): *Jazz Maturity* (NYC, 4,5 June): *Afro Cuban Jazz Moods* (Montreux, 16 July): *The Trumpet Kings* (LA, 19,20 November): *Bahiana*
Jimmy Giuffre (NYC, April): *Riverchant*
Benny Goodman (NYC, 15,23 September, 14 November): *Seven come eleven*
Dexter Gordon (Copenhagen, 21,22,23 February): *More than you know* (Copenhagen, 10 March): *Stablemates* (Zurich, 23,24 August): *Swiss Nights Vols 1,2,3* (Copenhagen, 13 September): *Something Different* (Copenhagen, 14 September): *Bouncin' with Dex*
Lars Gullin (Berlin, 26 May): *Quintet in Concert*
Al Haig (NYC, 27 March): *Strings attached* (NYC, 7,8 July): *Chelsea Bridge*
Jim Hall (NYC, April): *Concierto* (Toronto, June): *Live!*

Jake Hanna (Concord, July): *Live at Concord*
Billy Harper (Paris, 21,22 July): *Black Saint*
Barry Harris (NYC, 4 June): *Plays Tadd Dameron*
Beaver Harris (NYC, 20 January/11 February/11 December): *From Ragtime to No Time*
Hampton Hawes (SF, June): *Live at the Great American Music Hall*
Jimmy Heath (NYC, 22 September): *Picture of Heath*
Heath Brothers (Oslo, 22 October): *Marchin' On*
Julius Hemphill (NYC, 29 January): *Coon Bid'ness*
Joe Henderson (Berkeley, Spring & Autumn): *Black Miracle*
John Hicks (London, 21 May): *Hell's Bells*
Andrew Hill (NYC, 20 January): *Spiral* (NYC, 19,20 May, 31 July): *Hommage* (NYC, 10 July): *Divine Revelation* (Montreux, 20 July): *Live at Montreux*
Freddie Hubbard (Tokyo, 17 March): *Gleam*
Milt Jackson (Montreux, 17 July): *Milt Jackson at the Montreux Jazz Festival* (LA, 25 August): *The Big Three*
Keith Jarrett (Köln, 24 January): *The Köln Concert* (NYC): *Mysteries* (NYC): *Shades* (Ludwigsburg, October): *Arbour Zena*
Leroy Jenkins (NYC, 30 January): *For Players Only*
Plas Johnson (SF, September): *The Blues*
Elvin Jones (Kent, NY): *Elvin Jones is on the Mountain* (NYC): *New Agenda*
Hank Jones (NYC, 14,15 July): *Hanky Panky*
Clifford Jordan (Paris, 26 March): *Night of the Mark VII* (Amsterdam, 29 March): *On Stage Vols 1,2,3* (Munich, 18 April): *Firm Roots / The Highest Mountain*
Duke Jordan (Copenhagen, 2 March): *Truth* (NYC, 30 June): *Misty Thursday* (NYC, 18 November): *Duke's Delight / Lover Man*
Stan Kenton (Chicago, 3-5 December): *Kenton '76*
Barney Kessel (LA, April): *Barney plays Kessel*
Rahsaan Roland Kirk (NYC): *The Case of the Three-sided Dream in Audio Color*
Eric Kloss (NJ, 24,25 June): *Bodies' Warmth*
Lee Konitz (NYC, January): *Oleo* (NYC, 6 May): *Chicago 'n' all that jazz*
Lee Konitz/Hal Galper (NYC, 6 November): *Windows*
Joachim Kuhn (Ludwigsburg, 2-4 November): *Hip Elegy*

Photo: *David Redfern*

Steve Lacy (Berlin, 1 April): *Stabs – Solo in Berlin* (Paris, 12-15 May): *Steve Lacy's Dreams* (Tokyo, 7 June): *Stalks* (Tokyo, 8 June): *Solo at Mandara* (Kyoto, June): *Torments* (Tokyo, 24 June): *Distant Voices* (Como, September): *Axieme Vols 1&2*

Oliver Lake (NYC, January/February): *Heavy Spirits*

Dave Liebman (LA, 25,27,29,30 July): *Sweet Hands* (NYC, 18-20 November): *Forgotten Fantasies*

Jack McDuff: *Magnetic Feel*

Ken McIntyre (Copenhagen, 23 June): *Home* (Copenhagen, 19 November): *Open Horizon*

Charles McPherson (NYC, 12 August): *Beautiful*

Shelly Manne (LA): *Hot Coles*

Ronnie Mathews (Tokyo, 7,9 July): *Trip to the Orient*

Pat Metheny (Ludwigsburg, December): *Bright Size Life*

Gerry Mulligan (Milan, 16,17 October): *Gerry Mulligan meets Enrico Intra*

Oliver Nelson (Tokyo, 6 March): *Stolen Moments*

Sam Noto (NYC, 2 March): *Entrance* (NYC, 1 December): *Act One*

Horace Parlan (Copenhagen,10 December): *No Blues*

Joe Pass (Montreux, 17,18 July): *Joe Pass at the Montreux Jazz Festival*

NHO Pedersen (Copenhagen, 9,10 September, 10 December): *Jaywalkin'*

Art Pepper (LA, 9 August): *Living Legend*

Marvin 'Hannibal' Peterson (Ludwigsburg, 1,2 July): *Hannibal and the Sunshine Orchestra*

Oscar Peterson (Paris, 17 March): *Oscar Peterson & Joe Pass* (LA, 18 May): *Oscar Peterson & Clark Terry* (NYC, 5 June): *Oscar Peterson & Jon Faddis* (Montreux, 16 July): *Oscar Peterson Big 6 at Montreux*

Left: Multi-instrumentalist Roland Kirk at the Montreux Jazz Festival.

Right: Billy Butterfield at the 100 Club in London.

Below: Benny Goodman recreates his sextet for a Chicago TV show. Also visible are Red Norvo (vibes), George Benson (guitar) and Milt Hinton (bass).

Flip Phillips (NYC, August): *Phillips' Head*

Dave Pike (LA, 13,14 October): *Time out of Mind*

The Pollwinners (LA, 12 July): *Straight Ahead*

Jean-Luc Ponty (LA, December): *Aurora*

Don Pullen (NYC, 16,17 October): *Capricorn Rising*

Sammy Price (Paris, 12 May/Berne, 25 May): *Boogie and Jazz Classics*

Jimmy Raney (NYC, 2 September): *The Influence*

Dannie Richmond Rome, 28 July): *Jazz a Confronto*

Howard Riley (London, 3 July): *Intertwine*

Red Rodney (NYC, 30 September, 2 October): *The Red Tornado*

Sonny Rollins (Berkeley, 2-5 September): *Nucleus*

Frank Rosolino (Munich, 10 May): *Conversation / Just Friends*

Hilton Ruiz (NYC, 10 July): *Piano Man*

Patrice Rushen (Berkeley, August): *Before the Dawn*

Joe Sample (LA, 28 November): *The Three*

Woody Shaw (NYC, November): *Love Dance*

Photo: *Reg Peerless*

George Shearing (Villingen, October): *Continental Experience*

Archie Shepp (NYC, 12 April): *There's a Trumpet in my Soul* (Montreux, 18 June): *Montreux One & Montreux Two*

Wayne Shorter: *Native Dancer*

Horace Silver (LA): *Silver'n'Brass*

Zoot Sims (NYC, 6 June): *Zoot Sims & the Gershwin Brothers*

Martial Solal (Villingen, 7 April): *Nothing but piano* (Paris, 28 December): *Martial Solal plays Duke Ellington*

Louis Stewart (London, October): *Baubles, Bangles and Beads*

Sonny Stitt (NYC, 14 February): *Mellow* (NYC, 16 May): *In Walked Sonny* (NYC, 2 July): *My Buddy* (NYC, 3,4 December): *Blues for Duke*

Ralph Sutton (Zurich, 13 November): *Suttonly it jumped*

Buddy Tate: *The Texas Twister / Jive at Five*

Cal Tjader (LA, June): *Amazonas*

Charles Tolliver (NYC, 17 January): *Impact*

Stan Tracey (London, 3 November): *Captain Adventure*

Mickey Tucker (NYC, 22 December): *Triplicity*

Joe Turner (NYC, 11,18,25 February): *King of Stride*

Stanley Turrentine (Berkeley, July): *Have you ever seen the rain?*

Joe Venuti/Earl Hines (NYC,22 October): *Hot Sonata*

Joe Venuti/Zoot Sims (NYC, May): *Joe Venuti & Zoot Sims*

Leroy Vinnegar (LA): *Glass of Water*

Sadao Watanabe (Montreux, 18 July): *Swiss Air*

Bill Watrous (NYC): *The Tiger of San Pedro*

Randy Weston (Paris, 4 April): *African Rhythms* (Paris, 21 September): *African Nite*

Mary Lou Williams (NYC, November): *Live at the Cookery*

Phil Wilson (Dallas, August): *The Sound of the Wasp*

Phil Woods/Michel Legrand (London,February): *Images*

Phil Woods (London): *Floresta Canto* (NYC, October-December): *The New Phil Woods Album*

Photo: *Rollo Phlecks* Courtesy: *Hank O'Neal*

1976

Count Basie (72) has a heart attack.

Don Ellis (42) reforms his big band and starts playing trumpet again.

Charlie Mingus (54) makes a six week European tour in August and September, looks tired and weak.

25th Anniversary Reunion Concert by the Dave Brubeck Quartet in March, with Paul Desmond, Gene Wright and Joe Morello.

DEATHS
Gösta Theselius (53) 24 January
Jesse Fuller (78) 28 January
Ray Nance (63) 28 January
Vince Guaraldi (47) 6 February
Bob Short (64) 4 April
Jimmy Garrison (42) 7 April cancer
Carlos Krahmer (62) 20 April
Jim Robinson (84) 4 May
Lars Gullin (48) 17 May
Willie Maiden (48) 29 May
Bobby Hackett (61) 7 June alcoholic complications triggering diabetes
Johnny Mercer (66) 25 June
Buddy Featherstonhaugh (66) 12 July
Jerry Gray (61) 10 August
Bernard Peiffer (53) 7 September
Quentin Jackson (67) 2 October
Herb Flemming (76) 3 October
Victoria Spivey (70) 3 October
Rudy Powell (69) 30 October
Al Jones (45)

BOOKS
Whitney Balliett: New York Notes: a journal of jazz 1972-75
Ole Brash & Dan Morgenstern: Jazz People
Cab Calloway & Bryant Rollins: Of Minnie the Moocher and me
Bill Cole: John Coltrane
Graham Collier: Cleo and John: a biography of the Dankworths
Roger Cotterell (ed): Jazz Now: The Jazz Centre Society Guide
Brian Davis: John Coltrane Discography
Mark Evans: Scott Joplin and the Ragtime Years
Leonard Feather: The Pleasures of Jazz
Leonard Feather & Ira Gitler: Encyclopaedia of Jazz in the Seventies
Bud Freeman: If you know of a better life, please tell me
Jim Godbolt: All This and 10%
Benny Green: Swingtime in Tottenham
Jonathan Green: Glenn Miller and the Age of Swing
Max Harrison: A Jazz Retrospect
Mileham Hayes, Ray Scribner & Peter Magee: The Encyclopaedia of Australian Jazz^
Nat Hentoff: Jazz Is
Genie Iverson: Louis Armstrong
Hettie Jones: Big Star Fallin' Mama
Tom Lord: Clarence Williams
Albert Murray: Stomping the Blues
Giles Oakley: The Devil's Music: a history of the blues
Michael Ondaatje: Coming through Slaughter (novel based on life of Buddy Bolden)
Jan Scobey: He Rambled 'til Cancer cut him down
Eric Townley: Tell Your Story: a dictionary of jazz and blues recordings 1917-1950
Terry Waldo: This is Ragtime
Earl Wilson: Sinatra, an unauthorised biography

FILMS
Leadbelly (127mins): film bio of Huddie Ledbetter
Scott Joplin (96mins): film bio with appearances by Eubie Blake & Taj Mahal
Sven Klang's Kvintett (109mins): Swedish feature film about an amateur jazz group

RECORDS
John Abercrombie (Oslo, May): Sargasso Sea
George Adams (Rome, 28 July): Suite for Swingers
Nat Adderley (LA): Hummin' (NYC, 9 August): Don't Look Back
Air (NYC, 15 July): Air Raid
Toshiko Akiyoshi/Lew Tabackin (Tokyo, 30 January, 7,8 February): Road Time (LA, 22,23,24 June): Insights (LA, 19,20,21 July): Dedications
Joe Albany (Paris, 10 November): This is for my friends

Monty Alexander (Montreux, 10 June): Montreux Alexander
Mose Allison (NYC, 5,7,8,9 April): Your Mind is on Vacation
Amalgam (London, 21,23 June): Another Time
Benny Bailey (Germany, December): Serenade to a Planet
Gato Barbieri (Beverly Hills): Caliente
Count Basie (NYC, 12,13,14 January): I told you so (LA, 6 May): Basie Jam Nos 2&3
George Benson (6,7,8 January): Breezin'
Bill Berry (Concord): Hello Rev
Walter Bishop Jr (NYC, 25 May): Old Folks (NYC, 21 October): Soliloquy
Art Blakey (NYC, 15,16 March): Backgammon
Paul Bley (Japan, 25 July): Japan Suite
Joanne Brackeen (Holland, 14 July): Invitation (Holland, 15 July): New True Illusion
Ruby Braff (NYC, 23,24 March): Them There Eyes
Dollar Brand (NYC, 27 January): The Children of Africa (Cape Town, 30 August): Black Lightning
Anthony Braxton (NYC, February): Anthony Braxton Creative Orchestra Music 1976
Anthony Braxton/George Lewis (Moers, June): Elements of Surprise
Marion Brown (NYC, 8,9,14 July): Awofofora (NYC, 16 November): Zenzile
Dave Brubeck Quartet (Michigan, 10 March): 25th Anniversary Reunion
Ray Bryant (NYC, 10,12 January): Here's Ray Bryant (NYC, 21 December): Solo Flight
Gary Burton ((Oslo, November): Passengers
Charlie Byrd (Buffalo, June): Triste
Benny Carter (NYC, November): Wonderland
Ron Carter (NYC, May): Yellow and Green
Buck Clayton (NYC, 13 September): Buck Clayton Jam Session Vol 3
Don Cherry (NYC, December): Hear and Now
Al Cohn (NYC, 22 October): Silver Blue / True Blue (NYC, 6 December): Al Cohn's America
Dolo Coker (LA, 26 December): Dolo! (LA, 27 December): California Hard
Richie Cole (Maryland, 24 June): Starburst (NYC, 13 October): New York Afternoon
Ornette Coleman (Paris, 19 December): Body Meta
Chick Corea (Colorado, February): Romantic Warrior (Burbank, October/November): My Spanish Heart
Ronnie Cuber (NYC, 20 August): Cuber Libre!
Ted Curson (NYC, 1 July): Ted Curson & Co (Philadelphia, 16,17 October): Jubilant Power
Eddie 'Lockjaw' Davis (Copenhagen, March): Swingin' till the girls come home
Wild Bill Davison (Copenhagen, 6-8 August): Sweet and Lovely
Elton Dean (London, 22 March): Oh for the Edge (London,18 November): They'll all be on this old road
Jack De Johnette (Oslo, February): Untitled (Oslo, February): Pictures
Vic Dickenson (NYC, 31 March): Plays Bessie Smith – Trombone Cholly
Walt Dickerson (Philadelphia,11 August): Serendipity
Harry Edison (LA, 5 May): Edison's Lights
Teddy Edwards (NYC, 25 June): The Inimitable Teddy Edwards
Bill Evans (Berkeley, May): Quintessence
Jon Faddis (NYC, 8,9 January): Youngblood
Tal Farlow (Concord, August): On Stage (SF, 2 August): A Sign of the Times (NYC, 14,21 September): Trilogy
Art Farmer (NYC, 12,13 May): The Summer Knows (NYC, 14,15 May): At Boomer's (LA, 26,28 July, 16 August): On the Road
Tommy Flanagan (NYC, October, November): Positive Intensity
Frank Foster (NYC, June): Here and Now
Chico Freeman (Chicago, 8 September): Morning Prayer
Hal Galper (NYC, 11 November): Reach Out
Jan Garbarek (Oslo, December): Dis

Dizzy Gillespie (LA,15,16 September): Dizzy's Party
Dizzy Gillespie/Benny Carter (27 April): Carter Gillespie Inc
Dexter Gordon (Copenhagen, 15 June): Lullaby for a Monster (NYC, 9 November): Biting the Apple (Village Vanguard, NYC, 11,12 December): Homecoming
Grant Green (NYC, March): The Main Attraction
Al Grey (NYC, 30 August): Struttin' and Shoutin'
Johnny Griffin (Tokyo, 23 April): Live in Tokyo
Al Haig (LA, 24,25 February): Piano Interpretations (NYC,6 May): Duke'n'Bird (LA,16 November): Interplay
Jim Hall (NYC, 1,10,11,21,22 June, 1 July): Commitment (Tokyo, 28 October): Live in Tokyo (Tokyo, 1 November): Jazz Impressions of Japan
Herbie Hancock (SF): Secrets (Newport JF, 29 June): Herbie Hancock VSOP
Jake Hanna (LA, April): Kansas City Express (NYC, 14,15 December): Jake takes Manhattan
Tom Harrell (NYC, 24 June): Aurora
Barry Harris (Tokyo, 1,12,14 April): Live in Tokyo
Beaver Harris (NYC, 8,9 March): In: sanity
Hampton Hawes (LA, 14 August): Killing me softly with his song
Louis Hayes (NYC, 5 May): Ichi-Ban
Julius Hemphill (NYC, 28 May): Live in New York
Andrew Hill (Tokyo, 25 January): Nefertiti
Bobby Hutcherson (SF): Waiting (SF,4,5,6 August): The View from the Inside
Milt Jackson (Tokyo, 22,23 March): Milt Jackson at the Kosei Nenkin (LA, 12,13,14 April): Feelings
Illinois Jacquet (Nice, 16 July): Jacquet's Street
Ahmad Jamal (Vancouver): Live at Oil Can Harry's
Keith Jarrett (Germany, April): The Survivor's Suite (Paris, May): Staircase (Austria, May): Eyes of the Heart (Kyoto, November): Sun Bear Concerts
Elvin Jones: The Main Force
Hank Jones (Tokyo, 24 January): Satin Doll (NYC, 22 May): Love for Sale (SF, 8 October): Jones-Brown-Smith (NYC, 28 October): Arigato
Sam Jones (NYC, 5 January): Cello Again
Thad Jones/Mel Lewis (Munich, 9 September): Live in Munich
Clifford Jordan (NYC,18,19 May): Remembering Me-me
Duke Jordan (Japan, 20 September): Duke Jordan Trio Live in Japan (Tokyo, 25 September): Flight to Japan
Stan Kenton (LA,16-18 August): Journey into Capricorn
Barney Kessel (SF, 25 August): Soaring
Barney Kessel/Herb Ellis (SF): Poor Butterfly
Rahsaan Roland Kirk (Paris, November): Vibration Society Paris 1976
John Klemmer (LA, April/May): Barefoot Ballet
Eric Kloss/Richie Cole (NYC, 26,27 March): Battle of the Saxes
Eric Kloss/Barry Miles (NYC, 19,20 July): Together
Jimmy Knepper (8 November): Cunningbird
Lee Konitz (Rome, 17 January): Jazz Confronto 32 (London, 15 March): London Concert (London, 21 May): Lee Konitz Meets Warne Marsh Again (NYC, 13,18 October): The Lee Konitz Nonet (NYC, 20 October): Figure and Spirit
Joachim Kuhn (Munich, April): Springfever (Hamburg): Charisma
Steve Lacy (Italy, 20 February): Clangs (NYC, 11,14 March): Trickles (Montreal, 24 March): Chops (Oslo, 1 September): Sidelines (Italy, 5 December): Trio Live
LA4 (15,16 October): Pavane pour une infante defunte
Oliver Lake (NYC, March): Holding Together (NYC, 14-23 May): The New York Loft Jazz Sessions
Oliver Lake/Joseph Bowie (Toronto, 10,11 April): Oliver Lake and Joseph Bowie
Mel Lewis (NYC, 8,9 June): Mel Lewis and Friends
Mike Longo (NYC, January): Talk With The Spirits
Mundell Lowe (California,16,17 October): Guitar Player
Humphrey Lyttelton (London, 13 May): Hazy, Crazy and Blue
Jack McDuff (NYC): Sophisticated Funk
Howard McGhee (NYC,30 March): Here comes Freddy
Ken McIntyre (NYC, 30 October): Introducing the Vibrations
Marian McPartland (Tokyo, 27 January): Live in Tokyo
Charles McPherson (Tokyo, 14 April): Live in Tokyo
Junior Mance (NYC, 3,4 May): Holy Mama
Shelly Manne (LA, 6 May): Rex: Shelly Manne plays Richard Rodgers
Warne Marsh (Chicago, 21 February): All Music (LA, October): Tenor Gladness

Pat Martino (NYC, 10 February): *Exit* (NYC, 13,17 February): *We'll be together again*
Billy Mitchell (NYC): *Now's the Time*
Blue Mitchell (LA): *Funktion Junction*
Red Mitchell (Malmo, 17,18 December): *Blues for a crushed soul* (Copenhagen, 21 December): *Chocolate Cadillac*
Tete Montoliu (Copenhagen, 15,16 February): *Tootie's Tempo*
Sam Most (LA): *But Beautiful* (NYC, 27 May): *Mostly Flute* (NYC, 28 December): *Flute Flight*
Gerry Mulligan (NYC, 23 November): *Idle Gossip*
Phineas Newborn (LA, 7,8 December): *Look Out... Phineas is back*
Jimmy Owens (NYC, 4,5,6 May): *Young Man on the Move*
Joe Pass (LA,14 September, 26 October): *Virtuoso No2*
Cecil Payne (NYC, 2 February): *Bird gets the Worm*
NHO Pederson (Copenhagen, 15,16 February): *Double Bass* (Copenhagen, 4,5 December): *Pictures*
Art Pepper (LA, 15,16 September): *The Trip*
Houston Person (NYC, 29 April): *Stolen Sweets* (NYC, 20 May): *The Big Horn*
Marvin 'Hannibal' Peterson (Berlin, 11 November): *Hannibal in Berlin*
Oscar Peterson/Joe Pass (LA, 26 January): *Oscar Peterson & Joe Pass*
Don Pullen (NYC, April): *Healing Force*
Jimmy Raney (Tokyo, 12,14 April): *Live in Tokyo* (NYC, 20 December): *Solo*
Enrico Rava (Oslo, August): *The Plot*
Sam Rivers (Milan, 12,13 March): *The Quest* (Italy, 24 July): *Black Africa/Villabago* (Italy, 25 July): *Black Africa/Perugia* (Amsterdam, 2 September): *Essence*
Red Rodney (Stockholm, 4,5 March): *Yard's Pad* (NYC, 11,12 May): *Red, White and Blues*
Sonny Rollins (Berkeley, August, October): *The Way I Feel*
Frank Rosolino (Toronto, 21,23 April): *Thinking about you*
Charlie Rouse (NYC): *Cinnamon Flower*
Jimmy Rowles (NYC, March): *Grandpaws* (NYC, March): *Paws that refresh* (NYC, 22 December): *Music's the only thing that's on my mind*
Roswell Rudd (NYC, 27,28 March): *Blown-bone* (NYC, 21 May): *Inside Job*
Patrice Rushen (Berkeley): *Shout It Out*
David Sanborn (NYC): *Sanborn*
Bud Shank (California, January): *Sunshine Express*
Woody Shaw (NYC, 29 June): *Little Red's Fantasy*

George Shearing/Stephane Grapelli (Villingen, 11 April): *The Reunion*
George Shearing (Villingen, April): *The many facets of George Shearing*
Archie Shepp (Nuremburg, 14 May): *Steam*
Horace Silver (NYC, 24 September, 1 October): *Silver'n'Voices*
Zoot Sims (NYC, 8,9 January): *Soprano Sax* (NYC, August): *Summun* (LA, 20,21 September): *Hawthorne Nights*
Jimmy Smith (LA): *Sit on it!*
Martial Solal (Villingen, 26 April): *Movability*
Soprano Summit (NYC, 30 March/2 April): *Chalumeau Blue*
James Spaulding (NYC, 1,2 December): *Plays the Legacy of Duke Ellington*
Lou Stein (NYC, 20,21 March): *Tribute to Art Tatum*
Sonny Stitt (LA): *I remember Bird* (NYC): *Stomp off, let's go*
Kathy Stobart (London, 8 March): *Saxploitation*
Frank Strozier (White Plains): *Dance, dance* (NYC, 10 November): *Remember me*
Monette Sudler (NYC, 7 November): *Time for a change*
Idrees Sulieman (Weesp, 16,17 February): *Now is the time* (Copenhagen, 10 December): *Bird's Grass*
Sun Ra (Paris, August): *Cosmos*
Lew Tabackin (LA, 31 August, 3 September): *Dual Nature* (LA, 3 September): *Trackin'*
Buddy Tate/Jay McShann/Paul Quinichetter (NYC, 19,24 March): *Kansas City Joys*
Cecil Taylor (Yugoslavia, 18 June): *Dark to themselves* (Austria, 20 August): *Air above mountains, buildings within*
Clark Terry (Hamburg): *Wham*
Cal Tjader (SF, 22 May): *At Grace Cathedral* (Berkeley, September): *Guarabe*
Stan Tracey (London, 29 November): *The Bracknell Connection*
Stanley Turrentine (Berkeley, March): *Everybody come on out* (NYC, 25,28 August, 27,28 September): *The man with the sad face*
McCoy Tyner (Berkeley, 4,7 August): *Focal Point*
Warren Vaché (NYC): *First Time Out*
Leroy Vinnegar (Santa Monica): *The Kid*
Mal Waldron (Tokyo, 12 April): *Like Old Times*
Cedar Walton (NYC, 17 May): *The Pentagon*
Sadao Watanabe (NYC, 22 May): *I'm Old Fashioned*
Chuck Wayne (NYC, 12,21 December): *Traveling*
Weather Report (LA): *Black Market* (LA): *Heavy Weather*

Dick Wellstood (Berne, 17 June): *Swingin' on a Baby Grand*
Randy Weston (Milan, 28 January): *Randy Weston meets himself* (NYC, 14 December): *Perspective*
Jiggs Whigham (Cologne, 24 January): *Hope*
Phil Wilson (NYC): *Wilson – that's all*
Teddy Wilson (NYC, 23,24 June): *Teddy Wilson & his All Stars* (Nice, 14 July): *Three Little Words*
Chris Woods (Paris, 27 March): *Black & Blue F33100*
Phil Woods (Silver Springs, November): *Live from the Showboat*

Below: Bill Evans relaxes in the London studio of photographer David Redfern.

Bottom: Weather Report in concert, featuring co-founders Joe Zawinul (keyboards) and Wayne Shorter (saxophones).

Photo: Andrew Putler / Redferns

1977

20th anniversary of the Monterey Jazz Festival (September).

Mingus undertakes another long European tour despite worsening health. In November his illness is diagnosed as amyotrophic lateral sclerosis.

Arnett Cobb (59) is a big hit at the Nice and Montreux festivals.

The World Saxophone Quartet is formed by David Murray (tenor sax), Hamiett Bluiett (baritone sax), Oliver Lake & Julius Hemphill (alto saxes).

BIRTHS
Jason Marsalis (drums) 4 March

DEATHS
Erroll Garner (54) 2 January
Doc Evans (69) 10 January
Edgar Battle (69) 6 February
Buddy Johnson (62) 9 February
Armand Hug (66) 19 March
Hymie Schertzer (67) 22 March
Bennie Green (53) 23 March
Benny Moten (60) 27 March *heart attack*
Julius Watkins (55) 4 April
Moon Mullens (60) 7 April
Joe Garland (73) 21 April
Walter Johnson (73) 26 April
Hampton Hawes (49) 24 May
Paul Desmond (52) 30 May *cancer*
Ken Wray (52) 13 June *a fall*
Richie Kamuca (46) 22 July *cancer*
Milt Buckner (62) 27 July
Art Mardigan (54) August
Ethel Waters (80) 1 September
George Barnes (56) 5 September
Johnny Wiggs (78) 9 October
Bing Crosby (73) 14 October *heart attack*
Milt Raskin (61) 16 October
Eva Taylor (82) 31 October
Sonny Criss (50) 19 November *suicide*
Rahsaan Roland Kirk (41) 6 December *stroke*
Sammy Weiss (67) 18 December
Marlowe Morris (62)
J C Moses (40)

BOOKS
Anthony Agostinelli (ed): *The Newport Jazz Festival in Rhode Island 1954 – 1971*
Whitney Balliett: *Improvising: Sixteen Jazz Musicians and their Art*
Tom Bethell: *George Lewis, a jazzman from New Orleans*
Matthew Bruccoli & C.E. Clark (eds): *Conversations with Jazz Musicians*
Samuel Charters: *Sweet as the Showers of Rain*
Sid Colin: *And the Bands played on*
Stanley Dance: *The World of Earl Hines*
Frank Driggs: *Women in Jazz*
Burt Goldblatt: *Newport Jazz Festival: the Illustrated History*
Bill Gutman: *Duke: the musical life of Duke Ellington*
John Hammond: *John Hammond on Record*
James Haskins: *The Cotton Club*
Art Hodes & Chadwick Hansen: *Selections from the Gutter*
Edgar Jackson: *The World of Big Bands: The Sweet and Swinging Years*
Derek Jewell: *Duke – a portrait of Duke Ellington*
David Meeker: *Jazz in the Movies*
George Melly: *Rum, Bum and Concertina*
Leroy Ostransky: *Understanding Jazz*
John Ridgway: *The Sinatra File*
William Schafer & Richard Allen: *Brass Bands and New Orleans Jazz*
Arnold Shaw: *Honkers and Shouters*
Arnold Shaw: *52nd Street: the street of jazz* (new edition of *The Street that never slept* see 1971)
Austin Sonnier: *William Geary 'Bunk' Johnson: The New Iberia Years*
Frank Tirro: *Jazz: A History*
Joel Vance: *Fats Waller, His Life and Times*
Maurice Waller & Anthony Calabrese: *Fats Waller*
Valerie Wilmer: *As Serious as your Life*

FILMS
New York, New York: feature movie of the big band era starring Robert de Niro. Music by George Auld.

RECORDS
John Abercrombie (Oslo, July): *Gateway 2* (Oslo, November): *Characters*
Pepper Adams (France, 4 November): *Live in Europe*
Air (NYC, 17,18 November): *Air Time*
Akiyoshi/Tabackin (NYC): *March of the Tadpoles / The Big Apple* (NYC, 29 June): *Live at Newport*
Joe Albany (LA, 5 July): *The Albany Touch*
Monty Alexander (Laren, 10 March): *Live in Holland* (LA, 1,2 June): *Soul Fusion* (Villingen, 8,9 September): *Cobilimbo*
Barry Altschul (NYC, 8,9 February): *You can't name your own tune*
Amalgam (London, 26 January): *Samanna* (London, 17 November): *Deep*
Cat Anderson (Paris, 4 June): *Cat Speaks*
Derek Bailey (London, 26 May): *Company 5* (Holland, 14,17 December): *K'Ploeng*
Chet Baker (NYC, 20 February): *Once upon a Summertime* (Paris, 8,9 March): *Flic on voyou*
Eddie Barefield (NYC): *The Indestructible E.B.*
George Barnes (SF, 17 April): *Plays so good*
Count Basie (LA, 18,19,20 January): *Prime Time* (Montreux, 14 July): *Basie Jam* (Montreux, 15 July): *Montreux '77*
Count Basie/Dizzy Gillespie (Las Vegas, 3 February): *The Gifted Ones*
Gordon Beck (November): *Conversation Piece*
Borah Bergman (NYC, 25-27 March): *Burst of Joy*
Bill Berry (LA, 11,12 January): *Ellington All-Stars*
Louis Bellson (LA,21,22,23 December): *Sunshine Rock*
Walter Bishop Jr (NYC, June): *Soul Village* (NYC, 3,4,5 November): *I Remember Bebop*
Art Blakey (NYC, 14,17,28 February, 1 March): *Gypsy Folk Tales* (NYC, 29 December): *In my Prime*
Paul Bley (NYC, 1-3 July): *Axis*
Hamiett Bluiett (NYC): *Birthright, a solo blues concert* (NYC, 15 August): *SOS* (NYC, 21 November/1 December): *Resolution*
Joanne Brackeen (NYC,20 March,9 May): *Tring-a-ling* (NYC, 30 December): *Aft*
Ruby Braff/Dick Hyman (NYC,Spring): *Fats Waller's Heavenly Jive*
Dollar Brand (NYC, 18 September): *The Journey* (NYC, 20 September): *Streams of Consciousness*
Anthony Braxton (Chicago, 22 September): *For Trio*
Bridgewater Brothers (NYC, 10 December): *Lightning & Thunder*
Nick Brignola (NYC,22 December): *Baritone Madness*
Marion Brown (NYC, 2 July): *Solo Saxophone*
Ray Brown (LA, 22,23,24 June): *Something for Lester* (Tokyo, 29 November): *The Most Special Joint* (SF, 22 December): *As Good as it gets*
Dave Brubeck (Montreux, 17 July): *The New Dave Brubeck Quartet Live at Montreux*
Ray Bryant (Montreux, 13 July): *Live in Montreux*
John Bunch (NYC): *Slick Funk* (NYC): *John's Other Bunch*
Kenny Burrell (SF, 23 March): *Tin Tin Deo*
Frank Butler (LA, 19 November): *The Stepper*
Ron Carter (NYC,25 March): *Piccolo* (Tokyo,13 July): *Third Plane*
June Christy (LA, 7-9 June): *Impromptu*
Al Cohn/Jimmy Rowles (NYC,5 March): *Heavy Love*
Dolo Coker (California, 18 November): *Third Down* (NYC, 28 November): *All Alone*
Richie Cole (NJ, December): *Alto Madness*
Earl Coleman (9 September): *A song for you*
George Coleman (NYC, 2,3 November): *Big George*
George Coleman/Tete Montoliu (Holland, 20 February): *Meditation*
Ornette Coleman (NYC, 30 January): *Soapsuds*
Junior Cook (NYC, 1,2 November): *Pressure Cooker*
Chick Corea (NYC,20,21 May): *Return To Forever Live*
Stanley Cowell (NYC,6,8 July): *Waiting for the Monster*
Eddie Daniels (NYC, 11 July): *Brief Encounter*
Richard Davis (NYC, 3,16 May): *Harvest* (Berkeley, 30 June,): *Way Out West* (Berkeley, 30 June, 1

July): *Fancy Free*
Walter Davis: *Abide with me*
Wild Bill Davison/Ralph Sutton (23 May): *Together Again*
Elton Dean (February): *The Cheque is in the mail* (London, 26 July): *Happy Daze*
Buddy de Franco (Quebec, January & May): *Waterbed* (NYC): *Love affair with a clarinet*
Jack De Johnette (Ludwigsburg, May): *New Rags*
Walt Dickerson (NYC, 9 February): *Divine Gemini* (Copenhagen, 6 November): *Shades of Love*
Bruce Ditmas (NYC, 26 October/5 November): *Aeray Dust*
Kenny Drew (Germany, 3 February): *In Concert* (NYC, 6 February): *Lite Flite* (Copenhagen, 23 August): *Ruby, My Dear*
Jon Eardley (London, 12,13 August): *Namely Me*
Jon Eardley/Mick Pyne (London, 12 September): *Two of a Kind*
Charles Earland (NYC): *Mama Roots / Smokin'*
John Eaton (NYC, August/September): *It seems like old times*
Harry Edison (September): *Simply Sweets*
Don Ellis (Montreux, July): *Live at Montreux* (LA): *Star Wars*
Herb Ellis (NYC, October): *Windflower*
Bill Evans (LA, 23,24,25 August): *You must believe in Spring*
Gil Evans (NYC, 13 May): *Priestess*
Tal Farlow (LA, 15 September): *Tal Farlow 78*
Art Farmer (NYC, January): *Crawl Space* (Tokyo, 27 April): *Art Farmer meets Jackie McLean* (NYC, July): *Something you got*
Tommy Flanagan (NYC, 4 February): *Eclypso* (Montreux, 13 July): *Montreux 77* (NYC, 8 December): *Alone Too Long*
Chuck Flores (LA): *Drum Flower*
Ricky Ford (NYC, 16 June): *Loxodonta Africana*
Frank Foster (Tokyo, 29,30 November): *Manhattan Fever*
Chico Freeman (NYC): *Chico* (LA, 21-23 June): *Beyond The Rain* (NYC, September): *Kings of Mali*
Von Freeman (Laren,12 August): *Young and Foolish*
Don Friedman (NYC, 12 September): *Jazz Dancing*
Dave Frishberg (LA, 25,26 January): *Getting some fun out of life*
Eric Gale (NYC): *Multiplication*
Hal Galper (NYC, 15 February): *Now Hear This*
Jan Garbarek/Keith Jarrett (Oslo,November): *My Song*
Red Garland (Berkeley, 2 December): *Red Alert*
Dizzy Gillespie (1,2 February): *Free Ride* (Montreux, 14 July): *Montreux 77*
Gil Goldstein (NYC, 14-16 November): *Pure as Rain*
Dexter Gordon (NYC, 21,22 June): *Sophisticated Giant*
Al Grey/Arnett Cobb (Nice, 11 July): *Al Grey & Arnett Cobb*
Tiny Grimes (NYC, 7,9 April): *One is never too old to swing*
Al Haig (NYC, 18 February): *Serendipity* (NYC, 18 February/12 July): *Manhattan Memories* (NYC, 11 July): *A portrait of Bud Powell* (NYC, 22 July): *Reminiscence* (London, 16 September): *Stablemates* (Paris, 23 September): *Al in Paris* (Paris, 23 September): *Parisian Thoroughfare* (NYC, 5 November): *Plays Dizzy Gillespie*
Bengt Hallberg (Sweden, May): *Hallberg's Happiness*
Scott Hamilton (NYC): *Swinging Young Scott*
Lionel Hampton (NYC, 8,9 July): *Blackout*
Lionel Hampton/Gerry Mulligan (NYC, 19,29 October): *Giants of Jazz* (NYC, 29 October): *Lionel Hampton presents Gerry Mulligan*
Lionel Hampton/Buddy Rich(NYC): *Lionel Hampton presents Buddy Rich*
Billy Harper (NYC, 27,29,30 June): *Love on the Sudan* (NYC, 15,17 December): *Soran-Bushi B.H.*
Beaver Harris (Paris, 26 May): *African Drums*
Earl Hines (Chicago, 9 September/17 October): *Boogie Woogie on the St Louis Blues* (Chicago, 22 September): *East of the Sun* (New Orleans, 7 November): *Earl Hines in New Orleans* (NYC, 30 December): *Texas Ruby Red*
Terumasa Hino (NYC, 7 May): *May Dance* (Tokyo, 10,11 August / NYC, 15 December): *Hip Seagull*
Red Holloway (NYC, November): *Just Friends*
Milt Jackson (LA, 1,2 June): *Soul Fusion*
Willis Jackson (NYC, 8 March): *The Gator Horn*
Leroy Jenkins (NYC, 11 January): *Solo Concert* (NYC, 11 March): *Lifelong Ambition*

JJ Johnson/Nat Adderley (Japan): *The Yokohama Concert*

Hank Jones (LA, 27,28 June): *Just for Fun* (Paris, 28 July): *I remember you* (Germany, 1,2 August): *Have you met this Jones?*

Philly Joe Jones (NYC, 6,7 April): *Mean what you say*

Sam Jones (NYC, 14 September): *Changes & Things*

Max Kaminsky (NYC, 2,3 November): *Blame it on my Youth*

Barney Kessel (Tokyo, 23 February): *Live at Sometime*

Lee Konitz (NYC, January/July): *Tenor Lee* (NYC, 11 June): *Pyramis* (NYC, 18 July): *The Lee Konitz Quintet* (NYC, 19-21 September): *Nonet* (Rome, 29 November): *Duplicity*

Steve Kuhn (Ludwigsburg, January): *Motility*

Steve Lacy (NYC, 29 January): *Raps* (Berlin, 11 April): *Follies – Live in Berlin* (NYC, 19 May): *Threads* (Milan): *Straws* (Basle, 9 June): *Clinkers* (Rome, 17 September): *Catch* (Paris, 15 October): *Shots*

Hugh Lawson (NYC, 20 October): *Prime Time*

George Lewis (NYC): *Chicago Slow Dance*

Cecil McBee (NYC, 3 March): *Compassion* (NYC, 2 August): *Music from The Source*

Howard McGhee (NYC, 19 October): *Jazz Brothers*

Dave McKenna (NYC, 1,2 June): *Dave 'Fingers' McKenna* (NYC, 2,3 October): *McKenna* (NYC): *No Holds Barred*

Charles McPherson (NYC, 28 September): *New Horizons*

Jay McShann (Copenhagen, 12 April): *After Hours*

Shelly Manne (LA, 5,6 July): *Essence*

Shelly Manne/Lee Konitz (11 November): *French Concert*

Warne Marsh (14,15 May/5 June): *Warne Out*

Turk Mauro (NYC, 17,18 October): *The Underdog*

Pat Metheny (Oslo, February): *Watercolours*

Barry Miles (NYC, November): *Fusion Is*

Charles Mingus (Europe, July): *Charles Mingus Memorial Album* (NYC, 6 November): *The Music of Charles Mingus*

Sal Mosca (March/August): *Sal Mosca Music*

Paul Motian (Ludwigsburg, September): *Dance*

Alphonse Mouzon (Stuttgart, November): *In Search of a Dream*

David Murray (NYC, 31 December): *Live at the Lower Manhattan Ocean Club*

Red Norvo (NYC): *Red in New York*

Horace Parlan (15 February): *Hi Fly*

Joe Pass (LA, 4 February): *Quadrant* (May/June): *Virtuoso 3*

N H O Pedersen (Copenhagen, 2,3 October): *Trio*

Art Pepper (LA, 26 March): *No Limit* (NYC, 28-30 July): *More for Les at the Village Vanguard*

Julian Priester (January): *Polarization*

Don Pullen (Montreux, July): *Montreux Concert*

Doug Raney (Copenhagen, September): *Doug Raney*

Freddie Redd (LA, 3 December): *Straight Ahead*

Waymon Reed (NYC, 25 May): *46th and 8th*

Buddy Rich (NYC, October): *Class of 78*

Sam Rivers (Paris, 18 April): *Paragon* (Milan, 28 April): *Rendez-vous*

Red Rodney (NYC, 19 December): *Home Free*

Charlie Rouse (NYC, 20 October): *Moments' Notice*

Jimmy Rowles : *The Peacocks*

Hilton Ruiz (NYC, 8 February): *New York Hilton*

John Scofield (Munich, 4 November): *John Scofield Live*

Ronnie Scott (London, 18 October): *Serious Gold*

Charles 'Bobo' Shaw/Lester Bowie (NYC, 5 February): *Bugle Boy Bop*

Woody Shaw (NYC, 15,17,19 December): *Rosewood*

Archie Shepp (Copenhagen, 25 April): *Goin' Home* (Massachusetts, 7 May): *Ballads for Trane* (NYC, 3 June): *Day Dream* (Rome, 12 October): *The Tradition* (NYC, 28 November): *On Green Dolphin Street*

Carol Sloane (Tokyo, 16 October): *Sophisticated Lady*

Soprano Summit (NYC, 12 September): *Crazy Rhythm*

Jess Stacy (NYC, 19,20 July): *Stacy's Still Swinging*

Lou Stein/Ray McKinley (NYC, 25,26 May): *Stompin' 'em down*

John Stevens (London, 23 May): *No Fear*

Monette Sudler (NYC, 7 November): *Brighter Days for you*

Sun Ra (NYC, 20 May): *Solo Piano, Vol1* (NYC, 3 July): *St Louis Blues* (USA, July): *Somewhere over the rainbow* (Philadelphia, 14 October): *Some blues but not the kind that's blue* (NYC, 24,29 October): *Unity*

Buddy Tate/Dollar Brand (NYC, 25 August): *Buddy Tate Meets Dollar Brand*

John Tchicai (Denmark, 15,29 March): *Darktown Highlights*

Clark Terry (London, September): *Clark after Dark*

Mickey Tucker (NYC, 28 March): *Sojourn*

Stanley Turrentine (NYC, June/July): *Nightwings*

McCoy Tyner (Berkeley, 9-12 April): *Supertrios*

Warren Vaché (NYC, November): *Blues Walk*

Sarah Vaughan (Rio, November): *I Love Brazil*

Charlie Ventura (NYC): *Chazz 77*

Joe Venuti/Dave McKenna (NYC, 27,28 April): *Alone at the Palace*

VSOP (California, 16,18 July): *The Quintet*

Cedar Walton (Copenhagen, 1 October): *First Set / Third Set*

Sadao Watanabe (NYC, 4 May): *Bird of Paradise*

Bob Wilber/Scott Hamilton (NYC, 30 June/1 July): *Bob Wilber & the Scott Hamilton Quartet*

Jack Wilkins (NYC, 31 October): *You can't live without it*

Claude Williamson (May/July): *Holography*

Teddy Wilson: (NYC, 6,12,16,17 June): *Revamps Rodgers & Hart* (NYC): *Cole Porter Classics*

Phil Woods (London, March): *I Remember* (NYC, 9 November): *Song for Sisyphus*

Right: Maxine Sullivan (66) at the 100 Club in London.
Below Left: Dollar Brand (Abdullah Ibrahim) at the Lincoln Center in New York.
Below Right: Sonny Rollins (48).

1978

Charlie Mingus (56) is guest of honour at an all-star concert (18 June) on the lawns of the White House. Dexter Gordon (55), Roy Eldridge (67), Illinois Jacquet (55), Dizzy Gillespie (61), Lionel Hampton (70), Max Roach (54), Billy Taylor (57) Stan Getz (51) and Ornette Coleman (48) are all featured. President Carter embraces the weeping Mingus.

Johnny Griffin (50) returns to US for the first time in 15 years to play at the Monterey Festival in September.

Don Ellis dies in December, aged 44.

DEATHS

Chuck Peterson (62) 21 January
Gregory Herbert (30) 31 January
Alix Combelle (65) 27 February
Joe Marsala (71) 4 March
Louis Cottrell Jr (67) 21 March
Harold 'Money' Johnson (60) 28 March
Larry Young (37) 30 March
Ray Noble (74) 2 April
Teddy Hill (68) 19 May
Shad Collins (68) June
Matty Matlock (71) 14 June
Quinn Wilson (69) 14 June
Lennie Hastings (51) 14 July stroke
Teddy Bunn (69) 20 July
Joe Venuti (74) 14 August cancer
Irene Kral (46) 15 August
Louis Prima (65) 24 August
Beryl Booker (56) 30 September
Abbie Brunies (78) 2 October
Jimmy Nottingham (52) 16 November
Lennie Tristano (59) 17 November
Frank Rosolino (52) 26 November suicide
Walt Yoder (64) 2 December
Blanche Calloway (76) 16 December
Don Ellis (44) 17 December
Erskine Tate (82) 17 December
Happy Cauldwell (75) 29 December
Freddie Jenkins (72)
Alton 'Slim' Moore (70)

BOOKS

Joachim Berendt: The Story of Jazz
Michael Budds: Jazz in the Sixties
Ray Charles & David Ritz: Brother Ray
Jerry Coker: Listening to Jazz
James Lincoln Collier: The Making of Jazz
Julie Coryell & Laura Friedman: Jazz-Rock Fusion
Brian Case & Stan Britt: The Illustrated Encyclopaedia of Jazz
Vince Danca: Bunny: a bio discography of Jazz Trumpeter Bunny Berigan
Mercer Ellington & Stanley Dance: Duke Ellington in Person
Mark Gridley: Jazz Styles
James Haskins & Kathleen Benson: Scott Joplin
David Jasen & Trebor Tichenor: Rags and Ragtime
Jimmy Lyons & Ira Kamin: Dizzy, Duke, the Count and Me: the story of the Monterey Jazz Festival
Donald Marquis: In Search of Buddy Bolden
Donald Marquis: Finding Buddy Bolden
Leroy Ostransky: Jazz City: the impact of our cities on the development of jazz
Nat Shapiro: An Encyclopaedia of Quotations about Music
Harold Sill: Misbehavin' with Fats (novel for children based on the life of Fats Waller)
Maurice Summerfield: The Jazz Guitar: its evolution and its players
Leo Walker: The Big Band Almanac
Mark White: The Observer's Book of Jazz

RECORDS

George Adams (NYC, 21 December): Paradise Space Shuttle
Pepper Adams (NYC, 14 June): Reflectory
Nat Adderley/Johnny Griffin (Berkeley, 18,19 September): A little New York Midtown Music
Air (NYC, 21,22 February): Open Air Suit
Toshiko Akiyoshi (LA,3,4 April): Plays Billy Strayhorn (SF,8 May): Finesse (LA,5,6 December): Plays Toshiko
Akiyoshi/Tabackin (LA, 15,16 November): Salted Ginko Nuts
Monty Alexander (LA, 15,16 June): Jamento
Laurindo Almeida (LA, 27,28 March): Concierto de Aranjuez (LA, September): Chamber Jazz

Neil Ardley (London, July, September): Harmony of the Spheres
Art Ensemble of Chicago (Germany,May): Nice Guys
Harold Ashby (Paris, 17 May): Scufflin' (NYC, 7 August): Presenting Harold Ashby
Chet Baker (Laren, 30 November): Live at Nick's (Paris, 28 December): Broken Wing (Paris, 29 December): Two a day
Benny Bailey (Germany, April): East of Isar (NYC, 14 October): Grand Slam
Bill Barron (NYC, August): Jazz Caper
Count Basie/Oscar Peterson (LA, 21,22 February): Yessir, that's my baby / Night Rider
Louis Bellson (January): Sunshine Rock / Prime Time
Bill Berry (LA,11,12 January): For Duke (LA): Shortcake
Walter Bishop Jr (NYC, 21 June): Cubicle
Art Blakey (SF, 8 May): In this Korner (Holland, 4 December): Reflections in Blue (NYC, 29 December): In my Prime
Carla Bley (NYC, August-November): Musique Mechanique
Lester Bowie/Phillip Wilson (NYC,19 January): Duet
Lester Bowie (Rome, 16 April): African Children
Joanne Brackeen (NYC, 13 August): Trinkets and things (NYC, August): Prism (Villingen, 25,26 September): Mythical Magic
Ruby Braff (NYC, 4,5 May): Pretties
Nick Brignola (NYC, 30 October): New York Bound
Bob Brookmeyer (NYC, 23,25 May): Back Again (July): Live at Sandy's
Marion Brown (NYC, 3 July): Passion Flower (NYC, 14,15 November): Soul Eyes
Marion Brown/Gunther Hampel (NYC, 30 January): Reeds'n'Vibes
Dave Brubeck (LA, 27,28 February): A Cut Above
Ray Bryant (NYC, 10 April): All Blues
Monty Budwig (January): Dig
Kenny Burrell (NYC, 28 February, 1 March): Hand crafted (SF, September): When Lights are Low (NYC, 15 December): In New York / Live at the Village Vanguard
Gary Burton/Chick Corea (Oregon,23,25 October): Duet
Frank Butler (LA, 22 October): Wheelin' and Dealin'
Jaki Byard (NYC, 28 April, 1 May): Family Man
Charlie Byrd (California, August): Blue Bird
Capp/Pierce Juggernaut (LA, 14 July): The Capp/Pierce Juggernaut
Ron Carter (NYC, June): A Song For You (Tokyo, 30 July): Carnaval (NYC, December): Pick 'em
Arnett Cobb (August): Live at Sandy's
Richie Cole (NJ, 6 September): Keeper of the Flame
George Coleman (NYC, 29 December): Amsterdam after dark
Chick Corea (LA): The Mad Hatter (LA): Friends
Chick Corea/Lionel Hampton (Paris, January): Chick & Lionel Live at Midem
Stanley Cowell (Berkeley, 28-30 November): Equipoise / New World
Ted Curson/Dizzy Reece (NYC,9 June): Blowin' Away
Albert Dailey (13 July): That Old Feeling
Kenny Davern (NYC, 30 May): Unexpected
Walter Davis (NYC, 15 December): Night Song
Eddie 'Lockjaw' Davis/Harry Edison (Paris, 30 November): All of me
Buddy de Franco: Listen and sit-in
Jack De Johnette (Oslo, June): New Directions
Walt Dickerson (NYC, 6 July): To my Queen Revisited (NYC, 11 July): Visions (Copenhagen, 29 September): Trio: for my son
Arne Domnerus/Bengt Hallberg (NYC, 5,6 September): Two Swedes in New York
Kenny Drew (LA, 15 October): Home is where the soul is (LA, 16 October): For sure!
Ted Dunbar (NYC, 24 January): Opening Remarks
Charles Earland (NYC, 19 April): Infant Eyes (NYC, 19 April): Pleasant Afternoon

Herb Ellis (SF, August): Soft and Mellow
Rolf Ericson/Johnny Griffin (Berlin, 26,27 May): Sincerely Ours
Bill Evans (NYC,January/February): New Conversations (NYC, 30,31 October, 1,2 November): Affinity
Gil Evans (London): Live at the Royal Festival Hall (29 July): Parabola
Jon Faddis (NYC, August/September): Good and Plenty
Art Farmer/Jim Hall (NYC, February): Big Blues
Joe Farrell (LA): Night Dancing
Tommy Flanagan/Hank Jones (Berkeley, 28 January): Our Delight
Tommy Flanagan (Berkeley, 30 January): Something Borrowed, Something Blue (NYC, 15 November): Ballads & Blues (NYC, 21 November): The Super Jazz Trio
Ricky Ford (NYC, 1 August): Manhattan Plaza
Jimmy Forrest/Shirley Scott (Grand Rapids, 28 December): Heart of the Forrest
Frank Foster (Helsinki, July): Twelve Shades of Black (NYC, 27,28 November): Shiny Stockings (NYC, 7 December): Roots, Branches and Dances
Don Friedman (NYC, 21 March): The Progressive (NYC, 26 June): Hot Kneppers and Pepper (NYC, 30 August): Gone with the wind (NYC, 12 September): Love Music
Dave Frishberg (LA, 10 July): You're a Lucky Guy
Curtis Fuller (NYC, 18 September): Four on the Outside (NYC, 6 December): Fire and Filigree
Jim Galloway/Dick Wellstood (Toronto, 16,17 November, 29 December): Walking on Air
Ganelin Trio (Moscow, March): Strictly for our friends
Jan Garbarek (Oslo, December): Photo with...
Red Garland (NYC, 15 May): Feelin' Red (Berkeley, 4,5 August): Equinox
Terry Gibbs (California, 12 March): Live at the Lord (California, 30 July): Smoke 'em up!
Dexter Gordon (NYC): Manhattan Symphonie (Carnegie Hall, NYC,23 September): Great Encounter
Stephane Grapelli (NYC,5 April): Live at Carnegie Hall
Al Grey/Jimmy Forrest (Chicago,July): Live at Rick's
Johnny Griffin (Berkeley, 17 October): Return of the Griffin (Berkeley, 18,19 October): Bush Dance
Charlie Haden/Christian Escoude (Paris, 22 September): Gitane
Al Haig (NYC): Plays the Music of Jerome Kern (London, 14 October): Expressly Ellington
Jim Hall/Red Mitchell (NYC, 20,21 January): Live at Sweet Basil
Scott Hamilton/Warren Vaché (NYC): With Scott's Band in New York City
Scott Hamilton/Buddy Tate (SF, September): Back to Back
Lionel Hampton (NYC,July): All Star Band at Newport
Herbie Hancock (Tokyo, 17,18 October): Direct Step (Tokyo, 25,26 October): The Piano
Bill Hardman (NJ, 10 January): Home
Barry Harris (NYC, 17 January): Plays Barry Harris
Andrew Hill (12 October): From California With Love
Earl Hines/Harry Edison (Berne, 26 April): Earl Meets Harry (Berne, 30 April): Earl Meets Sweets and Jaws
Shirley Horn (9 July): A Lazy Afternoon
Freddie Hubbard: Super Blue
Dick Hyman (Washington): Music of Jelly Roll Morton
Abdullah Ibrahim (Tokyo, 10 June): Anthem for the New Nations (Lyon, 18 June): Autobiography (Stuttgart, 4 October): Nisa
Milt Jackson/Count Basie (LA, 18 January): Milt Jackson/Count Basie
Milt Jackson (LA, 20 January, 18,19 September): Soul Believer
Willis Jackson/Pat Martino (NYC, 26 April): Single Action
Willis Jackson/Von Freeman (Laren, 11 August): Lockin' Horns
Illinois Jacquet (Paris, March): God Bless my Solo
Leroy Jenkins (Milan, July): The Legend of Al Glatson (NYC, August/September): Space Minds, New Worlds, Survival of America
Elvin Jones (Stuttgart, 3,4,5 February): Remembrance (8,9 April): Live in Japan
Etta Jones (NYC, 21 June): If you could see me now
Hank Jones (NYC, 25 January): Groovin' High (NYC, 5 April): Milestones (17 July): Compassion (Berkeley, 5,6 August): Ain't Misbehavin'
Jonah Jones (Paris, 21 July): Confessin'
Philly Joe Jones (Berkeley, 10-12 October): Drum Song / Advance!

1978

Sam Jones (NYC, 20 March): *Visitation*

Clifford Jordan (NYC, 9 February): *The Adventurer* (NYC, 25 July): *Hello Hank Jones*

Duke Jordan (NYC, 30 June): *Duke's Artistry / The Great Session*

Roger Kellaway (LA, 18-20 September): *The Nostalgia Suite*

Eric Kloss (NYC, 4,5 January): *Now*

Jimmy Knepper (NYC, 20 October): *Just Friends*

Steve Kuhn (Ludwigsburg, April): *Non-Fiction*

Guy Lafitte (Paris, 29 March): *Corps et Ame*

Steve Lacy (Amsterdam, 9,10 December): *High, Low and Order*

LA4 (LA): *Watch what happens / Just Friends*

Oliver Lake/Julius Hemphill (NYC, 16 February): *Life Dance of Is* (Toronto, 1 March): *Buster Bee*

John Lewis (Brignoles, 19 July): *Mirjana*

Dave Liebman (NYC, 4,5 February): *Pendulum*

Humphrey Lyttelton (London, 18 October): *Spreadin' Joy* (Chichester, October): *Humphrey's About*

Howard McGhee (10,11 March): *Live at Emerson's*

Howard McGhee/Benny Bailey (NYC, 11 October): *Home Run*

Ken McIntyre (NYC, 7 July): *Chasing the Sun*

Jackie McLean (NYC,6,7 April): *New Wine, Old Bottles*

Marian McPartland (SF, December): *From this moment on*

Charles McPherson (NYC, 23 October): *Free Bop!*

Jay McShann (Toronto, 20,21 June): *Kansas City Hustle*

Albert Mangelsdorff (Stuttgart, 25-29 August): *A Jazz Tune I Hope*

Shelly Manne (LA): *Jazz Crystallizations* (LA, 15 December): *The Manne we love*

George Masso (NYC, 16 October): *Choice NYC Bone*

Ronnie Mathews (NYC, 7 December): *Roots, Branches and Dances*

George Melly (London): *Melly sings Hoagy*

Charles Mingus Band (NYC, 18,23 January): *Something like a bird* (NYC, 19,23 January): *Me, Myself an eye*

Billy Mitchell (NYC, 18 April): *The Colossus of Detroit*

Louis Moholo (London, 24 January): *Spirits Rejoice*

David Murray (Milan, February): *Interboogieology* (London, 11 August): *The London Concert* (3 September): *3-D Family*

Joe Newman (London, 20 July): *I love my baby*

Maggie Nichols/Julie Tippetts (London, June): *Sweet and S'ours*

Sal Nistico (NYC, 3 November): *Neo/Nistico*

Walter Norris (NYC, 17 July): *Stepping on Cracks*

Charles Owens (LA, 24 February): *Two Quartets*

Jimmy Owens (NYC): *Headin' Home*

Evan Parker (30 April): *Monoceros* (London, 29,30 July): *Circadian Rhythm* (Berkeley, 2 November): *At the Finger Palace*

Horace Parlan (Oslo, 15 February): *Hi-Fly* (Copenhagen, 13 November): *Blue Parlan*

Joe Pass (LA, 8 May): *Tudo Bem*

Joe Pass/Niels Pederson (London,19 November): *Chops*

Art Pepper (LA, 2 September): *Among Friends* (Berkeley, 1,2 December): *Today*

Bill Perkins (LA, 3,7 October): *Bill Perkins plays Lester Young* (LA, 20 November): *Confluence*

Oscar Peterson (5 October): *The Paris Concert* (21 October): *The London Concert*

Flip Phillips/Woody Herman (LA,5 January): *Together*

Nat Pierce (LA, 21 May): *5400 North*

Dave Pike (LA,22,23 March): *Let the Minstrels play on*

Pony Poindexter (San Luis Obispo, March): *Poindexter*

Dudu Pukwana (2-5 September): *Yi Yole*

Don Pullen (Milan, December): *Milano Strut*

Doug Raney (Copenhagen,17 August): *Cuttin' Loose*

Dewey Redman (California, 17-19 October): *Musics*

Dizzy Reece (NYC, 17 January): *Manhattan Project* (NYC, 9 June): *Blowin' Away*

Sam Rivers (NYC, August): *Waves*

Max Roach (Paris, 10 June): *Confirmation* (Milan, September): *Birth and Rebirth*

Sonny Rollins (SF, 13-15 April): *Don't stop the Carnival* (SF, New Haven, Madison, September, October): *Milestone Jazz Stars*

Frank Rosolino (30 August): *In Denmark*

Jimmy Rowles (NYC, 4 April): *We could make such beautiful music together* (NYC, 27 May): *Isfahan* (SF): *As good as it gets* (Paris, 21 July): *Shade and Light / Nature Boy / Scarab / Red'n'me*

Marshall Royal: *First Chair*

Hilton Ruiz (NYC, 9 December): *Fantasia*

Sal Salvador (NYC, 24 March): *Starfingers* (NYC, 5 September): *Juicy Lucy*

David Sanborn (NYC, January): *Heart to Heart*

John Scofield (Stuttgart,27 November): *Rough House*

Bud Shank (California, 19 December): *Heritage*

Woody Shaw (NYC, 5,6 July): *Stepping Stones* (NYC): *Woody III*

Archie Shepp (NYC, 7 December): *Lady Bird*

Archie Shepp/Dollar Brand (Tokyo, 5 June): *Duet*

Bobby Shew (4 March, 16 April): *Telepathy*

Zoot Sims (NYC, 18,19 September): *Warm Tenor* (NYC, 28,29 November): *The Sweetest Sounds*

Zoot Sims/Harry Edison (LA, 18,20 December): *Just Friends*

Martial Solal (Villingen, 28 February): *The Solo Solal*

John Stevens (London, 25 February): *Integration* (London, 31 August): *Application, Interaction And*

Sonny Stitt (NYC, 25 April): *Meets Sadik Hakim*

Kathy Stobart (London,28 February, 1 March): *Arbeia*

Monette Sudler (Copenhagen, 8 June): *Live in Europe*

Ira Sullivan (Berkeley, 20,21 September): *Peace*

Sun Ra (Rome, 2,7 January): *New Steps*

Supersax (Villingen, 24-28 April): *Supersax Dynamite*

Buddy Tate/Bob Wilber (29 January): *Sherman Shuffle*

Buddy Tate (Toronto,16 July): *The Buddy Tate Quartet*

Joe Temperley/Jimmy Knepper (NYC, 20 October): *Just Friends*

Clark Terry (July): *Out of Nowhere*

Barbara Thompson: *Jubiaba*

Eddie Thompson (London, 23 September): *Ain't She Sweet*

Cal Tjader (22,23 March): *Huracan*

Mickey Tucker (NJ, 23 June): *Mister Mysterious* (NJ, 15,16 November): *Theme for a boogie-woogie*

Norris Turney (France, 16 May): *I Let a Song*

Stanley Turrentine (Philadelphia, June, July): *What about you?*

McCoy Tyner (Tokyo, 28 July): *Passion Dance* (Berkeley, 31 August, 3 September): *Together*

James 'Blood' Ulmer (NYC, 5 December): *Tales of Captain Black*

Rene Urtreger (Paris): *Recidive*

Warren Vaché (SF, November): *Jillian* (Chester, NJ, 31 December): *Jersey Jazz at Midnight*

Sarah Vaughan (25 April): *How long has this been going on?*

Eddie 'Cleanhead' Vinson (LA, 22 February): *The Clean Machine* (August): *Live at Sandy's*

Mal Waldron (6,8 May): *Moods*

Bill Watrous (LA): *Watrous in Hollywood*

Dick Wellstood (NYC, January): *Ain't Misbehavin'*

Bob Wilber (NYC, 15,16 November): *Original Wilber*

Buster Williams (NYC,28,30 March,3 April): *Heartbeat*

Claude Williamson (NYC, 22 March, 8 June): *New Departure*

Kai Winding (Rome, 17 NOvember): *Duo Bones*

Mike Wofford (LA, 30 January): *Afterthoughts*

Chris Woods (Copenhagen): *Modus Operandi*

Phil Woods (London, March): *I Remember* (Austin, Texas, 23,26 May): *More Live*

Richard Wyands (NYC,12 October): *Then, Here and Now*

Snooky Young/Marshall Royal (LA): *Snooky & Marshall's Album*

Barry Zweig (8 January): *Desert Vision*

Mike Zwerin (Paris, 31 October, 1 November): *Not Much Choice*

Left: Art Blakey (59) and Dizzy Gillespie (61) backstage at the Middlesbrough Jazz Festival.

Below: **Chick Corea.**

Photo: *David Redfern*

Photo: *David Redfern*

Charlie Mingus dies in Mexico on 5 January aged 56.

Red Mitchell (52) returns to the US after 11 years resident in Sweden.

Stan Kenton dies on 25 August aged 67.

First Paris Jazz Festival.

Jack De Johnette (37) forms Special Edition, with Arthur Blythe (39) and David Murray (24) on saxophones.

DEATHS

Charlie Mingus (56) 5 January *sclerosis*
Sabu Martinez (48) 13 January
Fred Elizalde (71) 16 January
Sonny Payne (53) 29 January
Grant Green (47) 31 January
Peanuts Holland (68) 7 February
Zbigniew Seifert (32) 15 February
Raymond Fol (51) 1 May
Eddie Jefferson (60) 9 May *shot outside Detroit club*
Vernon Brown (72) 18 May
Bill Rank (74) 20 May
Blue Mitchell (49) 21 May *cancer*
Pee Wee Hunt (72) 22 June
Alton Redd (75) June
Henry Goodwin (69) 2 July
Matthew Gee (53) 18 July
Stan Kenton (67) 25 August
Wilbur Ware (56) 9 September
John Simmons (61) 19 September
Corky Corcoran (55) 3 October
David Izenson (47) 8 October
Henry Coker (59) 23 November
Edgar Hayes (75)

BOOKS

Stanley Baron: *Benny, King of Swing*
Joachim Berendt: *Jazz: A Photo History*
Sandy Brown: *The McJazz Manuscripts*
John Chilton: *Teach Yourself Jazz*
Dizzy Gillespie & Al Fraser: *To Be or not to Bop*
Chris Goddard: *Jazz away from home*
William Gottlieb: *The Golden Age of Jazz*
Kitty Grime: *Jazz at Ronnie Scott's*
Sheldon Harris: *Blues Who's Who*
Humphrey Lyttelton: *The Best of Jazz: Basin Street to Harlem*
Humphrey Lyttelton: *Jazz & Big Band Quiz*
Charles Nanry: *The Jazz Text*
Art Pepper: *Straight Life: The Story of Art Pepper*
Al Rose: *Eubie Blake*
Ronnie Scott: *Some of my best friends are blues*
Michael Ullman: *Jazz Lives*

RECORDS

John Abercrombie (Oslo, 19,20 March): *Straight Flight* (Oslo, November): *Abercrombie Quartet*
Muhal Richard Abrams (NYC, July): *Spihumonesty*
George Adams (Ludwigsburg, May): *Sound Suggestions* (NYC, 21 December):*Paradise Space Shuttle*
George Adams/Don Pullen (Milan, 2,3 November): *Don't lose control / All that funk / More funk*
Pepper Adams (Paris, June): *Bebop*
Air (NYC, 11,12 May): *Air Lore*
Joe Albany (NYC, 4 January): *Bird Lives*
Monty Alexander (Tokyo, 22 January): *In Tokyo* (Villingen, May): *The way it is* (SF, August): *Facets* (Geneva, 7 October): *So what*
Mousey Alexander (NYC): *The Mouse Roars*
Barry Altschul (NYC, 18 February): *For Stu* (Moers, 2 June): *Somewhere else*
Amalgam (November): *Wipe out*
Derek Bailey/Tony Coe (London, 23,24 April): *Time*
Chet Baker (Stuttgart, 8,9 January): *Ballads for two* (Copenhagen, 21 June): *The touch of your lips* (London, 4,5 September): *Rendezvous* (London, 5 September): *All Blues* (Stockholm, 2 October): *No Problem* (Copenhagen, 4 October): *Daybreak / This is Always*
Billy Bang/John Lindberg (LA, 29 September): *Duo*
Chris Barber (Ludwigsburg, 17 October): *Come Friday*
Mike & Gary Barone (LA, 27,28 December): *Blues & Other Happy Moments*
Count Basie (Montreux, 12 July): *On the Road*
Gordon Beck (London, 21-23 June): *Seven Steps to Evans* (Paris, June, July): *Sun Bird*

Louis Bellson (Concord, August): *Dynamite!*
Art Blakey (Tokyo, 12 February): *Night in Tunisia* (Milan, 4 November): *One by one*
Arthur Blythe (NYC): *In the tradition*
Joe Bonner (Copenhagen, 8 February): *Parade*
Joanne Brackeen (NYC): *Keyed in*
Anthony Braxton (Willisau, 1 September): *Performance for Quartet 1979*
Nick Brignola (Chicago, 19 June): *The Burn Brigade* (LA, 17 October): *L.A. Bound*
Marion Brown (NYC,June): *November Cotton Flower*
Ray Brown (Concord, August): *Live at the Concord Jazz Festival*
Ray Brown/Jimmy Rowles (SF, October): *Tasty!*
Dave Brubeck (Concord, August): *Back Home*
Dave Burrell (Basle, 13 September): *Windward Passages*
Kenny Burrell (SF, December): *Moon and Sand*
Charlie Byrd (Concord, August): *Sugarloaf Suite*
George Cables (LA, 17-19 December): *Cables' Vision*
Jackie Cain & Roy Kral (NYC, October): *Star Sounds*
Ron Carter (NJ, March): *Parade*
Doc Cheatham/Sammy Price (Toronto, 31 October): *Black Beauty*
John Coates (Tokyo, 28 November): *Tokyo Concert*
Al Cohn (NYC, 18 December): *No Problem*
Richie Cole (25 April): *Hollywood Madness*
George Coleman (Ronnie Scott's, London, April): *Playing Changes*
Ornette Coleman (NYC, April): *Of Human Feelings*
Cal Collins (SF, April): *Blues on my mind* (SF, December): *By Myself*
Junior Cook (NYC, 7 June): *Good Cookin'*
Bob Cooper (LA, 6 May): *Tenor Sax Jazz Impressions*
Chick Corea/Gary Burton (Zurich, 28 October): *In Concert*
Ted Curson (NYC, 3 January): *The Trio*
Andrew Cyrille (Milan, June): *Nuba*
Eddie Daniels (Milan, October): *Demoiselle*
Harold Danko (NYC, April): *Coincidence* (NYC): *Chasin' the bad guys*

Eddie 'Lockjaw' Davis (NYC, 18 January): *The Heavy Hitter*
Walter Davis Jr (Milan, 22 November): *A being such as you* (Milan, 23 November): *Blues Walk* (Paris, December): *400 years ago tomorrow*
Kenny Davern (1 July): *The Hot Three*
Kenny Davern/Ralph Sutton (NYC, 12,13 December): *Kenny Davern/Ralph Sutton Trio*
Rein de Graaf (NYC, 6 February): *New York Jazz*
Jack De Johnette (NYC, March): *Special Edition* (Switzerland, June): *New Directions in Europe*
Jimmy Deuchar (Edinburgh, 24 April): *The Scots Connection*
Dorothy Donegan (Paris,15,16 March):*Makin' Whoopee*
Joe Douglas (London, 23,24 January): *Visage*
Herb Ellis (Montreux, July): *Montreux Summer '79*
Ensemble Muntu (NYC):*The Evening of the Blue Men*
Bill Evans (Berkeley, 11-13 May): *I will say goodbye* (NYC, 6-9 August): *We will meet again Paris, 26 November):* The Paris Concerts
Digby Fairweather (28-30 November, 1 December): *Goin' out steppin'*
Art Farmer (NYC, April): *Yama* (Tokyo, 25 May): *Something Tasty*
Joe Farrell (LA, 29 January): *Skateboard Park* (LA, 27,28 November): *Sonic Text*
Malachi Favors (Cologne, 5 June): *African Magic*
Clare Fischer (June): *Clare Fischer & the Ex-42*
Ella Fitzgerald (Montreux, 12 July): *Basie & Ella*
Tommy Flanagan (NYC, 14-17 November): *Communication*
Frank Foster (Belgium, 24 February): *Chiquito Loco / A blues ain't nothin' but a trip*
Panama Francis (Paris, 31 January, 11 February): *Gettin' in the Groove*
Chico Freeman (Milan, 8,9 June): *No Time Left* (NYC, September): *Spirit Sensitive*
Don Friedman (Ludwigsburg, 20 May): *Themes and Variations* (NYC, 12 November): *Avenue of the Americas*
Red Garland (Berkeley, 9,10 July): *Stepping out* (Berkeley, 11,12 July): *Strike up the band*
Stan Getz (Holland, November): *Forest Eyes*
Dexter Gordon (SF, 23,24,27 March): *Nights at the Keystone*
Liz Gorrill (NYC): *I feel like I'm home*
Stephane Grappelli (Copenhagen, 6 July): *At the Tivoli Gardens*
Stephane Grappelli/Hank Jones (London, 20 July): *London Meeting*
Dave Green (Hatfield, 29 May): *Fingers remember Mingus*
Al Grey/Tony Coe (London, April): *Get it together*

Photo: *David Redfern*

1979

Johnny Griffin (Village Vanguard, NYC, 6,7 July): *NYC Underground* (NYC, 27,28 November): *To the Ladies*
Charlie Haden (Oslo, July): *Magico*
Scott Hamilton (SF, December): *Tenor Shoes*
Scott Hamilton/Warren Vache (NYC, July): *Skyscrapers*
Scott Hamilton/Buddy Tate (SF): *Back to Back*
Lionel Hampton (Holland,20 May): *Hamp in Haarlem*
Herbie Hancock (Tokyo, 29 July): *Five Stars*
Roland Hanna (Nice, 14 July): *Impressions* (Tokyo, 6 September): *Sunrise, sunset*
Billy Harper (Milan,24,25 January):*Quintet in Europe* (Paris, 29 January): *The Awakening*
Beaver Harris (Massachusetts, 7 December): *Negcaumongus*
Louis Hayes (NYC): *Variety is the Spice*
Roy Haynes (Paris,21 December):*Live at the Riverbop*
Heath Brothers (NYC): *Live at the Public Theatre / In Motion*
Joe Henderson (LA, 20 August, 29 December): *Relaxin' at Camarillo*
Woody Herman (Monterey, 15 September): *Woody and Friends*
John Hicks (NYC, 5,6 January): *After the Morning*
Billy Higgins (Milan, 21 January): *Soweto* (NYC, 3 December): *The Soldier*
Freddie Hubbard (LA, December): *Skagly*
Helen Humes: *Helen Humes and the Muse All-Stars*
Abdullah Ibrahim (Stuttgart, 11 March): *Africa/Tears and Laughter* (Ludwigsburg,7 September): *Echoes from Africa* (NYC, December): *African Marketplace*
Milt Jackson/Sonny Stitt (Milan, 11 November): *Loose Walk*
Oliver Jackson (France, 28 February): *Oliver Jackson Trio*
Keith Jarrett (Ludwigsburg, November): *The Moth and the Flame*
Leroy Jenkins (NYC, 22,23 March): *Mixed Quintet*
Dick Johnson (SF, May): *Dick Johnson Plays*
J.J. Johnson (California,17-19 September): *Pinnacles*
Elvin Jones (NJ, 13,14,20 June): *Very R.A.R.E.*
Hank Jones (Tokyo, 17,20 April): *Easy to Love* (Kagoshima, 2 May): *Live in Japan* (London, 22 July): *Bluesette*
Sam Jones (NYC, 3 January): *The Bassist* (NYC, 4 June): *Something New*
Thad Jones (Copenhagen, 17,18 September): *Eclipse*
Duke Jordan (Copenhagen): *Midnight Moonlight* (Copenhagen, 11 July, 29 October): *Thinking of you* (Copenhagen, 29 October): *Change a pace*
Sheila Jordan (NYC, July): *Playground*
Eric Kloss (NYC, 6,7 January): *Celebration*

Jimmy Knepper (Holland, 14 August): *Tell me*
Lee Konitz (17 April): *Yes, Yes, Nonet*
Steve Lacy (Basle, 23 January): *The Way* (Rome, 19 February): *Eronel* (Milan, 24,25 May): *Troubles* (Paris,14 December): *Tips* (NYC,29 December): *Capers*
Guy Lafitte/Hank Jones (Paris, July): *Happy*
LA4 (Montreux, July): *Live at Montreux*
Yusef Lateef (May): *In a Temple Garden*
John Lewis/Hank Jones (NYC, 25,26 January, 8,9 February): *An evening with two grand pianos*
John Lewis (France, 19 July): *Mirjana* (Paris, 29 November): *Piano, Paris 1979*
Mel Lewis (NYC,20,21 March):*Naturally* (Saalfelden, 9 September): *The New Mel Lewis Quintet Live*
Dave Liebman (NYC, August): *Doin' it again* (NYC, September): *Dedications*
Humphrey Lyttelton (July): *Sir Humph's Delight*
Cecil McBee (NYC): *Alternate Spaces*
Howard McGhee/Teddy Edwards (California, 4-6 October): *Young at Heart*
Dave McKenna (SF, May): *Giant Strides* (SF, December): *Left Handed Compliment*
Jackie McLean (NYC, January): *Monuments*
Jim McNeely (NJ,4 May, 27 June): *The Plot Thickens*
John McNeil (NYC, 16 April): *Faun*
Ronnie Mathews (NYC, 21 September): *Legacy*
Don Menza (LA, 1,2 May): *Horn of Plenty*
Butch Miles (NYC): *Salutes Chick Webb*
Mingus Dynasty (NYC, 9,10 July): *Chair in the Sky*
Grover Mitchell (LA,18 March):*Meet Grover Mitchell*
J.R. Monterose (Albany, NY, May): *Live in New York*
Danny Moss/Geoff Simkins (London, 15 October): *Straighten up and fly right*
Sam Most/Joe Farrell (LA,23,24 January):*Flute Talk*
David Murray (Milan, 4,5 December): *Sweet Lovely*
Joe Newman/Jimmy Rowles (London,14 July):*Duets*
Horace Parlan (Copenhagen, 26 November): *Musically Yours / The Maestro*
Joe Pass (LA, 17 February): *I remember Charlie Parker* (The Hague, July): *Northsea Nights* (Montreux, 12 July): *Digital 3 at Montreux*
Cecil Payne (London, 20 July): *Bright Moments*
N.H.O. Pedersen (Copenhagen, 3,4 July): *Dancing on the tables*
Art Pepper (NYC, 23 February): *So in Love* (Tokyo, 16,23 July): *Landscape – Art Pepper Live in Tokyo / Besame Mucho* (Berkeley,21 September):*Straight Life*
Oscar Peterson (Toronto, 11,12 April): *Night Child* (Montreux, 16 July): *Digital at Montreux*
Oscar Peterson/Stephane Grappelli (Copenhagen, 6 July): *Skol*
Jimmy & Doug Raney (NYC, 19 April): *Stolen Moments* (NYC, 21 April): *Duets*

Don Rendell (London, 18 June): *Earth Music*
Red Richards (21,22 February): *In a Mellow Tone*
Dannie Richmond (Milan, 23,24 November): *Ode to Mingus*
Howard Riley (Ludwigsburg, April): *Endgame*
Sam Rivers (Ludwigsburg, December): *Contrasts*
Max Roach (Willisau, 30 August): *The Long March* (Willisau, 31 August): *One in Two/Two in One* (Milan, 10,11,17 September): *Pictures in a Frame*
Max Roach/Cecil Taylor (NYC, 15 December): *Historic Concerts*
Howard Roberts (LA,6 November):*Turning to Spring*
Red Rodney (NYC, 13,14 March): *The 3 R's*
Sonny Rollins (15-18 May): *Don't Ask*
Jimmy Rowles (Warsaw, 26,27 April): *My Mother's Love* (London, 19 December): *Ellington by Rowles*
Roswell Rudd (Rome, 6 March): *The Definitive Roswell Rudd*
Teddy Saunders (LA, 12,13 January): *Sue Blue*
Dave Schnitter (NYC, 10 July): *Glowing*
John Scofield (Brooklyn): *Who's Who*
Bud Shank (California, October): *Crystal Comments*
George Shearing (Villingen, 19-21 September): *Getting in the swing of things / On Target* (Washington, 2-7 October): *Blues Alley Jazz*
Jack Sheldon (LA): *Singular*
Archie Shepp (Paris, 9 January): *Things have got to change* (Paris, 25 January): *Bird Fire* (Tokyo, 11 April): *Tray of Silver*
Bobby Shew (LA, 1 May, 3 July): *Outstanding in his field...*
Zoot Sims (LA, 14 August, 10,11 December): *Passion Flower* (LA, 10,11 December): *The Swinger*
Louis Smith (NYC, 13 April): *Prancin'*
Martial Solal/Lee Konitz (Villingen, May): *Four Keys*
Peter Sprague (LA, 8 June): *Dance of the Universe*
Louis Stewart (Dublin, 15 August): *Alone together* (Dublin & London): *I thought about you*
Sonny Stitt (Paris, 12 November): *Back to my own home town*
Sun Ra (Philadelphia): *Sound Mirror*
Ralph Sutton/Ruby Braff (NYC, 29,30 October): *Ralph Sutton & Ruby Braff*
Ralph Sutton (NYC, 10,11 December): *The Other Side of Ralph Sutton*
Lew Tabackin (LA, August): *Black & Tan Fantasy*
Horace Tapscott (NYC, 5 January): *In New York*
Martin Taylor (London): *Taylor Made*
Clark Terry (NYC, 15,16 March): *Ain't Misbehavin'*
Joe Thomas (April): *Raw Meat*
Cal Tjader (SF, July): *La onda va bien*
Ross Tompkins (Concord, August):*Concord All-Stars*
Mickey Tucker (NYC, 16 May): *The Crawl*
McCoy Tyner (NJ, 24,25 April): *Horizon*
Rene Urtreger (Paris): *Urtreger-Michelot-Humair*
Warren Vaché (NYC): *Polished Brass*
Sarah Vaughan (LA, 15,16 August, 12,13 September): *Duke Ellington*
V.S.O.P. (26 July): *Live under the sky*
Mal Waldron (Belgium, 28 February): *Mingus Lives*
Jack Walrath (NYC,21,22 August): *Demons in Pursuit*
Cedar Walton (NYC, 19 December): *Eastern Rebellion 3* (NYC): *Animation*
Benny Waters (29,30 March): *Bouncin' Benny*
Bill Watrous (LA, 26,27 March): *Funk'n'Fun*
Don Weller (London, 3-5 July): *Commit no nuisance*
Bobby Wellins (London): *Dreams are free*
Mike Westbrook (Hamburg,13-17 June):*Mama Chicago*
Bob Wilber (30,31 May): *In the mood for swing*
Claude Williamson (NYC, 6 August): *La Fiesta*
Jack Wilson (15,29 March): *Margo's Theme*
Kai Winding/Curtis Fuller (Copenhagen, 23,24 November): *Giant Bones*
Phil Woods (California, Summer): *Crazy Horse*
Richard Wyands (NYC,12 October):*Then, here and now*
Snooky Young: *Horn of Plenty*
Trummy Young (Hawaii, April): *Struttin' with some barbecue*
Attila Zoller (NYC, 6 May): *Common Cause*

Chet Baker plays at the Camden Jazz Festival (opposite page) while the Capitol Jazz Festival plays host to mainstream stars George Duvivier (bass), Pee Wee Erwin (cornet) and Bucky Pizzarelli (guitar).

1980

Miles Davis (54) returns to playing and records *The Man with the Horn*.

Pianist Bill Evans dies in September aged 51.

Steps, a group led by Mike Mainieri (vibes) and Mike Brecker (tenor sax), make their recording debut in December.

Wynton Marsalis (18) joins the Art Blakey Jazz Messengers.

DEATHS

Ed Garland (95) 22 January
Babs Gonzales (60) 23 January
Jimmy Crawford (70) 28 January
Charlie Fowlkes (63) 9 February *heart attack*
Norman Keenan (63) 12 February
Shorty Sherock (65) 19 February
Bobby Jones (51) 6 March
Ronnie Boykins (45) 20 April
Herman Autrey (75) 14 June
Barney Bigard (74) 27 June
Duke Pearson (47) 4 August *multiple sclerosis*
Jimmy Forrest (60) 25 August *liver illness*
Bill Evans (51) 15 September
Chauncey Morehouse (78) 31 October
Skip Hall (71) November
Keith Christie (49) 16 December
Alec Wilder (73) 24 December
Peck Kelley (82) 26 December *Parkinson's disease*
Lennie Felix (60) 29 December *knocked down by car*
Robert Pete Williams 31 December
Stu Martin

BOOKS

Rodney Dale: *The Story of Jazz*
Alexis De Veaux: *Don't Explain – a song of Billie Holiday*

RECORDS

John Abercrombie (November): *M*
Muhal Richard Abrams (NYC, 16,19 June): *Mama and Daddy*
George Adams/Don Pullen (Holland, 3,5 August): *Earth Beams*
George Adams/Dannie Richmond (Milan, 13,14 February): *Hand to hand*
Air (NYC, 28 December): *Air mail*
Monty Alexander (SF, August): *Trio*
Barry Altschul (NYC, 23 January): *Brahma*
Ernestine Anderson (SF, August): *Never make your move too soon*
Art Ensemble of Chicago (NYC, January): *Full force* (Munich, May): *Urban Bushman* (Italy, August): *Among the People*
Chet Baker (Paris, 25 June): *Live in Paris-Nightbird* (Paris, July); *Salsamba*
Billy Bang (NYC, 28 June/27 December): *Changing Seasons*

Kenny Barron (NYC, 4,18 April): *Golden Lotus*
Count Basie (April): *Kansas City Shout*
Gordon Beck (Paris, December 1979 & January 1980): *The Things You See*
Art Blakey (Florida, 11 October): *Live at Bubba's Jazz Restaurant*
Arthur Blythe (NYC): *Illusions*
Dollar Brand (Montreux, 18 July): *Dollar Brand at Montreux* (Switzerland, 12 October): *Matsidiso* (Switzerland, 12 November): *South African Sunshine*
Brecker Brothers (NYC): *Straphangin'*
Marion Brown (Paris, 14 February): *Back to Paris*
Kenny Burrell (NYC, 9,10 December): *Listen to the dawn*
Gary Burton (Ludwigsburg, June): *Easy as pie*
George Cables (LA, 18,19 February): *Some of my favourite things*
Jackie Cain/Roy Kral (San Francisco): *East of Suez*
Judy Carmichael (LA,4,29 April): *Two-handed stride*
Benny Carter (August): *Summer Serenade*
Ron Carter (NYC, 19,20 May): *Patrao* (NYC, 29 September): *Parfait*
Jay Clayton (NYC, October): *All out*
Billy Cobham (Europe): *Live: Flight Time*
Bill Coleman (Toulouse, 15 May): *Really I do*
Bob Cooper (LA, 31 July): *Plays the music of Michel Legrand*
Ted Curson (NYC, 5 January): *I Heard Mingus* (NYC): *Snake Johnson*
Miles Davis (NYC): *The man with the horn*
Elton Dean (Ludwigsburg, February): *Boundaries*
Brian Dee (London, 29 April): *Swing Doodle*
Buddy de Franco (Buenos Aires, 27 November): *Mood Indigo*
Jack De Johnette's Special Edition (Ludwigsburg, September): *Tin Can Alley*
Kenny Drew (Copenhagen, 29 November): *Afternoon in Europe*
Ted Dunbar (NYC, 12 June): *Secundum Artem*
Teddy Edwards (Copenhagen, 5 December): *Out of this world*
Don Ewell/Herb Hall (New Orleans, 3 March): *Don Ewell/Herb Hall Quartet*
Tommy Flanagan/Red Mitchell (NYC, 24 February): *You're me*
Ricky Ford (NYC, 24 April): *Flying colours*
Bud Freeman (London, May): *The dolphin has the message*

Chico Freeman (LA, 6,7 March): *Peaceful heart, gentle spirit*
Ganelin Trio (Leningrad, 15,16 November): *Ancora da Capo, Pts 1&2*
Jan Garbarek (Oslo, December): *Eventyr*
Russell Garcia (LA, 2 June): *I lead a charmed life*
Red Garland (Tokyo, 5 February): *Wee small hours*
Stan Getz: *Live at Midem '80*
Benny Golson (LA,20-22 October): *California Message*
Stephane Grappelli/Martial Solal (Paris, 17,18 February): *Happy reunion*
Scott Hamilton/Buddy Tate (San Francisco, August): *Scott's Buddy*
Billy Harper (NYC, 15 February): *The Believer* (Warsaw, 26 October): *Live in Warsaw 1980*
Ted Harris (NYC, 31 March): *Presents Five Giants of Jazz*
Johnny Hartman (NYC,11 August):*Once in every life*
Julius Hemphill (Milan,4,5 June):*Flat-out Jump Suite*
Billy Higgins (Bologna, 25 May): *Once More*
Andrew Hill (Milan, 13,14 June): *Faces of Hope*
Terumasa Hino (NYC, March/April): *Daydream*
Freddie Hubbard (The Hague, July): *Live at North Sea 1980*
Helen Humes (NYC, 17,19 June): *Helen*
Ronald Shannon Jackson (NYC): *Eye On You*
Willis Jackson (France, 26 January): *Ya understand me?* (NYC, 20 June): *Nothing Butt*
Illinois Jacquet (NYC,June):*Illinois Jacquet All Stars*
Ahmad Jamal (Florida, 20 March): *Live at Bubba's*
Keith Jarrett (March): *The Celestial Hawk* (Ottobeuren Abbey, October): *Invocations*
Dick Johnson/Dave McKenna (San Francisco, April): *Spider's blues*
Thad Jones (Copenhagen, 15,16 September): *Thad Jones' Eclipse Live*
Joe Kennedy Sr (Nice, 19 July): *Magnifique!*
Steve Khan (NYC, July): *Evidence*
John Klemmer (LA, 10 December): *Finesse*
Jimmy Knepper: *Primrose path*
Eiji Kitamura/Concord All Stars (Tokyo): *Dear Friends*
Lee Konitz/Martial Solal (Berlin, 30 October): *Live at the Berlin Jazz Days 1980*
Steve Lacy (18 December): *Ballets*
LA4 (London, June): *Zaca*
Oliver Lake (NYC, 11,12 August): *Prophet*
Jeannie Lambe (Sussex, 5 September): *Jeannie Lambe with Danny Moss Quartet*
Milcho Leviev/Art Pepper (Ronnie Scott's, London, 27,28 June): *Blues for the fisherman* (28,29 June): *True blues*
Mel Lewis (Village Vanguard, NYC, February): *Bob Brookmeyer, Composer, Arranger*
Dave Liebman (14 July): *If They Only Knew*
Didier Lockwood (Montreux, 28-30 July): *Live in Montreux*
London Jazz Composers Orchestra (26 March):*Stringer*

Jimmy Lyons (Paris, 13,14 September): *Riffs*
Humphrey Lyttelton (20 February): *One day I met an African*
Teo Macero (NYC): *Impressions of Charles Mingus*
Charlie Mariano (Helsinki, August): *Tea for Four*
Wynton Marsalis (Florida, 11 October): *First recordings/The All-American Hero*
Don Menza (LA): *Burnin'*
Pat Metheny (Oslo, 26-29 May): *80/81*
Pat Metheny/Lyle Mays (September): *As falls Wichita, so falls Wichita Falls*
Billy Mitchell (Dakar, 14,19 March): *Night Flight to Dakar* (NYC, 26 June): *De Lawd's Blues*
Tete Montoliu (22 March): *I wanna talk about you*
Bob Moses (NYC): *Visit with the Great Spirit*
David Murray (Switzerland, 30 May): *Solo Live, Vols 1&2* (NYC, 25,28 July): *Ming*
Evan Parker/George Lewis (London, 18 May): *From saxophone and trombone*
Paz (London, Summer): *Paz are back*
Charlie Persip (NYC): *Superband*
Oscar Peterson Big Four (LA, 10 March): *The Trumpet Summit meets*
Oscar Peterson (Holland): *Live at the North Sea Jazz Festival*
Michel Petrucciani (France, 11-13 August): *Flash*
Jean-Luc Ponty (LA, 6 July): *Civilized Evil*
Quadrant (LA, 21 January): *Quadrant toasts Duke Ellington*
Alvin Queen (Switzerland, 8 February): *In Europe*

Dewey Redman/Ed Blackwell (Willisau, 31 August): *Red and Black*
Rufus Reid (NYC, 27 January): *Perpetual Stroll*
Red Richards (Paris, 21 May): *It's a wonderful world*
Dannie Richmond (Bologna, 18 August): *Plays Charlie Mingus* (NYC, 24 September); *Dannie Richmond Quintet*
Howard Riley (London, 2 May): *Facets*
Red Rodney (NYC): *Hi Jinx at the Village Vanguard*
Marshall Royal (LA, March): *Royal Blue*
Pharoah Sanders (SF): *Journey to the One*
John Scofield (NYC, August): *Bar talk*
George Shearing/Carmen McRae (NYC, June): *Two for the Road*
Jack Sheldon (LA, 21,22 February): *Angel wings* (LA, 13,14 November): *Playin' it straight*
Archie Shepp (Copenhagen, 6 February): *Trouble in Mind* (Copenhagen, 7 February): *Looking at Bird*
Jimmy Smith (LA, July): *The Cat Strikes Again*
Leo Smith (NYC, 19 January): *Go in numbers*
Peter Sprague (LA, 5,6 September): *The Path*
Steps (Tokyo, 8-10 December): *Step By Step* (Tokyo, 14 December): *Smokin' in the Pit*
Sonny Stitt (NYC, 7 April): *Sonny's back*
Sun Ra (Willisau, 24 February): *Sunrise in Different Dimensions*
Ray Swinfield (London, 18-20 March): *Rain curtain*
Cecil Taylor (Germany, 14 September): *Fly! Fly! Fly! Fly! Fly!*
Toots Thielemans/Joe Pass/Niels Pederson (Hague, 13 July): *Live in the Netherlands*
Eddie Thompson/Roy Williams (London, 23 March): *When lights are low*
McCoy Tyner (NJ, 3,5,6 March/29 May): *4 X 4*
James 'Blood' Ulmer (NYC, 17 January): *Are you glad to be in America?*
Edward Vesala (NYC, May): *Heavy Life*
Eddie 'Cleanhead' Vinson (London, May): *Fun in London*
Miroslav Vitous (Oslo, July): *Miroslav Vitous Group*
Cedar Walton/Abbey Lincoln (LA, 15 December): *The Maestro*
Sadao Watanabe (Tokyo, 2-4 July): *How's Everything?*
Bill Watrous (December): *Coronary tronbossa*
Weather Report (LA): *Night Passage*
Phil Wilson (NYC, 6 February): *Boston-New York Axis*
Jimmy Witherspoon (25 May): *Jimmy Witherspoon & Panama Francis' Savoy Sultans*
Phil Woods (Italy, 7 November): *The Macerata Concert* (Perugia, 12 November): *European Tour Live*
World Saxophone Quartet (Paris, 14 October): *Revue*

Opposite page: **Panama Francis (drums) and the Savoy Sultans swing out at the Kool Jazz Festival at Waterloo Village in New Jersey.**

Below: **The Brecker Brothers – Mike (tenor sax) and Randy (trumpet).**

Photo: *David Redfern*

1981

Miles Davis (55) forms a working band including Bill Evans (saxophone), Mike Stern, Marcus Miller and Al Foster and performs in public again at the Newport Jazz Festival at Avery Fisher Hall, NYC (July). In September the band goes to Japan.

The Modern Jazz Quartet reform after 20 years and play the Monterey Jazz Festival Tour of Japan.

14 year old Tommy Smith wins the Best Musician Trophy at the Edinburgh International Jazz Festival.

DEATHS

Chink Martin (94) 7 January
Sinclair Traill (76) 10 January
Russell Procope (72) 21 January
Ray Biondi (75) 28 January
Cozy Cole (71) 29 January
Joe Carroll (61) 1 February *heart attack*
Don Frye (78) 9 February
Frank Froeba (73) 10 February
Joe 'Cornbread' Thomas (78) 18 February
Matty Malneck (77) 25 February
Ike Isaacs (57) 27 February
Red Saunders (69) 4 March
Tampa Red (77) 19 March
Sonny Red (48) 20 March
King Pleasure (58) 21 March *heart attack*
Dick Katz (64) 30 March
Carmen Mastren (67) 31 March *heart attack*
Eddie Sauter (66) 21 April *heart attack*
Cat Anderson (64) 29 April
Frank Socolow (57) 29 April
Joe Yukl (72) April
Mary Lou Williams (71) 28 May *cancer*
Pee Wee Erwin (68) 20 June
Floyd 'Candy' Johnson (59) June
Jim Buffington (59) 20 July
Snub Mosley (75) 21 July
Tommy Turk (54) 4 August *shot in a bar*
Bill Coleman (77) 24 August
Jorgen-Grunnet Jepsen (54) 24 August
Walter 'Foots' Thomas (74) 26 August
Helen Humes (68) 13 September
Harry Warren (87) 22 September
Furry Lewis (88) September
Will Hudson (73) September
Hazel Scott (61) 2 October
Johnny Windhurst (54) 2 October *heart attack*
Al Cooper (70) 5 October
Oscar Moore (68) 8 October *heart attack*
Louis Metcalf (76) 27 October
Bardu Ali (75) 29 October
Bob Eberle (65) November
Taft Jordan (66) 1 December
Walter 'Shakey' Horton () 8 December
Sam Jones (57) 15 December *cancer*
Hoagy Carmichael (82) 27 December
Irving Townsend (?) December *heart attack*
Bertie King (69)
Will Hudson (73)

BOOKS

Gary Giddins: *Riding on a Blue Note*
Humphrey Lyttelton: *The Best of Jazz–Enter the Giants*

RECORDS

Muhal Richard Abrams (Milan, 20,21,27 July): *Blues forever*
Pepper Adams (NYC, 30 September): *Urban Dreams*
Akiyoshi/Tabackin (LA, 24,25 March): *Tanuki's Night Out*
Franco Ambrosetti (NYC,10,11 February):*Heartbop*
Chet Baker (Cologne, 23 May): *I remember you*
Billy Bang/Charles Tyler (NYC, March): *Live at Green Space*
Gato Barbieri (June): *Gato.. Para Los Amigos*
Kenny Barron (NYC, 13 February): *At the Piano*
Count Basie (September): *Warm Breeze*
Tim Berne (NYC,1 July):*Songs and rituals in real time*
Art Blakey (SF, June): *Straight Ahead*
Carla Bley (SF, 19-21 August): *Live!*
Hamiett Bluiett (NYC, 9 April): *Dangerously Suite*
Arthur Blythe (NYC): *Blythe Spirit*
Lester Bowie (Ludwigsburg,June):*The Great Pretender*
Joanne Brackeen (NYC,8,9 December):*Special identity*
Anthony Braxton (NYC, 21,22 October): *Six Compositions: Quartet*
Nick Brignola (NYC, 24,25 June): *Groovin'*

Dave Brubeck (SF, September): *Paper Moon*
Kenny Burrell (NYC, 14,15 July): *Groovin' High*
Jaki Byard (Milan, 27 May): *To them – to us*
George Cables (LA, 13,14 February): *Whisper Not*
Capp/Pierce Juggernaut (LA, October/November): *Juggernaut strikes again*
Ron Carter (NYC, 14,15 April): *Super Strings* (NYC, December): *Heart and Soul*
Al Casey/Gene Rodgers (London, Summer). *Six swinging strings*
Billy Cobham (London, 18 March): *Stratus*
Al Cohn/Scott Hamilton/Buddy Tate (Tokyo, August): *Tour de Force*
Richie Cole (Tokyo, 7,8 February): *Cool'C'*
Chick Corea (LA, November): *Corea/Vitous/Haynes*
Larry Coryell (Stuttgart, April): *Bolero*
Lol Coxhill (Paris, 6 November): *The Dunois Solos*
Albert Dailey (New Jersey, 4 June): *Textures*
Eddie 'Lockjaw' Davis (Munich,February):*Jaw's Blues*
Bill Dobbins/Red Mitchell (NYC, 3 May): *Where one relaxes, Vol.1*
Lou Donaldson (January): *Sweet Poppa Lou*
Kenny Drew (Milan, 23 November): *It might as well be spring* (Milan, 25,26 November): *Your soft eyes*
Eddie Durham (July): *Blue 'bone*
Johnny Dyani (Glasgow, February): *Mbizo*
Herb Ellis (June): *Herb Mix*
Lars Erstrand (Sweden, 27 January): *Mine Forever*
Tal Farlow (NYC): *Chromatic palette*
Art Farmer (Milan, 29,30 November): *Manhattan*
Feather (LA, 25 November): *Chen Yu Lips*
Tommy Flanagan (NYC, 2,3 June): *The Magnificent Tommy Flanagan*

Bob Florence (LA, 3 March): *Westlake*
Ricky Ford (NYC, 6 April): *Tenor for the times*
Chico Freeman (LA,29,20 October): *Destiny's Dance*
Dave Frishberg (Pa, 29,30 April): *The Dave Frishberg Songbook, Vol.1*
Jim Galloway/Jay McShann (Toronto, 15,16 June): *Thou swell*
Ganelin Trio (Moscow, 27 August): *Vide* (Leningrad, 15 November): *Baltic Triangle*
Jan Garbarek (Oslo, December): *Paths, prints*
Stan Getz (SF, May): *The Dolphin* (Paris, 4 November): *Billy Highstreet Samba*
Dizzy Gillespie (Montreux, 17 July): *Musician-Composer-Raconteur*
Benny Golson (LA,19,20 August): *One more mem'ry*
Jimmy Gourley (Paris, 9 July): *No more*
Marty Grosz (NYC, 25,26 June/2 July): *I hope Gabriel likes my music*
Lionel Hampton (Japan, 2,3,6 September): *Aurex Jazz Festival 1981*
Roland Hanna (Chicago, 27 July): *The New York Jazz Quartet in Chicago*
Herbie Harper (LA,6,7 May):*Herbie Harper revisited*
Heath Brothers (NYC,29,30 December):*Brotherly love*
Marc Hemmeler (Paris, 17,18 March): *Easy does it*
Woody Herman (Chicago, 6 March): *Live in Chicago* (NYC, July): *Four Others* (California, 15 August): *Live at the Concord Jazz Festival 1981*
John Hicks (SF): *Some Other Time*
Terumasa Hino (February/March): *Double Rainbow*
Art Hodes/Milt Hinton (NYC, 26August): *Just the two of us*
Shirley Horn (The Hague, 10,11,12 July): *Violets for your furs*
Freddie Hubbard (NYC, 16,17 March): *Outpost*
Peanuts Hucko (NYC,15 July):*Peanuts Hucko Quartet*
Abdullah Ibrahim (Stuttgart, 8 June / Berlin, 6 July): *Duke's Memories*
Milt Jackson (NYC, 30 November): *Ain't but a few of us left*
Ronald Shannon Jackson (NYC, 23,27 March): *Nasty* (NYC, 13-16 June): *Street Priest*
Joseph Jarman/Don Moye (Milan, 16,17 February): *Earth passage density*

Photo: *Brian Foskett*

1981

Keith Jarrett (Bregenz, 28 May): *Concerts*
Rodney Jones/Tommy Flanagan (NYC, 21 December): *My Funny Valentine*
Clifford Jordan/Von Freeman (Chicago, 5 September): *Hyde Park After Dark*
George Kawaguchi/Art Blakey (NYC, 4 December): *Killer Joe*
Barney Kessel (SF, April): *Solo*
Steve Khan (NYC, November): *Eyewitness*
Eiji Kitamura (SF, August): *Seven stars*
Joachim Kuhn (NYC, April): *Nightline New York*
Peter Kuhn (NYC, 12 January/20 December): *The kill*
Steve Kuhn (NYC, April): *Last Year's Waltz*
Steve Lacy (Paris, 28,29 January): *Songs (with Brion Gysin)*
Steve Lacy/Mal Waldron (Paris, 4 August): *Shake out* (Paris, 15 August): *Herbe de l'oubli*

LA4 (LA, April): *Montage*
Oliver Lake (Milan, 13,14 April): *Clevont Fitzhubert* (NYC): *Jump Up*
Harold Land (LA, 22 October): *Xocia's dance*
Didier Lockwood (Holland, September): *Fasten Seat Belts*
Jimmy Lyons/Andrew Cyrille (NYC, 13 February): *Something in Return*
Humphrey Lyttelton (London, 1 July): *Echoes of Harlem*
Dick Meldonian/Sonny Igoe Big Band (NYC, 4 May): *Plays Gene Roland Music*
Don Menza (California, 2,3 October): *Hip Pocket*
Eddie Miller/Ralph Sutton (NYC, 10,11 September): *Live at Hanratty's*
Roscoe Mitchell (Milan, 16,17 February): *3 X 4 Eye*
MJQ (Tokyo): *Re-union at Budohkan*

Jemeel Moondoc (NYC, 24 October): *Kostanze's Delight* (NYC, 9 November): *Judy's bounce*
Lanny Morgan (LA, 7,8 September): *It's About Time*
Jimmy Mosher (LA, May/September): *A Chick from Chelsea*
Paul Motian (Hamburg, December): *Psalm*
Mark Murphy (LA, 12 March): *Bop for Kerouac*
David Murray (NYC, 31 October/1 November): *Home*
Horace Parlan (Munich, 11 February): *Pannonica*
Joe Pass (LA, 23 November): *Joe Pass loves Gershwin*
Art Pepper (LA, 15 August): *Roadgame*
Marvin 'Hannibal' Peterson (NYC, 15,19 February): *The Angels of Atlanta* (London, 2 November): *Poem Song*
Oscar Peterson (Toronto, 15 April/London, 24,25 April): *A Royal Wedding Suite*
Michel Petrucciani (Holland, 3,4 April): *Michel Petrucciani*
Alvin Queen (White Plains, NY, 18 August): *Ashanti*
Jimmy Raney (Holland, 27 February): *Raney 81*
Enrico Rava (W.Germany, December): *Opening night*
Emily Remler (SF, April): *Firefly*
Howard Riley (London, 22 May): *First Encounter* (London, 1 June): *Duality*
Sammy Rimington/Sing Miller (New Orleans, 15 January): *Songs of the south*
Sam Rivers (Paris, 4 April): *Crosscurrent*
Spike Robinson (LA, 18 November): *The Music of Harry Warren*
Red Rodney (NYC, 15,16 June): *Night and Day*
Sonny Rollins (California, 9-15 December): *No problem*
Jimmy Rowles (NYC, June): *Plays Duke Ellington & Billy Strayhorn*
Pharoah Sanders (NYC/SF): *Rejoice*
Maxim Saury (LA, 27 August): *In Los Angeles*
John Scofield (Munich, 12 December): *Shinola* (Munich, 14 December): *Out like a light*
Woody Shaw (NYC): *United*
Archie Shepp (Toronto, 11 February): *I Know About The Life* (Paris, 3 November): *My Man*
Lou Stein (October): *Live at the Dome*
Steps (NYC): *Paradox*
Slam Stewart/Major Holley (NYC, 6 December): *Shut Yo' Mouth*
Sonny Stitt (Fort Lauderdale, 11 November): *Sonny's Last Recordings*
Ira Sullivan (NYC, 14 September): *Does it all!*
Maxine Sullivan (Sweden): *The Queen with her Swedish All Stars Vol.1*
Ralph Sutton/Jack Lesberg (NYC, 1,2 October): *Ralph Sutton & Jack Lesberg*
Buddy Tate (Toronto, 12,13 June): *The Ballad Artistry* (NYC): *The Great Buddy Tate*
Cecil Taylor (Basle, 16 November): *Garden*
Martin Taylor/Peter Ind (London): *Triple Libra*
Keith Tippett (Berlin, 3,4 December): *Mujician*
Bruno Tommaso (Rome, April): *Ten Variations on a theme of Jerome Kern*
Ralph Towner/John Abercrombie (Oslo, March): *Five years later*
Warren Vaché (NYC): *Iridescence*
Mal Waldron/Steve Lacy (Paris, 13-15 August): *Let's Call This*
Jack Walrath (NYC, 23 May): *Revenge of the fat people*
Benny Waters (April): *On the sunny side of the street*
Dick Wellstood (NYC, 18 September): *Live at Hanratty's*
Dick Wellstood/Kenny Davern/Bob Rosengarden (NYC, 9,10 September): *The Blue Three*
Mike Westbrook Brass Band (Paris, May): *The Paris Album*
Bob Wilber (Washington, 10 May): *The Music of King Oliver's Creole Jazz Band*
Bob Wilber & the Bechet Legacy (UK, 24 November): *On the road*
Roy Williams/Eddie Thompson (London, 16 May/27 July): *Something wonderful*
Jimmy Witherspoon (London, June): *Big Blues*
Phil Woods/Tommy Flanagan/Red Mitchell (NYC, 6,7 January): *Three for all*
World Saxophone Quartet (6 November): *Live in Zurich*
Denny Zeitlin/Charlie Haden (SF, July): *Time remembers one time once*

Photo: *Brian Foskett*

Dexter Gordon (left) and Art Pepper (opposite page) at the Capital Radio Jazz Festival, Knebworth Park.

1982

Miles Davis (56) suffers a mild stroke (January). He recovers sufficiently to tour Europe in April with John Scofield (31) added to the band.

The Blue Note club opens on 3rd Street in New York.

Wynton Marsalis (20) emerges as the new super-hero of jazz.

Charlie Rouse (58) forms Sphere, a band dedicated to the music of Thelonious Monk, with Kenny Barron (39), Buster Williams (40) and Ben Riley (49). Their debut album is recorded 17 February, ironically on the very day of Monk's death.

Art Farmer (54) and Benny Golson (53) reform the Jazztet with Curtis Fuller (48).

The Modern Jazz Quartet undertake a European tour.

DEATHS

Tommy Bryant (52) 3 January
Vido Musso (68) 9 January
Don de Michael (53) 4 February
Kurt Edelhagen (61) 8 February
Thelonious Monk (64) 17 February
Gabor Szabo (45) 26 February
Charlie Spivak (75) 1 March
Sonny Greer (78) 25 March
Bob Ysaguirre (85) 27 March
Fatty George (54) 29 March
Floyd Smith (65) 29 March
Ann Richards (46) 1 April
Dan Minor (62) 11 April
Dave Wilborn (78) 25 April
Murray McEachern (66) 28 April
Jimmy Jones (63) 29 April
Cal Tjader (56) 5 May
Bernie Glow (56) 8 May
Monk Montgomery (60) 20 May
Art Pepper (56) 15 June
Alex Welsh (52) 25 June
Wingy Manone (82) 9 July
Candy Finch (48) 13 July
Sonny Stitt (58) 23 July
Wingy Manone (78) July
Gene Roland (60) 11 August *cancer*
Natty Dominique (86) 30 August
Shelly Manne (64) 26 September
Ray Draper (42) 1 November *killed during robbery*
Al Haig (59) 16 November *heart attack*
Bobby Plater (68) 20 November *heart attack*

BOOKS

Berger & Patrick: *Benny Carter, A Life in American Music*
Ian Cruickshank: *The Guitar Style of Django Reinhardt & the Gypsies*
Frank Driggs & Harris Lewine: *Black Beauty, White Heat*
Sally Placksin: *American Women in Jazz*
Arthur Taylor: *Notes and Tones*
Billy Taylor: *Jazz Piano – a jazz history*

RECORDS

George Adams/Don Pullen (NYC, 6,9 June): *Melodic Excursions*
Air (23,24 January): *80° Below '82*
Toshiko Akiyoshi/Lew Tabackin (LA, 21,22 September): *European Memoirs*
Monty Alexander/Ray Brown/Herb Ellis (Osaka, March): *Triple Treat* (Tokyo, March): *Overseas Special*
Chet Baker (NYC, 23 February): *Peace*
Billy Bang (Milan, 13,14 April): *Invitation* (Willisau, 29 August): *Bangception*
Chris Barber (London, 20 April): *Barbican blues*
Kenny Barron (Tokyo, 9 June): *Imo Live* (Tokyo, 21 June): *Spiral*
Count Basie (May): *Farmers Market Barbecue*
Bob Berg (Italy, 8 December): *Steppin': live in Europe*
Dick Berk (LA, 19,20 October): *The Rare One*
Art Blakey (SF, January): *Keystone 3* (NYC, 11 April): *Art Blakey & the All Star Jazz Messengers* (Holland, 20 May): *Oh – by the way*
Arthur Blythe (NYC): *Elaborations*
Lester Bowie (Ludwigsburg, June): *All the magic*
Ruby Braff/Dick Hyman (Pennsylvania, 24 April): *America, the Beautiful*
Dollar Brand (Ludwigsburg, 7 June): *African Dawn*
Anthony Braxton (Ludwigsburg, 18 March): *Open aspects '82*
Mike Brecker (NYC, 4-8 January): *Cityscape*
Ray Brown (SF, February): *A Ray Brown 3*

Dave Brubeck (Concord, August): *Concord Summer Night*
Gary Burton (NYC, January): *Picture this*
George Cables (LA, 11,12 January): *Old Wine, New Bottle* (LA, 13,14 December): *Wonderful LA*
Jackie Cain/Roy Kral (SF, February): *High standards*
Baikida Carroll (NYC, 13,20 January): *Shadows and reflections*
Betty Carter (NYC): *Whatever happened to love?*
Doc Cheatham (NYC, 26,26 October): *I've got a crush on you* (NYC, 25,26 October): *Too marvellous for words* (NYC, 6,7 December): *It's a good life*
Vladimir Chekasin (Odessa, 9 July/Leningrad, 16 November): *Exercises*
Don Cherry/Ed Blackwell (Ludwigsburg, February): *El Corazon*
Arnett Cobb (The Hague, 13 November): *Live*
Al Cohn (NYC, April): *Overtones*
Richie Cole (SF, 31 July): *Alto Annie's Theme*
Johnny Coles (Holland, 19 December): *New Morning*
Chick Corea/Gary Burton (LA, September): *Lyric Suite for Sextet*
Marilyn Crispell (Berlin, 4 November): *Live in Berlin*
Charles Davis (NYC, 12 January): *Super 80*
Eddie 'Lockjaw' Davis (Zurich, 19,20 March): *Live at the Widder*
Jack De Johnette (NYC, September): *Inflation Blues*
Vic Dickenson (NYC, 20 September): *With Ralph Sutton*
Arne Domnerus (Sweden, 4,5,6 June): *Fragment*
Lou Donaldson (Paris): *Back Street*
Bob Dorough (France, March): *Devil May Care*
Ted Dunbar (NYC, 29 July): *Jazz Guitarist*
Allen Eager (March): *Renaissance*
Peter Erskine (NYC, June): *Peter Erskine*
Kevin Eubanks (NYC, May-August): *Guitarist*
Tal Farlow (NYC): *Cookin' on all burners*
Art Farmer (NYC, 18,19 September): *Mirage*
Joe Farrell (LA, 23 March): *Someday*
Wally Fawkes (London, 27 November): *Wally Fawkes & the Rhythm Kings*
Clare Fischer/Gary Foster (LA,23 November): *Starbright*
Ella Fitzgerald (LA, 4,5 February): *The Best is Yet to Come*
Tommy Flanagan (17,18 February): *Giant steps*
Ricky Ford (NYC, 22 February): *Interpretations*
Chico Freeman (NYC): *Tradition in transition*
Bill Frisell (Oslo, August): *In Line*
Curtis Fuller (Rome, 23 December): *Meets Roma Jazz Trio*
Slim Gaillard (London, 30 October): *Anytime, anyplace, anywhere*
Vyacheslav Ganelin (26 June): *New Wine*
Stan Getz (SF, January/NYC, February): *Pure Getz*
Globe Unity Orchestra (Paris,4 June): *Intergalactic blow*
Bill Goodwin (Pennsylvania, Autumn): *Network*
Dexter Gordon (Philadelphia, 8 March/NYC, 16 March): *American Classic*
Great Guitars (Washington DC, August): *At Charlie's Georgetown*
Charlie Haden (Ludwigsburg, November): *The Ballad of the Fallen*
Jim Hall/Ron Carter (NYC, November): *Live at Village West*
Bengt Hallberg (NYC, 23 September): *In New York*
Lionel Hampton (NYC): *The boogie woogie album* (Tokyo, 1,3 June): *Made in Japan*
Tom Harrell (NYC, 11 February): *Play of Light*
Woody Herman (Japan, September): *World Class*
Eddie Higgins (Florida, 6 June): *Once in a While*
Earl Hines (NYC): *Deep Forest*
Freddie Hubbard/Oscar Peterson (LA, 24 May): *Face to face*
Bobby Hutcherson (SF,10,11 July): *Farewell Keystone*

Milt Jackson (Ronnie Scott's, London, 23,24 April): *A London Bridge* (Ronnie Scott's, London, 28 April): *Memories of Thelonious Sphere Monk*
Oliver Jackson (NYC, 27 September): *Presents Le Quartet*
Ronald Shannon Jackson (NYC, June): *Mandance*
Elvin Jones (NYC, 10 February): *Earth Jones* (NYC, October): *Brother John*
Sheila Jordan/Harvie Swartz (NYC, 15 October): *Old Time Feeling*
George Kelly (UK, 11 October/NYC, 10 December): *Fine and dandy* (NYC, November): *Live at the West End Café*
Peter King (London, 23 June/15 July): *New beginning*
Lee Konitz (LA, 18,19 January): *High Jingo*
Lee Konitz/Michel Petrucciani (Paris, May): *Toot Sweet*
Karin Krog/Bengt Hallberg (Oslo, 15-17 April): *Two of a kind*
Joachim Kuhn (Hamburg, June): *Quartet*
Peter Kuhn (NYC, 12 January/30 December): *The Kill*
Steve Lacy (Milan, 18,19 January): *The Flame* (Paris, 1,2 November): *Prospectus*
Guy Lafitte/Wild Bill Davis (Paris, 15 January): *Three Men on a Beat*
LA4 (SF, June): *Executive Suite*
Don Lanphere (Seattle, 13,14 June): *Out of Nowhere*
Lou Levy (LA, 27,28 November): *The Kid's Got Ears!*
John Lewis (NYC, 4,5 November): *Slavic Smile*
Kirk Lightsey (NYC, 22 September/5 October): *Lightsey 1*
Charles Lloyd (Montreux, July): *Montreux '82*
Pat Longo & his Super Big Band (LA): *Billy May for President*
Cecil McBee (NYC): *Flying out*
John McLaughlin (Paris,June/July): *Music spoken here*
Jay McShann/Al Casey (London,April): *Best of Friends*
Machito (The Hague, 18 July): *Live at North Sea 82*
Albert Mangelsdorff (Oberursel, 23 February): *Solo*
Michael Mantler (NYC,February/June): *Something there*
Tania Maria (SF, August): *Come with me*
Warne Marsh (Monster, 14 August): *Star Highs*
George Masso (NYC, July): *Pieces of Eight*
Butch Miles (NYC, January): *Salutes Gene Krupa* (NYC, August): *Hail to the Chief!*
Mingus Dynasty (Milan, 5-7 April): *Reincarnation*
Red Mitchell (Sweden, 27,28 January): *Soft and warm and swinging*
MJQ (Montreux, 25 July): *Together again*
David Murray (Milan, 14 May/19 July): *Murray's Steps*
Nathen Page (NYC, 27 September): *Page-ing Nathen*
Paraphernalia (London, Summer): *Mother Earth*
Errol Parker (NYC, 4 May): *Tribute to Thelonious Monk*
Joe Pass (LA, 25 May/8 July): *Eximious*
Oscar Peterson Big Four (Tokyo, 20,21 February): *Freedom song*
Pat Peterson (NYC, 21 February): *Introducing Pat Peterson*
Michel Petrucciani (Rome, 29,30 March): *Estate* (Paris, 18 October): *Oracle Destiny*
Flip Phillips (Sweden, 14 June): *Symphony*
Alvin Queen (NYC, 29 July): *Glidin' and stridin'*
Doug Raney (Copenhagen,28 July): *I'll close my eyes*
Dewey Redman (NYC,January): *The struggle continues*
Emily Remler (NYC, June): *Take two*
Howard Riley (27 July): *For Four on Two Two*
Sam Rivers (Milan, 13 September): *Colours*
Max Roach/Connie Crothers (26 February): *Swish*
Max Roach (Milan, 22,23 July): *In the Light*
Red Rodney/Ira Sullivan (NYC,3,4 November): *Sprint*
Roswell Rudd (Milan, 25,26 June): *Regeneration*
George Russell (NYC, 30,31 July): *Live in an American Time Spiral*
Sal Salvador (NYC, November): *In our own sweet way*
Pharoah Sanders (Keystone Corner, SF, 23 January): *Heart is a Melody* (LA): *Live*
Lalo Schifrin (LA, 29,30 March): *Ins and outs*
Woody Shaw (NYC, 7 January): *Lotus Flower* (NYC, 25 February): *Master of the art / Night Music*
George Shearing/Mel Tormé (SF, 15 April): *An evening with...*
Archie Shepp (Villingen, 5 February): *Mama Rose* (NYC, 25 February): *Night Music* (Cologne, 1 December): *Soul Song*
Zoot Sims (NYC, 9 March): *The Innocent Years*
Carol Sloane (Tokyo, 29 August): *As time goes by*
Carrie Smith (19 April): *Negro Spirituals & Gospel Songs*
Jimmy Smith (NYC, 2 June): *Off the top*

Sphere (NYC, 17 February): *Four in one*
Spirit Level (London): *Mice in the wallet*
John Stevens (Bracknell, July): *Freebop*
Sonny Stitt (NYC, 8,9 June): *The Last Stitt Sessions*
Maxine Sullivan (Sweden): *The Queen with her Swedish All Stars Vol.2*
Sun Ra (NYC, September): *Celestial Love*
John Surman (Oslo, December): *Such Winters of Memory*
Horace Tapscott (LA, June/September/November): *The Tapscott Sessions, Vols 2&4*
Joe Thomas/Jay McShann (NYC, 9,10 December): *Blowin' in from K.C.*
Butch Thompson (Minnesota, February/April): *A 'Solas*
John Tirabasso (Pasadena, 28 July): *Live at Dino's*
Cal Tjader/Carmen McRae (SF, January): *Heatwave*
Ross Tomkins (LA, April): *Street of dreams*
Warren Vaché (NYC): *The Warren Vaché Trio – Midtown Jazz*
Sarah Vaughan (LA,1,2 March): *Crazy and mixed up*
Eddie 'Cleanhead' Vinson (NYC, 27 January): *Roomful of blues*
Miroslav Vitous (Oslo, July): *Journey's end*
Larry Vuckovich (SF, October): *Cast Your Fate*
Mal Waldron (Tokyo, 23 April): *In Retrospect*
Bennie Wallace (NYC, 4,5 May): *The Bennie Wallace Trio with Chick Corea*
Jack Walrath (Copenhagen, 22 July): *In Europe* (NYC, September): *A plea for sanity*
Bill Watrous (London, 22 March): *In London* (NYC, July): *Roaring back into New York NY*
Eberhard Weber (Ludwigsburg, March): *Later that evening*
Bob Wilber & the Bechet Legacy (NYC, 5,6 August): *Ode to Bechet*
James Williams (NYC, February): *Arioso*
Gerald Wilson (LA, 29 November/6 December): *Jessica*

Below: Freddie Hubbard and Tony Williams at the Capital Radio Jazz Festival, Knebworth Park.
Bottom: Benny Goodman meets Scott Hamilton at the same festival. Also on hand are Chris Flory (guitar) and Phil Flanigan (bass).

Photo: Brian Foskett

Photo: Brian Foskett

The compact disc is launched.

Humphrey Lyttelton starts his own record label, Calligraph.

Gil Evans (71) forms a regular band to play Monday nights at Sweet Basil (April).

George Russell (60) debuts his composition *The African Game* (18 June) in Boston's Emmanuel Church.

Tommy Smith (16) makes his recording debut (August).

The inaugural Floating Jazz Festival aboard the SS Norway, produced by Hank O'Neal and Shelley Shier, sails out of Miami in October. Musicians on board include Zoot Sims, Clark Terry, Bucky Pizzarelli, Adam Macowicz and Wild Bill Davison.

Miles Davis (57) tours Europe and Japan in the spring. In November, he is fêted at Radio City Music Hall in New York when Bill Cosby hosts 'MilesAhead: a Tribute to an American Music Legend'.

DEATHS
Barry Galbraith (63) 13 January
Sweet Emma Barrett (85) 28 January
Moses Allen (75) 2 February
Eubie Blake (100) 12 February
Bob Shoffner (82) 5 March
Ernie Royal (62) 16 March
Gigi Gryce (55) 17 March
Wallace Jones (76) 23 March
Kenny Kersey (66) 1 April
Jim Lanigan (81) 9 April
Dolo Coker (55) 13 April
Earl Hines (77) 22 April *heart attack*
Jimmy Mundy (75) 24 April
Muddy Waters (68) 30 April
Pat Smythe (60) 6 May
Kai Winding (60) 7 May *heart attack following treatment for a brain tumour*
Paul Quinichette (67) 25 May
Mort Herbert (57) 5 June
Al Lucas (66) 19 June
Sadik Hakim (Argonne Thornton) (63) 20 June
Sandy Mosse (54) 1 July
Harry James (67) 5 July *lymphatic cancer*
Lammar Wright Jr (55) 8 July
Don Ewell (66) 9 August *stroke*
Willie Bobo (49) 15 September
Johnny Hartman (60) 15 September
Preston Jackson (81) 12 November
Waymon Reed (43) 25 November
Marshall Brown (62) 13 December
Jimmy McLin (75) 15 December
Big Chief Russell Moore (71) 15 December
Nat Shapiro (61) 15 December
Harry Miller (42) 16 December *car crash*
Frank Orchard (69) 27 December
Lucille Armstrong

BOOKS
Thomas DeLong: *Pops: Paul Whiteman, King of Jazz*
Ted Fox: *Showtime at the Apollo*
S.F. Starr: *Red and Hot: the fate of jazz in the Soviet Union 1917-1980*

RECORDS
Muhal Richard Abrams (NYC, 8,10,25 January): *Rejoicing with the light*
George Adams/Don Pullen ·Holland, 27,28 March): *City Gates* (NYC, 19 August): *Live at the Village Vanguard Vols 1&2*
George Adams/Dannie Richmond (NYC, 11,12 January): *Gentleman's Agreement*
Pepper Adams (NYC, 19,20 August): *Live at Fat Tuesday's*
Nat Adderley (Keystone Corner, SF): *On the Move*
Monty Alexander (Villingen, 29 March): *The Duke Ellington Songbook* (Stuttgart): *Reunion in Europe*
Ray Alexander (NYC, October): *Cloud Patterns*
Laurindo Almeida (SF, April): *Artistry in Rhythm*
Barry Altschul (Milan, 12 February): *Irina*
Franco Ambrosetti (NYC, 1,2 December): *Wings*
Ernestine Anderson (SF, February): *Big City*
Svend Asmussen (NYC, 18,19 August): *June Night*
Chet Baker (Holland, 25 May): *Mr B* (Gothenburg, 29 September): *Live in Sweden*
Bill Barron (NYC, 23,24 August): *Variations in Blue*
Kenny Barron (Monster, 9 July): *Green Chimneys*
Count Basie (LA, 11,12 May): *88 Basie Street* (NYC, 11,12 May/11 November): *Fancy Pants*

Sathima Bea Benjamin (NYC, 7 October): *Memories and Dreams*
Richie Beirach (NYC, 5 July): *Continuum*
Borah Bergman (NYC, 14,15 April): *A New Frontier*
Tim Berne (NYC, 19 February): *The Ancestors* (Milan, 5,6 March): *Mutant Variations*
Ed Bickert (Toronto, January): *At Toronto's Bourbon Street*
Ran Blake (NYC, 28,29 September): *Suffield Gothic*
Art Blakey (NYC, April): *Caravan*
Carla Bley (NYC, 11-13 January): *I hate to sing* (Willow, NY, September/October): *Heavy Heart*
Paul Bley (Milan, 21 May): *Tango Palace*
Arthur Blythe (NYC, 27 January): *Light Blue*
Joe Bonner (Copenhagen, 20 February): *Devotion*
Bobby Bradford (LA, 7,8 June): *Lost in LA*
Ruby Braff/Scott Hamilton (NYC, 15 December): *Mr Braff to you*
Dollar Brand (Ludwigsburg, 29 May): *Zimbabwe* (NJ, 17 November): *Ekaya*
Anthony Braxton (Milan, 9,10 March): *Four Compositions (Quartet) 1983* (Stuttgart, 6 December): *Composition 113*
Nick Brignola (Utica NY, 21 June): *Signals...in from somewhere*
Gordon Brisker (LA, February): *Cornerstone*
Kenny Burrell (NYC, 23 August): *A La Carte*
George Cables (LA, 19, 20 May): *Sleeping Bee*
Tommy Chase (London, 13,14 November): *Hard!*
Doc Cheatham (NYC, 16,17 November): *The Fabulous Doc Cheatham*
Vladimir Chekasin (17 November): *Nostalgia*
Coe, Oxley & Co (Willisau, 28 August): *Nutty on Willisau*
Al Cohn (LA, November): *Standards of Excellence*
Chris Connor (NYC, 12,19 September): *Love is here with you*
Chick Corea (Ludwigsburg, July): *Children's Songs*
Lol Coxhill (Chantenay Villedieu,2 September): *Coucou*
Harold Danko (NYC, 20 September): *Ink and Water*
Harold Danko/Kirk Lightsey (NYC, 19,21 July): *Shorter by Two*
Eddie 'Lockjaw' Davis (Paris, February): *That's All* (Copenhagen, 28 August): *All of me*
Miles Davis (NYC): *Star People*
Buddy de Franco (Scotland, 28 September): *On Tour – UK*
Neville Dickie (NYC, 21 April): *Taken In Stride*
Kenny Drew (Milan, 21 February): *And Far Away*
Johnny Dyani (Copenhagen, 1 October): *Afrika* (Stockholm, 18 November): *Born under the heat*
Gil Evans (Bradford,18 March): *The British Orchestra*
Digby Fairweather (London,29 July):*Songs for Sandy*
Art Farmer (NYC, April): *Maiden Voyage* (Tokyo, October/November): *Ambrosia*
Art Farmer/Benny Golson Jazztet (Milan, 30,31 May): *Moment to Moment*
Joe Farrell/Louis Hayes Quartet (Holland, 15 November): *Vim 'n' Vigor*
Claudio Fasoli (Milan, 22,24 February): *Lido*
Vic Feldman (LA, 7,8 May): *To Chopin with love*
Tommy Flanagan (NYC, 16,17 June): *The master trio* (NYC, 16,17 June): *Blues in the closet*
Bob Florence (LA, 29,30 November): *Magic Time*
Helen Forrest (NYC, January): *Now and Forever*
Frank Foster/Frank Wess (Connecticut, 11,12 October): *Two for the blues*
Ganelin Trio (Moscow, 20 November): *Con Affeto*
Jan Garbarek (Oslo, March): *Wayfarer*

Stan Getz (Stockholm, 18 February): *The Stockholm Concert*
Stan Getz/Al Dailey (NYC, 12 January): *Poetry*
Jimmy Giuffre (Connecticut, 14,15 January): *Dragonfly*
Benny Golson (NYC, 20,21 December): *This is for you, John*
Stephane Grappelli (Vancouver, June): *Stephanova*
Anita Gravine (NYC, 12,13 September): *Dream Dancing*
Bengt Hallberg/Arne Domnerus (Stockholm, 30 September/3 October): *Powerhouse-Kraftwerk*
Scott Hamilton (Tokyo, January): *The Second Set* (Tokyo, June): *In Concert*
Woody Herman (California, April): *Presents a Great American Evening, Vol.3*
Art Hodes (Toronto,29 November):*South side memories*
Dave Holland (Ludwigsburg, October): *Jumpin' In*
Freddie Hubbard (NYC, 13,14 June): *Sweet Return*
Milt Jackson (NYC, 30 November/1 December): *Soul Route*
Milt Jackson/JJ Johnson/Ray Brown (LA, 25,26 May): *Jackson/Johnson/Brown & Company*
Milt Jackson/Oscar Peterson (NYC, 20 January): *Two of the few*
Ronald Shannon Jackson (NYC, March): *Barbecue Dog*
Keith Jarrett (NYC, January): *Standards, Vols 1&2* (NYC, January): *Changes*
JJ Johnson/Al Grey: *Things are getting better all the time*
Plas Johnson (LA): *LA55*
Etta Jones (NYC, 19 September): *Love me with all your heart*
Hank Jones/Tommy Flanagan (Villingen, 7 May): *I'm all smiles*
Philly Joe Jones/Dameronia (NYC, 11 July): *Look Stop and Listen*
Duke Jordan (Copenhagen): *Plays Standards Vol 1: Autumn Leaves* (Holland, 8,9 June): *Blue Duke*
Peter King (London, 29 January): *East 34th Street*
Lee Konitz (NYC, 25,27 February): *Dovetail*
Lee Konitz/Albert Mangelsdorff (Villingen, 8-10 June): *The Art of the Duo*
Steve Lacy (Paris, 1,3 November): *Prospectus*
Don Lanphere (22 August/26 December): *Into Somewhere*
Barbara Lashley (California, 22,23 June): *How long has this been going on?*
Hugh Lawson (NYC, 15 January): *Colour*
Jay Leonhart (NYC, 19,29 March): *Salamander Pie*
Mark Levine (SF, June): *Concepts*
Kirk Lightsey (Holland, 14 February): *Isotope* (Holland, March): *Everything Happens to me*
Charles Lloyd (Copenhagen, 11 July): *A night in Copenhagen*
Humphrey Lyttelton (Toronto, 26,27 July): *Humphrey Lyttelton in Canada* (London, 28 September): *It Seems Like Yesterday*
Rob McConnell (Toronto): *All in good time*
Dave McKenna (Bloomington, May): *A Celebration of Hoagy Carmichael*
John McNeil (Copenhagen, 30 August): *Things we did last summer*
Charles McPherson (LA, 18 April): *The Profet*
Jay McShann (Toronto, 24 August): *Just a lucky so and so*
Junior Mance (NYC, 1 April): *The tender touch* (NYC, 13 December): *Truckin' and Trackin'*
Tania Maria (California): *Love Explosion*
Branford Marsalis (NYC, 18,19 April /28,29 November): *Scenes in the City*
Wynton Marsalis (NYC, October): *Think of one*
George Masso (NYC): *George Masso Sextet*
Bill Mays (LA, 24 January): *Tha's Delight*
Dick Meldonian (NYC, 15 March): *It's a Wonderful World*
Pat Metheny (NYC, November): *Rejoicing*
Harry Miller (3 March): *Down South*
Pete Minger (Fort Lauderdale, 31 October): *Straight from the source*
Roscoe Mitchell (Milan, 2,3 June): *The Sound & Space Ensembles*
Paul Motian (Milan,27,28 July):*The Story of Maryam*
Jim Mullen (April): *Thumbs Up*
Gerry Mulligan (NYC): *Little Big Horn*
Mark Murphy (SF,21,22 March/2,4 August): *Brazil Song* (8-10 October/1 November): *Sings Nat's Choice*

David Murray (NYC, 25,26,30 September): *Morning Song*

Amina Claudine Myers (Milan, 3,4 February): *The Circle of Time*

New Air (Montreal, July): *Live at Montreal International Jazz Festival*

James Newton (NYC): *Luella*

Red Norvo/Bucky Pizzarelli (NYC, 8,9 August): *Just Friends*

Evan Parker (London, 7 January): *Tracks*

Joe Pass/JJ Johnson (October): *Together again*

Jaco Pastorius (Japan): *Invitation*

Jim Pepper (NYC,12 May/22,23 June):*Comin'and Goin'*

Oscar Peterson (California, 9 January): *If you could see me now* (California, 8 November): *A Tribute to my Friends*

Michel Petrucciani (NYC, June): *100 Hearts*

Jean-Luc Ponty (NYC,March/May):*Individual Choice*

Eddie Prevost (Bracknell, 3 July): *Continuum*

Dudu Pukwana (Bracknell/Willisau): *Live in Bracknell & Willisau*

Don Pullen (NYC, 28,29 September): *Evidence of Things Unseen*

Alvin Queen/Dusko Goycovich (Holland, 23 March): *A Day in Holland*

Enrico Rava (Milan, 6,7 May): *Andanada*

Reflexionen (Holland, 22 November): *Reflexionen*

Emily Remler (NYC, October): *Transitions*

Dannie Richmond (Milan, 30 May): *Dionysius*

Max Roach (Munich, 7 November): *Double Quartet Live at Vielharmonie*

Shorty Rogers/Bud Shank (LA, June): *Yesterday, Today and Forever*

Michele Rosewoman (Milan, 26 April): *The Source*

Rova Saxophone Quartet (Milan, 15-17 November): *Favourite Street*

Jimmy Rowles/Michael Hashim (NYC, 14 June): *Peacocks*

George Russell (Boston, 18 June): *The African Game*

Paul Rutherford (Bracknell, 2 July): *Bracknell '83*

David Sanborn (NYC): *Backstreet*

Woody Shaw (Bologna, 1 June): *Time is Right* (NYC, December): *Setting Standards*

George Shearing/Mel Tormé (SF,March): *Top drawer*

Jack Sheldon (LA, March): *Stand By for the Jack Sheldon Quartet*

Horace Silver (LA, 1 September): *There's no need to struggle*

Jimmy Smith (Atlanta, September): *Keep on Coming*

Tommy Smith (Glasgow, August): *...Taking Off*

Peter Sprague (SF, September): *Musica Del Mar*

Steps Ahead (NYC): *Steps Ahead*

Ralph Sutton/Bob Barnard (NYC, 25 August): *Partners in Crime*

Horace Tapscott (LA, March): *The Tapscott Sessions,Vol 3*

Martin Taylor (Edinburgh, August): *A Tribute to Art Tatum*

Eddie Thompson (London, 19 October): *Memories of you*

Mel Tormé/George Shearing (Georgetown, October): *An Evening at Charlie's*

Big Joe Turner (NYC, 26 January): *Blues Train*

29th Street Saxophone Quartet (Utrecht,19 November/ Amsterdam, 25 November): *Pointillistic Groove*

McCoy Tyner (NYC, October): *Dimensions*

James 'Blood' Ulmer (Montreux, July): *Part Time*

Michael Urbaniak (Copenhagen, 11 November): *A Quiet Day in Spring*

Mal Waldron (NYC, 28,29 June): *Breaking new ground* (Japan, 9 December): *You and the night and the music*

Cedar Walton (Holland, May): *Eastern Rebellion 4*

Bobby Watson (NYC, April): *Jewel* (Milan, November): *Perpetual Groove*

Weather Report (NYC): *Procession*

Randy Weston (Seattle, March): *Blue*

Kenny Wheeler (NYC, May): *Double, double you*

Putte Wickman/Claes Crona (Stockholm, 12 December): *Double Play*

Bob Wilber/Bodeswell Strings (NYC, 8-10 June): *Reflections*

Roy Williams (Stockholm, 14-16 December): *Again! Roy Williams in Sweden*

Glenn Zottola (NYC, December): *Stardust*

Photo: Rollo Phlecks Courtesy: Hank O'Neal

Right: **Ruby Braff recording for Phontastic with John Bunch (piano), Phil Flanigan (bass) and guitarist Chris Flory (December).**

Below: **Steps Ahead, featuring Mike Mainieri (vibes) and Mike Brecker (tenor sax).**

Photo: *David Redfern*

1984

Peter Ind opens the Bass Clef club in London.

MJQ record for Pablo.

Arthur Blythe (44), Lester Bowie (43), Chico Freeman (35) and Don Moye (38) get together to form *The Leaders*.

Guitarist Stanley Jordan (25) causes a sensation at the Kool Jazz Festival in New York City with his revolutionary 'hammering-on' technique which enables him to sound like two guitarists. He signs with Blue Note and records *The Magic Touch*.

Miles Davis (58) receives the Leonie Sonning Music Foundation Prize in Copenhagen (December). Plays an hour long piece titled *Aura* composed in his honour by Palle Mikkelborg.

DEATHS
Alexis Korner (55) 1 January
Claude Hopkins (80) 19 February
Ina Ray Hutton (67) 19 February
Fred Robinson (83) 11 April
Machito (72) 15 April
Mabel Mercer (84) 21 April
Red Garland (60) 23 April *heart attack*
Juan Tizol (84) 23 April
Count Basie (79) 26 April
Jean-Louis Viale (51) 10 May
Ray Copeland (57) 18 May
John Hardee (65) 18 May
Santo Pecora (82) 29 May
Dill Jones (60) 22 June *throat cancer*
Al Dailey (46) 26 June *respiratory infection*
Don Elliott (57) 5 July
Frank Butler (56) 24 July
Babe Russin (73) 4 August
Joe Thomas (75) 6 August
Esther Phillips () August
Trummy Young (72) 10 September *heart attack*
Shelly Manne (64) 26 September
Alberta Hunter (89) 17 October
Budd Johnson (73) 20 October
Vic Dickenson (78) 16 November
Denis Rose (62) 22 November
Rollie Culver (76) 8 December
Gene Ramey (71) 8 December *heart attack*
Charlie Teagarden (71) 10 December
Bill Pemberton (66) 13 December
Viola Wells (82) 22 December
Elmon Wright (54)
George Orendorff (78)

BOOKS
Linda Dahl: *Stormy Weather: the music and lives of a century of jazzwomen*
James M Doran: *Erroll Garner: the most happy piano*
Dave Gelly: *Lester Young*
Raymond Horricks: *Gil Evans*
Raymond Horricks: *Dizzy Gillespie*
Burnett James: *Coleman Hawkins*
Burnett James: *Billie Holiday*
Alun Morgan: *Count Basie*
Richard Palmer: *Oscar Peterson*
Alan Plater: *The Beiderbecke Affair* (novel)

RECORDS
Muhal Richard Abrams (NYC, 22,27 September):, *View from Within*
George Adams/Hannibal Peterson (Zurich, 9 September): *More Sightings*
George Adams/Don Pullen (Netherlands, 2,3 February): *Decisions*
Toshiko Akiyoshi Jazz Orchestra (LA, 24,25 May): *Ten Gallon Shuffle*
Howard Alden/Jack Lesberg (NYC, February/March): *No Amps Allowed*
Lorez Alexandria (Monterey, 27 March): *Harlem Butterfly*
Ernestine Anderson (SF, August): *When the sun goes down*
Art Ensemble of Chicago (Ludwigsburg, June): *The Third Decade*
Chet Baker (Monster, 30 September): *Blues for a reason*
Billy Bang (NYC, 19,29 September): *The Fire from Within*
Carlos Barbosa-Lima (NYC, January): *Plays Luiz Bonfa & Cole Porter*
Kenny Barron (NYC, 23,24 April): *1+1+1* (NYC, 14 December): *Autumn in New York*

Gordon Beck (Bracknell, 7 July): *Celebration*
Gene Bertoncini/Michael Moore (NYC): *Close Ties*
Terence Blanchard/Donald Harrison (NYC, December): *Discernment*
Art Blakey (Mikell's, NYC, May): *New York Scene*
Hamiet Bluiett (NYC, 1,2,13 February): *Ebu* (Berlin, November): *The Clarinet Family*
Karel Boehlee (Holland, 26 February): *Switch*
Anthony Braxton (NYC, 10,11 September): *Six Compositions (Quartet) 1984*
Nick Brignola (NYC, 3 July): *Northern Lights*
Ray Brown (SF, August): *Soular Energy*
Dave Brubeck (Concord, August): *Iola*
Kenny Burrell/Grover Washington (NYC, April): *Togethering*
Gary Burton (Ludwigsburg, November): *Real Life Hits*
Jaki Byard/Howard Riley (London, 29 August): *Live at the Royal Festival Hall*
Charlie Byrd (NYC, March): *Isn't it romantic*
Joe Carter/Art Farmer (NYC, 25,26 October): *My Foolish Heart*
Ron Carter/Jim Hall (California, August): *Telephone*
Jeannie & Jimmy Cheatham (LA, September): *Sweet Baby Blues*
Chick Corea (LA, October): *Septet*
Chick Corea/Steve Kujala (Ludwigsburg, July): *Voyage*
Chick Corea/Miroslav Vitous/Roy Haynes (Willisau & Reutlingen, September): *Trio Music Live in Europe*
Larry Coryell (New Jersey, 7 February): *Comin' Home*
John Critchinson (London): *New Night*
Laila Dalseth (Oslo, August): *Day Dreams*
Kenny Davern/Dick Wellstood (Annapolis, USA,): *Live Hot Jazz*
Buddy de Franco (NYC): *Mr Lucky* (London, 24 October): *Groovin'*
Jack de Johnette (NYC, June): *Album Album*
Gene DiNovi/Ruby Braff (Toronto): *My Funny Valentine*
Lou Donaldson (Bologna, January): *Live in Bologna*
Ray Drummond (White Plains, NY, 17,19 July): *Susanita*
Gil Evans (Sweet Basil, NYC, 27 August): *Live at Sweet Basil*
Digby Fairweather/Stan Barker (Southport): *Let's Duet*
Tal Farlow (LA, September): *The legendary Tal Farlow*
Art Farmer (NYC, 13,15 December): *You make me smile*
Pierre Favre (Willisau, May): *Singing Drums*
Ricky Ford (NYC, 28 August): *Shorter Ideas*
Bruce Forman (SF, May): *Full Circle*
Forward Motion (Berklee, November): *The Berklee Tapes*
Frank Foster/Frank Wess (NYC, December): *Frankly Speaking*
Chico Freeman (NYC, 9 April): *The Pied Piper*
Bill Frisell (NYC, August): *Rambler*
Steve Gadd (NYC, July): *Gaddabout*
Vyacheslav Ganelin: *Inverso*
Jan Garbarek (Oslo, December): *It's OK to listen to the gray voice*
Herb Geller (W.Germany, 24 November): *Hot house*
Dizzy Gillespie (NYC, California, Miami): *Closer to the Source*
Egberto Gismonti/Nana Vasconceles (Oslo, June): *Duas Vozes*
Liz Gorrill (NYC, 13 December): *True Fun*
Stephane Grappelli/Marc Fosset (Paris, April): *Looking at you*
Steve Grossman (Milan, 23,24 July): *Way Out East*
Bengt Hallberg (Sweden, 12,13 December): *Trio con Tromba*

Barry Harris (NYC, 2 March): *For the moment*
Ted Harris (NYC, 10 November): *New Jersey Jazz Festival*
Mark Helias (NYC, 29 August): *Split Image*
Dave Holland (Ludwigsburg, November): *Seeds of Time*
Richard 'Groove' Holmes (St Louis, August): *Swedish Lullaby*
Milt Hinton (NYC, 3 September): *Back to Bass-ics*
Bobby Hutcherson (Berkeley, 9,10 August): *Good Bait*
Milt Jackson (NYC, July): *It don't mean a thing if you can't tap your feet to it*
Oliver Jackson (Paris, 28 February/29 October): *Billie's Bounce*
Andy Jaffe (NYC,24 January): *Manhattan Projections*
Khan Jamal (Copenhagen, 30 September): *Dark Warrior*
Leroy Jenkins (NYC, 2 January): *Urban Blues*
Budd Johnson/Phil Woods (NYC, 4 February): *The Ole Dude and the Fundance Kid*
Thad Jones (Copenhagen, 4 October): *Three and One*
Clifford Jordan (NYC, 3 August): *Dr Chicago*
Clifford Jordan/Junior Cook (Monster, 1 October): *Two Tenor Winner*
Duke Jordan (Copenhagen): *Tivoli One/Tivoli Two*
Sheila Jordan (NYC, 1,2 October): *The Crossing*
Stanley Jordan (): *The magic touch*
Don Joseph (NYC, 2,3 June): *One of a Kind*
Dick Katz (NYC, 7,8 May): *In high profile*
George Kelly (NYC, August): *Plays the music of Don Redman*
Carol Kidd (Pencaitland, January): *Carol Kidd*
Peter King (France, 4 March): *Hi Fly* (Oxford, March): *90˚ of one per cent*
Jimmy Knepper (NYC, 10,11 February): *I dream too much*
Lee Konitz (Glasgow, 29,30 March/3 April): *Wild as Springtime*
Steve Lacy (Paris,19,20 November): *Futurities Parts 1&2*
Oliver Lake (NYC, 17,20 September): *Expandable Language*
Jeannie Lambe (London): *The Midnight Sun*
Don Lanphere (Washington, 21-24 October): *Don loves Midge*
Andy Laverne (NYC, 30,31 October): *Liquid Silver*
Jay Leonhart/Joe Beck (NYC, June-August): *There's gonna be trouble*
Kim Lesley (London): *Store it up til morning*
Dave Liebman (Toronto, March): *Sweet Fury*
Frank Lowe (NYC, 24,28 September): *Decision in Paradise*
Les McCann (Washington, 25-27 May): *Music Box*
Rob McConnell (Toronto, 17,25 May): *Old Friends / New Music*
Dave McKenna (SF, August): *The Key Man*
John McLaughlin (Paris, April/May): *Mahavishnu*
Carmen McRae: *You're lookin' at me*
Manhattan Jazz Quintet (NYC, 11 July): *Manhattan Jazz Quintet*
Fabrizio Marchesi (Milan, 4 December): *Soul*
Tania Maria (SF, September): *The Real Tania Maria – Wild!*
Wynton Marsalis (NYC, May): *Hot house flowers*
M'Boom (NYC, 16-18 October): *Collage*
Mike Melillo (Milan, 3,9 March): *Sepia*
Grover Mitchell (NYC, 20,21 April): *Live at the Red Parrot*
Tete Montoliu (California, 25 April): *Carmina*
Paul Motian (Milan, 26-28 March): *Jack of Clubs* (Ludwigsburg, July): *It should've happened a long time ago*
David Murray (NYC, 24-26 August): *Live at Sweet Basil* (NYC, 27 October/15 November): *Children*
Amina Claudine Myers (Ludwigsburg, March): *Jumping in the Sugar Bowl*
Joe Newman/Joe Wilder (NYC, May): *Hangin' Out*
Nexus (Sweden, 8,9 March): *Meets Enrico Rava*
Horace Parlan (Copenhagen, 30 July): *Glad I found you*
Joe Pass (California, January): *Live at Long Beach City College*
Dave Pell (LA, 13,14 August): *The Dave Pell Octet Plays Again*
Michel Petrucciani (NYC, 16 March): *Live at the Village Vanguard* (Paris, 5 October): *Notes'n'Notes*
Enrico Pieranunzi (Rome, 17 February): *New Lands*
Tito Puente (SF, May): *El Rey*
Joe Puma (June): *Shining Hour*
Sue Raney (California, 23,24 May/4 June): *Ridin' high*

Rufus Reid (NYC, 25 November): *Seven Minds*
Emily Remler (SF, August): *Catwalk*
Howard Riley/Keith Tippett (London, 13 June): *In focus*
Max Roach (Milan, 31 May): *Scott Free* (NYC, 19-21 October): *Survivors*
Spike Robinson (London, 9 August): *London Reprise*
Spike Robinson/Eddie Thompson (Southend, 28 July): *At Chesters*
Bernt Rosengren/Nisse Sandstrom (Stockholm, 22, 23 January): *Summit Meeting*
Charlie Rouse (NYC, 21, 22 January): *Social Call*
Hilton Ruiz (NYC, November): *Cross Currents*
Sal Salvador (NYC, November): *Plays Gerry Mulligan*
David Sanborn (NYC): *Straight to the heart*
Nisse Sandstrom (Stockholm, 8, 9 January): *Young Forever*
Sandvik Big Band (Vancouver): *Sandvik Big Band in Vancouver*
Bill Saxton (White Plains, NY, 12, 16 April): *Beneath the Surface*
Loren Schoenberg (NYC, 19, 20 July): *That's the way it goes*
John Scofield (NYC, April/May): *Electric Outlet*
Don Sebesky (NYC): *Full Cycle*
Bud Shank (NYC, 14 November): *This Bud's for you*
Archie Shepp (NYC, 5-8 February): *Down Home New York* (Massachusetts): *The Good Life* (Germany, 6 October): *African Moods*
Charlie Shoemake (NYC, 8 March): *Incandescents*
Alan Simon (NYC, 14 August): *Rainsplash*
Zoot Sims (LA, 20, 21 March): *Quietly there*
Rudy Smith (Stockholm, 28, 29 March): *Still Around*
Spirit Level (Wokingham, 10, 11 March): *Proud Owners*
Steps Ahead (NYC, January/February): *Modern Times*
Irwin Stokes/Oliver Jackson (Paris, 28 February): *Irwin Stokes/Oliver Jackson*
John Stubblefield (NYC, 18, 21 September): *Confessin'*
Maxine Sullivan (NYC, 6, 7 November): *Great Songs from the Cotton Club*
Bob Summers (LA, 6 February): *Inside Out*
Sun Ra (Athens, 27 February): *Live at Praxis 84*
Horace Tapscott (LA, January): *The Tapscott Sessions, Vol 5*
Rusty Taylor (London, 29 January/5 February): *Give me a call*
John Tchicai (Switzerland, 7 February): *Timo's Message*
Barbara Thompson (London, 23 January): *Pure Fantasy*
Butch Thompson/Hal Smith (Minnesota, 6-8 March): *Echoes from Storyville Vol 1*
Butch Thompson (Minnesota, 8 March/17 October): *Echoes from Storyville Vol 2*
Sir Charles Thompson (Toronto, 18 March): *Portrait of a Piano*
Don Thompson (NYC, January): *A Beautiful Friendship*
Keith Tippett (Exeter, 25 October): *A Loose Kite*
Cal Tjader (Concord): *Good Vibes*
Stan Tracey (London, 2 June): *The Poet's Suite*
Joe Turner (LA, 14 February): *Kansas City here I come*
Stanley Turrentine (NYC, 24 November/7 December): *Straight Ahead*
Phil Upchurch (LA, August/September): *Companions*
Michael Urbaniak (Copenhagen, 21 August): *Take good care of my heart*
Allan Vaché (Texas, 12 February): *High Speed Swing*
Mal Waldron (Seattle, 18 March): *Encounters*
Bennie Wallace (NYC, March): *Sweeping through the city*
Bobby Watson (Tubingen, 8 August): *Advance*
Weather Report (Osaka/Pasadena): *Domino Theory*
Eberhard Weber (Ludwigsburg, September): *Chorus*
Mike Westbrook (Amiens, 12 May): *On Duke's Birthday*
Putte Wickman (Stockholm, 24, 26 April): *Desire*
Bob Wilber/Dick Wellstood (NYC, 27, 28 March/22 May): *Bob Wilber & Dick Wellstood*
James Williams (NYC, 19, 20 July): *Alter Ego*
Gerald Wilson (California, 29, 30 November): *Calafia*
Phil Woods (Bologna, April): *Integrity*

Photo: *David Redfern*

Top: Hamiet Bluiett (baritone sax), co-founder of the World Saxophone Quartet.

Right: Gerry Mulligan (baritone sax), Dave McKenna (piano), Zoot Sims (tenor sax) and Al Cohn (tenor sax) in concert.

Photo: *Rollo Phlecks* Courtesy: *Hank O'Neal*

1985

The Blue Note label is reactivated by Bruce Lundvall and Michael Cuscuna at Capitol Records and relaunched at a mammoth concert in New York's Town Hall on 22 February. *One Night with Blue Note* features Herbie Hancock, McCoy Tyner, Ron Carter, Tony Williams, Jackie McLean, Charles Lloyd, Joe Henderson, Bobby Hutcherson, Cecil Taylor, Bennie Wallace, Kenny Burrell, Grover Washington, Lou Donaldson, Stanley Turrentine, Art Blakey, Johnny Griffin, Freddie Hubbard, Jimmy Smith and Stanley Jordan.

Thad Jones (62) becomes leader of the Count Basie Orchestra (February).

Harold Ashby (60) stars at the Nice Jazz Festival in July.

Chick Corea (44) forms his Elektric Band.

Dexter Gordon (62) stars in the feature film *'Round Midnight.*

Mel Lewis (56) celebrates 20 years of Monday nights at the Village Vanguard.

DEATHS
Papa Joe Assunto (79) 5 January
Johnny Guarnieri (67) 7 January
Cié Frazier (80) 10 January
Kenny Clare (55) 11 January *cancer*
Kenny Clarke (71) 26 January
Ray Ellington (70) 28 February
Zoot Sims (59) 23 March *cancer*
Irving Mills (99) 21 April
Joe Darensbourg (78) 24 May
Skeeter Best (70) 27 May
Lonnie Hillyer (45) 1 July
Chris Woods (59) 4 July
George Duvivier (64) 11 July
George Kelly (69) 15 July
Dick Vance (69) July/August
Sam Wooding (90) 1 August
Nick Ceroli (45) 11 August
Cedric Wallace (76) 19 August
Rudi Blesh (86) 25 August
Philly Joe Jones (62) 30 August *heart attack*
Jo Jones (73) 3 September
Little Brother Montgomery (79) 6 September
Charlie Holmes (75) 12 September
Cootie Williams (77) 15 September *kidney complaint*
Ed Lewis (76) 18 September
Richard Williams (54) 5 November
Dicky Wells (78) 12 November
Derek Jewell () November
Big Joe Turner (74) 23 November
Rex Harris (81) November
Calvin Jackson (66) 9 December
Benny Morton (78) 28 December

BOOKS
Count Basie & Albert Murray: *Good Morning Blues*
Barney Bigard: *With Louis and the Duke*
Ron Brown with Cyril Brown: *Georgia on my mind: the Nat Gonella Story*
Red Callender & Elaine Cohen: *Unfinished Dream: the musical world of Red Callender*
Sid Colin: *Ella: the life and times of Ella Fitzgerald*
Gary Giddins: *Rhythm-a-ning*
Ira Gitler: *Swing to Bop*
Leslie Gourse: *Every Day: the story of Joe Williams*
John E Hasse (ed): *Ragtime: the history, composers and music*
Adrian Ingram: *Wes Montgomery*
Piet Klaasse, Mark Gardner & J Bernlef: *Jam Session*
Herman Leonard: *The Eye of Jazz*
Paul S Machlin: *Stride: the music of Fats Waller*
Lewis Porter: *Lester Young*
Mike Zwerin: *La Tristesse de Saint Louis: swing under the Nazis*

FILMS
'Round Midnight: feature film starring Dexter Gordon

RECORDS
John Abercrombie (Oslo, September): *Current Events*
George Adams/Don Pullen (Copenhagen, 4,5 April): *Live at Montmartre*
Monty Alexander *Full Steam Ahead* (Florida, October): *Friday Night* (Maryland, October): *The River* (Milan, 30 November/2 December): *Threesome*
Barry Altschul (Milan, 25,26 November): *That's Nice*
Ray Anderson (NYC, 14,15 June): *Old Bottles – New Wine* (Ludwigsburg, November): *You Be*
Meredith d'Ambrosio (NYC, 27,28 March): *It's your dance*

Franco d'Andrea (Montpellier, November): *My Shuffle*
Azimuth (London): *Azimuth '85*
Derek Bailey (London, April/July): *Notes*
Chet Baker (Dallas, 13,14 January): *My Foolish Heart / Misty / Time after Time* (Holland, June): *Chet's Choice* (Sweden, 30 June): *Candy* (Holland, 2,6 October): *Sings again* (Italy, 24 November): *Live from the Moonlight*
Kenny Barron (NYC, 11 March): *Scratch*
Count Basie Orchestra (NYC, 24,25 June): *Long Live the Chief*
John Basile (NYC): *Very Early*
Harry Beckett (London): *Pictures of You*
Ed Bickert/Lorne Lofsky (Toronto, 27 January): *The Ed Bickert/Lorne Lofsky Quartet*
Art Blakey (London, 25 February): *Live at Ronnie Scott's* (Holland, 17 March): *Blue Night* (SF, April): *Live at Kimball's*
Carla Bley (NYC, June-August): *Night-Glo*
Paul Bley (Lush Life, NYC, 10 March): *Hot*
Lillian Boutté (New Orleans): *A Fine Romance*
Lester Bowie (NYC, February): *I only have eyes for you*
Joanne Brackeen (NYC, June): *Havin' fun*
Ruby Braff/Scott Hamilton (NYC, February): *A Sailboat in the Moonlight*
Ruby Braff/Dick Hyman (NYC, 3 December): *Manhattan Jazz*
Anthony Braxton (London, 13 November): *Quartet (London) 1985*
Randy Brecker/Eliane Elias (NYC, May): *Amanda*
Gordon Brisker (NYC, 14,15 February): *About Charlie*
Ray Brown (May): *Don't Forget the Blues* (Blue Note, NYC, November/December): *The Red Hot Ray Brown Trio*
Ted Brown (NYC, 23 December): *In Good Company*
Dave Brubeck (Connecticut, December): *Reflections*
Michel Camilo (NYC, 25-27 February): *Why Not?*
Judy Carmichael (NYC, September): *Pearls*
Benny Carter (SF, August): *A Gentleman and his Music*
Doc Cheatham/George Kelly (NYC, 12 December): *Highlights in Jazz*
Jeannie & Jimmy Cheatham (LA, November): *Midnight Mama*
Jay Clayton/Jerry Granelli (Seattle, December): *Sound Songs*
Ornette Coleman & Prime Time (Fort Worth): *Opening the Caravan of Dreams*
Steve Coleman (NYC, March): *Motherland Pulse*
Graham Collier (Hong Kong, December): *Something British*
Ken Colyer (Harlow, 24 February): *Too Busy*
Willie Cook (Sweden): *Christl Mood*
Larry Coryell (NYC, 8 January): *Equipoise*
Stanley Cowell (Toronto, 26 June): *Live at Café des Copains*
Lol Coxhill (8-10 August): *The Inimitable*
Marilyn Crispell/Doug James (Woodstock, 7-9 March): *And your ivory voice sings*
Dardanelle (North Carolina, 2,3 May): *Down Home*
Kenny Davern (Harlow, 10 November): *Live and Swinging*
Kenny Davern Big Three (London, 25 November): *Playing for Kicks*
Kenny Davern/Humphrey Lyttelton (London, 10 December): *This old gang of ours*
Miles Davis (Copenhagen, February/March): *Aura*

Elton Dean (Bologna, 18 April): *The Bologna Tape*
Buddy DeFranco/Oscar Peterson (Berkeley, 30 April): *Hark!*
Charlie Earland (New Jersey, 15,16 May): *Third Degree Burn*
Harry Edison/Claes Crona (Stockholm, 12 February): *Meeting in Stockholm*
Art Ellefson (Toronto, 16 November): *Quartet featuring Tommy Flanagan*
Bill Evans (NYC, January-May): *The Alternative Man*
Jon Faddis (NYC, August): *Legacy*
Mary Fettig (SF, January): *In good company*
Carl Fontana (NYC, 5,6 September): *The Great Fontana*
Bruce Forman/George Cables (SF, February): *Dynamics*
Forward Motion (Oslo, 13,14 June): *Progressions*
Ganelin Trio (Nickelsdorf, 19 October): *Ttango...in Nickelsdorf*
Frank Gordon (NYC, 6,10 June): *Clarion Echoes*
Stan Greig (London, 25 March): *Blues every time*
Keith Greko (Tucson): *Last Train outta Flagstaff*
Steve Grossman (Milan, May): *Love is the thing*
Slide Hampton (Holland, 17 April): *Roots*
Tom Harrell (NYC, 22 December): *Moon Alley*
Craig Harris (NYC): *Tributes*
Gene Harris (NYC, November/December): *Gene Harris Trio Plus One*
Billy Hart (NYC): *Oshumare*
Jimmy Heath (NYC, 18,20 June): *New Picture*
Joe Henderson (NYC, 14-16 November): *Live at the Village Vanguard* (NYC, November): *The State of the Tenor*
Milt Hinton (NYC,): *We Three: Live in New York*
Wayne Horvitz (NYC, 25,26 November): *The Sonny Clark Memorial Quartet / Voodoo*
Freddie Hubbard/Woody Shaw (NYC, 21,22 November): *Double Take*
Abdullah Ibrahim (Montreux, July): *South Africa* (NYC, October): *Water from an Ancient Well*
Ahmad Jamal (Dallas): *Digital Works*
Keith Jarrett (New Jersey, May/July): *Spirits, Vol 1&2* (Paris, 2 July): *Standards Live*
Jane Jarvis (NYC): *Cut Glass*
Oliver Jones (Montreal, 3 July/9 September): *Speak Low, Swing Hard* (Canada, 2,3 November): *Requestfully Yours*
Duke Jordan (Holland, 29 July): *As time goes by*
Karin Krog (Oslo, August): *Freestyle*
Kronos Quartet (California, Autumn): *Music of Bill Evans*
Steve Lacy (Milan, 20,21,24 June): *The Condor* (Milan, 29-31 July): *Only Monk*
Birelli Lagrene (Freiburg, 1,2 June): *Live with Vic Juris*
Peter Leitch (NYC, 16 November): *Red Zone*
Uli Lenz (Berlin, 30,31 October): *Midnight Candy*
Mark Levine (SF, November): *Smiley & Me*
Mel Lewis Orchestra (NYC, 20-22 March): *20 Years at the Village Vanguard*
Dave Liebman/Richard Beirach (Copenhagen, 21 April): *Double Edge*
Dave Liebman & Tolvan Big Band (Malmo, December): *Guided Dream*
Didier Lockwood (NYC, April): *Out of the blue*
Jimmy Lyons (Milan, 6,7 March): *Give it up*
Humphrey Lyttelton (London, 15 November): *Humph at the Bull's Head*
Rob McConnell (Toronto, 11,12 March): *Boss Brass and Woods*
Dave McKenna (SF, August): *Dancing in the dark and other music of Arthur Schwartz*
Marian McPartland (NYC, January): *Willow Creek and other ballads*
Jay McShann (Canada, 9 August): *Airmail Special*
Manhattan Jazz Quintet (NYC, 3 March): *Autumn Leaves* (NYC, 20 November): *My Funny Valentine*
Michael Mantler (NYC, July): *Alien*
Guido Manusardi (Milan, 17 May/3 June): *Down Town*
Tania Maria (NYC): *Made in New York*
Wynton Marsalis (NYC, December): *J Mood*
Warne Marsh (NYC, 15 March): *Posthumous*
Ronnie Mathews (NYC, 26 August): *So Sorry Please*
Mike Melillo (Milan, March): *Live and Well*
Pat Metheny (NYC, 12-14 December): *Song X*
Steve Miller (London, 11 November): *Miller's Tale*
Bob Mintzer (NYC, 1,2 April): *Incredible Journey*
Jemeel Moondoc (NYC, 24 November): *Nostalgia in Times Square*

Ralph Moore (NYC, 21 December): *Round Trip*

Mark Murphy (NYC, 10,11 September): *Beauty and the Beast*

David Murray (NYC, 8 October): *New Life*

NYJO (London, 20 January): *Full Score* (London, 22 June/14 September): *Concrete Cows*

Johnny O'Neal (Baker's Keyboard Lounge, Detroit, 13 July): *Live at Baker's*

OTB (NYC, 7,8 June): *Out of the Blue*

Jeff Palmer (NYC, 16 July): *Laser Wizzard*

Paris Reunion Band (Stockholm, 3 July): *French Cooking*

Errol Parker (NYC, 12 April): *Live at the Wollman Auditorium*

Kim Parker (Milan, 28,29 May): *Sometimes I'm Blue*

Cecil Payne (NYC, 27 February): *Casbah*

Pete Peterson (Dallas, 28,29 September): *Playin' in the Park*

Billy Pierce (NYC,29,30 May): *William the Conqueror*

Valery Ponomarev (NYC, 14 April): *Means of Identification*

Tito Puente (SF, May): *Mambo Diablo*

Don Pullen (NYC, 12,13 June): *The Sixth Sense*

Alvin Queen (NYC, 24,25 August): *Jammin' Uptown*

Alvin Queen/Lonnie Smith (Paris, 28 May): *Lenox and Seventh*

Jimmy Raney (NYC, 30 December): *Wistaria*

Reflexionen (Switzerland, November): *Reflexionen Live*

Buddy Rich (NYC, 7 November): *The Cinch*

Max Roach (Brooklyn, 4,7,8 January): *Easy Winners*

Spike Robinson (London, 17 July): *Spring can really hang you up the most* (London, 20 July): *It's a Wonderful World*

Claudio Roditi (NYC, 27 January): *Claudio!*

Terje Rypdal (Oslo, May): *Chaser*

Jordan Sandke (NYC, June): *Rhythm is our business*

John Scofield (NYC, June): *Still Warm*

Bud Shank/Shorty Rogers (California, 19 May): *California Concert*

George Shearing (SF, May): *Grand Piano*

George Shearing/Mel Tormé (SF, May): *An Elegant Evening*

Archie Shepp (Sacramento, 22 May): *California Meetings* (Milan, 11-13 December): *Little Red Moon*

Wayne Shorter (LA): *Atlantis*

Cees Slinger (Holland, 22 April): *Sling Shot!*

Rudy Smith (Stockholm, 9 October): *Stretching Out*

Sphere (Bologna, November): *On Tour*

Peter Sprague (LA, February): *Na Pali Coast*

Leni Stern (NYC, 16,17 December): *Clairvoyant*

Harvie Swartz (NYC, February): *Urban Earth*

Claude Tissendier (France, October): *Tribute to John Kirby*

Nabil Totah (NYC, June): *Double Bass*

Ralph Towner/Gary Burton (Ludwigsburg, May): *Slide Show*

Joe Turner/Jimmy Witherspoon (LA, 11 April): *Patcha, Patcha, All Night Long*

29th Street Saxophone Quartet (NYC, Spring): *Watch your step*

McCoy Tyner (SF): *Just Feelin'*

James 'Blood' Ulmer (Hamburg, September): *Got Something Good For You*

Michal Urbaniak (NYC, January): *Friday Night at the Village Vanguard*

Miroslav Vitous (Ludwigsburg, September): *Emergence*

Mal Waldron (Holland, 21 April): *Bluesville Time*

Mal Waldron/David Friesen (Milan, 18 November): *Dedication*

Bennie Wallace (NYC): *Twilight Time*

Cedar Walton (Holland, 16 April): *Cedar Walton Trio* (Holland, 21 April): *Bluesville Time*

Sadao Watanabe (Tokyo, 13 July): *Parker's Mood* (Tokyo, July): *Tokyo Dating*

Bobby Watson (Milan, 5 February): *Appointment in Milano* (Milan, 6 February): *Round Trip*

Trevor Watts (Birmingham, 20 January): *Trevor Watts' Moiré Music Live*

Weather Report (LA, December): *This is This*

Dick Wellstood (Toronto, 29 May): *Live at Café des Copains*

Mike Westbrook (Paris, 7,8 December): *Love for Sale*

Tommy Whittle/Alan Barnes (London, November): *Straight Eight*

Putte Wickman (Copenhagen, June): *Mr Clarinet* (Stockholm, 24-27 June): *Songs without words*

James Williams (NYC, 22,24 May): *Progress Report*

John Williams (Woodcray Manor, 19,20 May): *Year of the Buffalo*

Cassandra Wilson (NYC, December): *Point of View*

World Saxophone Quartet (NYC, 6,7 December): *Live at Brooklyn Academy of Music*

John Zorn (NYC, 21 October): *Cobra*

Photo: *Rollo Phlecks* Courtesy: *Hank O'Neal*

60-year-old Al Cohn *(above)* **and 78-year-old Benny Carter** *(right)* **enjoy the fresh air and sunshine aboard the SS Norway during the 3rd annual Floating Jazz Festival (October).**

Photo: *Rollo Phlecks* Courtesy: *Hank O'Neal*

1986

George Russell (63) makes his first British tour (February) leading an Anglo-American Orchestra.

Ella Fitzgerald (68) has coronary by-pass surgery.

Robert Parker's Jazz Classics in Stereo issued.

The American Jazz Orchestra, brainchild of writer Gary Giddins, makes its debut at New York's Cooper Union (June), recreating the great bands of jazz.

Benny Goodman dies on 13 June aged 77.

Teddy Wilson dies on 31 July aged 73.

Woody Herman 50th Anniversary Concert at the Hollywood Bowl (July).

Condon's club closes in New York (July).

Frank Foster (58) takes over leadership of the Count Basie Orchestra following the resignation of Thad Jones.

Miles Davis (59) acts in TV's *Miami Vice*.

DEATHS
Joe Farrell (48) 10 January *bone cancer*
Ken Moule (60) 27 January
Everett Barksdale (75) 29 January
Bob Casey (77) 9 April
Dorothy Ashby (53) 13 April
Teddy Kotick (57) 17 April
Fred Hunt (62) 25 April *cancer*
Cliff Leeman (72) 29 April *kidney failure*
Wallace Bishop (80) 2 May
Clyde Bernhardt (80) 20 May
Hank Mobley (55) 30 May *double pneumonia*
Benny Goodman (77) 13 June
Curley Russell (69) 3 July
Eddie Shu (67) 4 July
Joe Thomas (77) 3 August
Teddy Wilson (73) 31 July
Thad Jones (63) 21 August
Pete Daily (75) 23 August
Joe Tarto (84) 24 August
Bennie Payne (79) 2 September
Billy Taylor (80) 2 September
Knocky Parker (68) 3 September
Pepper Adams (55) 10 September *cancer*
Emmanuel Sayles (79) 5 October
Johnny Dyani (40) 24 October
Alan Branscombe (50) 27 October
Eddie 'Lockjaw' Davis (65) 3 November
Eddie Thompson (61) 6 November *heart attack*
Marky Markowitz (62) 11 November
Sippie Wallace (88) November
Paul Bascomb (74) 2 December
Slam Stewart (72) 10 December
Fred Stone (51) 10 December

BOOKS
K Abé: *Jazz Giants*
Clyde Bernhardt, Sheldon Harris: *I remember*
Roy Carr, Brian Case, Fred Dellar: *The Hip*
Bruce Crowther & Mike Pinfold: *The Jazz Singers*
John Fordham: *Let's join hands and contact the living: the story of Ronnie Scott and his club*
Jim Godbolt: *All This and 10%*
Robert Gordon: *Jazz West Coast*
Gerard Herzhaft: *Long Blues in A minor (novel)*
Lowell D Holmes & John W Thomson: *Jazz Greats: Getting better with age*
Raymond Horricks: *Gerry Mulligan*
Barry McRae: *The Jazz Handbook*
Michel Ruppli: *The Clef/Verve Labels: a discography*
Steve Voce: *Woody Herman*

FILMS
Round Midnight ( ): feature film starring Dexter Gordon

RECORDS
John Abercrombie/Don Thompson (Toronto, 24-25 June): *Witchcraft*
Muhal Richard Abrams (NYC, 19 December): *Colors in Thirty-Third*
Howard Alden-Dan Barrett (NYC, September): *Swing Street*
Lew Anderson (NYC): *All American Big Band*
Franco Ambrosetti (NYC, 24,25 November): *Movies*
Art Ensemble of Chicago (NYC, 25-27 July): *Naked*

Derek Bailey/Anthony Braxton (Canada, 4 October): *Moment Precieux*
Chet Baker (Copenhagen, 23 February): *When Sunny gets blue* (Ronnie Scott's, London, 6 June): *Nightbird*
Billy Bang (NYC, 23 November): *Live at Carlos 1*
Bob Barnard (London, 3 November): *Class!*
Kenny Barron (NYC, 17 February): *What If*
Guido Basso (LA, 19,20 June): *Guido Basso*
George Benson (Windsor, Ontario, 12,13 May): *Swings & Swings & Swings*
Karl Berger (NYC, 25,26 August): *Transit*
Totti Bergh/Al Cohn (Oslo, 9-10 August): *Tenor Gladness*
Tim Berne (NYC, July): *The Little Trumpet of Petra*
Warren Bernhardt (NYC, 17-21 October): *Hands On*
Eddie Bert (One Bone – Four Strings)
Ran Blake (Massachusetts, 26 August): *Short Life of Barbara Monk*
Lester Bowie (Ludwigsburg, March): *Avant Pop*
Joanne Brackeen (NYC, October): *Fi-fi goes to Heaven*
Bobby Bradford (Florida, 11 November): *One Night Stand*
Anthony Braxton (Milan, 2,3 July): *Five Compositions (Quartet) 1986*
Joshua Breakstone (NYC, 19 February): *Echoes*
Randy Brecker (NYC, 19,20 October): *In the Idiom*
Dee Dee Bridgewater (Paris, 24,25 November): *Live in Paris*
Dave Brubeck (SF, November): *Blue Rondo*
Kenny Burrell (NYC, 24,25 October): *Pieces of Blue and the Blues*
Gary Burton (Ludwigsburg, June): *Whiz Kids*
Charlie Byrd (Baltimore, April): *Byrd & Brass*
Benny Carter/Oscar Peterson (LA, 14 November): *Benny Carter meets Oscar Peterson*
Michael Carvin (NYC, 7 October): *First Time*
Philip Catherine (Freiburg, 24,25 November): *Transparence*
Richie Cole (NYC, November): *Pure Imagination*
Steve Coleman (NYC, January): *On the Edge of Tomorrow* (NYC, November): *World Expansion*
Marilyn Crispell (Paris, 19 December): *Quartet Improvisations – Paris 1986*
Jim Cullum (San Antonio, 21,22 October): *Super Satch*
Laila Dalseth/Al Cohn (Oslo, 9,10 August): *Travelling Light*
Maxine Daniels (London): *Every night about this time*
Miles Davis (NYC): *Tutu*
Wild Bill Davison (Ludwigsburg, 19 October): *Wild Bill Davison All Stars*
Niels Lan Doky (Copenhagen, 17 January): *Here or There*
Dorothy Donegan (Zurich, December): *Live at the Widder Bar*
Bob Dorough (France, May): *Clankin' on Tin Pan Alley*
Eliane Elias (NYC, 22-24 October): *Illusions*
Peter Erskine (NYC, 16,17 October): *Transition*
Gil Evans (NYC, 1,22 December): *Farewell Gil Evans*
Art Farmer/Benny Golson Jazztet (Sweet Basil, NYC, 21,22 February): *Real Time*
Claudio Fasoli (Milan, 6 May): *Welcome*
Wally Fawkes (London, 21 July): *Whatever Next!*
Boulou Ferre (Copenhagen, 25 May): *Boulou Ferre Quartet*
First Brass (Hamburg): *First Brass*

Tommy Flanagan (NYC, 18,19 October): *Nights at the Vanguard*
Bob Florence (LA, 24,25 November): *Trash Can City*
Bruce Forman (SF, August): *There are times*
Chico Freeman (Ronnie Scott's, London): *Groovin' Late*
Dave Friedman (NYC, 24,25 April): *Shades of Change*
Vyacheslav Ganelin (Leningrad, 10 February): *Con Amore*
Jan Garbarek (Oslo, August): *All those born with wings*
Herb Geller (Hamburg, 24,25 January): *Birdland Stomp*
Stan Getz (California, 9 March): *Voyage*
Tiziana Ghiglione (Milan, 28,29 April): *Somebody special*
Terry Gibbs (Berkeley, 9,10 May): *The Latin Connection*
Dizzy Gillespie/Phil Woods (Holland, 14 December): *Dizzy Gillespie meets the Phil Woods Quintet*
Rowland Greenberg (Oslo, 14,15 November): *How about you*
Al Grey/Jesper Thilo (Copenhagen, 10 August): *Al Grey & Jesper Thilo Quintet*
Marty Grosz (NYC, 20,22 May): *Sings of Love and Other Matters*
Charlie Haden (LA, 22,23 December): *Quartet West*
Scott Hamilton (NYC, 23 January): *The Right Time* (Boston, May): *Major League*
Eddie Harris (Holland, 27 February): *Eddie Who?*
Donald Harrison/Terence Blanchard (NYC, 28-31 January): *Nascence*
Gijs Hendriks/Beaver Harris (Holland, March): *Sound Compound*
Woody Herman (SF, March): *50th Anniversary Tour*
Eddie Higgins (NYC, 5 August): *By Request*
Andrew Hill (Milan, 3,4 July): *Shades* (Milan, 5 July): *Verona Rag*
Jeff Hittman (NYC, 14 November): *Mosaic*
Peanuts Hucko (Monster, 8 July): *Tribute to Louis Armstrong/Benny Goodman*
Human Chain (London, Spring): *Human Chain*
Dick Hyman (NYC, 25 June): *Gulf Coast Blues*
Dick Hyman/Dick Wellstood (NYC, 19 July): *Stridemonster*
Ronald Shannon Jackson & the Decoding Society (Fort Worth): *Live at the Caravan of Dreams*
Khan Jamal (Philadelphia, 7 October): *Thinking of you*
Keith Jarrett (Munich, 13 July): *Still Live* (Ludwigsburg, July): *Book of Ways*
Clifford Jordan (NYC, 23 December): *Royal Ballads*
Jimmy Knepper (NYC, 3 April): *Dream Dancing*
Lee Konitz (Milan, 22,23 July): *Ideal Scene*
Steve Kuhn (Village Vanguard, NYC, 28-30 March): *Life's Magic*
Steve Lacy (NYC, 16-18 July): *The Gleam*
Birelli Lagrene (2,3 May): *With Special Guests*
Last Exit (Paris, 16 February): *Last Exit*
The Leaders (California, 11,12 June): *Mudfoot*
Peter Leitch (Holland, November): *On a misty night*
Kirk Lightsey (Holland, 23 April): *First Affairs*
Loose Tubes (London, July/August): *Delightful Precipice*
Dave McKenna (California, August): *My Friend the Piano*
Adam Macowicz (Stockholm, March): *Interface*
Manhattan Jazz Quintet (Tokyo, 21 April): *Live at Pitt Inn*
Guido Manusardi/Lee Konitz (Italy, Autumn): *Velvet Soul*
Branford Marsalis (NYC, March/July): *Royal Garden Blues*
Wynton Marsalis (NYC, 29,30 May/24,25 September): *Marsalis Standard Time* (Washington DC, 19,20 December): *Live at Blues Alley*
Warne Marsh (NYC, 31 March): *Back Home*
Helen Merrill (Paris, March): *Music Makers*
Butch Miles (NYC, 15,22 April): *Jazz Express*
Red Mitchell/Kenny Barron (Stockholm, 19 August): *The Red Barron Duo*
Roscoe Mitchell (Chicago, 29 June/7 September): *The flow of things*
Tete Montoliu (Milan, 1 December): *The music I like to play*
Frank Morgan (Berkeley, 21,22 April): *Lament* (Village Vanguard, NYC, 14,15 December): *Bebop Lives!*
Paul Motian (Milan, 14-16 July): *Misterioso*

1986

Bob Mover (Montreal, 22 January): *The Night Bathers*
Gerry Mulligan/Scott Hamilton (NYC, January): *Soft Lights & Sweet Music*
Turk Murphy (Concord, 10 August): *Concert in the Park*
David Murray (Boston, 1 March): *I want to talk about you* (NYC, 3,4 September): *In our style* (NYC, 29 November): *The Hill*
New Air (Milan, 2,3 June): *Air Show No1*
James Newton (NYC, 20,21 August): *Romance and Revolution*
Keith Nichols & Red Hot Syncopators (London, 7 January): *Doctor's Jazz*
Anita O'Day (London,): *Wave*
Paris Reunion Band (Stockholm, 23,24 October): *For Klook*
Horace Parlan (Monster, 10 July): *Joe meets the Rhythm Section*
Bill Perkins (Pasadena): *Remembrance of Dino's*
Michel Petrucciani (Montreux, 14 July): *Power of Three*
Dave Pike (Holland, 5 February): *Pike's Groove*
Courtney Pine (London, July & August): *Journey to the Urge Within*
Bucky Pizzarelli (NYC): *Solo Flight*
John Pizzarelli (NYC, November): *Sing! Sing! Sing!*
Enrico Rava (Milan, 7,8 July): *Secrets* (Ludwigsburg, October): *Volver*
Max Roach (NYC, 1,2 October): *Bright Moments*
Spike Robinson (London, 23 October): *In Town with Elaine Delmar*
Terje Rypdal (Oslo, November): *Blue*
Arturo Sandoval (Ronnie Scott's, London, August): *No Problem*
John Scofield (NYC, September): *Blue Matter*
Bud Shank (Berkeley, 17,18 February): *That old feeling* (Seattle, 16-18 December): *At Jazz Alley*
Bud Shank/Bill Perkins (Berkeley, 2-4 December): *Serious Swingers*
George Shearing (SF, October): *More Grand Piano*
Lew Soloff (NYC, 15,16 September): *Yesterdays*
Sphere (Perugia, 14 July): *Live at Umbria Jazz*
Mike Stern (NYC, March & April): *Upside Downside*
String Trio of New York (Milan, 1,2 April): *Natural Balance*
Rory Stuart (NYC, 13,14 May): *Hurricane*
Maxine Sullivan (Tokyo, September): *Swingin' Sweet*
Sun Ra (Berlin, 28 June): *A night in East Berlin* (Milan, 18,19 December): *Hours After*
Buddy Tate/Humphrey Lyttelton (London, 16 December): *Long Tall Tenor*
Cecil Taylor (Berlin, 9 April): *For Olim*
Clark Terry/Jon Faddis (NYC, 27 February/Zurich, 19 May): *Take Double*
Eje Thelin (Gothenburg, 26,27 July): *E.T.Project*
Thelonious (Burbank, November): *Thelonious*
Jesper Thilo (Copenhagen, 2,16 February): *Featuring Harry Edison*
Clark Tracey (London, February): *Suddenly Last Tuesday*
Stan Tracey (London, 6 July): *Plays Duke Ellington*
McCoy Tyner (NYC, 7,9 June): *Double Trios*
Warren Vaché (NYC, December): *Easy Going*
Nana Vasconcelos (London): *Bush Dance*
Vibration Society (NYC, 14,15 January): *The Music of Rahsaan Roland Kirk*
Mal Waldron/Steve Lacy (Milan, 17 February): *Sempre Amore*
Mal Waldron/Jackie McLean (Tokyo, 1 September): *Left Alone '86*
Mal Waldron/Jim Pepper (Munich, 5 April): *Art of the Duo*
Mal Waldron (Milan, 10 March): *Update* (Village Vanguard, NYC, 16 September): *The Seagulls of Kristiansund* (Sweet Basil, NYC, 3,4 October): *Fire Waltz* (Germany): *Mal Waldron plays the blues*
Bennie Wallace (7,8 September): *Brilliant Corners*
Jack Walrath (NYC, 15 March/1 April): *Wholly Trinity* (England, 12,13 May): *Killer Bunnies*
Cedar Walton (LA, 29,30 September): *Plays the music of Billy Strayhorn*
Kazumi Watanabe (London, October/November): *The Spice of Life*
Trevor Watts Moiré Music (England, 23 October): *Saalfelden Encore*
Michael Weiss (NYC, 4 April): *Presenting Michael Weiss*
Mike Westbrook (Zurich, 11,12 November): *Westbrook-Rossini*
Putte Wickman (Stockholm, 19 November): *Miss Oidipus*
Jessica Williams (California, 26 February): *Nothin' but the truth*
Tony Williams (California, 24-26 November): *Civilization*
Claude Williamson (Barcelona, 17 May): *The Sermon*
Norma Winstone (Oslo, July): *Somewhere called home*
Phil Woods (NYC, 19 June): *Gratitude*
Reggie Workman (Philadelphia, 15 June): *Synthesis*
Attila Zoller (Leverkusen, 1 November): *Overcome*

Photo: *Rollo Phlecks* Courtesy: *Hank O'Neal*

Above: **Flip Phillips (71) and Woody Herman (73) are reunited at the Floating Jazz Festival aboard the SS Norway (October).**

Right: The Floating Jazz Festival also marks the temporary return to jazz of Mel Powell (63).

Photo: *Rollo Phlecks* Courtesy: *Hank O'Neal*

1987

Buddy Rich (69) undergoes an operation to treat a brain tumour on 17 March. He dies on 2 April.

Andy Sheppard makes his first recording under his own name (July).

Buck Clayton (76) forms a big band to play his own compositions and arrangements.

Dizzy Gillespie tours the world with his '70th Birthday Big Band'.

Ray Charles (57) receives 'Lifetime Achievement Award' from President Reagan.

Bob Wilber (59) forms a big band to stage recreations of Benny Goodman's 1938 Carnegie Hall Concert, including a performance at London's Royal Festival Hall on 8 October.

DEATHS

Alton Purnell (75) 14 January
Harry Dial (79) 25 January
Spike Hughes (78) 2 February
Alfred Lion (78) 2 February *congestive heart failure*
John Malachi (67) 11 February
Bola Sete (63) 14 February
Freddie Green (75) 1 March
Eddie Durham (78) 6 March
Bill McGuffie (59) 22 March *cancer*
Moustache (58) 25 March *car crash*
Buddy Rich (69) 2 April *cancer*
David Burnett James (67) 3 April
Maxine Sullivan (75) 7 April *brain tumour*
Heinie Beau (76) 19 April
Irving Ashby (66) 22 April
Wilbur Little (59) 4 May
Vic Feldman (53) 12 May *asthma attack*
Turk Murphy (71) 30 May *bone cancer*
Booty Wood (67) 10 June *emphysema*
Kid Thomas Valentine (91) 16 June
Frank Rehak (60) 26 June *cancer of oesophagus*
Doug Dobell (69) 10 July
John Hammond (76) 10 July
Howard McGhee (69) 17 July
Dick Wellstood (59) 24 July *heart attack*
Steve Davis (58) 21 August
Jaco Pastorius (35) 22 September *from injuries sustained in a brawl*
Gene Rodgers (77) 23 October
Willis 'Gator' Jackson (59) 25 October
Woody Herman (74) 29 October
Albert McCarthy (67) November
Harold Vick (51) 13 November
Slam Stewart (73) 10 December
Warne Marsh (60) 18 December *heart attack*

BOOKS

Bruce Crowther: *Gene Krupa*
Max Jones: *Talking Jazz*
Marian McPartland: *All in good time*
Arnold Shaw: *The Jazz Age: Popular music in the 1920's*
John White: *Billie Holiday: her life & times*

FILMS

Celebrating Bird (60 mins): documentary about Charlie Parker by Gary Giddins
A Night in Havana: Dizzy Gillespie

RECORDS

John Abercrombie (NYC, April): *Getting There*
Monty Alexander (Santa Monica, June): *Triple Treat III*
Lorez Alexandria with Gordon Brisker Band (LA, 24 March/14 April): *Dear to my heart*
Mose Allison (NYC, 11,12,21 May/2 June): *Ever since the world ended*
Meredith d'Ambrosio (NYC, 27,28 October): *The Cove*
Ray Anderson (NYC, 31 January/1 February): *It just so happens*
Chet Baker (Tokyo, 14 June): *Memories*
Alan Barnes (London, 14 July/1 September): *Affiliation*
Dan Barrett (NYC, June): *Strictly Instrumental*
Bass Desires (Oslo, March): *Second Sight*
Louie Bellson (Chicago, October): *Live at Joe Segal's Jazz Showcase*
Bob Berg (NYC, March): *Short Stories*
Dick Berk & the Jazz Adoption Agency (California, 28,29 January): *Play the Music of Rodgers & Hart*
Eddie Bert & Impuls (Holland, 14,17 June): *TNT*
Gene Bertoncini & Michael Moore (NYC): *Strollin'*
Cindy Blackman (NYC, 8 August/23 December): *Arcane*
Paul Bley/Paul Motian (Milan, 3,4 July): *Notes*
Paul Bley (Oslo, November): *Quartet*
Hamiet Bluiett (NYC, 7 July): *Nali Kola*

Lester Bowie's Brass Fantasy (NYC, April): *Twilight Dreams*
Charles Brackeen (Dallas, 13 February): *Bannar* (Dallas, 28 November): *Worshippers come nigh* (Dallas, 29 November): *Attainment*
Anthony Braxton (Milan, 30 June/1 July): *Six Monk's Compositions (1987)*
Joshua Breakstone (NYC, 11 December): *Evening Star*
Alan Broadbent (LA, 2,3 July): *Another time*
Deborah Brown (Holland, 22 July): *Deborah!*
Donald Brown (NYC, 4,5 June): *Early Bird*
Dave Brubeck (Moscow, March): *Moscow Night*
Ray Bryant (NYC, 15,16 February): *Plays Basie and Ellington*
John Bunch (NYC, June): *The best thing for you*
Donald Byrd (NYC, 22,24 September): *Harlem Blues*
Jackie Cain/Roy Kral (NYC, 19,20 March): *One More Rose*
Benny Carter (NYC, August): *Central City Sketches* (NYC, 9,11 November): *In the Mood for Swing*
Doc Cheatham (Sweden, 13,14 May): *A tribute to Billie Holiday*
Jeannie & Jimmie Cheatham (LA, January): *Homeward Bound*
George Chisholm (London, 11 June): *That's-a-plenty*
Clarinet Summit (Atlanta, 29 March): *Southern Bells*
Dave Cliff (London, November): *The Right Time*
Al Cohn & the Jazz Seven (London, 28 May): *Keeper of the Flame*
Al Cohn (June): *Rifftide*
Richie Cole/Hank Crawford (France, 16 July): *Bossa International*
George Coleman (SF, August): *At Yoshi's*
Larry Coryell (NYC, 8 September): *Toku Do*
Larry Coryell/Miroslav Vitous (West Germany, 13 May): *Quartet*
Marilyn Crispell (NYC, 15 March): *Gaia*
Connie Crothers/Richard Tabrik (NYC, 21 March): *Duo Dimension*
The Cunninghams/Dick Berk (LA, 7,8 July): *Make me a sweet potato pie*
Maxine Daniels (London, 9,10 March): *A Pocketful of Dreams* (London, 8 September): *My very good friend*
Danish Radio Big Band (Glasgow, 22 February/York, 24 February): *First UK Tour/Crackdown*
Dardanelle (Georgia, 11 January): *That's my Style*
Nathan Davis (London, 17,18 August): *London by night*
Al Dimeola (NYC, April): *Tirami Su*
District Six (England, June): *To be free*
Eliane Elias (NYC, 16-21 March): *Cross Currents*
Gil Evans/Laurent Cugny (Paris, 2,3,26 November): *Rhythm-a-ning*
Gil Evans/Steve Lacy (Paris, 30 November/1 December): *Paris Blues*
Clare Fischer (LA, 13,24 June): *Tjaderama*
Ricky Ford (NYC, 4 September): *Saxotic Stomp*
Stan Getz (Copenhagen, 6 July): *Anniversary*
Terry Gibbs/Buddy de Franco (Chicago, 24-26 July): *Chicago Fire*
Benny Golson/Freddie Hubbard (NYC, 22,23 June): *Stardust*
Eddie Gomez (NYC, November): *Power Play*
Dusko Goykovich (London, 18 August): *Celebration*
Marty Grosz (NYC, 29 January/5,12 March): *Keepers of the Flame*
George Gruntz (Fort Worth, 16,17 October): *Happening Now!*
Charlie Haden/Paul Motian/Geri Allen (NYC, 14,15 September): *Etudes*
Charlie Haden (Rome, 11,12 November): *Silence*
Bengt Hallberg (Stockholm, 25,26 March/18,20 November): *Hallberg's Yellow Blues*
Sir Roland Hanna/Jesper Thilo (Copenhagen, 17,18 June): *This time it's real*

Gene Harris All Star Big Band (Burbank, March/June): *Tribute to Count Basie*
Mark Helias (NYC, 4,5 March): *The Current Set*
Joe Henderson/Charlie Haden/Al Foster (Genova Jazz Festival, July): *An Evening with...*
Woody Herman (Concord, March): *Woody's Gold Star*
Art Hodes (Canada, 20 April/17 June): *Joy to the Jazz World – Yuletide Piano Solos*
Dave Holland (Ludwigsburg, February): *The Razor's Edge*
Red Holloway (SF, January): *And Company*
Bill Holman (LA, 30 November/1 December): *Bill Holman Band: World Class*
Shirley Horn (Maryland, October): *Softly*
Freddie Hubbard (NYC, 23,24 January): *Life Flight*
Freddie Hubbard/Woody Shaw (NYC, 11,12 June): *The Eternal Triangle*
Peter Ind (London): *Jazz Bass Baroque*
Irakere (Ronnie Scott's, October): *In London*
Ronald Shannon Jackson (Dallas, 9-11 April): *Texas*
Keith Jarrett (Tokyo, 11 April): *Dark Intervals* (Tokyo, April): *Personal Mountains* (USA, October): *Changeless*
Billy Jenkins (London): *Scratches of Spain*
Oliver Jones (NYC, 3 September): *Cookin' at Sweet Basil*
Roger Kellaway/Red Mitchell (NYC, 10 February): *Fifty Fifty*
Barney Kessel (Berkeley, 20-22 February): *Spontaneous Combustion*
Carol Kidd (Scotland, January): *Nice Work*
Pete King/Dick Morrissey/Martin Taylor (London): *Live at the Bull*
Pat LaBarbera (Montreal, April): *Virgo Dance*
Steve Lacy (Ludwigsburg, 21,22 April): *Explorations* (Paris, 20-22 May): *Momentum* (Milan, 30,31 July): *The Window* (Liverpool, 16 October): *Image*
Birelli Lagrene (NYC, July): *Inferno*
Lawson-Haggart Band (Atlanta, 25 March): *Go to New Orleans*
The Leaders (Paris, 18,19 February): *Out here like this...*
Dave Liebman (NYC, 27,28 January): *Homage to John Coltrane* (NYC, 1,2 May): *Trio + One*
Kirk Lightsey/Freddie Hubbard (Monster, 5,6,13 June): *Temptation*
Abbey Lincoln (NYC, 6,7 November): *A Tribute to Billie Holiday*
Loose Tubes (London, December): *Open Letter*
Humphrey Lyttelton (London, 11,12 August): *Gigs*
Chris McGregor (London, 18 August): *Blue Note from Johnny*
Marian McPartland (NYC, March): *Plays the music of Billy Strayhorn*
Carmen McRae (California, December): *Fine and Mellow*
Guido Manusardi (Italy, 14,15 March): *Bra Session*
Branford Marsalis (LA, 25-28 January): *Renaissance* (Tokyo, 12,13 August): *Random Abstract*
Warne Marsh (Sherman Oaks, 4,5 June): *Two days in the life of...* (Oslo, 21-23 September): *For the time being*
Turk Mauro (Paris, 11 May/5 November): *Live in Paris*
Mike Melillo/Massimo Urbani (Italy, 23 March): *Duets for Yardbird*
Pat Metheny (NYC, March/April): *Still Life (Talking)*
Mulgrew Miller (NYC, 11 May): *Wingspan*
Mingus Dynasty (NYC, 29,30 September): *Mingus' Sounds of Love*
Grover Mitchell (NYC, 26 September): *Truckin'*
Charnett Moffett (NYC): *Net Man*
James Moody (New Jersey, 10,11 September/18 November): *Moving Forward*
Ralph Moore (NYC, 27 February): *623 C Street*
Airto Moreira/Flora Purim (West Germany, November): *The Colours of Life*
Mark Morganelli (NYC, 24,25 February/5 March): *Five is Bliss*
Paul Motian (Milan, 21,22 September): *One time out*
David Murray/Randy Weston (NYC, 26 September): *The Healer*
Buell Neidlinger (Milan, 24,25 July): *Locomotive*
Bjarne Nerem (Oslo, 29,30 August): *More than you know*
Eduardo Niebla/Antonio Forcione (London, September): *Celebration*
Paris Reunion Band (Ronnie Scott's, London, 27,28 November): *Hot Licks*
Horace Parlan (Milan, 12,13 March): *Little Esther*

1987

John Patitucci: *Patitucci*
Gary Peacock (Oslo, March): *Guamba*
Ken Peplowski (NYC, December): *Double Exposure*
Jim Pepper (NYC, 14 January): *Dakota Song*
Flip Phillips/Scott Hamilton (NYC, March): *A Sound Investment*
Billy Pierce (NYC, 6 June/24 October): *Give and take*
Marlene Ver Planck (NYC, June): *Pure & Natural*
Mel Powell (aboard SS Norway, October): *The Return of Mel Powell*
Power Tools (NYC, 8-10 January): *Strange Meeting*
Tito Puente (SF, January): *Un Poco Loco*
Mick Pyne (London, 23 July): *A Little Blue*
Dudu Pukwana/John Stevens (England,14 January): *They shoot to kill*
Quest (Copenhagen, 21,22 April): *Midpoint: Live at Montmartre*
Enrico Rava (Milan, 2-5 June): *Animals*
Reflexionen (Ludwigsburg, 23,24 February): *Remember to remember*
Mike Renzi (NYC, 9 May): *A Beautiful Friendship*
Red Richards/George Kelly (NYC, 28 August): *I'm shooting high*
Spike Robinson (London, 20,21 October): *With Strings*
Spike Robinson/Al Cohn (NYC, 17 June): *Henry B. meets Alvin G.*
Sonny Rollins (Berkeley, 15 September): *Dancing in the Dark*
Charlie Rouse (London,16 October): *Playin' in the Yard*
Rova Saxophone Quartet (Milan, 13-15 April): *Beat Kennel*
Ellyn Rucker (Denver, 2,3 September): *Ellyn*
Hilton Ruiz (NYC, 15 October): *El Camino*

Akio Sasajima/Joe Henderson (Chicago, 16,17 May): *Akio*
Diane Schuur (LA, 26 February): *And the Count Basie Orchestra*
Jon Scofield (Tokyo, 7 October): *Pick Hits* (NYC, December): *Loud Jazz*
Mark Shane (NYC): *Blueberry Rhyme*
Woody Shaw (Zurich, 7 February/ Bern, 8 February): *In my own sweet way* (NYC, 24 June): *Imagination*
George Shearing (NYC, May): *Breakin' Out* (Japan): *Dexterity*
Jack Sheldon (California, September): *Hollywood Heroes*
Andy Sheppard (London, 21,25 July): *Andy Sheppard*
Archie Shepp/Horace Parlan (Monster, 4 May): *Splashes* (Monster, 5 May): *Reunion*
Archie Shepp/Jasper Van't Hof (Monster, 7,8 May): *The Fifth of May*
Ben Sidran (Minneapolis, October): *Too hot to touch*
Marvin 'Smitty' Smith (March): *Keeper of the Drums*
Jim Snidero (NYC, 24 December): *Mixed Bag*
Mark Soskin (NYC, December): *Overjoyed*
John Stubblefield (NYC, 27,28 May): *Countin' on the Blues*
Stan Sulzmann/John Taylor (London): *Everybody's Song but my own*
John Surman (Oslo, December): *Private City*
Neil Swainson (Toronto, May): *Quintet*
Cecil Taylor (Bologna, 3 November): *Live in Bologna* (Vienna, 7 November): *Live in Vienna*
Gary Thomas (NYC, 3,4 April): *Seventh Quadrant*
Henry Threadgill (NYC, 20,21 September): *Easily

slip into another world*
Mel Tormé/George Shearing (Saratoga, August): *A Vintage Year*
Jean Toussaint (Holland, 23 July): *Impressions of Coltrane*
Clark Tracey (London, 5 October): *Stiperstones*
Steve Turre (NYC, 7,8 February): *Viewpoint*
James Blood Ulmer (NYC): *America – do you remember the love?*
Mal Waldron (NYC, 28,29 August): *Live at Sweet Basil* (Munich, 25 November): *Mal, Dance and Soul*
Bennie Wallace (NYC, 7,8 February): *The Art of the Saxophone* (NYC, June): *Border Town*
Jan Wallgren (Stockholm, 22 April): *Blueprints*
Jazz Warriors (London, 13,14 March): *Out of many, one people*
Benny Waters (NYC, 26 June): *Hearing is convincing*
Ernie Watts LA,14,15 December): *Ernie Watts Quartet*
Kenny Wheeler (Milan, 26,27 May): *Flutter by, Butterfly*
Glenn Wilson (NYC, 17 December): *Elusive*
Mike Wofford (LA, 28,29 September): *Funkallero*
Phil Woods (Tokyo, November): *Bouquet* (Tokyo, November): *Bop Stew*
George Young (NYC, 16 November): *Oleo*

Left: 20-year-old Tommy Smith in action at the Edinburgh Jazz Festival (August).
Below: Sarah Vaughan.
Bottom: Kenny Davern and Flip Phillips join forces at the Floating Jazz Festival aboard the SS Norway (October).

Photo: Brian Foskett

Photo: Rollo Phlecks Courtesy: Hank O'Neal

1988

Bob Wilber leads the Loren Schoenberg Orchestra at a 50th anniversary recreation of Benny Goodman's historic Carnegie Hall concert (16 January).

New Orleans City Council decree that Lillian Boutté is the Official Music Ambassador of New Orleans.

Eighteen-year-old alto saxophonist Christopher Hollyday attracts attention with his recording 'Reverence',

Gil Evans dies of peritonitis in March at the age of 79. His regular Monday night big band gig at New York's Sweet Basil continues under the leadership of his son, Miles.

Chet Baker (58) falls to his death from a hotel window in Amsterdam.

DEATHS

Joe Albany (63) 11 January
Ray Bauduc (78) 15 January
Al Hall (72) 18 January
Don Patterson (61) 10 February
Al Cohn (62) 15 February *liver cancer*
Charles Delaunay (77) 16 February
Memphis Slim 72) 24 February
Peck Morrison (68) 25 February
Ken Colyer (59) 8 March
Dannie Richmond (52) 15 March
Billy Butterfield (71) 18 March *cancer*
Gil Evans (75) 20 March
Tommy Potter (69) March
Pony Poindexter (62) 14 April
Nappy Lamare (80) 8 May
Chet Baker (58) 13 May *fell out of hotel window*
Emmanuel Paul (84) 23 May
Sy Oliver (77) 28 May
Eddie 'Cleanhead' Vinson (70) 2 July *heart attack*
Lawrence Brown (81) 5 September
Sam Woodyard (63) 20 September
J. C. Heard (70) 28 September *heart attack*

BOOKS

Garvin Bushell with Mark Tucker: *Jazz from the beginning*
Bruce Crowther & Mike Pinfold: *The Big Band Years*
Michael Cuscuna & Michel Ruppli: *The Blue Note Label*
Ron Frankl: *Duke Ellington*
Peter Gamble & Peter Symes: *Focus on Jazz*
Christopher Hillman: *Bunk Johnson: his life & times*
Milt Hinton & David G Berger: *Bass Line*
Barry Kernfeld (editor): *The New Grove Dictionary of Jazz*
Bud Kliment: *Ella Fitzgerald*
Gene Lees: *Oscar Peterson: the will to swing*
Gene Lees: *Singers and the Song*
Barry McRae: *Dizzy Gillespie: his life & times*
Mike Pinfold: *Louis Armstrong: his life & times*
Harry Shapiro: *Waiting for the Man; the story of drugs and popular music*
Alyn Shipton: *Fats Waller: his life & times*
Peter Silvester: *A Left Hand like God: A study of boogie woogie*
Mel Tormé: *It wasn't all velvet*

FILMS

Bird (154 mins): feature film about Charlie Parker, produced and directed by Clint Eastwood

RECORDS

John Abercrombie (Boston, 21 April): *John Abercrombie/Marc Johnson/Peter Erskine*
Howard Alden/Jack Lesberg (NYC, February/March): *No Amps Allowed*
Monty Alexander (NYC, February, March): *Jamboree*
Harry Allen (NYC, 30 June): *How long has this been going on?*
Franco Ambrosetti (NYC, 22,23 March): *Movies, Too*
Ray Anderson (NYC, 27,28 March): *Blues bred in the bone*
Harold Ashby (Oslo, 4 August): *The Viking*
Benny Bailey (London, 27,28 November): *For Heaven's Sake*
Chet Baker (Italy, 29 February): *The Heart of the Ballad* (Italy, 1,2 March): *Little Girl Blue* (Hanover, 28 April): *My Favourite Songs*
Iain Ballamy (Cornwall, December): *Balloon Man*
Chris Barber (Monster, 16 May): *Stardust*
John Barnes (London, 28,29 September): *Fancy our meeting*

Kenny Barron (NYC,15,16 January):*Live at Fat Tuesday's*
Gary Bartz (NYC, 5 April): *Monsoon* (NYC, 22 November): *Reflections of Monk*
Bob Berg (NYC, 17-19,25,26 June): *Cycles*
Jerry Bergonzi (Milan, May): *Jerry on Red*
Walter Bishop Jr (NYC, 10 September): *Just in Time*
Art Blakey (Milan, 19 March): *Not Yet* (Sweet Basil, NYC, 5 September): *Standards* (Milan, 11 November): *I get a kick out of Bu*
Carla Bley (Copenhagen, 14-16 November): *Fleur Carnivore*
Carla Bley/Steve Swallow (NYC, Summer): *Duets*
Bone Structure (London, 19-22 April/5 May): *Bone Structure*
Joe Bonner (Copenhagen, 3 August): *New Life*
Ruby Braff (NYC, June): *Me, Myself and I / Bravura Eloquence*
Randy Brecker (NYC, 18-20 November): *Live at Sweet Basil*
Nick Brignola (NYC, 12,13 September): *Raincheck*
Donald Brown (NYC, June): *The Sweetest Sounds*
Ray Brown (California, July): *Summer Wind* (Tokyo, December): *Bam Bam Bam*
Gary Burton (NYC): *Times like these*
Jaki Byard (NYC, 25 August): *Foolin' Myself*
Charlie Byrd/Scott Hamilton (NYC, August): *It's a Wonderful World*
Jackie Cain/Roy Kral (LA, 31 May/1,2 June): *Full Circle*
Michel Camilo (NYC, 30 January/1 February): *Michel Camilo*
Ian Carr (London, April/May): *Old Heartland*
Barbara Carroll (NYC, May/July): *Old Friends*
Benny Carter (Berkeley, 20 August): *My Kind of Trouble* (NYC, 5,6,9 October): *Cookin' at Carlos 1* (NYC, 18,19 October): *Over the Rainbow*
Doc Cheatham/Sammy Price (New Orleans, 23 April): *In New Orleans*
Jeannie & Jimmy Cheatham (California, November): *Back to the neighbourhood*
Don Cherry (NYC, 27,28,30 August): *Art Deco*
Stanley Clarke (NYC): *If this bass could only talk*
Buck Clayton Swing Band (Gulliver's, New Jersey, 23 October): *A Swingin' Dream*
Tony Coe (London, 28,29 November): *Canterbury Song*
Buddy Collette/James Newton (Milan, 4,5 July): *Flute Talk*
John Colianni (NYC, August): *Blues-o-matic*
Junior Cook (NYC, 23 November): *The Place to be*
Larry Coryell (Paris, 4 June): *Air-Dancing*
Eddie Daniels (NYC): *Blackwood*
Harold Danko (NYC, March): *The First Love Song*
Kenny Davern (NYC, January): *One Hour Tonight / I'll see you in my dreams*
Walter Davis Jr (NYC): *Illumination*
Buddy De Franco (Philadelphia): *Born to Swing!*
Trudy Desmond (Toronto, 24,25 November): *RSVP*
Garry Dial/Dick Oatts (NYC, 9-11 September / 11,17,18 October): *Dial and Oatts*
Kenny Drew (NYC, May): *The Rainbow Connection*
Herb Ellis/Red Mitchell (Santa Monica, March): *Doggin' Around*
Peter Erskine (NYC, 25 April-1 May): *Motion Poet*
Robin Eubanks (NYC, June): *Different Perspectives*
Gil Evans Orchestra (Umbria & Sicily, 8-24 July): *Tribute to Gil*
Art Farmer (NYC, 4,8 February): *Blame it on my youth*
Maynard Ferguson (LA): *High Voltage*
Chris Flory (NYC, January): *For all we know*
Bruce Forman (SF, October): *Pardon me!*
Pete Fountain (Nashville): *Live at the Ryman*

Johnny Frigo (NYC,16 November): *Live from Studio A*
The Gadd Gang (NYC, March): *Here & Now*
Jan Garbarek (Oslo, July): *Legend of the Seven Dreams*
Kenny Garrett (NYC, 21-23 September): *Garrett 5*
Tiziana Ghiglioni (Milan, 24-26 March): *Yet Time*
Mike Gibbs (Boston, NYC, London): *Big Music*
Terry Gibbs (Berkeley, 22,23 August): *Holiday for Swing*
Benny Green (NYC, 22 February): *Prelude*
Al Grey (NYC, 16,17 May): *The New Al Grey Quintet*
Marty Grosz (NYC, 6-8 June/20 July): *Swing it!*
Jim Hall & Tom Harrell (NYC, 9,10 February): *These Rooms*
Lionel Hampton (NYC, 10 March/8 April): *Mostly Blues*
Tom Harrell (NYC, 26,27 January): *Stories*
Art Hodes (Frankfurt, 17 April): *The Music of Lovie Austin* (London, 4 November): *Pagin' Mr Jelly*
Art Hodes/Jim Galloway (Café des Copains, Toronto, 25 September): *Live from Toronto*
Holly Hofmann (San Diego, October): *Take Note!*
Dave Holland (NYC, March): *Triplicate*
Christopher Hollyday (NYC): *Reverence*
Shirley Horn (NYC, 14-16 November); *Close enough for love*
Freddie Hubbard/Art Blakey (Monster, 31 October/1 November): *Feel the Wind*
Chris Hunter (NYC, 26 June): *This is Chris*
Bobby Hutcherson (Berkeley, 15,16 April): *Cruisin' the Bird*
Abdullah Ibrahim (NYC, 7,8 March): *Mindif*
Ronald Shannon Jackson (NYC): *Taboo*
Keith Jarrett (Paris, 17 October): *Paris Concert*
Barbara Jay (London): *Memories of you*
Lillette Jenkins (NYC, 12 January/29,30 November): *The Music of Lil Hardin Armstrong*
Hank Jones Great Jazz Trio (Netherlands, 18-20 April): *Standard Collection*
Geoff Keezer (NYC, 16,17 September): *Waiting in the Wings*
Roger Kellaway/Red Mitchell (Stockholm, 2,3 July): *Alone Together*
Barney Kessel (Berkeley, 15-17 March): *Red Hot & Blues*
Peter King (London, 20,30 April): *Brother Bernard*
Lee Konitz/John Taylor (NYC, 15,16 June): *Songs of the Stars*
Lee Konitz (Rome, 3 December): *Blew*
Steve Lacy (Paris, 4,5 July): *The Door*
Jeannie Lambe (London): *My Man*
Duncan Lamont (London, January): *Blues in the Night*
Yank Lawson (Atlanta, 14 March): *Something old, something new, something borrowed, something blue* (Milton Keynes, 28,29 May, with Dave Barrett): *A Yank at Cambridge*
The Leaders (NYC, 28,29 May): *Heaven Dance*
Mike LeDonne (NYC, 11 January): *'Bout Time*
Peter Leitch (NYC, 30 December): *Portraits and Dedications*
Uli Lenz/Cecil McBee/Joe Chambers (NYC, 1 September): *Live at Sweet Basil*
Mel Lewis Jazz Orchestra (Village Vanguard, NYC, 11-15 February): *The Definitive Thad Jones / Soft Lights and Hot Music*
Joe Lovano (NYC, 7-9 June): *Village Rhythm*
Humphrey Lyttelton (London, 24 May/15 June): *The Dazzling Lillian Boutté*
Susannah McCorkle (NYC, October): *No More Blues*
Bobby McFerrin (NYC): *Simple Pleasures*
Dave McKenna (SF, June): *No more ouzo for Puzo*
Chris McGregor's Brotherhood of Breath (London, January): *Country Cooking*
Manhattan Jazz Quintet (NYC, 15,16 January): *Plays Blue Note* (NYC, 9,10 December): *Caravan*
Branford Marsalis (NYC, 3,4 January): *Trio Jeepy*
Wynton Marsalis (NYC, 27,28 October): *The Majesty of the Blues*
Greg Marvin (NYC, 5 January): *Workout!*
Bob Mintzer (NYC, 4,5 January): *Spectrum*
Buddy Montgomery (Berkeley, 19 July/12 August): *So why not?*
Marian Montgomery (Ronnie Scott's, London): *I gotta have to sing...*
Ralph Moore (NYC, 19 February): *Rejuvenate!* (NYC, 15,17 December): *Images*
Frank Morgan (Berkeley, 10,11 January): *Yardbird Suite*

Dick Morrissey (London, 9 December): *Resurrection Ritual*

David Murray (NYC, January): *Deep River* (NYC, January): *Ballads* (Munich, 25 September): *Luck Four*

David Newton (Glasgow, 6 February): *Given Time*

Greg Osby (NYC, May): *Mindgames*

Jackie Paris (NYC, 11,12 July): *Nobody else but me*

Joe Pass (Berkeley, 2,3 February): *Blues for Fred* (LA, 28 December): *One for my Baby*

Houston Person (NYC, September): *We owe it all to love*

Ralph Peterson (NYC, 19,20 April): *V*

Billy Pierce (NYC, 2 January): *Equilateral*

Dave Pike/Charles McPherson (Monster, 17 October/7 November): *Bluebird*

Valery Ponomarev (NYC, 11 April): *Trip to Moscow*

Sammy Price (Canada, 26-28 February): *Paradise Valley Duets*

Don Pullen (NYC, 16 December): *New Beginnings*

Colin Purbrook/Peter King (Frognal, 22 September): *Blues for Buddy*

Quest (NYC, 21,22 March): *NY Nites – Standards*

Sun Ra (NYC, 5 December): *Blue Delight*

Doug Raney (Denmark, 9 September): *Doug Raney*

Emily Remler (NYC, May): *East to Wes*

Howard Riley (London, 10 January): *Feathers*

Marcus Roberts (NYC, 26,27 July): *The Truth is spoken here*

Spike Robinson/Harry Edison (LA, 19 September): *Jusa Bit o' Blues*

Spike Robinson/Rob Mullins (Denver, 8 November): *The Odd Couple*

Red Rodney (Copenhagen, 6,7 April): *Red Giant* (Copenhagen, 11,12 July): *One for the Bird*

Wallace Roney (NYC, 6 January): *Intuition*

Charlie Rouse (SF, 10 October): *Epistrophy*

Hilton Ruiz (NYC, 30 November/1 December): *Strut*

Arturo Sandoval (London, 15,16 August): *Just Music*

John Scofield (NYC, December): *Flat Out*

Avery Sharpe (NYC, January): *Unspoken Words*

Archie Shepp/Chet Baker (Frankfurt, 13 March/Paris, 14 March): *In Memory of*

Alan Skidmore (London, 18,19 February): *Tribute to 'Trane*

Carol Sloane (NYC, 6,7,28 October): *Love You Madly*

Lonnie Smith (NYC, 23 July): *Think*

Tommy Smith (NYC, 7,8 September): *Step by Step*

James Spaulding (NYC, 25 November): *Brilliant Corners*

Leni Stern (NYC, 24 September-1 October): *Secrets*

Markus Stockhausen/Gary Peacock (Oslo, March): *Cosi Lontano...Quasi Dentro*

Superblue (NYC, 26 April): *Superblue*

Duncan Swift (Birmingham, March): *Out looking for the Lion*

Billy Taylor (NYC, 13,14 June): *White Night and Jazz in Leningrad*

Rusty Taylor (London, 13,14 June/18 July): *Let's Misbehave*

Clark Terry (NYC, 16 December): *Portraits*

Clark Terry/Red Mitchell (Stockholm, 7 July): *Jive at Five*

Henri Texier (Amiens, 16-18 May): *Izlaz*

Toots Thielemans (NYC, April, May): *Only trust your heart*

Gary Thomas & Seventh Quadrant (NYC, 20,21,25,25 July): *Code Violations*

Barbara Thompson's Paraphernalia (London): *A cry from the heart: Live in London*

Butch Thompson (Hampshire, 13 July): *King Oliver Centennial Band*

Henry Threadgill (December): *Rag, Bush and all*

Claude Tissendier (Paris, 4 January): *Saxomania*

Charles Tolliver (Berlin, 21,22 July): *Live in Berlin at the Quasimodo*

Giovanni Tommasso (Rome, February): *To Chet*

Mel Tormé (LA, August): *Reunion* (Tokyo, December): *In Concert Tokyo*

Stan Tracey/Don Weller (Sydney, 24 February): *Play Duke, Monk and Bird*

Stan Tracey (London, 6 December): *We still love you madly*

Steve Turre (NYC, 5,6 February): *Fire and Ice*

29th Street Saxophone Quartet (Italy, July): *Live*

McCoy Tyner (NYC, 25-27 October): *Revelations* (Blue Note, NYC, 25,26 November): *Uptown/Downtown*

Dave Valentin (NYC, 31 May/1 June): *Live at the Blue Note*

Mal Waldron (Munich, 1-3 November): *No More Tears (for Lady Day)*

Jack Walrath (NYC, 19,21 August): *Neohippus*

Benny Waters (London, 22,23 September/15 November): *Memories of the Twenties*

Bobby Watson & Horizon (NYC, 1 May): *No question about it*

Trevor Watts (Rye Festival, 8 September): *With One Voice*

Eberhard Weber (Ludwigsburg, May/August): *Orchestra*

Putte Wickman/Red Mitchell (Stockholm, December 1987/ 23 January 1988): *The very thought of you*

Tony Williams (NYC, 4-6 April): *Angel Street*

Cassandra Wilson (NYC, February): *Blue Skies*

Mike Wofford (California, 6 September/6 October): *Plays Gerald Wilson*

Phil Woods (NYC, May): *Evolution* (Rome, 15 November): *Phil's Mood* (NYC, 20,21 December): *Here's to my lady*

John Zorn (NYC, 18,19 August): *Spy vs Spy: the music of Ornette Coleman*

The Floating Jazz Festival aboard the SS Norway once again plays host to the greatest names in jazz (October).
Far left: Illinois Jacquet (66) leads his powerhouse big band.
Left: Dexter Gordon (65) answers questions about his Oscar-winning performance in the 1985 movie *Round Midnight*.
Above: Benny Carter (81) and Clark Terry (67).

Frank Foster's *Count Basie Jazz History Suite* is premiered at the National Association of Jazz Educators Convention in San Diego (January).

Woody Shaw (44) dies on 9 May. He had lost his left arm in January when he fell under a subway train, and had been in a coma ever since.

Jazz Messengers past and present, including Terence Blanchard, Walter Davis Jr, Curtis Fuller, Benny Golson, Freddie Hubbard and Jackie McLean, assemble in Leverkusen, West Germany, to celebrate Art Blakey's 70th birthday (October).

Wynton Marsalis (28) headlines at the 20th Annual New Orleans Jazz & Heritage Festival.

DEATHS
Eddie Heywood (73) 2 January
Roy Eldridge (78) 26 February
Billy Moore (71) 28 February
Tiny Grimes (72) 4 March *meningitis*
Arnett Cobb (70) 24 March
Woody Shaw (44) May
Phineas Newborn Jnr (57) May
Steve McCall (56) 25 May
John Kendall (56) 10 June *brain haemorrhage*
Will Bradley (78) July
Nesuhi Ertegun (71) 15 July
Irv Cottler (71) 8 August *heart attack*
Sahib Shihab (64) 24 October
Burt Bales (73) 26 October
Lu Watters (77) 5 November
Kenneth 'Pancho' Hagood (62) 9 November
Jeremy French (57) 11 November
Rose Murphy (?) 16 November
Freddy Clayton (62) November
Wild Bill Davison (83) November
Ann Burton (?) 29 November *cancer*
Eric Dixon (59)
Freddy Waits (46)
Reunald Jones
Jimmy Shirley (76)

BOOKS
Stan Britt: *Long Tall Dexter*
James Lincoln Collier: *Benny Goodman & the Swing Era*
Michael Doane: *The Surprise of Burning*
Peter Gammond & Peter Clayton: *Bluff your way in Jazz*
Ted Gioia: *The Imperfect Art: reflections on jazz and modern culture*
Jim Godbolt: *A History of Jazz in Britain 1950-1970*
Chris Hillman: *Bunk Johnson, his life and times*
Keith Keller: *Oh, Jess – a jazz life*
Graham Lock: *Forces in Motion*
Barry McRae: *Ornette Coleman*
Barry McRae: *Miles Davis*
Francois Postif: *Les Grandes Interviews de Jazz Hot*
Gunther Schuller: *The Swing Era: The Development of Jazz 1930-1945*
Alyn Shipton: *Fats Waller, his life and times*
Sam Tanenhaus: *Louis Armstrong*

RECORDS
John Abercrombie (Oslo, October): *Animato*
Muhal Richard Abrams (NYC, 17,18 January): *The Hearinga Suite*
George Adams (NYC, May/June/July): *America*
Alden/Barrett Quintet (NYC, June): *The ABQ salutes Buck Clayton*
Laurindo Almeida/Carlos Barbosa-Lima/Charlie Byrd (California, May): *Music of the Brazilian Masters*
Meredith d'Ambrosio (Florida, 26 February): *South to a Warmer Place*
Ernestine Anderson/Clayton-Hamilton Orchestra (LA, September): *Boogie Down*
Ray Anderson (NYC,16-18 December): *What Because*
Art Ensemble of Chicago (Chicago, January): *The Alternate Express*
Charlie Antolini (14 April): *Cookin'*
Kenny Baker (London, 5–18 November): *The Louis Armstrong Connection Vol 7*
Guy Barker (London, 6,7 March): *Holly J*
Kenny Barron/John Hicks (NYC, 3 September): *Rhythm-a-ning*
Louis Bellson (Berne, 30 April): *Jazz Giants*
David Benoit (LA, 5 February/25 May): *Waiting for Spring*
Jerry Bergonzi (Massachusetts, 19 October): *Standard Gonz*

Warren Bernhardt (Connecticut, 1-5 March): *Heat of the Moment*
Gene Bertoncini/Michael Moore (NYC, 10,20 March): *Two in Time*
Ed Bickert (NYC, January): *Third Floor Richard*
Ed Bickert/Lorne Lofsky (Toronto, December): *This is new*
Lillian Boutté (London, 13,14 November): *Having a good time!*
Lester Bowie (Brooklyn, 4-6 April): *Serious Fun*
Joanne Brackeen (Berkeley, June): *Live at Maybeck Recital Hall*
Anthony Braxton/Marilyn Crispell (Vancouver, 30 June): *Duets, Vancouver 1989*
Joshua Breakstone (NYC, 18 January): *Self-Portrait in Swing*
Randy Brecker (Stamford, August): *Toe to Toe*
Nick Brignola (New Jersey, 25 September): *On a different level*
Ruth Brown (NYC, 12,13 June): *Blues on Broadway*
Thierry Bruneau/Mal Waldron (Belgium, 13,14 September): *Live at De Kave*
Gary Burton (NYC, 6-10 May): *Reunion*
Donald Byrd (NYC, 10,12 October): *Getting down to business*
Janusz Carmello (Edinburgh, 2,3 June): *Portrait*
George Chisholm/Maxine Daniels (London, 25 July): *Swinging down Memory Lane*
James Clay (NYC, 20 January): *I let a song go out of my heart*
Clayton/Hamilton Jazz Orchestra (California, 18,19 April): *Groove Shop*
Harry Connick Jr (NYC, 6,12,19 June): *When Harry met Sally*
Junior Cook (NYC, June): *On a Misty Night*
Larry Coryell (NYC, 20 October): *Shining Hour*
Stanley Cowell (NYC, July): *Back to the Beautiful*
Hank Crawford/Jimmy McGriff (NYC, 4 April/9 August): *On the Blue Side*
Marilyn Crispell (SF, 20 October/Vancouver, 30 June/NYC, 8 July): *Live in San Francisco*
Tony Crombie (London, 5,19 January): *Tony Crombie and Friends*
Connie Crothers/Lennie Popkin (NYC, 4 December): *New York Night*
Eddie Daniels (NYC, 6,7,9 December): *Nepenthe*
Maxine Daniels (London, 20,21 June): *That's All*
Richard Davis (NYC, 6,7 July): *One for Frederick*
Buddy de Franco (NYC, 11 March): *Like Someone in Love*
Barbara Dennerlein (Vienna,18 January): *Live on Tour*
Christian Minh Doky (Copenhagen, 26,27 November/3,4 December): *The Sequel*
Niels Lan Doky (NYC, 22,23 August): *Dreams*
Kenny Drew (Copenhagen, 14,15 May): *Recollections* (NYC, June): *Third Phase*
Paquito d'Rivera (June/August): *Tico! Tico!*
Ray Drummond (NYC, 28 December): *Camera in a Bag*
John Eaton (NYC, July/August): *Indiana on our minds*
Eliane Elias (NYC, December): *Plays Jobim*
Kevin Eubanks (NYC, 13-19 November): *Promise of Tomorrow*
Bill Evans (Tokyo, 9 September): *Let the Juice Loose*
Ella Fitzgerald (LA, March): *All that jazz*
Tommy Flanagan (NYC, 17,19 January): *Jazz Poet*
Bob Florence (California): *State of the Art*
Ricky Ford (NYC, 24 February): *Hard Groovin'* (NYC, 4 May): *Manhattan Blues*
Chico Freeman (Paris, 18 May): *Brainstorm*
Chico Freeman/Arthur Blythe (Ronnie Scott's, London, 25 February): *Luminous*
Hal Galper (NYC, February): *Portrait*
Ray Gelato (London): *Giants of Jive*
Jimmy Giuffre/Paul Bley/Steve Swallow (NYC, 16,17 December): *The Life of a Trio: Saturday / Sunday*

Liz Gorrill/Charley Krachy (NYC, 13 October): *A Jazz Duet*
Danny Gottlieb (NYC): *Whirlwind*
Grand Union Orchestra (London, February): *Freedom Calls*
Benny Green Trio (NYC, 29 December 1988/2 January 1989): *In this Direction*
Marty Grosz (NYC, August/September): *Extra! The Orphan Newsboys*
George Gruntz Concert Jazz Band (Zurich, 7,8 May): *First Prize*
Chico Hamilton (London): *Euphoria* (Milan, 28,29 June): *Reunion*
Scott Hamilton (NYC, March): *Plays Ballads*
Roy Hargrove (NYC, December): *Diamond in the Rough*
Harper Brothers (Village Vanguard, NYC, 8,9 September): *Remembrance*
Tom Harrell (NYC, 22,23 March): *Sail Away*
Gene Harris (Sausalito, March): *Listen here!*
Gene Harris & Philip Morris Superband (NYC, 23 September): *Live at Town Hall, NYC*
Louis Hayes (Holland, 21 April): *Light and Lively* (NYC, 14 October): *The Crawl* (14 December): *Una Max*
Mark Helias (NYC, 1,2 April): *Desert Blue*
Eddie Henderson (20 April): *Phantoms* (December): *Think of me*
Fred Hersch (NYC, 4,5 December): *Heartsongs*
Terumasa Hino (NYC, 19,21 September): *Bluestruck*
Jay Hoggard (NYC, 22 June): *Overview*
Dave Holland (NYC, September): *Extensions*
Red Holloway/Clark Terry (LA,June): *Locksmith Blues*
Christopher Hollyday (NYC, 25,26 January): *Christopher Hollyday*
Chris Hunter (NYC,19,20 August): *Scarborough Fair*
Bobby Hutcherson (Berkeley, August/September): *Ambos Mundos*
Abdullah Ibrahim (NYC, 1 June): *African River*
Keith Jarrett (Cologne, October): *Tribute*
Hank Jones (NYC, July): *Lazy Afternoon*
Oliver Jones/Clark Terry (Montreal, January): *Just Friends*
Geoff Keezer (NYC, 22 June): *Curveball*
Roger Kellaway/Putte Wickman/Red Mitchell (Stockholm, 27,28 June): *Some o' this and some o' that*
Steve Khan (NYC, January): *Public Access*
Peter King (London, 4-9 March): *Crusade*
Karin Krog (Copenhagen, June): *Something Borrowed...Something New*
Steve Kuhn (Paris, 20,21 September): *Oceans in the Sky*
Steve Lacy (Milan, 18,19 April): *More Monk* (Paris, 27,28 June): *Anthem*
Christof Lauer (Germany, April): *Christof Lauer*
Barbara Lea & The Legendary Lawson-Haggart Jazz Band (Atlanta, 21 February): *You're the Cats!*
The Leaders (NYC, 19,20 December): *Unforeseen Blessings*
Mel Lewis (NYC, 11,12 April): *The Lost Art*
David Liebman/Richard Beirach (Germany, July): *Chant*
Lighthouse All-Stars (Hermosa Beach, 12 February): *Jazz Invention*
Charles Lloyd (Oslo, July): *Fish out of Water*
Ron McClure (21 December): *McJolt*
Dave McKenna (Berkeley, November): *Live at Maybeck Recital Hall*
Jim McNeely (NYC, 6 July): *Winds of Change*
Jay McShann/Ralph Sutton (NYC, March): *Last of the Whorehouse Piano Players*
Herbie Mann (NYC, December 88/January 89): *Opalescence*
Guido Manusardi (Milan, 21,22 March): *Acqua Fragia*
Rick Margitza (NYC, April/May): *Color*
Sherrie Maricle/John Mastroianni (NYC, 4 January): *Cookin' on all burners*
Mike Melillo (Italy, 25 October): *Recycle*
Vince Mendoza (NYC, 13,14 November): *Start Here*
Pat Metheny (NYC, Spring): *Letter from home*
Pat Metheny/Dave Holland/Roy Haynes (NYC, 21 December): *Question & Answer*
Mulgrew Miller (Berkeley, 15,16 August): *The Countdown*
Bob Mintzer (NYC, 24-26 February/2-5 March): *Urban Contours*
Charnett Moffett (NYC): *Beauty Within*
Tete Montoliu/Peter King (Barcelona, 1 January): *New Year's Morning '89*
Frank Morgan (NYC, 26,27 June): *Mood Indigo*

Paul Motian (NYC, September): *On Broadway – Vol 2*
Gerry Mulligan (Connecticut, March/September): *Lonesome Boulevard*
Steve Nelson (NYC, 8 October): *Full Nelson*
David 'Fathead' Newman (NYC, 3 September): *Blue Head*
Newport Jazz Festival All-Stars (Bern, July): *Bern Concert '89*
Greg Osby (NYC, July): *Season of Renewal*
Roberto Ottaviano (Italy, May): *Sotto il Sole Giaguaro* (Milan, 17,18 June/14 July): *Six Mobiles – Portrait in Six Colours*
Paris Reunion Band (Switzerland, 19,20 May): *We Remember Klook*
Errol Parker (NYC, 2 June): *Compelling Force*
Ken Peplowski (NYC, January): *Sonny Side*
Ralph Peterson (NYC, 27,28 February): *Volition* (NYC, 22,23 December): *Presents the Fo'tet*
Courtney Pine (NYC,17-19 January): *The Vision's Tale*
Marlene Ver Planck (NY, 1,11 December): *A Quiet Storm*
Dewey Redman (NYC, 13,14 September): *Living on the Edge*
Irene Reid (London, 19 April): *The Lady from Savannah*
Rufus Reid (New Jersey, 5 March): *Corridor to the Limit*
Sam Rivers (Monster, 9,10 October): *Lazuli*
Marcus Roberts (NYC, 8,9,12 October): *Deep in the Shed*
Spike Robinson/Louis Stewart/Janusz Carmello (London, 15 July): *Three for the Road*
Sonny Rollins (NYC, 2 June/5 August/9September): *Falling in love with Jazz*

Renée Rosnes (NYC, 4 February): *Renée Rosnes*
Jimmy Rowles (London): *Remember when*
Hilton Ruiz (NYC, 9-11 November): *Doin' it right*
Mongo Santamaria (SF, May): *Olé Ola*
John Scofield (NYC, 19-21 November): *Time on my hands*
Bobby Scott (NYC, 3-5April): *For Sentimental Reasons*
Bud Shank (Washington, 2,3 December): *Tales of the Pilot*
George Shearing (NYC, February): *George Shearing in Dixieland* (SF, May): *Piano*
Andy Sheppard (London, 6-9 November): *Soft on the inside*
Jim Snidero (Italy, July): *Live*
Leni Stern (NYC, December): *Closer to the Light*
Mike Stern (NYC, February): *Jigsaw*
Sun Ra (NYC): *Purple Night*
Lew Tabackin (NYC, December): *Desert Lady*
Horace Tapscott (LA, 14–17 December): *The Dark Tree Vol 1*
Cecil Taylor (NYC, 8 June): *In Florescence*
Clark Terry Spacemen (NYC,13 February): *Squeeze Me*
Toots Thielemans (NYC, 19,20 December): *Footprints*
Ed Thigpen (NYC, 20,21 March): *Young Men and Olds*
Butch Thompson (Massachusetts, 1–3 March): *New Orleans Joys / Chicago Breakdown / Good Old New York*
Claude Tissendier/Saxomania (Paris, 24,25 April): *Presenting Spike Robinson*
Mickey Tucker (NYC,June): *Blues in Five Dimensions*
McCoy Tyner (Sweet Basil, NYC, 19,20 May): *Live at Sweet Basil* (NYC, 2,27 November): *Things ain't what they used to be*
James 'Blood' Ulmer (Germany, May): *Blues all night*

Warren Vaché/Beaux Arts String Quartet (NYC, June): *Warm Evenings*
Larry Vuckovich (California, August): *Tres Palabras*
Mal Waldron (Innsbruck, 25,26 October): *Quadrologue at Utopia*
Bobby Wellins (UK): *Birds of Brazil*
Kenny Werner (NYC, 6,7 March): *Introducing the Trio*
Frank Wess/Harry Edison (Tokyo, November): *Dear Mr Basie*
Randy Weston (Paris, 4 June): *Portraits of Duke Ellington*
Jiggs Whigham (Washington, 26 July): *The Jiggs up*
Bob Wilber (New Orleans, 19,20 November): *Dancing on a Rainbow*
Buster Williams (NYC, 8,9 March): *Something More*
Joe Williams (LA, 19,21 January): *In Good Company*
Rod Williams (NYC, 1 May): *Hanging in the Balance*
Tony Williams (NYC, 11-13 September): *Native Heart*
Larry Willis (NYC, February): *My Funny Valentine* (NYC, 7 July): *Just in Time* (December): *Heavy Blues*
Cassandra Wilson (Brooklyn, July/August): *Jump World*
Gerald Wilson (LA, 27,28 June): *Jenna*
Phil Woods (NYC, April): *Flash*
Working Week (London): *Fire in the Mountain*
Reggie Workman (NYC, 31 January/July): *Images*
George Young (NYC, 30 March): *Yesterday and Today* (NYC, 12,13 September): *Old Times*

Left: Mulgrew Miller.
Below: Jay McShann.
Bottom: Harry 'Sweets' Edison meets Philip Harper, one of the new trumpet generation, at the Jazz Party in Amsterdam.

Photograph: *Brian Foskett*

Photograph: *Brian Foskett*

Photo: Rollo Phlecks Courtesy: Hank O'Neal

1990

Doc Cheatham celebrates his 85th birthday during the 10th year of his long-running Sunday brunch gig at New York's Sweet Basil club.

Nineteen-year-old trumpeter Roy Hargrove causes a stir with the release of 'Diamond in the Rough', his debut album as a leader.

DEATHS
George Auld (70) 7 January
Clarence 'C' Sharpe (53) 28 January
Mel Lewis (60) 3 February *cancer*
Russell Jacquet (72) 4 March
Al Sears (80) 23 March
Sarah Vaughan (66) 3 April *lung cancer*
Dave Dexter Jr (74) 19 April
Dexter Gordon (67) 25 April
Emily Remler (32) 4 May *heart attack*
Frank Wright (54) 17 May *heart attack*
Chris McGregor (53) 26 May *lung cancer*
Walter Davis Jr (57) 2 June
June Christy (64) 21 June *kidney failure*
Dudu Pukwana (51) 29 June
Joe Turner (82) 21 July
Chester Zardis (90) 14 August
Pearl Bailey (72) 17 August
Louis Vola (88) August
Phil Napoleon (89) 30 September
Art Blakey (71) 16 October *lung cancer*
Major Holley (66) 25 October
Peter Schilperoort (71) 17 November
Dave Wilkins (76) 26 November
Bill Hardman (58) 6 December *cerebral haemorrhage*
Lee Castle (75) 10 December

BOOKS
Miles Davis with Quincy Troup: *Miles – the Autobiography*
John Chilton: *The Song of the Hawk: the life and recordings of Coleman Hawkins*
Bud Freeman: *Crazeology*
John Gibbon: *Gibb's Club Files, Vol.1*
Lionel Hampton with James Haskins: *Hamp: an autobiography*
Frances Hanly & Tim May (eds): *Rhythms of the World*
Mike Hennessey: *Klook: the story of Kenny Clarke*
Woody Herman & Stuart Troup: *The Woodchopper's Ball*
Andy Kirk: *Twenty Years on Wheels*
Bud Kliment: *Billie Holiday*
Stephen Longstreet: *Jazz from A to Z: a graphic dictionary*
Stuart Nicholson: *Jazz: the Modern Resurgence*
Jeff Nuttall: *The Bald Soprano*
Paul Oliver: *The Blackwell Guide to Blues Records*
Sammy Price: *What do they want?*
Brian Rust: *My Kind of Jazz*
Valerie Wilmer: *Mama said there'd be days like this*

RECORDS
Alex Acuna (SF, February/March): *Alex Acuna & the Unknown*
Nat Adderley (NYC, 8,9 November): *Talkin' About You*
Howard Alden (NYC, April): *Snowy Morning Blues*
Geri Allen (NYC, 5,6 January): *The Nurturer*
Ernestine Anderson (Concord, 18 August): *Live at the 1990 Concord Jazz Festival – Third Set*
Ray Anderson (NYC, December): *Wishbone*
Peter Appleyard (Barbados, 17,18 February): *Barbados Heat / Barbados Cool*
Art Ensemble of Chicago (NYC, December 89 / January 90): *America South Africa*
Roy Ayers (Ronnie Scott's, London, May): *Searchin'*
Benny Bailey (Oslo, 22,23 April): *While My Lady Sleeps*
Kenny Barron (Berkeley, 3 December): *Live at Maybeck Recital Hall* (NYC, 20 December): *Invitation*
Gary Bartz (NYC, 31 March): *W42nd Street*
Django Bates (31 January-2 February): *Music for the Third Policeman*
Ran Blake (Zurich, 3,4 July): *That Certain Feeling (George Gershwin Songbook)*
George Benson/Count Basie Orchestra (NYC): *Big Boss Band*
Bob Berg (NYC): *In the Shadows*
Nathan Berg (LA, 21 August): *Fish With No Fins*
Totti Bergh (Oslo, 12 August): *Major Blues*
Tim Berne (Ludwigsburg, November): *Pace Yourself*
Warren Bernhardt (NYC, 19,20 April): *Ain't Life Grand*
Walter Bishop Jr (NYC, 25 October): *What's New*

Art Blakey (NYC, 1,2 February): *Chippin' In*
Carla Bley (Ludwigsburg, 29,30 October): *The Very Big Carla Bley Band*
Paul Bley (Switzerland, 23,24 May): *12 (+6) In a Row*
Lester Bowie's Brass Fantasy (NYC, 22-30 January): *My Way*
Ruby Braff/Dick Hyman (NYC, 12,13 June): *Younger than Swingtime*
Nick Brignola (NYC, 9 October): *What It Takes*
Gary Burton/Paul Bley (Copenhagen, 29 March): *Right Time, Right Place*
Betty Carter (NYC, 25,26 May/7 June): *Droppin' Things*
Jeannie & Jimmy Cheatham (LA, May): *Luv in the Afternoon*
Steve Coleman (NYC, February): *Rhythm People* (NYC, December): *Black Science*
Cal Collins (Cincinnati, November): *Ohio Style*
Joyce Collins (LA, 9,25-27 April): *Sweet Madness*
Stanley Cowell (Berkeley): *Live at Maybeck Hall, Vol.5*
Meredith d'Ambrosio (NYC, 19,20 December): *Love is Not a Game*
Kenny Davern/Bob Wilber (NYC, May): *Summit Reunion*
Elton Dean/Howard Riley (London, 21 June): *All the Tradition*
Barbara Dennerlein (Germany, 6-8 June): *Hot Stuff*
Gary Dial/Dick Oatts (NYC, 2-4 February/29,30 March): *Brassworks*
Niels Lan Doky (NYC, 18 August/Copenhagen, 9 September): *Friendship*
Dorothy Donegan (S/S Norway, October/November): *Live at the 1990 Floating Jazz Festival*
Paquito d'Rivera/Arturo Sandoval (Ludwigsburg, August): *Reunion*
Ray Drummond (NYC, 8,9 October): *The Essence*
Charles Earland (NJ, 23 May): *Whip Appeal*
Harry Edison (NYC, 27,28 April): *Swing Summit*
Robin Eubanks (NYC, May): *Karma*

Tommy Flanagan (Holland, 29,30 April): *Beyond the Bluebird*
Ricky Ford (NYC, 2 June): *Ebony Rhapsody*
Tomas Franck (NYC, 4 December): *Tomas Franck in New York*
Chico Freeman (London, April): *Sweet Explosion*
Larry Gales (NYC, 9 June): *A Message From Monk*
Hal Galper (Berkeley, July): *Live at Maybeck Recital Hall, Vol 6* (NYC, 18 November): *Invitation to a Concert*
Jan Garbarek (Oslo, August): *I took up the runes*
Kenny Garrett (NYC): *African Exchange Student*
Benny Golson (NYC, 20,21 June): *Benny Golson Quintet*
Stephane Grappelli (NYC): *Piano My Other Love* (Tokyo, 4 October): *In Tokyo*
Benny Green (NYC, 30 January/2 February): *Lineage*
Al Grey (S/S Norway, 22,23,25 October): *Live at the 1990 Floating Jazz Festival*
Johnny Griffin (NYC, 29 October/1 November): *The Cat*
Don Grolnick (NYC): *Weaver of Dreams*
Steve Grossman (Paris, 16 September): *Reflections* (Italy, 17 December): *My Second Prime*
Marty Grosz (NYC, 25-27 June): *Laughing at Life*
Marty Grosz/Keith Ingham (NYC, January/February): *Unsaturated Fats*
Scott Hamilton (NYC, February): *Radio City*
Scott Hamilton/Gene Harris (SF, May): *At Last*
Roy Hargrove (NYC, October): *Public Eye*
Barry Harris (Berkeley, 12 March): *Live at Maybeck Recital Hall*
Eddie Harris (NYC, 9 May): *There Was a Time (Echoes of Harlem)*
Gene Harris & Philip Morris Superband (Sydney, 18 October): *World Tour 1990*
Donald Harrison (NYC, 14 May): *Full Circle* (NYC, 9,10 November): *For Art's Sake*
Michael Hashim (NYC): *The Billy Strayhorn Project*
Charlie Hearnshaw (London, 9,10 January): *So Slam it*
Dick Heckstall-Smith (London): *Woza Nasu*
Eddie Henderson / Laurent De Wilde (NYC, 7,8 March): *Colors of Manhattan*
Vincent Herring (NYC, 29 June/2 July): *Evidence*
John Hicks (NYC, 10 May): *The Power Trio* (Berkeley, August): *Live at Maybeck Recital Hall, Vol 7*

Photograph: *David Redfern*

166

1990

Andrew Hill (NYC, 12,13 July/16 September): *But Not Farewell*
Milt Hinton (NYC, October 89–March 90): *Old Man Time*
Christopher Hollyday (NYC, 16,17 January): *On Course*
Shirley Horn (NYC): *You Won't Forget Me*
Dick Hyman (Berkeley, 14 February): *Music of 1937*
Keith Ingham (Toronto, 30 November/2 December): *Out of the Past*
Milt Jackson (NYC, 10,11 December): *The Harem*
Pete Jolly (LA): *Gems*
Oliver Jones (Montreal, June/September): *Northern Summit*
George Kawaguchi (Tokyo, 2 November): *Jazz Battle*
Carol Kidd (Edinburgh, 12,13 February): *The night we called it a day...*
Steve Kuhn (NYC, October): *Looking Back*
Steve Lacy (Vienna, 26-28 November): *Itinerary*
Guy Lafitte (Toulouse, 17,18 August): *The Things We Did Last Summer*
Birelli Lagrene (Paris, July): *Acoustic Moments*
Don Lanphere/Larry Coryell (Seattle, 11,12 April): *Lanphere/Coryell*
Barbara Lea (Atlanta, 6 March): *Sweet and Slow*
Mike LeDonne (NYC, 2 January): *The Feeling of Jazz*
Peter Leitch (NYC, January): *Mean what you say*
Kirk Lightsey (NYC, 28 November): *From Kirk to Nat*
Humphrey Lyttelton/Helen Shapiro (London, 7,8 November): *I Can't Get Started*
Rob McConnell (Toronto, August): *Rob McConnell Jive Five*
Susannah McCorkle (NYC, February): *Sabia*
Dave McKenna (California, March): *Shadows 'N' Dreams*
Marian McPartland (LA, January): *Plays the Benny Carter Songbook*
Herbie Mann (NYC, March): *Caminho de Casa*
Rick Margitza (NYC, June): *Hope*
Branford Marsalis (NYC, 10 January/8 February/1 March): *Crazy People Music*
Ellis Marsalis (NYC, 18 March): *Ellis Marsalis Trio*
George Masso (NYC, August): *Just For A Thrill*
Ronnie Mathews (NYC, 26 October): *Dark Before the Dawn*
David Matthews (NYC, 23 September): *American Pie*

Mulgrew Miller (NYC, March): *From day to day*
James Moody (NYC, October): *Honey*
Mark Morganelli (NYC, 13 June): *Speak Low*
Paul Motian (NYC, May): *Bill Evans*
David Murray (NYC, 30 July): *Remembrances*
David Newton (Edinburgh, 13 February/London, 14 May): *Victim of Circumstance*
Paolo Nonnis Big Band (LA, 26,27 June): *Just In Time*
Walter Norris (Berkeley, April): *Live at Maybeck Recital Hall, Vol 4* (SF, 13,14 September): *Lush Life*
NYJO (London, 4,5 January): *Portraits* (London, July/August): *Cookin' with Gas*
Greg Osby (NYC, October/November): *Man-Talk for Moderns*
Ken Peplowski (NYC, February): *Mr Gentle and Mr Cool* (NYC, 20,21 November): *Illuminations*
Oscar Peterson (NYC, 16 March): *The Legendary Oscar Peterson Trio Live at the Blue Note*
Courtney Pine (NYC, 20,21 January): *Within The Realms of Our Dreams*
Pinski Zoo (Derby, January): *East Rail East*
John Pizzarelli (NYC, 6,7 February): *My Blue Heaven*
Don Pullen (NYC, 23 March): *Random Thoughts*
Jason Rebello (London): *A Clearer View*
Trevor Richards (Frankfurt, 18-20 June): *New Orleans Trio*
Howard Riley (London, 9 April): *Procession*
Marcus Roberts (New Orleans, 3-5 June/NYC, 22 September): *Alone with the Blues*
Spike Robinson (Edinburgh, 5 October): *Stairway To The Stars*
Claudio Roditi (NYC, 24,25 September): *Two of Swords*
Renee Rosnes (NYC, 15,16 February): *For the Moment*
Gonzales Rubalcaba (Montreux, 15 July): *Discovery*
Pharoah Sanders (France, 17-19 July): *Welcome To Love*
Rob Schneiderman (NYC, 28 February): *Smooth Sailing*
Ronnie Scott (London, October/November): *Never Pat a Burnning Dog*
Jim Self (LA, June): *Tricky Lix*
Tad Shull (NYC, 24 November): *Deep Passion*
Louis Smith (22 March): *Ballads for Lulu*
Tommy Smith (Oslo, 9-13 January): *Peeping Tom*
Gary Smulyan (NYC, 7 December): *The Lure of Beauty*
String Trio of New York (NYC, 24,25 June): *Ascendant*
John Surman (Oslo, April): *The Road to St Ives*

Ralph Sutton (Woking, 7 April): *Eye Opener*
Tana/Reid (NYC, September): *Yours and Mine*
Martin Taylor (London, 27,28 September): *Don't Fret!*
Clark Terry (NYC, 19,20 November): *Live at the Village Gate*
Jesper Thilo (Copenhagen, 7-9 September): *Shufflin'*
Gary Thomas (NYC, May): *While The Gate Is Open*
Danny Thompson & Whatever (London): *Elemental*
Henry Threadgill (NYC, 19-21 November): *Spirit of Nuff...Nuff*
Sumi Tonooka (NYC, 9 November): *Taking Time*
Mel Tormé (Concord, August): *Night at the Concord Pavilion*
Mel Tormé/George Shearing (Saratoga, 2,3 September): *Mel & George 'Do' World War II*
James 'Blood' Ulmer (NYC, 24,25 October/6,7 November): *Black And Blues*
Bobby Watson & Horizon (NYC, 17,18 December): *Post-Motown Bop*
Trevor Watts (Venezuela, 2,4,10 November): *Live in Latin America Vol 1*
Dave Weckl (LA & St Louis): *Master Plan*
Kenny Werner (NYC, 10,11 January): *Uncovered Heart*
Frank Wess (Tokyo, 11 November): *Entre Nous*
Kenny Wheeler (London & Oslo, January): *Music for Large and Small Ensembles* (Oslo, February): *The Widow in the Window*
Gerry Wiggins (Berkeley, August): *Live at Maybeck Recital Hall*
Barney Wilen (Monster, 2 October): *Movie Themes from France*
Cassandra Wilson (NYC, July-December): *She Who Weeps*
Val Wiseman (Birmingham, 20-22 February): *Lady Sings the Blues*
Jimmy Witherspoon (NYC, 24,25 May): *Live at Condon's*
Phil Woods (NYC, June): *All Bird's Children* (NYC, 27,28 September): *Real Life*

Opposite page: David Murray (tenor sax) at the Brecon Jazz Festival.
Below: Freddie Hubbard (trumpet) and the rising young tenor sax star Ralph Moore, together at the North Sea Jazz Festival.

Photograph: *Brian Foskett*

Index of musicians

Al Aarons (trumpet) [1932-]
Ahmed Abdul-Malik (bass) [1927-]
Mike Abene (piano) [1942-]
John Abercrombie (guitar) [1944-]
Don Abney (piano) [1923-]
Lee Abrams (drums) [1925-]
Muhal Richard Abrams (piano) [1930-]
Ray Abrams (tenor sax) [1920-]
George Adams (tenor sax) [1940-1992]
Pepper Adams (baritone sax) [1930-1986]
Cannonball Adderley (alto sax) [1928-1975]
Nat Adderley (trumpet) [1931-]
Nat Adderley Jr (piano) [1955-]
Bernard Addison (guitar) [1905-]
Toshiko Akiyoshi (piano) [1929-]
Pheeroan Ak Laff (drums) [1955-]
Manny Albam (composer) [1922-]
Joe Albany (piano) [1924-1988]
Alvin Alcorn (trumpet) [1912-]
Howard Alden (guitar) [1958-]
Tony Aless (piano) [1921-]
Monty Alexander (piano) [1944-]
Mousie Alexander (drums) [1922-]
Roland Alexander (tenor sax) [1935-]
Lorez Alexandria (vocals) [1929-]
Rashied Ali (drums) [1935-]
Geri Allen (piano) [1957-]
Harry Allen (tenor sax) [1966-]
Henry Allen Sr (cornet) [1877-1952]
Henry 'Red' Allen (trumpet) [1908-1967]
Moses Allen (bass/tuba) [1907-1983]
Vernon Alley (bass) [1915-]
Mose Allison (piano/vocals) [1927-]
Laurindo Almeida (guitar) [1917-]
Trigger Alpert (bass) [1916-]
Barry Altschul (drums) [1943-]
Danny Alvin (drums) [1902-1958]
Hayes Alvis (bass) [1907-1972]
Franco Ambrosetti (trumpet) [1941-]
Albert Ammons (piano) [1907-1949]
Gene Ammons (tenor sax) [1925-1974]
Curtis Amy (tenor sax) [1929-]
Arild Andersen (bass) [1945-]
Cat Anderson (trumpet) [1916-1981]
Ernestine Anderson (vocals) [1928-]
Ivie Anderson (vocals) [1905-1949]
Ray Anderson (trombone) [1952-]
Wayne Andre (trombone) [1931-]
Chuck Andrus (bass) [1928-]
Ray Anthony (trumpet) [1922-]
Peter Appleyard (vibes) [1928-]
Tony Archer (bass) [1939-]
Jimmy Archey (trombone) [1902-1967]
Neil Ardley (composer) [1937-]
Louis Armstrong (trumpet) [1901-1971]
Sidney Arodin (clarinet) [1901-1948]
Georges Arvanitas (piano) [1931-]
Marvin Ash (piano) [1914-]
Vic Ash (tenor sax) [1930-]
Dorothy Ashby (harp) [1932-1986]
Harold Ashby (tenor sax) [1925-]
Irving Ashby (guitar) [1920-1987]
Bill Ashton (leader) [1936-]
Svend Asmussen (violin) [1916-]
Frank Assunto (trumpet) [1932-1974]
Fred Assunto (trombone) [1929-1966]
Papa Joe Assunto (trombone) [1905-1985]
Georgie Auld (tenor sax) [1919-1990]
Lovie Austin (piano) [1887-1972]
Herman Autrey (trumpet) [1904-1980]
George Avakian (record producer) [1919-]
Roy Ayers (vibes) [1940-]
Albert Ayler (tenor sax) [1936-1970]
Don Ayler (trumpet) [1942-]

Harry Babasin (bass) [1921-]
Roy Babbington (bass) [1940-]
Alice Babs (vocals) [1924-]
Louis Bacon (trumpet) [1904-1967]
Achille Bacquet (clarinet/saxes) [1885-1956]
George Bacquet (clarinet) [1883-1949]
Don Bagley (bass) [1927-]
Benny Bailey (trumpet) [1925-]

Buster Bailey (clarinet) [1902-1967]
Colin Bailey (drums) [1934-]
Dave Bailey (drums) [1926-]
Derek Bailey (guitar) [1932-]
Donald Bailey (drums) [1933-]
Mildred Bailey (vocals) [1907-1951]
Pearl Bailey (vocal) [1918-1990]
Chet Baker (trumpet) [1929-1988]
Ginger Baker (drums) [1940-]
Harold 'Shorty' Baker (trumpet) [1914-1966]
Kenny Baker (trumpet) [1921-]
Red Balaban (bass) [1929-]
Kenny Baldock (bass) [1932-]
Burt Bales (piano) [1916-]
Kenny Ball (trumpet) [1930-]
Ronnie Ball (piano) [1927-]
Iain Ballamy (saxes) [1964-]
Butch Ballard (drums) [1917-]
Whitney Balliett (writer) [1920-]
Gabe Baltazar (alto sax) [1929-]
Billy Bang (violin) [1947-]
Danny Bank (baritone sax) [1922-]
Billy Banks (vocals) [1908-1967]
Paul Barbarin (drums) [1899-1969]
Bill Barber (tuba) [1920-]
Chris Barber (trombone) [1930-]
Gato Barbieri (tenor sax) [1934-]
Dave Barbour (guitar) [1912-1965]
Danny Barcelona (drums) [1929-]
Eddie Barefield (saxes) [1909-1991]
Blue Lu Barker (vocals) [1913-]
Danny Barker (guitar) [1909-]
Thurman Barker (drums) [1948-]
Everett Barksdale (guitar) [1910-1986]
George Barnes (guitar) [1921-1977]
John Barnes (saxes) [1932-]
Charlie Barnet (saxes) [1913-1991]
Gary Barone (trumpet) [1941-]
Mike Barone (trombone) [1936-]
Dan Barrett (trombone) [1955-]
Sweet Emma Barrett (piano/vocals) [1897-1983]
Ray Barretto (conga) [1929-]
Bill Barron (tenor sax) [1927-]
Kenny Barron (piano) [1943-]
Benny Barth (drums) [1929-]
Gary Bartz (saxes) [1940-]
Dud Bascomb (trumpet) [1916-1972]
Paul Bascomb (tenor sax) [1912-1986]
Count Basie (piano) [1904-1984]
Django Bates (piano) [1960-]
Edgar Battle (trumpet/arranger) [1907-1977]
Ray Bauduc (drums) [1909-1988]
Billy Bauer (guitar) [1915-]
Mario Bauza (trumpet) [1911-]
Yolande Bavan (vocals) [1940-]
Charlie Beal (piano) [1908-]
Floyd Bean (piano) [1904-1974]
Heinie Beau (saxes) [1911-1987]
Sidney Bechet (clarinet/soprano sax) [1897-1959]
Gordon Beck (piano) [1936-]
Joe Beck (guitar) [1945-]
Pia Beck (piano/vocals) [1925-]
Fred Beckett (trombone) [1917-1946]
Harry Beckett (trumpet) [1935-]
Ronnie Bedford (drums) [1931-]
Bix Beiderbecke (cornet) [1903-1931]
Aaron Bell (bass) [1922-]
Louis Bellson (drums) [1924-]
Tex Beneke (tenor sax) [1914-]
Tommy Benford (drums) [1905-]
Joe Benjamin (bass) [1919-1974]
Betty Bennett (vocals) [1921-]
Lou Bennett (organ) [1926-]
Max Bennett (bass) [1928-]
Tony Bennett (vocals) [1926-]
Han Bennink (drums) [1942-]
Sammy Benskin (piano) [1922-]
George Benson (guitar) [1943-]
Walter Benton (tenor sax) [1930-]
Joachim-Ernst Berendt (writer/record producer) [1922-]
Bob Berg (tenor sax) [1951-]
Karl Berger (vibes) [1935-]
Chuck Berghofer (bass) [1937-]

Bunny Berigan (trumpet) [1908-1942]
Dick Berk (drums) [1939-]
Sonny Berman (trumpet) [1925-1947]
Clyde Bernhardt (trombone) [1905-1986]
Milt Bernhardt (trombone) [1926-]
Warren Bernhardt (piano) [1938-]
Artie Bernstein (bass) [1909-1964]
Bill Berry (trumpet) [1930-]
Chu Berry (tenor sax) [1910-1941]
Emmett Berry (trumpet) [1915]-
Eddie Bert (trombone) [1922-]
Vic Berton (drums) [1896-1951]
Gene Bertoncini (guitar) [1937-]
Jimmy Bertrand (drums) [1900-1960]
Denzil Best (drums) [1917-1965]
Johnny Best (trumpet) [1913-]
Skeeter Best (guitar) [1914-1985]
Keter Betts (bass) [1928-]
Ed Bickert (guitar) [1932-]
Barney Bigard (clarinet) [1906-1980]
Acker Bilk (clarinet/leader) [1929-]
Ray Biondi (guitar) [1905-1981]
Chris Biscoe (saxes) [1947-]
Wallace Bishop (drums) [1906-1986]
Walter Bishop Jr (piano) [1927-]
Gus Bivona (clarinet) [1915-]
Dave Black (drums) [1928-]
Ed Blackwell (drums) [1929-1992]
Eubie Blake (piano/composer) [1883-1983]
Jerry Blake (saxes) [1908-1961]
Ran Blake (piano) [1935-]
Andrew Blakeney (trumpet) [1898-1992]
Art Blakey (drums) [1919-1990]
Terence Blanchard (trumpet) [1962-]
Jimmy Blanton (bass) [1918-1942]
Rudi Blesh (writer/record producer) [1899-1985]
Carla Bley (piano) [1938-]
Paul Bley (piano) [1932-]
Sandy Block (bass) [1917-]
Johnny Blowers (drums) [1911-]
Arthur Blythe (alto sax) [1940-]
Hamiet Bluiett (saxes) [1940-]
Willie Bobo (percussion) [1934-1983]
Peter Bocage (cornet/violin) [1887-1967]
Phil Bodner (saxes) [1919-]
George Bohannon (trombone) [1937-]
Steve Bohannon (drums) [1947-]
Francy Boland (piano) [1929-]
Buddy Bolden (cornet/leader) [1877-1931]
Walter Bolden (drums) [1925-]
Claude Bolling (piano) [1930-]
Sharkey Bonano (trumpet) [1904-1972]
Jimmy Bond (bass) [1933-]
Joe Bonner (piano) [1948-]
Beryl Booker (piano) [1922-1978]
Walter Booker (bass) [1933-]
Lester Boone (saxes) [1904-]
Richard Boone (trombone/vocals) [1930-]
Sterling Bose (trumpet) [1906-1958]
Earl Bostic (alto sax) [1913-1965]
Johnny Bothwell (alto sax) [1919-]
Lillian Boutté (vocals) [1949-]
Lester Bowie (trumpet) [1941-]
Dave Bowman (piano) [1914-1964]
Patti Bown (piano) [1931-]
Nelson Boyd (bass) [1928-]
Ronnie Boykins (bass) [1935-1980]
Joanne Brackeen (piano) [1938-]
Bobby Bradford (trumpet) [1934-]
Clea Bradford (vocalist) [1936-]
Perry Bradford (piano) [1893-1970]
Will Bradley (trombone/leader) [1912-1989]
Tiny Bradshaw (leader) [1905-1958]
Ruby Braff (cornet) [1927-]
Dollar Brand (piano) [1934-]
Alan Branscombe (piano/vibes/alto sax) [1936-1986]
Oscar Brashear (trumpet) [1944-]
Wellman Braud (bass) [1891-1966]
Anthony Braxton (alto sax) [1945-]
Mike Brecker (tenor sax) [1949-]
Randy Brecker (trumpet) [1945-]

Willem Breuker (saxes) [1944-]
Percy Brice (drums) [1923-]
Cecil Bridgewater (trumpet) [1942-]
Dee Dee Bridgewater (vocals) [1950-]
Ronnell Bright (piano) [1930-]
Nick Brignola (saxes) [1936-]
Jack Brokensha (vibes/drums) [1926-]
Bob Brookmeyer (valve trombone) [1929-]
Roy Brooks (drums) [1938-]
Tina Brooks (tenor sax) [1932-1974]
Peter Brötzmann (tenor sax) [1941-]
Boyce Brown (alto sax) [1910-1959]
Cameron Brown (bass) [1945-]
Cleo Brown (piano/vocals) [1909-]
Clifford Brown (trumpet) [1930-1956]
Garnett Brown (trombone) [1936-]
Gerry Brown (drums) [1951-]
Lawrence Brown (trombone) [1907-1988]
Les Brown (bandleader) [1912-]
Marion Brown (alto sax) [1935-]
Marshall Brown (valve trombone) [1920-1983]
Oscar Brown Jr (vocals) [1926-]
Pete Brown (alto sax) [1906-1963]
Pud Brown (saxes) [1917-]
Ray Brown (bass) [1926-]
Ruth Brown (vocals) [1928-]
Sandy Brown (clarinet) [1929-1975]
Sonny Brown (drums) [1936-]
Steve Brown (bass) [1890-1965]
Tom Brown (trombone) [1888-1958]
Vernon Brown (trombone) [1907-1979]
Chris Brubeck (trombone/bass) 1952
Danny Brubeck (drums) [1955-]
Darius Brubeck (keyboards) [1947-]
Dave Brubeck (piano) [1920-]
Bill Bruford (drums) [1949-]
Philippe Brun (trumpet) [1908-]
Georg Brunis (trombone) [1902-1974]
Bobby Bryant (trumpet) [1934-]
Ray Bryant (piano) [1931-]
Tommy Bryant (bass) [1930-1982]
Willie Bryant (vocals/leader) [1908-1964]
Beryl Bryden (vocals) [1926-]
Milt Buckner (organ) [1915-1977]
Teddy Buckner (trumpet) [1909-]
Errol Buddle (saxes) [1928-]
Dennis Budimir (guitar) [1938-]
Monty Budwig (bass) [1929-1992]
Papa Bue (trombone) [1930-]
John Bunch (piano) [1921-]
Larry Bunker (drums/vibes) [1928-]
Teddy Bunn (guitar) [1909-1978]
Vinnie Burke (bass) [1921-]
Roy Burnes (drums) [1935-]
Dwayne Burno (bass) [1970-]
Dave Burns (trumpet) [1924-]
Ralph Burns (piano/arranger) [1922-]
Jon Burr (bass) [1953-]
Kenny Burrell (guitar) [1931-]
Alvin Burroughs (drums) [1911-1950]
Gary Burton (vibes) [1943-]
Lennie Bush (bass) [1927-]
Garvin Bushell (saxes) [1902-1991]
Joe Bushkin (piano) [1916-]
Sam Butera (tenor sax) [1927-]
Frank Butler (drums) [1928-1984]
Billy Butterfield (trumpet) [1917-1988]
Don Butterfield (tuba) [1923-]
Jimmy Butts (bass) [1917-]
Jaki Byard (piano) [1922-]
Don Byas (tenor sax) [1912-1972]
Billy Byers (trombone/composer) [1927-]
Charlie Byrd (guitar) [1925-]
Donald Byrd (trumpet) [1932-]
Bobby Byrne (trombone) [1918-]

George Cables (piano) [1944-]
Ernie Caceres (baritone sax) [1911-1971]
Jackie Cain (vocals) [1928-]
Happy Caldwell (tenor sax) [1903-1978]
Eddie Calhoun (bass) [1921-]
Red Callender (bass) [1918-1992]
Cab Calloway (vocals) [1907-]

Index of musicians

169

Index of musicians

Ziggy Elman (trumpet) [1914-1968]
Alan Elsdon (trumpet) [1934]
Bob Enevoldsen (trombone) [1920-]
Bill English (drums) [1925-]
Rolf Ericson (trumpet) 1922
Peter Erskine (drums) [1954-]
Ahmet Ertegun (record producer) [1923-]
Nesuhi Ertegun (record producer) [1917-1989]
Booker Ervin (tenor sax) [1930-1970]
Pee Wee Erwin (trumpet) [1913-1981]
Ralph Escudero (bass/tuba) [1898-1970]
Kevin Eubanks (guitar) [1957-]
Julian Euell (bass) [1929-]
Bill Evans (piano) [1929-1980]
Bill Evans (tenor sax) [1958-]
Doc Evans (cornet) [1907-1977]
Gil Evans (composer) [1912-1988]
Herschel Evans (tenor sax) [1909-1939]
Stump Evans (saxes) [1904-1928]
Sue Evans (percussion) [1951-]
Don Ewell (piano) [1916-1983]
Streamline Ewing (trombone) [1917-]
Billy Exiner (drums) [1910-]

Jon Faddis (trumpet) [1953-]
Don Fagerquist (trumpet) [1927-1974]
Al Fairweather (trumpet) [1927-1993]
Digby Fairweather (trumpet) [1946-]
Jack Fallon (bass) [1915-]
Tal Farlow (guitar) [1921-]
Addison Farmer (bass) [1928-1963]
Art Farmer (trumpet) [1928-]
Joe Farrell (tenor sax) [1937-1986]
Nick Fatool (drums) [1915-]
Malachi Favors (bass) [1937-]
Pierre Favre (drums) [1937-]
Wally Fawkes (clarinet) [1924-]
Irving Fazola (clarinet) [1912-1949]
Leonard Feather (writer) [1914-]
Buddy Featherstonhaugh (saxes) [1909-1976]
Morey Feld (drums) [1915-1971]
Wilton Felder (tenor sax) [1940-]
Vic Feldman (vibes/ piano) [1934-1987]
Lennie Felix (piano) [1920-1980]
Maynard Ferguson (trumpet) [1928-]
Glenn Ferris (trombone) [1950-]
Herbie Fields (saxes) [1919-1958]
Kansas Fields (drums) [1915-]
Otis 'Candy' Finch (drums) [1934-1982]
Bill Finegan (arranger) [1917-]
Barry Finnerty (guitar) [1951-]
Clare Fischer (piano) [1928-]
Arnold Fishkin (bass) [1919-]
Ella Fitzgerald (vocal) [1918-]
Roberta Flack (vocals) [1940-]
Tommy Flanagan (piano) [1930-]
Phil Flanigan (bass) [1956-]
Marty Flax (saxes) [1924-1972]
Brick Fleagle (guitar) [1906-]
Herb Flemming (trombone) [1900-1976]
Bob Florence (arranger) [1932-]
Chuck Flores (drums) [1935-]
Chris Flory (guitar) [1953-]
Med Flory (alto sax) [1926-]
Hubert Fol (alto sax) [1925-]
Raymond Fol (piano) [1928-1979]
Carl Fontana (trombone) [1928-]
Ricky Ford (tenor sax) [1954-]
Robben Ford (guitar) [1951-]
Reginald Foresythe (piano/composer/leader) [1907-1958]
Michael Formanek (bass) [1958-]
Jimmy Forrest (tenor sax) [1920-1980]
Sonny Fortune (alto sax) [1939-]
Al Foster (drums) [1944-]
Frank Foster (tenor sax) [1928-]
Gary Foster (saxes) [1936-]
George 'Pops' Foster (bass) [1892-1969]
Herman Foster (piano) [1928-]
Pete Fountain (clarinet) [1930-]
Vernel Fournier (drums) [1928-]
Charlie Fowlkes (baritone sax) [1916-1980]
Charles Fox (writer/broadcaster) [1921-1991]

Panama Francis (drums) [1918-]
Aretha Franklin (vocals) [1942-]
Cié Frazier (drums) [1904-1985]
Bud Freeman (tenor sax) [1906-1991]
Chico Freeman (tenor sax) [1949-]
Russ Freeman (piano) [1926-]
Von Freeman (tenor sax) [1922-]
Don Friedman (piano) [1935-]
David Friesen (bass) [1942-]
Bill Frisell (guitar) [1951-]
Dave Frishberg (piano/vocal/songwriter) [1933-]
Frank Froeba (piano/leader) [1907-1981]
Tony Fruscella (trumpet) [1927-1969]
Don Frye (piano) [1903-1981]
Curtis Fuller (trombone) [1934-]
Walter Fuller (trumpet/vocal) [1910-]
Walter 'Gil' Fuller (composer/arranger) [1920-]

Steve Gadd (drums) [1945-]
Al Gafa (guitar) [1941-]
Slim Gaillard (piano/guitar/vocal) [1916-1991]
Charlie Gaines (trumpet) [1900-]
Barry Galbraith (guitar) [1919-1983]
Eric Gale (guitar) [1938-]
Larry Gales (bass) [1936-]
Jim Galloway (saxes) [1936-]
Hal Galper (piano) [1938-]
Al Gandee (trombone) [1900-1944]
Vyacheslav Ganelin (piano) [1944-]
Allan Ganley (drums) [1931-]
Jan Garbarek (saxes) [1947-]
Dick Garcia (guitar) [1931-]
Russ Garcia (arranger/trumpet) [1916-]
Ed Garland (bass) [1885-1980]
Joe Garland (saxes/arranger) [1903-1977]
Red Garland (piano) [1923-1984]
Erroll Garner (piano) [1921-1977]
Carlos Garnett (tenor sax) [1938-]
Donald Garrett (bass) [1932-]
Kenny Garrett (alto sax) [1960-]
Michael Garrick (piano) [1933-]
Arv Garrison (bass) [1922-1960]
Jimmy Garrison (bass) [1934-1976]
Leonard Gaskin (bass) [1920-]
Vic Gaskin (bass) [1934-]
Michel Gaudry (bass) [1928-]
Hal Gaylor (bass) [1929-]
Wilton 'Bogey' Gaynair (tenor sax) [1927-]
Matthew Gee (trombone) [1925-1979]
Herb Geller (alto sax) [1928-]
Lorraine Geller (piano) [1928-1958]
Chuck Gentry (baritone sax) [1911-]
Fatty George (saxes) [1927-1982]
Karl George (trumpet) [1913-]
Squire Gersh (bass) [1913-]
Stan Getz (tenor sax) [1927-1991]
Mike Gibbs (composer/trombone) [1937-]
Terry Gibbs (vibes) [1924-]
Andy Gibson (arranger) [1913-1961]
Gary Giddins (writer) [1948-]
Gene Gifford (guitar) [1908-1970]
Dizzy Gillespie (trumpet) [1917-1993]
John Gilmore (tenor sax) [1931-]
Steve Gilmore (bass) [1943-]
Egberto Gismonti (guitar) [1947-]
Ira Gitler (writer) [1928-]
Jimmy Giuffre (saxes) [1921-]
Eddie Gladden (drums) [1937-]
Ralph Gleason (writer) [1916-1975]
Tyree Glenn (trombone) [1912-1974]
Bernie Glow (trumpet) [1926-1982]
A G Godley (drums) [1900-1973]
Dusko Gojkovic (trumpet) [1931-]
Harry Gold (saxes) [1907-]
Sanford Gold (piano) [1911-]
Don Goldie (trumpet) [1930-]
Larry Goldings (organ) [1968-]
Jean Goldkette (piano/leader) [1899-1962]
Benny Golson (tenor sax) [1929-]
Eddie Gomez (bass) [1944-]
Nat Gonella (trumpet) [1908-]
Paul Gonsalves (tenor sax) [1920-1974]

Babs Gonzales (vocal) [1919-1980]
Coleridge Goode (bass) [1914-]
Benny Goodman (clarinet) [1909-1986]
Bill Goodwin (drums) [1942-]
Henry Goodwin (trumpet) [1910-1979]
Bob Gordon (baritone sax) [1928-1955]
Dexter Gordon (tenor sax) [1923-1990]
Joe Gordon (trumpet) [1928-1963]
Danny Gottlieb (drums) [1953-]
Frank 'Big Boy' Goudie (tenor sax/clarinet) [1899-1964]
Jimmy Gourley (guitar) [1926-]
Brad Gowans (trombone) [1903-1954]
Conrad Gozzo (trumpet) [1922-1964]
John Graas (french horn) [1924-1962]
Bob Graettinger (composer) [1923-1957]
Bill Graham (alto sax) [1918-]
Kenny Graham (tenor sax/arranger) [1924-]
Jerry Granelli (drums) [1940-]
Norman Granz (impresario) [1918-]
Stephane Grappelli (violin) [1908-]
Milford Graves (drums) [1941-]
Glen Gray (saxes) [1906-1963]
Jerry Gray (composer/arranger) [1916-1976]
Wardell Gray (tenor sax) [1921-1955]
Ronnie Greb (drums) [1938-]
Buddy Greco (vocals) [1926-]
Bennie Green (trombone) [1923-1977]
Benny Green (tenor sax/writer) [1927-]
Benny Green (piano) [1963-]
Bill Green (alto sax) [1928-]
Charlie Green (trombone) [1900-1936]
Dave Green (bass) [1942-]
Freddie Green (guitar) [1911-1987]
Grant Green (guitar) [1931-1979]
Lil Green (vocal) [1922-]
Urbie Green (trombone) [1926-]
Burton Greene (piano) [1937-]
Charles Greenlee (trombone) [1927-]
Sonny Greer (drums) [1903-1982]
Max Greger (tenor sax) [1926-]
Stan Greig (piano/drums) [1930-]
Al Grey (trombone) [1925-]
Chris Griffin (trumpet) [1915-]
Johnny Griffin (tenor sax) [1928-]
Malcolm Griffiths (trombone) [1941-]
Henry Grimes (bass) [1935-]
Tiny Grimes (guitar) [1917-]
Steven Grossman (saxes) [1951-]
Marty Grosz (guitar) [1930-]
Carl Grubbs (alto sax) [1944-]
Earl Grubbs (tenor sax) [1942-]
George Gruntz (piano) [1932-]
Dave Grusin (composer/ piano) [1934-]
Gigi Gryce (alto sax) [1927-1983]
Vince Guaraldi (piano) [1928-1976]
Johnny Guarnieri (piano) [1917-1985]
John Guerin (drums) [1939-]
Roger Guerin (trumpet) [1926-]
Phil Guilbeau (trumpet) [1926-]
Friedrich Gulda (piano/composer) [1930-]
Lars Gullin (baritone sax) [1928-1976]
Onaje Allen Gumbs (piano/arranger) [1949-]
Tommy Gumina (accordion) [1931-]
Trilok Gurtu (percussion) [1951-]
Barry Guy (bass) [1947-]
Fred Guy (banjo/guitar) [1897-1971]
Joe Guy (trumpet) [1920-1961]
Tommy Gwaltney (clarinet) [1921-]

Eddie Haas (bass) [1930-]
Bobby Hackett (cornet) [1915-1976]
Charlie Haden (bass) [1937-]
Shafi Hadi (tenor sax) [1929-]
Dick Hafer (tenor sax) [1927-]
Bob Haggart (bass) [1914-]
Jerry Hahn (guitar) [1940-]
Al Haig (piano) [1924-1982]
Omar Hakim (drums) [1959-]
Sadik Hakim (piano) [1919-1983]
Corky Hale (piano / harp) [1931-]
Adelaide Hall (vocals) [1909-]
Al Hall (bass) [1915-1988]
Edmond Hall (clarinet) [1901-1967]

Herb Hall (clarinet) [1907-]
Jim Hall (guitar) [1930-]
Minor 'Ram' Hall (drums) [1897-1959]
Skip Hall (piano) [1909-1980]
Tubby Hall (drums) [1895-1946]
Bengt Hallberg (piano) [1932-]
Lenny Hambro (alto sax) [1923-]
Chico Hamilton (drums) [1921-]
Jeff Hamilton (drums) [1953-]
Jimmy Hamilton (clarinet/tenor sax) [1917-]
John 'Bugs' Hamilton (trumpet) [1911-1947]
Scott Hamilton (tenor sax) [1954-]
Jan Hammer (keyboards) [1948-]
John Hammond (record producer/critic) [1910-1987]
Lionel Hampton (vibes) [1913-]
Slide Hampton (trombone) [1932-]
Herbie Hancock (piano) [1940-]
George Handy (piano/arranger) [1920-]
Captain John Handy (alto sax) [1900-1971]
John Handy (alto sax) [1933-]
W C Handy (cornet/composer/leader) [1873-1958]
Jake Hanna (drums) [1931-]
Roland Hanna (piano) [1932-]
Ole Kock Hansen (piano) [1945-]
Bob Hardaway (tenor sax) [1928-]
John Hardee (tenor sax) [1918-1984]
Wilbur Harden (trumpet) [1925-]
Lil Hardin (piano) [1902-1971]
Buster Harding (piano) [1917-1965]
Bill Hardman (trumpet) [1933-1990]
Otto Hardwicke (alto sax) [1904-1970]
Emmett Hardy (cornet) [1903-1925]
Al Harewood (drums) [1923-]
Rufus Harley (bagpipes) [1936-]
Billy Harper (tenor sax) [1943-]
Herbie Harper (trombone) [1920-]
Tom Harrell (trumpet) [1946-]
Joe Harriott (alto sax) [1928-1973]
Barry Harris (piano) [1929-]
Beaver Harris (drums) [1936-]
Benny Harris (trumpet) [1919-1975]
Bill Harris (trombone) [1916-1973]
Eddie Harris (tenor sax) [1936-]
Gene Harris (piano) [1933-]
Joe Harris (drums) [1926-]
Donald Harrison (alto sax) [1960-]
Jimmy Harrison (trombone) [1900-1931]
Billy Hart (drums) [1940-]
Clyde Hart (piano) [1910-1945]
Johnny Hartman (vocals) [1923-1983]
Eddie Harvey (trombone/piano) [1925-]
Stan Hasselgard (clarinet) [1922-1948]
Lennie Hastings (drums) [1927-1978]
Bob Havens (trombone) [1930-]
Dickie Hawdon (trumpet) [1927-]
Hampton Hawes (piano) [1928-1977]
Coleman Hawkins (tenor sax) [1904-1969]
Erskine Hawkins (trumpet) [1914-]
Clancy Hayes (banjo) [1908-1972]
Harry Hayes (saxes) [1909-]
Louis Hayes (drums) [1937-]
Tubby Hayes (tenor sax) [1935-1973]
Herbie Haymer (tenor sax) [1915-1949]
Roy Haynes (drums) [1926-]
Lenny Hayton (piano/arranger) [1908-1971]
Cedric Haywood (piano) [1914-1969]
Monk Hazel (drums) [1903-1968]
J.C. Heard (drums) [1917-1988]
John Heard (bass) [1938-]
Albert Heath (drums) [1935-]
Jimmy Heath (tenor sax) [1926-]
Percy Heath (bass) [1923-]
Ted Heath (trombone/leader) [1900-1969]
Spike Heatley (bass) [1933-]
Dick Heckstall-Smith (tenor sax) [1934-]
Neal Hefti (trumpet/composer) [1922-]
Lucille Hegamin (vocal) [1894-1970]
Mark Helias (bass) [1950-]
Bob Helm (clarinet) [1914-]
Julius Hemphill (alto sax) [1940-]

Index of musicians

Sheldon Hemphill (trumpet) [1906-1959]
Bill Henderson (vocals) [1930-]
Eddie Henderson (trumpet) [1940-]
Fletcher Henderson
  (piano/arranger/leader) [1897-1952]
Horace Henderson (piano) [1904-]
Joe Henderson (tenor sax) [1937-]
Michael Henderson (electric bass)
  [1951-]
Rick Henderson (saxes) [1928-]
Wayne Henderson (trombone) [1939-]
Jon Hendricks (vocal) [1921-]
Al Hendrickson (guitar) [1920-]
Ernie Henry (alto sax) [1926-1957]
Haywood Henry (saxes) 1913-]
Nat Hentoff (writer) [1925-]
Gregory Herbert (saxes) [1947-1978]
Mort Herbert (bass) [1925-1983]
Peter Herbolzheimer
  (trombone/leader) [1935-]
Skeets Herfurt (saxes) [1911-]
Woody Herman (clarinet/leader)
  [1913-1987]
Eddie Heywood (piano) [1915-1989]
Al Hibbler (vocal) [1915-]
John Hicks (piano) [1941-]
J.C. Higginbotham (trombone) [1906-1973]
Billy Higgins (drums) [1936-]
Eddie Higgins (piano) [1932-]
Willie Hightower (cornet/leader)
  [1889-1959]
Andrew Hilaire (drums) [c1900-c1936]
Alex Hill (piano/arranger) [1906-1937]
Andrew Hill (piano) [1937-]
Bertha 'Chippie' Hill (vocals) [1905-1950]
Ernest 'Bass' Hill (bass) [1900-1964]
Freddie Hill (trumpet) [1932-]
Teddy Hill (tenor sax/bandleader)
  [1909-1978]
Lonnie Hillyer (trumpet) [1940-1985]
Earl Hines (piano) [1903-1983]
Motohiko Hino (drums) [1946-]
Terumasa Hino (trumpet) [1942-]
Milt Hinton (bass) [1910-]
Chris Hinze (flute) [1938-]
Jutta Hipp (piano) [1925-]
Al Hirt (trumpet) [1922-]
Jon Hiseman (drums) [1944-]
Les Hite (alto sax) [1903-1962]
André Hodeir (writer) [1921-]
Art Hodes (piano) [1904-1993]
Johnny Hodges (alto sax) [1906-1970]
George Hoefer (writer) [1909-1967]
Granville T.Hogan (drums) [1929-]
Jay Hoggard (vibes) [1954-]
Allan Holdsworth (guitar) 1946
Allan Holdsworth (guitar) 1948
Billie Holiday (vocal) [1915-1959]
Clarence Holiday (guitar) [1900-1937]
Dave Holland (bass) [1946-]
Peanuts Holland (trumpet) [1910-1979]
Major Holley (bass) [1924-1990]
Kenneth Hollon (tenor sax) [1909-1974]
Bill Holman (tenor sax/composer) [1927-]
Charlie Holmes (alto sax) [1910-1985]
Richard 'Groove' Holmes (organ)
  [1931-1991]
Isaac 'Red' Holt (drums) [1932-]
Bill Hood (baritone sax) [1924-]
Stix Hooper (drums) [1938-]
Elmo Hope (piano) [1923-1967]
Claude Hopkins (piano) [1903-1984]
Fred Hopkins (bass) [1947-]
Lightning Hopkins (guitar/vocals)
  [1912-1982]
Paul Horn (saxes) [1930-]
Shirley Horn (piano/vocals) [1934-]
Lena Horne (vocal) [1917-]
David Horowitz (keyboards) [1942-]
Clint Houston (bass) [1946-]
Avery 'Kid' Howard (trumpet) [1908-1966]
Darnell Howard (saxes) [1895-1966]
Noah Howard (alto sax) [1943-]
Michael Howell (guitar) [1943-]
Freddie Hubbard (trumpet) [1938-]
Ed Hubble (trombone) [1928-]

Ralf Hübner (drums) [1939-]
Peanuts Hucko (clarinet) [1918-]
Will Hudson (composer/bandleader)
  [1908-1981]
Armand Hug (piano) [1910-1977]
Jim Hughart (bass) [1936-]
Bill Hughes (trombone) [1930-]
Spike Hughes (bass/composer/writer)
  [1908-1987]
Daniel Humair (drums) [1938-]
Derek Humble (alto sax) [1931-1971]
Helen Humes (vocals) [1913-1981]
Bobbi Humphrey (flute) [1950-]
Paul Humphrey (drums) [1935-]
Percy Humphrey (trumpet) [1905-]
Willie Humphrey Jr (clarinet) [1900-]
Lex Humphries (drums) [1936-]
Roger Humphries (drums) [1944-]
Fred Hunt (piano) [1923-1986]
Pee Wee Hunt (trombone) [1907-1979]
Alberta Hunter (vocals) [1895-1984]
Chris Hunter (alto sax) [1957-]
Clyde Hurley (bass) [1916-1963]
Clarence Hutchenrider (saxes) [1908-1991]
Bobby Hutcherson (vibes) [1941-]
Ina Ray Hutton (bandleader) [1916-1984]
Margie Hyams (vibes) [1923-]
Dick Hyman (piano) [1927-]

Sonny Igoe (drums) [1923-]
Wes Ilcken (drums) [1923-1957]
Peter Ind (bass) [1928-]
Keith Ingham (piano) [1942-]
Tony Inzalaco (drums) [1938-]
Charlie Irvis (trombone) [c1899-c1939]
Cecil Irwin (saxes) [1902-1935]
Dennis Irwin (bass) [1951-]
Ike Isaacs (bass) [1923-1981]
Frank Isola (drums) [1925-]
Chuck Israels (bass) [1936-]
David Izenson (bass) [1932-1979]

Calvin Jackson (piano) [1919-1985]
Chip Jackson (bass) [1950-]
Chubby Jackson (bass) [1918-]
Cliff Jackson (piano) [1902-1970]
Duffy Jackson (drums) [1953-]
Franz Jackson (tenor sax) [1912-]
Javon Jackson (tenor sax) [1965-]
Mahalia Jackson (vocals) [1911-1972]
Milt Jackson (vibes) [1923-]
Oliver Jackson (drums) [1933-]
Preston Jackson (trombone) [1902-1983]
Quentin Jackson (trombone) [1909-1976]
Ronald Shannon Jackson (drums) [1940-]
Rudy Jackson (clarinet) [1901-c1968]
Tony Jackson (piano/composer) [1876-1921]
Willis 'Gator' Jackson (tenor sax)
  [1932-1987]
Pim Jacobs (piano) [1934-]
Pete Jacobsen (piano) [1950-]
Illinois Jacquet (tenor sax) [1922-]
Russell Jacquet (trumpet) [1917-]
Ahmad Jamal (piano) [1930-]
Khan Jamal (vibes) [1946-]
Billy James (drums) [1936-]
Bob James (piano) [1939-]
George James (tenor sax) [1906-]
Harry James (trumpet) [1916-1983]
Michael James (writer) [1932-]
Stafford James (bass) [1946-]
Conrad Janis (trombone) [1928-]
Joseph Jarman (saxes) [1937-]
Keith Jarrett (piano) [1945-]
Clifford Jarvis (drums) [1941-]
Bobby Jaspar (tenor sax) [1926-1963]
Frankie 'Half Pint' Jaxon
  (vocals/composer) [1895-]
Eddie Jefferson (vocal) [1918-1979]
Hilton Jefferson (alto sax) [1903-1968]
Ron Jefferson (drums) [1926-]
Paul Jeffrey (tenor sax) [1933-]
Herb Jeffries (vocal) [1916-]
Freddie Jenkins (trumpet) [1906-1978]
John Jenkins Jr (alto sax) [1931-]
Leroy Jenkins(violin) [1932-]

Pat Jenkins (trumpet) [1914-]
Jack Jenney (trombone) [1910-1945]
Jorgen-Grunnet Jepsen
  (discographer) [1927-1981]
Antonio Carlos Jobim (piano/guitar)
  [1927-]
Alphonso Johnson (bass) [1951-]
Bill Johnson (bass) [1874-1972]
Budd Johnson (tenor sax) [1910-1984]
Buddy Johnson (piano/leader) [1915-1977]
Bunk Johnson (trumpet) [1889-1949]
Charlie Johnson (piano/leader) [1891-1959]
Dick Johnson (alto sax) [1925-]
Dink Johnson (piano/clarinet/drums)
  [1892-1954]
Floyd 'Candy' Johnson (tenor sax)
  [1922-1981]
Gus Johnson (drums) [1913-]
Harold 'Money' Johnson (trumpet)
  [1918-1978]
Howard Johnson (baritone sax) [1941-]
James P Johnson (piano/composer)
  [1894-1955]
Jimmie Johnson (drums) [1930-]
J. J. Johnson (trombone) [1924-]
Keg Johnson (trombone) [1908-1967]
Ken 'Snakehips' Johnson (leader)
  [1917-1941]
Lem Johnson (tenor sax) [1909-]
Lonnie Johnson (guitar/vocal) [1889-1970]
Manzie Johnson (drums) [1906-1971]
Osie Johnson (drums) [1923-1966]
Pete Johnson (piano) [1904-1967]
Plas Johnson (tenor sax) [1931-]
Reggie Johnson (bass) [1940-]
Walter Johnson (drums) [1904-1977]
Pete Jolly (piano/ accordion) [1932-]
Al Jones (drums) [1930-c1976]
Bobby Jones (tenor sax) [1928-1980]
Buddy Jones (bass) [1924-]
Carmell Jones (trumpet) [1936-]
Claude Jones (trombone) [1901-1962]
Clifford 'Snags' Jones (drums) [1900-1947]
Dill Jones (piano) [1923-1984]
Eddie Jones (bass) [1929-]
Elvin Jones (drums) [1927-]
Etta Jones (vocals) [1928-]
Hank Jones (piano) [1918-]
Harold Jones (drums) [1940-]
Isham Jones (piano/composer/leader)
  [1894-1956]
Jimmy Jones (piano) [1918-1982]
Jo Jones (drums) [1911-1985]
Jonah Jones (trumpet) [1908-]
LeRoi Jones (writer) [1934-]
Max Jones (writer) [1917-1993]
'Sirone' Norris Jones (bass) [1940-]
Oliver Jones (piano) [1934-]
Philly Joe Jones (drums) [1923-1985]
Quincy Jones (trumpet) [1933-]
Reunald Jones (trumpet) [1910-]
Richard M Jones (piano/composer/
  arranger) [1892-1945]
Rodney Jones (guitar) [1956-]
Rufus Jones (drums) [1936-]
Rusty Jones (drums) [1932-]
Sam Jones (bass) [1924-1981]
Thad Jones (trumpet) [1923-1986]
Wallace Jones (trumpet) [1906-1983]
Willie Jones (drums) [1929-]
Wilmore 'Slick' Jones (drums) [1907-1969]
Clifford Jordan (tenor sax) [1931-]
Duke Jordan (piano) [1922-]
Louis Jordan (alto sax/vocals) [1908-1975]
Sheila Jordan (vocals) [1928-]
Stanley Jordan (guitar) [1959-]
Steve Jordan (guitar) [1919-]
Taft Jordan (trumpet) [1915-1981]
George Joyner *Jamil Nasser* (bass)
  [1932-]

Tiny Kahn (drums) [1923-1953]

Max Kaminsky (trumpet) [1908-]
Richie Kamuca (tenor sax) [1930-1977]
Dick Katz (piano) [1924-]
Dill Katz (bass) [1946-]
Fred Katz (cello) [1919-]
Lee Katzman (trumpet) [1928-]
Connie Kay (drums) [1927-]
Carol Kaye (electric bass) [1935-]
Nate Kazebier (trumpet) [1912-1969]
Shake Keane (trumpet) [1927-]
Norman Keenan (bass) [1916-1980]
Orrin Keepnews (record producer)
  [1923-]
Geoff Keezer (piano) [1971-]
Roger Kellaway (piano) [1939-]
Peck Kelley (piano/leader) [1898-1980]
George Kelly (tenor sax) [1915-1985]
Guy Kelly (trumpet) [1906-1940]
Red Kelly (bass) [1927-]
Wynton Kelly (piano) [1931-1971]
Hal Kemp (alto sax/leader) [1905-1940]
Charlie Kennedy (alto sax) [1927-]
Dick Kenney (trombone) [1920-]
Stan Kenton (piano/bandleader) [1911-1979]
Robin Kenyatta (alto sax) [1942-]
Freddie Keppard (cornet) [1890-1933]
Brooks Kerr (piano) [1951-]
Kenny Kersey (piano) [1916-1983]
Barney Kessel (guitar) [1923-]
Steve Khan (guitar) [1947-]
Karl Kiffe (drums) [1927-]
Masabumi Kikuchi (piano) [1940-]
Al Killian (trumpet) [1916-1950]
Deane Kincaide (arranger/saxes) [1911-]
Morgana King (vocals) [1930-]
Peter King (alto sax) [1940-]
Stan King (drums) [1900-1949]
Teddi King (vocals) [1929-]
Tony Kinsey (drums) [1927-]
John Kirby (bass) [1908-1952]
Andy Kirk (saxes/leader) [1898-]
Roland Kirk (saxes) [1936-1977]
Kenny Kirkland (piano) [1955-]
Don Kirkpatrick (piano/arranger)
  [1905-1956]
Eiji Kitamura (clarinet) [1929-]
Harry Klein (baritone sax) [1928-]
Manny Klein (trumpet) [1908-]
John Klemmer (tenor sax) [1946-]
Al Klink (tenor sax) [1915-1991]
Eric Kloss (saxes) [1949-]
Irv Kluger (drums) [1921-]
Earl Klugh (guitar) [1954-]
Jimmy Knepper (trombone) [1927-]
Freddie Kohlman (drums) [1918-]
Hans Koller (tenor sax) [1921-]
Lee Konitz (alto sax) [1927-]
Alexis Korner (guitar/vocals) [1928-1984]
Teddy Kotick (bass) [1928-1986]
Carlo Krahmer (drums) [1914-1976]
Irene Kral (vocalist) [1932-1978]
Roy Kral (piano/vocal) [1921-]
Carl Kress (guitar) [1907-1965]
Karin Krog (vocals) [1937-]
Gene Krupa (drums) [1909-1973]
Joachim Kuhn (piano) [1944-]
Rolf Kuhn (clarinet) [1929-]
Steve Kuhn (keyboards) [1938-]
Billy Kyle (piano) [1914-1966]

Joe La Barbera (drums) [1948-]
John La Barbera (trumpet) [1945-]
Pat La Barbera (tenor sax) [1944-]
Steve Lacy (soprano sax) [1934-]
Tommy Ladnier (trumpet) [1900-1939]
Scott la Faro (bass) [1936-1961]
Guy Lafitte (tenor sax) [1927-]
Bireli Lagrene (guitar) [1966-]
Alfred 'Baby' Laine (cornet) [1895-1957]
Cleo Laine (vocals) [1927-]
Papa Jack Laine (drums/leader) [1873-1966]
Rick Laird (bass) [1941-]
Oliver Lake (alto sax) [1942-]
Nappy Lamare (guitar) [1907-1988]
John Lamb (bass) [1933-]
Dave Lambert (vocal) [1917-1966]

Index of musicians

Don Lamond (drums) [1920-]
Harold Land (tenor sax) [1928-]
Harold Land Jr (piano) [1950-]
Eddie Lang (guitar) [1902-1933]
Jim Lanigan (bass) [1902-1983]
John La Porta (saxes) [1920-]
Ellis Larkins (piano) [1923-]
Pete La Roca (drums) [1938-]
Prince Lasha (alto sax) [1929-]
Yusef Lateef (saxes) [1920-]
Chris Laurence (bass) [1949-]
Cy Laurie (clarinet) [1926-]
Arnie Lawrence (alto sax) [1938-]
Azar Lawrence (tenor sax) [1953-]
Elliot Lawrence (piano/arranger) [1925-]
Hubert Laws (flute) [1939-]
Ronnie Laws (tenor sax) [1950-]
Hugh Lawson (piano) [1935-]
Yank Lawson (trumpet) [1911-]
Dill Lee (bass) [1920-]
David Lee Jr (drums) [1941-]
George E Lee (vocal/baritone
    sax/leader) [1896-1958]
Jeanne Lee (vocals) [1939-]
John Lee (bass) [1952-]
Julia Lee (piano, vocals) [1902-1958]
Peggy Lee (vocal) [1920-]
Tony Lee (piano) [1934-]
Will Lee (bass) [1950-]
Cliff Leeman (drums) [1913-1986]
Gene Lees (writer) [1928-]
Wade Legge (piano) [1934-1963]
Carmen Leggio (saxes) [1927-]
Michel Legrand (piano/composer) [1932-]
Min Leibrook (bass/tuba) [1903-1943]
Bernie Leighton (piano) [1921-]
Elaine Leighton (drums) [1926-]
Pete Lemer (keyboards) [1942-]
Brian Lemon (piano) [1937-]
Harlan Leonard (saxes) [1904-1983]
Jay Leonhart (bass) [1940-]
Bill le Sage (vibes) [1927-]
Jack Lesberg (bass) [1920-]
Johnny Letman (trumpet) [1917-1992]
Didier Levallet (bass) [1944-]
Stan Levey (drums) [1925-]
Milcho Leviev (piano) [1937-]
Marc Levin (flute/cornet) [1942-]
Mark Levine (piano/trombone) [1938-]
Alan Levitt (drums) [1932-]
Rod Levitt (trombone) [1929-]
John Levy (bass) [1912-]
Lou Levy (piano) [1928-]
Ed Lewis (trumpet) [1909-1985]
George Lewis (clarinet) [1900-1968]
George Lewis (trombone) [1952-]
Herbie Lewis (bass) [1941-]
Jimmy Lewis (bass) [1918-]
John Lewis (piano) [1920-]
Meade Lux Lewis (piano) [1905-1964]
Mel Lewis (drums) [1929-1990]
Ramsey Lewis (piano) [1935-]
Sabby Lewis (piano/bandleader) [1914-]
Ted Lewis (clarinet/leader) [1892-1971]
Vic Lewis (guitar/leader) [1919-]
Willie Lewis (saxes) 1905-1971]
Dave Liebman (tenor sax) [1946-]
Kirk Lightsey (piano) [1937-]
Harry Lim (record producer) [1919-]
Abbey Lincoln (vocals) [1930-]
Abe Lincoln (trombone) [1907-]
Nils Lindberg (piano) [1933-]
John Lindsay (bass/trombone) [1894-
    1950]
Ray Linn (trumpet) [1920-]
Alfred Lion (record producer) [1908-
    1987]
Melba Liston (trombone) [1926-]
Booker Little (trumpet) [1938-1961]
Wilbur Little (bass) [1928-1987]
Fud Livingston (saxes) [1906-1957]
Ulysses Livingston (guitar) [1912-]
Charles Lloyd (saxes) [1938-]
Jerry Lloyd (trumpet) [1920-
Eddie Locke (drums) [1930-]
Didier Lockwood (violin) [1956-]
Tricky Lofton (trombone) [1930-]
Giuseppi Logan (saxes) [1935-]

Clyde Lombardi (bass) [1922-c1975]
Mike Longo (piano) [1939-]
Eddie Louiss (piano/organ) [1941-]
Jacques Loussier (piano) [1934-]
Joe Lovano (tenor sax) [1952-]
Herbie Lovelle (drums) [1924-]
Leroy Lovett (piano) [1919-]
Frank Lowe (tenor sax) [1943-]
Mundell Lowe (guitar) [1922-]
Henry Lowther (trumpet) [1941-]
Herman Lubinsky (record producer)
    [1896-1974]
Al Lucas (bass) [1916-1983]
Lawrence Lucie (guitar) [1907-]
Jimmie Lunceford (leader) [1902-1947]
Jesper Lundgaard (bass) [1954-]
Claude Luter (clarinet) [1923-]
Gloria Lynne (vocalist) [1931-]
Jimmy Lyons (alto sax) [1933-1986]
Jimmy Lytell (clarinet) [1904-1972]
Johnny Lytle (vibes) [1932-]
Humphrey Lyttelton (trumpet) [1921-]

Harold Mabern (piano) [1936-]
Cecil McBee (bass) [1935-]
Christian McBride (bass) [1972-]
Lennie McBrowne (drums) [1933-]
Mary Ann McCall (vocal) [1919-]
Steve McCall (drums) [1933-1989]
Les McCann (piano) [1935-]
Albert McCarthy (writer) [1920-1987]
Ron McClure (bass) [1941-]
Rob McConnell (trombone) [1935-]
Bob McCracken (clarinet) [1904-1972]
Roy McCurdy (drums) [1936-]
Dick McDonough (guitar/banjo) [1904-
    1938]
Brother Jack McDuff (organ) [1926-]
Murray McEachern (trombone) [1915-
    1982]
Teo Macero (tenor sax/record producer)
    [1925-]
Eddie McFadden (guitar) [1928-]
Gary McFarland (vibes/ composer)
    [1933-1971]
Bobby McFerrin (vocals) [1950-]
Lou McGarity (trombone) [1917-1971]
Brownie McGhee (guitar) [1915-]
Howard McGhee (trumpet) [1918-1987]
Chris McGregor (piano) [1936-1990]
Jimmy McGriff (organ) [1936-]
Machito (bandleader) [1912-1984]
Adrian Macintosh (drums) [1942-]
Tom McIntosh (trombone) [1927-]
Earl McIntyre (trombone) [1953-
Hal McIntyre (alto sax) [1914-1959]
Ken McIntyre (alto sax) [1931-]
Billy Mackel (guitar) [1912-]
Dave McKenna (piano) [1930-]
Red McKenzie (vocals) [1899-1948]
Al McKibbon (bass) [1919-]
Ray McKinley (drums) [1910-]
William McKinney (drums/leader)
    [1895-1969]
Hal McKusick (alto sax) [1924-]
John McLaughlin (guitar) [1942-]
Jackie McLean (alto sax) [1932-]
Jimmy McLin (guitar) [1908-1983]
Harold McNair (flute / saxes) [1931-
    1971]
Jim McNeely (piano) [1949-]
Dick McPartland (guitar) [1905-1957]
Jimmy McPartland (trumpet) [1907-
    1991]
Marian McPartland (piano) [1920-]
Charles McPherson (alto sax) [1939-]
Tommy McQuater (trumpet) [1914-]
Barry McRae (writer) [1935-]
Carmen McRae (vocal) [1922-]
Teddy McRae (tenor sax/arranger/
    composer) [1908-]
Jay McShann (piano) [1916-]
Jack McVea (tenor sax) [1914-]
Willie McWashington (drums) [1908-
    1938]
Bob Magnusson (bass) [1947-]
Gildo Mahones (piano) [1929-]
Willie Maiden (tenor sax) [1928-1976]

Joe Maini (saxes) [1930-1964]
Mike Mainieri (vibes) [1938-]
Bob Maize (bass) [1945-]
Adam Makowicz (piano) [1940-]
John Malachi (piano) [1919-1987]
Matty Malneck (violin) [1903-1981]
Tom Malone (trombone) [1947-]
Junior Mance (piano) [1928-]
Henry Mancini (piano/composer)
    [1924-]
Johnny Mandel (trombone/composer)
    [1925-]
Manuel Manetta (piano/cornet/saxes)
    [1889-1969]
Albert Mangelsdorff (trombone) [1928-]
Chuck Mangione (trumpet) [1940-]
Gap Mangione (piano) [1938-]
Herbie Mann (flute) [1930-]
Tony Mann (drums) [1942-]
Shelly Manne (drums) [1920-1984]
Wingy Manone (trumpet) [1900-1982]
Ray Mantilla (percussion) [1934-]
Mike Mantler (trumpet) [1943-]
Fate Marable (piano/leader) [1890-1947]
Lawrence Marable (drums) [1929-]
Steve Marcus (tenor sax) [1939-]
Art Mardigan (drums) [1923-1977]
Arif Mardin (composer) [1932-]
Paul Mares (trumpet) [1900-1949]
Sam Margolis (tenor sax) [1923-]
Charlie Margulis (trumpet) [1903-1967]
Tania Maria (piano/vocals) [1948-]
Charlie Mariano (alto sax) [1923-]
Marky Markowitz (trumpet) [1923-1986]
Dodo Marmarosa (piano) [1925-]
Lawrence Marrero (banjo) [1900-1959]
Joe Marsala (clarinet) [1907-1978]
Marty Marsala (trumpet) [1909-1975]
Branford Marsalis (tenor sax) [1960-]
Delfeayo Marsalis (trombone) [1965-]
Jason Marsalis (drums) [1977-]
Wynton Marsalis (trumpet) [1961-]
Warne Marsh (tenor sax) [1927-1987]
Eddie Marshall (drums) [1938-]
Jack Marshall (guitar) [1921-]
John Marshall (drums) [1941-]
Kaiser Marshall (drums) [1899-1948]
Wendell Marshall (bass) [1920-]
Chink Martin (bass/tuba) [1886-1981]
Sara Martin (vocals) [1884-1955]
Skip Martin (saxes) [1916-]
Sabu Martinez (percussion) [1930-1979]
Pat Martino (guitar) [1944-]
Barry 'Kid' Martyn (drums) [1941-]
Hugh Masakela (trumpet) [1939-]
Harvey Mason (drums) [1947-]
George Masso (trombone) [1926-]
Carmen Mastren (guitar) [1913-1981]
Mat Mathews (accordion) [1924-]
Ronnie Mathews (piano) [1935-]
Ron Mathewson (bass) [1944-]
Matty Matlock (clarinet) [1907-1978]
Sleepy Matsumoto (tenor sax) [1926-]
Dave Matthews (saxes) [1911-]
Onzy Matthews (piano/ arranger) [1936-]
Benny Maupin (tenor sax) [1940-]
Turk Mauro (baritone sax) [1944-]
Leroy Maxey (drums) [1904-]
Billy Maxted (piano) [1917-]
Jimmy Maxwell (trumpet) [1917-]
Billy May (trumpet/arranger) [1916-]
Earl May (bass) [1927-]
Gene Mayl (bass) [1928-]
Bill Mays (piano) [1944-]
Lyle Mays (keyboards) [1953-]
Marilyn Mazur (percussion) [1955-]
Dick Meldonian (saxes) [1930-]
Mike Melillo (piano) [1939-]
Gil Melle (sax) [1931-]
George Melly (vocal) [1926-]
Frank Melrose (piano/bandleader)
    [1907-1941]
Mike Melvoin (piano) [1937-]
Don Menza (tenor sax) [1936-]
Johnny Mercer (songwriter) [1909-1976]
Chucho Merchan (bass) [1953-]
Helen Merrill (vocals) [1930-]
Jymie Merritt (bass) [1926-]

Paul Mertz (piano) [1904-]
Louis Metcalf (trumpet) [1905-1981]
Pat Metheny (guitar) [1954-]
Doug Mettome (trumpet) [1925-1964]
Mezz Mezzrow (clarinet) [1899-1972]
Pierre Michelot (bass) [1928-]
Wilfred Middlebrooks (bass) [1933-]
Velma Middleton (vocal) [1917-1961]
Jay Migliori (tenor sax) [1930-]
Palle Mikkelborg (trumpet) [1941-]
Barry Miles (drums) [1947-]
Butch Miles (drums) [1944-]
Lizzie Miles (vocals) [1895-1963]
Bubber Miley (trumpet) [1903-1932]
Eddie Miller (tenor sax) [1911-1991]
Glenn Miller (trombone) [1904-1944]
Harry Miller (bass) [1941-1983]
Marcus Miller (bass guitar) [1959-]
Mulgrew Miller (piano) [1955-]
Punch Miller (trumpet/vocals) 1894-
    1971]
Sing Miller (piano) [1914-]
Lucky Millinder (leader) [1900-1966]
Irving Mills (impresario) [1884-1985]
Jackie Mills (drums) [1922-]
Dom Minasi (guitar) [1943-]
Johnny Mince (saxes) [1912-]
Harold Minerve (alto sax) [1922-1992]
Charles Mingus (bass) [1922-1979]
Dan Minor (trombone) [1909-1982]
Bob Mintzer (saxes) [1953-]
Billy Mitchell (tenor sax) [1926-]
Blue Mitchell (trumpet) [1930-1979]
Dwike Mitchell (piano) [1930-]
George Mitchell (cornet) [1899-1972]
Grover Mitchell (trombone) [1930-]
Red Mitchell (bass) [1927-1992]
Roscoe Mitchell (saxes) [1940-]
Whitey Mitchell (bass) [1932-]
Danny Mixon (piano) [1949-]
Hank Mobley (tenor sax) [1930-1986]
Paul Moer (piano) [1916-]
Charles Moffett (drums) [1929-]
Louis Moholo (drums) [1940-]
Miff Mole (trombone) [1898-1961]
Grachan Moncur (bass) [1915-]
Grachan Moncur III (trombone) [1937-]
Toots Mondello (alto sax) [1912-]
Joe Mondragon (bass) [1920-]
Thelonious Monk (piano) [1917-1982]
Ade Monsbourgh (saxes) [1917-]
J.R. Monterose (tenor sax) [1927-]
Buddy Montgomery (vibes) [1930-]
Little Brother Montgomery
    (piano/vocals) [1906-1985]
Marian Montgomery (vocals) [1934-]
Monk Montgomery (electric bass)
    [1921-1982]
Wes Montgomery (guitar) [1923-1968]
Tete Montoliu (piano) [1933-]
Jack Montrose (tenor sax) [1928-]
James Moody (saxes) [1925-]
Joe Mooney (accordion) [1911-1975]
Alton 'Slim' Moore (trombone) [1908-
    1978]
Billy Moore (piano/arranger) [1917-
    1989]
Brew Moore (tenor sax) [1924-1973]
Danny Moore (trumpet) [1941-]
Dudley Moore (piano) [1935-]
Eddie Moore (drums) [1940-]
Freddie Moore (drums) [1900-]
Glen Moore (bass) [1941-]
Michael Moore (bass) [1945-]
Monette Moore (vocals) [1902-1962]
Oscar Moore (guitar) [1912-1981]
Pee Wee Moore (baritone sax) [1928-]
Big Chief Russell Moore (trombone)
    [1912-1983]
Herb Morand (trumpet) [1905-1952]
Chauncey Morehouse (drums) [1902-
    1980]
Airto Moreira (percussion) [1941-]
John Morell (guitar) [1946-]
Marty Morell (drums) [1944-]
Joe Morello (drums) [1928-]
Al Morgan (bass) [1908-1974]
Alun Morgan (writer) [1928-]

Index of musicians

Frank Morgan (alto sax) [1933-]
Lanny Morgan (alto sax) [1934-]
Lee Morgan (trumpet) [1938-1972]
Russ Morgan (trombone/arranger) [1904-1969]
Dan Morgenstern (writer) [1929-]
Marlowe Morris (piano) [1915-c1977]
Peck Morrison (bass) [1919-1988]
Dick Morrissey (tenor sax) [1940-]
Buddy Morrow (trombone/leader) [1919-]
George Morrow (bass) [1925-1992]
Ella Mae Morse (vocals) [1924-]
Benny Morton (trombone) [1907-1985]
Jelly Roll Morton (piano/composer/ leader) [1890-1941]
Ray Mosca (drums) [1932-]
Sal Mosca (piano) [1927-]
Bob Moses (drums) [1948-]
J C Moses (drums) [1936-1977]
Snub Mosley (trombone) [1905-1981]
Danny Moss (tenor sax) [1927-]
Sandy Mosse (tenor sax) [1929-1983]
Abe Most (clarinet) [1920-]
Sam Most (flute/alto sax) [1930-]
Bennie Moten (piano/leader) [1894-1935]
Benny Moten (bass) [1916-1977]
Paul Motian (drums) [1931-]
Ken Moule (piano/composer/arranger) [1925-1986]
Alphonse Mouzon (drums) [1948-]
Bob Mover (alto sax) [1952-]
Don Moye (drums) [1946-]
George Mraz (bass) [1944-]
Bheki Mseleku (piano/saxes) [1955-]
Idris Muhammad [Leo Morris] (drums) [1939-]
Jim Mullen (guitar) [1945-]
Moon Mullens (trumpet) [1916-1977]
Gerry Mulligan (baritone sax) [1927-]
Jimmy Mundy (tenor sax/arranger) [1907-1983]
Joe Muranyi (clarinet) [1928-]
Mark Murphy (vocalist) [1932-]
Spud Murphy (alto sax/arranger/ composer) [1908-]
Turk Murphy (trombone) [1915-1987]
David Murray (tenor sax) [1955-]
Don Murray (clarinet/saxes) [1904-1929]
Sunny Murray (drums) [1937-]
Vido Musso (tenor sax) [1913-1982]
Romano Mussolini (piano) [1927-]
Boots Mussulli (saxes) [1917-1967]
Amina Claudine Myers (piano/vocals) [1943-]
Bumps Myers (tenor sax) [1912-1968]
Wilson Myers (bass) [1906-]

Zbigniew Namyslowski (alto sax) [1939-]
Ray Nance (trumpet/violin) [1913-1976]
Joe 'Tricky Sam' Nanton (trombone) [1904-1946]
Marty Napoleon (piano) [1921-]
Phil Napoleon (trumpet) [1901-1990]
Teddy Napoleon (piano) [1914-1964]
Kenny Napper (bass) [1933-]
Dick Nash (trombone) [1928-]
Ted Nash (tenor sax) [1922-]
Ted Nash (tenor sax) [1956-]
Jamil Nasser George Joyner (bass) [1932-]
Fats Navarro (trumpet) [1923-1950]
Ray Neapolitan (bass) [1940-]
Buell Neidlinger (bass) [1936-]
Bob Neloms (piano) [1942-]
Dave Nelson (trumpet/piano/arranger) [1905-1946]
Big Eye Louis Nelson (clarinet) [1880-1949]
Oliver Nelson (saxes/ composer) [1932-1975]
Bjarne Nerem (tenor sax) [1923-1991]
Sammy Nestico (arranger/composer) [1924-]
Oscar Castro Neves (guitar) [1940-]
Calvin Newborn (guitar) [1933-]
Phineas Newborn (piano) [1931-]

David 'Fathead' Newman (saxes) [1933-]
Joe Newman (trumpet) [1922-1992]
Frankie Newton (trumpet) [1906-1954]
James Newton (flute) [1953-]
Albert Nicholas (clarinet) [1900-1973]
Big Nick Nicholas (tenor sax) [1922-]
Wooden Joe Nicholas (cornet/clarinet) [1883-1957]
Herbie Nichols (piano) [1919-1963]
Keith Nichols (piano) [1945-]
Maggie Nicols (vocal) [1948-]
Red Nichols (cornet) [1905-1965]
Lennie Niehaus (alto sax) [1929-]
Gerry Niewood (saxes) [1943-]
Jack Nimitz (baritone sax) [1930-]
Phil Nimmons (clarinet) [1923-]
Sal Nistico (tenor sax) [1940-1991]
Ray Noble (leader/composer/arranger) [1903-1978]
Michael Nock (piano) [1940-]
Paolo Nonnis (drums) [1950-]
Jimmie Noone (clarinet/leader) [1895-1944]
Jimmie Noone Jr (clarinet) [1938-1991]
Walter Norris (piano) [1931-]
Red Norvo (vibes) [1908-]
Sam Noto (trumpet) [1930-]
Jimmy Nottingham (trumpet) [1925-1978]
Alcide 'Yellow' Nunez (clarinet) [1884-1934]
Adam Nussbaum (drums) [1955-]

Floyd O'Brien (trombone) [1904-1968]
Anita O'Day (vocal) [1919-]
Chico O'Farrell (composer) [1921-]
Claus Ogerman (composer/piano) [1930-]
King Oliver (cornet/leader) [1885-1938]
Paul Oliver (writer) [1927-]
Sy Oliver (trumpet) [1910-1988]
Hank O'Neal (record producer) [1940-]
Frank Orchard (trombone) [1914-1983]
John Ore (bass) [1933-]
George Orendorff (trumpet) [1906-1984]
Tony Ortega (saxes) [1928-]
Kid Ory (trombone/leader) [1890-1973]
Mary Osborne (guitar) [1921-1992]
Mike Osborne (alto sax) [1941-]
Greg Osby (saxes) [1960-]
Harold Ousley (tenor sax) [1929-]
Hall Overton (piano/composer) [1920-1972]
Charles Owens (tenor sax) [1939-]
Jimmy Owens (flugelhorn) [1943-]
Tony Oxley (drums) [1938-]
Makoto Ozone (piano) [1961-]

Nathen Page (guitar) [1937-]
Oran 'Hot Lips' Page (trumpet) [1908-1954]
Walter Page (bass) [1900-1957]
Marty Paich (piano) [1925-]
Jimmy Palao (violin) [1885-1925]
Earl Palmer (drums) [1924-]
Roy Palmer (trombone) [1892-1963]
Singleton Palmer (bass) [1912-]
Remo Palmieri (guitar) [1923-]
Hugues Panassié (writer) [1912-1974]
Tony Parenti (clarinet) [1900-1972]
Tiny Parham (piano) [1900-1943]
Truck Parham (bass) [1911-]
Jackie Paris (vocals) [1926-]
Charlie Parker (alto sax) [1920-1955]
Evan Parker (tenor sax) [1944-]
Johnny Parker (piano) [1929-]
Knocky Parker (piano) [1918-1986]
Leo Parker (baritone sax) [1925-1962]
Horace Parlan (piano) [1931-]
David Parlato (bass) [1945-]
Jack Parnell (drums) [1923-]
Avery Parrish (piano) [1917-1959]
Hermeto Pascoal (piano/flute/guitar) [1936-]
Jerome Don Pasquall (saxes) [1902-1971]
Joe Pass (guitar) [1929-]
Tony Pastor (saxes/leader) [1907-1969]
Jaco Pastorius (bass) [1951-1987]
Don Patterson (organ) [1936-1988]

Ottilie Patterson (vocals) [1932-]
Big John Patton (organ) [1935-]
Emmanuel Paul (tenor sax) [1904-1988]
Alcide 'Slow Drag' Pavageau (bass) [1888-1969]
Benny Payne (piano/vocals) [1907-1986]
Cecil Payne (baritone sax) [1922-]
Don Payne (bass) [1933-]
Sonny Payne (drums) [1926-1979]
Gary Peacock (bass) [1935-]
Dick Pearce (trumpet) [1951-]
Duke Pearson (piano) [1932-1980]
Nat Peck (trombone) [1925-]
Santo Pecora (trombone) [1902-1984]
Guy Pedersen (bass) [1930-]
Niels-Henning Orsted Pederson (bass) [1946-]
Beverly Peer (bass) [1912-]
Bernard Peiffer (piano) [1922-1976]
Dave Pell (tenor sax) [1925-]
Bill Pemberton (bass) [1918-1984]
Ralph Pena (bass) [1927-1969]
Ralph Penland (drums) [1953-]
Ken Peplowski (reeds) [1959-]
Art Pepper (alto sax) [1925-1982]
Armando Peraza (percussion) [1924-]
Manuel Perez (cornet/leader) [1871-1946]
Bill Perkins (tenor sax) [1924-]
Carl Perkins (piano) [1928-1958]
Walter Perkins (drums) [1932-]
Gene Perla (bass/composer) [1940-]
Mimi Perrin (vocals/piano) [1926-]
Ray Perry (violin/alto sax) [1915-1950]
André Persiany (piano) [1927-]
Charlie Persip (drums) [1929-]
Houston Person (tenor sax) [1934-]
Aake Persson (trombone) [1932-1975]
Bent Persson (cornet) [1947-]
Hannibal Peterson (trumpet) [1948-]
Oscar Peterson (piano) [1925-]
Ralph Peterson (drums) [1962-]
Buddy Petit (trumpet/leader) [c1897-1931]
Michel Petrucciani (piano) [1962-]
Oscar Pettiford (bass) [1922-1960]
Benny Peyton (drums) [c1890-1965]
Dave Peyton (piano/arranger) [c1885-1956]
Barre Phillips (bass) [1934-]
Esther Phillips (vocals) [1925-]
Flip Phillips (tenor sax) [1915-]
Sid Phillips (clarinet) [1907-1973]
Walter 'Fats' Pichon (piano/vocal/ arranger) [1906-1967]
Alphonse Picou (clarinet) [1878-1961]
Billie Pierce (vocals/piano) [1907-1974]
Billy Pierce (tenor sax) [1948-]
Dede Pierce (trumpet) [1904-1973]
Nat Pierce (piano) [1925-1992]
Dave Pike (vibes) [1938-]
Hayes Pillars (tenor sax/leader) [1906-]
Courtney Pine (tenor sax) [1964-]
Ward Pinkett (trumpet) [1906-1937]
Armand J Piron (violin/leader) [1888-1943]
John Pisano (guitar) [1931-]
Bucky Pizzarelli (guitar) [1926-]
John Pizzarelli (guitar) [1960-]
Ray Pizzi (saxes) [1943-]
Bobby Plater (alto sax) [1914-1982]
Lonnie Plaxico (bass) [1960-]
King Pleasure (vocal) [1922-1981]
Pony Poindexter (alto sax) [1926-1988]
Ed Polcer (cornet) [1937-]
Ben Pollack (drums) [1903-1971]
Terry Pollard (piano/vibes) [1931-]
Danny Polo (saxes) [1901-1949]
Jimmy Ponder (guitar) [1946-]
Valery Ponomarev (trumpet) [1943-]
Jean-Luc Ponty (violin) [1942-]
Odean Pope (trumpet) [1938-]
Al Porcino (trumpet) [1925-]
Gene Porter (saxes/clarinet) [1910-]
Roy Porter (drums) [1923-]
Yank Porter (drums) [c1895-1944]
Tommy Potter (bass) [1918-1988]
Benny Powell (trombone) [1930-]

Bud Powell (piano) [1924-1966]
Jimmy Powell (alto sax) [1914-]
Mel Powell (piano) [1923-]
Richie Powell (piano) [1931-1956]
Rudy Powell (alto sax/clarinet) [1907-1976]
Seldon Powell (tenor sax) [1928-]
Specs Powell (drums) [1922-]
Ollie Powers (drums/vocals/leader) [c1890-1928]
Chano Pozo (conga) [1915-1948]
Don Prell (bass) [1929-]
Eddie Preston (trumpet) [1928-]
Andre Previn (piano) [1929-]
Eddie Prévost (drums) [1942-]
Jesse Price (drums) [1909-1974]
Sammy Price (piano) [1908-1992]
Julian Priester (trombone) [1935-]
Brian Priestley (piano/writer) [1946-]
Louis Prima (trumpet/vocals) [1911-1978]
Roland Prince (guitar) [1946-]
Bernie Privin (trumpet) [1919-]
George Probert (clarinet) [1927-]
Russell Procope (alto sax) [1908-1981]
Clarence Profit (piano) [1912-1944]
Carl Pruitt (bass) [1918-]
Dudu Pukwana (alto sax) [1938-1990]
Don Pullen (piano) [1941-]
Joe Puma (guitar) [1927-]
Colin Purbrook (piano) [1936-]
Bernard 'Pretty' Purdie (drums) [1939-]
Flora Purim (vocals/guitar) [1942-]
Alton Purnell (piano) [1911-1987]
Keg Purnell (drums) [1915-1965]
Maurice Purtill (drums) [1916-]
Jack Purvis (trumpet) [1906-1962]
Chris Pyne (trombone) [1939-]
Mick Pyne (piano) [1940-]

Chelsea Quealey (trumpet) [1905-1950]
Ike Quebec (tenor sax) [1918-1963]
Alvin Queen (drums) [1950-]
Benoit Quersin (bass) [1927-]
Howdy Quicksell (banjo) [1901-1953]
Gene Quill (alto sax) [1927-]
Paul Quinichette (tenor sax) [1916-1983]

Steve Race (piano/broadcaster) [1921-]
Don Rader (trumpet) [1935-]
John Rae (drums) [1934-]
Boyd Raeburn (bandleader) [1913-1966]
Henry Ragas (piano) [1891-1919]
Junior Raglin (bass) [1917-1955]
Chuck Rainey (bass) [1940-]
Ma Rainey (vocals) [1889-1939]
Gene Ramey (bass) [1913-1984]
Ram Ramirez (piano/composer) [1913-]
Frederick Ramsey (writer) [1915-]
Freddy Randall (trumpet) [1921-]
Don Randi (piano) [1937-]
Irving 'Mouse' Randolph (trumpet) [1909-]
Doug Raney (guitar) [1957-]
Jimmy Raney (guitar) [1927-]
Bill Rank (trombobe) [1904-1979]
Milt Raskin (piano) [1916-1977]
Enrico Rava (trumpet) [1943-]
Casper Reardon (harp) [1907-1941]
Pat Rebillot (piano) [1935-]
Sonny Red (alto sax) [1932-1981]
Freddie Redd (piano) [1928-]
Vi Redd (alto sax/vocals) [1928-]
Dewey Redman (tenor sax) [1931-]
Don Redman (saxes/composer/arranger) [1900-1964]
Joshua Redman (tenor sax) [1969-]
Dizzy Reece (trumpet) [1931-]
Waymon Reed (bass) [1940-1983]
Tony Reedus (drums) [1959-]
Della Reese (vocalist) [1932-]
Reuben Reeves (trumpet) [1905-1975]
Frank Rehak (trombone) [1926-1987]
Bill Reichenbach (drums) [1923-]
Bill Reichenbach (trombone) [1949-]
Rufus Reid (bass) [1944-]
Django Reinhardt (guitar) [1910-1953]
Emily Remler (guitar) [1957-1990]

Index of musicians

Index of musicians

Index of musicians

Walt Yoder (bass) [1914-1978]
Eldee Young (bass) [1936-]
Larry Young (organ) [1940-1978]
Lee Young (drums) [1917-]
Lester Young (tenor sax) [1909-1959]
Snooky Young (trumpet) [1919-]
Trummy Young (trombone) [1912-1984]
Bob Ysaguirre (bass/tuba) [1897-1982]
Joe Yukl (trombone) [1909-1981]

Zeke Zarchy (trumpet) [1915-]
Chester Zardis (bass) [1900-1990]
Joe Zawinul (piano) [1932-]
Denny Zeitlin (piano) [1938-]
Monica Zetterlund (vocals) [1938-]
Ronnie Zito (drums) [1939-]
Attila Zoller (guitar) [1927-]
Bob Zurke (piano) [1912-1944]
Barry Zweig (guitar) [1942-]
Mike Zwerin (bass trumpet) [1930-]